The Rorschach: A Comprehensive System, in two volu
  by John E. Exner, Jr.
Theory and Practice in Behavior Therapy
  by Aubrey J. Yates
Principles of Psychotherapy
  by Irving B. Weiner
Psychoactive Drugs and Social Judgment: Theory and Research
  edited by Kenneth Hammond and C. R. B. Joyce
Clinical Methods in Psychology
  edited by Irving B. Weiner
Human Resources for Troubled Children
  by Werner I. Halpern and Stanley Kissel
Hyperactivity
  by Dorothea M. Ross and Sheila A. Ross
Heroin Addiction: Theory, Research and Treatment
  by Jerome J. Platt and Christina Labate
Children's Rights and the Mental Health Profession
  edited by Gerald P. Koocher
The Role of the Father in Child Development
  edited by Michael E. Lamb
Handbook of Behavioral Assessment
  edited by Anthony R. Ciminero, Karen S. Calhoun, and Henry E. Adams
Counseling and Psychotherapy: A Behavioral Approach
  by E. Lakin Phillips
Dimensions of Personality
  edited by Harvey London and John E. Exner, Jr.
The Mental Health Industry: A Cultural Phenomenon
  by Peter A. Magaro, Robert Gripp, David McDowell, and Ivan W. Miller III
Nonverbal Communication: The State of the Art
  by Robert G. Harper, Arthur N. Wiens, and Joseph D. Matarazzo
Alcoholism and Treatment
  by David J. Armor, J. Michael Polich, and Harriet B. Stambul
A Biodevelopmental Approach to Clinical Child Psychology: Cognitive Controls and
Cognitive Control Theory
  by Sebastiano Santostefano
Handbook of Infant Development
  edited by Joy D. Osofsky
Understanding the Rape Victim: A Synthesis of Research Findings
  by Sedelle Katz and Mary Ann Mazur
Childhood Pathology and Later Adjustment: The Question of Prediction
  by Loretta K. Cass and Carolyn B. Thomas
Intelligent Testing with the WISC-R
  by Alan S. Kaufman
Adaptation in Schizophrenia: The Theory of Segmental Set
  by David Shakow
Psychotherapy: An Eclectic Approach
  by Sol L. Garfield
Handbook of Minimal Brain Dysfunctions
  edited by Herbert E. Rie and Ellen D. Rie
Handbook of Behavioral Interventions: A Clinical Guide
  edited by Alan Goldstein and Edna B. Foa
Art Psychotherapy
  by Harriet Wadeson
Handbook of Adolescent Psychology
  edited by Joseph Adelson
Psychotherapy Supervision: Theory, Research and Practice
  edited by Allen K. Hess

D1237248

Continued on back

FAILURES IN
BEHAVIOR THERAPY

FAILURES IN BEHAVIOR THERAPY

Edited by

EDNA B. FOA
Temple University School of Medicine
Philadelphia, Pennsylvania

PAUL M. G. EMMELKAMP
Academic Hospital
Department of Clinical Psychology
Groningen, The Netherlands

A WILEY-INTERSCIENCE PUBLICATION
JOHN WILEY & SONS
New York • Chichester • Brisbane • Toronto • Singapore

Library of Congress Cataloging in Publication Data:
Main entry under title:

Failures in behavior therapy.

(Wiley series on personality processes)
Includes index.
1. Behavior therapy—Evaluation. I. Foa, Edna B.
II. Emmelkamp, Paul M. G., 1949– . III. Series.
[DNLM: 1. Behavior therapy. WM 425 F161]

RC489.B4F34   1983   616.89'142   82-17644
ISBN 0-471-09238-X

Printed in the United States of America

10 9 8 7 6 5 4 3 2 1

Contributors

DAVID K. AHERN, PH.D., *Program Co-ordinator, Miriam Hospital, Providence, Rhode Island*

ROBERT E. ALBERTI, PH.D., *Counseling Psychologist, Impact Consultants, San Luis Obispo, California*

JOHN D. BURCHARD, PH.D., *Professor, Department of Psychology, University of Vermont, Burlington, Vermont*

DIANE L. BYTHELL, M.A., *Department of Psychology, State University of New York at Buffalo, Buffalo, New York*

R. LORRAINE COLLINS, PH.D., *Assistant Professor, Department of Psychology, State University of New York at Stony Brook, Stony Brook, New York*

ROBERT DITOMASSO, PH.D., *Assistant Professor, Department of Psychiatry, The University of Pennsylvania, Tatem-Brown Family Practice Center, Philadelphia, Pennsylvania*

HARVEY G. DOPPELT, PH.D., *Psychology Intern, Temple University School of Medicine, Philadelphia, Pennsylvania*

PATRICIA M. DUBBERT, M.D., *Assistant Professor, Veterans Administration Medical Center, Jackson, Mississippi*

ALBERT ELLIS, PH.D., *Executive Director, Institute for Rational-Emotive Therapy, New York, New York*

PAUL M. G. EMMELKAMP, PH.D., *Associate Professor, Department of Clinical Psychology, Academic Hospital, Groningen, The Netherlands*

MICHAEL L. EMMONS, PH.D., *Co-Director, Holos Center, Los Osos, California*

RENEE C. EPSTEIN, *Department of Educational Psychology, New York University, New York, New York*

WALTER T. A. M. EVERAERD, PH.D., *Professor of Psychology, University of Utrecht, Utrecht, The Netherlands*

EDNA B. FOA, PH.D., *Professor, Department of Psychiatry, Temple University School of Medicine, Philadelphia, Pennsylvania*

MICHAEL J. FOLLICK, PH.D., *Assistant Professor of Psychiatry, Miriam Hospital, Providence, Rhode Island*

v

JANEL GAUTHIER, PH.D., *Associate Professor, Ecole de Psychologie, University of Laval, Quebec City, Quebec, Canada*

THOMAS GILES, PSY.D., *Post-Doctoral Fellow, University of Alabama School of Medicine, Birmingham, Alabama*

IRIS GOLDSTEIN-FODOR, PH.D., *Professor of Psychology, New York University, New York, New York*

JONATHAN B. GRAYSON, PH.D., *Assistant Professor, Department of Psychiatry, Temple University School of Medicine, Philadelphia, Pennsylvania*

ANTHONY M. GRAZIANO, PH.D., *Professor and Director of Graduate Training Program in Clinical-Community Psychology, State University of New York at Buffalo, Buffalo, New York*

STANTON L. JONES, PH.D., *Assistant Professor, Psychology Department, Wheaton College, Tempe, Arizona*

ALAN E. KAZDIN, PH.D., *Professor of Psychiatry, University of Pittsburgh, Pittsburgh, Pennsylvania*

JULIE M. KUEHNEL, PH.D., *Assistant Research Psychologist, University of California at Los Angeles School of Medicine, Los Angeles, California*

THEODORE W. LANE, *Department of Psychology, University of Vermont, Burlington, Vermont*

ROBERT P. LIBERMAN, M.D., *Professor of Psychiatry, University of California at Los Angeles, Chief Rehabilitation Medical Services, Brentwood Veterans Administration Medical Center, Los Angeles, California*

G. ALAN MARLATT, PH.D., *Professor of Psychology, University of Washington, Seattle, Washington*

W. L. MARSHALL, PH.D., *Professor of Psychology, Queen's University, Kingston, Ontario, Canada*

JOHN S. MARZILLIER, PH.D., *Regional Tutor in Clinical Psychology, The Warneford Hospital, Birmingham, England*

MICHAEL PERTSCHUK, M.D., *Assistant Professor of Psychiatry, University of Pennsylvania, Philadelphia, Pennsylvania*

LIZETTE PETERSON, PH.D., *Assistant Professor, Department of Psychology, University of Missouri-Columbia, Columbia, Missouri*

STANLEY J. RACHMAN, PH.D., *Professor, University of British Columbia, Vancouver, British Columbia, Canada*

A. JOHN RUSH, M.D., *Associate Professor, Department of Psychiatry, University of Texas, Dallas, Texas*

BRIAN F. SHAW, PH.D., *Associate Professor of Psychology, University of Western Ontario, London, Ontario, Canada*

GAIL S. STEKETEE, M.S.S., *Social Worker, Temple University School of Medicine, Philadelphia, Pennsylvania*

RALPH M. TURNER, PH.D., *Assistant Professor, Department of Psychiatry, Temple University School of Medicine, Philadelphia, Pennsylvania*

ADA VAN DER HOUT, *Clinical Psychologist, Academic Hospital, Groningen, The Netherlands*

EUGENIE G. WHEELER, M.S.W., *Senior Psychiatric Social Worker, Ventura County Mental Health Department, Los Angeles, California*

G. TERENCE WILSON, PH.D., *Professor of Psychology, Rutgers University, Piscataway, New Jersey*

KEITH WINTER, M.S., *Principal Clinical Psychologist, Barnsley Hall Hospital, Worcester, England*

ANTONETTE M. ZEISS, PH.D., *Assistant Professor, Veterans Administration Hospital, Palo Alto, California*

ROBERT E. ZITTER, PH.D., *Assistant Professor, Rush-Presbyterian-St. Luke Hospital, Chicago, Illinois*

Series Preface

This series of books is addressed to behavioral scientists interested in the nature of human personality. Its scope should prove pertinent to personality theorists and researchers as well as to clinicians concerned with applying an understanding of personality processes to the amelioration of emotional difficulties in living. To this end, the series provides a scholarly integration of theoretical formulations, empirical data, and practical recommendations.

Six major aspects of studying and learning about human personality can be designated: personality theory, personality structure and dynamics, personality development, personality assessment, personality change, and personality adjustment. In exploring these aspects of personality, the books in the series discuss a number of distinct but related subject areas: the nature and implications of various theories of personality; personality characteristics that account for consistencies and variations in human behavior; the emergence of personality processes in children and adolescents; the use of interviewing and testing procedures to evaluate individual differences in personality; efforts to modify personality styles through psychotherapy, counseling, behavior therapy, and other methods of influence; and patterns of abnormal personality functioning that impair individual competence.

IRVING B. WEINER

University of Denver
Denver, Colorado

Preface

The birth of this book took place two years ago in a small cafe in Paris, where the authors first met. At the time we both had already been heavily involved in investigating behavioral treatment procedures for anxiety disorders. We shared the realization that, although behavioral therapy had developed rapidly in the last decade, few new ideas had been advanced recently. Available treatment procedures for anxiety-based disorders had been found effective with approximately 75 percent of the patients; attempts to further enhance efficacy by devising new variants of existing procedures or by implementing combinations of them had not proven fruitful.

We felt a critical examination of the state of the art for behavior therapy could lead to the generation of new hypotheses and the exploration of novel ideas. A natural beginning would be to study our failures. This is how the idea of devoting an entire book to the analysis of failures in behavior therapy was born. To maximize the value of this effort we approached scholars who are prominent in their respective areas and asked them to participate in this endeavor. At first we were quite hesitant: who would want to admit his or her ineffectiveness? Surprisingly, most of those whom we contacted shared our enthusiasm. A few, however, refused. A friend who had devised a widely recognized procedure regretfully admitted he had had no failures. Another scholar was plainly not interested in those who fail; he was content with the present advances. Several of our colleagues wanted to contribute but, having limited their observation to group means, they had not collected data that would have allowed them to investigate their failures. It is hoped that the present volume will influence future designs and analyses of outcome studies so that data on failures will be systematically collected.

This volume is not a criticism of behavior therapy. Rather, it intends to help students acquire a critical and inquisitive attitude on the application of psychotherapeutic intervention. Clinicians who have been instructed in behavioral procedures and who strive to increase treatment effectiveness with their clients may find the book helpful. Thus the present volume is a natural companion to guides on the application of behavioral procedures. Finally, the book is intended as a source of stimulation for those who have devoted their careers to the advancement of knowledge in our science.

We would like to extend our thanks to all the authors whose efforts made this volume possible. It was not easy to collaborate across the ocean; a vast amount of correspondence was involved. This burden was carried by our respective secretaries, Margaret Altomare and Greetje Hollander, to whom we express our deep appreciation.

EDNA B. FOA
PAUL M. G. EMMELKAMP

Philadelphia, Pennsylvania
Groningen, The Netherlands
January 1983

Contents

1. FAILURES ARE A CHALLENGE,   1

   Paul M. G. Emmelkamp and Edna B. Foa

2. TREATMENT OF OBSESSIVE-COMPULSIVES: WHEN DO WE
   FAIL?   10

   E. B. Foa, G. Steketee, J. B. Grayson, and H. G. Doppelt

3. OBSTACLES TO THE SUCCESSFUL TREATMENT OF
   OBSESSIONS,   35

   S. Rachman

4. FAILURE IN TREATING AGORAPHOBIA,   58

   Paul M. G. Emmelkamp and Ada van der Hout

5. FAILURES IN FLOODING,   82

   W. L. Marshall and Janel Gauthier

6. LIMITATIONS OF THE TREATMENT FOR SOCIAL
   ANXIETY,   104

   John S. Marzillier and Keith Winter

7. FAILURE: WINNING AT THE LOSING GAME IN
   ASSERTIVENESS TRAINING,   121

   Michael L. Emmons and Robert E. Alberti

8. ASSERTIVENESS TRAINING FOR WOMEN: WHERE ARE WE
   FAILING?   137

   Iris Goldstein-Fodor and Renee C. Epstein

9. FAILURES IN RATIONAL-EMOTIVE THERAPY,   159

   Albert Ellis

10. FAILURES IN SELF-CONTROL,   172

Lizette Peterson

11. BEHAVIORAL TREATMENT OF DEPRESSION: EXAMINING
TREATMENT FAILURES,   197

Antonette M. Zeiss and Stanton L. Jones

12. FAILURES IN TREATING DEPRESSION BY COGNITIVE
BEHAVIOR THERAPY,   217

A. John Rush and Brian F. Shaw

13. FAILURES IN THE TREATMENT OF ADDICTIVE
BEHAVIORS,   229

R. Lorraine Collins and G. Alan Marlatt

14. CONTROLLED DRINKING,   245

Michael Pertschuk

15. FAILURES IN BEHAVIOR THERAPY FOR OBESITY: CAUSES,
CORRELATES, AND CONSEQUENCES,   263

Patricia M. Dubbert and G. Terence Wilson

16. FAILURES IN THE TREATMENT OF INSOMNIA: A PLEA FOR
DIFFERENTIAL DIAGNOSIS,   289

Ralph M. Turner, Robert Di Tomasso, and Thomas Giles

17. FAILURES IN THE OPERANT TREATMENT OF CHRONIC
PAIN,   311

Michael J. Follick, Robert E. Zitter, and David K. Ahern

18. FAILURE OF PERSONS TO RESPOND TO THE TOKEN
ECONOMY,   335

Alan E. Kazdin

19. FAILURE TO MODIFY DELINQUENT BEHAVIOR: A
CONSTRUCTIVE ANALYSIS,   355

Theodore W. Lane and John D. Burchard

20. FAILURES IN BEHAVIORAL MARITAL THERAPY,   378

Robert Paul Liberman, Eugenie G. Wheeler, and Julie M. Kuehnel

21. FAILURE IN TREATING SEXUAL DYSFUNCTIONS, 392

    Walter T. A. M. Everaerd

22. FAILURES IN CHILD BEHAVIOR THERAPY, 406

    Anthony M. Graziano and Diane Lee Bythell

    AUTHOR INDEX, 425

    SUBJECT INDEX, 439

CHAPTER 1

Failures Are a Challenge

PAUL M. G. EMMELKAMP
EDNA B. FOA

The authors both grew up in the midst of great developments in behavior therapy, during a period characterized by the invention of numerous new techniques. The attitude of those who started the behavioral movement was exceedingly optimistic, almost verging on a sense of omnipotence. Influential books such as Bandura's (1969), Ullman and Krasner's (1969), and Wolpe's (1958) fostered the belief that given a carefully planned treatment program and an appropriate choice of behavioral techniques most—if not all—human misery could be alleviated. This enthusiasm is natural to a new movement.

The eagerness of behavior therapists to demonstrate the power of their techniques led to the development of two research strategies. The first employed group designs to test the effectiveness of treatment procedures or of single components included in them (Paul, 1967). In so doing the main emphasis was on group means, with a disregard for what happened to the individual patient. Within-group variance was perceived as an unfortunate occurrence rather than as a major source of relevant information. The second strategy involved a methodology appropriate to the study of single cases (Yates, 1970; Hersen, & Barlow, 1976). This latter strategy focused on the responsiveness of an individual to a given intervention, but it did not provide information about the generalizability of the results obtained, be they success or failure.

A convergence of the generalization and individualization approaches is found in some experimental designs that examine the interaction between treatment factors and individuals characteristics. An example of this line of research is provided by Öst, Jerremalm, and Johansson (1981). Socially anxious patients were divided into behavioral and physiological reactors. The results showed that for the behavioral reactors social skills training was superior to relaxation, whereas the reverse was true for the physiological reactors. Unfortunately, this approach requires a large number of subjects. Inasmuch as the number of patients available for any given study is often limited, the application of this strategy to outcome studies has been rare. An alternative strategy is to calculate group means to obtain information about the generality of the findings and at the same time to examine the responses of the individuals who participated in the study. In this way information is gained on the clinical significance of the results as well as on their generalizability. For example, Jacobson (1977) compared the efficacy of behavioral marriage therapy with a control group; in addition, a single-subject design was employed for each couple who participated in the treatment group. It is regrettable that only few clinical outcome studies followed this latter strategy.

The predominant type of outcome research in behavior therapy involved between-group studies comparing different procedures or treatment components. These studies have provided a vast amount of information about the general efficacy of behavioral techniques for the "average" patient. However, they have taught us little about the individual cases and particularly about those who did not improve.

Scarcity of reports on treatment failure is not unique to behavior therapy. First, there are very few studies with acceptable methodology on the efficacy of some widely used psychotherapeutic interventions such as psychoanalysis. Second, when outcome studies were conducted they often did not employ an adequate methodology for the investigation of failures and successes. Often, neither the population nor the techniques were homogeneous, and the measurement used to assess poorly defined treatment effects were frequently inadequate (e.g., personality scales). As stated by Garfield (1978): "A host of idiosyncratic studies of poorly defined populations with vaguely described therapies and exceedingly variable outcome criteria will not produce findings of any substance" (p. 225). Even in the last decade when much effort has been directed towards investigating the comparative efficacy of different therapeutic schools the flaws mentioned above still existed (Sloane et al., 1975).

Despite these methodological limitations, the investigation of prognostic variables related to failure has not been totally ignored (e.g., Luborsky et al., 1979). An interesting attempt to study differences between patients who benefited from treatment and those who failed to show change has been provided by Strupp (1980 a,b,c,d). In a series of case studies, he investigated patient's and therapist's variables that differentiated success from failure, with an emphasis on the therapeutic process. This line of investigation is encouraging. However, these studies do not answer a question of great relevance to the clinician: "What type of treatment should be given to what patient in order to minimize therapeutic failures?"

The picture presented by behavior therapy may look brighter at first sight. Aware of the weaknesses of psychotherapy outcome studies, investigators in behavior therapy have attempted to use homogeneous populations, specified procedures, and more specific measures of outcome. However, homogeneity is always relative to the state of the knowledge at a given time. For example, whereas several years ago phobics were considered a homogeneous group, there is increasing agreement at present that agoraphobics differ from simple phobics, and each of these groups requires a different treatment program. Another problem stems from the fact that, in an attempt to avoid heterogeneity, behavioral researchers tended to utilize analogue populations (mostly college student volunteers). The generalizability of the results thus obtained to patient populations is questionable (e.g., Bandura, 1978; Borkovec & Rachman, 1979; Emmelkamp, 1980; Kazdin, 1978).

The literature on behavior therapy provides us with little or no information with respect to the number of patients who failed to benefit; neither does it furnish us with information about factors related to failures. It is amazing that researchers will invest vast efforts in collecting data on long-term follow-up, while neglecting to report *how many* patients failed to benefit from treatment (e.g., Munby & Johnston, 1980).

But, of course, failures always exist; they are just not reported that often. Contact with clients has taught us that clinical practice is not as simple as that portrayed in textbooks. After thorough assessment and application of the appropriate techniques we still fail occasionally. What has made this realization even more painful is the fact that failures have not been openly discussed. This reticence fostered the belief that if one encounters a treatment failure, then one is a failure as a therapist. For, if the therapist had made a correct behavioral analysis and subsequently applied adequately the appropriate procedures, success would have been inevitable. This might be a reason for the scarce literature on failures and for the little attention given to the few that exist. It seems that once a technique was endorsed as effective, it became almost taboo to admit that sometimes the expected positive results were not obtained.

Various other reasons militate against reporting failures. First, journals discourage reports of negative results. This is true with respect to group studies as well as with single case reports. Second, in the face of criticism from traditional schools of psychotherapy, behaviorists felt compelled to demonstrate the efficacy of their procedures rather than question them and thus provide the "enemy" with ammunition. Third, researchers prefer to report their successes rather than relating their failures. For one, we all tend to conveniently forget that we occasionally fail. And often when we fail we don't understand why. A report on failure without advancing some hypothesis for it (other than declaring lack of motivation on the part of the patient) is unlikely to enhance our knowledge. We hope that as we become more comfortable with the advancement of our science we will be more inclined to critically examine our failures. Rather than being a source of discomfort, failures may then become an invaluable source of information for elucidating the mechanisms underlying our interventions, for perfecting existing procedures, and for inventing new ones.

If one endorses the position that the study of failures is essential for the advancement of behavioral psychotherapy, then several central issues should be examined. Are there different types of treatment failures? How will failure be defined? How can we identify sources of failure?

A CLASSIFICATION OF FAILURE

Given that we have a set of procedures that proved reasonably effective in ameliorating a specified problem, failure might occur even before any interaction between the client and the helper has occurred. We specifically refer here to problems inherent in dissemination of information about our treatment programs. For example, an agoraphobic who after much hesitation applied for treatment, told her therapist that she was reluctant to seek behavioral treatment as a result of horrifying stories she heard about the "torture" involved in treatment by exposure in vivo in meetings of The Phobic Society, a self-help group in The Netherlands. Although this patient overcame her reluctance, one wonders how many individuals who belong to similar groups have deprived themselves of the opportunity to resume a more functional life. Others might not have sought behavioral therapy simply because they never heard about it.

Refusals

Another type of pretreatment failure involves patients who apply for treatment but later refuse to follow through. We can hardly ignore this problem. Garfield (1980) reported that one third of individuals coming to a psychotherapy clinic refused the treatment offered to them and Marks (1978) reported that one fourth of those who applied for behavioral therapy did not pursue the treatment. Failure to benefit from treatment due to refusal may not always be dependent on the prospective patient. Family members might be the decision makers. Sometimes communities may hinder the application of an effective treatment; Lane and Burchard (Chapter 19, this volume) report of communities who refuse to permit the establishment of treatment facilities for delinquents.

Dropouts

Patients who do not complete a course of treatment considered to be adequate by the therapist are defined as dropouts and generally are labeled failures. Although it is likely that most of these patients will not greatly benefit from therapy, some may drop out simply because they have achieved their goal. An agoraphobic who became able to drive alone for 10 miles might be content with this achievement and, therefore, terminate treatment before the therapist's more ambitious goals have been reached. Other patients may have changed their treatment goal during the course of treatment and thus may feel that further therapy directed at the original goal is not required. Much of our information on treatment outcome is acquired in controlled studies, where the number of treatment sessions is usually determined; therefore, any patient who terminates therapy before completing the prescribed full course is considered a dropout. Ideally, in the clinical setting a patient should be defined as a dropout only when the treatment goals agreed upon by both the therapist and the patient have not been achieved and when the therapist believes that additional sessions are essential and, indeed, will result in further improvement. When patients terminate treatment before reaching the agreed-upon goal, they should be considered nonresponders if no expectation for further improvement exists on the part of the therapist.

Nonresponders

This category is the most commonly used for treatment failures. Patients belonging to this category have received what is considered by the therapist to be adequate treatment, yet they fail to reach the agreed-upon criteria for improvement. The choice of criteria for labeling a patient as a nonresponder is not without problems. We will elaborate on this issue when discussing criteria for failure.

Relapses

There is an assumption in psychotherapy that the processes underlying the changes that occurred during therapy should persist after the termination of treatment, preferably as long as the patient lives. If such permanence does not occur, the patient becomes "a relapse" and thus a treatment failure. This assumption is not always justified. There may be psychological conditions that require continued intervention or booster treatment as is often the case in many medical problems. For example, at the present state of knowledge nobody expects that severe hypertension will not recur when medication is discontinued; although blood pressure will increase with termination of drug treatment, the patient will not be considered a treatment failure. Yet, despite our often weak interventions, we expect behavior therapy to produce durable changes. If a certain set of unwanted behaviors are maintained by environmental reinforcements that persist after termination of treatment, why should we expect that these behaviors will not be resumed when the patient returns to his or her natural environment?

CRITERIA FOR FAILURES

In order to define a patient as a treatment failure, the desirable outcome should be determined in advance. First, a set of goals should be set up. Ideally, these goals should be reached by a consensus between the patient or the social system on the one hand, and the therapist on the other. The choice of a treatment goal may be a simple process in some cases but quite complex in others. For example, should the focus of the treatment of an agoraphobic who does not have assertiveness skills when interacting with his or her spouse or parents be to increase mobility, or should we also strive to alter the patient's communication style? If it is agreed upon that changes in both areas are necessary, then two sets of interventions should be employed and two sets of measurements should be used. In case of multiple goals, no simple dichotomy between success and failure is feasible. Obviously, when treatment fails to ameliorate one problem area but leads to change in the other, then the person is a failure in the former and a success in the latter.

   Another complication may stem from the fact that goals may change in the course of treatment. For example, treatment of obesity may result in the expected loss of weight, but at the same time may create unforeseen negative consequences such as irritability, deprivation, and depression (Dubbert & Wilson, Chapter 15, this volume). Is this patient a success or failure? With respect to the original goal one could consider this case a success. But if the overall well-being of the patient is a major criteria for success, then this case will be a failure. Whether negative "side effects" that emerge during treatment will render the patient a failure depends upon their nature and severity.

Once the goals are defined, a treatment program can be devised and adequate assessment procedures be selected. In the state of the art of psychotherapy, outcome measurements constitute a major problem involving many facets. First, who should assess the treatment outcome? The patient, the therapist, or—in the case of a delinquent—society. As noted by Marzillier and Winter (Chapter 6, this volume): "Failure is also relative. What is perceived by one party as failure is perceived by another as success."

A second issue is the choice of measurements. After a long tradition of using global measurements and personality inventories with questionable reliability and validity, it is no wonder that behavioral researchers have emphasized the use of objective behavioral assessment procedures. But, in an effort to devise reliable assessment we might have overlooked issues of external validity (Emmelkamp, 1981). For example, is the ability of a couple to resolve an argument in the lab without destroying the furniture indicative of their ability to do so at home? Or, will an obsessive-compulsive who can endure contamination in the lab or clinic without emitting his or her rituals be able to refrain from ritualizing at home? A case in point is the agoraphobic who can travel long distances with the "observing" therapist, but may not be able to drive a mile alone. We are not advocating a romantic naturalistic approach to measurement nor do we suggest complete reliance on self-report, although in some instances this still may be the most valid measure. Rather, one could perceive the natural environment and the artificiality of the lab as opposite poles of a continuum. It is up to the individual researcher to judge at which point the objectiveness achieved in the laboratory situation ceases to reflect reality.

Once an observer has been chosen and the measures of assessing the goal behavior has been selected, how little change will qualify a patient as a failure? Presently, the cutoff point is decided arbitrarily by each researcher. Ideally, this point should correspond to the absence of meaningful clinical changes. There is a clear need for research to address the issue of external validity of cutoff points.

SOURCES OF FAILURE

The readers of this volume may find that the sources for failure are quite limited. Indeed, the same source often appears again and again in different contexts under the pen of different authors. A factor often discussed is diagnostic error which leads to the employment of a potentially powerful procedure while omitting the adoption of a more useful one. This happens, for example, when the therapist attributes psychological causes to a behavior that is caused by organic factors. For example, patients with endogeneous depression respond to medication, whereas the effect of psychological interventions has not yet been proven success-ful with this subpopulation (Rush & Shaw, Chapter 12). A most distressing exam-ple of misdiagnosis has been provided by Follick, Zitter, and Ahern (Chapter 17) concerning a patient who was treated with an operant-based treatment for a pain caused by cancer that was diagnosed as psychogenic.

Another type of error in diagnosis stems from failure to conduct an accurate functional behavioral analysis; there are many examples of this error throughout the book. A common flaw is failure to deal with factors in the patient's environ-ment that maintain the problem behavior. The procedures used may be appropri-ate but treatment fails because of negligence in changing the environmental condi-tions. The social system in which the patient lives may indeed contribute to failure. This issue is discussed by Emmelkamp and van der Hout for agoraphobia (Chapter 4), Zeiss and Jones for depression (Chapter 11), Dubbert and Wilson for obesity (Chapter 15), and Follick et al. for pain (Chapter 17). An erroneous conceptualization of the problems presented by the patient is yet another source of failure that may lead to employment of an inappropriate procedure; this factor is discussed by Turner, di Tomasso, and Giles (Chapter 16).

A common source of failure is the inadequate application of a treatment pro-gram that would have resulted in success had it been carried out properly. For example, when exposure to anxiety-evoking stimuli is too short, failure to extin-guish the phobia could be expected. Likewise, as noted by Kazdin (Chapter 18), when stimuli that would constitute potent reinforcement are not used in an oper-ant program, failure is expected. These examples refer to inadequacies on the therapist's part, but inadequate treatment may also be due to the patient's lack of compliance with the treatment program.

Variables related to long-term maintenance of gain (or relapse) may differ from those involved in changes that occurred during therapy. For example, when an addiction is controlled by interpersonal anxiety or stressful life events, it is reason-able to assume that the effects of treatment directed at the addictive behavior will not be maintained if the controlling factors are not removed. A relapse may also stem from lack of generalization from one setting to another. Often, when treat-ment is conducted in institutional settings, the gains are not carried into the pa-tient's natural environment (see Chapter 18 by Kazdin, and Chapter 19 by Lane and Burchard).

Several authors reported that certain patients' personality characteristics were related to failure. However, any one characteristic has not proven to be a powerful predictor of outcome inasmuch as it accounts for only 5 to 10 percent of the vari-ance (Luborsky et al., 1979). The processes that operate in any therapeutic inter-vention are so complex that no one variable can be expected to account for a large proportion of the variance of outcome. Therefore, we should develop predictive models based upon the interaction among several variables (see Foa et al., Chap-ter 2, this volume).

Some authors have suggested that a negative therapeutic relationship may lead to failure. However, the data available at present are far from being conclusive. Likewise, aspects of therapist's behavior that are related to failure are yet to be identified. Perhaps the recognition of the relevance of therapeutic relationship to outcome of behavioral procedures will provide a bridge between behavior therapy and other schools of psychotherapy.

SUMMARY AND CONCLUSIONS

Several types of failure probably exist in each problem area; but it seems that some types are more prominent in one disorder than in another. In disturbances for which a high initial success rate is achieved, it might be more important to focus on relapses rather than on nonresponders. For example, there is a clear need for maintenance programs for addictive behaviors that show 80 percent relapse after one year (Collins & Marlatt, Chapter 13, this volume). In other areas where relapse is less of a problem (e.g., phobias) the investigation of dropouts and nonresponders should take precedence.

It seems that the replication of studies utilizing behavioral techniques whose effects have already been established for the "average" patient are not likely to produce new knowledge. We suggest that more effort be directed at elucidating factors associated with failure. As a science, behavior therapy will mature when it acknowledges its shortcomings and investigates its sources. It is hoped that data so obtained will foster critical evaluation and fruitful research. As knowledge about failures becomes available it should be incorporated into the training of behavior therapists, replacing the often rigid indoctrination of our students.

We believe that research in behavior therapy has made a considerable contribution to clinical practice. To further develop our science, we should critically analyze our failures. We hope that the present volume will provide impetus towards this goal.

REFERENCES

Bandura, A. (1969) *Principles of behavior modification.* New York: Holt, Rinehart & Winston.

Bandura, A. (1978) On paradigms and recycled ideologies. *Cognitive Therapy and Research,* **2,** 79–103.

Borkovec, T. D., & Rachman, S. (1979) The utility of analogue research. *Behaviour Research and Therapy,* **17,** 253–261.

Emmelkamp, P. M. G. (1980) Relationship between theory and practice in behavior therapy. In W. de Moor & J. Wijngaarden (Eds.), *Psychotherapy: Research and training.* Amsterdam: Elsevier.

Emmelkamp, P. M. G. (1981) The current and future status of clinical research. *Behavioral Assessment,* **3,** 249–253.

Garfield, S.L. (1978) Research on client variables in psychotherapy. In S.L. Garfield and

A.E. Bergin (Eds.), *Handbook of psychotherapy and behavior change*, 2nd ed. New York: Wiley.

Garfield, S. L. (1980) *Psychotherapy: An eclectic approach.* New York: Wiley.

Hersen, M., & Barlow, D. H. (1976) *Single case experimental designs: Strategies for studying behavior change.* New York: Pergamon.

Jacobson, N. S. (1977) Problem solving and contingency contracting in the treatment of marital discord. *Journal of Consulting and Clinical Psychology, 45,* 92–100.

Kazdin, A. E. (1978) Evaluating the generality of findings in analogue research. *Journal of Consulting and Clinical Psychology, 46,* 673–686.

Luborsky, L., Mintz, J., & Christoph, P. (1979) Are psychotherapeutic changes predictable? Comparison of a Chicago counseling center project with a Penn psychotherapy project. *Journal of Consulting and Clinical Psychology, 47,* 3, 469–473.

Marks, I. (1978) Behavioural psychotherapy of adult neurosis. In S. L. Garfield & A. E. Bergin (Eds.), *Handbook of psychotherapy and behavior change.* New York: Wiley.

Munby, M., & Johnston, D. W. (1980) Agoraphobia: The long-term follow-up of behavioural treatment. *British Journal of Psychiatry, 137,* 418–427.

Öst, L. G., Jerremalm, A., & Johansson, J. (1981) Individual response patterns and the effects of different behavioural methods in the treatment of social phobia. *Behaviour Research and Therapy, 19,* 1–16.

Paul, G. L. (1967) Strategy of outcome research in psychotherapy. *Journal of Consulting Psychology, 31,* 109–118.

Sloane, R. B., Staples, F. R., Cristol, A. H., Yorkston, N. J., & Whipple, K. (1975) *Psychotherapy versus behavior therapy.* Cambridge, Mass.: Harvard.

Strupp, H. H. (1980a) Success and faiure in time-limited psychotherapy: A systematic comparison of two cases: Comparison 1. *Archives of General Psychiatry, 37,* 595–603.

Strupp, H. H. (1980b) A systematic comparison of two cases: Comparison 2. *Archives of General Psychiatry, 37,* 708–716.

Strupp, H. H. (1980c) With special reference to the performance of a lay counselor. *Archives of General Psychiatry, 37,* 831–841.

Strupp, H. H. (1980d) Further evidence (comparison 4). *Archives of General Psychiatry, 37,* 947–954.

Ullmann, L. P., & Krasner, L. (1969) *A psychological approach to abnormal behavior.* Englewood Cliffs, N.J.: Prentice-Hall.

Wolpe, J. (1958) *Psychotherapy by reciprocal inhibition.* Stanford: Stanford.

Yates, A. J. (1970) *Behavior therapy.* New York: Wiley.

CHAPTER 2

Treatment of Obsessive-Compulsives: When Do We Fail?

E. B. FOA
G. STEKETEE
J. B. GRAYSON
H. G. DOPPELT

In the utopic state of the art of psychotherapy for each patient we will be able to specify which set of interventions should be applied, once the behaviors chosen for change are specified and the relevant characteristics of the patient are assessed. We will also be able to detect early unresponsiveness to treatment, to identify its roots, and to modify the treatment procedures accordingly. We are far from reaching this state. However, by studying our failures we have made some advances with respect to obsessive-compulsive disorders.

The search for predictors of failure for a given diagnostic group becomes fruitful only after effective treatments have been developed. It is only then that the investigation of the differences between those who succeed and those who fail can throw light on the mechanisms involved in the treatment and provide cues for the development of more effective techniques. At present we can confidently state that obsessive-compulsives are best treated by an intervention that includes both deliberate exposure and some manner of response prevention. Variants of this treatment intervention have been applied to a large number of patients of whom 60 to 85 percent were improved (e.g., Boersma, den Hengst, Dekker, & Emmelkamp, 1976; Boulougouris & Bassiakos, 1973; Catts & McConaghy, 1975; Foa & Goldstein, 1978; Marks, Hodgson, & Rachman, 1975; Mills, Agras, Barlow, & Mills, 1973; Rachman, Cobb, Grey, McDonald, Mawson, Sartory, & Stern, 1979; Roper, Rachman, & Marks, 1975).

In pursuing the study of those who failed to benefit from behavioral treatment, we have focused on the relationship among outcome, treatment components, pa-

The authors wish to thank Uriel G. Foa for his helpful comments on earlier versions of this manuscript. Our thanks are extended to Ralph M. Turner and Paul R. Latimer who acted as independent assessors for many of the patients whose data were reported here. We are indebted to Richard A. Roemer, Michael Frese, and Leo Rigsby for their assistance with the statistical analyses.

tient characteristics, and patient responses during exposure. In this paper we will summarize what we have learned from this line of investigation.

Our observations about treatment failures are based on nearly 100 patients treated at the Department of Psychiatry, Temple University, all of whom met the DSM III criteria for obsessive-compulsive disorder. (For an extensive discussion of the definition, see Foa & Steketee, 1979.) Seventy-two of these patients participated in various research projects. All had symptoms of at least one-year duration and engaged in obsessions and rituals for at least one hour per day. Fifty percent of the subjects were female. Two thirds had primarily washing rituals and one third checking rituals. The mean age for the sample was 34 years (S.D. = 10.6 years). Average symptom duration was 11.1 years (S.D. = 10.6 years). Fifty-eight patients were followed for periods ranging from three months to three years with a mean of one year (S.D. = .72 years).

Each patient had received 10 to 20 daily sessions of one of the following treatments: exposure in imagination, exposure in vivo, response prevention, a combination of the latter two, or a combination of all three. (For a detailed description of these procedures, see Foa & Tillmanns, 1980.) Such intensive treatment is often stressful and requires an extensive time commitment from patients. It is most appropriate when the obsessive-compulsive symptoms are severe, interfering with patients' general functioning. Indeed, the vast majority of our patients manifest severe symptoms. Therefore, our clinical observations and the analysis of the factors associated with failure reported here apply to severe obsessive-compulsives, and may not be applicable to mild cases.

TYPES OF FAILURE

The process of therapy begins when an individual seeks to change behaviors or emotions.* Whether the changes sought by the individual call for psychological treatment is a decision determined by one's definition of "normality" and how much deviation constitutes psychopathology. When both the patient and therapist agree that treatment is appropriate, the behaviors, cognitions, and emotions to be changed are delineated. A process of applying certain procedures designed to produce long lasting effects in the designated symptoms is then instituted. Failure may occur at any time throughout the course of this process.

1. *Refusals.* After the available treatment procedures are described, the patient may refuse to undergo therapy. The procedures may be perceived as too demanding, too frightening, or not credible. If we have an effective treatment but the patient refuses it, we have failed.

---

*It is generally accepted that the goal of therapy is inducement of change. In clinical trials we expect the control group to evince little or no change and the experimental group to show a large change. But change may not necessarily need to be the goal of the treatment group. One can conceive of a situation where lack of treatment would result in worsening of symptoms and treatment would maintain the status quo. The goal of treatment, then, would be to maintain the patients' present state rather than alter it.

2. *Dropouts.*   Even when we succeed in convincing the patient to partake of treatment, he or she may opt out of it prematurely, that is, before the therapist feels that an adequate trial has been provided.

3. *Treatment failures.*   Patients are considered failures when they do not respond to a procedure within a time period that normally would be expected to result in improvement. This may occur when the procedures are inappropriate given the presenting problem, when they are not carried out properly, or when particular characteristics of the patient hinder his or her ability to respond.

4. *Relapses.*   Finally, a patient may improve immediately after treatment but may not maintain his or her gains. Inasmuch as treatment is supposed to effect a long-term change, relapses are considered to be treatment failures.

REFUSALS AND DROPOUTS

Emmelkamp and his colleagues (Emmelkamp, van der Helm, van Zanten, & Ploch, 1980; Emmelkamp & Kraanen, 1977) and Foa and Goldstein (1978) reported that relatively few obsessive-compulsives (5 to 13 percent) refused to participate in exposure and response prevention treatment. A higher rate of refusal of help, 25 percent, was reported for two large samples of obsessive-compulsives treated at the Maudsley (Marks, Hodgson, & Rachman, 1975; Rachman et al., 1979). This rate is in accord with our current finding. We are presently in the process of contacting these individuals in order to investigate their reasons for refusing our treatment, the status of their symptoms during the intervening period, and whether they sought other types of treatment elsewhere. At present we can only draw on our clinical impressions.

The rate of dropouts from behavioural treatment is surprisingly low. Emmelkamp reported no dropouts in one study (Emmelkamp, & Kraanen, 1977) and a 12 percent dropout rate in a second (Emmelkamp et al., 1980). Marks, Hodgson, and Rachman (1975) and Rachman et al. (1979) report a 6 percent dropout rate in a total sample of 130 patients. In our center only 3 patients out of the 80 who participated in various studies (3 percent) did not complete their trial. Possible reasons for refusing to enter treatment and for failure to complete it are discussed below.

Attitude Toward Treatment

Some patients seek treatment because of family pressure rather than because of a conviction that they should rid themselves of their symptoms. One such patient came to the initial interview accompanied by an angry and desperate husband. During the past 20 years, at the wife's insistence, the family had moved frequently from one residence to another to escape contamination and to start anew in a "clean" environment. Each time, within several months, the family ended up living exclusively in the dining room, eating and sleeping there. This was done at the request of the patient in order to prevent contamination of the entire house and the resulting excruciating cleaning activities. The husband pleaded for help while the patient remained aloof and disinterested throughout the interview. There was little doubt that her refusal of help reflected lack of interest in altering her behavior.

In contrast to this patient, others express intense distress regarding their symptoms. Yet, after learning about the nature of the treatment and the potential discomfort they will have to undergo, they lack the courage to proceed. They either choose to live with the severe restrictions imposed by the disorder or they seek a less rigorous, "more comfortable," treatment elsewhere. A patient who feared contamination by people critical of her, particularly her husband, was quite impatient with her extremely restrictive lifestyle. She had been in psychoanalytic treatment for eight years to no avail. As she proceeded through four sessions of preliminary interviews, she became increasingly apprehensive about the agony she anticipated would ensue from exposure and prevention treatment. She finally refused treatment. A year later she called to inquire about "new developments"; she was hoping that we had found a way of curing obsessive-compulsives without torturing them.

An illustration of the extent to which exposure and response prevention can terrify patients is found in a woman who felt contaminated by death-associated objects and locations, such as coffins, funeral homes, and cemeteries. At the time she sought treatment she had been confined to bed, avoiding any contact with the external world and permitting only her husband to feed her. She rejected exposure treatment and instead chose to undergo psychosurgery. Her choice was dictated by the fact that she feared psychosurgery less than confrontation of her contaminants. Only when surgery failed to produce changes did she finally return for behavioral treatment.

In summary, when the commitment to overcome the obsessive-compulsive fears exceeds the anticipatory fear of the treatment procedures, the patient is ready to submit to the uncomfortable set of interventions that we offer. In fact, a number of individuals who refused treatment for this reason have returned at a later time when their motivation to change overrode their fear of treatment.

Expectations regarding the efficacy of treatment is yet another factor influencing the patient's decision to reject or undergo treatment. Realizing that by the end of treatment their entire environment will be contaminated, patients are justified in asking "What if it doesn't work? How will I ever restore the state of cleanliness necessary for me to feel comfortable again?" Those who lack confidence that treatment will substantially reduce their fears of contamination find the risk of undergoing exposure and response prevention too great.

A belief that exposure and/or response prevention will increase the *realistic* probability that feared future catastrophes will materialize is yet another factor

---

*We assume here that severity of symptoms was among the 21 variables that Rachman et al. found unrelated to outcome.

in rejection of treatment. One prospective patient, a 21-year-old male, avoided contact with bathroom germs and feared that if he was dirty, he would not be able to register important information he might be told. He refused treatment on the grounds that his safety measures were necessary to maintain his health and mental faculties. In his mind, response prevention would endanger him. Elsewhere we have labeled this type of reasoning "overvalued ideation" (Foa, 1979).

In summary, lack of motivation to improve, lack of courage to undergo a stressful treatment, and disbelief in the efficacy and safety of treatment interfere with willingness to avail oneself of treatment.

Situational Constraints

The regimen we offer is quite demanding of the patients' time and effort. In practice we request that their lives revolve almost entirely around treatment for a period of three to four weeks. They receive two hours of treatment daily as well as homework exercises for an additional four hours per day. Inasmuch as we require that response prevention be supervised, patients are asked to enlist the support and constant presence of a family member or friend throughout the treatment period. Hospitalization is required of those who come from out of town or who do not have adequate arrangements for supervision. These demands can be easily accommodated by persons who have few everyday obligations. For those who, despite severe symptoms, manage to hold jobs or carry out family responsibilities, such requirements are difficult to meet and may lead to a refusal to enter treatment. On the other hand, the ostensible rejection of treatment because of lack of time or other logistical reasons, may reflect low motivation or fear of treatment. Most patients who legimately reject treatment because of such constraints enter therapy at a later point after they have made all of the required arrangements.

Therapist Characteristics

During the past several years six therapists have treated the vast majority of our 80 obsessive-compulsive patients. Most refusals of treatment took place at preliminary interviews with the therapist. Of six patients who dropped out during this information-gathering phase, four had been assigned to the same therapist. This therapist also treated one of the two patients who terminated therapy midway through behavioral treatment. We have not assessed our therapists' characteristics or patients' perception of their therapists. However, subjective judgment of the interaction between this therapist and patients suggested a lack of warmth and empathy and an arrogant attitude.

Hadley and Strupp (1976) have reported the therapist to be an oft-cited source of negative effects in psychotherapy. But, as suggested by Mathews, Johnston,

*This research was supported by Grant MH-31634 from the Clinical Research Branch of the National Institute of Mental Health awarded to Edna B. Foa.

Shaw, and Gelder (1973), the personal qualities of the therapist, which appear to be central to outcome of psychotherapy, have less impact on the more precisely formulated techniques of behavioral therapy. It is likely that the more powerful the therapeutic procedure employed, the less potent will be the effect of the therapist. However, during the preliminary stages of information gathering (which are more similar to traditional psychotherapeutic interventions), the interaction between the therapist and the patient may determine whether the patient will give us the opportunity to provide him or her with proper treatment.

Interestingly, once they begin the intensive phase of the treatment program, obsessive-compulsives seldom terminate prematurely. As noted above, only three of our sample of patients dropped out. This is a startling finding especially if one contrasts it with the high rate of premature dropouts in another group of severe anxiety neurotics, agoraphobics (see Chapter 4). One explanation is that in order to undergo the rigorous treatment program required of them, our patients have made quite elaborate arrangements, thereby strengthening their commitment and making it a "public" one. It is also possible that inasmuch as the program is of brief duration, even those who are quite apprehensive and who experience considerable initial discomfort may feel they can tolerate this state on a short-term basis. Finally, obsessive-compulsives may have a strong sense of responsibility and, once committed to the program, feel compelled to follow through. Whatever the reason, premature termination of treatment has not presented a problem in our experience.

TREATMENT FAILURES AND RELAPSES

How Do We Define Treatment Failure?

The widely accepted definition of failure as a lack of noticeable change and/or lack of maintenance of change over time is not without problems. The first problem lies in defining the goals of treatment. Consider a situation in which at the end of treatment the patient still washes much more than a normal individual but improved her relationship with her husband and resumed her job. Another patient after treatment washes her hands briefly only five times per day; yet, her lifestyle remains restricted, her marriage is still unhappy, and she feels unable to resume the career she left because of her symptoms. Who benefited more from treatment? Many obsessive-compulsives experience a general difficulty in making decisions and are imbued with doubts in numerous aspects of their functioning. If this cognitive style does not change with the reduction of the compulsive rituals, have we failed to "cure" the obsessive-compulsive symptoms?

The first issue in defining failure, then, relates to the delineation of treatment goals. Despite existing relationships between various behaviors in the same individual, it is inconceivable that any single procedure will affect a variety of divergent behaviors. For instance, there is no reason to expect treatment by exposure to contaminants to improve the patient's social skills. Therefore, a successful procedure is one that alters the set of behaviors toward which it is directed. As Cawley (1974) notes, "It is clear that in assessing treatment the hypotheses must be meaningful within the terms of what is claimed for the treatment in question" (p. 278). If several sets of behaviors require change, several techniques known to affect each should be employed. The success and failure of each technique should then be measured separately. Here, our main focus will be on the obsessive-compulsive symptomatology, that is, fears (obsessions) and ritualistic behavior (compulsions).

Assuming we have the proper tools to accurately assess the specified behavior (and it is hoped we will improve upon these with time), how much change is required for treatment to be considered successful? Conversely, how little change constitutes failure? One patient used to wash her hands 40 times a day using five bars of soap; at the end of treatment she washed 12 times and used two bars of soap. Is she a success or a failure? The answer will vary from one therapist to another, from one researcher to another. Moreover, there is often a discrepancy between the patient's definition of success and that of the therapist. For example, a patient who had engaged in washing rituals for about four hours per day defined herself as much improved with three hours of ritualizing. We considered her a failure.

There are several ways in which treatment success and failure can be examined. One way is to observe the state of the symptomatology after treatment. This is exemplified by Foa and Goldstein (1978) who divided their sample of 21 patients into four discrete categories: absent, mild, moderate, and severe symptoms, the last category representing the failures. Alternately, responsiveness to treatment can be defined by the degree of change from pretreatment to posttreatment. For example, Marks, Hodgson, and Rachman (1975) divided their sample into three categories: "much improved" were those who showed a change score of 4 or more points on a 9-point scale, the "improved" group evidenced a change of 2 to 3.9 points and the "not improved" patients changed less than 2 points. Similarly, Emmelkamp and van de Hout (see Chapter 4) dichotomized their sample of agoraphobics on the basis of change scores; patients with change scores of 3 points or less on a 9-point scale were identified as failures and the remainder were considered successes. The choice of how much change marks a success and how little a failure is often arbitrary. Ideally, the researcher will use cutoff points that correspond to a clinically significant change.

Another way of examining treatment outcome is to compute the relative rather than the absolute degree of change from pretreatment baseline. In investigating the differences between success and failure we have chosen to define outcome by the percentage of change from pretreatment scores. Those who improved 30 percent or less are classified as failures, those who improved 70 percent or more are considered successes, and the remaining patients are categorized as improved. This method is not without disadvantages. For example, is a 50 percent symptom reduction in patients who improved from 8 to 4 equivalent to a 50 percent reduction in those who began at 4 and reduced to 2? The former changed more in absolute terms than the latter, yet both will be put in the same category by our criterion. Still we feel that this type of data transformation conveys most accurately the concept of improvement.

Failure Due to Inadequate Treatment

Altogether, five different treatment programs were implemented in our center: (1) imaginal exposure only; (2) exposure in vivo only; (3) response prevention only; (4) exposure in vivo and response prevention; (5) imaginal exposure, in vivo exposure, and response prevention. Which treatments are most likely to lead to failure? More specifically, are treatments that include both exposure and response prevention less likely to result in failure than treatment by a single component? To answer this question the five programs were collapsed into two categories: combined versus single-component treatments. The combined treatments were comprised of treatments 4 and 5 above; the remaining treatments constituted the single-component group.

Measurements

Treatment outcome was measured as follows: Two independent assessors rated each patient on a 9-point scale with regard to severity of obsessions and of compulsions. These ratings were obtained before treatment, at posttreatment, and at follow-up. The ratings of the assessors were averaged so that for each patient two scores were obtained at each rating point, one for obsessions and one for compulsions. These were again averaged, resulting in a single measure of obsessive-compulsive symptoms at each assessment. The posttreatment and follow-up ratings were then transformed into percent change scores from the pretreatment score.

Treatment with Single or Combined Components

As noted earlier, the 72 obsessive-compulsives whose data were analyzed for the present study were divided into three groups: "much improved" (gains of 70 percent or more), "improved" (gains of 31 to 69 percent), and "failures" (30 percent or less). The data was then tabulated in a 2 (type of treatment) $\times$ 3 (degree of improvement) table for posttreatment and for follow-up (see Tables 2.1 and 2.2). At posttreatment, 12.5 percent failed to benefit from either single or combination treatments, 44 percent were improved and 43.5 percent were much improved. Of those who failed, the majority (78 percent) had received a single treatment. At follow-up with 58 patients, 33 percent failed to benefit, 17 percent were improved, and 50 percent were much improved. Of those who received combined treatments, only about 25 percent failed, in contrast to 66 percent failures among those who had single-component treatments. The mean percent improvements for the combined treatment was .72 at posttreatment and .61 at follow-up. By contrast, the corresponding means for the single-component treatments were .43 and .25, respectively. [For posttreatment, $F(1, 69) = 22.43, p < .001$; for follow-up, $F(1, 55) = 7.21, p < .01$]. In general, then, patients receiving the single components did significantly worse than those receiving combined treatments.

Table 2.1.   Comparison of Outcome at Posttreatment by Treatment Program

	Much Improved	Improved	Failures	
Combined treatment	29	19	2	50
Single components	2	13	7	22
	31	32	9	72

Table 2.2.   Comparison of Outcome at Follow-Up by Treatment Program

	Much Improved	Improved	Failures	
Combined treatment	27	8	11	46
Single components	2	2	8	12
	29	10	19	58

Why is treatment by a single component more likely to lead to failure than treatment by exposure and response prevention? What happened to the obsessions and the compulsions of patients who were treated by either exposure or response prevention? Successful treatment should result in both reduction of anxiety to feared stimuli (e.g., contaminants) and amelioration of ritualistic behavior. Foa, Steketee, and Milby (1980) found that obsessive-compulsive washers who were treated by response prevention only (with no deliberate exposure) evinced very little reduction in anxiety when confronted with their most feared contaminant, whereas ritualistic behavior was successfully eliminated by this technique. The opposite pattern was observed for those who received in vivo exposure but no response prevention. Their fears were greatly reduced but they failed to show substantial decrease in compulsions. Treatment in which both deliberate exposure and response prevention was implemented affected both the anxiety and the rituals.

The theoretical implications of the differential effects of exposure and response prevention are discussed elsewhere (Foa, Steketee, & Milby, 1980; Steketee, Grayson, & Foa, 1981). Their clinical implications are quite clear: Because response prevention does not greatly reduce anxiety to contaminants, urges to wash persist. Refraining from rituals, then, is accomplished only through extensive avoidance of contaminants. When avoidance fails to protect the patient from anxiety, a relapse is likely to occur. However, we observed that the implementation of response prevention alone motivated some patients to deliberately expose themselves (and face contaminants courageously). If these patients continued to refrain from ritualizing, anxiety eventually decreased. Thus, whether planned by a therapist or self-induced, both prolonged exposure and response prevention should take place in order to successfully treat the obsessive-compulsive symptoms.

Imaginal Exposure

The use of imaginal exposure in the treatment of obsessive-compulsives has been limited. This is in line with the general disenchantment with imaginal procedures in the treatment of anxiety-based disorders following the findings that exposure in fantasy does not result in as much change as in vivo exposure (e.g., Emmelkamp, & Wessels, 1975; Rabavilas, Boulougouris, & Stefanis, 1976). But the fears of some obsessive-compulsives, in particular, checkers, center around responsibility for potential catastrophes (e.g., causing fire, killing one's child). Will neglecting to expose patients to such fears (by imaginal exposure) result in their failure to benefit from treatment? To answer this question, 15 obsessive-compulsives with checking rituals were divided into two groups. Seven were treated with a combination of imaginal exposure, in vivo exposure, and response prevention. The remaining eight did not receive imaginal exposure and thus were not exposed systematically to their feared "disasters." Immediately after treatment, both groups improved to an approximately equal extent. At follow-up, however, those who did not have imaginal exposure relapsed considerably, whereas the group who were exposed to their feared catastrophes maintained their gains. Thus the omission of imaginal exposure seems to increase the probability of a relapse (Foa, Steketee, Turner, & Fischer, 1980).

Response to Treatment and Maintenance of Gains

The patient's state at the termination of treatment and how he or she does one year later are quite related ($r = .57, p < .001$). A crosstabulation of the results at posttreatment and at follow-up again indicated a highly significant relationship [$\chi^2 (4) = 2.16, p < .002$]. Both those who were much improved or who failed at the end of treatment remained so at follow-up. None of the failures improved with time and only 23 percent of the successes deteriorated, 10 percent relapsing completely. In contrast to the relative stability of the extreme groups, partial improvement proved an unstable state. Only 24 percent of this group remained in this category at follow-up, 28 percent improved further, and 48 percent relapsed. Thus, those who are only partly improved after treatment are likely to become failures within a short time.

In summary, in order to both ameliorate anxiety and decrease ritualistic behavior, treatment for obsessive-compulsives should include at least a combination of in vivo exposure and response prevention. Partial treatment produces failures or at best partial improvement; the latter, in turn, are likely to become failures at follow-up. Therefore, to establish long-term maintenance of gains, we should not be content with partial treatments; ways to enhance success must be developed. One possible method is to increase the number of treatment sessions. We have *not* improved our average success rate by increasing the number of sessions from 10 to 15, but these findings do not necessarily mean that individual patients will not benefit from additional sessions. Further, the number of relapses may be reduced with the addition of imaginal exposure for those who fear the disastrous consequences of not ritualizing.

Despite our efforts to tailor treatment individually to patients, some simply do not get better. What do we know about these individuals?

Failure and Attitude Toward Treatment

Expectancy

Among the most studied of the nonspecific variables in treatment is the patient's expectation of improvement (Kazdin & Wilcoxon, 1976; Rosenthal & Frank, 1958). Generally, those who believe that treatment will help do better than those who lack faith in it. Our obsessive-compulsives followed this rule to some extent ($r = .46$, $p = .03$). Positive expectancy alone is unlikely to result in successful treatment unless the appropriate treatment procedure has been applied. Amongst our patients, the mean expectancy of those who received "good" treatment did not differ from that of those who received inadequate procedures, yet the former benefited more.

Commitment

The most common reason for unresponsiveness to exposure and response prevention treatment reported by the Maudsley investigators was lack of compliance with treatment procedures. In discussing failures, Rachman and Hodgson (1980) note that

> The first and most common, it seems, is inability or unwillingness on the part of the patient to suspend or delay carrying out his or her rituals. The second type of failure arises from inability to tolerate the stress of the exposure treatment sessions . . .at the end of three weeks of daily treatment they (those who cannot tolerate exposure) may have progressed no further than the ability to touch two or three contaminated items with the tip of one finger. (p. 327)

These observations that a failure to comply with either the exposure or the response prevention instructions interferes with treatment gains are congruent with our findings regarding treatment by single components. It is conceivable that patients who do not adhere to the procedural requirements of treatment are even more likely to fail than those who receive partial treatment; in addition to permitting only partial treatment, their noncommitment may reflect other factors (e.g., low expectancy) that may impede success.

Nonadherence to the treatment program is the most obvious manifestation of lack of commitment. More subtle ones exist. Some patients comply with the "letter of the law" as laid down by the therapist, yet continue to avoid any feared stimuli not explicitly assigned for exposure. Others may refrain from washing their hands but will use hand lotion or will symbolically wipe off their hands to decrease contamination. Some patients are able to make a short-term but not a long-term commitment; they pledge (to themselves) to comply with the stringent demands of a brief treatment, but as expressed by one of our patients, "In the back of my mind, I always knew I would start washing as soon as the treatment was over." This patient was, indeed, considerably improved at the end of treatment but relapsed within a short period of time. The first type of lack of commitment, failure to comply with the treatment requirements, results in immediate failure; the more subtle forms seem to lead to relapse after a period of improvement.

It is clear why patients who do not adhere to a treatment program fail to benefit from it. Such cases do not present a theoretical challenge to our current treatment of obsessive-compulsives. Yet, they pose a serious problem common to all treatment techniques that require high levels of motivation. Although we do know how to manipulate some cognitive variables, such as expectancy about treatment effects, we have little success in our attempts to convert the uncommitted into enthusiasts. We do not possess the knowledge of how to manipulate the degree of commitment, an essential prerequisite for success.

Characteristics of Those Who Fail

Earlier attempts to identify prognostic variables have not been very fruitful. In correlating 21 pretreatment variables with five outcome criteria, Rachman and his colleagues found no "pointers" (Rachman & Hodgson, 1980). By contrast, in our sample of 72 patients we have found several variables to be associated with outcome.

Depression

Several authors have noted that the presence of severe depression hinders the effectiveness of treatment by exposure and response prevention (e.g., Foa, 1979; Foa, Steketee, & Groves, 1979; Marks, 1973, 1977). Likewise, the temporary interference of depressive mood with progress during treatment, resulting at times in loss of previous gains, was described by Rachman and Hodgson (1980, p. 80). Foa, Steketee, and Groves (1979) treated a severely depressed obsessive-compulsive with exposure and response prevention without success; only after the introduction of imipramine did anxiety associated with contaminants dissipate. In a sample of 15 patients, Boulougouris (1977) found a high negative correlation between patients' self-ratings of depression and their follow-up scores on the Leyton, although not with their scores on the main obsession.

A strong relationship between initial depression (averaged patient's and assessor's ratings on a 9-point scale) and treatment outcome was found by Foa, Grayson, and Steketee (1981). Forty-seven obsessive-compulsives were divided into three groups according to severity of depression. The highly depressed patients improved less than did the low depressed ones on obsessions and on compulsions both at posttreatment and at follow-up. Moreover, the severely depressed patients evinced a greater relapse rate than did the other two groups.

We further explored the association between depression and treatment outcome in our sample of 72 obsessive-compulsives. This time patients were divided into three groups according to their response to treatment, as well as according to three levels of depression. Those whose depression rating was greater than 1 S.D. above the mean were labeled severely depressed, those with a rating greater than 1 S.D. below the mean were called mildly depressed, and the remainder were classified as moderately depressed. The relationship between depression and outcome was then explored by crosstabulating the two variables at posttreatment [χ^2 (4) = 15.99, $p < .003$] and at follow-up [χ^2 (4) = 12.54, $p < .01$]. Patients who evinced mild depression did not fail; most were highly successful. On the other hand, severely depressed patients improved moderately at posttreatment and tended to relapse at follow-up. Those with moderate depression also tended to show moderate improvement at the end of treatment; some had relapsed at follow-up.

Anxiety

It is often claimed that in neurotic populations measures of anxiety and depression may reflect the same variable. Indeed, we have found a sizeable correlation (.53) between these two variables. Is anxiety related to outcome in the same manner found for depression? To answer this question patients were divided into three groups according to their level of anxiety (in the same manner as for depression). Anxiety was then crosstabulated with outcome at posttreatment [χ^2 (4) = 10.53, $p < .03$] and at follow-up [χ^2 (4) = 9.56, $p < .05$]. Although both depression and anxiety were found to be related to treatment outcome, two distinct patterns emerged. Patients who evinced initial mild anxiety were much improved and retained their gains at follow-up. However, unlike the highly depressed obsessive-compulsives, those with high anxiety were not necessarily doomed to fail. In fact, both the highly and moderately anxious patients responded nearly identically both at the end of treatment and at follow-up. Thus low anxiety facilitated success but high anxiety did not hinder it.

In summary, patients showing initial low depression and low anxiety are very likely to benefit most from treatment. Those with high depression regardless of their anxiety levels will fail or relapse, and patients with high anxiety and low depression may go either way.

Age at Symptom Onset.

In addition to depression and anxiety, age at symptom onset was found highly negatively correlated with outcome at follow-up ($r = -.49$, $p < .001$) but not at posttreatment. That is, the younger the individual was when symptoms began, the better he or she maintained improvement. It is important to note that *duration* of symptoms was unrelated to response to treatment, nor was the patient's *age* at the time of treatment associated with outcome. Perhaps age of symptom onset is associated with maintenance of treatment gains through its relationship to other personality variables. Would early onsetters show better ability to cope with their symptoms? Will they manifest less of the "obsessional personality" characterized by indecisiveness and doubts? Do they have better social skills? At this point we cannot answer these questions. However, onset age may be a pointer to other possible predictors.

Obviously, we are unable to alter age of onset but we may be able to identify the personality characteristics associated with it. We may, then, be able to modify these "traits" or behaviors and possibly improve outcome. In the meantime, we should attempt to reduce the degree of anxiety and of depression that patients experience by psychological or pharmacological means in an effort to improve a patient's odds of responding to treatment.

In addition to depression, anxiety, and age at symptom onset, we also explored other factors that we expected to predict outcome. Surprisingly, we did not find them to be related to degree of responsiveness to treatment.

Overvalued Ideation

Foa (1979) proposed that patients who strongly believe that their fears are *realistic* and that their ritualistic behavior prevents the occurrence of *actual* disasters fail to benefit from treatment. Consequently, we have devised a self-administered scale to measure what we have labeled "overvalued ideation." No relationship between treatment outcome and scores on this measure were detected. However, the validity of this method of assessing overvalued ideation is questionable, inasmuch as patients evidenced difficulty in following the instructions. Many patients included "being very anxious" as a disaster and, of course, rated it as a highly probable occurrence. In this manner, some patients with little or no true overvalued ideations received high scores on our measure. On the basis of our experience we have revised the questionnaire and will again explore the relationship between the strength of belief and failure to benefit from behavioral treatment.

Duration and Severity of Symptoms

Based on theoretical considerations (Walton & Mather, 1963), we expected both long duration and great severity of obsessive-compulsive symptomatology to be associated with poor response to treatment. The longer a patient has engaged in compulsive behavior and the more he or she emits these behaviors, the stronger should be the habit, and thus the more resistance to extinction should be evident. Surprisingly, no such relationships have been found by other researchers (Boulougouris, 1977; Meyer, Levy, & Schnurer, 1974; Rachman, Marks, & Hodgson, 1973) nor by us in our sample of 72 patients. We should remember, however, that very few of our patients had their symptoms for less than three years. It could well be that by this time the habit is quite established. Likewise, one of our primary criteria for patient selection was high severity of symptoms. It is entirely possible that in a sample with a wider range of initial severity and duration of symptoms, these two factors would be associated with outcome. It is clear, however, that neither long duration nor severe symptomatology necessarily increase the probability of failure to respond to treatment.

Type of Rituals

Clinical observations have led researchers to distinguish between patients manifesting checking rituals and those engaging in washing rituals (Rachman, & Hodgson, 1980). The former were found to be more resistant to change by Boulougouris (1977) and by Rachman and Hodgson (1980). However, Foa and

Goldstein (1978) reported that their seven checkers benefited as much from treatment as did their 14 washers. With a sample of 24 checkers and 48 washers we again found that the type of rituals was not related to treatment outcome.

Can the Therapist Impede Success?

It has been demonstrated that a major involvement of the therapist is not a necessary factor for exposure treatment to effect change (e.g., Emmelkamp & Kraanen, 1977). Yet many obsessive-compulsives find themselves unable to implement exposure and response prevention on their own. A very articulate patient provided the following insight on this issue:

> It is very difficult to stick with an object when you feel contaminated, are sick inside, and your panic keeps increasing, if you do not know that the feeling will pass. There must be a depth of trust in the therapist the patient can feel that will permeate the barrier of doubt and fear as the treatment moves along. It seems that the therapist is important during the high anxiety periods because the anxiety makes one want to return to one's usual way of dealing with anxiety—avoidance. (Foa & Goldstein, 1978)

Informal observations have also led Marks, Hodgson, and Rachman (1975) to suggest that "this treatment requires a good *patient–therapist working relationship,* and a sense of humor helps patients over difficult situations" (p. 360). Some of their patients also commented that they could contaminate themselves following the therapist's instructions, although they could not do so previously when urged by their spouses.

Therapist qualities of warmth, support, and empathy have long been recognized as important in any psychotherapeutic treatment (e.g., Truax & Carkuff, 1967). Our clinical observations have led us to suggest that, indeed, these qualities facilitate the execution of treatment by exposure and response prevention but, in addition, firmness and insistence are necessary (Foa & Tillmanns, 1980). A prospective study by Rabavilas, Boulougouris, and Perissaki (1979) confirmed these observations. In their study phobic and obsessive-compulsive patients who had been treated by exposure in vivo were asked to rate their therapists on 16 variables related either to the therapist's attitude or to the way in which he or she conducted treatment. Patients who rated their therapists as respectful, understanding, interested, encouraging, challenging, and explicit improved more. On the other hand, gratification of dependency needs, permissiveness, and tolerance were negatively related to outcome.

How Do Failures Respond During Exposure?

Most psychotherapies share a common assumption that confrontation with discomfort-evoking material is central to the therapeutic process. In this regard, prolonged or repeated exposure has been found to be a powerful manipulation for effecting change in anxiety-based disorders. We know it brings about habituation (i.e., response decrement) of psychophysiological and subjective manifestations of anxiety (e.g., Foa & Chambless, 1978; Watson, Gaind, & Marks, 1972). It also decreases avoidance behaviors and urges to ritualize in obsessive-compulsives (Likierman & Rachman, 1980; Rachman, de Silva, & Roper, 1976). If exposure brings about a decrement in anxiety, why do some patients fail to benefit from exposure treatments? Moreover, why do some individuals fail to benefit from naturally occurring environmental exposures?

Proponents of treatment by exposure postulate that the greater the number of relevant cues included in the exposure and the greater the emotional reactivity to these cues, the more complete will be the *emotional processing* and thus the better will be the outcome. Lang, Melamed, and Hart (1970), in a study of process and outcome variables in desensitization, were among the first to provide information supporting the above proposition. In brief, they found that greater initial psychophysiological responses to imaginal presentations of phobic situations were associated with greater habituation and better treatment outcome. They interpreted these results as evidence that greater processing of the phobic scenes took place in subjects who benefited from treatment. Since then other researchers have corroborated and extended these findings (e.g., Borkovec & Sides, 1979; Grayson & Borkovec, 1978). In a recent thought-provoking paper, Rachman (1980) discussed the concept of emotional processing: "Emotional processing is regarded as a process whereby emotional disturbances are absorbed and decline to the extent that other experiences and behavior can proceed without disruption."

We propose that the normal course of successful absorption of a disturbing experience is gradual. Individuals gauge their ability to tolerate upsetting stimuli, confronting only that information which they can successfully process. When a highly stressful event occurs (such as loss of loved one, rape, serious accident, etc.), one begins to process it by engaging only parts of the associated cues, perhaps the least painful ones. When responses to these habituate, more upsetting cues, hitherto too painful to approach, lose some of their impetus through a process of generalization. They are then confronted (thought about, talked about, visualized, etc.) and eventually processed as well. This procedure continues until all the relevant disturbing cues are successfully processed; that is, exposure to them no longer evokes undue disturbance.

A set of second mechanisms that may take place concurrently with habituation during emotional processing is cognitive. We suggest that as a result of exposure, disturbing events are reclassified (relabeled) and their perceived meaning changes as they become less emotionally laden. These cognitive changes, in turn, are responsible for long-term (between sessions) habituation. (For further discussion see Foa, 1979.)

Failures in Emotional Processing

When emotional processing breaks down, habituation fails to occur, cognitions do not change, and the stimuli continue to be anxiety or discomfort provoking. At least two paths may lead to such a breakdown. The first is excessive behavioral or cognitive avoidance; the individual prevents himself or herself from experiencing enough of the significant disturbing cues or from responding emotionally to them to allow processing to take place. The second is excessive arousal in the presence of feared stimuli. Such an excessive fear response will impede both habituation and the cognitive changes necessary for emotional processing.

Let us turn to the first cause of unsuccessful processing: excessive avoidance. Advocates of exposure have expended much time in developing techniques to increase the amount of exposure to the discomfort-evoking stimuli. However, patients who are accustomed to emotionally blocking unpleasant experiences may continue to do so even when deliberately confronted in vivo with disturbing stimuli. As Borkovec and Grayson (1980) have suggested,

> Objective presentation of stimuli does not guarantee functional exposure to those stimuli . . .events which interfere with or facilitate the subjects' awareness and/or processing of the information (the feared stimuli) will critically influence the effect of those procedures on a targeted emotional behavior. (p. 117)

Exposure that proved to be nonfunctional (cognitively avoided) is exemplified by one of our patients. During exposure sessions, her main contaminant (urine) was put on several places on her arms. Initially she was overwhelmed with anxiety but calmed down very quickly. In response to our inquiry about her rapid drop in reported discomfort, she related a curious avoidance technique: she "froze" the contaminated spot in her mind, thereby preventing the spread of the contamination to other parts of her body. Once under control, her feelings of contamination and associated anxiety decreased. In her case, the observed rapid reduction in discomfort did not reflect successful emotional processing but rather successful avoidance. Habituation between sessions was minimal and she made little progress. Obviously, in cases of excessive avoidance we need to develop attention-focusing techniques to enhance exposure.

Let us turn now to the second reason for failure of emotional processing: excessive reactivity in the presence of disturbing stimuli. Will exposure treatment enhance emotional processing under such conditions? Some findings lead to the prediction that this will not be the case. Lader and Wing (1966) reported that complex phobics (agoraphobics, social phobics, anxiety states, etc.) showed greater general arousal (evidenced by more spontaneous fluctuations, higher skin conductance level, higher pulse rate) and less habituation of evoked skin conductance responses to neutral stimuli than did simple phobics; the latter, in turn, were more aroused when confronted with phobic stimuli and habituated more slowly than normals, whereas subjects with agitated depression evidenced greater arousal and slower habituation. These results have been replicated in other populations with differing anxiety levels (e.g., Katkin & McCubbin, 1969; Lykken & Venables, 1972). Further support for the contention that initial high levels of anxiety hinder habituation comes from Grey, Sartory, and Rachman (1979) who studied phobic subjects. These authors found that subjects who were exposed to situations that aroused moderate anxiety evidenced greater habituation on subjective ratings of anxiety than did those exposed to highly disturbing situations. Other investigators have observed that high intensity stimuli appear to hinder habituation in animals (Davis & Wagner, 1969; Groves & Thompson, 1970), as well as in humans (Grayson, 1979; O'Gorman, & Jamieson, 1975). Patients whose arousal levels are extremely high may then fail to habituate. Too much reactivity may produce such a failure by impeding an individual's ability to process incoming information about the feared stimuli.

Indirect evidence that processing of disturbing events is optimal with moderate reactivity comes from Gur, Reivich, Rosen, Alavi, Greenberg, and Gur (1981) who measured metabolic activity in the frontocortical region of the brain. It was suggested that this region had a major involvement in the regulation of anxiety and negative affect. The metabolic rate of subjects undergoing an unpleasant medical procedure was plotted against their state anxiety score on the Spielberger State-Trait Inventory. A curvilinear relationship was found: Metabolic rates in the frontocortical regions of the brain increased as a function of anxiety up to a point above which greater anxiety was associated with decreased metabolic activity. This pattern was not observed in other regions not hypothesized to regulate anxiety. If metabolic rate can be taken as an indicator of the amount of information processed, then Gur et al.'s findings might indicate that both high and low anxious individuals process anxiety-related information less than do those who are moderately aroused. The optimal state for successful processing, then, may be one of moderate arousal.

The idea that emotional processing is best achieved under a moderate degree of arousal is embedded in Rachman's (1980) list of factors that impede or promote this process. Among the promoting factors are "engaged exposure," no distraction, and vivid presentations. All of these are expected to enhance emotional response. However, relaxation, which is designed to reduce emotional reactivity, is also considered a factor that promotes processing. Among the impeding factors are avoidance behavior, distractions, and unresponsive autonomic reactions, all of which seem to relate to emotional response. But Rachman also included excessively large "chunks" among the factors impeding emotional processing, perhaps because they lead to excessive reactivity.

Depression, Arousal, Habituation, and Outcome

Failure to habituate within exposure sessions as well as between (across) sessions has been reported by Foa (1979) and by Foa, Steketee, and Groves (1979) in severely depressed obsessive-compulsives. At that time we suggested that the failure of depressed individuals to benefit from exposure and response prevention treatment was due to their failure to habituate. But the picture emerging from further investigation of this proposition is more complex.

Habituation between sessions and, to a lesser degree, habituation within sessions was found to be positively related to treatment outcome, but the relationship between depression and habituation between sessions was weaker than expected ($r = -.35$). Nevertheless, we found that when first presented with the most feared situation, severely depressed patients reacted with a higher level of anxiety than did mildly depressed patients ($r = .61$). This level of initial reactivity, in turn, was negatively correlated with habituation across sessions ($r = -.54$). Further analysis seemed to suggest that the relationship between depression and intersession habituation is mediated by the level of reactivity (Foa, Grayson, & Steketee, 1981). Perhaps, then, it is the greater reactivity manifested by the depressed patients that hinders their emotional processing and impedes the effectiveness of treatment.

Further support for the association of treatment failure, habituation, and initial reactivity was provided by Foa, Grayson, Steketee, and Doppelt (1981). Habituation within and between sessions were both found to be greater in the most improved group at posttreatment. At follow-up habituation between sessions (but not within sessions) was related to treatment outcome. As expected, the degree of reactivity was also found associated with outcome at posttreatment but not at follow-up. These results suggest that very high (excessive) reactivity to disturbing material hinders rather than facilitates successful emotional processing as indicated by the degree of habituation of subjective anxiety; this, in turn, results in inferior outcome. Depressed individuals seem to have a greater tendency to respond with excessive reactivity and thus show poorer outcome. Lang et al's (1970) high reactors, who habituated more and benefited more from treatment, were volunteers and may not have been as aroused as our reactive group of patients. If the former were moderately aroused, a linear relationship between level of arousal, habituation, and treatment outcome would be expected, as was found by Lang et al., rather than the curvilinear association suggested here.

The preceding discussion suggests that in planning our exposure treatment sessions we should strive to increase the reactivity of "avoiders" and decrease the arousal level of "overreactors." It may also be important to control the state of arousal throughout and immediately after treatment in order to ensure that a relapse does not occur due to excessive arousal when the patient returns to a normal routine and responsibilities. Techniques by which the arousal level is regulated will probably vary from one patient to another. By now a few, such as relaxation and "habituation training" (Rachman, 1980), are available. Cognitive procedures have not yet proven successful with obsessive-compulsives (Emmelkamp et al., 1980). Clomipramine has been found helpful in enhancing the effects of behavioral treatment with depressed obsessive-compulsives (Marks et al., 1980), perhaps by decreasing initial reactivity and thereby promoting habituation. Whether antianxiety agents will also be of help is yet to be studied.

SUMMARY AND CONCLUSIONS

Treatment by exposure and response prevention benefits about 75 percent of the obsessive-compulsives who are willing to partake of it. In this paper we have attempted to delineate variables associated with failures. We hope that this information can be utilized to improve our treatments. Approximately 25 percent of those who are suitable for behavioral treatment reject it. Many of these patients refuse treatment because they fear the suffering it imposes. Perhaps we can reduce the number of failures by providing more information and support in the initial interviews. We definitely cannot make the treatment process less painful by neglecting to include any of its components. By omitting deliberate exposure, habituation of anxiety is impeded; the failure to institute response prevention results in continuation of ritualistic behavior; neglecting to include imaginal exposure may invite relapse (at least for checkers).

On the whole, the immediate response to treatment is strongly related to how one fares over time. More specifically, those who are much improved tend to maintain their gains and those who fail do not improve their lot with time. In contrast, moderate improvement is not a stable state. Most patients who fall into this category tend to relapse. Contentment with partial improvement is, therefore, unjustified; ways to enhance immediate treatment gains are needed. In our investigation of possible prognostic indicators for those who undergo an adequate trial of exposure and response prevention, we have found that severe depression prior to treatment was directly related to treatment outcome; the more depressed the patient, the poorer the immediate, as well as the longer term responsiveness to treatment. The relationship between depression and treatment outcome is linear: Those with high depression fail and those with low depression succeed. Such a pattern was not found for initial anxiety. Low initial anxiety was strongly related to successful outcome but high anxiety did not necessarily lead to failure. Although neither severity of symptoms nor their duration was associated with treatment gain, the age at which the obsessive-compulsive symptoms started was strongly related to outcome at follow-up, but not at posttreatment. We suggest that age of symptom onset may be related to personality variables which, in turn, are associated with maintenance of treatment effects. It is hoped that these characteristics will be identified in future investigations.

At least two processes have been found to take place during exposure: habituation (response decrement) of anxiety within sessions (which might be related to inhibitory mechanisms such as fatigue) and habituation between sessions (which might be related to mechanisms underlying cognitive change) (e.g., Foa & Chambless, 1978). Those who fail at posttreatment habituate less, both within and between sessions. The amount of habituation, in turn, is negatively related to the degree of reactivity to fear-arousing stimuli, and the latter is positively related to initial depression.

We have found that two types of factors, patient characteristics before entering treatment and their response during treatment, are related to responsiveness to treatment. On the basis of the foregoing results we have developed a prognostic model for obsessive-compulsives undergoing behavioral treatment which we hope will lead to early detection of potential treatment failures. This model, derived by path analysis, depicts the interrelationship among the seven variables that are associated with treatment outcome (see Figure 2.1). The time sequence of the variables is indicated by the arrows. The strength of each association is expressed by the size of the correlation coefficient next to each arrow. Technical aspects of the model are discussed in Foa, Grayson, Steketee, Doppelt, Turner, and Latimer (1981).

It is important to note that the variables included in the model occur within a time sequence that allows us to infer causality. For example, the model suggests that the more depressed one is, the greater will be one's reactivity on first introduction of feared stimuli. Some factors in the model are predicted by variables that occur earlier in time. They, in turn, predict succeeding ones. For example, pretreatment anxiety, type of treatment, and habituation between sessions predicts posttreatment response which then becomes a predictor of response at follow-up. The model proposes that some predictors have both direct and indirect effects; the level of depression directly affects initial reactivity and indirectly affects intrasession habituation through its effect upon the former. Finally, the predictive capability of the model is far from perfect. The multiple correlation of posttreatment outcome with its predictors is .70 ($p < .001$). It is likely then that other variables and paths not yet identified will be found.

Posttreatment response is a *direct* function of three variables: habituation between sessions, treatment type, and initial anxiety. As suggested by Foa (1979) and Foa, Grayson, and Steketee (1981) these results indicate that habituation between sessions plays an important role in determining the effectiveness of expo-

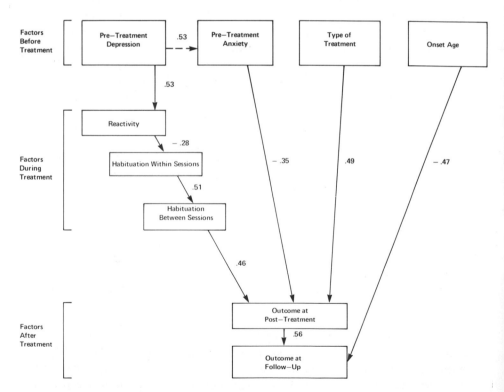

Figure 2.1. A model for predicting response to behavioral treatment of obsessive-compulsives.

sure treatment. A second factor directly related to outcome at posttreatment is the type of treatment (single versus composite), which was not found to affect process variables. Inasmuch as the main difference between the single and combination treatments was the addition of response prevention, it seems that the latter does not facilitate habituation but affects outcome through some other mechanism not yet investigated. The third variable associated with outcome is pretreatment anxiety. Contrary to our expectations, it does not do so through its interference with habituation either within or between sessions. The mechanism whereby pretreatment anxiety affects posttreatment responses is then unclear. Finally, a fourth variable, depression, has an impact on initial reactivity, thereby indirectly affecting habituation within and between sessions and, ultimately, posttreatment outcome. We also propose that depression promotes anxiety. The dashed arrow indicates that the directionality of the relationship is only inferred inasmuch as both variables are assessed simultaneously. This proposal is derived from the finding that almost all of our highly depressed patients were anxious but not all of our highly anxious patients were depressed.

With respect to follow-up, we found a multiple correlation of all the predictors to be .78, accounting for 61 percent of the variance. Depression, anxiety, and type of treatment, as well as the process variables, indirectly influence outcome at follow-up through their effect upon posttreatment response. In addition, age of symptom onset has a direct impact on long-term outcome. As discussed earlier, we suspect that this variable may reflect personality characteristics not yet examined.

In conclusion, we have proposed a model that brings together several variables found related to treatment outcome. It is hoped that this model will assist us not only in detecting prospective failures but also in identifying possible reasons for such failure and ways to overcome them.

REFERENCES

Boersma, K., Den Hengst, S., Dekker, J., & Emmelkamp, P. M. G. (1976) Exposure and response prevention: A comparison with obsessive-compulsive patients. *Behaviour Research and Therapy,* **14**, 19–24.

Borkovec, T. D., & Grayson, J. B. (1980) Consequences of increasing the functional impact of internal emotional stimuli. In K. Blankstein, P. Pliner, & H. Polivey (Eds.), *Advances in the study of communication and affects* (Vol. 3). New York: Plenum.

Borkovec, T. D., & Sides, J. (1979) The contribution of relaxation and expectancy to fear reduction via graded imaginal exposure to feared stimuli. *Behaviour Research and Therapy,* **17**, 529–540.

Boulougouris, J. C. (1977) Variables affecting the behaviour modification of obsessive-compulsive patients treated by flooding. In J. C. Boulougouris and A. D. Rabavilas (Eds.), *The treatment of phobic and obsessive-compulsive disorders.* Oxford: Pergamon.

Boulougouris, J. C., & Bassiakos, L. (1973) Prolonged flooding in cases with obsessive-compulsive neurosis. *Behaviour Research and Therapy*, **11**, 227–231.

Catts, S., & McConaghy, N. (1975) Ritual prevention in the treatment of obsessive-compulsive neurosis. *Australian and New Zealand Journal of Psychiatry*, **9**, 37–41.

Cawley, R. (1974) Psychotherapy and obsessional disorders. In H. R. Beech (Ed.), *Obsessional states.* London: Methuen.

Davis, M., & Wagner, A. R. (1969) Habituation of the startle response under incremental sequence of stimulus intensities. *Journal of Comparative and Physiological Psychology*, **67**, 486–492.

Emmelkamp, P. M. G., & van de Hout, A. (1983) Failure in treating agoraphobia. In E. B. Foa, & P. M. G. Emmelkamp (eds.), *Failures in behavior therapy.* New York: Wiley.

Emmelkamp, P. M. G., van der Helm, M., van Zanten, B. L., & Ploch, I. (1980) Contributions of self-instructional training to the effectiveness of exposure *in vivo:* A comparison with obsessive-compulsive patients. *Behaviour Research and Therapy*, **18**, 61–66.

Emmelkamp, P. M. G., & Kraanen, J. (1977) Therapist-controlled exposure *in vivo* vs. self-controlled exposure *in vivo:* A comparison with obsessive-compulsive patients. *Behaviour Research and Therapy*, **15**, 491–496.

Emmelkamp, P. M. G., & Wessels, H. (1975) Flooding in imagination and flooding *in vivo:* A comparison with agoraphobics. *Behaviour Research and Therapy*, **13**, 7–15.

Foa, E. B. (1979) Failure in treating obsessive-compulsives. *Behaviour Research and Therapy*, **17**, 169–179.

Foa, E. B., & Chambless, D. L. (1978) Habituation of subjective anxiety during flooding in imagery. *Behaviour Research and Therapy*, **16**, 391–399.

Foa, E. B., & Goldstein, A. (1978) Continuous exposure and complete response prevention in the treatment of obsessive-compulsive neurosis. *Behaviour Therapy*, **9**, 821–829.

Foa, E. B., Grayson, J. B., Steketee, G., Doppelt, H. G., Turner, R. M., & Latimer, P. R. Success and failure in the treatment of obsessive-compulsives. Journal of Consulting and clinical Psychology, in press.

Foa, E. B., Grayson, J.B., & Steketee, G. (1981) Depression, habituation and treatment outcome in obsessive-compulsives. In J. C. Boulougouris (Ed.), *Practical applications of learning theories in psychiatry.* New York: Wiley.

Foa, E. B., Grayson, J. B., Steketee, G., & Doppelt, H. G. (1981) *Predictors for success and failure in treatment of obsessive-compulsives.* Paper presented at the American Psychological Association Convention, Los Angeles, August.

Foa, E. B., & Steketee, G. S. (1979) Obsessive-compulsives: Conceptual issues and treatment interventions. In M. Hersen, R. M. Eisler, & P. M. Miller (Eds.), *Progress in behavior modification* (Vol. 8). New York: Academic.

Foa, E. B., Steketee, G., & Groves, G. A. (1979) The use of behavioral therapy and imipramine in a case of obsessive-compulsive neurosis with severe depression. *Behavior Modification*, **3**, 419–430.

Foa, E. B., Steketee, G., & Milby, J. B. (1980) Differential effects of exposure and response prevention in obsessive-compulsive washers. *Journal of Consulting and Clinical Psychology*, **48**, 71–79.

Foa, E. B., Steketee, G., Turner, R. M., & Fischer, S. C. (1980) Effects of imaginal exposure to feared disasters in obsessive-compulsive checkers. *Behaviour Research and Therapy,* **18**, 449–455.

Foa, E. B., & Tillmanns, A. (1980) The treatment of obsessive-compulsive neurosis. In A. Goldstein, & E. B. Foa (Eds.), *Handbook of behavioral interventions: A clinical guide.* New York: Wiley.

Grayson, J. B. (1982) The elicitation and habituation of orienting and defensive responses to phobic imagery and the incremental stimulus intensity effect. Psychophysiology, 19, 104–111.

Grayson, J. B., & Borkovec, T. D. (1978) The effects of expectancy and imagined response to phobic stimuli on fear reduction. *Cognitive Therapy and Research,* **1**, 11–24.

Grey, S., Sartory, G., & Rachman, S. (1979) Synchronous and desynchronous changes during fear reduction. *Behaviour Research and Therapy,* **17**, 137–148.

Groves, P. M., & Thompson, R. F. (1970) Habituation: A dual-process theory. *Psychological Review,* **77**, 419–450.

Gur, R. C., Reivich, M., Rosen, A. D., Alavi, A., Greenberg, J., & Gur, R. E. (1981) *Anxiety and local glucose metabolism in frontocortical limbic projections in man.* Paper presented at the International Neuropsychologica Society, Atlanta.

Hadley, S. W., & Strupp, H. H. (1976) Contemporary views of negative effects in psychotherapy: An integrated account. *Archives of General Psychiatry,* **33**, 1291–1302.

Katkin, E. S., & McCubbin, R. J. (1969) Habituation of the orienting response as a function of individual differences in anxiety and autonomic lability. *Journal of Abnormal Psychology,* **73**, 54–60.

Kazdin, A. E., & Wilcoxon, L. A. (1976) Systematic desensitization and non-specific treatment effects: A methodological evaluation. *Psychological Bulletin,* **83**, 729–758.

Lader, M. H., & Wing, L. (1966) Physiological measures, sedative drugs and morbid anxiety. *Maudsley Monograph,* London: Oxford.

Lader, M. H., & Wing, L. (1969) Physiological measures in agitated and retarded depressed patients. *Journal of Psychiatric Research,* **7**, 89–100.

Lang, P. M., Melamed, B. G., & Hart, J. (1970) A psychophysiological analysis of fear modification using an automated desensitization procedure. *Journal of Abnormal Psychology,* **76**, 220–234.

Likierman, H., & Rachman, S. J. (1980) Spontaneous decay of compulsive urges: Cumulative effects. *Behaviour Research and Therapy,* **18**, 387–394.

Lykken, D. T., & Venables, P. H. (1972) Direct measurement of skin conductance: A proposal for standardization. *Psychophysiology,* **8**, 656–672.

Marks, I. M. (1973) New approaches to the treatment of obsessive-compulsive disorders. *Journal of Nervous and Mental Disease,* **156**, 420–426.

Marks, I. M. (1977) Clinical studies in phobic, obsessive-compulsive and allied disorders. In W. S. Argas (Ed.), *Behavior therapy in clinical psychiatry.* Boston: Little, Brown.

Marks, I. M., Hodgson, R., & Rachman, S. (1975) Treatment of chronic obsessive-compulsive neurosis by *in vio* exposure. *British Journal of Psychiatry*, **127**, 349–364.

Marks, I. M., Stern, R. S., Mawson, D., Cobb, J., & McDonald, R. (1980) Clomipramine and exposure for obsessive-compulsive rituals. *British Journal of Psychiatry,* **136,** 1–25.

Mathews, A. M., Johnston, D. W., Shaw, P. M., & Gelder, M. G. (1973) Process variables and the prediction of outcome in behavior therapy. *British Journal of Psychaitry,* **123,** 445–462.

Meyer, V., Levy, R., & Schnurer, A. (1974) A behavioral teatment of obsessive-compulsive disorders. In H. R. Beech (Ed.), *Obsessional states.* London: Methuen.

Mills, H. L., Agras, W. S., Barlow, D. H. & Mills, J. R. (1973) Compulsive rituals treated by response prevention. *Archives of General Psychiatry,* **28,** 524–529.

O'Gorman, J., & Jamieson, R. (1975) The incremental stimulus intensity effect and habituation of autonomic responses in man. *Physiological Psychology,* **3,** 385–389.

Rabavilas, A. D., Boulougouris, J. C., & Perissaki, C. (1979) Therapist qualities related to outcome with exposure *in vivo* in neurotic patients. *Journal of Behavior Therapy and Experimental Psychiatry,* **10,** 293–299.

Rabavilas, A. D., Boulougouris, J. C., & Stefanis, C. (1976) Duration of flooding sessions in the treatment of obbessive-compulsive patients. *Behaviour Research and Therapy* , **14,** 349–355.

Rachman, S. (1980) Emotional processing. *Behaviour Research and Therapy,* **18,** 51–60.

Rachman, S. J., Cobb, J., Grey, S., McDonald, B., Mawson, D., Sartory, G., & Stern, R. (1979) The behavioural treatment of obsessional-compulsive disorders with and without clomipramine. *Behaviour Research and Therapy,* **17,** 462–478.

Rachman, S. J., de Silva, R., & Roper, G. (1976) The spontaneous decay of compulsive urges. *Behaviour Research and Therapy,* **14,** 445–453.

Rachman, S., & Hodgson, R. (1980) *Obsessions and compulsions.* Englewood Cliffs, N.J.: Prentice Hall.

Rachman, S., Marks, I. M., & Hodgson, R. (1973) The treatment of obsessive-compulsive neurotics by modelling and flooding *in vivo. Behaviour Research and Therapy,* **11,** 463–471.

Roper, G., Rachman, S., & Marks, I. M. (1975) Passive and participant modelling in exposure treatment of obsessive-compulsive neurotics. *Behaviour Research and Therapy,* **13,** 271–279.

Rosenthal, D., & Frank, J. D. (1958) The fate of psychiatric clinic outpatients assigned to psychotherapy. *Journal of Nervous and Mental Disease,* **127,** 330–343.

Steketee, G., Grayson, J. B. & Foa, E. B. (1981) *Effects of exposure and response prevention on obsessive-compulsive symptoms.* Paper presented at the American Psychological Association Convention, Los Angeles, August.

Truax, C. B. & Carkuff, R. R. (1967) *Toward effective counceling in psychotheraoy: Training and practice.* Chicago: Aldine.

Walton, D. & Mather, M. D. (1963) The application of learning principles to the treatment of obsessive-compulsive states in the acute and chronic phases of illness. *Behaviour Research and Therapy,* **1,** 163–174.

Watson, J. P., Gaind, R., & Marks, I. M. (1972) Physiological habituation to continuous phobic stimuli. *Behaviour Research and Therapy,* **10,** 269–278.

CHAPTER 3

Obstacles to the Successful Treatment of Obsessions

S. RACHMAN

The main obstacle to the successful treatment of obsessions is the absence of effective techniques. Fruitful contemplation of the causes of therapeutic failures can be undertaken only against a background of successes. Examining our failures against such a background may lead to the discovery of an important omission or a flaw in our techniques, but the contemplation of failures in isolation leads to a renewed search for effective alternatives, and with good fortune, may in the interim offer assistance to practicing clinicians.

When treatment methods fail, we can resort to ad hoc inventiveness or clinical intuition, or we can carry out basic re-analyses of the intransigent problem in the hope of forming some fresh alternatives. Exploration of two fresh perspectives, the 3-systems analysis and the concept of emotional processing, forms the theoretical substance of this chapter. Before turning to this challenging task, however, some observations on failures in general are offered, and these are followed by a practical-minded discussion of specific cases of failure.

THE NATURE OF OBSESSIONS

For purposes of this chapter the definitions set out by Rachman and Hodgson (1980) will be adopted.

An obsession is an intrusive, repetitive thought, image or impulse that is unacceptable and/or unwanted and gives rise to subjective resistance. It generally produces distress. Obsessions are difficult to remove and/or control. It is said that during calm periods the person acknowledges the senselessness of the thought or impulse. The content of an obsession is repugnant, worrying, blasphemous, obscene, nonsensical—or all of these—and frequently takes the form of doubting. The following are clinical examples of obsessional thoughts: "Am I a lesbian?" "Did I kill the old lady?" "Christ was a bastard." Examples of obsessional impulses are the following "I might expose my genitals in public"; "I am about to shout obscenities in public"; "I feel I might strangle a child". Examples of obsessional images include mutilated corpses, decomposing foetuses, my husband involved in a serious motor accident, my parents being violently assaulted. Obsessional impulses often are accompanied or preceded by a fear of losing control—in fact, the impulses are rarely acted upon. (p. 10)

In a majority of instances these obsessions are associated with stereotyped and compulsive activities that are recognized by the person to be excessive and/or exaggerated, or senseless. Like obsessions, they often provoke subjective resistance and are followed by distress.

Obsessions are distinguished from morbid preoccupations (see Rachman, 1973), even though both phenomena involve intrusive repetitive cognitions. Unlike morbid preoccupations, characteristic obsessions are at least partly irrational, often unrealistic in content, usually associated with subjective resistance, and often are repugnant and ego-dystonic.

ON FAILURES IN GENERAL

Some slight consolation can be drawn from therapeutic failures and, paradoxically, it is the serious failures rather than the technical failures that are most likely to offer such consolation. The serious failures are those in which little or no therapeutic progress is achieved even though the chosen technique has been given an adequate trial. The consequences of failures in which the appropriate technique is known but not given a fair trial, are limited to the patient concerned. Few conclusions can be drawn from technical failures of this character.

The serious failures, those in which the unexpected occurs, or more often, those in which the expected fails to occur, add new information and may help to expand our understanding of the technique and/or of the disorder. There is a good deal of truth in the claim that everyday therapeutic successes, like technical failures, add little to our knowledge. Serious failures are likely to be the most educational.

The list of potential causes (and types) of therapeutic failure in dealing with obsessions and/or compulsions is alarmingly long. One might even conclude from such a list that the prospects of helping anyone to overcome his or her obsessions are poor indeed. Hence it is best to open by stating that some slight progress has been made and more can be expected. Moreover, recent successes in treating the associated, and far more common, disorder of obsessional compulsive behavior give reason to be optimistic. In one sense, the remaining intransigence of pure obsessions can be regarded as a matter of mopping up the smaller remnants of a larger problem. Given that presently we are in the much stronger position to modify compulsive behavior than we are to change pure obsessions, it might be expected that patients who present obsessions accompanied by compulsions are more likely to be helped. This question has not been the subject of systematic investigation but my view, based on unsystematic clinical observations, is that obsessions associated with compulsions are, indeed, easier to modify than "pure" obsessions, that is, those not accompanied by overt compulsive acts. It is an intellectually challenging problem and one that is distressing for the people affected, but it is not a problem of great magnitude.

A major reason for our slow progress in dealing with the problem can be traced to the nature of obsessions, which are essentially cognitive. Contemporary clinical psychologists, with their behavioral heritage, are more at ease and more familiar with observable, manipulable, and measureable behavior. We are ill prepared and ill equipped to deal with what Henry Maudsley (1895) described as these "haunting horrors" that persistently intrude into the mind "despite the most earnest wish to turn and keep them out" (p. 170).

The following discussion of failures rests on an uncertain basis for the reason given above. Providing that one remembers the scarcity of successes, the comments and analyses may be of some assistance to clinicians pending the growth of effective methods. Current patients require the best available ideas and methods.

Technical Failures

The main forms of technical or practical failure are relatively easy to enumerate. In the first place, failures may occur because of the therapist's incorrect identification of the problem. For example, if a schizophrenic delusion is mistakenly regarded as an obsessional rumination, then the application of methods designed to tackle the latter sort of problem are bound to end in failure. Similarly, mistakenly identifying schizophrenic thoughts that the patient is convinced are being inserted by some outside agent or force, for an obsession as defined above, precludes the possibility of effective treatment along the lines used for dealing with neurotic manifestations.

A second set of failures, certainly more common than the incorrect identification of the problem arises from the patient's unwillingness to accept the interpretation and/or the therapeutic suggestions offered by the therapist. For example, if the therapist construes the obsessional problem in psychodynamic terms of an unduly fanciful or spectacular character, the patient may feel disinclined to proceed. Another possibility is that the therapist makes a plausible construal of the problem, and even goes so far as to propose a plausible plan of action, but for other reasons the patient is unwilling to follow the advice provided. There is a range of possible reasons that might explain such refusals. The patient may be so demoralized by earlier therapeutic failures or by the debilitation of a serious and prolonged affective disturbance, that he or she is unwilling or unable to make the effort required. These possibilities can be illustrated by reference to the following two cases.

In the first case, a man who had been troubled by a repugnant set of violent thoughts declined the offer of a course of relaxation and thought-stopping on the understandable grounds that he had already tried (and failed to benefit from) no less than six therapeutic attempts, not including the 12 different psychotropic drugs which he had tried without success. With these failures behind him, it was difficult to understand why he had sought the original consultation, and the answer was that he had been persuaded to do so by his wife who was at the end of her endurance. The therapeutic plan was not adopted and the patient left in an unchanged state. This unfortunate failure is classed as a technical failure, and one from which very little could be learned.

In a second case, a 32-year-old woman who was tortured by aggressive thoughts and impulses directed towards her two children accepted the explanation of her abhorrent obsessions but was at the time so deeply depressed that she felt, perhaps correctly, that she would be incapable of the exertions required by a course of treatment. Her sleep and appetite were disturbed, and she was persistently and deeply unhappy and found that even getting out of bed in the morning required a major effort. On a number of occasions, the effort proved to be too great and she lay in bed seemingly inert throughout the entire day and night. In the circumstances it was agreed to postpone introduction of treatment until the patient experienced some relief from her oppressive dysphoria. An attempt was made to put into operation the therapy plan, but her periods of remission from severe depression were so brief and erratic as to make the direct treatment of her obsession impractical.

A third and more frustrating type of technical failure occurs when a patient is unwilling or unable to adhere to the agreed upon therapeutic program. Problems of this kind tend to appear fairly early in the program; the first problems are encountered in obtaining satisfactory baseline data. For one reason or another the records are kept irregularly, are incomplete, or so inaccurate as to be of little value. These difficulties are then added to by the patient's failure to carry out the required assignments or between-session practice periods. A recent example of this type of poor adherence was encountered in a young man with a set of aggressive obsessions directed mainly towards members of his immediate family. On returning for his second treatment session, it was found that his baseline data were so sparse as to be worthless. The boy explained that he had had difficulty in rating the quality or duration of the obsessions, and hence made very few entries in his daily diary. An attempt to use a simplified system also ended in failure. The next problem that arose was that the relaxation exercises provided in the early treatment sessions were not practised at home, and as a result the patient's unacceptably high level of tension remained an impediment to progress. The planned treatment program staggered from one watered-down compromise to the next until it came to a dismal and premature conclusion. There is, of course, a considerable and growing literature on the subject of noncompliance with treatment of various kinds, but there is nothing in our experience of treating obsessional patients that enables us to make a useful addition to the subject at this stage.

The next set of failures may be exclusively technical or a combination of a technical failure and what has been defined as a more serious failure. Sometimes, when the patient presents a set of several related problems, gratifying progress is made in dealing with one or more of the problems while others remain provocatively inert. For example, we can refer to a 24-year-old psychiatric nurse who was troubled by a severe and almost continuous set of obsessions on the theme of her body image, about which she remunated for prolonged periods each day. She was plagued by a senseless uncertainty about the coherence and connectedness of her various bodily parts. In addition, she was troubled by a range of mild to moderate checking compulsions, severe social anxiety, and episodic depression of severe intensity. The treatment of this patient was a partial success, or for those of gloomy outlook, a partial failure. The intensity and frequency of the depressive episodes were diminished to some extent (seemingly by antidepressant medication), her social anxiety was substantially reduced by a course of relaxation and in vivo desensitization, her checking compulsions were modified by a program of response prevention, but her prolonged obsessions were never removed. After a course of satiation training, sometimes supplemented by thought-stopping, she was able to reduce the duration of the obsessional activity by a significant amount, but there were very few days on which she was free of these distressing intrusive thoughts. The reason for the undue persistence of the obsessions, even in the face of a range of other improvements, remains unexplained, but there was in this case no question of a lack of application. The patient worked long and hard at overcoming all of her problems and was successful in part, despite her persisting distress from obsessional thoughts.

Relapses can occur for technical reasons but might indicate a more serious failure. The reappearance of obsessions after a patient has been exposed to unusually stressful events is not unexpected and may present few problems once the stresses have diminished. A good example of this course of events was observed in a young married woman whose blasphemous and aggressive thoughts responded successfully to a course of satiation treatment but then returned in a slightly dampened form two years later during the course of her mother's serious illness. Shortly after her mother made a satisfactory recovery, the patient's level of tension diminished and it was then possible to give her a short and successful course of booster treatment. Other technical relapses may arise if a period of depression occurs, it being borne in mind that there is a close relationship between depression and obsessions (see Rachman & Hodgson, 1980). Given that in some cases the depression appears to mediate the obsessions, it is reasonable to expect that the appearance or return of an affective disturbance will be followed by the return of obsessional activity; by the same token, however, the successful treatment of the depressive episode should be followed by relief from the obsessional activities or by their becoming more amenable to direct treatment. The relationship between depression and obsessions is of major importance and will be returned to later in this chapter.

Serious Failures

We can now turn to what have been described as serious failures, that is, failures that occur against prediction. To take one notable example from our own experience, repeated attempts to use the normally successful method of exposure and response prevention to treat a patient who was partly disabled by repetitive checking compulsions failed to produce any significant change in her problem. The patient was well-motivated, fully cooperative, and entirely rational in her approach to the problem and her understanding of the treatment rationale. After the failure of the first attempt, using what one might call the standard form of exposure and response prevention, we explored the potential value of minor and major variations in technique, but had transitory success at the best of times. Contrary to prediction, the patient's obsessive-compulsive problems were *not* modified by the treatment technique or its variations. We were unable to explain the failure at the time and still have no satisfactory explanation. It is worth mentioning that we made several attempts to deal with the problem, spanning a period of more than four years. On one occasion, when we were examining the considerable bulk of data that we had collected over the years one of the more persistent therapists, Dr. R. Hodgson, made the consoling interpretation that the information could perhaps be regarded as the longest baseline ever collected from a single patient.

In coming to grips with failures that occur in the treatment of predominantly obsessional problems, one has to contend with an additional impediment. Unlike the position prevailing in respect to the treatment of predominantly compulsive disorders, we are not in possession of a reasonably dependable form of treatment for obsessions. It follows that even when predictions can be made, they rest on a weaker basis. As a result, it is less easy to conclude that the failure of a particular course of treatment falls into the serious or the technical category. So, for example, if a patient with an obsessional problem fails to benefit from a course of thought-stopping treatment, the explanation might be that the technique itself is of limited power, or that the therapist or patient were not using the method appropriately. For example, Stern, Lipsedge, and Marks' (1973) failure to produce therapeutic benefits with thought-stopping methods has been criticized on the grounds that they used tape-recorded therapeutic instructions, provided insufficient therapy, and had inadequate evidence on which to judge whether the patient had implemented the technique. The other explanation is that thought-stopping is an ineffective technique.

Because of the special difficulties that arise in evaluating failures to help obsessional patients, the serious failures will be considered from the following perspectives. First, consideration is given to some of the factors that might impede successful modification of these difficulties and, second, the various techniques that have been brought into play in the hope of modifying the problems are briefly evaluated.

Depression

The freshest approach to therapeutic failures comes from the recent research of Foa (1979), and even though her work has been concerned with obsessional-compulsive problems rather than pure obsessions, it provides the best starting point for this discussion. In brief, she argued that there are at least two impedi-

ments to therapeutic success when using behavioral techniques to overcome obsessional-compulsive problems: severe depression or the presence of over-valued
ideas.

Describing her results with two small groups of obsessional-compulsive patients, Foa (1979) identified two reasons for failure: the presence of a "strong
conviction that their fears were realistic" or the manifestation of "severe depression." In the first group of patients she observed that habituation to the feared
stimulus occurred within treatment sessions, but these gains were lost between
sessions. In the case of the second group, however, habituation was not seen to
occur either within or between sessions. These failures were in contrast to those
observed in patients who responded successfully to comparable forms of treatment, and who showed both forms of habituation; that is, within and between
sessions. In a later report on a larger group of patients, Foa, Grayson, and Steketee (1980) confirmed that highly depressed patients show less improvement
than mildly depressed patients, both in respect to their improvement on compulsions *and* obsessions. These differences were apparent at the end of treatment
and at the follow-up assessment. Furthermore, in the highly depressed group
there was a significant increase in obsessions during the period intervening between the completion of treatment and the follow-up assessment. In respect to
both obsessions and compulsions, the "highly depressed patients gained less from
treatment than low depressed patients. Moreover, they relapsed more than did
either the low or moderately depressed ones."

In regard to the observation reported in her first paper, to the effect that the
presence of severe depression appears to impede habituation, Foa, Grayson, and
Steketee found that there was a nonsignificant trend for the highly depressed patients to show less habituation within the session, and a similar nonsignificant
trend was observed in respect to habituation between sessions. A modest negative
correlation between habituation and depression was calculated ($-.33$ for within
session changes and $-.35$ for between session changes).

These authors also reported one additional finding of some interest. Habituation between sessions correlated significantly with the percentage of change in
obsessions, both at the completion of treatment and at follow-up. They go on
to observe, however, that the failures among their patients cannot be attributed
solely to their failure to habituate (because of the modest correlations). They rule
out the possibility that their results can be explained by differences in pretreatment severity. The correlation between initial severity of obsessions and percentage of improvement was not significant. However, when they turned their attention to anxiety, they found a significant negative correlation between habituation
and the initial level of anxiety provoked by the most feared items. For various
reasons given by the authors, these findings and the conclusions that might be
drawn from them must be regarded with caution, subject to replication. With
this caution in mind, their summary seems fully justified: "In summary, the relationship between depression and inter-session habituation seems due to the fact
that both are related to initial anxiety. . . .Habituation and depression seem to

affect outcome independently." This interesting and somewhat unexpected conclusion, however tentative its status, is of particular interest in the light of a recently completed experiment by Parkinson and Rachman (1981), who found evidence of a relation between anxiety and intrusive cognitions.

Stress

Following on the work of Horowitz (1975), they investigated the effects of an uncontrived stress on the formation of intrusive cognitions. The experiences of a group of mothers whose children were being admitted to a hospital for elective surgery were compared with those of a comparable group of mothers whose children were not awaiting medical or surgical treatment. In the course of confirming their prediction of a considerable increase in intrusive cognitions, which can for many purposes be regarded as similar to clinical obsessions (see Rachman & Hodgson, 1980), they found a significant correlation between the presence of anxiety and intrusive cognitions; a little surprisingly, the relationship between intrusive cognitions and dysphoria was not significant. A second piece of information that is in keeping with the emerging emphasis on the role of anxiety in the production and maintenance of intrusive cognitions comes from another experiment by Parkinson and Rachman (1980). In an investigation of habituation processes affecting intrusive thoughts, they obtained strong evidence of the facilitative effect of relaxation.

Given the central role attached to the interplay between arousal levels, relaxation, and habituation in the maximal habituation model originally proposed by Lader and Wing (1966), these recent findings hang together fairly comfortably. The following connections appear to be emerging from the clinical and experimental findings briefly referred to here—it should, of course, be clear that at this stage elaboration would be premature.

As things stand, however, the following chain of events is worth considering: Exposure to stressful events gives rise to an increase in anxiety that, in turn, is followed by an increase in intrusive cognitions including obsessions. The continued presence of high levels of anxiety impedes the occurrence of habituation that might otherwise take place "spontaneously." If, on the other hand, the stressors are removed and/or the person's level of anxiety diminishes, then presumably the process of habituation can proceed satisfactorily. From a therapeutic or experimental point of view, the process of habituation to external stressors or to intrusive cognitive events can be facilitated by the introduction of procedures or agents that induce relaxation. Hence in the case of persisting intrusive cognitions, one might facilitate their removal by the induction of relaxation training, the use of suitable drugs, and so on. It should be noted that this change in perspective, in which greater emphasis is to be placed on the role of anxiety than was formerly the case, does not necessarily rule out the importance of the part played by dysphoria.

As has been remarked on many occasions, there is an intimate and significant association between depression and obsessions (see Rachman, & Hodgson, 1980).

Moreover, the controlled clinical trial on 40 obsessional-compulsive patients reported by Rachman et al. (1979) confirms the significant part played by depression and its dissipation in the treatment of patients with these types of problems. In that trial, however, patients whose major complaints were of obsessional activity were excluded and the results can be regarded only as a pointer to what might be observed among patients with purely obsessive problems. It nevertheless is of interest that those patients who had significantly elevated levels of depression responded well to clomipramine, which appears to have dissipated the depression, and that change was, in turn, followed by an alleviation of the obsessional-compulsive problems, even in anticipation of direct behavioral treatment.

Despite the absence of persuasive confirmatory evidence, the recent study by Foa, Grayson, and Steketee (1980), shows that it would be unwise to dismiss the potential role of depression in impeding therapeutic progress with obsessional patients. It should be remembered that Lader (1969) reported that depressed patients show very little or no habituation even to neutral stimulation and that Foa, in her first report in 1979, produced convincing clinical illustrations of depressed patients failing to habituate within or between treatment sessions. To this we can add some clinical observations of our own, in which patients with fluctuating levels of depression were observed to make little or no progress in overcoming their obsessions by means of satiation treatment during those periods when they were most deeply depressed. In contrast, in those periods when they were less deeply affected by dysphoria, they appeared to make reasonably rapid progress in dealing with their obsessions.

Over-Valued Ideas

The second subgroup of patients identified by Foa (1979) as being recalcitrant to behavioral treatment were characterized by what she described as "overvalued ideation." As with the earlier subgroup of patients, those suffering from severe depression, Foa's clinical descriptions are convincing and recognizable to clinicians accustomed to dealing with obsessional-compulsive problems. At the outset it should be said that many patients who display evidence of overvalued ideation would not be offered a course of behavioral treatment. Instead, they are likely to attract a diagnosis of "psychosis," either affective or schizophrenic and, in consequence, are more likely to be provided with drug treatment in preference to behavioral retraining. The fact that these are the most common diagnostic and treatment decisions does not provide sufficient justification of such a course of action. Even if on the present evidence, the conventional approach, based on drugs, is plausible, it should not preclude attempts to proceed as if the abnormal ideas and accompanying behavior are variants of obsessional disorders. A fuller examination of the similarities and differences between obsessions and overvalued ideas can be found in Rachman and Hodgson (1980) and will not be pursued here. Let us instead consider what happens when patients displaying at least some of the characteristics of obsessional disorders turn out to be fettered by the rigidities of a circumscribed and irrational idea.

According to Foa (1979), patients suffering from severe depression show little or no habituation either within or between sessions. However, the pattern for patients with overvalued ideas was different. Here Foa observed habituation *within* the session but this was followed by a return of subjective discomfort for the beginning of the subsequent session (i.e., the intrasession gains were lost in the period intervening between sessions). Foa remarks, "it seems that while the mechanism underlying short-term habituation is intact, in the overvaluing idea the second mechanism is blocked. Their rigid belief system may prevent changes of expectation and retention on the habituation experience, thus resulting in absence of gains between sessions" (p. 174). For some reason, perhaps because of the reassurance provided by the therapist as suggested by Foa, these patients are sometimes able to maintain progress within the session. Although it is true that we have made unsystematic observations consonant with those of Foa, some exceptions have been encountered. To begin with the similarities: One of the patients described by Foa was a 26-year-old woman who had an excessive and irrational fear of tetanus. During the course of exposure and response prevention treatment, the patient "reported decrement of discomfort as the sessions proceeded . . . however, no generalization was evident from one day to the next" (p. 173). By what may be no more than a remarkable coincidence, we experienced a comparable failure some years ago when trying to assist a fully qualified young nurse who had developed an intense and irrational fear of contracting tetanus. Despite some progress within sessions, her fears tended to make a disappointing reappearance whenever we began a new session of treatment. Her irrational belief, made even more remarkable by the fact that she was a qualified and highly competent nurse, failed to weaken despite the temporary improvements in her behavior which were apparently mediated by a reduction in fear. The belief and the fear responded independently. Attempts to weaken the belief by direct treatment, including demonstrations and appeals to medical authority, failed to have any effect.

A slightly different pattern has been encountered in other patients with overvalued ideation, but I cannot recall the fully successful treatment of any such patient. In a recent case, a moderate amount of success was achieved with a woman who had an intense and irrational fear of contracting skin disease. After completing a course of exposure and response prevention, supplemented by antidepressant drug treatment, her affective disorder diminished at roughly the same time as her fear and avoidance behavior. Nevertheless, despite the virtual disappearance of her depression, she continued to believe that she was at some risk of developing skin diseases. The difference here was that on some occasions at least, she was prepared to recognize the irrational basis of the belief. For the most part, however, and even during the partially successful conquest of her fear, she continued to defend her irrational belief that she was running an elevated risk of contracting disease, probably cancer.

A third patient, whom we were unable to help to any useful extent, complained of an unusual obsession. This middle-aged man had for a number of years been tormented by an incident in which he observed a distant acquaintance displaying a strange facial expression for a brief period. The patient found that later on the day of the incident he began to wonder how it was possible for the acquaintance to distort his face in the manner observed, and the patient even went so far as to make attempts to mimic the abnormal facial expression. The thoughts and associated compulsions became increasingly troublesome and preoccupying. At no stage were we able to get the patient to agree that the thought was essentially nonsensical and the accompanying actions wasteful and useless. Having failed to shift the beliefs and associated behavior, we made a direct attack on the obsessions themselves. Attempts at thought-stopping, habituation training, and satiation all failed to produce any benefit, either within or between sessions. In other words, the pattern observed in this failure was much closer to that described by the severely depressed patients treated by Foa. It should be added that our patient was not at the time of treatment, or in the period preceding it, suffering from significant depression.

Given that the observation is valid, and that patients suffering from overvalued ideation do not respond to the available methods of treatment, what might the explanation be? Although she does not state it explicitly, it would appear from Foa's descriptions that she attributes the within-session habituation to the reassuring presence of the therapist. She also goes on to observe that some of the patients "seemed to attach a magic power to their therapist's rules . . .and required continuous reassurance via frequent telephone calls to the therapist." She also notes in passing that these patients were willing and able to follow the "rules of safety" devised by the therapist, even though they were dissonant with the patient's belief. Within the sessions the patients behaved as if the therapist's rules were satisfactory, although the patients were "never fully convinced of their validity." This description bears a remarkable similarity to our own experiences. In the case of the patient with a fear of skin disease described above, she stated that she was willing to be guided by our statements regarding the probability of infection, even though she retained serious doubts about their validity. Within sessions she was willing to be guided by our constant reassurance, but as in the case described by Foa, the power of the reassurance faded and had constantly to be refreshed. My suspicion is that we have here a phenomenon of considerable interst and one that would repay close investigation. Regrettably, there is very little that can be said about it at present and certainly not much can be offered in the way of practical advice for therapists. Presumably, the presence and actions of the therapist suffice to reduce the patient's fear and discomfort, while leaving the irrational belief unchanged. Among other possibilities raised by the emergence of this phenomenon is the relationship between affective states, especially anxiety, and the strength of irrational beliefs. Are these two phenomena in some form of reciprocal balance? Can a reduction in the level of anxiety, where present, mediate a weakening of irrational belief? On the other side, might an increase in the strength of the irrational belief mediate an elevation of anxiety? And in respect to the irrational belief, what is the relationship between the degree of irrationality and affective state, and between the strength of the conviction and the affective state? Questions of these kinds are intrinsically intersting (see Rachman, 1981) and it is to be hoped that clarification of their significance might, in turn, lead to the development of more effective ways of modifying obsessional and other disorders in which overvalued ideas play a prominent part. As things stand at present, however, we can do little further than going beyond the somewhat pessimistic prediction that the presence of a significant overvalued idea associated with, or part of, an obsessional disorder is predictive of long-term failure, even if temporary improvements can be achieved.

In addition to the two observations made by Foa, there is a third set of conditions that may predict therapeutic failure. Given the probable association between affective problems and the emergence and/or maintenance of obsessional activity, it is reasonable to expect that increases in affective problems are likely to undermine therapeutic progress. In plain speech, if the person is suffering from a significant degree of depression or is living under stressful conditions that are likely to give rise to anxiety, progress towards overcoming the obsessional problems will be slow or impossible to achieve. Recent research into the nature and precipitants of intrusive unwanted cognitions has produced evidence of a close connection between the arousal of anxiety and a significant increase in intrusive cognitions (Parkinson, & Rachman, 1981). If we extrapolate from this research on the effects of an uncontrived stress, in this instance the effect on others of having their children admitted to a hospital for elective surgery, one can say that exposure to stress, especially of an anxiety-provoking kind, is likely to result in a significant increase in obsessional activities. If a patient in treatment is under stress, treatment may be impeded either within sessions (because an elevated level of arousal retards habituation) or between sessions because new obsessional activities are being provoked by repeated exposures to stress.

As far as the practicing clinician is concerned, the persistent exposure of their patients to anxiety-provoking or other stressful conditions is likely to retard progress and they would be well advised to take whatever steps are possible to remove or mitigate the current stresses. For therapists who favor the supplementary use of drugs, it means, of course, that one might in these circumstances have to consider the possible use not only of antidepressant medication, but also of anxiety-reducing drugs.

Before introducing a fresh perspective on these problems, it might be useful to summarize the arguments so far and to suggest some remedies. Leaving aside what have been termed the technical failures, we are left to contend with therapeutic failures that might be attributable to one of three factors, or some combination of these three factors. In the first place, the presence of severe depression is likely to retard habituation and hence overall progress as well. Secondly, the presence of overvalued ideas may permit within-session habituation and, therefore, transient improvements, but will retard between-session improvements and long-term changes. The third possibility is that if the patient is repeatedly or continuously exposed to stresses, especially those that provoke anxiety, therapeutic progress might be interrupted both within sessions and between sessions. Possible solutions to the first and third of these problems are not too difficult to identify. In the case of severe depression, there is a range of techniques that might be used.

On present knowledge the most effective alternative probably is antidepressant medication, using clomipramine or some similar drug (e.g., Rachman et al., 1979). There are other physical methods that might be adopted, and recent progress in the application of cognitive methods of therapy to combating depression promises further assistance. As far as the interference caused by persisting stress is concerned, one might turn to environmental manipulations, drug supplements, or some of the standard fear-reducing techniques such as desensitization, modeling, and so forth. The second probable cause of therapeutic failure, overvalued ideas, presents the most difficult problem, and there is regrettably little that can be added at present.

FRESH PERSPECTIVES

It has been remarked that the contemplation of therapeutic failures against an absence of successes is of limited value, but that it may help to promote a fresh approach to the nature of the problem and how best to modify it. Two novel perspectives will be considered.

Emotional Processing

The problems of obsessions can be reexamined in terms of a three-system analysis, along the lines set out by Rachman (1980) and in terms of the concept of emotional processing (Rachman, 1981).

Beginning with the concept of emotional processing, it is proposed that

> Emotional disturbances are absorbed and decline to the extent that other experiences and behavior can proceed without disruption . . .if an emotional disturbance is *not* absorbed satisfactorily, some signs become evident . . .the central indispensible index of unsatisfactory emotional activity, such as obsessions, nightmares, pressure of talk, phobias, inappropriate expressions of emotion that are out of context or out of proportion, or simply out of time. (p. 51)

Reexamined from this perspective, Foa's (1979) two types of failure can be reconstrued. The first is a failure of processing, in the case of excessively depressed patients. In cases of failure attributed to the presence of overvalued ideas, one can speak of a partial failure of emotional processing. Some emotional processing is completed in the early stages, but the intrusive signs of emotional activity, in the form of obsessions or compulsions in these cases, return after an interval. Without losing sight of the fact that Foa was dealing with problems that were predominantly compulsive rather than obsessional, it can be said that the depressed patients failed to process the emotional material at all.

Perhaps the depressed patients failed to process the material because they failed even to register the emotional input. No doubt, if the appropriate psychophysiological and other measures had been taken at the time, it would have been found that these patients failed to respond to the introduction of the pertinent emotional material. Here it can be recalled that Lang (1977, p. 863) has asserted that "the critical requirement . . .is that at least partial response components of the affective state must be present if an emotional image is to be modified" (p. 874). This view of Foa's observations leads to the addition of another circumstance in which emotional processing may fail—where there is an apparent failure to register the emotional material. The patients with overvalued ideas did not show this kind of failure. During the treatment sessions they displayed reducing emotional reactivity—plainly this was not a failure of registration. Instead, the failures in these cases took place between sessions, and can be regarded as failures of consolidation rather than of registration.

It may also be that Foa's observations on these obsessional-compulsive patients bear some resemblance to the phenomenon called "the return of fear" (Rachman, 1979). Given the transience of the intrasession reductions in fear that gave rise to the concept of "the return of fear," it was reasonable to suppose that these changes reflect the operation of fatigue-like processes. However, the first experimental analysis of this possibility, by Grey, Sartory, and Rachman (1981), failed to produce supporting evidence. If the return of fear, or in the case of Foa's patients, the return of compulsive problems, is not easily attributable to the generation of a fatigue-like state during the session (followed by its dissipation during the rest interval), then the next possibility is that the fear or the compulsive problems are *reinstated* during the intersession interval. And it is here that Foa's observations might be most useful. Given that her patients retained in substantially unchanged form their original false beliefs about the compulsive material, when no longer in the therapeutic setting they had ample opportunity to reconsider the events of the past treatment session and their false beliefs had free play to reinstate the related fears. It is perhaps for reasons of this kind that patients with overvalued ideas, such as those described by Foa and some encountered in our own clinical experience, constantly seek reassurance within the sessions and then with equal or increased vigor between sessions. Whatever the validity of these speculations, Foa's observations provide an excellent example of the intimate connections between cognitions and emotional reactions. Among patients with overvalued ideas, it would appear that the persistence of the false beliefs is capable of reviving the fear or compulsive activity at intervals. One might say that the fear is revived and hence sustained by the false belief. If this analysis is well founded, one is bound to give serious consideration to the need for therapeutic techniques that will enable us to modify the false belief that in these cases appears to play a controlling and decisive part in sustaining the abnormal behavior. Notwithstanding the encouraging early successes of cognitive behavior therapy (see Beck, 1976, and others), it has to be admitted that attempts to modify the kind of false belief described by Foa have not been notably successful (Watts et al., 1973). As with so many other examples, these clinical observations tell us more about the failures of emotional processing than of the conditions and circumstances in which emotional processing is satisfactorily completed (see Rachman for a full account, 1981).

Three-Component Analysis

Turning from the concept of emotional processing, we can now examine the second alternative perspective, developed from Lang's analysis of fear (1968, 1970). Obsessions can be said to comprise three main components—cognitive, behavioral, and physiological—each of which can be distinguished by its major features. Cognitive features are characterized by the unacceptability of the content of the thoughts, their immovability, their intrusive qualities, and the discomfort with which they are associated. The behavioral aspects are characterized by passive avoidance of potentially dangerous or distressing stimuli, active avoidance of situations in which threatening stimuli might be encountered, and internal neutralizing activities. The psychophysiological component, usually autonomic arousal, is assessed separately. The development of this analysis leads to a series of deductions about treatment tactics and their probable consequences. It is argued that the application of the appropriate treatment tactic is essential. For example, if one attempts to tackle the cognitive aspects of an obsession by predominantly behavioral tactics, the chances of success are lessened. Selection of a suitable cognitive procedure, or rather a procedure designed to deal specifically with the cognitive aspects of the problem, is more likely to be successful. A clear example of this approach is given by Ost et al. (1981) in their study of social anxiety.

The argument can be illustrated by reference to the case of a man who suffered from repetitive obsessions on the theme that he might incorrectly inform on an innocent person. These distressing thoughts led him to adopt a wide range of avoidance tactics, including the establishment of set patterns of traveling to and from work that enabled him to avoid going past any mailboxes. In this way he sought to protect himself from the possibility of unwittingly or inadvertently sending postal accusations to the authorities. In the early stages of treatment, direct attempts were made to reduce the intrusiveness and frequency of the obsessive thoughts themselves. A small amount of progress was made but there was no significant modification of the avoidance behavior until active steps were taken to ensure that the patient deliberately and repeatedly approached all of those stimuli and situations that he was customarily avoiding. In the early stages of this exposure part of the treatment he experienced the expected arousal of anxiety, but equally expectedly, he showed a steady and successful habituation to the stimuli and circumstances he had been avoiding.

The general conclusion to be drawn from this construal of obsessions, in terms of the 3-component analysis, is that the major treatment tactic should be chosen on the basis of a 3-component analysis. If the patient's problem is primarily a difficulty in dismissing the intrusive thoughts, then a tactic designed specifically to improve dismissal capacity should be given priority. If, on the other hand, the

3-system analysis leads one to conclude that the problem is mainly of frequency of intrusions, rather than duration, one would experiment with methods of distraction or of thought-blocking rather than thought-dismissal. An obsessional problem in which the psychophysiological reaction to the intrusive cognition is the patient's major problem would require the use of a tactic that has a major effect on the physiological reactions; for example, one may consider using a relaxation technique or a drug supplement. Table 3.1 sets out the components of obsessions and their relation to treatment tactics, and Table 3.2 gives the detailed predictions for each treatment tactic. The argument that the particular treatment tactic should be selected by a rational analysis of the nature of the presenting problem seems to us plausible, but it should not disguise the shortage of validated treatment tactics. At present we have very few treatment techniques of assured value.

In the analysis carried out by Rachman (1978), the treatment techniques set out in Table 3.2 were considered: habituation training, satiation training, cognitive restructuring, dismissive tactics, desensitization, modeling, counseling, paradoxical intention, response prevention and exposure, and thought-stopping. A modestly optimistic assessment of these possibilities is given in Rachman and Hodgson (1980) but those considered by Beech and Vaughan (1978) received a more severe and harsh evaluation. In the view of the latter writers, none of the presently available tactics has achieved respectability. Rather than restate and rehearse the evidence and arguments relating to each of these techniques (in fact, most of the debate is about the effects of thought-stopping), we will instead give an account of some recent laboratory and clinical research that bears on the subject.

Following on the analysis set out by Rachman in 1978, a test of the therapeutic value of habituation training was carried out on 60 nonpsychiatric subjects who reported experiencing unwanted, unacceptable, intrusive thoughts that are said to bear similarity to clinical obsessions (see Rachman & de Silva, 1978). In this experiment by Parkinson and Rachman (1980) it was found that habituation training, which consisted of getting the subject repeatedly to form the relevant intrusive thought to instruction, was followed by a decrease in the amount of discomfort and stressfulness associated with the thought. Moreover, the supplementary use of relaxation training appeared to facilitate the progress of habituation training, or even to substitute for it. Armed with this encouraging result, Likierman and Rachman (in press) carried out a small clinical trial in which they compared the effects of habituation training and thought-stopping in the treatment of the obsessions of 12 psychiatric patients. The results of the laboratory experiment by Parkinson and Rachman are shown in Figure 3.1 and can be compared with the disappointing results obtained in the clinical trial by Likierman and Rachman (1981) shown in Figures 3.2 and 3.3, in which the induced changes proved to be too transient to be of therapeutic value.

Even if it is conceded that we have made some useful progress in the analysis of obsessions, we are not yet in sight of a treatment tactic or tactics of proven value. The case for following a 3-component analysis and for seeking to develop

Table 3.1. The Components of Obsessions in Relation to Treatment Possibilities

	Cognitive				Behavioral-Cognitive Responses		
	Discomfort	Acceptability	Intrusiveness	Immovability	Overt Avoidance	Neutralizing	Psychophysiological Disturbances
Direct treatments (plus, secondary tactics, given in parentheses)	Habituation/satiation training (relaxation, cognitive restructuring, dismissive, desensitization, modeling)	Cognitive restructuring	Distractive (desensitization, modeling, stress-reducers)	Dismissive	Response prevention after exposure (direct instruction, satiation)		Habituation training (relaxation, cognitive restructuring, dismissive)
Conventional, current methods—primary action	Drugs, counseling	Paradoxical intention, counseling	Counseling ("occupy yourself")	Thought-stopping			Drugs, leucotomy

Primary and secondary behavioral treatment tactics appropriate to each feature of the three components, plus notes on conventional tactics.

Table 3.2. Predicted Effects of Treatment Approaches: Primary and Secondary

Habituation/Satiation Training (±Relaxation)	Response Prevention (after exposure)	Distraction Training	Dismissal Training	Cognitive Restructuring	Fear-Reduction (modeling, desensitization)
Primary effects					
Reduced psychophysiological disturbance	Reduced frequency of overt avoidance	Reduced frequency of obsessions	Reduced duration of obsessions	Increased acceptability	Reduced fear
Reduced subjective discomfort	Reduced frequency of neutralizing activities	Reduced duration of obsessions		Generality of changes	Reduced discomfort
Note, specificity of changes					
Secondary effects					
Increased acceptability	Cognitive restructuring	Reduced discomfort	Reduced discomfort	Reduced discomfort	Reduced frequency and duration
Reduced duration of obsession			Reduced frequency	Reduced avoidance and neutralizing	
Reduced frequency					

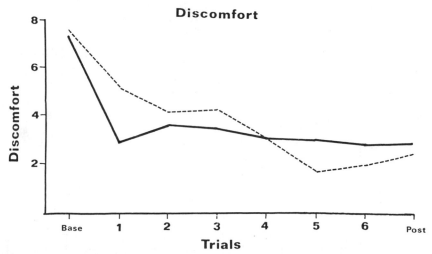

Figure 3.1. Subjective discomfort scores, trial by trial for 60 subjects. The results shown in the solid line are for subjects who had relaxation training plus habituation training, and the dotted line shows the scores for subjects who had habituation training without relaxation (from Parkinson, & Rachman, 1980).

tactics that will be appropriate to the findings that emerge from component analyses seems to us to be plausible, but its value remains to be demonstrated and, of course, such a demonstration must itself await the development of sufficiently robust treatment tactics. Except insofar as the present analysis and the associated arguments are of some value, it can be said that discussions of failures to help obsessional patients are premature. One's failures should not be taken too seriously—until they can be examined against the glow of successes.

SUMMARY AND CONCLUSIONS

The main obstacle to the successful treatment of obsessions is the absence of robust proven techniques. It is argued that the adoption of fresh perspectives, namely, a 3-component analysis of obsessions and the introduction of the concept of emotional processing, may facilitate the search for, and development of, new methods of treatment.

In the interim, some tentative guidelines are offered to practicing clinicians. Following Foa's analysis of compulsive problems, it is possible that the presence of significant depression will block therapeutic progress, and the presence of overvalued ideas will prevent enduring progress. Also, the presence of stress or anxiety will retard progress. Attempts should be made to reduce these interfering conditions but at present there is no sure way of unraveling overvalued ideas.

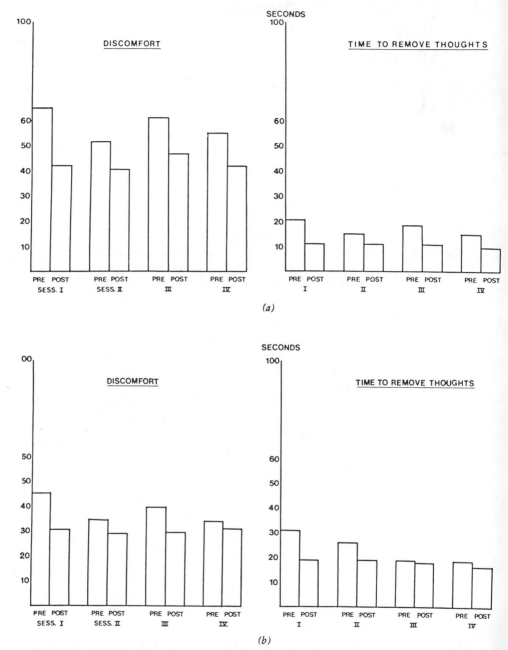

Figure 3.2. Subjective discomfort, pre- and post-sessions for treatment groups: (*a*) thought-stopping and (*b*) habituation training (from Likierman, & Rachman, 1981).

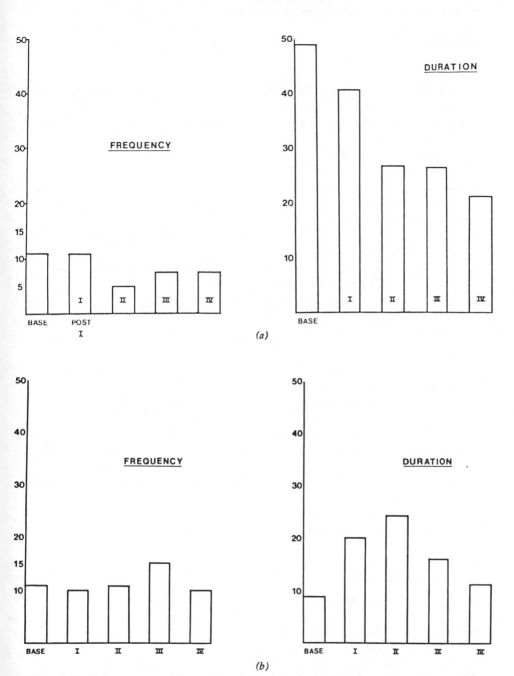

Figure 3.3. Daily measures of frequency and duration of obsessions, for treatment groups: (*a*) thought-stopping and (*b*) habituation (from Likierman, & Rachman, 1981).

REFERENCES

Beck, A. (1976) *Cognitive therapy and the emotional disorders.* New York: International Universities Press.

Beech, H., & Vaughan, M. (1978) *Behavioural treatment of obsessional states.* New York: Wiley.

Foa, E. (1979) Failures in treating obsessive compulsives. *Behaviour Research & Therapy,* **17,** 169–176.

Foa, E., Grayson, J., & Steketee, G. (1980) *Depression, habituation, and treatment outcome in obsessive compulsives.* Symposium on "Practical Applications of Learning Theories in Psychiatry", Crete, April.

Grey, S., Sartory, G. & Rachman, S. (1981) The return of fear: The role of inhibition. *Behaviour Research and Therapy.*

Horowitz, M. (1975) Intrusive and repetitive thoughts after experimental stress. *Archives of General Psychiatry,* **32,** 1457–1463.

Lader, M. (1969) Physiological measures in agitated and retarded depressed patients. *Journal of Psychiatric Research,* **7,** 89–100.

Lader, M., & Wing, L. (1966) *Physiological measures, sedative drugs & morbid anxiety.* London: Oxford.

Lang, P. (1968) Fear reduction and fear behavior. In J. Schlien (Ed.), *Research in psychotherapy.* Washington D.C.: American Psychological Association (Vol. 3), pp. 90–103.

Lang, P. (1970) Stimulus control, response control and the desensitization of fear. In D. Levis (Ed.), *Learning theory approaches to therapeutic behavior.* Chicago: Aldine.

Lang, P. (1977) Imagery in therapy. *Behavior Therapy,* **8,** 862–886.

Likierman, H., & Rachman, S. (in press). The treatment of obsessions by habituation training or thought stopping.

Maudsley, H. (1895) *The pathology of mind.* (Reprinted in 1979 by *Behavioral Psychotherapy.* Friedmann Publishers, London.)

Ost, L., Jerremalm, A., & Johannson, J. (1981) Individual response patterns and the effects of behavioral methods in treating social phobics. *Behaviour Research & Therapy,* **19,** 1–16.

Parkinson, L., & Rachman, S. (1980) Are intrusive thoughts subject to habituation? *Behaviour Research and Therapy,* **18,** 409–418.

Parkinson, L., & Rachman, S. (1981) Intrusive thoughts: The effects of an uncontrived stress. *Advances in Behaviour Research and Therapy,* **3,** 111–118.

Rachman, S. (1973) Some similarities and differences between obsessional ruminations and morbid preoccupations. *Canadian Psychiatric Association Journal,* **18,** 71–74.

Rachman, S. (1978) An anatomy of obsessions. *Behaviour Analysis & Modification,* **2,** 253–278.

Rachman, S. (1979) The return of fear *Behaviour Research and Therapy,* **17,** 164-166.

Rachman, S. (1981) Emotional processing. *Behaviour Research & Therapy,* **18,** 51–60.

Rachman, S., & de Silva, P. (1978) Abnormal and normal obsessions. *Behaviour Research & Therapy,* **16,** 233–248.

Rachman, S., Cobb, J., MacDonald, B., Mawson, D., Sartory, G., & Stern, R. (1979) The behavioural treatment of obsessional compulsive disorders, with and without clomipramine. *Behaviour Research and Therapy,* **17,** 467–478.

Rachman, S., & Hodgson, R. (1980) *Obsessions and compulsions.* Englewood Cliffs, N.J.: Prentice-Hall, Century Series.

Stern, R., Lipsedge, M., & Marks, I. (1973) Obsessive ruminations: A controlled trial of a thought-stopping technique. *Behaviour Research & Therapy,* **11,** 659–662.

Watts, F., Powell, G., & Austin, S. (1973) The modification of abnormal beliefs. *British Journal of Medical Psychology,* **46,** 359–363.

CHAPTER 4

Failure in Treating Agoraphobia

PAUL M.G. EMMELKAMP
ADA VAN DER HOUT

Agoraphobics have been reported to be very difficult to treat by therapists of different theoretical orientations. Systematic desensitization has only small effects on agoraphobics. In the studies by Evans and Kellam (1973), Gelder, Marks, and Wolff (1967), and Marks, Boulougouris, and Marset (1971), agoraphobics improved less than specific phobics with systematic desensitization. Agoraphobics are characterized by high neuroticism scores, more spontaneous fluctuations in skin conductance, and a slowed GSR habituation rate to repeated auditory stimuli as compared with subjects with specific phobias and normals. There is some evidence that habituation rate and palmar skin conductance is related to improvement with systematic desensitization (Lader, Gelder, & Marks, 1967). In contrast with other phobics, most agoraphobics have other problems besides the phobia including free-floating anxiety, panic attacks, and depression, which also may hinder progress with treatment by systematic desensitization.

The meager results of systematic desensitization with agoraphobics have led to treatment innovations. There are now numerous studies demonstrating that exposure in vivo might be highly effective. The exposure in vivo procedures can be divided roughly into two categories: prolonged exposure in vivo and self-controlled exposure in vivo. The studies in this area have been recently reviewed elsewhere (Emmelkamp, 1979; Emmelkamp, in 1982 a) and this will not be reiterated here. Studies comparing individual and group exposure in vivo found no clear differences in effectiveness (Emmelkamp & Emmelkamp-Benner, 1975; Hafner & Marks, 1976). However, group exposure in vivo offers the advantage of being more economical in that it might save therapist time and is now conducted in a number of treatment centers.

Another recent innovation concerns cognitive restructuring. Cognitive re-

Completion of this chapter was facilitated by Grant 56-153 from the Netherlands Organization for the Advancement of Pure Research.

structuring was found to be less effective than prolonged exposure in vivo in a study by Emmelkamp, Kuipers, and Eggeraat (1978). However, both treatments involved five sessions and were conducted in one week. It may be that insufficient time was allowed for all the effects of cognitive restructuring to appear. It is conceivable that the response to cognitive restructuring follows a longer time course than that by prolonged exposure in vivo. In a replication study, Emmelkamp and Mersch (1982) found that cognitive restructuring might have delayed effects comparable to that of prolonged exposure in vivo.

It has gradually become clear that in many instances it is insufficient to focus exclusively on the modification of phobic anxiety and avoidance. Inasmuch as in a number of patients agoraphobia is associated with other problems, the latter may become therapeutic goals on their own. For example, Andrews (1966) considers such patients as generally shy, anxious, and dependent in many other situations than the typically phobic situations. Behavioral approaches that focus on such broader therapeutic targets include cognitive restructuring and assertive training. A recent study (Emmelkamp, 1980a) demonstrated that assertive training may be helpful with respect to the interpersonal functioning of agoraphobics; assertive training had less effect with respect to the improvement of phobic anxiety and avoidance.

Several follow-up studies of treated agoraphobics have been conducted (Emmelkamp & Kuipers, 1979; McPherson, Brougham, & McLaren, 1980; Munby & Johnston, 1980). Generally, improvements brought about by the treatment were maintained over a follow-up period that ranged from four years (Emmelkamp & Kuipers; McPherson et al.) up to nine years (Munby & Johnston, 1980). However, although behavioral treatment led to considerable improvements, relatively few patients were completely free of agoraphobic symptoms. Figure 4.1 presents the results on the anxiety and avoidance scales at pretest, posttest, and four-year follow-up in the Emmelkamp and Kuipers (1979) study. Although 75 percent of patients turned out to have improved on the main phobia, improvement was far from complete. There proved to be a great variation in the improvement achieved. Some patients were symptom free, some were moderately improved, and a few patients did not benefit at all. Similarly, McPherson et al. (1980) reported that only 10 percent of the sample was completely symptom free: "The majority (66%) reported that their symptoms had stabilised at a level which, while occasionally causing them slight distress, could easily be tolerated and affected their every day lives only slightly, if at all" (p. 151).

PROGNOSTIC VARIABLES

Several studies have looked for predictors of treatment outcome. Generally, pretreatment measures prove to be poor predictors of outcome (e.g., Hafner & Marks, 1976). Heightened physiological arousal before treatment (Stern &

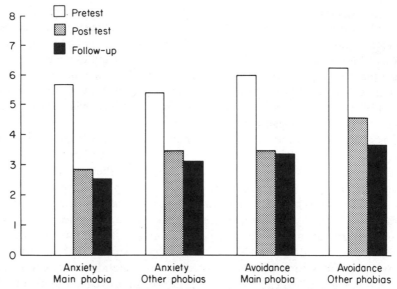

Figure 4.1.   Mean phobic anxiety and avoidance rating at pretest, posttest, and follow-up. (Reprinted with permission from *British Journal of Psychiatry*, 1979.)

Marks, 1973; Watson & Marks, 1971), initial severity of phobia (Stern & Marks, 1973), "emotional stability" and duration of phobia (Mathews, Johnston, Lancashire, Munby, Shaw, & Gelder, 1976), and expectancy of therapeutic gain (Emmelkamp & Emmelkamp-Benner, 1975; Emmelkamp & Wessels, 1975) may all be associated with outcome. The few relationships that have been found between variables at the start of treatment and outcome can be partially explained by chance and have little clinical utility.

Johnston, Lancashire, Mathews, Munby, Shaw, and Gelder (1976) found that predictive power improved as treatment progressed. However, they pointed out that: "These correlations do not achieve useful levels until about eight weeks have passed, and this is rather too long for it to be of practical value" (p. 374). Emmelkamp and Kuipers looked for prognostic variables for result of treatment at four-year follow-up. The following prognostic variables, measured at the start of treatment, were investigated: (1) duration of phobia, (2) locus of control, (3) social anxiety, and (4) depression. None of these variables showed a clear relationship with results at follow-up. Munby and Johnston (1980) correlated patients' scores on the main measures of agoraphobic severity prior to treatment with follow-up results (ranging from five to nine years after treatment). The correlations showed that phobia rating prior to treatment were poor predictors of long-term outcome.

In summary, studies in which pretreatment measures were related with short-term and long-term outcome have not been particularly useful in providing cues with respect to the issue of treatment failures.

INTERPERSONAL CONFLICT

Both psychodynamically oriented and system-theoretic oriented therapists hold that agoraphobia is the result of conflict. Psychodynamically oriented clinicians regard the phobic symptoms as deriving from interpersonal and intrapersonal conflicts that are recapitulations of early childhood patterns. These conflicts may manifest themselves in the interpersonal relationships of phobic patients. Thus proponents of this view hold that phobic symptoms are "dynamically" related to faulty interpersonal relationships.

According to the system theories, phobic symptoms should be regarded as a result of inadequate interactions. There have evolved a number of different system theories, the most influential being the communication oriented approach of the Palo Alto Group (Watzlawick, Beavin, & Jackson, 1967). A basic assumption for communication theorists is that psychiatric symptoms have interpersonal meaning in relationships. Thus it is assumed that the phobic symptoms reflect relationship conflict.

Several behavior therapists also stressed the importance of interpersonal conflicts in the development of agoraphobia. Goldstein and Chambless (1978) found some evidence that agoraphobia onset was related to high interpersonal conflict. They proposed that the phobic symptoms are the result of psychological avoidance behavior in conflict situations:

> Usually because of his/her unassertiveness the agoraphobic has found himself/herself in an unhappy seemingly irresolvable relationship under the domination of a spouse or parent. The urges to leave and the fears of being on her/his own balance out, and the agoraphobic is trapped in this conflict, unable to move and lacking the skills to change the situation. (Chambless & Goldstein, 1980, p. 324)

If agoraphobia has an important function in the system of the patient, one could hypothesize that any isolated modification of the patient's symptoms should lead to the emergence of new symptoms in the patient or to changes in the partner. Further, a behavioral approach of the phobic symptoms that does not take into account the interpersonal meaning of the symptoms would be expected to lead to treatment failure.

In several studies an attempt has been made to examine the emergence of new symptoms after behavior therapy. In a study by Crisp (1966), new symptoms did not emerge in a series of mixed neurotic patients who were treated with behavior therapy: "A number of patients whose symptoms improved during treatment remained improved over the follow-up period and did not themselves produce new symptoms" (p. 191). In a follow-up study on 70 agoraphobic patients who had been treated with behavior therapy four years previously, Emmelkamp and Kuipers (1979) found no evidence of new symptom emergence. Similarly, neither in the follow-up study of Munby and Johnston (1980) nor in the study of McPherson et al. (1980) was there evidence of the development of new symptoms. Hafner (1976) examined the emergence of fresh symptoms after prolonged exposure in vivo on 39 agoraphobic patients. His criterion for fresh symptom emergence was an increase over pretreatment scores on any scale of the Middlesex Hospital Questionnaire (MHQ) or Fear Survey Schedule (FSS) on more than one of the five posttreatment assessments. One third of the patients did well on almost any criteria, one third responded well to treatment on only one criterion: that of symptoms directly treated but "was actually worse twelve months after treatment" (p. 381) on three of the four remaining measures. The results of the third group of patients was between the other two groups. Unfortunately, the results of this study are difficult to interpret due to the lack of a control group and Hafner's definition of fresh symptom emergence. Of 39 patients, 26 met the criterion of fresh symptom emergence. However, it should be noted that the MMQ and FSS consist of 13 subscales and that any increase over pretreatment scores on two out of five occasions was already defined as a fresh symptom. Thus the finding of fresh symptoms in this study might be at least partly attributed to chance.

Three types of studies are relevant with respect to the partner of phobic patients. First, studies sought to investigate whether partners of agoraphobics do have psychiatric pathology themselves. Second, a series of studies examined the influence of interpersonal problems on the outcome of behavior therapy. Finally, a few studies addressed themselves to the issue of whether improvement of the phobic patient led to negative changes in the partner or in the marital relationship.

1. *The partners of agoraphobics.*   Several authors (e.g., Fry, 1962; Hafner, 1979; Webster, 1953) suggested that partners of (agora)phobic patients are psychologically abnormal or have phobic symptoms themselves. In contrast, in studies by Agulnik (1970), Buglass, Clarke, Henderson, Kreitman, and Presley (1977), and Hafner (1977a) no evidence was found that the phobic partners were neurotic.

2. *Interpersonal problems.*   Several studies investigated the extent to which interpersonal problems affect the outcome of exposure in vivo procedures. Hudson (1974), working with agoraphobics who received prolonged exposure in vivo treatment, found that patients from "sick families" showed much less improvement than patients from "well adjusted" families. Milton and Hafner (1979) treated 18 patients with prolonged exposure in vivo and found that patients whose marriages were rated as unsatisfactory before treatment improved less during treatment, and were significantly more likely to relapse during follow-up than those patients with satisfactory marriages. Bland and Hallam (1980) related the level of marital satisfaction with response to exposure in vivo treatment and found a significant difference between "good marriage" and "poor marriage" groups with respect to phobic severity. At three-month follow-up, the "poor marriage" group showed a significantly greater tendency to relapse compared with the "good marriage" group. Interestingly, improvement was found to be associated with the patient's satisfaction with spouse. Spouse's dissatisfaction with the patient was *not* related to outcome of treatment. Finally, Emmelkamp (1980b) distinguished two types of interpersonal problems: problems with the spouse, and

unassertiveness. Agoraphobics were divided in low and high marital satisfaction and in low and high assertiveness on the basis of their scores on questionnaires. All patients were treated with self-controlled exposure in vivo. After four treatment sessions, almost no significant differences between groups were found. Low-assertive patients improved as much as high-assertive patients; patients with low marital satisfaction improved as much as patients with high marital satisfaction. Neither at the posttest nor at one-month follow-up was self-controlled exposure in vivo influenced by the interpersonal problems of agoraphobics. The finding of this study is in contrast to the findings of Bland and Hallam (1980) Hudson (1974) and Milton and Hafner (1979). The contradictory findings might be explained by a number of differences. First, in the Emmelkamp (1980b) study, treatment consisted of self-controlled exposure in vivo rather than prolonged exposure in vivo. Further, the assessment of marital satisfaction varied from study to study and may not be directly comparable. Finally, Emmelkamp (1980b) assessed only short-term effects, whereas the differences in outcome between "good" and "bad" marriage groups tended to become greater at three-month (Bland & Hallam, 1980) and six-month (Milton & Hafner, 1979) follow-ups. Thus although little differences may be found immediately after treatment, maritally dissatisfied patients may relapse and maritally satisfied patients may show further improvement several months after treatment.

   3. *Adverse treatment effects.*   Several studies investigated whether treatment has adverse effects on the patient's spouse and the marital relationship. Hand and Lamontagne (1976) reported that in some cases improvement of phobias was followed by a marital crisis. Hafner (1977b) found that a deterioration of the most hostile husbands at follow-up coincided with a maximum improvement in their wives' phobic symptoms. Some spouses were adversely affected by their wives' improvement, but improved when their partner relapsed. Milton and Hafner (1979) reported that: "the marriages of nine (out of 15) patients appeared to be adversely influenced by their symptomatic improvement" (p. 807). However, inspection of their data (Milton, & Hafner, Table 1, p. 808) reveals a totally different picture: Both patients and their partners show an improvement rather than a deterioration on marital and sexual adjustment. Thus the idea of a worsening of the marriage was based on clinical anecdotal material, rather than on the more objective measures used. In contrast to the conclusions of Milton and Hafner, Bland and Hallam (1980) found that phobia removal led to a reduction in the spouse's dissatisfaction with the patient. In summary, although clinical anecdotes suggest that phobia removal might lead to an exacerbation of interpersonal problems, little or no objective data are provided to support this idea.

FACTORS RELATED TO FAILURE

The present study was undertaken with the aim of investigating factors that might be associated with treatment failures. Before presenting some data with respect to our treatment failures, we will provide results of a survey that we conducted on patients who did ot accept our treatment offer and on patients who prematurely discontinued the treatment.

Nonacceptance of Treatment

A number of patients do not accept the treatment offered to them. Garfield (1978, 1980) reviewed studies that investigated nonacceptance of psychotherapy and found that approximately one third or more of the patients refused the psychotherapy offered to them. Marks (1978) reported that approximately one fourth of patients who were offered behavioral treatment did not accept it. Very few studies have investigated factors related to this nonacceptance of therapy and results are inconclusive (Garfield, 1980).

Inasmuch as we were interested in learning the reasons why patients refused treatment, we recently undertook a focused investigation into the problem of nonacceptance of therapy. Twenty-five consecutive referrals to our department who did not accept the behavioral treatment offered to them were asked to participate. Treatment that was offered consisted of prolonged exposure in vivo, sometimes preceded by cognitive restructuring, both conducted in groups. Patients were requested to fill in a questionnaire containing 22 questions pertaining to factors that could be related to their nonacceptance of therapy. Although the questions were presented in random order, they clustered around the following headings:

1. Patient already improved (no need for treatment)
2. External circumstances (e.g., inconvenient time: no baby-sitter available)
3. Discongruent treatment expectations (e.g., medication, individual treatment)
4. Frightened of treatment
5. Therapist
6. Family
7. Other reasons

Patients had to rate each question as to whether it was: (1) not applicable, (2) somewhat applicable, or (3) very much applicable. Sixteen agoraphobics returned completed questionnaires. Summary statements of the questions and the number of persons that responded affirmatively to each question are listed in Figure 4.2.

About half of the patients reported that they were already (somewhat) improved at the start of treatment. Presumably, we have to take this answer with a grain of salt, inasmuch as most of these patients also gave other reasons for their failure to accept therapy. A number of patients blamed external circumstances for the nonacceptance of therapy and some of these patients intended to contact us for treatment in the future. The findings that patients' expectations of therapy did not fit our offer and that a number of patients reported to be frightened of the proposed treatment indicate that more attention should be given to

Improved

1. already improved

2. no longer troubled by phobia

   External circumstances

3. inconvenient time

4. certain circumstances

5. physical condition

   Discongruent expectations

6. proposed treatment did not appeal

7. group treatment not suited

8. expect more benefits from pills

   Frightened of treatment

9. location (psychiatric hospital)

10. treatment

11. having to stop taking pills

12. previous interview

    Therapist

13. not understood by therapist

14. too young

15. didn't like therapist

    Family

16. treatment too heavy burden for family

17. partner found treatment unnecessary

18. partner is of considerable assistance

19. applied for treatment because of family

    Other reasons

20. "You have to overcome your fears on your own"

21. Phobia will pass off with time

22. Attention worsens problem

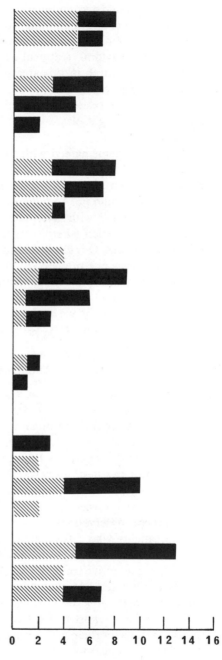

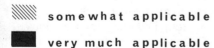 somewhat applicable

very much applicable

0 2 4 6 8 10 12 14 16

Figure 4.2. Number of patients responding affirmatively to questions regarding their nonacceptance of treatment.

the introduction of treatment to the patients. A number of studies have been carried out with reference to preparing the patients for psychotherapy and the results suggest that pretherapy training might be useful (see Heitler, 1976, for a review of this work). Whether such an approach is helpful for the preparation of agoraphobics for behavioral treatment needs to be demonstrated. The present findings suggest that research in this area is needed.

Surprisingly, characteristics of the therapist who held the first interview seemed not to be related to the failure to accept therapy. In contrast, therapist characteristics might play an important part in failure of therapy which will be discussed later on.

Thirteen patients agreed with the slogan: "You have to overcome your fears on your own." Inasmuch as eight of these patients also reported that their partners were of considerable assistance when they were anxious, one may wonder whether this should not be taken to indicate that at least for these patients, "on your own" means "with my partner." A total of 10 patients responded affirmatively to the question whether the partner was of considerable assistance when they were anxious. Our clinical impression is that with a number of agoraphobics the "secondary gain" provided by the partner is an important factor contributing to refusal of treatment. Although the responses to this question are compatible with this view, one should be cautious in inferring too much from the present survey. Unfortunately, we do not have data from a control group of patients who did accept the treatment.

Early Termination of Treatment

Although dropout of therapy is a serious problem, relatively little attention has been paid to this issue by behavior therapists. Inasmuch as we were interested in the reasons for early termination, we sent questionnaires to 15 agoraphobics who dropped out of group treatment during the previous two years. The questionnaire consisted of questions that were also used in the "nonacceptance" study supplemented by questions pertaining to the specific treatment received. Because of the variety of treatment procedures used and the small number of completed questionnaires returned to us ($n = 8$), we will have to limit our discussion to a few general observations.

The patients who returned the questionnaire dropped out of the following treatments: prolonged exposure in vivo (PE, $n = 4$), cognitive restructuring (CR, $n = 2$), and assertive training (AT, $n = 2$). Most patients terminated treatment after one or two sessions, except for two patients in the exposure group who terminated treatment after the fifth and sixth treatment sessions respectively.

Most patients reported that treatment had made them anxious. Four patients gave as reasons for their early termination that the group had made them anxious (two from AT, one from PE, and one from CR). Discongruent treatment expectations also played a part with five persons. Two persons preferred a less "aggressive" approach. One patient wanted "to talk with a doctor and nothing further," another patient wanted pills and "something else," and the last patient—although dissatisfied—could not state which kind of treatment he preferred. Obviously, when a patient's expectancies are incongruent with what occurs in therapy, he or she is likely to become dissatisfied and might prematurely terminate treatment.

As to therapist characteristics, three patients found the therapist too young. In addition, two patients reported that the therapist did not understand their feelings. Discongruent treatment expectations and rating of therapist's characteristics seemed not to be related to any treatment in particular.

Two of the four patients from the exposure group reported that they were often unable during the treatment session to stay in the phobic situation until anxiety declined. In addition they stated that prolonged exposure to these situations did not lead to anxiety reduction. Another patient from the exposure treatment found that there had been too little time to discuss her feelings in the group.

Both patients who dropped out of assertive training reported that having to participate in role-playing made them anxious; being looked at by the other patients was a terrible experience. One of these patients remarked that the treatment did not focus on her problem.

Both patients who had received cognitive restructuring were unable to reduce their anxiety by cognitive means and became disappointed in the treatment. One of these patients felt that everyone in the group looked at him which made him very anxious. The other patient found that the treatment was not directed at her problems.

Taken together, the experiences of the patients who dropped out of treatment suggest that we have to modify our interventions in order to offer these patients more adequate treatment. The following points should be viewed as suggestions that might be worthwhile investigating in further studies and are by no means exhaustive.

1.   More attention should be paid to the individual problems of each patient. A standardized group program, although efficient and successful for a number of patients, might have adverse effects on others. Further studies should shed some light on the issue of those for whom such programs are helpful and for whom not. An important question for further study is whether dropout from treatment can be predicted.

2.   Pretherapy training might also be helpful in preventing dropouts. Emmelkamp and Emmelkamp-Benner (1975) investigated the effect of pretherapy training on 34 agoraphobics. Before treatment, half of the patients saw a video recording which lasted 25 minutes (self-controlled exposure in vivo), the other half of the patients did not see the film. In the film, three "ex agoraphobics" were interviewed about their experiences with the same treatment. Although the videofilm did not increase the effect of treatment, it was notable that patients dropped out only in the condition without video ($n = 3$).

3.   Social cohesion might also be an important factor in preventing dropout. Hand, Lamontagne, and Marks (1974) compared two different group conditions when conducting prolonged exposure in vivo. In their structured groups, cohesion was fostered; in their unstructured groups, interaction between the group

members was kept to a minimum, thus minimizing group cohesion. Cohesive groups yielded fewer dropouts and fewer relapses.

4.   Another line which might be profitable to follow is to use former phobics as cotherapists (Ross, 1980). When, for example, exposure in vivo is conducted by former phobics, patients might feel better understood and experience such treatment as less "harsh" than when conducted by a behavior therapist. Similarly, former phobics might be better able to convince patients of the relevance of cognitive restructuring and assertive training for their presenting problems than therapists. Often patients feel they are being ridiculed or not taken seriously when told by a therapist that their fears are irrational, which might be less of a problem when former phobics conduct cognitive restructuring. Obviously, not all former phobics will be suitable therapists. Studies are needed to investigate whether the use of former phobics as therapists might offer a solution for the problem of dropout.

5.   A final suggestion to prevent premature termination is to have the partner of the phobic patient participate in the treatment. Several studies on agoraphobics (Mathews, Janoun, & Gelder, 1979; Mathews, Teasdale, Munby, Johnston, & Shaw, 1977) and obsessive-compulsives (Emmelkamp, 1982 b) indicate that the partner might be employed as cotherapist but it should be noted that the use of the partner as a cotherapist may not be without problems (Emmelkamp, 1982 c).

Failure of Exposure in Vivo

In the next study to be reported, we investigated whether failure of prolonged exposure in vivo was related to such variables as initial severity, depression, assertiveness, marital complications, and illness phobias. In addition, we studied whether failures were differentiated from successful cases by age, previous treatment, previous use of psychotropic medication, and duration of phobia.

For this study we used the data of 16 agoraphobics who had received group treatment (prolonged exposure in vivo) at our department (approximately 10 sessions). Failure was defined as less than a 3-point change on a 0–8 scale for anxiety and avoidance. Patients had to rate the following situations: (1) walking away from the hospital, (2) walking down a busy main street, (3) traveling on a bus, (4) shopping in a supermarket, and (5) sitting in a restaurant (Emmelkamp et al., 1978). The patient's ratings for anxiety and avoidance were combined. Using this rather strict criterion of failure, 11 patients were categorized as successful cases and 5 as failures.

Initial Severity, Depression, and Assertiveness

Results revealed that initial severity (as measured by anxiety and avoidance rating, behavioral measure, Fear Survey Schedule, and anxious mood) did not differentiate failures from successful cases. Further, neither pretreatment depression (SDS; Zung, 1965) nor assertiveness (ASES; Gay, Hollandsworth, & Galassi, 1975) did so. The data were analyzed using 2-tailed t tests for independent samples and on none of these variables was a significant difference between groups found ($p < .05$). The finding that initial depression did not differentiate failures from successes is of some importance, inasmuch as several authors found a relationship between agoraphobia and depression (Bowen & Kohout, 1979; Marks, 1969; Schapira, Kerr, & Roth, 1970). The present finding is consistent with the results of Emmelkamp and Kuipers (1979), who also could not find a relationship between initial depression and success of exposure treatment at four-year follow-up. Finally, unassertiveness seems not to be related to failure and corroborates the finding of Emmelkamp (1980b).

Marital Complications

In the studies that examined a relationship between marital satisfaction and treatment outcome, marital satisfation was assessed before the start of treatment. It is conceivable that patients might find it difficult to admit dissatisfaction with their partner before a therapeutic relationship has developed. Therefore, a patient's account of the relationship in the course of treatment might give a more accurate picture of satisfaction with the spouse than pretreatment indices of marital satisfaction. In the present study the information with respect to marital satisfaction was gathered retrospectively from the therapists' files. It was hypothesized in advance that patients who complained about their partners during treatment were more likely to become treatment failures with exposure in vivo as compared with patients who did not complain about their partners. Results revealed that complaints about the partner did differentiate failures from successful cases (1-tailed Fisher test, $p < .05$).

Illness Phobias

As discussed elsewhere (Emmelkamp, 1982 c) agoraphobia is often associated with illness phobias and hypochondriasis. In a study on disease-phobic patients Bianchi (1971) found that approximately 35 percent of these patients also suffered from agoraphobia, whereas none of the controls did. If the avoidance behavior of agoraphobics is motivated by fear of having a serious disease, it is unlikely that exposure in vivo to agoraphobic situations will lead to an improvement of the agoraphobia, inasmuch as the treatment does not deal with the underlying cause of the disorder. Foa (1979) suggested that "overvalued ideation" might hinder successful treatment by exposure in vivo. She found that obsessive-compulsive patients who showed strong beliefs that their fears were realistic failed to benefit significantly from treatment. Although, normally, habituation occurs both within and between sessions a different pattern was found with patients with "overvalued ideation": "the decrement in subjective anxiety within sessions still appeared but there was no evidence for habituation between sessions. Whatever was gained during a session was apparently lost during the time lapse between sessions" (p. 172). In order to test whether agoraphobics who had *realistic* fears that they had a serious disease failed to benefit from treatment by exposure in vivo, we rated our cases with respect to this "overvalued ideation." The information was gathered from therapists' files. The extent to which patients were rated to have "overvalued ideation" did *not* differentiate successes from failures (Fisher test). It should be noted, however, that our information was gathered retrospectively which obviously limits the conclusions to be drawn. Further, it is doubtful whether "overvalued ideation" as expressed in hypochondrical fears is comparable to that found among obsessive-compulsives.

Other Variables

On none of the other variables (age, duration of agoraphobia, previous treatment, and previous use of medicaton) were statistically significant differences between groups found.

In summary, the present analysis revealed little differences between failures and successful cases of exposure in vivo. It should be noted, however, that the failure group was relativey small ($n = 5$). Nevertheless, most of the negative findings are in agreement with other studies that sought to investigate predictors of success of treatment. The only significant difference between failures and successes was found on marital satisfaction, failures complaining significantly more about their partners than successful cases. The finding is consistent with the results of Bland and Hallam (1980) and Milton and Hafner (1979) which also indicated that the effects of prolonged exposure in vivo were negatively influenced by marital conflict.

Therapeutic Relationship

Psychotherapists assume that the therapeutic relationship is an important vehicle to achieve therapeutic changes in the patient. Client-centered therapists hold that such therapist's dimensions as empathy, nonpossessive warmth, and genuineness are necessary and essential conditions in psychotherapy (Truax & Carkhuff, 1967). There is little purpose in either listing or reviewing the studies that showed that the therapeutic relationship is an important factor contributing to the outcome of therapy. The literature in this area was recently reviewed by Mitchell, Bozarth, and Krauft (1977) and Parloff, Waskow, and Wolfe (1978). Mitchell et al. (1977) come to the following conclusion: "The recent evidence, although equivocal, does seem to suggest that empathy, warmth, and genuineness are related in some way to client change but that their potency and generalizability are not as great as once thought" (p. 483).

The relationship between therapist and patient has been neglected in the behavioral literature (De Voge & Beck, 1978), despite the finding of some studies in the early 1960s that the therapeutic relationship might be of paramount importance in the process of behavior therapy. For example, Meyer and Gelder (1963) pointed out that the therapeutic relationship might be crucial in the behavioral treatment of agoraphobia. After having given an account of the treatment by behavior therapy of five agoraphobics they state: "the single factor which seems most relevant to the outcome of behaviour therapy is this relationship" (p. 26), and they go on to suggest that "feelings which the therapist forms in relation to patient influence the course of treatment just as the countertransference does in psychotherapy" (p. 27). One of the first studies that examined systematically the influence of the therapeutic relationship in behavior therapy was conducted by Crisp (1966). Using a modification of Kelly's Repertory Grid Technique, Crisp attempted to assess the positive and negative feelings of the patient for the therapist throughout the behavioral treatment of eleven patients including agoraphobics. He found a consistent relationship between such "transference" feelings and the clinical course of the treatment: "the major clinical changes during treatment are often associated with or occasionally preceded by . . .appropriate change in 'transference' " (p. 182).

Generally, studies into the effects of various behavioral procedures with agoraphobics neglected the possible influence of the therapeutic relationship upon the outcome of therapy. Usually, patients were randomly assigned across various therapists in an attempt to control for a possible "therapist" factor. Mathews et al. (1973) compared flooding, desensitization, and control treatment and found no evidence that one therapist was more effective than others. They suggest: "the personal qualities which appear to influence the results of counseling procedures are less important when the more precisely formulated techniques of flooding, desensitization, and the special control treatment are used" (p. 459). However, subsequent studies (Mathews et al., 1976; Mathews et al., 1979) found a significant therapist effect, indicating that the improvements achieved could not be ascribed solely to technical procedures. In the Mathews et al. (1976) study, patients were asked to rank eight features of the treatments in order of their perceived helpfulness. The results showed that "all patients attributed important effects to the therapists' encouragement and sympathy, and to a slightly lesser extent the practice component and learning to cope with panic" (p. 369). Further, even with systematic desensitization in an analogue context, therapist variables appeared to be of importance. For example, analogue studies by Morris and Suckerman (1974a, b) demonstrated that a warm therapeutic voice produced significantly better results than a cold voice.

Recently, Rabavilas and Boulougouris (1979) investigated the influence of perceived therapists' qualities on the outcome of behavioral treatment. Phobic and obsessive-compulsive patients who had been treated with exposure in vivo rated the following therapists' qualities at follow-up: warmth, acceptance, respect, understanding, interest, liking, objectivity, and gratification of dependency needs. Results indicated that therapists' respect, understanding, and interest was positively related to outcome. However, gratification of patient's dependency needs was negatively related to outcome.

Hadley and Strupp (1976) undertook an investigation into the problem of negative effects in psychotherapy by soliciting the opinions of a great number of expert psychotherapists, spanning a wide range of theoretical orientations. They reported that the therapist himself or herself was one of the most often cited sources of negative effects in psychotherapy. Considering the growing interest in the therapeutic relationship as a factor contributing to failure in psychotherapy we attempted to explore whether the therapeutic relationship was related to success of behavioral treatment of agoraphobia.

Subjects were agoraphobics who recently had participated in a group treatment. Twenty-three persons were asked to participate in this study but for a variety of reasons only 13 persons cooperated. A number of persons refused to cooperate because they considered the information requested by the questionnaire too confidential. All patients had undergone group exposure in vivo treatment. In addition, some of them had received six sessions of cognitive restructuring.

Patients had to fill in a Dutch version of The Relationship Inventory (Barrett-Lennard, 1973) as modified by Lietaer (1976). An advantage of this scale is that it assesses the patient's reported experience rather than measures technically accurate therapist responses that are considered helpful (Bergin & Lambert, 1978). The version used consists of the following subscales: (1) empathy, (2) positive regard, (3) incongruity, (4) negative regard, (5) unconditionality, (6) transparency, and (7) directivity. The directivity subscale measures an authoritarian attitude, which expresses itself in not respecting the privacy of the patient and trying to change the patient in the direction of the therapist's own feelings and behavior. In an attempt to measure directivity as characteristic of behavior therapists, another subscale was constructed by us and added to the inventory. Inasmuch as there proved to be almost no variance among patients on the latter subscale, it was not used in the data analysis.

Lietaer (1976) suggested combining the subscales empathy, positive regard, incongruity, and negative regard after some necessary transformations to the EPIN scale. This EPIN scale is a "global measure of the quality of the relationship" (Lietaer, p. 83). In the present study two measures of the therapeutic relationship were used: EPIN scale and directivity subscale.

Inasmuch as only one patient could be considered a failure as defined in the previous study, only correlational analyses could be conducted. Correlations were compared between patients' scores on the combined phobic anxiety and avoidance scales at the posttest on the one hand, and the EPIN scale and directivity subscale on the other. Pearson's product moment correlation coefficient was $r = .61$ ($p < .05$) for the EPIN scale and $r = -.69$ ($p < .01$) for the directivity subscale. Thus there was a significant relationship between outcome of therapy and such "good" therapist characteristics as empathy, positive regard, and congruity. Further, results indicated that directivity as defined from a client-centered point of view was negatively related to outcome.

The findings of the present study corroborate the results of Boulougouris and Rabavilas. Both studies found a relationship between perceived therapists' characteristics and outcome of exposure in vivo treatment. It is tempting to consider the results of this study to be support for the view that therapists' characteristics play an important part in the behavioral treatment of agoraphobics. Alternatively, the patients' rating of outcome and therapist may be reflections of the patient's overall satisfaction with the treatment. If the latter is the case, one may not conclude that the therapists' characteristics were causal in effecting the favorable outcome inasmuch as the favorable outcome of therapy might have influenced the patients' recall of their therapists' characteristics (Parloff et al., 1978). Nevertheless, the results are intriguing and indicate that the therapeutic relationship deserves more attention by behavior therapists.

Perceived Parental Characteristics

Several authors suggested that agoraphobic persons are very dependent and hold that a parental overprotective concern for the child that is not necessarily affectionate may account for the development of the phobia (Terhune, 1949; Webster, 1953). Studies that have investigated parental characteristics of phobic patients have provided conflicting results. Solyom, Silberfeld, and Solyom (1976) hypothesized that agoraphobia is a reactivation of early attachment behavior: "The potential for such reactivation may be enhanced by having an overprotective mother whose constant presence not only reduces anxiety but also reduces the number of opportunities for developing more adequate responses" (p. 109). In an attempt to test this hypothesis the mothers of agoraphobics were assessed on a Maternal Overprotection Questionnaire and the results were compared with normative data. Results indicated that the mothers of agoraphobics were more overprotective than controls. On the other hand, Buglass et al. (1977) found no difference between agoraphobics and controls with respect to premorbid dependency.

Parker (1979) studied parental characteristics of agoraphobics ($n = 40$) and social phobics ($n = 41$) using the Parental Bonding Instrument developed by Parker, Tupling, and Brown (1979). This questionnaire measures two dimensions: parental care and parental overprotection. The phobic patients scored their parents as less caring and more overprotective than controls. Further analyses revealed that parental rearing practices may have differed for agoraphobics and social phobics respectively: "Social phobics scored both parents as low on care and high on over-protection, while agoraphobics differed from controls only in lower maternal care" (p. 559). Another striking contrast was that higher agoraphobic scores were associated with less maternal care and less maternal overprotection, whereas higher social phobic scores were associated with greater maternal care and greater maternal overprotection.

In the present study we investigated whether parental characteristics were associated with failure of treatment. To assess the perceived parental characteristics we used a Dutch version of the EMBU (own memories of childrearing experiences) developed by Perris, Jacobsson, Lindström, von Knorring, and Perris (1980). This questionnaire contains 15 subscales. Factor analysis revealed four factors. In the present study the following three factors were used (Perris et al., 1980):

Controlling. This factor consists of the subscales (1) abusive, (2) depriving, (3) punitive, (4) shaming, (5) overinvolved, (6) performance oriented, (7) guilt engendering, and (8) "unspecified."

Rejection. This is a bipolar factor consisting of the subscales (1) rejecting, (2) affectionate, (3) stimulating, and (4) tolerant.

Overprotective. This variable emerged as a separate factor only concerning the mothers' behavior and not the fathers' (Perris et al., 1980).

The questionnaire contains two additional questions that also were used in the present analysis, one concerned with the degree of *"consistency"* in parental behavior and the other with *"strictness"* of parental discipline.

Nineteen agoraphobics for whom we had completed questionnaires participated in this study. Patients were categorized in successes and failures as defined
previously. Failures were differentiated from successes on the "strictness" dimension. Failures perceived their mothers as more strict than did the patients whose
treatment had been successful [$t(17) = -1.78$, $p < .05$]. The other differences
were not statistically significant.

The results of this study are inconclusive. No evidence was provided of a relationship between "overprotective," "controlling," and "rejecting" parental characteristics on the one hand and failure of treatment on the other. However, the
relationship between strictness of parental discipline and failure of treatment suggests that parental discipline might be an important prognostic factor. Obviously,
this finding has to be cross validated before conclusions can be drawn.

Patients' Accounts of Reasons Why Treatment Failed

We were interested to hear from the patients themselves which factors they
thought to be related to the failure of the treatment. We selected a number of
patients who were considered to be treatment failures by the supervisor (senior
author).

A semistructured interview was conducted by the second author, who had had
no previous contact with the patients. The interview centered around the following topics:

1. Current state of the agoraphobia
2. Patients' experiences with respect to the treatment
3. Relationship with the therapist
4. Family relationship

The patients were contacted by letter and invited either to visit the hospital or
to be visited at home when they were unable to visit the hospital. Ten patients
were invited to cooperate in this study and eight of them were willing to do so.
One person refused to cooperate but provided us with some information by
phone. Another person failed to show up for the appointment. Of the remaining
eight persons, only two were able to come on their own to our department, two
had to be accompanied by their partner and the other four had to be visited at
home. For present purposes, we will discuss only the patients who were treated
by more than one behavioral technique, leaving seven persons. The characteristics
of the patients and the treatments are summarized in Table 4.1.

Current State of the Agoraphobia

Generally, the patients were as agoraphobic as they had been when treatment
was finished. Most patients had undergone treatment elsewhere after the unsuccessful treatment at our department but this apparently had not led to improvements with respect to the agoraphobia. Only one patient was somewhat improved,
which was related to the fact that her husband threatened to divorce her.

Table 4.1.   Sample Characteristics of Treatment Failures

	Age	Duration of Agoraphobia (years)	Treatment	Group or Individual	Number of Sessions	Duration of Treatment (months)
Patient A	59	1	Exposure in vivo Assertive training	Both	20	6
Patient B	33	2	Exposure in vivo Assertive training	Both	17	8
Patient C	37	2	Exposure in vivo Cognitive restructuring Assertive training	Both	34	9
Patient D	47	25	Exposure in vivo Cognitive restructuring Assertive training	Both	68	17
Patient E	28	2	Exposure in vivo Cognitive restructuring Assertive training Conjoint marital therapy	Both	41	13
Patient F	54	30	Exposure in vivo Conjoint marital therapy	Group	20	6
Patient G	32	4	Exposure in vivo Cognitive restructuring Assertive training	Both	30	13

Experiences of Treatment

The patients who had received group prolonged exposure in vivo were dissatisfied with this treatment as expressed in the following quotations:

"Treatment was a torment; anxiety did not reduce when I had to walk on the streets." (Patient F)

"Having to walk on the streets was terrible; that was the most awful experience; it lasted much too long. I was afraid that I never could return to the hospital." (Patient D)

"If you get a panic attack, anxiety will not reduce till you have returned safely to the hospital." (Patient G)

"When you still feel terrible at the end of the exposure session, it is nonsense that the therapists are enthusiastic about your achievements." (Patient E)

Although the other two patients who received group exposure in vivo were also dissatisfied, they found that treatment had been helpful to them in some way.

"In the beginning the exercises were terrible. I thought, what do they want with me, leave me in peace. However, it put me in a fair way, otherwise, I still would have been totally housebound." (Patient A)

"The exercises during the treatment sessions were much easier than when I had to do it on my own, but that did not influence my feelings." (Patient C)

Most patients found that the pace of the exercises had been too fast and preferred a more gradual approach. One patient remarked that the therapists had been technique rather than patient oriented: "It didn't matter how you felt, but what you had done, and how long you had persisted: the treatment was performance oriented." (Patient E)

Six patients had received assertive training and most of them experienced treatment as helpful, but not with respect to the agoraphobic complaints. None of the patients saw a relationship between their unassertiveness and the agoraphobic complaints.

Therapists

Generally, patients found that the therapists did not show that they really understood their feelings. One patient (F) remarked: "People who suffer from phobias always feel lonely, no one understands their feelings." In addition, three patients found the therapists too young. For this reason two of these patients did not discuss certain difficulties (e.g., sexual problems). Four of the six patients who had received individual treatment were dissatisfied with their therapists. One patient found that "she was not taken seriously," another was afraid that the therapist "could ridicule her," and the third had experienced the therapist as authoritarian, "as if she knew everything." It is remarkable that all four patients who were dissatisfied with their therapists had received cognitive restructuring (Rational Emotive Therapy). The other patients who were individually treated and who were satisfied with their therapists did not receive cognitive restructuring. Presumably, Rational Emotive Therapy is more likely to lead to such negative evaluations of the therapists than other approaches.

Family

One patient was divorced and will not be discussed here. Although the patients did mention tension in the marital relationship only in passing, our clinical ipression was that there was often serious marital distress. All married patients (n = 6) felt they were not understood by their husbands. With five of these patients the partner did all the shopping and accompanied the patient when she had to go somewhere, which suggests that "secondary gain" might be involved. The husband of the other patient (B) threatened to divorce her, if she did not overcome her fears. She took this seriously and started to expose herself in vivo to several phobic situations with some success.

Although far from conclusive, the present observations are consistent with previous findings that agoraphobia may play a functional role in the relationship of patients and suggest that more attention should be devoted to this factor in the future.

SUMMARY AND CONCLUSIONS

The present study revealed several factors that may be associated with failure in treating agoraphobia. Rather than repeat these factors, a few additional recommendations will be made:

1.   A functional analysis of the behavior of the agoraphobic patient is very important. However, it is unlikely that such an analysis will prevent failure in all cases. For example, with the failures interviewed in the present study, a functional analysis had been made but treatment was nevertheless unsuccessful. As stated elsewhere (Emmelkamp, 1981), research into reliability, validity, and utility of the functional analysis is in an embryonic stage and needs to be developed.

2.   Not every patient is suited for group treatment. Some patients are better off with an individualized treatment program from the start. For example, there is now some evidence, although far from conclusive, that such an individualized approach may be necessary for patients with marital complications.

3.   It should be noted that prolonged exposure in vivo does not always lead to anxiety reduction. When overt or covert avoidance is involved, this has to be dealt with (see Emmelkamp, 1982 c). However, if anxiety still doesn't reduce after repeated prolonged exposures to the phobic situations there seems little sense in continuing the program. A reanalysis of the case is then necessary in order to decide whether a more gradual approach or focusing on other therapeutic goals is needed.

4.   The therapeutic relationship seems to be of paramount importance. For some patients it may take a considerable time before a "good" therapeutic relationship develops. With this subgroup of patients, premature exposure in vivo may be at best a waste of time and at worst a "torment" that can lead to dropout of treatment. The finding of the present study that perceived strictness of mothers' discipline was related to failure of exposure in vivo may have a bearing on the issue of the therapeutic relationship. It is conceivable that patients with such rearing experiences are particularly sensitive to the "strictness" of the therapist during exposure in vivo. This proposed "transference" is, of course, highly speculative but the present findings are interesting enough to warrant further study.

5.   Finally, in a majority of cases, agoraphobia is associated with hyperventilation and in some cases hyperventilation may need special consideration (e.g., breathing exercises; see Emmelkamp, 1982 c). In some other cases, agoraphobia is associated with mitral valve prolapse syndrome (Kantor, Zitrin, & Zeldis, 1980). Information about this disorder may help these patients to adjust to their palpitations with less anxiety.

In conclusion, this overview is not a definitive summary of factors related to failure in treating agoraphobia. Nevertheless, it is to be hoped that the foregoing discussion affords some direction for further research. There undoubtedly will be many complex and difficult issues to resolve before it may be possible to devise treatments for patients who presumably need therapeutic help most: our failures.

REFERENCES

Agulnik, P. (1970) The spouse of the phobic patient. *British Journal of Psychiatry,* **117,** 59–67.

Andrews, J.D.W. (1966) Psychotherapy of phobias. *Psychological Bulletin,* **66,** 455–480.

Barrett-Lennard, G.T. (1973) *Relationship inventory: Experimental form OSS-42.* Unpublished manuscript, Waterloo, Ontario: University of Waterloo.

Bergin, A.E., & Lambert, M.J. (1978) The evaluation of therapeutic outcomes. In S. L. Garfield, & A. E. Bergin (Eds.), *Handbook of psychotherapy and behavior change.* New York: Wiley.

Bianchi, G.N. (1971) Origins of disease phobia. *Australian and New Zealand Journal of Psychiatry,* **5,** 241–257.

Bland, K., & Hallam, R. S. (1980) *Investigation of agoraphobic patients' response to exposure in vivo treatment in relation to marital satisfaction.* Unpublished manuscript, Maudsley Hospital, London.

Bowen, R.C., & Kohout, J. (1979) The relationship between agoraphobia and primary affective disorders. *Canadian Journal of Psychiatry,* **24,** 317–322.

Buglass, D., Clarke, J., Henderson, A.S., Kreitman, N., & Presley, A.S. (1977) A study of agoraphobic housewives. *Psychological Medicine,* **7,** 73–86.

Chambless, D.L., & Goldstein, A. (1980) The treatment of agoraphobia. In A. Goldstein, & E. Foa (Eds.), *Handbook of behavioral interventions.* New York: Wiley.

Crisp, A.H. (1966) 'Transference' 'symptom emergence' and 'social repercussion' in behaviour therapy. *British Journal of Medical Psychology,* **39,** 179–196.

De Voge, J.T., & Beck, S. (1978) The therapist–client relationship in behavior therapy. In M. Hersen, R.M. Eisler, & P.M. Miller (Eds.), *Progress in behavior modification* (Vol. 6) New York: Academic.

Emmelkamp, P.M.G. (1979) The behavioral study of clinical phobias. In M. Hersen, R.M. Eisler, & P.M. Miller (Eds.), *Progress in behavior modification* (Vol. 8). New York: Academic, 55–125.

Emmelkamp, P.M.G. (1980a) *The effectiveness of exposure in vivo, cognitive restructuring and assertive training in the treatment of agoraphobia.* Paper read at the conference of the American Association of Behavior Therapy, New York, November.

Emmelkamp, P.M.G. (1980b) Agoraphobics' interpersonal problems: Their role in the effects of exposure in vivo therapy. *Archives of General Psychiatry,* **37,** 1303–1306.

Emmelkamp, P.M.G. (1981) The current and future status of clinical research. *Behavioral Assessment,* **3,** 249–253

Emmelkamp, P.M.G. (1982a) In vivo treatment of agoraphobia. In D.L. Chambless and

A.J. Goldstein (Eds.), *Agoraphobia: Multiple Perspectives on theory and treatment.* New York: Wiley, 43–75.

Emmelkamp, P.M.G. (in 1982 b) Recent developments in the behavioral treatment of obsessive-compulsive disorders. In J. Boulougouris (Ed.), *Learning theory approaches to psychiatry.* New York: Wiley.

Emmelkamp, P.M.G. (1982 c) *Phobic and obsessive-compulsive disorders: Theory, research, and practice.* New York: Plenum.

Emmelkamp, P.M.G., & Emmelkamp-Benner, A. (1975) Effects of historically portrayed modeling and group treatment on self-observation: A comparison with agoraphobics. *Behaviour Research and Therapy,* **13,** 135–139.

Emmelkamp, P.M.G., & Kuipers, A. (1979) Agoraphobia: A follow-up study four years after treatment. *British Journal of Psychiatry,* **134,** 352–355.

Emmelkamp, P.M.G., Kuipers, A., & Eggeraat, J. (1978) Cognitive modification versus prolonged exposure in vivo: A comparison with agoraphobics. *Behaviour Research and Therapy,* **16,** 33–41.

Emmelkamp, P.M.G., & Mersch, P.P. (1982) Cognition and exposure in vivo in the treatment of agoraphobia: Short-term and delayed effects. *Cognitive Therapy and Research,* **6,** 77–90.

Emmelkamp, P.M.G., & Wessels, H. (1975) Flooding in imagination vs flooding in vivo: A comparison with agoraphobics. *Behaviour Research and Therapy,* **13,** 7–16.

Evans, P.D., & Kellam, A.M.P. (1973) Semi-automated desensitization: A controlled clinical trial. *Behaviour Research and Therapy,* **11,** 641–646.

Foa, E.B. (1979) Failure in treating obsessive-compulsives. *Behaviour Research and Therapy,* **17,** 169–176.

Fry, W.F. (1962) The marital context of an anxiety syndrome. *Family Process,* **1,** 245–252.

Garfield, S.L. (1978) Research on client variables in psychotherapy. In S.L. Garfield, & A.E. Bergin (Eds.), *Handbook of psychotherapy and behavior change.* New York: Wiley.

Garfield, S.L. (1980) *Psychotherapy: An eclectic approach.* New York: Wiley.

Gay, M.L., Hollandsworth, J.G., & Galassi, J.P. (1975) An assertiveness inventory. *Journal of Counseling Psychology,* **22,** 340–344.

Gelder, M.G., Marks, I.M., & Wolff, H.H. (1967) Desensitization and psychotherapy in the treatment of phobic states: A controlled enquiry. *British Journal of Psychiatry,* **113,** 53–73.

Goldstein, A.J., & Chambless, D.L. (1978) A reanalysis of agoraphobia. *Behavior Therapy,* **9,** 47–59.

Hadley, S.W., & Strupp, H.H. (1976) Contemporary views of negative effects in psychotherapy. *Archives of General Psychiatry,* **33,** 1291–1302.

Hafner, R.J. (1976) Fresh symptom emergence after intensive behaviour therapy. *British Journal of Psychiatry,* **129,** 378–383.

Hafner, R.J. (1977a) The husbands of agoraphobic women: Assortative mating or pathogenic interaction? *British Journal of Psychiatry,* **130,** 233–239.

Hafner, R.J. (1977b) The husbands of agoraphobic women and their influence on treatment outcome. *British Journal of Psychiatry,* **131,** 289–294.

Hafner, R.J. (1979) Agoraphobic women married to abnormally jealous men. *British Journal of Medical Psychology,* **52,** 99–104.

Hafner, R.J., & Marks, I.M. (1976) Exposure *in vivo* of agoraphobics: Contributions of diazepam, group exposure, and anxiety evocation. *Psychological Medicine,* **6,** 71–88.

Hand, I., & Lamontagne, Y. (1976) The exacerbation of interpersonal problems after rapid phobia-removal. *Psychotherapy: Theory, Research and Practice,* **13,** 405–411.

Hand, I., Lamontagne, Y., & Marks, I.M. (1974) Group exposure (flooding) in vivo for agoraphobics. *British Journal of Psychiatry,* **124,** 588–602.

Heitler, J.B. (1976) Preparatory techniques in initiating expressive psychotherapy with lower-class, unsophisticated patients. *Psychological Bulletin,* **83,** 339–352.

Hudson, B. (1974) The families of agoraphobics treated by behaviour therapy. *British Journal of Social Work,* **4,** 51–59.

Johnston, D.W., Lancashire, M., Mathews, A.M., Munby, M., Shaw, P.M., & Gelder, M.G. (1976) Imaginal flooding and exposure to real phobic situations: Changes during treatment. *British Journal of Psychiatry,* **129,** 372–377.

Kantor, J.S., Zitrin, C.M., & Zeldis, S.M. (1980) Mitral valve prolapse syndrome in agoraphobic patients. *American Journal of Psychiatry,* **137,** 467–469.

Lader, M.H., Gelder, M.G., & Marks, I.M. (1967) Palmar skin-conductance measures as predictors of response to desensitization. *Journal of Psychosomatic Research,* **11,** 283–290.

Lietaer, G. (1976) Nederlandstalige revisie van Barrett-Lennard's Relationship Inventory voor individueel therapeutische relaties. *Psychologia Belgica,* **16,** 73–94.

Marks, I.M. (1969) *Fears and phobias.* New York: Academic.

Marks, I.M. (1978) Behavioural psychotherapy of adult neurosis. In S.L. Garfield, & A.E. Bergin, *Handbook of psychotherapy and behavior change.* New York: Wiley.

Marks, I.M., Boulougouris, J., & Marset, P. (1971) Flooding versus desensitization in the treatment of phobic patients: A cross-over study. *British Journal of Psychiatry,* **119,** 353–375.

Mathews, A., Janoun, L., & Gelder, M. (1979) *Self-help methods in agoraphobia.* Paper presented at the Conference of the European Association of Behaviour Therapy, Paris.

Mathews, A.M., Johnston, D.W., Shaw, P.M., & Gelder, M.G. (1973) Process variables and the prediction of outcome in behavior therapy. *British Journal of Psychiatry,* **123,** 445–462.

Mathews, A.M., Johnston, D.W., Lancashire, M., Munby, M., Shaw, P.M., & Gelder, M.G. (1976) Imaginal flooding and exposure to real phobic situations: Treatment outcome with agoraphobic patients. *British Journal of Psychiatry,* **129,** 362–371.

Mathews, A.M., Teasdale, J.D., Munby, M., Johnston, D.W., & Shaw, P.M. (1977) A home-based treatment program for agoraphobia. *Behavior Therapy,* **8,** 915–924.

McPherson, F.M., Brougham, L., & Mc Laren, S. (1980) Maintenance of improvement in agoraphobic patients treated by behavioural methods—a four-year follow-up. *Behaviour Research and Therapy,* **18,** 150–152.

Meyer, V., & Gelder, M.G. (1963) Behaviour therapy and phobic disorders. *British Journal of Psychiatry,* 109, 19–28.

Milton, F., & Hafner, J. (1979) The outcome of behavior therapy for agoraphobia in relation to marital adjustment. *Archives of General Psychiatry,* **36,** 807–811.

Mitchell, K.M., Bozarth, J.D., & Krauft, C.C. (1977) A reappraisal of the therapeutic effectiveness of accurate empathy, nonpossessive warmth, and genuineness. In A.S. Gurman, & A.M. Razin (Eds.), *Effective psychotherapy: A handbook of research.* Oxford: Pergamon.

Morris, R.J., & Suckerman, K.R. (1974a) Therapist warmth as a factor in automated systematic desensitization. *Journal of Consulting and Clinical Psychology,* **42,** 244–250.

Morris, R.J., & Suckerman, K.R. (1974b) The importance of the therapeutic relationship in systematic desensitization. *Journal of Consulting and Clinical Psychology,* **42,** 147.

Munby, M., & Johnston, D.W. (1980) *Agoraphobia: The long-term follow-up of behavioral treatment.* Unpublished manuscript, University of Oxford.

Parker, G. (1979). Reported parental characteristics of agoraphobics and social phobics. *British Journal of Psychiatry,* **135,** 555–560.

Parker, G., Tupling, H., & Brown, L.B. (1979) A parental bonding instrument. *British Journal of Medical Psychology,* **52,** 1–10.

Parloff, M.B., Waskow, I.E., & Wolfe, B.E. (1978) Research on therapist variables in relation to process and outcome. In S.L. Garfield, & A.E. Bergin (Eds.), *Handbook of psychotherapy and behavior change.* New York: Wiley.

Perris, C.J., Jacobsson, H., Lindström, H., von Knorring, L., & H. Perris. (1980) Development of a new inventory for assessing memories of parental rearing behaviour. *Acta Psychiatria Scandinavia,* **61,** 265–274.

Rabavilas, A.D., & Boulougouris, J.C. (1979) *Therapeutic relationship and long term outcome with flooding treatment.* Paper presented at the 9th Conference of the European Association of Behaviour Therapy, Paris.

Ross, J. (1980) The use of former phobics in the treatment of phobias. *American Journal of Psychiatry,* **137,** 715–717.

Schapira, K., Kerr, T.A., & Roth, M. (1970) Phobias and affective illness. *British Journal of Psychiatry,* **117,** 25–32.

Solyom, L., Silberfeld, M., & Solyom, C. (1976) Maternal overprotection in the etiology of agoraphobia. *Canadian Psychiatric Association Journal,* **21,** 109–113.

Stern, R., & Marks, I.M. (1973) Brief and prolonged flooding: A comparison in agoraphobic patients. *Archives of General Psychiatry,* **28,** 270–276.

Terhune, W.B. (1949) The phobic syndrome. *Archives of Neurology and Psychiatry,* **62,** 162–172.

Truax, B.B., & Carkhuff, R.R. (1967) *Toward effective counseling and psychotherapy.* Chicago: Aldine.

Watson, J.P., & Marks, I.M. (1971) Relevant and irrelevant fear in flooding—a cross-over study of phobic patients. *Behavior Therapy,* **2,** 275–293.

Watzlawick, P., Beavin, J.H., & Jackson, D.D. (1968). *Pragmatics of human communication.* London: Faber and Faber.

Webster, A.S. (1953) The development of phobias in married women. *Psychological Monographs,* **67,** 367.

Zung, W.W.K. (1965) A self-rating depression scale. *Archives of General Psychiatry,* **12,** 63–70.

CHAPTER 5

Failures in Flooding

W.L. MARSHALL
JANEL GAUTHIER

The consideration of failures in flooding therapy is something of a novelty, and as with any novel venture there is little in the way of empirical evidence, direct or indirect, on which to base our appraisal. In the first place it is not at all clear that failures, in the sense of a complete absence of behavioral change, have occurred with sufficient frequency in flooding to warrant concern. Although success rates as high or higher than 80 percent have been reported, it is usually impossible to infer from group averages the degree of change in particular subjects. Some subjects may have shown remarkable benefits whereas others failed to profit from treatment, or all may have improved to a limited degree. In one of our early studies (Marshall, Gauthier, Christie, Currie, & Gordon, 1977) we found that one of the advantages flooding had over desensitization was the uniformity of its effects across subjects; all improved substantially!

Perhaps some failures, especially those who cannot be persuaded to enter or remain in treatment, are excluded from consideration in research reports and, no doubt, part of the problem concerns just what it is we mean when we speak of failures. We will take a broad definition in this chapter to include not only those who are not helped by treatment, but also those who resist entry into treatment, who drop out during treatment, or who, despite immediate gain, subsequently relapse.

In its broad conceptualization this chapter represents a logical analysis of when and how failures might occur with some of that reasoning being based on an understanding of the experimental determination of the factors that control flooding efficacy. Inasmuch as there is no more than a limited explicit documentation of failures in flooding we will rely heavily on our own clinical experience as well as on the informal observations kindly provided by friends and colleagues.

THE NATURE OF FLOODING THERAPY

In a sense, any deliberate attempt to expose clients to unpleasant stimuli so as to reduce the power of these stimuli to elicit such responses, may be described as flooding. However, we have restricted the definition of flooding to include only those procedures that involve prolonged exposure to the most distressing aspects of the stimuli: Flooding is a generic term for procedures that have as their goal the extinction of classes of maladaptive responses to aversive stimuli by exposure to high-intensity subsets of these aversive stimuli for prolonged periods in the absence of actual physical injurious consequences (Marshall, Gauthier, & Gordon, 1979, p. 215).

This definition draws attention to a number of factors, but perhaps the most important for the present discussion is that flooding is a procedure with a limited goal, that is, the reduction of maladaptive responding to emotionally distressing stimuli. For the client who presents with anxiety, and for whom flooding is the chosen treatment, we would expect reductions in the client's feelings of anxiety, a diminution in his or her physiological arousal to the stimuli, and less avoidance behavior after the intervention. If the client is also depressed, has poor marital relations, sexual problems, or other dysfunctions, there is no reason to suppose that flooding, aimed at reducing anxiety to specific stimuli, will have any effect on these difficulties. It may happen that these problems will also improve, and this would be welcome, but there is no reason to expect generalization of such a remarkable degree, or bemoan its absence, *unless specific additional procedures are included in treatment* (Baer, Wolf, & Risley, 1968).

Flooding, then, is a procedure, the restricted aim of which is to reduce distressful emotional reactions. Other benefits may result from the intervention, but they will be fortuitous and will not be a matter of concern in the assessment of the success or failure of flooding therapy.

EXTENT OF THE PROBLEM

Before we consider how it is that failures may occur in flooding therapy, we will summarize the evidence concerning the extent of the problem.

We need first of all to dismiss the common, but for the most part unfounded, idea that flooding is potentially dangerous. The authors of many texts and articles have cautioned against the use of flooding procedures (e.g., Bandura, 1969; Coleman, 1976; Morganstern, 1973; Rimm & Masters, 1974; Singer, 1974; Wolpe, 1969), although they adduce no evidence in support of such warnings.

In a case involving the most serious possible consequence to therapy, Boyce (unpublished case material cited by Hafner, in press) reports the death by suicide of a man treated by in vivo exposure. This severely obsessional patient was unable, for fear of contamination, to touch or be touched by anyone, and this was particularly distressing to his family. A flooding and response prevention procedure effectively eliminated this problem. However, three weeks later the man took his life, leaving a note describing loneliness and existential despair. In an analysis of this case, Hafner (in press) suggests that a more effective treatment program might have focused on these problems including the marital and family relationships, rather than the avoidance behavior alone. Hafner argues that the use of flooding was inappropriate, serving only to highlight this unfortunate man's problems, indicating that it was the therapist's judgment, rather than the technique, which was at fault.

Other reports have suggested that harmful effects may occasionally accompany flooding treatment, but again it is often not clear that the application of the exposure procedure was wisely selected. In other cases unwanted effects appear to be transitory. For example, Barrett (1970) observed "runaway imagery" of a serious nature between treatment sessions in two patients treated by implosive therapy. In these two patients images of a vivid and compelling nature proved to be very distressful, but they disappeared when treatment became effective. On the other hand, Marks (1978) has observed sensitization in 3 percent of his patients treated with flooding even though they cooperated, were seemingly well motivated, and completed an appropriate course of treatment. Likewise, Hafner (1979) described the appearance of an acute and persisting psychotic disorder after the successful elimination of agoraphobia by flooding, despite the patient's willing cooperation and the welcome reception by her family of the initial improvement. However, even these unfortunate cases do not represent grounds for extreme concern of the kind sometimes expressed.

Perhaps the most serious effort to examine the possible harmful effects of floodinglike procedures was carried out by Shipley and Boudewyns (1980) who conducted a mail survey of known practitioners of these techniques. Seventy practitioners, representing an 83 percent return rate, reported the use of flooding or implosion with 3,493 clients. Only 6 of the 70 respondents reported "serious negative side effects," and these were limited to only 9 patients. Four of these patients were said to have suffered "acute psychotic reactions," whereas the other five experienced "brief panic reactions." Two of those who showed "psychotic reactions" were described as having a history of paranoid schizophrenia, and all four responded rapidly to phenothiazine medication. Of those who displayed "panic reactions," three ultimately responded well to flooding, one "recovered" prematurely, and the remaining patient received only one session, and, not surprisingly, failed to benefit from treatment. Eighty-seven percent of the therapists said that the side effects of flooding were similar to, and no worse than, those resulting from other behavioral interventions. Shipley and Boudewyns concluded that flooding was a safe procedure and, although this represents only one study, we think it is proper to accept their conclusion until evidence (not argument) is provided to the contrary.

A search of the literature revealed four reports (Foa, 1979; Hafner, in press; Marks, Hodgson, & Rachman, 1975; Rachman & Hodgson, 1980) that discussed failures where flooding therapy was the prime treatment. Foa (1979) reported that 10 patients from her series of treatment studies either failed to benefit from treatment or relapsed shortly after completion of therapy despite their having complied with treatment demands. It is difficult to infer precisely just what percentage this represents, although her reported overall success rate is 85 percent (Foa & Goldstein, 1978). However, this implied failure rate of 15 percent may include failures of compliance, dropouts, or those who refused treatment. Marks et al. (1975) point to 5 of 20 patients who failed to respond to in vivo exposure procedures, and although Rachman and Hodgson (1980) provide an illuminating discussion of failures, they do not report the rate of occurrence of such problems. Hafner's (in press) discussion is too general to infer specific rates.

In addition to these published remarks, we received personal communications of a rather informal nature from 24 practitioners and researchers who have written articles dealing with flooding therapy. None of these correspondents indicated that failures were more than a minor problem, and some said they were hard-pressed to identify any complete failures. Several mentioned difficulties or delays in obtaining satisfactory change, but all seemed to agree that failures were not more likely with flooding than with any other technique, and at least four claimed that flooding resulted in fewer failures. Our experience agrees with the latter remarks. Nevertheless, failures do occur, and we can usually learn more about a behavior or a treatment procedure when we are unsuccessful in producing benefits. The following, then, will involve a consideration of where flooding might go wrong, with the hope that these observations might be valuable for both the clinical application and the experimental analyses of treatment.

ERRORS OF IMPLEMENTATION

It is our contention that the proper tactic in analyzing failures is to hold ourselves (i.e., the therapists) responsible rather than the patient. This forces us to scrutinize and, we hope as a consequence, modify our behavior. Thus we may be able to alter the way in which we construe the problem, change the steps we take to prepare treatment, and modify the procedural specifics of our use of flooding.

Errors in Conceptualization

Our view is that the therapist's conceptualizations of problems are basic to designing effective treatment and it is, therefore, crucial that such theorizing be made explicit. We believe that assumptions, however vaguely held, guide the behavior

Table 5.1.   Factors That Influence Outcome in Flooding Therapy

Conceptualizations
> General perspective—behavioral analytic
> Problem perspective—theories of anxiety, etc.
> Individual perspective—specific client difficulties

Preparation for treatment
> Therapist factors—knowledge, confidence, interpersonal skills, etc.
> Individual factors—understanding of procedure, motivation, additional difficulties
> Environmental factors—relatives/friends

Implementation
> Controlling variables—duration of exposure, content of stimuli, client's responses, etc.
> Individual variables—adherence to instructions, adjustment of procedures to fit client, etc.

of therapists so that it is only by becoming aware of these notions that we can evaluate their validity and abandon or modify them when necessary.

Certain levels of conceptualization may be distinguished in the approach to the modification of specific behaviors. First, there is our general view of the processes that generate, maintain, and modify human behavior. Second, we should be concerned with an understanding of the type of problem behaviors we wish to modify. Finally, we must formulate a theory concerning the nature of the problem(s) facing our individual client.

General Perspective

Marshall (1982a) has pointed to the range of factors (external and internal) that, in general, appear to contribute to the development and maintenance of dysfunctional behavior. He notes that the specific contribution of any set of factors, in any particular case, will be most easily discerned when we are guided by a theory concerning the problem in question as well as an understanding of the individual. Marshall further argues that the most effective tactic throughout this process will be to adopt a "behavioral analytic" approach. A general perspective, then, is essentially defined by one's theoretical preferences.

In a general sense behavioral analysis refers to the ongoing process of gathering information, formulating a theory or hypothesis regarding the client's problem(s), testing that hypothesis by implementing treatment, and in light of the results, perhaps reformulating the problem(s), and introducing additional tests until the goals of treatment are met to the satisfaction of both client and therapist. Behavioral analysis, then, is a specific and applied form of what is usually understood as the scientific process. In this sense, inasmuch as science is an ongoing process of refining our control over the variables in question, it makes little sense to speak of failures except as delays, or as the result of either the therapist giving up or the client leaving prematurely. When a specific technique such as flooding does not produce the desired results, this may simply mean that the behavioral analysis is incomplete. This is not to deny that there are certain general procedural features that will affect the efficacy of flooding; there certainly are such features and ignorance of them in the implementation of flooding may very well lead to failures. Nor does our view suggest there will be no advantages to adjusting the general established form of flooding to suit the specifics of each client's problem.

Problem Perspective

At the second level of conceptualization we are concerned with theories dealing with particular problem behaviors. Marshall (1981a; 1982) has drawn attention to a variety of different perspectives of phobias and other anxiety-based behaviors, and Gauthier and Marshall (1977a) have outlined a theory of "pathological grief" that has implications for treatment. The reader is referred to these sources for examples of a behavioral approach to phobias. However, we would also like to draw attention to certain aspects of that body of literature not usually considered within a behavioral perspective that might, nevertheless, have relevance for a more expansive view of problems. For example, it is known that certain physiological dysfunctions commonly occur in anxiety disorders. Pariser, Jones, Pinta, Young, and Fontana (1979) observed cardiovascular irregularities (mitral valve prolapse) in a significant number of patients who experienced frequent panic attacks, and Kantor, Zitrin, and Zeldis (1980) were able to demonstrate identical problems in 11 of 25 agoraphobic females. Likewise, Venkatesh, Pauls, and Crowe (1978) found a significant relationship between the presence of mitral valve prolapse and whether a patient was diagnosed as "anxiety neurotic." It has also been shown that stress produces cardiac arrhythmias in mitral valve prolapse patients, but not in normals subjected to identical levels of stress (Coombs, Shah, & Shulman, 1977). Taken together, these data suggest a possible physiological vulnerability in anxiety-prone patients to the occurrence of panic attacks in response to stress.

Klein's (1980) extensive research aimed at refining our conceptualization and treatment of anxiety, also points to the role of panic attacks in the genesis and maintenance of certain phobic responses, including agoraphobia. He has found that whereas flooding or the use of sedatives and alcohol reduces anticipatory anxiety in phobics, these procedures do not modify the panic attacks. Imipramine, on the other hand, eliminates panics but has no effect upon the anticipatory anxiety, whereas a combination of imipramine and flooding effectively resolved these patients' difficulties (Zitrin, Klein, & Woerner, 1980). Those phobics who did not have panic attacks were not helped by imipramine (Klein & Rabkin, 1980).

Individual Perspective

Inadequacies in our conceptualizations of patients' problems may lead us to focus on limited aspects of clients' difficulties, or to utilize incomplete or inappropriate treatment procedures. Factors may be omitted from consideration, whereas others may be inappropriately understood.

Several authors (Fodor, 1974; Goldstein, 1970, 1973; Hafner, in press) have suggested that, among other difficulties, agoraphobics are afraid of being independent, and both Hafner (1977) and Hudson (1974) have provided evidence that these patients are often involved in marital relationships that support their housebound behaviors and punish improvements. However, these relationship factors are common not only among agoraphobics but also in depression (Mayo, 1979), obsessional disorders (Pollitt, 1957), and in other anxiety-based problems (Jackson & Yalom, 1965; Marshall & Neill, 1977). Clearly the same may be true for other phobic and emotionally distressful conditions, although family, marital, and relationship problems are frequently overlooked by behavioral therapists.

Recently we were asked to assist in the treatment of a young woman suffering from advanced Hodgkin's disease that required regular chemotherapy. This procedure commonly produces anticipatory distress and subsequent nausea, which with this patient developed into a conditioned aversion of sufficient intensity that she could not tolerate intravenous chemotherapy. Unfortunately, this placed her life in jeopardy. The hospital behavior therapist had exposed the patient to in vivo flooding in the setting where chemotherapy was administered, and with all the paraphernalia present. Throughout this treatment, the patient displayed extreme distress which remained constant for the whole eight-hour period. This either reflected a remarkable capacity to maintain high levels of arousal for long periods, or cast some doubt on the authenticity of her emotional display. She showed no subsequent benefits, and refused to go through the procedure again.

In our evaluation we found that the patient greatly admired the physician in charge of her case, who she had to see far more frequently than did his other patients, because of her difficulty in receiving intravenous chemotherapy. In addition to these visits she was seeing the chief psychiatrist and the behavior therapist, both of whom she spontaneously described as "attractive and nice." All three professionals, she said, were the only people capable of appreciating her difficulties, whereas her family and friends treated her as an invalid and actively discouraged any possible romantic relationships.

These observations, plus the fact that she seemed determined to display her fears during interviews, suggested that her "fears" may have been less substantial than she claimed, and may have served to secure attention from attractive males. One might question this proposition given the danger in which this behavior placed her. However, it appeared that the idea of her imminent death was remote to her, and simply provided yet another opportunity to gain attention and sympathy. Accordingly, a program was suggested that made access to these key hospital staff contingent upon progress in accepting intravenous administrations. In conjunction with this we suggested training in interpersonal skills. Unfortunately, all of our suggestions were rejected by the presiding physician so that their validity was not tested.

In considering factors that influence individuals' responses to treatment, much has been made of the relevance of particular client characteristics, or the individual's "personality." Unfortunately, much of the research in this area seems to be predicated on the nonbehavioral assumption that these characteristics are relatively intractable traits whose elucidation should serve at best as guidelines for matching patients rather than behaviors with treatment, or, more frequently, as a basis for rejecting clients in advance as unable to profit from treatment. In any event the influence of these factors does not appear to be either profound or consistent. For example, Mathews, Johnston, Shaw, and Gelder (1974) found a slight trend suggesting that high scores on extraversion were associated with a positive response to both flooding and desensitization, and Hallam (1976) reported data that offered rather modest support for the idea that the phobic reactions of extraverts underwent more rapid extinction than did the reactions of introverts. On the other hand, Horne (1974) found just the opposite to be true. Introverts demonstrated greater gains than extraverts irrespective of the treatment procedure.

Perhaps a more profitable suggestion for the role of idiosyncratic factors is that offered by Rachman (1981). He proposes that failures in flooding may be more frequent in those patients "who have initially a very high level of reactivity," and Rachman and Hodgson (1980) point to the value of pharmacological agents in allowing such patients to tolerate exposure sessions more easily. Although the benzodiazepines have been shown to effectively reduce anxiety (Rickels, 1980), it is also known that their effects are not retained after withdrawal of the medication. Presumably, taking drugs does not teach patients how to manage anxiety for themselves. Inasmuch as the data indicate that whereas benzodiazepines reduce tension, fears, worries, and anxiety, but do not beneficially affect those behavioral strategies of the individual that maintain emotional problems (Rickels, Downing, & Winokur, 1978), the best procedure may combine a gradual fading out of drug use while continuing to employ behavioral procedures that enhance independent functioning. Indeed, Munjack (1975) found that the gradual withdrawal of Brevital during prolonged exposure facilitated transfer of the antianxiety effects to the nondrugged state.

The point we have been trying to make throughout this section is that the therapist's conceptualizations are often the reason for failures in treatment. Making these assumptions explicit may help to reduce such errors. Of course, there are other sources of possible problems, not the least of which are the procedures employed preparatory to treatment.

Preparation for Treatment

Marks (1978) indicates that as many as 23 percent of the 300 patients who were offered behavioral treatment in his unit during a four-year period refused to accept the therapy. As Marks notes, this refusal rate compares favorably with that of other treatment approaches (Garfield & Kurz, 1952; Rosenthal & Frank, 1959). Marks suggests that these refusals are due to motivational factors, and proposes that these factors relate to, or are influenced by, social pressure, credibility of the therapist, and what he calls "suggestion." All of these seem to be, at least to some degree, open to therapist manipulation. Proper preparation for treatment, then, may be expected to reduce refusal rates. Of course, proper preparation should also reduce dropouts, secure greater cooperation during treatment, facilitate learning, and maximize determination to change.

We have come, over the years, to spend a good deal of time on preparing for treatment and have very few refusals; certainly no more than five percent.

Preparing the Therapist

In an earlier paper (Marshall, 1981a) it was suggested that it is not only the client who needs to be prepared for the possible stresses of flooding therapy; the therapist himself or herself may be distressed, and even at times unnerved by the degree of discomfort displayed by some patients. Although this does not happen often in anxiety disorders, the therapist should have the stamina to persist until the client's anxiety has abated, otherwise the rare harmful effects may ensue. In the course of training therapists to use flooding, we have found that the most difficult task is to get them to persist when a patient becomes distressed.

In the course of an experimental project we once exposed a spider-phobic woman to a live tarantula without apparently adequately preparing her or ourselves. As soon as she saw the insect she began to scream very loudly and fled from the room, much to the dismay of those in the building who witnessed the episode, not to mention the embarrassment we experienced or the distress of our hapless client. We were quite unprepared for this outcome and her subsequent marked increase in fear. Fortunately, treatment eventually removed her phobia altogether (Keltner & Marshall, 1975).

Preparing the Client

It is often claimed that the client's positive motivation to change is crucial to successful outcome. However, we should be careful in attributing failures to a lack of motivation on the part of the client, inasmuch as this diverts attention from the need to change what we are doing.

Similarly, we should not suppose that a client who is positively motivated to seek our help and who is favorably disposed toward a behavioral approach will automatically succeed. Indeed, some clients may be overly optimistic. We once had a patient who had several fears, one of which concerned his feelings of terror when confronted by an attractive female. The referring psychiatrist had, in the hope of persuading this man to accept our treatment, convinced him that behavior therapy was so powerful that one or two sessions would "cure" him. Not surprisingly this did not happen, and the client left us in disgust only to return several weeks later when his problem had finally worn him down. We should have spent more time properly preparing him by working to reduce his overly optimistic view of our talents, rather than being flattered by his positive remarks and attempting to fulfill his unrealistic expectations.

Rachman and Hodgson (1980), in their excellent book dealing with obsessions and compulsions, specifically address the issue of failures. Among other proposals, they suggest enhancing the patient's motivation by way of "a more intensive therapeutic preparation" before exposure procedures are undertaken. Contrary to this proposal, Marks (1976), although agreeing that the client's motivation is crucial, advocates simply describing the procedure to prospective clients in an objective manner and leaving it to them to choose whether to continue. Given such a strategy, it is no surprise that he has a rather high refusal rate. Colleagues working within the framework of more traditional psychotherapy often attribute failures in treatment to the patient's lack of motivation (Baekland & Lundwall, 1975; Strupp, (1980), and although some psychotherapists see these as relatively refractory features of these clients (Cartwright, Lloyd, & Vicklund, 1980; Fiester & Rudestam, 1975; Taulbee, 1958), others recommend pretreatment training procedures to overcome some obstacles (Hoen-Sarie, Frank, Imber, Nash, Stone, & Battle, 1964; Orne & Wender, 1968).

At least some aspects of this very general notion of client motivation may be influenced by the way in which the therapist presents himself or herself and the proposed treatment. For instance, anything that makes the client feel more positive and optimistic about the likely outcome will enhance the client's participation in, and enthusiasm for, the intervention program. Similarly if the therapist and his or her general approach to the problem encourage confidence, then we might expect the client to be more committed to obtaining a successful outcome. Given Marks's (1976) rather bland presentation of flooding to prospective clients, we might expect those who do accept treatment to be rather less than optimistic regarding its benefits and, therefore, rather likely to drop out of therapy. However, Marks et al. (1975) report only 5 of 82 patients withdrew after treatment was initiated, and this is only slightly higher than our own figures despite our enthusiastic presentation of flooding. We have already noted that one of our patients dropped out of treatment for a period because he did not make sufficiently rapid progress, and another man terminated treatment against our advice because he believed he had overcome his difficulty. Of course we have had other withdrawals but not for these nonspecific reasons. A shift in residence for one man led to withdrawal, and a failure to secure cooperation in two women resulted in their dropping out of treatment.

The influence of some of these factors, usually described as "nonspecifics" inasmuch as they are not thought of as the specific elements of any particular treatment procedure, has been elucidated within the context of systematic desensitization (Borkovec & O'Brien, 1976; Emmelkamp, 1975; Kazdin & Wilcoxon, 1976; Wilkins, 1979). Interest in the role of these factors in flooding therapy, on the other hand, has been rather slow to develop. Even the research in desensitization is only now coming to a sufficiently precise delineation of the various nonspecific influences to allow meaningful statements to be made regarding both the effects of nonspecific factors, and the appropriate methods for inducing these influences. In fact it appears likely, for certain designated behaviors at least (e.g., small animal phobias), that nonspecific factors may account for all of the effects resulting from desensitization. Whether the same will be true for flooding remains to be seen, but we have tentative data suggesting that this may be the case (Segal & Marshall, 1980).

The nonspecific factors that we assume contribute to positive outcome concern such things as: (1) providing the client with an overall perspective that promotes optimism regarding the possibility of change; (2) providing specific details regarding the actual procedure with its associated logical, theoretical, and empirical underpinnings, as well as the therapist's own experience with the techniques; (3) the induction of appropriate demands for change; and (4) the therapist's confidence and interpersonal skills.

Lack of attention to any of these details may retard progress in treatment, or may even turn the patient away altogether. Some years ago we had difficulty persuading a patient who had a variety of specific anxieties, obsessions, and compulsions that flooding made any sense. She had spent the previous nine years with a therapist who cast her problems in psychoanalytic terms, and even though those nine years were spent in the fruitless pursuit of her psyche leaving her difficulties unchanged, her attitudes were fixed. Generally, in such cases it is valuable to have the client adopt a "scientific" perspective by simply trying the procedure and evaluating its benefits (Mahoney, 1974). However, even under these conditions she and her husband made only a halfhearted effort at the home-practice in vivo exposure we recommended. Treatment was then transferred to the office where imaginal flooding of an associated obsessive thought (that if she cleaned the house—the initial in vivo procedure—the resultant stirring up of germs would contaminate her children) proved effective. This led the client to change her perspective of the procedure, and encouraged her to initiate the in vivo practice.

Preparing the Environment

In the case just described we also found that it was necessary to spend time preparing the patient's husband. For instance, it was necessary for the therapist to supervise the first two sessions at home before the husband was convinced of the value of the approach so that his cooperation as an assistant therapist was secured. In addition, as Hafner (in press) and others have noted, spouses may actually resist beneficial changes in their dependent mates, and this resistance may arise from fears concerning the nature of the possible changes and their effects on the relationship. Properly preparing relatives for the effects of therapy and securing their support and cooperation may, therefore, be essential to the attainment of treatment goals.

A man in his early thirties was referred for treatment at a time when he was completely unable to drive any vehicle including his bicycle. Although he was otherwise not restricted in his ability to leave home and work, so that he could not be characterized as agoraphobic, he was, nevertheless, entirely dependent upon his wife and mother for transport. Indeed, the three of them appeared to be mutually dependent to a degree that did not seem functional. Our analyses suggested that the most valuable approach would be imaginal exposure followed by graduated in vivo exposure (initially accompanied but not driven by the therapist, then accompanied but not driven by his wife or mother, which was to be faded to driving alone). We also attempted to initiate family-counseling sessions, but we failed at first to properly prepare the family for the radical changes that improvement would produce in their relationships. Signs of growing independence were met with hostility on the part of the wife and mother with this anger being directed at both the patient and therapist. It took some considerable time and persuasion to win back their confidence and cooperation, but once this was done, and the consequences of change were made clear, the family became an important and effective agent in this man's subsequent improvement.

Thus, preparation for treatment is an important element in effectively modifying behavior, and just as errors in conceptualization may prevent the attainment of a successful outcome in the use of flooding therapy, so also might inadequate preparation. A final area where errors may arise concerns the actual application of treatment.

Errors in Application

There are two areas of concern here. The first has to do with our knowledge of the factors that control effective flooding therapy in general, and the second involves the adaptation of the procedure to the problems of specific clients.

Treatment Variables

Marshall et al. (1979) reviewed a substantial body of literature dealing with the efficacy of flooding and were able to identify several factors that were either known to control its effects or were thought to be likely controlling elements. We do not need to consider all of these features here, and the reader is referred to that review for a more thorough appraisal. We will, however, draw the reader's attention to some of the most important characteristics of flooding that must be considered when applying treatment.

Perhaps the single most important factor that influences the effectiveness of flooding is the duration of exposure to the stimuli that induce distress. After considering a number of studies that manipulated exposure duration, Marshall et al. (1979) concluded that all one could say regarding this evidence was that longer exposures were more effective than shorter ones. They argued, however, that the designation of exposure as "long" or "short" depending on arbitrarily set time intervals, was erroneous. Exposure duration, Marshall et al. claimed, should be determined by the subject's responses, particularly those indicative of distress. Gauthier and Marshall (1977b) demonstrated that terminating exposure, contingent upon the subjects reporting that their fear had subsided, produced both longer exposures and more beneficial effects than using habituation of physiological responses as the criterion. Subsequently, Marshall and Nadolny (1979) were able to show that ending exposure when acrophobics were still fearful resulted in a failure to obtain benefits at least in terms of the average change in behavior in the group. Extending this study, and providing more detailed individual analyses (Marshall, 1981b), revealed that although all but 1 of 30 subjects profited from exposure that continued until their anxiety diminished, the results obtained with brief exposures were mixed: some subjects remained unchanged, the fears of others were exacerbated, and a few improved. For those who improved, distress during treatment (as revealed by their inability to tolerate exposures) progressively declined across exposures and across sessions. In those subjects whose fear was worse after the series of brief exposures, the data reflected either the opposite effect (i.e., fear became more intense across exposures and sessions), or very little change was evident, although there were considerable fluctuations over the series.

These data, plus our earlier findings with phobics (Gauthier & Marshall, 1977b), suggest that it is important to end the exposure session when the patient is at a low level of arousal. Whenever we have done otherwise, either deliberately in our research projects or inadvertently in treatment, the clients or subjects have usually either failed to improve, or become more distressed as a result of the experience. Obviously, the easiest way to guarantee success is to keep arousal low throughout exposure, but such a recommendation is contrary to the views of implosive therapists (Stampfl & Levis, 1973) who consider it essential to maximize anxiety. The evidence on this issue suggests that either highly arousing scenes interfere with effective treatment (Marshall et al., 1977), or there is no difference between "high-" or "low-arousing" themes (Mathews & Shaw, 1973).

In addition to exposure duration we must be concerned with the kind of stimuli used in flooding. Studies of anxiety reduction employing various procedures have consistently shown an advantage for in vivo forms of treatment over imaginal procedures. This is true for systematic desensitization (Mathews, 1978), modeling (Thelen et al., 1979), and covert versus overt reinforcement procedures (Kazdin & Smith, 1979) as well as flooding (Emmelkamp & Wessels, 1975). However, Mathews (1978) suggested that imaginal flooding may serve to effectively prepare the patient for the stresses of in vivo exposure, and this was confirmed by Sherry and Levine (1980).

It is certainly true that flooding in imagination is the only possible mode of exposure for emotional distresses induced exclusively by thoughts (imaginal fears, obsessions, ruminations, etc.) or by dreams. We found that grief is effectively treated by imaginal flooding (Gauthier & Marshall, 1977a), and it is hard to see how one could otherwise extinguish all of the grief-related responses. Similarly, Foa and her colleagues (Foa & Steketee, 1977; Foa, Steketee, & Milby, 1980) demonstrated that imaginal flooding was essential to eliminate the distress induced by ritual-related obsessive thoughts in their patients. It may well be that distressing thoughts often arise independently of the external stimuli that are usually included in flooding treatments, and this appears to be similar to the contentions of the implosive therapists (Levis & Hare, 1977). Lack of consideration of these factors may lead to apparent treatment failure.

The observations of Foa, concerning obsessions and compulsions, suggest that in addition to exposing clients to the eliciting stimuli (be they imaginal or real), treatment must also modify the patient's overt responses. We have made similar observations in our treatment of both public-speaking distress (Marshall, Stoian, & Andrews, 1977) and height phobia (Marshall & Nadolny, 1979). For deficient public speakers, we found that anxiety reduction needed to be accompanied by training in overt skills if the goals of treatment were to be secured, and similar benefits were obtained by modifying anxiety-exacerbating self-speech. Although we found no immediate benefits, over and above those secured by our usual treatment package, from training our public speakers to emit coping self-statements, such training resulted in greater maintenance of treatment effects over time (Marshall, Cooper, & Parker, 1979). In the case of acrophobia, training clients to emit coping self-statements both enhanced the immediate effects of in vivo flooding and bolstered maintenance (Marshall & Nadolny, 1979).

An illustration of the importance of training in coping skills (both self-statements and overt behavior) is provided in the following case description.

Hospitalized for a variety of problems, a woman in her midthirties complained of being unable to enter the cafeteria due to excessive social fear. Inasmuch as we could not persuade her to engage in in vivo exposure, we implemented an imaginal procedure. However, she showed no sign of habituation either within or between sessions. Further analyses suggested that as soon as our patient approached the cafeteria, or imagined herself approaching it, she would become very tense and engage in negative thinking. For example, she would think to herself, "I am going to be overcome by fear"; "I am going to fail yet again"; "I am always a failure"; and so on. The development of tension, no doubt exacerbated by the negative self-appraisals, apparently interfered with the extinction of fear both in treatment and in real life. Training her to emit more constructive self-statements (see Meichenbaum, 1977) and to engage in relaxation as a coping skill (Russell & Sipich, 1974), radically changed the patient's ability to participate in, and profit from, flooding. After two more sessions of imaginal flooding, during which rapid habituation occurred, she was able to enter the cafeteria and quickly extinguish her remaining fear.

Another factor that deserves attention is the content of flooding. With respect to in vivo flooding there are not likely to be errors in stimulus content, inasmuch as any mistakes should become apparent immediately exposure begins. However, when flooding is conducted in imagination the patient may readily be led astray by the therapist's theoretical convictions regarding the meaning of fears and the like, or by the therapist's mistaken conclusions regarding the nature of the provocative stimuli. The implosive therapists (Levis & Hare, 1977; Stampfl & Levis, 1973) have attempted to combine psychodynamic theory with a conditioning view in their analyses of phobic behavior. This leads them to make specific and testable propositions about the content of flooding scenes. In the first place they propose that people acquire phobias to particular objects or to some aspects of situations rather than others because of the symbolic significance of the cues. These additional features of the phobic object, which they describe as "hypothesized" cues, must, they declare, be included in treatment if the phobia is to be completely resolved. Secondly, their interpretation of extinction processes demands that the client be made to experience maximal anxiety during exposure. From this position they were led to conclude that exaggerated forms of the feared cues (called "horrific" cues by others) must be included in treatment if extinction is to be rapid and permanent. Of course to accommodate both these requirements, the therapist must chose imaginal exposure, and yet we have seen that in vivo procedures are more effective. In fact, there is little evidence concerning the value of stimulus content, but what there is suggests that psychodynamically symbolic cues are irrelevant to treatment effectiveness (Prochaska, 1971), whereas "horrific" cues appear to retard or eliminate benefits (Foa, Blau, Prout, & Latimer, 1977; Marshall et al., 1977).

Some Examples

Now that we have noted the main general rules for the use of flooding, we will consider some examples where these rules were not appropriately adapted to individual cases. Again we remind readers that these errors reflect incomplete behavioral analyses.

Procedural variations that may be advantageous with particular individuals are suggested by the following case. This woman complained of a phobia of spiders that markedly restricted her life. She described herself as generally quite tense and unable to concentrate on any topic for more than a few minutes. We decided to start with imaginal exposure because this woman expressed considerable distress at the prospect of in vivo flooding so we thought she needed the preparation that the imaginal procedure provides. Initial attempts at imaginal flooding were, however, ineffective. No changes were evident in overt behavior, and the woman complained that the treatment procedure was not suitable. The problem appeared to be her inability to maintain attention to the stimuli during treatment. In turn, this failure to attend seemed to be exaggerated by high levels of muscular tension that caused her discomfort. Relaxation training was ineffective until we were able to modify her attentional behavior so that she could concentrate long enough to learn the skills. Once her concentration was satisfactory and she was able to relax on cue, we introduced real life flooding, and she responded very well. However, again there was little or no transfer to her extratherapeutic experience. This time the problem was, she said, due to the fact that, "When the therapist is present I feel in control but when I am at home I do not." We therefore modified the procedure in order to directly induce control by the client. Three harmless spiders were placed in a room which the subject was to enter. She was to seek out the spiders, pick them up, and place them in their cage. Once she was able to master this, we placed one of the insects on her person leaving her to remove it. Finally, we dropped a spider on her lap unexpectedly during conversation although, of course, we had secured her agreement to this procedure beforehand. During the course of these variations the patient showed quick increases in anxiety, but also rapid extinction which transferred immediately to her everyday life situation. We would certainly not recommend such procedures as routine applications, and it is crucial when they are used to adequately prepare the client for the experience.

Another example may serve to illustrate a procedural error in selecting the content of flooding stimuli. A man in his forties complained that he had suddenly developed a fear of riding in automobiles which proved to be incapacitating inasmuch as he lived outside the city some 10 miles from his work and beyond available bus routes. The patient saw this fear as a general problem of riding in or driving automobiles, and it seemed a straightforward case that should respond to direct in vivo exposure. We chose, for convenience, to drive about with him in the city as the initial in vivo exposure, inasmuch as we agreed that the problem was an undifferentiated fear of driving. However, several hours of riding around the city streets failed to elicit distress, and also failed to modify his behavior. Further detailed analyses of the problem did not turn up anything of significance until he remembered that approximately one month before the onset of his difficulties he had awoken in a panic after dreaming that he had been involved in an automobile accident. In his dream our client lost control of his car while driving on the country road from his home to the city. Prolonged in vivo exposure to driving on this particular country road led to considerable immediate distress, but rapid extinction. Four such accompanied exposures to country rather than city driving, produced sufficient gains so that the client was able to complete a successful self-managed treatment.

ABSOLUTE FAILURES

In both cases discussed immediately above, and in those mentioned earlier, had we been unwilling to learn from the initial disappointment in treatment, or had we not used it as a prompt to look further, we would no doubt have recorded a failure. Our experience has been, then, that absolute failures are rare because we rarely abandon a case as a result of an initial unsuccessful attempt at modifying behavior. We expect such problems just as we find similar frustrations in experimental research and in the development of scientific understanding.

From our clinical records we could find only one case where flooding appeared to be appropriately applied and yet benefits were not evident. A young woman presented with a fear of those earthworms that appear on the surface of the ground after heavy rains. On these occasions she was unable to go outdoors. As it does not rain at the convenience of therapists, and as just the thought of these creatures upset her, we decided to conduct flooding in imagination. This procedure initially elicited strong anxiety that dissipated over six one-hour sessions just as it should. Unfortunately, there were no corresponding effects on her behavior; the next rainy day made her equally housebound and afraid to even look out the window. She seemed, if anything, worse, and even her distress at discussing the creatures had returned.

We then collected a number of these worms and placed them on a table in front of her. Again this elicited considerable distress that dissipated over five sessions. Unfortunately, there were no effects on in vivo behavior, and again after direct exposure all her imaginal fears returned to full strength. We finally combined preparatory relaxation training with an extended session of imaginal flooding, followed immediately by an extended session of exposure to captured worms, followed immediately by an attempt to have her go outside in the rain when she expected the grass to have numerous worms on it (we waited for a rainy day). Even though her distress extinguished to the imaginal and captured worms, she was struck by terror when she attempted to leave the building and could not go outside. No amount of persuasion on our part could get her to even continue to look out the door or window. Neither subsequent desensitization, our version of Rational Emotive Therapy, nor benzodiazepines were of any help in ameliorating this woman's problem despite her clear determination to overcome the fear. We are at a loss to explain this failure. Perhaps if we had used benzodiazepines in the way we suggested earlier (i.e., as preparatory to and accompanying treatment with their gradual withdrawal over flooding sessions) we might have helped this woman, but it was hard to escape the conclusion that this fear meant more than the patient was prepared to admit.

FAILURES TO COOPERATE AND RELAPSES

In our experience the most difficult problems involve those patients who do not carry out recommended home practice, which we consider to be essential to ensure generalization of treatment benefits to the patient's day-to-day circumstances. In one case a compulsive house cleaner would not allow someone as "messy" as the therapist (W.L.M.) to enter her home to demonstrate the procedures. In fact, she was so upset by this prospect that we could not persuade her to return to treatment. Usually, however, the problem concerns the patient's continued diligent practice (or rather lack of it) once direct therapist supervision is withdrawn. When we were somewhat more naive we relied on patients' reports, which all too often proved to be inaccurate overestimates of the amount of home practice they had completed. We now attempt to secure the cooperation of a spouse, relative, or friend.

Marks et al. (1975) discuss two obsessive-compulsives who refused to permit their homes to be contaminated, and who consequently failed to benefit from treatment. For another patient it was impossible to arrange essential home visits due to the remoteness of her residence, and another patient was unable to resist engaging in rituals between treatment sessions. These observations suggest that home practice is essential for treatment to be effective, and the evidence confirms this suggestion (Jannoun, Munby, Catalan, & Gelder, 1980; Mathews, Teasdale, Munby, Johnston, & Shaw, 1977).

We noted earlier the necessity of preparing family members and friends for the changes that occur in treatment, and we now point to our use of these people as monitors of home practice. In addition to this role, it is useful to involve family and friends as much as possible in treatment. Some years ago, one of us was having difficulty making progress in reducing a fear of shopping in a young married woman who appeared to be very cooperative. Her husband was asked to cooperate by ensuring that she carried out her prescribed self-directed practice. This he did enthusiastically but she was still unable to get further than the initial steps. Although she had never mentioned the matter, the therapist suspected that she craved more attention from her husband. Accordingly, he was asked to accompany her during home practice and within two weeks she was shopping free of anxiety at large supermarkets. Whether she was originally phobic is hard to tell, but it is certainly clear that involving the husband was an effective step.

Of course, we are not the first to note these benefits. Marks et al. (1975) formed "an obsessive family group" within which several patients and their relatives met to discuss problems and solutions and spouses were trained to act more effectively. Hand, Lamontagne, and Marks (1974) used a similar group program for agoraphobics. These types of procedures may enhance cooperation during treatment and provide sufficient support and demands to carry out essential extratherapeutic practice.

Such procedures may also help to reduce relapses. Indeed, Mathews et al. (1977) found that the home-practice procedure resulted in immediate benefits equivalent to a larger number of clinic-based sessions, and that patients exposed to this procedure continued to show gains throughout the follow-up period. Generally speaking, clinic-based treatment does not produce gains after therapy ends, and if anything there appears to be some loss at follow-up assessments (Gelder, 1977). Although we have found some losses in the specified responses of our patients after formal treatment is over, this rarely occurs when home practice is part of the program, and gains have always been reinstated with either additional therapist-administered treatment or a reinitiation of the self-managed practice. Of course, we are not able to keep track of all our patients so these remarks refer only to those who stay in contact.

SUMMARY AND CONCLUSIONS

Flooding describes procedures that expose clients for prolonged periods to stimuli eliciting distressful emotional reactions, so that these unpleasant reactions will be extinguished. Flooding may have other beneficial effects, but we cannot expect these gains unless we deliberately expand treatment to include the modification of various behaviors additional to the distressful emotional responses.

There does not seem to be substantial evidence to support the often expressed concern that flooding may exacerbate rather than extinguish fears, nor are any significant other side-effects at all common. The literature and the comments of clinicians and researchers suggest that failures are no more common in flooding than they are in the use of other anxiety-management procedures, and may even be less frequent.

We understand behavioral analysis to refer to the whole process by which a scientist-practitioner translates empirical knowledge and theoretical perspectives into clinical practice. Table 5.1 outlines the initial aspects of this process, which would customarily be followed by an assessment of the value of the application, the outcome of which should indicate the need to reappraise the process or to end treatment. From this perspective it is clear that errors could occur at any one of the steps (or substeps) described in the table. Such errors within a careful behavioral analysis should be readily identified, and should lead to self-correcting responses finally resulting in satisfactory outcome.

Absolute failures, in the sense of no apparent benefits despite the patient's co-operation in an apparently adequate treatment program, appear to be rare. Failures as a result of the patient not cooperating, dropping out, or relapsing seem to be uncommon, and sometimes result from factors beyond the therapist's control.

REFERENCES

Baekland, F., & Lundwall, L. (1975) Dropping out of treatment: A critical review. *Psychological Bulletin*, **82**, 728–783.

Baer, D.M., Wolf, M.M., & Risley, T.R. (1968) Some current dimensions of applied behavior analysis. *Journal of Applied Behavior Analysis*, **1**, 91–97.

Bandura, A. (1969) *Principles of behavior modification*. New York: Holt, Rinehart & Winston.

Barrett, C.L. (1970) "Runaway imagery" in systematic desensitization therapy and implosive therapy. *Psychotherapy: Theory, Research and Practice*, **7**, 233–235.

Borkovec, T.D., & O'Brien, G.T. (1976) Methodological and target behavior issues in analogue therapy outcome research. In M. Hersen, R.M. Eisler, & P.M. Miller (Eds.), *Progress in behavior modification* (Vol. 3). New York: Academic.

Cartwright, R., Lloyd, S., & Vicklund, J. (1980) Identifying early dropouts from psychotherapy. *Psychotherapy: Theory, Research and Practice*, **17**, 263–267.

Coleman, J.C. (1976) *Abnormal psychology and modern life* (5th ed.). Glenview, Ill.: Scott Foresman.

Coombs, R., Shah, P., & Shulman, R. (1977) Effects of psychological stress on click and rhythm in mitral valve prolapse. *American Heart Association Monograph,* No. 57, Part II, **56**(4), III–111.

Emmelkamp, P.M.G. (1975) Effects of expectancy on systematic desensitization and flooding. *European Journal of Behavioural Analysis and Modification,* **1**, 1–11.

Emmelkamp, P.M.G., & Wessells, H. (1975) Flooding in imagination vs flooding *in vivo:* A comparison with agoraphobics. *Behaviour Research and Therapy,* **13**, 7–15.

Fiester, A., & Rudestam, K. (1975) A multivariate analysis of the early dropout process. *Journal of Consulting and Clinical Psychology,* **43**, 528–535.

Foa, E.B., & Goldstein, A. (1978) Continuous exposure and complete response prevention in the treatment of obsessive-compulsive neurosis. *Behavior Therapy,* **9**, 821–829.

Foa, E.B., Blau, J.S., Prout, M., & Latimer, P. (1977) Is horror a necessary component of flooding (implosion)? *Behaviour Research and Therapy,* **15**, 397–402.

Foa, E.B., & Steketee, G. (1977) Emergent fears during treatment of three obsessive compulsives: Symptom substitution or deconditioning? *Journal of Behavior Therapy and Experimental Psychiatry,* **8**, 353–358.

Foa, E.B., Steketee, G., & Groves, G. (1979) Use of behavioral therapy and imipramine: A case of obsessive-compulsive neurosis with severe depression. *Behavior Modification,* **3**, 419–430.

Foa, E.B., Steketee, G., & Milby, J.B. (1980) Differential effects of exposure and response prevention in obsessive-compulsive washers. *Journal of Consulting and Clinical Psychology,* **48**, 71–79.

Foa, E.B., Steketee, G., Turner, R.M., & Fischer, S.C. (1980) Effects of imaginal exposure to feared disasters in obsessive-compulsive checkers. *Behaviour Research and Therapy,* **18**, 449–455.

Fodor, I.G. (1974) The phobic syndrome in women. In V. Franks, & V. Burtle (Eds.), *Women in therapy.* New York: Brunner/Mazel.

Garfield, S.L., & Kurz, M. (1952) Evaluation of treatment and related procedures in 1216 cases referred to a mental hygiene clinic. *Psychiatric Quarterly,* **26**, 414–424.

Gauthier, J., & Marshall, W.L. (1977a) Grief: A behavioral/cognitive analysis. *Cognitive Therapy and Research,* **1**, 39–44.

Gauthier, J., & Marshall, W.L. (1977b) The determination of optimal exposure to phobic stimuli in flooding therapy. *Behaviour Research and Therapy,* **15**, 403–410.

Gelder, M. (1977) Behavioral treatment of agoraphobia: Some factors which restrict change after treatment. In J. Boulougouris, & A. Rabavilas (Eds.), *Phobic and obsessive compulsive disorders.* Oxford: Pergamon.

Goldstein, A.J. (1970) Case conference: Some aspects of agoraphobia. *Journal of Behavior Therapy and Experimental Psychiatry,* **1**, 305–313.

Goldstein, A.J. (1973) Learning theory insufficiency in understanding agoraphobia. In J.C. Brengelman, & W. Turner (Eds.), *Behavior Therapy.* Munich: Urban & Schwarzenberg.

Hafner, R.J. (1977) The husbands of agoraphobic women and their influence on treatment outcome. *British Journal of Psychiatry,* **131**, 289–294.

Hafner, R.J. (1979) Behavior therapy as a test of psychoanalytic theory. *American Journal of Psychiatry,* **136,** 88–90.

Hafner, R.J. (in press) Behaviour therapy for the neuroses: Some conceptual and practical problems. *Australian and New Zealand Journal of Psychiatry.*

Hallam, R.S. (1976) The Eysenck personality scales: Stability and change after therapy. *Behaviour Research and Therapy,* **14,** 369–372.

Hand, I., Lamontagne, Y., & Marks, I.M. (1974) Group exposure (flooding) in vivo for agoraphobics. *British Journal of Psychiatry,* **124,** 588–602.

Hoen-Sarie, R., Frank, J., Imber, S., Nash, E., Stone, A., & Battle, M. (1964) Systematic preparation of patients for psychotherapy. 1. Effects on therapy behavior and outcome. *Journal of Psychiatric Research,* **2,** 267–281.

Horne, A.M. (1974) Effect of personality type in reducing specific anxiety with behavioral and psychodynamic therapy. *Journal of Counseling Psychology,* **21,** 340–341.

Hudson, B. (1974) The families of agoraphobics treated by behavior therapy. *British Journal of Social Work,* **4,** 51–59.

Jackson, D., & Yalom, I. (1965) Conjoint family therapy as an aid to intensive psychotherapy. In A. Burton (Ed.), *Modern psychotherapeutic practice: Innovations in technique.* San Francisco: Science and Behavior.

Jannoun, L., Munby, M., Catalan, J., & Gelder, M. (1980) A home-based treatment program for agoraphobia: Replication and controlled evaluation. *Behavior Therapy,* **11,** 294–305.

Kantor, J., Zitrin, C., & Zeldis, S. (1980) Mitral valve prolapse syndrome in agoraphobic patients. *American Journal of Psychiatry,* **137,** 467–469.

Kazdin, A.E., & Smith, G.A. (1979) Covert conditioning: A review and evaluation. *Advances in Behaviour Research and Therapy,* **2,** 57–98.

Keltner, A., & Marshall, W.L. (1975) Single-trial exacerbation of an anxiety habit with second-order conditioning and subsequent desensitization. *Journal of Behavior Therapy and Experimental Psychiatry,* **6,** 323–324.

Klein, D.F. (1980) Anxiety reconceptualized. *Comprehensive Psychiatry,* **21,** 411–427.

Klein, D.F., & Rabkin, J.G. (1980) *Anxiety revisited.* New York: Raven.

Lazarus, A.A. (1971) *Behavior therapy and beyond.* New York: McGraw-Hill.

Levis, D.J., & Hare, N. (1977) A review of the theoretical rationale and empirical support for the extinction approach of implosive (flooding) therapy. In M. Hersen, R.M. Eisler, & P.M. Miller (Eds.), *Progress in behavior modification* (Vol. 4). New York: Academic.

Mahoney, M.J. (1974) *Cognition and behavior modification.* Cambridge, Mass.: Ballinger.

Marks, I.M. (1976) The current status of behavioral psychotherapy: Theory and practice. *American Journal of Psychiatry,* **133,** 253–261.

Marks, I.M. (1978) Behavioral psychotherapy of adult neurosis. In S.L. Garfield, & A.E. Bergin (Eds.), *Handbook of psychotherapy and behavior change* (2nd Ed.). New York: Wiley.

Marks, I.M., Hodgson, R., & Rachman, S. (1975) Treatment of chronic obsessive-compulsive neurosis by *in vivo* exposure. *British Journal of Psychiatry,* **127,** 349–364.

Marshall, J., & Neill, J. (1977) The removal of a psychosomatic symptom: Effects on the marriage. *Family Process,* **16,** 273–280.

Marshall, W.L. (1981a) Behavioral treatment of phobic and obsessive-compulsive disorders. In L. Michelson, M. Hersen, & S.M. Turner (Eds.), *Future perspectives in behavior therapy.* New York: Plenum.

Marshall, W.L. (1981b) *The effects on acrophobics of repeated, brief in vivo exposures to high intensity stimuli.* Unpublished manuscript, Queen's University, Kingston, Ontario, Canada.

Marshall, W.L. (1982a) A model of dysfunctional behavior. In A.S. Bellack, M. Hersen, & A.E. Kazdin (Eds.), *International handbook of behavior modification and therapy (Vol. 1). New York: Plenum.*

Marshall, W.L., Cooper, C.M., & Parker L. (1979) Self-instructions, anxiety management, and skills training with public-speakers paper presented at the 13th Annual Convention of the Association for the Advancement of Behavior Therapy, San Francisco.

Marshall, W.L., Gauthier, J., Christie, M.M., Currie, D.W., & Gordon, A. (1977) Flooding therapy: Effectiveness, stimulus characteristics, and the value of brief *in vivo* exposure. *Behaviour Research and Therapy,* **15,** 79–87.

Marshall, W.L., Gauthier, J., & Gordon, A. (1979) The current status of flooding therapy. In M. Hersen, R.M. Eisler, & P.M. Miller (Eds.), *Progress in behavior modification* (Vol. 7). New York: Academic.

Marshall, W.L., & Nadolny, A. (1979) *Exposure duration in flooding therapy with acrophobics.* Paper presented at the 13th Annual Convention of the Association for the Advancement of Behavior Therapy, San Francisco.

Marshall, W.L., Stoian, M.S., & Andrews, W.R. (1977) Skills training and self-administered desensitization in the reduction of public speaking anxiety. *Behaviour Research and Therapy,* **15,** 115–117.

Mathews, A.M. (1978) Fear reduction research and clinical phobias. *Psychological Bulletin,* **85,** 390–404.

Mathews, A.M., Johnston, D.W., Shaw, P.M., & Gelder, M.G. (1974) Process variables and the prediction of outcome in behaviour therapy. *British Journal of Psychiatry,* **125,** 256–264.

Mathews, A.M., & Shaw, P.M. (1973) Emotional arousal and persuasion effects in flooding. *Behaviour Research and Therapy,* **11,** 587–598.

Mathews, A.M., Teasdale, J.D., Munby, M., Johnston, D.W., & Shaw, P.M. (1977) A home-based treatment program for agoraphobia. *Behavior Therapy,* **8,** 915–924.

Mayo, J. (1979) Marital therapy with manic-depressive patients treated with lithium. *Comprehensive Psychiatry,* **20,** 419–426.

Meichenbaum, D. (1977) *Cognitive-behavior modification: An integrative approach.* New York: Plenum.

Morganstern, K.P. (1973) Implosive therapy and flooding procedures: A critical review. *Psychological Bulletin,* **79,** 318–334.

Munjack, D.J. (1975) Overcoming obstacles to desensitization using in vivo stimuli and Brevital. *Behavior Therapy,* **5,** 543–546.

Orne, M., & Wender, P. (1968) Anticipatory socialization for psychotherapy: Method and rationale. *American Journal of Psychiatry,* **124,** 1202–1212.

Pariser, S.F., Jones, B.A., Pinta, E.R., Young, E.A., & Fontana, M.E. (1979) Panic attacks: Diagnostic evaluations of 17 patients. *American Journal of Psychiatry,* **136,** 105–106.

Prochaska, J.O. (1971) Symptom and dynamic cues in the implosive treatment of test anxiety. *Journal of Abnormal Psychology,* **77,** 133–142.

Rachman, S. (1981) Personal Communication.

Rachman, S., & Hodgson, R. (1980) *Obsessions and compulsions.* New York: Prentice-Hall.

Rickels, K. (1980) Clinical comparisons. In Benzodiazepines 1980: Current update. *Psychosomatics (Supplement),* **21,** 4–8.

Rickels, K., Downing, R.W., & Winokur, A. (1978) Antianxiety drugs: Clinical use in psychiatry. In L.L. Iversen, S.D. Iversen, & S.H. Snyder (Eds.), *Handbook of psychopharmacology, Vol. 13. Biology of mood and antianxiety drugs.* New York: Plenum.

Rimm, D.C., & Masters, J.C. (1974) *Behavior therapy: Techniques, and empirical findings.* New York: Academic.

Rosenthal, D., & Frank, J.D. (1959) The fate of psychiatric clinic outpatients assigned to psychotherapy. *Journal of Nervous and Mental Disease,* **127,** 330–343.

Russell, R.K., & Sipich, J.F. (1974) Treatment of test anxiety by cue-controlled relaxation. *Behavior Therapy,* **5,** 673–676.

Segal, Z., & Marshall, W.L. (1980) *Predicted versus actual expectancies in flooding therapy.* Paper presented at the 14th Annual Convention of the Association for the Advancement of Behavior Therapy, New York.

Sherry, G.S., & Levine, B.A. (1980) An examination of procedural variations in flooding therapy. *Behavior Therapy,* **11,** 148–155.

Shipley, R.H., & Boudewyns, P.A. (1980) Flooding and implosive therapy: Are they harmful? *Behavior Therapy,* **11,** 503–508.

Singer, J.L. (1974) *Imagery and daydream methods in psychotherapy and behavior modification.* New York: Academic.

Stamfl, T.G., & Levis, D.J. (1973) *Implosive therapy: Theory and technique.* Morristown, N.J.: General Learning Press.

Strupp, H.H. (1980) Success and failure in time-limited psychotherapy: Further evidence (comparison 4). *Archives of General Psychiatry,* **37,** 947–954.

Taulbee, E. (1958) Relationship between certain personality variables and continuation in psychotherapy. *Journal of Consulting Psychology,* **22,** 83–89.

Venkatesh, A., Pauls, D., & Crowe, R. (1978) *Mitral valve prolapse in anxiety neurosis.* Paper presented at the 131st Annual Meeting of the American Psychiatric Association, Atlanta.

Wilkins, W. (1979) Expectancies in therapy research: Discriminating among heterogeneous nonspecifics. *Journal of Consulting and Clinical Psychology,* **47,** 837–845.

Wolpe, J. (1969) *The practice of behavior therapy.* Oxford: Pergamon.

Zitrin, C., Klein, D.F., & Woerner, M. (1980) Treatment of agoraphobia with group exposure *in vivo* and imipramine. *Archives of General Psychiatry,* **37,** 63–72.

CHAPTER 6

Limitations of the
Treatment for Social Anxiety

JOHN S. MARZILLIER
KEITH WINTER

The cult of success has dominated behavior therapy virtually since its beginnings and it is a refreshing change to be able to write a chapter on therapeutic failures. We have been aware for some time of the inadequacies of many of our attempts to treat socially anxious patients (see, e.g., Marzillier & Winter, 1978) and welcome the opportunity to share our difficulties and concerns in a more extensive analysis. Failure, like its counterpart success, is an elusive phenomenon which everyone knows but few acknowledge. Failure is also relative. What is perceived by one party as failure is perceived by another as success. A therapist may despair of a patient's ability to conquer his social anxieties and write him off as a "failure," only to find some years later that the patient is socializing successfully "thanks to the therapy." And the reverse, the capacity of therapists to perceive some light in the gloom is notorious! It is only the inexperienced or self-deluded therapist who is unable to look beyond the claims of his or her patient and see the risks and the dangers even in the most heralded success stories. An apparent outright failure may prove to be a salutary learning experience that eventually leads to the pursuit of more appropriate and rewarding goals. In discussing our "failure cases," therefore, we are hopeful that we shall arrive at a better understanding not only of the nature and treatment of social anxiety, but also of the values that underpin our approach to therapy, inasmuch as failure, like success, is ultimately an expression of the therapist's beliefs and ideals about normal and abnormal behaviour.

THE NATURE OF SOCIAL ANXIETY

It is not in itself abnormal to experience anxiety in social situations. All, except for the very blasé or the extremely confident, would experience feelings of at least moderate apprehension at the prospect of addressing a large and critical audience, for example. If pressed, most of us would admit to some anxiety on entering a room full of strangers, on passing by a gang of tough-looking youngsters, or during the vicissitudes of an intimate and difficult relationship. The experience of social anxiety is thus far from uncommon in our society; indeed, it is a normal accompaniment of many social encounters. It may even be a useful feature of social life, providing the dynamic force that energizes our interactions and drives us to seek out social stimulation. However, in its clinical manifestations, social anxiety is disruptive and unpleasant; it can be a source of continual and unremitting distress to some people with the result that social contact is shunned and a bleak solitary existence sought out. Later in the chapter we describe two clinical cases of severe social anxiety that illustrate the extent to which anxiety comes to dominate social life.

There is no accepted or satisfactory way of defining social anxiety. Marks (1969) used the term "social phobia" to define one of four categories of phobic anxiety. On the basis of 23 social phobics seen at the Maudsley Hospital, London, Marks drew attention to a number of key characteristics: fears of eating and drinking in public, fear of oneself vomiting or of seeing others vomit, excessive self-consciousness, over-concern with what other people may think, inappropriate or exaggerated worries about one's appearance, and such specific difficulties as inability to write in public and a fear of using the telephone. From 35 cases of "severe social anxiety" seen at a Somerset Hospital, Nichols (1974) extracted 12 features. Among these were low self-evaluation, heightened sensitivity to criticism, a feeling of being trapped in "socially enclosed" situations (i.e., ones in which escape was difficult), fears of losing control, and an exaggerated awareness of the somatic accompaniments of anxiety (e.g., blushing, trembling, shaking). Inasmuch as both descriptions of social anxiety were derived from small and selected clinical samples, their wider validity is uncertain. Many clinicians who have come into contact with socially anxious patients will recognize some of the features that Marks and Nichols have described. But how well this constellation of problems defines a recognizable category or personality characteristic has not been established.

In this chapter we shall not attempt to formulate our own definition of social anxiety as we remain unconvinced that a discrete and homogeneous category can be identified. Instead we shall use the term in a loose sense to describe a variety of clinical problems in which the experience of anxiety in social situations is a significant feature. Anxiety may be experienced as the primary complaint, or may be secondary to other problems. As will be evident from the cases that we discuss, our clinical experience of social anxiety has been largely derived from therapeutic work in hospital outpatient clinics and in health center and general practice settings. Therefore, our remarks are primarily directed at the socially anxious patients who seek help themselves and are functioning at a particular level in the community.

BEHAVIORAL TREATMENTS OF SOCIAL ANXIETY

Behavioral treatments of social anxiety can be divided into those that seek to reduce anxiety directly, as, for example, systematic desensitization, and those that seek to modify factors believed to be responsible for anxiety. Among the latter are assertive and social skills training methods and the more recent cognitive-behavioral approaches. Recent research studies have shown some support for anxiety management approaches (e.g., Öst, Jerremalm, & Johansson, 1981), skills training methods (e.g., Trower, Yardley, Bryant, & Shaw, 1978), and cognitive-behavioral treatments (Kanter & Goldfried, 1979). Inasmuch as the practicing clinician will generally use a combination of therapeutic procedures, we are thus keenly aware that findings reported in the research literature are often unrepresentative of the realities of clinical practice. It is our firm belief that individual patient differences are highly significant in determining the choice of any effective treatment strategy, a view that we have previously expressed and illustrated (Marzillier & Winter, 1978). Thus perhaps the most important clue to the treatment of socially anxious patients lies in the understanding and analysis of the problems they present from which the appropriate treatment strategies should emerge.

THE IMPORTANCE OF INITIAL ANALYSIS

The most likely single cause of failure in the behavioral treatment of social anxiety is an incomplete or faulty initial analysis of the problem. Most behaviorally oriented clinicians would now recognize that behavior therapy requires a detailed individual analysis followed by the selection of an appropriately tailored treatment strategy. However, the process of synthesizing the facts and observations derived from the clinical assessment is interpretive and may be error prone. Where treatment failure has occurred, it is possible that a more thorough examination of the problem or a revision of those facts and observations may generate alternative hypotheses about the treatment procedure to be employed. It has to be recognized from the outset that socially anxious people presenting as patients may be markedly different in the nature of their social problem, their desire to alter their social life, and, therefore, in the choice of an appropriate treatment strategy.

The typical clinical presentation of social anxiety is one of the habitual experience of discomfort or distress when encountering specified classes of social stimuli. Often this leads to avoidance of those situations or to the adoption of an alternative coping strategy such as consuming alcohol. Frequently the autonomic turmoil that makes up the somatic component of social anxiety appears of paramount importance to the patient, who may voice his or her complaint in terms of stomach churning, nausea, frequency of micturition, palpitations, dizziness, sweating, or tremor.

These unpleasant feelings will obviously need attention but a failure to examine associated or causative factors may well lead to failure in treatment in the longer term. Our clinical experience of social anxiety has led us to consider the following key features when arriving at a behavioral analysis.

Physiological Aspects of Social Anxiety

Acute physical discomfort can be experienced before, during, and after social interaction. This discomfort can take the form of general physiological signs of anxiety as previously described, or may be in the form of a quite specific symptom, such as "a choking sensation in the throat." The severity, intensity, and frequency of anxiety symptoms is, in our experience, highly variable. We have encountered patients whose emotional distress is so pervasive that their whole existence is dominated by the experience of anxiety and by methods of avoiding or escaping from that experience, and other patients whose specific anxiety symptoms occur in an otherwise socially active and well-adjusted individual.

Cognitive Aspects of Social Anxiety

Ruminative thoughts about previous, current, or anticipated social encounters are frequently reported by socially anxious patients. Typically these thoughts are worrying or repetitive in nature: "Am I making a fool of myself?" "Did I say the wrong thing and upset someone?" "I must look awful," and so on. These thoughts can often be related to the presence of underlying maladaptive beliefs. One of our patients had the firm belief that her head and her hands trembled which led her to feel excessively self-conscious on social occasions. She was convinced that other people could see the tremor although, in fact, no tremor could be observed. This led her to ruminate about the way she looked and the way others responded to her. The conviction that one is inferior to others, alienated from the rest of society, incapable of leading a normal social life, and other fundamental beliefs about oneself in relation to others can come to dominate thoughts and behavior. These convictions are not necessarily untrue or irrational; but if they exert a profound and negative influence on the course of the patient's life, they are clearly maladaptive. Awareness of the existence of such beliefs is vital in the analysis and treatment of social anxiety. We have found it helpful to consider in particular (1) the person's perception of himself or herself and (2) his or her perception of others. Misperceptions in both instances are all too frequent.

Motivational Factors

The experience of intense social anxiety, particularly if it is pervasive, can easily lead to the inhibition of social activity and a disinterest in social life. In this sense the patient may be seen as *unmotivated* to change his or her social behavior because the patient cannot conceive of social life as being other than anxiety-based. Although motivation to change may increase as anxiety decreases, it is often difficult to get such patients to accept the desirability of treatment in the first instance. They are simply too frightened to consider change. In other cases, depression and apathy can result from prolonged social isolation and the repeated failure of attempts to socialize such that any attempt at change, however small or unthreatening, is seen as doomed to fail. It is important for the clinician to assess the degree to which the patient is likely to participate in an active treatment program. Overzealous attempts at radical change can rebound if the patient's motivation is very uncertain.

Environmental Factors

The patient's social environment plays a significant part in any assessment. Socially anxious patients tend to lead fairly restricted social lives. The degree to which these will change depends not only on intrapersonal changes that result from therapy, but the accessibility of the social environment. A single, unemployed person living a lonely life in a one room apartment with no family or friends has to battle hard to make an impact on the social environment. Those with existing social ties and potential social outlets, such as at work or at leisure, have a head start in their attempts at socialization. However, it is also the case that some social environments reinforce withdrawal and isolation as when the family of a patient provides a safe and unthreatening alternative to a more independent social existence.

Social Skills

Social anxieties are often closely related to deficiencies in social skills. A patient may talk too little or too much, may be dull and boring to talk to, or may have little idea of how to initiate a pleasant conversation with another, or how to handle himself or herself in a group. These and other deficiencies in social skills provoke anxiety which, in turn, renders the social performance more ineffective. The reciprocal relationship between anxiety and poor social skills is readily recognizable in many patients. A thorough analysis needs to take the social performance of the patient into account.

Personal Appearance

A fact seldom noted in the literature is that many individuals suffering from social anxiety have problems with their appearance. Those who are physically unattractive, or those suffering from specific deformities, may find the process of socialization more difficult. Although physical apparance is to a large extent immodifiable except by cosmetic surgery, advice may be given on make-up, hairstyle, clothing, and other aspects of personal care.

FAILURE CASES

The six features of social anxiety described above serve as a general guide to the assessment and analysis of individual patients. We recognize that the process of behavioral analysis is a difficult and complicated one and that it is not easy for clinicians to understand the complexity of factors that describe and maintain social anxiety. We believe, however, that in many instances of treatment failure, the causes of failure reside in inadequate and often oversimplified analysis. The following two case histories have been selected to illustrate the ways in which the initial analysis proved incorrect or misleading.

Incorrect Analysis

CASE 1. FAILURE TO CONTROL ANXIETY, DUE TO REFUSAL TO INCREASE SOCIAL CONTACT

This case has been previously described by Marzillier and Winter (1978) and concerns a 29-year-old woman from an impoverished and punitive family background who was excessively fearful about meeting and interacting with unfamiliar people. She reported leaving at least 60 jobs, mainly residential domestic work, because of embarrassment caused by her inability to relate to people. Somewhere in the midst of this series she met a man whom she married, but this arrangement lasted only a few months because her husband was unable to tolerate her general fearfulness and refusal to mix with people. As far as could be determined, her social anxiety was lifelong.

When first seen, this lady was overtly very anxious, answering questions with the briefest of replies and describing her problem as "a fear of people." She reported feeling self-conscious about her height (5'9") and also about her appearance, which was, in fact, perfectly normal.

Behavioral assessment revealed a number of social skills deficits: short utterance, failing to initiate conversation, tense posture, insufficient eye contact, and a lack of expressive movement. General assessment revealed depression, low self-esteem, and extreme self-consciousness to be important features of the patient's problem. She was extremely socially isolated but did not feel that she wished to extend her social life beyond making one or two close friends that she could see once or twice a week. With the benefit of hindsight it may be said that the patient's limited social ambition was given too little weight in determining the nature and extent of the intervention.

It became clear that the patient's excessive anxiety would require treatment before social skills training or exposure to additional social interaction could commence. Even after several sessions she remained uneasy about remaining in the same room with the therapist, and too worried to properly comprehend or retain instructions. Inasmuch as enforced exposure to social interaction (flooding) would have been totally unacceptable to the patient, it was decided to commence with several sessions of deep muscle and differential relaxation training which she could also practice at home with the aid of cassette-recorded instructions.

At first it seemed that some relief was obtained by relaxation and it was agreed to proceed with social skills training with the initial target of increasing the frequency of question asking in a general conversation. Training consisted of modeling, rehearsal, and therapist feedback until she reported that the treatment sessions were once again causing intolerable anxiety that could not be controlled by relaxation. After a few more sessions in which treatment reverted to relaxation practice and imaginal desensitization, she stated that she did not wish to continue with treatment. Treatment was terminated by mutual agreement.

Three years after behavioral treatment was abandoned, the authors carried out a follow-up interview with this woman to discover her current situation. The former patient was found to be living on her own in an isolated studio apartment and still very frightened of meeting people. Her curtains were kept drawn, she was suspicious about her neighbors' attitude towards her, and felt that people were laughing at her appearance. She had made two suicidal attempts in the past three years and was lonely, bored, and frustrated. Her ideal social life would be to have regular contact with a few trusted friends but her fears prevented her from meeting people.

Reflecting on treatment, it emerged that she had been relieved when treatment stopped inasmuch as a high level of anxiety was associated with clinic attendance. It was not the building, the personality, or the sex of the therapist that concerned her, but the enforced interaction. In retrospect she claimed that her anxiety was never really controlled by relaxing and that she had no confidence in the technique. She did say that she was finding it somewhat easier to make conversation, possibly as a result of what little was achieved in the social skills training, but more probably by virtue of spending 12 months of communal living in a psychiatric after-care hostel (which she hated). At the time of the follow-up she was depending greatly on a combination of a tricyclic antidepressant and a benzodiazepine tranquilizer. She professed the latter drug to be the best means she had found for keeping her anxiety in check.

In this case treatment failed because the treatment session was itself aversive to the patient, and this in spite of the effort made to reduce tension by muscular control and by the adoption of a casual friendly approach. It may seem as though the step from anxiety management to social skills training was taken too rapidly and that further measures should have been applied to achieve control of this woman's anxiety. Perhaps the therapist could have proceeded more slowly, desensitizing the patient to the clinic setting before making any demands such as relaxation practice. To have stood any chance of success there would have to have been a low expectation of participation by the patient and this would have rendered the procedure slow and expensive, both in time and resources. An alternative may have been to secure calm by chemical means prior to the commencement of psychological treatment. However, it is by no means certain that either of these suggestions would have effected significant change.

Behavioral analysis of this case had (correctly, we believe) pinpointed excessive and intense anxiety as a central feature, yet attempts to reduce anxiety had been conspicuously unsuccessful. Why? What remained relatively unexplored in this patient's case was her motivation to change and, more particularly, the degree to which active attempts to reduce anxiety, thereby raising the expectation of further social change, were themselves a source of considerable anxiety. She was not "ready" for such a demanding treatment. Given her limited social ambition—the desire for regular contact with one or two close friends only—it would have perhaps been more productive for the therapist to have directed her towards a less threatening social goal, for example, finding an acquaintance with similar needs. Perhaps the establishment of an accepting and nonthreatening therapeutic relationship was necessary before any demands could be made on her, however small. The lessons we have drawn from this case are, first, the need to take into account the patient's limited social ambitions in planning treatment strategies, and second, the need to establish a basis for a more active treatment by developing a positive and mutually acceptable therapeutic relationship. Finally, for some cases of severe social anxiety it may be entirely unrealistic for the therapist to expect much more than a very limited social change at best and to create expectations of more radical change can be counterproductive and doomed to fail.

CASE 2.   WHOSE PROBLEM IS IT ANYWAY?

The second case in which the initial analysis proved inadequate is that of an 18-year-old girl who was referred for psychological help because her parents were worried about her increasing shyness, social anxiety, lack of friends, and the absence of a social life. Jenny, as we shall call her, had experienced feelings of anxiety and general insecurity since she was 14 years old. She felt excessively self-conscious in the presence of others and at times was convinced that she was talked about and laughed at behind her back. When first seen she had just begun training as a student nurse and was living in nursing accommodation, but very often returned to her parental home. She came from a prosperous middle-class family; her father was a successful businessman, her mother pursued an active social life, and she had two elder sisters. The impression of her from the initial interview was of a pleasant, if rather reserved and worried person, who had become increasingly cut off from social contact since leaving school, who now found it more and more difficult to build herself a fulfilling and independent social life. At first sight the prospects of guiding her to overcome her anxieties and lead a more fulfilling social life looked reasonably good.

Jenny was seen once weekly for an initial five weeks during which the strategy of tackling her social anxieties directly by anxiety management training was discussed and agreed, and the first steps of the strategy implemented. Relaxation training was carried out, specific social interactions selected, covert modeling introduced, role-playing of the requisite behavior carried out, and homework assignments set. After an initially promising response, Jenny began to find it increasingly difficult to generalize the skills and strategies learned in therapy to real life. She repeatedly failed to carry out homework assignments and became depressed and apathetic about the therapy program. Further, she suddenly gave up her work as a student nurse because she felt unable to cope with the social demands of the job and it was clear that her social anxieties had only been minimally affected by the treatment so far. After a 3-week gap occasioned by the intervention of a holiday period, she was seen twice more. There was no real improvement; if anything, Jenny had become more withdrawn, anxious, and depressed. By mutual agreement therapy was terminated with the understanding that it might be resumed at a later date, an option that Jenny did not take up.

Two years later Jenny was contacted again and agreed to be seen for a follow-up interview. She had a full-time job supervising blind people, which she valued, and had a boyfriend whom she met regularly. However, although superficially she was much better off, she still admitted to feeling insecure and socially anxious and was pessimistic about her future adjustment. She had met her boyfriend at a psychotherapy group which she had attended for three months and described them both as "broken reeds" who had drifted together. She still lived with her parents but, although wishing to get away, was too frightened to do so. Apart from the brief period of group psychotherapy, which had not been a success, she had not had any other treatment.

When asked about the behavioral treatment, Jenny reported that she felt it had placed too much demand upon her too early. Although it had been useful in the sense of suggesting specific things for her to do, it had had little impact because she had been unable to follow them through. She strongly felt that being seen only once a week was a severe limitation as she had found that experiences in the intervening period undermined what happened in the therapy sessions. Ideally she would want someone who could be contacted constantly for advice and help about problems when they arose. She also felt that a group approach offered more in the sense of sharing problems with others, allowing her to get in touch with people of her own age. However, the psychotherapy group that she had participated in had failed because of disruptive elements within the group. Finally, she admitted to feeling considerable anger towards her parents, whom she at times blames for failing her. After rows with them she would also feel guilty and upset.

Like the previous case, this case illustrates the need for the therapist to consider the patient's motivation very carefully at the outset. Jenny found it difficult to respond to a treatment program that placed even fairly small demands upon her. A key feature that was overlooked in the initial analysis was that Jenny had been referred because of her parents' worries and concern, not because she herself had sought help. Although she would have liked to be less anxious and insecure, she was not at that stage fully prepared to tackle her anxieties directly. In retrospect we feel that Jenny might have been more appropriately helped by a more extensive period of initial assessment in which her feelings about herself and her role in the family and outside it could have been explored with a view to establishing her expectations of change. In particular, the role of her parents in bringing her to therapy should have been fully discussed. Perhaps as a result of a more thorough initial preparation, Jenny's social anxieties might have been more successfully handled in therapy.

Another lesson that can be learned from this case is that once-weekly therapy sessions may have very little impact upon a socially anxious patient whose anxieties are continually being reinforced by experiences between sessions. More frequent therapy sessions in the initial phase of therapy may prove more effective. Alternatively, a period of intensive therapy, perhaps on an inpatient basis, may be necessary. Because of the nature of social anxiety, it is not easy for a relatively infrequent intervention carried out away from the source of distress to have much effect, at least at first. The problems of generalization and ineffectual treatment are also illustrated in the next example of failure.

Lack of Generalization

CASE 3.   FAILURE TO CONTROL ANXIETY, DEPENDENCE ON DRUGS AND ALCOHOL

The third of our failure cases is one in which the initial analysis correctly focused on excessive anxiety as the central feature, but despite extensive treatment, anxiety remained uncontrolled by behavioral means. The patient instead relied on a maladaptive way of coping with anxiety, which, although effective in the short term, led to long-term harmful consequences.

This patient was 21 years old when first referred for behavior therapy. The presenting problem was anxiety and tension occurring in company and an inability to talk to people. Exposure to social situations caused trembling, sweating, and a feeling of being tongue-tied. The patient felt that he blushed in the company of females, tended to stay in the background in any social group, and avoided interaction or escaped from it if the opportunity presented itself. He reported that three or four pints of beer alleviated his anxiety and allowed him to mix more freely. He had been prescribed minor tranquilizers and said that, although these helped, he was still nervous with people. The patient had worked as a machine press operator but had found contact with other employees difficult, had taken time off from work, and had subsequently been sacked.

Behavioral assessment in a conversational test with a stooge revealed social skills deficits in length of utterance, showing interest in the other, frequency of eye contact, variation in posture, and gesture. He provided a generally "nervous" and uncomfortable appearance. Treatment was attempted using a combination of strategies including social skills training, conversation practice with stooges, videotape feedback, relaxation training, graded exposure to social interactions of varying difficulty (e.g., male to female, individual to group), imaginal desensitization, and graded homework assignments. The patient was seen by two different therapists for an approximate total of 30 sessions, during the course of which he also attended an industrial therapy unit for rehabilitation in a sheltered work setting. At the end of six months no improvement had been achieved and the patient was referred to a regional inpatient unit catering to young people in a group therapy setting. At this point the authors lost contact with the patient until he was seen as part of a follow-up program three years later.

At follow-up this young man was holding down a job as a garage manager, was maintaining himself in his own apartment, had regular contact with a girl-friend and could visit bars, restaurants, the cinema, and go dancing. Superficially, this represented a considerable improvement, but it soon became clear that the gains were only maintained by high doses of tranquilizers or by heavy consumption of alcohol. If the month's allocation of tablets was used up in two or three weeks, then the patient survived the remainder of the month by consuming up to one bottle of spirits per day. If neither tablets nor alcohol were available, then he felt unable to go out and stayed away from work. The old feelings of self-consciousness, churning stomach, and sweating returned. His condition became miserable, one where death held no fears and suicide had been contemplated.

This patient's comments concerning the effectiveness of behavioral treatment were quite instructive. Although he found the social skills training sessions difficult at the time, he admitted that the techniques he had learned were useful to him now. However, the most beneficial ingredient of the treatment was said to be the videotape feedback which, at least at the time, convinced him that he appeared a normal person. Unfortunately, the benefit did not last. As for relaxation, he denied that this had ever been of help to him in social situations.

Subsequent to his treatment as an outpatient he was transferred to a small inpatient unit for younger adult patients. Here he received traditional group therapy for 12 months, developed friendships, and in particular, a relationship with one or two females. He described the 12 months as "fantastic," feeling relaxed and confident once settled in the new environment. However, when he was eventually discharged, moved to another district, and lost contact with his clinic friends, he quickly reverted to his previous, socially anxious nature. Once again his main problem was control of the physical manifestations of anxiety.

This case must again be considered a failure from the point of view of behavioral treatment. Although it is possible to hypothesize that the sequencing of treatment was wrong, that behavioral group therapy and communal living could have been combined over a longer period of time, there is no guarantee that the alternative mixture or ordering of the elements would have helped this patient to function comfortably outside the treatment setting. This case illustrates that, although a clinician may arrive at a correct initial analysis, it is still not always possible to achieve the desired therapeutic goal. The intensity of some patients' anxiety symptoms may be so overwhelming that behavioral or other psychosocial treatment has at best only a transient effect.

Effects of Social Environment

A further common reason for the failure of behavioral treatments in dealing with social anxiety is the extreme difficulty encountered in controling or modifying the patient's social environment. A cutting comment, a refusal to date, a rebuff of any kind will rapidly undermine the confidence painstakingly developed during the treatment sessions. These factors are usually outside the therapist's control. The group treatment setting is often a supportive social environment, but the outside world is less likely to be so. In fact, the world at large may be very punitive. The following case history illustrates the manner in which a behavioral treatment program can fail because of punishing environmental events.

Case 4. Failure to Improve Social Satisfaction and Self-Awareness

This patient was a 35-year-old married man who complained of difficulty in dealing with business interactions and social encounters. His work involved dealing with sales representatives, attending management conferences, and fairly frequent entertaining. He described typical features of somatic anxiety in the presence of others, difficulty in making conversation, and a fear that he was considered odd or ludicrous by other people. Behavioral assessment revealed poor conversation content, a lack of humor, a failure to show interest in the other person, a rigid inflexible posture, and profuse sweating.

The initial interviews and assessment had suggested problems in the areas of somatic anxiety, social skills, and self-perception. Consequently treatment was carried out that utilized relaxation training, imaginal desensitization, social skills training, videotape feedback, positive self-statements, and graded task-setting. By the end of six weeks of outpatient treatment, two sessions per week, progress was felt to be encouraging. However, just after this point the patient met with a series of minor reverses that shattered his confidence and led him to decline further treatment. The incidents were quite trivial. For example, a fellow museum visitor happened to express his amazement at a particular object but our patient walked away without taking the opportunity to reply. Afterwards he ruminated about this wasted opportunity to make casual conversation with a stranger and felt disappointed by his inadequacy. At about the same time he became convinced that his colleagues at work were laughing about him behind his back and held him as a figure of fun. In spite of many successful interactions, structured as part of his treatment program, and in spite of an obvious improvement in his ability to role-play simulated working interactions, this man felt that he was no better and that the treatment was not getting to the root of the problem. He has not been seen since as he refused further offers of treatment.

This case shows the difficulty often experienced by the therapist in determining the accuracy of the patient's account of extratherapeutic experience. Did the patient really miss a conversational opportunity in the museum? Were his colleagues indeed laughing at him at his place of work? An equally plausible interpretation is that this patient has formed distorted beliefs about others in his working environment and that his impressions of social situations are not accurate. If this is true, it has to be said that such verbal reassurance and videotape feedback as was provided in this case were not sufficient to overcome the problem.

If emerging social confidence is so easily lost at the hands of capricious experience, what more can the therapist do to maximize the likelihood of a successful intervention? One suggestion is that the patient should be prepared for rebuffs and failures as part of the treatment and that he or she should realize that some failures are inevitable. Indeed, potentially embarrassing situations could be role-played in therapy. This method could be described as an attempt to inoculate the individual against the unpleasant emotional effects of social failure.

The therapist and patient must also consider the desirability of changing the patient's social environment by changing employment, by moving to another district, or by taking up fresh social activities. Perhaps the businessman who dislikes business interactions coupled with entertaining is sometimes more simply advised to seek an alternative job. The next case illustration underlines the significance of environmental factors in achieving long-term relief from social anxiety and improved social satisfaction.

CASE 5.   SPONTANEOUS REMISSION DUE TO ENVIRONMENTAL CHANGES

This case could be described as an initial treatment failure which, reexamined three years later, turned out to be a success. The improvement may have been due not so much to the treatment program but to the beneficial changes which subsequently occurred in this individual's social life.

The patient was a 27-year-old single man, employed as a grinding machine operator and living with his parents. He described himself as a "loner" who found it difficult to mix with people and was disappointed that he had been unable to form lasting or permanent relationships with friends of either sex. He had a habit of drinking heavily, as a means of bolstering himself up to enter into social activities, such as dances, and had one conviction for pub-crawling. The assessment revealed social anxiety, social skills deficits, and a dissatisfaction with the level of social activity. The patient's appearance was presentable, his self-perception fairly accurate, and his problem drinking already controlled.

At the end of 3½ months of behavioral treatment, no consistent pattern of change was discernible. Ratings of social anxiety remained similar to the pretreatment level, and a social diary measure revealed no general increase or change in the type of social activities undertaken. A slight improvement in the level of social skills was noted in role-played conversation tests but the extent of generalization was unknown.

Three years later the patient had a steady girlfriend and was planning a wedding date. His ratings of social anxiety and social satisfaction both showed tremendous improvement, although some social skills deficits obviously remained. The patient said that behavioral treatment had given him a slight boost in confidence. Afterwards he had made a greater effort to socialize and realized that it was now up to him. Meeting a girl and going steady had made him much happier but even this was not the greatest single factor. The main reason for improvement was said to be the acquisition of a metal detector. The patient had become fascinated and devoted most of his spare time to this new hobby, finding that people frequently approached him to ask how he was faring or technical questions about the apparatus. Thus the metal detector attracted people to converse with him and, of course, became a practiced topic of conversation. This experience, repeated many times, had helped to reduce his anxiety in talking to strangers. The cure for social anxiety—buy a metal detector!

SUMMARY AND CONCLUSIONS

Experimental studies of behavioral treatments are unable to provide much information on the exigencies of practical casework and, therefore, our conclusions are based almost exclusively on our clinical experiences and as such are, of course, notoriously subjective.

The Need for an Extensive Period of Initial Assessment

An overriding conclusion that we draw from both successes and failures is the need for an extensive period of initial assessment and analysis. In particular, we believe that an initial analysis should be concerned with the following factors.

An Understanding of the Meaning of the Patient's Problems

A careful and thorough description of the problem in its personal and social context should be undertaken.

The Exploration of the Patient's Expectations About Himself or Herself and the Potential Costs and Benefits of Change

The goals of therapeutic involvement should emerge from such an exploration. It is not always the case that the elimination or even management of social anxiety is an appropriate goal for the patient, as was suggested for Cases 1 and 2. In some cases the therapist may be advised to work towards a limited goal, such as the introduction of the patient to a nonthreatening social group, or to a more productive social environment.

The Establishment of a Good "Working Alliance"

A longer period of initial assessment allows for the possibility of the establishment of a relationship of trust and understanding. In our opinion it is unlikely that a therapist will have much impact on a patient's social anxieties without this relationship. Case 2 illustrates how difficult it is to institute change in a patient who remains uncertain and skeptical about therapeutic involvement. We believe that the concept of a "working alliance" is an important one for behavior therapists inasmuch as it focuses directly on the therapeutic relationship as a potential aid to more specific change. By a working alliance we essentially refer to the need for the therapist to listen to and support the patient and to work out with him or her an agreed and understood basis for therapy. Thus the therapist should be prepared to spend part of the initial sessions in clarifying the patient's expectations about therapy, and in doing so avoid over-hasty commitment to techniques or treatment strategies. The therapist should be sympathetic and nonjudgmental, yet realistic about the potential changes that can be made. The patient should be encouraged to take responsibility for his or her own problems and for the changes that treatment may bring. Thus such as alliance gives the patient an important and active role in the process of therapy, which is very much part of the philosophy underlying contemporary behavior therapy.

The Need to Maximize the Impact of Therapy

As many practitioners are only too aware, treatment, however carefully related to initial assessment, often has only too little impact on the patient's problems. Our cases have suggested certain reasons why this might occur. Once-weekly sessions may be insufficient to counter the aversive effects of ordinary social life. The gains made in therapy are not easily transferred to the very different world outside. It may take time and experience for the insights and changes made in therapy to have a substantial impact. The emotional and somatic turmoil experienced by some patients may be just too intense to control. In order to maximize the impact of therapy, it may be necessary for the behavior therapist to consider the following suggestions.

Institution of Environmental as Well as Personal Changes

If the therapist can directly affect the social environment of the patient such that its more aversive effects are reduced and its positive features enhanced, then this may have more impact than many sessions of anxiety management or social skills training. In some of our cases temporary changes in their social environment proved only of temporary benefit, as when Case 1 stayed in an after-care hostel and Case 3 in a small inpatient treatment unit. Clearly, the best form of environmental change is one that will be lasting in its effect on the patient and can be integrated into his or her existing social life.

Greater Frequency and Closer Spacing of Therapy Sessions

The feedback that we received from some of our failure cases pointed to the value of having more frequent and closely spaced therapy sessions in the initial phase of therapy.

For some patients it may be necessary to maximize the impact of therapy by an intensive course of daily treatment over a weekly or two-weekly period, perhaps on a residential basis. Such a course is similar to that used by Masters and Johnson in their treatment of various sexual dysfunctions (Masters & Johnson, 1970).

Greater Reliance on Group Therapy

At least two of our failure cases had benefited, if only to a temporary extent, from group treatment. The advantage of a group is that it provides an existing form for practicing social interactions and for sharing experiences with others. However, the success of a group depends to a large extent upon the behavior of its members, and experiences of disruptive and hostile groups are only too common. A further difficulty arises if the group itself becomes a substitute for social life, as was the case for two of our patients.

Generalization and Enduring Social Change

A number of our failure cases experienced short-term improvement from intensive treatments only to relapse following their termination. We have these suggestions for improving generalization and maintaining treatment gains.

Homework Assignments

The patient and therapist should choose and plan social encounters that the patient will subsequently undertake between therapy sessions. Although most behavioral treatments incorporate some form of homework assignments, it is often the case that patients fail to carry them out. It is easy to underestimate the difficulties of carrying out homework tasks, and at times the demands we place on the patient may be unrealistic. This was illustrated in Case 2 where the young girl found even the simplest tasks too difficult. Thus homework assignments should be very carefully selected as a result of joint discussions between therapist and patient and graded such that the very easiest tasks are set at the outset. The feedback provided by the patient from the initial tasks is very important and should be used to ensure that further tasks are likely to be successfully achieved. Finally, we have often found it helpful to involve other people in homework assignments, for example, getting members of a social club to look after the patient at his or her first meeting, or getting friends, acquaintances, or relatives to participate in the assigned ventures.

Self-Help Social Groups

Following a course of group treatment, small groups of patients could continue to meet regularly in the form of a self-help social group, independent of professional involvement.

Friendship and Social Clubs

For people suffering from severe social anxieties, the provision of a nonthreatening friendship organization or social club may be desirable. If this were organized from a therapeutic rather than commercial standpoint, the risk of social failure or of exploitation would be lessened.

The Adaptive Value of Social Anxiety

An assumption implicit in most treatments of social anxiety is that it is, of necessity, maladaptive and, therefore, requires modification. However, at the introduction to this chapter we suggested that social anxiety is not in itself abnormal and is commonly experienced in our society. For some patients, social anxiety may be an expression of something significant in their current life and to seek its elimination or control runs the risk of ignoring its wider meaning. This possibility was brought home to us by another "failure case" who, after a considerable amount of therapeutic work on his social anxieties with only minimal benefit, was suddenly made redundant in his industrial job. The effect was to produce a dramatic improvement in his social anxieties, which had clearly been exacerbated by the dissatisfactions and frustrations he had been experiencing in his work. He spoke enthusiastically to his therapist about beginning a course of teacher training and was not at all dissuaded from this choice of a future career by the prospect of standing up in front of a large class, a situation that would normally have provoked considerable anxiety. Where social anxiety is a realistic expression of significant and serious social problems, attempts to reduce or control anxiety without any resolution of these problems are misdirected.

REFERENCES

Kanter, N.J., & Goldfried, M.R. (1979) Relative effectiveness of rational restructuring and self-control desensitization in the treatment of social anxiety. *Behavior Therapy,* **10,** 472–490.

Marks, I.M. (1969) *Fears and phobias.* London: Heinemann.

Marzillier, J.S., & Winter, K. (1978) Success and failure in social skills training: Individual differences. *Behaviour Research & Therapy,* **16,** 67–84.

Öst, L.-G., Jerremalm, A., & Johansson, J. (1981) Individual response patterns and the effects of different behavioural methods in the treatment of social phobia. *Behaviour Research & Therapy,* **19,** 1–16.

Trower, P., Yardley, K., Bryant, B., & Shaw, P. (1978) The treatment of social failure. A comparison of anxiety-reduction and skills acquisition procedures on two social problems. *Behaviour Modification,* **2,** 41–60.

CHAPTER 7

Failure: Winning at the Losing Game in Assertiveness Training

MICHAEL L. EMMONS
ROBERT E. ALBERTI

Assertive behavior therapy is a humanistic-behavioral procedure developed to overcome interpersonal anxiety and teach appropriate social skills. The process involves at least three elements, however it may be structured, whatever specific techniques are utilized, and whoever the trainees and trainer may be. These key elements include the following:

Skills training, in which specific behaviors are taught, practiced, and integrated into the trainee's behavioral repertoire.

Anxiety reduction, which may be achieved directly (e.g., through desensitization or other counterconditioning procedures), or indirectly, as a byproduct of skills training.

Cognitive restructuring, in which values, beliefs, cognitions, and/or attitudes may be changed by insight, exhortation, or behavioral achievements.

Therapeutic procedures used in assertive behavior therapy (also commonly identified in both popular and professional literature as *assertive training, assertion training, assertiveness training, AT, social skills training,* include the following: journal keeping; role-playing; psychodrama; behavior rehearsal; guided practice; role-reversal; mirroring; modeling; audio, video, and verbal feedback; token feedback; flooding; desensitization; covert practice; coaching; self-management; homework; contracting; nonverbal exercises; value clarification exercises; self-disclosure; small group discussion; group assignments; field trips; films; selected readings.

Readers who are unfamiliar with the assertive behavior training process are invited to seek further information in the references noted, in particular, Alberti (1977), Alberti and Emmons (1982), and Lange and Jakubowski (1976).

Little, if any, follow-up is conducted on outcomes of AT. We know of few long-term systematic follow-up studies in the AT literature. One such study was reported by Emmons (1978). Do we *know* or only *assume* that the thousands who have undergone assertive behavior training are really better off for that experience? Those follow-up studies that have been conducted—usually employing such very limited criteria as the capacity to resist a telephone solicitation—suggest some benefits up to two years following treatment.

This chapter will proceed from an examination of the AT model and its theoretical assumptions, through the steps of intervention—referral, assessment, treatment. Characteristics of both clients and therapists contribute to failure, and are viewed in turn. Finally, a holistic-eclectic alternative is offered, along with recommendations for therapist practice to minimize failure.

FAILURES DUE TO INADEQUACIES IN THE AT MODEL

Definition

There is no clear and generally agreed upon definition of assertiveness (Fiedler & Lee, 1976). Most behavior therapists accept a rough statement about self-affirming, direct behavior that doesn't attempt to hurt others. Much early debate in the field centered around the notion of assertiveness as a general trait versus situation-specific assertive behavior.

From the earliest beginnings of AT (Salter, 1949; Wolpe, 1958), the lure of a global trait theory has been great. As a result, and because much recent research demonstrated the shortcomings of such an approach, there exists much confusion about the nature of assertiveness. Nevertheless, rather than continue the search for semantic adequacy, therapists are concerned primarily with assessing client needs and presenting a program of AT selected to respond to those needs.

We have advocated a comprehensive model that defines assertive behavior in terms of four dimensions: situation *context, response* of the other person(s), *intent* of the act, and the *behavior* itself (Alberti & Emmons, 1982).

Behavioral Assumptions

Assertiveness training developed as a behavior therapy, and the theoretical assumptions underpinning AT, are those of learning theory. The process is viewed as one in which dysfunctional habits or behavioral deficits are replaced by new, better, and more effective behaviors. Although such a positive and short-intervention style does, in fact, work for many clients, it is clearly not enough for others. Many persons who seek to become more assertive want to know "why" they have assertive deficits. They want to know why others are more effective in social situations, and they want to know why the model works so simply.

Other clients are concerned with larger existential issues in their lives. Although difficulty in interpersonal functioning may well be due to skill deficits, anxiety, and/or attitudes about "polite behavior," deeper life issues may be important factors. In a recent and very important contribution to the literature of psychotherapy, Irvin Yalom (1980) analyzes the paradox that faces all brief psychotherapeutic interventions: the presenting complaint may be ameliorated, and therapy considered "successful"; nevertheless, more significant issues in the client's life are ignored, and a valid opportunity to help is missed. The existential question, "Who am I, really?" is not answered by simple skill training, or other standard AT interventions. Indeed, AT rarely deals directly with these broader and deeper life issues.

Client Choice and Motivation

"Personal power" is something of a *sine qua non* of the AT model, yet for many people, it is simply not a relevant concept. Therapists generally agree that self-directed lives are healthier, and the evidence of this is clear, by psychological standards. Yet, is it not a form of self-determination to choose to allow others to control one's life? What about those who adopt a religious faith that calls for submission to an all-powerful being? And what of those cultural norms that demand respect for and dominance by one's elders? Though it may risk "failure" by some therapeutic standards, therapists must allow each client freedom to choose such paths.

An implicit assumption in assertiveness training is that participants actually wish to change their lives. Often instead, they are merely following the latest treatment fad or have been urged on by a concerned relative, friend, or professional. Others may have started with a wish to change, but may alter their goals in the process of assertiveness training.

Finally, there are some clients who, in spite of participating in the program, *choose* not to change. Perhaps their shortcomings are well-reinforced by the status quo. Or, in some cases, they have adopted a view of themselves as inhibited or socially inadequate. Or social effectiveness may be seen as requiring other changes or responsibilities that are undesired. Does therapy "fail" when the client elects not to meet the *therapist's* expectations for change?

Transfer of Training

AT procedures, as most therapies, are predicated upon the assumption that what is learned in therapy will be available to the client in other life situations. Yet, the evidence is clear that such transfer of learning is difficult for many. Indeed, it has been widely reported in the behavior therapy literature that transfer is very limited between situations used in assertive behavior training. That is, trainees who learn to say "no" may not apply that learning to unreasonable requests from family members or bosses. Members of an AT group, after all, are of little long-term consequence in each other's lives. This issue is discussed further in the section on treatment.

Group Success Versus Individual Failure

Like most therapeutic procedures, assertive behavior therapy developed as a result of studies of training conducted in groups. Such procedures generate clean statistical analyses that are ideal for dissertations and publishable studies, but wash out results for *individuals* within the groups. Any given client may have failed to achieve his or her goals, or even the goals stated by the therapist, yet the group results look good (and hence publishable), and the procedure goes down in the literature as one more method which "enhances" AT practice.

Cheek (1976) has made it clear that AT was developed for a population of white, middle class, verbal clients. Can it be adequately adapted for other populations? His work suggests an affirmative answer; however, most AT is *not* explicitly modified for the unique individuals in the therapy situation. Cultural variables are but one of a number of individualizing factors that make a great deal of difference, and any attempt to measure "success" or "failure" must account for the applicability of the learning to the natural environment of the client.

FAILURES DUE TO INAPPROPRIATE REFERRAL AND INADEQUATE ASSESSMENT

Referral

When a professional realizes that a supplementary treatment method would further treatment outcome, referral is a logical conclusion. And indeed, many—perhaps most—AT clients are referred in some manner. Unfortunately, difficulties develop when the referring person has not familiarized himself or herself with the adjunctive treatment.

AT as a referral procedure seems especially prone to miscalculations by the referring individual. Often, the professional's image of AT is based on the popular media conception that it has something for everyone, is fast and easy, and cannot hurt anyone. Referral to AT is likely to be done, without much forethought, for any shy, inhibited, or socially inept person.

Inappropriate referral can be circumvented by proper screening by the assertiveness therapist. Screening should include some form of pre-AT participation questionnaire, with questions about reasons for participating, prior or current mental health difficulties, and prior or current psychological treatment. An AT assessment instrument may be administered and, ideally, each participant would be interviewed for one half to one hour.

Inadequate referrals can usually be detected in the initial meeting which typically includes an introduction to basic concepts and an explanation of the teaching process. Examples of the types of situations to be worked on are presented, with assurance that participation is voluntary, and there may be times a person will decide not to join in the videotaping or behavior rehearsal.

In one such opening meeting, a short self-introduction was modeled, critiqued, and then assigned to participants as their first behavioral exercise. This also provided group members a chance to become acquainted. When her turn came, one of the group members immediately began crying. She would not look up or say anything; the therapists moved quickly to the next person. After the session, Jane was asked to remain for a few moments, during which the leaders discovered that she had been referred by another therapist who felt the group would be good for her. Jane felt overwhelmed by the format of the group and believed that she was not ready to take part. After further questioning, her decision was accepted. The referring therapist was contacted, and after hearing Jane's reaction *and* what the group format included, he concurred.

In order to prevent inadequate referrals, referring professionals should become familiar with the basic components of the program and what should be expected of the participants.

Assessment

Any measurement presumes some relatively clear definition of the phenomenon to be measured. Assertiveness, as noted above, suffers from the absence of a single accepted definition (Frazier & Carver, 1975). As a result, a large number of assessment instruments have evolved over the years, most of them unvalidated, and each representing a slightly different concept of "assertiveness" (Galassi & Galassi, 1977). It is thus extremely difficult for the practitioner to really evaluate clients in a meaningful and comprehensive sense.

A promising recent assertive behavior evaluation device is the Interpersonal Behavior Survey (Mauger & Adkinson, 1980). Others widely researched include the Rathus Assertiveness Schedule (Rathus, 1973), and the Self-Expression Scales (Galassi et al., 1977). Several popular AT assessment devices were examined in a special issue of *ASSERT: The Newsletter of Assertive Behavior and Personal Development* (1979). Available instruments are perhaps best used as a structured interview, whenever possible, with attention to each item for each client, rather than as global measures of a vague phenomenon labelled "assertiveness."

Figure 7.1 suggests a schema for assessing various aspects of assertive behavior (Alberti, 1979). Inasmuch as it is clear that assertiveness is a complex phenomenon, facilitators who want to maximize the effectiveness of their AT interventions must view their clients from a multivariate perspective.

To help therapists systematize an approach to assessment, the model "intervention map" suggests that the trainer first determine the level of intervention needed (self-help, training, therapy), then measure the client's adequacy of (1) information about AT concepts, (2) attitudes toward assertive behavior, (3) assertive skills, and (4, 5, 6) various obstacles to effective assertiveness. Appropriate assessment devices may be selected for each dimension. Therapists may reduce the likelihood of failures by a precise assessment and prescriptive interventions, rather than "shotgun" procedures.

In selecting assessment tools, therapists ought to consider what goals are

"Intervention Map"

			Self Help	Training	Therapy
[1]	Information	Assessment			
		Intervention			
[2]	Attitudes	Assessment			
		Intervention			
[3]	Skills	Assessment			
		Intervention			
[4]	Environmental Obstacles	Assessment			
		Intervention			
[5]	Interpersonal Obstacles	Assessment			
		Intervention			
[6]	Intrapersonal Obstacles	Assessment			
		Intervention			

Figure 7.1. Schema for assessing aspects of assertive behavior.

expected to be reached by AT. Obviously, success or failure should be assessed according to therapeutic criteria (anxiety reduction, greater self-esteem, improved interpersonal functioning, greater independence, or increased awareness).

Contraindications

Factors that recommend against the use of assertiveness training have been largely overlooked in the literature, perhaps following the early "it's good for everybody" assumption. Nevertheless, a number of client characteristics suggest caution or exclusion from AT: extreme anxiety levels (which suggest desensitization as a prior procedure); highly aggressive behavior (particularly disruptive in groups); retarded or low verbal skill clients (who usually need individualized attention or special group work); clients with special cultural differences (which often require attention from a professional familiar with the culture); schizophrenics; individuals who demand the "center of attention" in groups (inasmuch as they monopolize group time, and AT is not the treatment of choice for their problem); clients with extreme skills deficits (who need gradual individual work, rather than "standard" models); individuals who have extremely hostile home environments that are likely to punish assertion (in this case, AT is likely only to increase the level of frustration until the home environment can be modified in some way or the client can leave the home).

FAILURES DUE TO INADEQUACIES IN TREATMENT

Unlike most therapies, carefully shepherded by a guru since their earliest beginnings, assertiveness training is the product of many contributors. A variety of styles and definitions of the procedure led to the inclusion of a wide range of techniques and considerable inconsistency in the training. Among those differences are varying emphases on cognitive dimensions (attitudes, information, self-statements, rational beliefs), skills (verbal and nonverbal behavioral repertoires), anxiety about interpersonal functioning, and environmental interventions. Each of these dimensions, of course, is a key aspect of the success of any individual assertive act, but the process of matching the needs of a client to a given therapist or trainer style may be virtually impossible.

In the 1970s, there was a flush of popular enthusiasm for AT, and many of us came to believe that it was "good for everybody." We often fail as therapists and trainers because we are busy teaching people to say "no" or to send back an overcooked steak, when their concerns are with vital life issues. Homework assignments frequently used by some trainers include going into a service station and asking to have the windshield washed without buying gasoline (probably not even possible today), and going into a restaurant and asking for a glass of water without intending to buy anything else, or to pay for the drink. Such procedures teach a distorted sense of rights, and take advantage of others who are providing services at considerable cost. Trainees know this, and are reluctant to commit themselves to a style that manipulates others.

Canned Procedures

An unfortunately large number of AT practitioners adopted a distortion of the popular "Gestalt prayer" that came out like this: "I'll do my thing, and if you get anything out of it, good for you!" Procedures were developed to meet trainer needs, rather than those of clients. Failures were commonplace under these conditions—more often associated with community-based training models, but also frequent in therapeutic settings.

Most AT practice assumes that all trainees start with the same readiness to learn. Moreover, it appears that much AT is conducted as though everyone can learn through its usual procedures: exhortation, modeling, rehearsal, feedback. Little attention is given to cognitive mapping, determination of the learning styles of group members. Many of us learn well through traditional lecture or demonstration methods, but others need more visual or aural stimuli.

Time is another confounding factor; the usual group pace may be boring to some quick trainees, impossibly fast for others, yet training is conducted as if everyone were following at the same pace. Although we talk of individualizing, it appears that most AT is canned procedure. We must expect, under these circumstances, that the middle two thirds of any group will do reasonably well, and that the third that falls one standard deviation above or below the mean will be less successful.

Inherent in AT is a certain degree of risk taking. Clients are asked to try out new behavioral styles and to thus risk rejection by others if they do not succeed. Particularly for those clients whose history of interpersonal relationships has been less than successful (most people who sign up for AT), that paradigm is quite threatening. Yet many trainers make a practice of pushing clients to perform beyond their level of readiness, with little sensitivity to the high anxiety that often results. Some encouragement is appropriate, of course, but considerable sensitivity is required to recognize how much a given client can handle.

Skills training is often used as the model of choice. Yet other procedures are equally important: cognitive restructuring, obstacle and environmental interventions, and anxiety reduction. Finally, the *level* of an AT intervention is important. Therapy, of course, involves more sensitive long-term individualized interventions to overcome severe deficits. Training is more superficial, didactic, usually conducted with larger groups, for a shorter term, and in a situational manner. There is a vast difference between them and a thorough assessment of individual client needs is the only means of determining which level is appropriate.

Nontransfer of Training

Do the gains in assertive behavior from participation in workshops, groups, or individual therapy hold up in real life? This is the key research issue facing assertiveness training today. Do good results transfer out of the laboratory or therapy setting into the person's actual everyday living situation?

To date, the results are equivocal. Some studies indicate success in generalization to real life, whereas others do not. Part of the difficulty involves setting up valid ways of measuring transfer. Gathering adequate follow-up information is crucial, yet doing so is difficult. Several studies discuss the topic thoroughly: Hersen, Eisler, and Miller (1974); Kirschner (1976); Rich and Schroeder (1976). Clinical experience indicates that training which is specific to a situation in the client's life has excellent carryover. Clients who attempt to move to situations not trained are more likely to fail. This type of failure is most noticeable in the early weeks of training or therapy, according to our observations.

Among college student clients, for example, stories of failure are common after a long weekend. Group members return home excited to try out their new skills with key individuals in the family. Unfortunately, these difficult close interpersonal situations often have not yet been dealt with in training. An example of such a "disaster" is the following.

Joe, a university freshman, decided to confront his mother over her strict rules for him at home. He had been away for two quarters and had become quite independent. Joe was dating, staying up quite late at times, and had started smoking. On previous weekends at home, his mother still "watched him like a hawk." She insisted he be home before midnight, and Joe knew that she did not allow smoking. In the past, his response was to "keep the peace" because his parents were paying for his education. He would grudgingly comply to the curfew and the smoking was kept a secret.

When Joe returned to the group after the first long weekend at home, he described "the big fight" with his mother. Careful questioning revealed that he had stayed out very late one night; his mother waited up and was upset. Joe defended himself by telling her to quit treating him like a baby, adding (yelling at her by now) that he was smoking. His mother stood up for her values for a while but soon was reduced to tears. Joe gave up and went to bed.

Joe's newly learned assertive skills had failed to generalize, and he had taken on a very difficult relationship problem before he was ready. Fortunately, the therapist and group members were able to offer instruction, support, and encouragement so that Joe resolved the issue at a later date.

Transfer to new, untrained, assertive situations will occur more frequently if the therapist focuses on a series of recommendations of Van Hasselt, Hersen, and Milliones (1978): (1) use concrete generalization instructions; (2) conduct precise assessment; (3) implement specific training procedures; (4) use highly relevant training situations; (5) employ a wide range of interpersonal situations; (6) include positive and negative assertions; (7) employ self-control, self-regulatory procedures.

Further, transfer might be facilitated (Shelton, 1977b) by using homework assignments. The generalization suggestions noted above also prove useful in fostering long-term assertiveness.

FAILURES DUE TO CLIENT CHARACTERISTICS

A number of client characteristics seems to be associated with failing to benefit from AT. They will be discussed below.

Resistance to Change

The general concept of resistance is that the client unintentionally, but purposefully, obstructs progress in therapy (Menninger, 1958). To our knowledge, no one has studied traditional psychoanalytic "resistance" in AT. Perhaps resistance is not thought to be of importance when one is using a behaviorally based method. We have observed the psychoanalytic form of resistance infrequently in our work with assertiveness. Nevertheless, resistances such as being late for appointments, not paying the therapist on time, failing to show up for appointments, attempting to evade sensitive issues, and not completing homework take place in AT just as in all therapies.

There are time-honored ways of handling these resistances. We see these behaviors more as indications of a weak commitment to therapy, or of specific fears of changing the life situation, rather than as conscious or unconscious attempts to foil the opportunity to change for the better. Persons who enter assertive behavior therapy are rarely seeking major "personality reorganization."

Our observation is that when clients manifest blocks there is an underlying fear. Certain clients resist learning assertive behavior because they so fear *appear-*

ing to be aggressive. These individuals have established nonassertive patterns as a reaction to aggression. This pattern may result from the client's own history of aggression, or from having had a mother or father who behaved aggressively. The client has decided not to identify with that type of behavior. The following case will exemplify this point.

When Susan was first asked to raise her voice volume in a group exercise, she stated emphatically that she could not. Later, she revealed that doing so reminded her of her mother, who repeatedly broke into outbursts of anger. Susan and her sister would be humiliated and reduced to tears. Susan resolved never to "act like that." Any "angry-type" behavior such as increased voice volume produced a marked negative reaction.

Another common fear which leads to resistance is that of *negative consequences.* "I will lose my friends"; "My spouse will divorce me"; "The children won't love me"; "Mother would disown me." Any type of fear or resistance in AT will cause failure if the individual does not acknowledge it, or if the therapist fails to recognize the fear. The very process inherent in assertiveness training—behavior rehearsal—may foster fears that need to be dealt with in order to assure appropriate growth. A recent intriguing case comes to mind.

George had read about various therapies before entering individual therapy. After participating in two assertiveness therapy sessions, he commented that the process was only focusing on his "outer behavior." He felt it was failing to resolve his deep problems from his upbringing. The therapist discussed dealing with current behavior versus understanding how one developed the problems. George was adamant about his beliefs and felt he should enter psychoanalysis. Other therapeutic procedures which dealt more with historical antecedents were offered to George. He maintained his stance and did not return.

Attitudes and Beliefs

Cognitive structures that put down assertive behaviors in favor of nonassertive or aggressive behaviors come in myriad forms. These range from the simple attitude that saying "no" will offend others, to the belief that women are not to be equal to men, to deeply ingrained religious or cultural belief systems. The pervasiveness of the problem has prompted many authors and trainers to develop long lists of rights for use with AT.

Many attitudes are amenable to change when new information is presented, and are easily removed as obstacles through the AT process of "cognitive restructuring." Closely held beliefs, of course, are more difficult to overcome. These are often a result of childhood learning and have the strength of years, as shown by the following example.

Sonny came to therapy complaining of being mistreated by his roommates. They taunted him about his religious convictions and passive "goody-two-shoes" behavior. The therapist felt that AT would be of help. Sonny reacted strongly to the explanation of AT and began quoting Biblical passages, such as "The meek shall inherit the earth," and "Love thy neighbor as thyself." Further explanations attempted were to no avail. Sonny left and did not return for further counseling.

Overvaluing assertiveness typically is easier to deal with in terms of failure. "Overzealous" trainees (i.e., overcritical) can give AT a bad name. Soon everyone tires of hearing how great AT is, not to mention the discomfort of dealing with the "compulsive" assertions of such individuals. Usually, it will be only a short time before such a person calms down.

Severe Skill Deficits

Some participants have had little socialization in basic interpersonal skills. This dearth of skill may be situation-specific, as with the person who has been raised by a single same-sex parent and schooled only in same-sex settings. Or the problem may be more global, as in the case of one who has been deprived because of severe mental or physical illness, isolated due to physical deformity, or shunned by peers. Once the therapist becomes aware of severe deficiency in skills, the person may be helped to decide upon a plan to avoid failure in remedying the problem.

High Levels of Interpersonal Anxiety

Wolpe's (1958) original premise regarding assertive responses was that they inhibit or weaken anxiety. His "reciprocal inhibition" theory suggests that assertive responses decrease one's anxiety responses. The AT outcome literature generally supports this conclusion, albeit not for the reasons advanced by Wolpe.

Assertive responses, of course, were only one of several anxiety inhibitors Wolpe proposed in the reciprocal inhibition treatment model. Others include sexual, relaxation, abreaction, and respiratory responses. Wolpe did not intend the use of AT to be the sole treatment, and later expressed concern about the popularization of AT as a separate therapy (Wolpe, 1974). He indicated that undertaking AT should not keep the therapist from exploring other sources of anxiety and other psychological difficulties, such as guilt or depression.

To minimize failures due to high anxiety levels, therapists conducting assertiveness training in workshop or group format could offer the following process.

1. Administer an anxiety assessment prior to beginning therapy or training and provide appropriate feedback to clients on the results.
2. Inform participants that high levels of anxiety may appear during their training.
3. Indicate that high anxiety levels may diminish or disappear as assertive responses are practiced.
4. Discuss the fact that when high levels of anxiety do not reduce that the individual is not a failure and that the AT process is not a failure (assuming it has truly been administered properly).

5. Review additional therapeutic approaches available for the client to deal with high levels of anxiety; offer treatment or referral.

Therapists specializing in AT with individual clients have the opportunity to provide a more comprehensive program. The individual therapist has the responsibility to conduct a thorough analysis of anxiety levels.

Chronic Aggressive or Nonassertive Styles

Although AT has produced success in helping clients overcome chronic behavior styles of an aggressive or nonassertive nature (Bartman, 1976; Finch & Wallace, 1977; Hanson & Bencomo, 1972), there are some who have great difficulty breaking out of those patterns. The areas discussed above, when applied to these individuals, will often help remedy the bondage. But we all know there will always be a few who seek help, but who do not respond to these approaches.

Cases that do not respond to the method discussed require a more in-depth psychological approach. In addition, it is suggested that medical or physical factors be examined. Individual psychotherapy will usually be the logical beginning step. If the assertiveness trainer discovers clients with chronic aggressive or nonassertive styles in workshop or group settings, transfer to individual therapy is probably advised. As therapy progresses, the client should again become an appropriate candidate for group AT, although one should proceed with caution.

The medical aspect of chronic cases has come to our attention in recent years. In several cases, such factors as mononucleosis, hypoglycemia, anemia, or acute infection have been found to be present. Undiscovered medical problems can cause high irritability and aggressive outbursts, or extremely low energy levels and little emotional responsiveness. A later section on holistic approaches will expand on this idea.

FAILURES DUE TO THERAPIST CHARACTERISTICS

AT seems more subject than most therapies to the dangers of unqualified trainers. Many professionals in human services are practicing AT, as are many laypersons with little or no behavioral science training. Shelton (1977a) deals with problems of the trainer in the AT process. One topic in the article is "The psychonoxious leader."

These excellent descriptive titles introduce Shelton's discussion of the tendency of AT to attract trainers who have shortcomings. Much of this attraction results from the proven value of AT; this may be both advantage and disadvantage of the method. Unfortunately, some leaders who gravitate to the method do more harm than good, and tend to produce more failures. These observations are particularly true for those trainers who practice outside traditional therapeutic environments, but the apparent simplicity of the method invites therapists, too, to attempt it without adequate preparation.

These circumstances set the stage for a proposal by eight leaders in the field to offer guidelines for ethical practice of AT (Alberti, 1977). Concern for widespread reported misuse of AT, failures in training, and a large number of practitioners with inadequate preparation led to a rather rigorous statement of qualifications for facilitators.

It is strongly recommended that any therapist or trainer involved in any level of AT read this material. Well qualified facilitators will reduce the number of failures in assertive behavior therapy.

Therapist Personality Factors

Even with the best of preparation, therapists may exhibit blind spots in administering the training, usually resulting from unresolved personality problems of their own. Examples include showing disdain toward clients who show key deficits in assertive behavior, and personal fears and problems that interfere with the training process. A particular problem occurs when the therapist is not adequately assertive in his or her own life.

When clients describe or exhibit aggressive behavior in a training setting, some therapists consider it necessary to squelch such behavior. Surely such behavior need be discouraged through appropriate behavioral and cognitive approaches, but it is unnecessary to "come down" too hard on the person. The trainer may have experienced such behavior in his or her personal life and developed an unnecessarily strong reaction against it.

FAILURES IN AT: SPRINGBOARD TO HOLISTIC-ECLECTIC TREATMENT

Emmons has discussed holistic-eclectic approaches to therapy in two previous papers (1977, 1978). In a holistic treatment paradigm, the therapist may analyze medical or physical complaints and patterns. He or she may discuss such areas as religious history and current beliefs and practices. Physical exercise and dietary habits are important. And a thorough look at psychological functioning is advocated.

Failures in assertive behavior therapy may be a signal to the therapist that it is time to look at the client in more depth, as defined by the holistic-eclectic approach. Behavior therapists are not expected to treat all manner of ailments; however, it is simply good practice to thoroughly assess client needs, treat those that we can, and refer when needed. The holistic-eclectic approach is illustrated in the following example.

Georgine was a member of an introductory AT group. At the end of the final session, she indicated she needed more help. One of the therapists agreed to see her individually. A thorough analysis of her failure in AT showed that she did quite well in group, but felt afraid to apply herself outside of the security of therapy. Key factors included a poor upbringing by a mentally ill mother, an extreme fear of rejection, and a poor diet.

A holistic treatment program was employed, involving systematic desensitization, meditative therapy, and nutritional counseling. After a period of 15 sessions, Georgine had begun asserting herself in most life situations. She reported feeling a new freedom and acknowledged that "assertion actually works!" Her evaluation of therapy gave high marks to all of the treatments administered.

SUMMARY AND CONCLUSIONS

Assertiveness training is a deceptively easy procedure. At first blush, failures would appear of minimal consequence. Notwithstanding this superficial appearance of ease, failures in AT are common, have been too long ignored, can be of major proportions in the lives of clients, and probably can be reduced by careful attention to the material analyzed in this paper.

The following specific recommendations summarize and conclude this chapter:

1. Adopt an individual working definition of assertive behavior, avoiding simplistic concepts.
2. Recognize that purely behavioral approaches will not respond to the needs of all clients.
3. Allow clients to choose their own goals for therapy.
4. Make special efforts to individualize assertive behavior therapy.
5. Become informed and inform colleagues about AT procedures, in order to facilitate effective referrals.
6. Find an assertiveness assessment instrument that works for you; use it as part of a comprehensive evaluation of client needs and progress (include information, attitudes, skills, obstacles).
7. Recognize contraindications to assertive behavior therapy and screen clients accordingly.
8. Select treatment approaches carefully, according to client needs.
9. Attempt to employ procedures that have maximum relationship to client lives.
10. Use a minimum of canned procedures.
11. Fully inform clients of procedures to be used in therapy.
12. Use appropriate caution in encouraging clients to take risks.
13. Follow up client outcomes insofar as possible.
14. Take steps to ensure maximum generalization from therapy to client life situations.
15. Recognize client characteristics that diminish therapeutic effectiveness.

16. Refer to other types of therapy when appropriate.

17. Examine therapist characteristics that may inhibit effectiveness, including preparation and personal variables.

18. Adopt a holistic frame of reference; assess, treat, and refer clients according to a holistic analysis of needs.

REFERENCES

Alberti, R. (Ed.) (1977) *Assertiveness: Innovations, applications, issues.* San Luis Obispo, Calif.: Impact.

Alberti, R. (1979) An "intervention map" for AT assessment. *Assert: The Newsletter of Assertive Behavior,* **28.**

Alberti, R., & Emmons, M. (1982) *Your perfect right: A guide to assertive behavior.* San Luis Obispo, Calif.: Impact.

Bartman, E. (1976) Assertive training with hospitalized suicide attempters. *Dissertation Abstracts International,* **37,** No. (3-B), September, 1425.

Cheek, D. (1976) *Assertive black—puzzled white.* San Luis Obispo, Calif.: Impact.

Emmons, M. (1977) Assertiveness training within a holistic-eclectic perspective. In R. Alberti (Ed.), *Assertiveness: Innovations, applications, issues.* San Luis Obispo, Calif.: Impact.

Emmons, M. (1978) Holistic health: The inner source and psychophysiospiritulogical wholeness. In M. Emmons (Ed.), *The inner source.* San Luis Obispo, Calif.: Impact.

Fiedler, D., & Lee, R. (1976). *On the decision to be assertive (Tech. Rep. 76-5).* Seattle, Wash. Department of Psychology, University of Washington. Office of Naval Research Contract N00014–76–C–0193.

Finch, B., & Wallace, C. (1977) Successful interpersonal skills training with schizophrenic in-patients. *Journal of Consulting and Clinical Psychology,* **45,** No. 5, 885–890.

Frazier, J., & Carver, J. (1975) Some comments on the problems of defining assertive training. *Comprehensive Psychiatry,* **16,** 369–373.

Galassi, J., & Galassi, M. (1977) Assessment procedures for assertive behavior. In R. E. Alberti (Ed.), *Assertiveness: Innovations, applications, issues.* San Luis Obispo, Calif.: Impact.

Hanson, R., & Bencomo, A. (1972) Adopting a structured assertion training program to a group of chronic psychiatric patients. *Newsletter for Research in Psychology,* **14,** 17–18.

Hersen, M., & Belack, A. (1976) Social skills training for chronic psychiatric patients: Rationale, research findings and future directions. *Comprehensive Psychiatry,* **17,** No. 4, 559–580.

Hersen, M., Eisler, R., & Miller, P. (1974) An experimental analysis of generalization in assertiveness training. *Behavior Research and Therapy,* **12,** 295–310.

Kirschner, N. (1976) Generalization of behaviorally oriented assertive training. *Psychological Record,* **26,** No. 1, 117–125.

Lange, A., & Jakubowski, P. (1976) *Responsible assertive behavior: Cognitive/behavioral procedures for trainers.* Champaign, Ill.: Research Press.

Mauger, P., & Adkinson, D. (1980) *Interpersonal behavior schedule manual.* Los Angeles: Western Psychological Services.

Menninger, K. (1958) *Theory of psychoanalytic technique.* New York: Basic.

Rathus, S. (1973) A 30-item schedule for assessing assertive behavior. *Behavior Therapy,* **4,** 398–406.

Rich, A., & Schroeder, H. (1976) Research issues in assertiveness training. *Psychological Bulletin,* **83,** No. 6, 1081–1096.

Salter, A. (1949) *Conditional reflex therapy.* New York: Farrar, Straus & Giroux.

Shelton, J.L. (1977a) Assertive training: Consumer beware. *Personnel and Guidance Journal,* April, 465–468.

Shelton, J.L. (1977b) Homework in AT: Promoting the transfer of assertive skills to the natural environment. In R.E. Alberti (Ed.), *Assertiveness: Innovations, applications, issues.* San Luis Obispo, Calif.: Impact.

Van Hasselt, V., Hersen, M., & Milliones, J. (1978) Social skills training for alcoholics and drug addicts: A review. *Addictive Behaviors,* **3,** 221–233.

Wolpe, J. (1958) *Psychotherapy by reciprocal inhibition.* Stanford: Stanford University Press.

Wolpe, J. (1973) *The practice of behavior therapy.* New York: Pergamon.

Wolpe, J. (1974) Personal communication.

Yalom, I. (1980) *Existential psychotherapy.* New York: Basic.

CHAPTER 8

Assertiveness Training
for Women:
Where Are We Failing?

IRIS GOLDSTEIN-FODOR
RENEE C. EPSTEIN

A FAILURE TO STUDY FAILURE

At first glance a chapter on assertiveness training for women would not seem to belong in this book on failures in behavior therapy. After all, doesn't everyone know the success of assertiveness training for women? This behavioral technique has achieved wide popularity and generated a substantial body of research literature, much of which specifically addresses women's issues (Stringer-Moore & Jack, 1981).

A review of such research findings suggests that most female participants in assertiveness training programs appear to derive at least short-term benefits from this training (both from self-report and behavioral measures) and there is growing evidence of positive generalization in terms of enhanced self-esteem and a feeling of greater control over their lives (Ball, 1976; Henderson, 1976). Thus, from the consumer's point of view, assertiveness training is generally judged to be a success and most therapists and researchers share their clients' positive appraisal.

However, the wide popularity and acclaimed success of assertiveness techniques for women during the past decade are reason enough to take a second look. What is most striking in a critical review of the literature is the large discrepancy between research programs and clinical practice. Most of the reported research projects involve short-term study of change after treatment and are typically focused within a narrow range of analogue situations. Clinicians, on the other hand, treat within their workshops a multitude of real life problems, while neglecting assessment and follow-up. Further, there is an emphasis in the literature on the success of assertiveness training and pointed neglect of the issue of dropouts and failures. With the exception of Linehan and Egan's (1979) unpublished work, there is little discussion of client motivation, problematic cases, the difficulty in implementing assertiveness techniques within the client's real life situations, and whether using assertiveness training is really beneficial to clients in achieving their goals.

In this chapter we shall examine the assumptions underlying the development of assertiveness training programs for women in order to specify exactly where these programs are failing. The assumption most basic to assertiveness training suggests that nonassertiveness is a deficit behavior for many women and programs can be constructed to develop appropriate assertiveness. It is further assumed that once women complete assertiveness training they will utilize these skills in their natural environment in order to achieve personal goals. Although there are, of course, many problems and undeveloped areas of assessment and program development, the major failure to study failure appears to occur in the implementation of these techniques by women in their natural environments following training. It is our hope that the examination of various types of failures in assertiveness training will stimulate trainers and researchers to move beyond repetition of successful therapeutic formulas in order to help train women in areas that are relevant and appropriate for their real life situations.

Assertiveness Training in Relation to the Women's Movement

Assertiveness training for women has its roots in behavior therapy as pioneered by Lazarus (1966), Salter (1949), and Wolpe (1958), among others, and the women's liberation movement that emerged in the 1970s. From experience in working with women's consciousness raising groups, such behavior therapists as Butler (1976), Jakobowski-Spector (1973), Osborn and Harris (1975) and Wolfe and Fodor (1975), conceptualized nonassertion as a socially conditioned feminine trait associated with passive, submissive, helpless, and altruistic behaviors in women. Assertiveness techniques were utilized in work with women's groups to provide an antidote to the traditional feminine nonassertive social programming. Further, expanding on Alberti and Emmon's (1970) definition* of assertiveness as a human right, feminist therapists hypothesized that women would use assertiveness training to develop their own personal power base in order to confront the male establishment and redress societal inequities.

That women have felt the need for assertiveness training is evidenced by the fact that since the early 1970s they have participated in large numbers (typically self-referred) in workshops all over the United States and a growing number in Europe. They have been the consumers of numerous popular self-help books on assertiveness training and have sought training not only from professional therapists but from trainers at a variety of community centers. Articles about assertiveness training have been written in almost every United States women's magazine as well as in the popular press.

In spite of the large number of assertiveness training participants, few studies have been conducted on who comes for AT and why. The majority of assertiveness training work has, in fact, been conducted with women coming to therapists

---

*Behavior which enables a person to act in his (her) best interest, to stand up for himself (herself) without feeling undue anxiety, to express his (her) honest feelings comfortably or to exercise his (her) rights without denying the rights of others" (Alberti, & Emmons, 1970, p. 2).

not with clinical symptoms (i.e., depression or phobias) but rather with women representative of those in the mainstream. They are, for the most part, young, white, and middle class.

In trying to understand why so many women have sought assertiveness training, it is important to emphasize that the past decade has been a transitional period for redefining women's roles and reassessing sex role inequities. Most women still do not have equal access to power or an economic base comparable with males. Yet, during the 1970s, middle-class women entered the workforce in increasing numbers and began forging into work arenas previously reserved for men. Additionally, a large number of women began to require independence and equity in their personal relationships (Weitz, 1977). Hence it would appear that assertiveness training programs have special appeal for women struggling to cope with new role alignments.

If women are indeed seeking assertiveness training to remedy stereotypic feminine behaviors, our discussion of failure must focus on the assumptions and goals underlying the feminist oriented assertiveness training package. By highlighting neglected areas of concern and failure, we hope we will point out directions for more effective alternative program construction.

Assumptions Underlying AT Programs for Women

1. Women have a deficit in assertiveness behavior.
2. Nonassertiveness is a behavioral deficit that can be replaced by appropriate assertive behaviors.
3. Assertiveness techniques train women to be more assertive.
4. Fear of being assertive is a result of prior female socialization history and is irrational; cognitive restructuring along with assertiveness training can eliminate such irrational fear.
5. Women will apply their newly acquired assertiveness skills to their real life problem situations.
6. Women will continue to use their skills and develop new assertive behaviors on their own over an extended period of time.
7. By becoming more assertive, women will be more successful in their personal relationships and work environments.

WHERE WE ARE FAILING

Assumption 1.   Women Have a Deficit in Assertiveness

Failure of Self-Report Measures to Delineate Specific Nature of Women's Assertiveness Deficit

Most clinical work on assertiveness is based on the assumption that females have deficits in assertiveness. Feminists are fond of quoting the study by Broverman,

Broverman, Clarkson, Rosenkrantz, and Vogel (1970) where mental health professionals rated assertiveness as an appropriate trait for a healthy male and its opposite, unassertiveness (passivity, submissiveness) as appropriate for a healthy female. Yet, the published research to date fails to demonstrate a significant difference between global ratings of assertiveness on self-report scales between males and females (Applebaum, 1976; Chandler, Cook & Dugovics, 1978; Hersen, Eisler, & Miller, 1974; Hollandsworth & Wall, 1977; Morgan, 1974; Orenstein, 1975; Stebbins, Kelly, Tolor, & Power, 1977).

Writers on assertiveness suggest that it is not a global trait but rather a situationally specific behavior. Yet the assessment scales and behavioral measures are generally global in nature and, furthermore, do not focus on issues relevant to women. Given the early socialization history of women in contemporary cultures, one might expect them to show specific assertion deficits centering around risk taking, expression of anger, and submissiveness in the face of authority, and to show fewer deficits in such feminine areas as giving compliments, expressing appreciation, and communicating positive feelings (Linehan & Egan, 1979). To date, however, there is only confirmation that when presented with tasks calling for refusal behaviors, women demonstrate conflict between acting in their own self-interest and being nurturant (Rathus & Nevid, in press). In another study, female college students who sought assertiveness training compared to those who sought vocational counseling scored higher on succorance, appeared more helpless, and demonstrated a greater need to be liked (Hartsook, Olch, & DeWolf, 1976).

Although clinicians suggest that many women seek assertiveness training for problems relating to the exercise of authority, particularly in work environments, very little research has been done to assess power issues as an underlying factor in female assertiveness problems. Hollandsworth and Wall (1977) found that women were less assertive than men on 6 of 12 items on the ASES Scale that dealt with persons in authority, but further assessments of authority issues are notably lacking in the research literature. Thus with the exception of refusal behavior, we have failed to adequately assess the nature of the assertiveness deficit for women, nor have we adequately defined female assertive strengths.

Failure to Assess Behavior Relevant to Women's Real Life Issues

Similar issues arise when we consider behavioral measures of assertiveness. Very little work has been done in isolating the specific skills deficits or strengths common to women entering assertiveness training programs (Blechman, 1980). Most researchers use analogue situations for assessment rather than the subject's own issues (thereby assuming that refusing to let a roommate borrow one's sweater is relevant to a client's actual assertiveness problem). A methodology does exist for uncovering and utilizing real life situations (Goldfried & D'Zurilla, 1969), but most investigators do not select out those situations that are genuinely problematic for individual participants in assertiveness training studies.

Role-play tests have become the standard means of assessing interpersonal behavior yet their validity has yet to be demonstrated.

Behavior in the role play test was not found to be highly related to behavior in the parallel in vivo situations . . .the process of role playing may be associated with unique response demands that produce an idiosyncratic response pattern. (Bellack, Hersen, & Turner, 1979)

Further, there is evidence that assertive subjects are better at role-play in general; nonassertivesubjectshavetroubleevenplayingsubmissiveroles(Atkinson,1977).

Assumption 2.   Nonassertiveness Is a Behavioral Deficit That Can Be Replaced by Appropriate Assertive Behavior

Failure to Define Criteria for Successful Assertiveness

The typical assertiveness training study for women involves screening via a self-report questionnaire, a behavioral test for assessing skills deficits (typically, an analogue refusal situation), and a set of training procedures (usually using modeling, role-play, coaching, and behavior rehearsal). Some studies may also include techniques for cognitive restructuring. Improvement at posttreatment is then assessed by self-report or behavioral rating in the same or similar analogue situation. If a follow-up is included in the program design, it usually occurs a week later.

Utilizing such procedures, assertiveness training for women is said to be very effective (Stringer-Moore & Jack, 1981). Yet, in examining the results of many of these studies the criteria for success need further questioning. Most of the data use group means as measures of compared change or the designs involve comparisons of different types of treatment packages. There is a failure to report data on individual responses to treatment, types of assertiveness deficits, and characteristics possessed by the more effective as compared to the less effective participants in assertiveness training programs.

Unlike successful therapeutic results in other clinical areas, such as phobias or obesity, where the measure of success is visible in loss of weight or confronting the feared object, success or failure in assertiveness training depends upon the perspective of both the client and her "significant others" (husband, therapist, mother, boss). Further, when one examines the content of the assertiveness training packages, it is hard to decide whether the programs have succeeded or failed, inasmuch as they are too often evaluated in terms of trivial, artificial, and irrelevant situations compared to the real life problems of clients. For example, there has been a marked overemphasis for women on training and evaluation in refusal situations to the neglect of other behaviors. Further, the measured "success" of assertiveness training packages often reflects only success at learning coached responses during the treatment program.

Failure to Determine "Appropriately Assertive" Responses

How do we know what is an appropriate response for a particular client? Who decides on effectiveness? Commonly buried in the footnotes of the research literature are notes to the effect that the "appropriate assertive responses" were judged by trained graduate psychology students. Inasmuch as assertiveness is a new area for women, how are we to know what are appropriate competencies?

CASE EXAMPLE

One of the authors was consulted by a young woman lawyer who was to have her first appearance in court. She had long been fearful of such an appearance and had successfully managed to avoid court for years. At her superior's insistence, she had to prepare for court presentations. We worked via role-play, behavior rehearsal, and desensitization on what seemed to both of us an effective courtroom style. The client went into court feeling more confident and prepared but was unnerved by the hard, attacking, abrasive style of the opposing male attorney. Even though she performed in the way we had rehearsed, she did not feel strong or effective and was often on the verge of tears.

In analyzing this failure, we see that we had overestimated our client's ability to handle herself under stress and shaped a response that she later felt was not up to the demands of the situation. If we focus on the issue of shaping an effective response for this particular situation, we are presented with many problems. If women do not wish to model the aggressive attacking mode of many male lawyers, what are the alternatives? As we proceed to help women begin to get in touch with their strengths, we need to develop strong female nonverbal components of assertiveness. At present the model is the male assertive style, but female voices and bodies and strengths are different (Serber, 1972). Clearly, before beginning an assertiveness training program, one needs to rethink the issue of what is appropriate assertive behavior. Perhaps it would be helpful to videotape assertive women in varying settings instead of assuming we know a priori what is best for a particular client in a particular situation.

Assumption 3.   Assertiveness Techniques Train Women to Be More Assertive

Failure of Training Methods

Role-play with behavior rehearsal and coaching is among the standard assertiveness training procedures. Yet, many realistic problems women encounter are not tapped by role-plays. For example, our female lawyer could not duplicate in the office the stress of the courtroom no matter how many times she practiced. Many clients have problems with high rates of anxiety, anger, irritability, and low frustration tolerance. Role-play situations in the office or workshop often do not elicit these emotions. A common remark heard by assertiveness training failures is, "When it really counts, I can't be assertive," or, "I just melt."

CASE EXAMPLE

A client complains about too frequent phone calls from an oversolicitous mother. We role-play a response to the mother. The following week, the client reports that her assertive behavior didn't work. In reviewing the problem again, it turns out that the client does not get upset or angry at the time she is speaking to her mother. Rather she is either pleasant, unconcerned, or even numb. Some time later she begins to burn and upset herself.

Many female clients are used to pushing problems under the rug and smiling placatingly when upset. These women clearly need more in vivo training to allow other feelings to develop while encountering the problematic situations. A major failure of assertiveness training research is that so few studies are conducted within the clients' natural environments; this prevents investigation of the emotional components of assertive responding and the development of coaching techniques that are specifically relevant to these aspects of assertive behavior.

Failure to Prepare Women for New Roles

Another objection to many of the assertiveness training studies in which women participate is the use of sex role stereotyping and the portrayal of women in conventional roles. For example, there are now numerous studies on attractiveness and assertiveness. Male college students are asked to rate pictures of "attractive" and "unattractive" female college students and are then asked to select students from whom they are willing to accept an assertive response (Jackson & Hudson, 1975; Stringer-Moore & Jack, 1981). The implications of this work for therapists might be that one should proceed with caution in shaping assertive behavior in "unattractive" women. Linehan & Egan (1979) cite one series of studies in which women are portrayed in role-play situations as waitresses, wives, and secretaries, whereas males are consistently bosses.

   Although such sex role stereotyping fails to address women's issues, it further precludes the development of programs to guide women in the development of new behaviors and role repertoires so often cited as the reasons for women entering assertiveness training workshops. Sex role discrimination issues are frequently brought up by women in workshops, but we have few guidelines for the most effective ways of handling many of these situations. Women now have legal recourse for the most blatant types of job discrimination (i.e., salary disparity for equivalent job descriptions), but can they use it? Where does the woman draw the line in assertive behavior? Does she risk losing her job, giving up her financial stability, and gaining a reputation as a "troublemaker" in fighting the stereotype and discrimination issues?

CASE EXAMPLE

A young woman with a PhD in communications is the only female on a small teaching staff in a management training program. After a very successful year on the job, she learns that she is being paid $10,000 less than her male colleagues for the same job description (it is quite common for women to find such discrepancies only after getting on the inside track of a job situation). Even with extensive assertiveness training involving role play of her confrontation with her boss, we questioned the outcome risks involved and the most effective role behavior appropriate to this problem.

Further, it may be even harder to learn effective ways of coping with the more subtle but equally frustrating instances of sex role discrimination women encounter daily. Topics frequently mentioned at assertiveness training workshops include the following: secretaries who are asked to run personal errands for bosses on their lunch hours, exclusion of female managers from male lunches or after work drinks, less favorable assignments for women reporters, sexist remarks and sexual harassment, disparaging comments about their competence and stamina reported by women surgical residents, being asked to present work relevant only to women's issues at professional meetings, tokenism (the few women at a particular level being pitted against each other for promotion).

There is a further question as to whether some of the behavioral problems reported by women at work can even be considered aspects of unassertiveness. Gambrill and Richey (1976) have studied the assertiveness problems of working women and report that many of them may be called "anxious performers" rather than unassertive women. Brockway (1976) further describes a group of professional women who have adequate assertiveness skills according to the standard assessment measures but who perceive themselves as inadequately assertive in dealing with the work pressures in male dominated occupations. Further research is necessary in order to devise techniques to meet the special needs of these women.

Another new role behavior neglected by assertiveness training programs is female initiation of social interactions. There is a vast literature on dating anxiety in males with multiple programs developed to shape up initiating behaviors (Curran & Gilbert, 1975; Stringer-Moore & Jack, 1981). Yet women are now initiating dates and very little research has been carried out to study implementation of dating behavior in females. One of the few studies of dating initiation in women involved studying males to see if they were willing to accept female initiation (50 percent of males were indeed willing; Muehlenhard, 1980).

Assumption 4.   Women's Fears of Being Assertive: Myth or Reality?

Failure of Cognitive Restructuring to Counter Real Discrimination

Most assertiveness trainers in working with women attribute women's failures to behave assertively to irrational beliefs or fear of the consequences of assertive behavior (Jakobowski-Spector, 1973; Wolfe & Fodor, 1975). There is a growing body of research suggesting that lack of assertiveness may be more like a performance anxiety than a skills deficit. That is, using the analogy of other performance anxieties (i.e., test anxiety), it is more of an anticipatory cognitive deficit that results in avoidance and possible nondevelopment of appropriate competencies than a primary skill deficit.

Research findings are beginning to support such a position. The Schwartz and Gottman (1976) study suggests that both assertive and nonassertive people know the appropriate behaviors, but the primary skill deficit in nonassertive persons may be their inability to *accurately estimate* the consequences of their assertion. If this is true,

> Greater emphasis must be placed on changing the person's cognitive expectations of the consequences . . .involving a process of teaching the client a new set of expectations about possible outcomes based on the characteristics of differing situations. (Eisler, Frederiksen, & Peterson, 1978)

To date, the addition of the cognitive component has had mixed findings. At best it may only slightly enhance the results of assertiveness training (Linehan, Goldfried & Goldfried, 1979) and lower slightly the client's anxiety rating (Wolfe & Fodor, 1977). Most clinical treatment packages now include cognitive restructuring but even after such training some clients are still afraid to risk behaving more assertively. What is lacking in many of the clinical studies are careful assessments of the interplay between cognitive appraisal, risk taking, and assertive behavior.

However, it may also be that as we follow our female clients from their training groups into the real world, we may find that beliefs inhibiting assertive responding are not so irrational or maladaptive (Fodor, 1980; Linehan & Egan, 1979; Wolfe & Fodor, 1975). Thus when Schwartz and Gottman (1976) speak of the deficit in nonassertive persons as the inability to accurately estimate the consequences of their assertions, as it applies to women it may be the *accuracy* of their perception of the consequences that truly inhibits their behavior.

There is now a growing body of research to suggest that there is a bias against assertive women. It may not be possible for female assertive behaviors to be judged independently of the sex of the participant and observer. Research by Bellack et al. (1979), among others, suggests that expert judges are influenced by the sex of the clients and, in particular, are biased against assertive behavior by women. Rich and Schroeder (1976) report that expert and peer male and female judges both identified comparable noncoercible behaviors when enacted by men as assertive but aggressive when performed by women.

Not only is there bias, but Fiedler and Beach (1978) suggest that behaviors encouraged by assertiveness training often are not rewarded but rather punished. A woman who is learning to be assertive may find that she was more highly valued by her spouse or employer when she was accommodating, self-denying, and passive. Her assertiveness may increase her self-respect, but she may be unwilling to live with the negative reactions of others to her behavior and, therefore, may cease to use her skills. Inasmuch as some female clients seeking assertiveness training appear to have a strong need to be liked (Hartsook et al., 1976), we may have a paradox in that they will maintain only those behaviors that are likely to be reinforced and thus will not risk assertive responding when likeability is at issue.

To return to the example of the woman lawyer, we may fail to help her develop an effective courtroom style if we adopt the male style as the assertive model which might be perceived as "too aggressive" and, therefore, ineffective for her; a softer female style, however, might reinforce the belief that women can't handle courtroom pressure or fight for their clients like men. When the client was near tears in court, she might have been reacting to a no-win situation wherein she knew that neither behavior would be effective for her.

Nowhere in the research literature are there studies that point out techniques designed to help women maintain assertive responding in the face of little environmental reinforcement, although the feminist literature speaks of the necessity for women's support networks to create alternative reinforcement systems. Our struggling lawyer may need to work with other women lawyers to develop effective styles, to bring more women into the courtroom, and to study the courtroom style of the too few forceful, respected women attorneys.

Failure to Study Nonassertive "Effective" Female Behaviors

As we begin to acknowledge that we are facing an uphill battle, it may be time to take a second look at some so-called nonassertive behaviors. Although it is important for a woman to try to develop herself fully in self-expressiveness and functional strength, when these assertive behaviors are not giving her what she wants, it may be time to examine some of the more "traditional" women's ways that have been pushed aside and devalued by assertiveness trainers and the women's movement.

There have been very few studies of what are considered the negative female modes of getting power—placating, manipulating, stroking, smiling through stress, and the like. We may need to study such techniques to try to cull some wisdom from the "feminine wiles" that have been effective for some women. Many women who fail to use their newly learned assertiveness skills do so because they are not willing to risk displeasing the important people in their lives. They would rather remain unassertive than be without a man, not be liked, or be passed over for promotion. In many ways, being diplomatic and charming is "phony" and not truly up front or honest, but these techniques may be essential to the women entering the "clubhouse." One common complaint heard from men after encountering women completing assertiveness training workshops is the shift from "being nice to being abrasive" (Jakobowski-Spector, 1973). Linehan and Egan (1979), among others, have begun research on the softer approaches for assertion and much more work needs to be done in this area. In a recent *New York Times* article, Betty Friedan suggested that the success of the first stage of the women's movement tended to polarize feminists and those women with "traditional" values. "We have to break through our own feminine mystique now and move into the second stage, no longer against men, but with them." Assertiveness training programs must be developed that accord with women's goals and utilize the most effective modes of assertive behavior.

Assumption 5.   Women Will Apply Their Newly Developed Assertiveness Skills to Their Real Life Problem Situations

Failures in Generalization

Most assertiveness training is conducted in a workshop, lab, or therapist's office. Typically, the clients must then apply these newly learned skills in their natural environments. From the authors' experience in working with women as they apply assertiveness techniques to their own problems, the following categories of failures often occur:

1. *Unwillingness to risk change.*   A woman who is economically dependent on her husband may want to be assertive in order to establish an equalitarian relationship. Treatment might not be effective, however, unless the woman is willing to be less economically dependent and to work on putting a firmer base under her independence.

2. *Unwillingness to accept an other's point of view.*   Another client insists that she is entitled to get what she wants and after assertiveness training begins to express her wants directly. She is incensed that the treatment "failed" because her spouse won't change enough or is unwilling to accommodate her wants. Again, she has learned the appropriate assertive behaviors, but they are repeated by rote in unsuccessful attempts to establish her rights and her unhappiness continues.

3. *Insisting one is right.*   A mother of a teenage girl comes to an assertiveness training workshop very upset about the late hours her daughter is keeping. The mother knows she is right about her daughter requiring more sleep on school days, but the daughter insists she is doing fine. The mother's continued assertion of being right creates oppositional insistence by the teenager and leads to a clear stalemate. Assertiveness training procedures for this woman must allow her to get past the "mother knows best" concept and learn expanded role options for maternal behaviors (Fodor & Wolfe, 1977).

4. *Collecting past grievances.*   After completing assertiveness training another client becomes aware of the many ways she has been mistreated in her marital relationship and begins to insist on better treatment. Her spouse agrees and actually begins to change, but she is so caught up in her past grievances and past anger that whatever he does in the present moment only aggravates her further inasmuch as even the change reminds her of her list of past grievances. How can one encourage clients to stay with the present, to take in the small changes others make as sufficient, and not demand continuous retroactive apologies?

5. *Failures in expecting too much too soon.*   Some women need many presentations and tremendous amounts of coaching and support in order to achieve small changes and then may be well satisfied with little, whereas other clients expect far too much from assertiveness training. They may be greedy for too much too soon or have a host of realistic life stresses and expect assertiveness training to solve all their problems. On behavioral measures, however, the second

client may show more positive behavioral changes but report greater dissatisfaction with treatment outcome.

6.   *Failure in teaching discrimination: when not to be assertive.*   Clients who have opened themselves to the nuances of assertiveness issues may need to become sensitive to the conditions under which inhibition of assertive responding may be appropriate. For example, a woman who has just become aware of the oppression of women begins to see sexist issues everywhere. Regardless of the accuracy of her perceptions, she responds to all instances of male chauvinism with her newly developed assertive skills. She quickly becomes labeled by her friends and colleagues as a "women's libber" and, given the prejudice in her environment, they may begin to take her less seriously. A better way to effect change may be to learn appropriate selection of situations for assertion.

Assumption 6.   Women Will Continue to Use Their Skills and Develop New Assertive Behaviors on Their Own Over an Extended Period of Time

Failure to Follow up Clients

Most assertiveness training is done on a short-term basis; a typical client might have one- to two-hour sessions over several weeks with at best a one-week follow-up. Homework assignments are usually given but the results are only monitored during treatment (53 percent of studies report no followup, 26 percent less than one month; Blechman, 1980). There is almost nothing in the assertiveness training literature on "booster" sessions for maintenance and continued change, although some clinics are now giving such sessions. There is a real need for study of the process of learning to be assertive inasmuch as it is a skill that must be practiced over a long period of time.

Failure of Trainers to Be Realistic in Expecting Changes From Short-Term Contacts

In individual work, many therapists are finding that learning to be assertive takes time, patience, and continued support and there are many setbacks.

CASE EXAMPLE

The first author has been following one young woman over the past four years with continued booster sessions when needed. At first, she was very shy and inhibited and allowed her relatives and friends to completely dominate her. She was in a dead-end clerical job despite the fact that she was an honors university graduate. Initially, we spent a great deal of time listening to her whine and complain about how hard life was; gradually she learned to express her needs better, first to her sister and mother, and then at work. After a year, social dating began and she became involved in a relationship with a very demanding man. She so devalued herself and her rights that another year passed before she had the courage to stand up to him and face the "singles" scene again. (During this period she might have been considered a treatment failure.) By the third year, she had many friendships and had taken a new job involving contact with people and was more confrontative and much less complaining. These changes occurred gradually with many setbacks and the therapist was available to rework each situation, to shore up old competencies, to train new ones, and to oversee the application of these skills as needed.

Assumption 7.   By Becoming More Assertive, Women Will Be More Successful in Their Personal Relationships and Work Environments

Failure to Assess Impact of Assertiveness Training on "Significant Others"

Another neglected area in follow-up, particularly inasmuch as so many workshop participants have very short treatment sessions and no contact with their trainer after treatment, is the impact of assertiveness training on "significant others." How is it perceived by others, how do they react, and do the clients get what they want from others by behaving more assertively? Issues involving personal relationships are among the most frequently discussed topics in assertiveness training workshops. The following are among typical treatment failures.

1.   *Failure to predict "significant other's" response.*   After living with a man for several years, a client worked in the group on asserting her wish to be married. She came into the group quite upset the following week. "It didn't work." What didn't work was that the "significant other's" response was not predicted and the client not only didn't get what she wanted but hadn't a clue as to how to respond to his withdrawal. Much more preparation for disappointment and deal-ing with aggressive, angry, punitive, or nonresponsive others needs to be built into assertiveness training procedures. The research training situations rarely go beyond the initial first shaping of a response. What one needs is replay and reply training.

2.   *Failure of "significant others" to appreciate assertive behavior.*   A com-mon problem women report in workshops is when having fully prepared what they consider an appropriate assertive response, they are met with, "Since you've gone to that women's group, you've become so aggressive." Not only is the woman facing the sex bias mentioned previously, but more likely a lack of under-standing of assertiveness. Leviton (1979) found that assertive behavior is often disapproved of by observers who may have trouble distinguishing assertive from aggressive behavior—(after all, they haven't all read Alberti and Emmons (1970) and don't know how to respond to what they perceive as confrontative behavior coming at them.)

3.   *Assertiveness training results in a power struggle.*   One of the most com-mon failures reported by clients, often formerly submissive, yielding women, is that after assertiveness training things seem to be worse in their relationships. In many cases, couples are locked into a power struggle and are fighting over

everything. The woman asserts herself ("I want to go away this weekend"), and the husband asserts himself ("I want to stay in the city this weekend"). Neither partner will yield, and, for the woman particularly, any backing off from her assertive stance means a return to her formerly unassertive self.

4. *Failure to include "significant others" in treatment.*   Much of the vast literature on assertion training for women has centered on individuals who come for assertiveness training for themselves and to work on their personal relationships. Yet, as the preceding case examples illustrate, one might avoid failure, unhappiness, or relationship disruption if one included "significant others" in the training process. There is now a growing body of research that suggests assertiveness training is helpful for couples in conflict and for families (Blau, 1978; Christenson & Nicol, 1980; Fodor and Wolfe, 1977; Gurman, 1980). Further, although many women believe that men do not want more assertive wives, husbands do report increased marital satisfaction following assertiveness training if such training includes empathic listening (Powell, 1978). Thus, in the case of the couple with the power struggle, individual work with the woman will most likely result in continued anger at the husband and an insistence that she get recognition for her newly acquired assertiveness skills. If such behavior persists, it is likely to lead to continued misery or breakup of the relationship. With both people in treatment, one could monitor the wife's assertive behavior as well as work with the husband in shaping more effective reply techniques. Perhaps empathic listening training is essential to replace the stalemate posed by each partner's asserting himself or herself without any movement.

Another "significant other" group who needs to be taken into consideration is mothers. Often older women are the targets of their daughters' newly learned assertiveness skills and are baffled, upset, and at a loss to know how to respond. Typically, these women do not come into workshops on their own and need some outreach. The first author has been working on assertiveness training programs for mothers and daughters and has found great value in including partners in lifelong relationships within the same workshops (Fodor & Wolfe, 1977).

Assertiveness Training for Battered Women: Failure Has Serious Consequences.

There is a growing literature on spouse abuse wherein assertiveness training is mentioned as the treatment of choice. The application of our techniques to this clinical area, however, presents some interesting problems. First of all, the presenting situation is almost always wife abuse (the husband is the batterer) and the treatment is mainly aimed at the victim (the wife) and not the husband. Secondly, although there are a few instances of spouse abuse where the husband is the victim (Steinmetz, 1978) that situation is the one typically portrayed as the subject of humor, for example, the comic strips are known for presenting spouse abuse as an aggressive wife battering a meek husband. In both cases, whether the woman is the victim or wielding the rolling pin, the focus of responsibility is on her. A too common occurrence (evidenced by growth nationally of shelters for battered women) is a woman who is submissive, unassertive, dependent, and frightened who is usually the subject of abuse. For example, Star (1978) found battered women to be more passive, timid, and less dominant than a control group of women.

There are contradictory findings offered about the instigation of wife abuse. Whitehurst (1971) suggests that the changing expectations of women result in increased violence, and Strauss (1974) believes that the expression of anger may increase the violence against women. On the other hand, Stahley (1978) stresses that feelings of powerlessness and submissiveness of the wives provoke violence, and Kaplan (1978) suggests that women not hitting back serves as provocation for further abuse. In many respects, the abused wife is the perfect example of the helpless female who needs assertiveness training. Yet, given the contradictory findings on triggers for husbands' abusive behaviors, there is high risk that if we train such women to be more assertive, we may be subjecting them to further abuse or possible marital breakup (the latter being quite a serious problem for many of these women as they are totally economically and emotionally dependent upon their husbands and have few other resources).

One of the tenets of assertiveness training is that our clients wish to act in their own self-interest and be in charge of their lives. When we are faced with women who remain in situations where they are not in charge and subject to abuse, we are often faced with women who have an intense conflict about what they really want.

CASE EXAMPLE

A battered wife who was receiving assertiveness training kept returning to her husband who clearly was not willing to stop using beatings as a way of handling conflicts. The therapist sees treatment as a failure because the client would not avoid the husband or insist on his participating in treatment as a condition for staying in the marriage.

Although the clinical writings stress assertiveness training as a treatment of choice for spouse abuse, it is important to recognize the enormous complexities involved in the application of assertiveness training to this population. There is a need for data-based research on the best way to handle provocation, how to motivate the husbands to participate in treatment, and the development of methods for assessing risk with possible treatment outcomes.

Assertiveness Training for Work-Related Issues: Failure to Follow Clients More Closely in Work Environments.

In focusing on the impact of assertiveness training on "significant others," more attention needs to be directed toward the clients' work settings. Often women in diverse professions have varying problems. For example, many women are still working in the traditional women's service professions, whereas others are entering arenas previously reserved for men. Obviously the problems of these two groups of professional women are quite different. Although management executives might be reinforced for assertive behaviors (and worry whether they are assertive enough), do doctors really appreciate assertive nurses or dietitians? Sherman (1978), in her work with nurses, and Fodor (1982) in similar work with dietitians, address the problems of women in the traditional service professions where they work in a hierarchical structure and often have very fixed roles.

CASE EXAMPLE

A young middle-class dietitian discussed her difficulty handling abusive remarks from the kitchen staff while on supervisory duty. In an assertiveness training group, the therapist and group helped her shape what seemed to everyone several effective responses to the harrassment and noncompliance with rules. On follow-up, however, the client reported that she was not able to carry out what she had practiced because her supervisor thought the situation should be handled differently. Naturally, we could work on an assertive response to the supervisor, but inasmuch as the problem was recurrent and a not uncommon one for dietitians, a better solution would be for the trainer to consult with the entire staff.

Unless assertiveness trainers begin to enter the workplace and work across disciplines, these types of failures will persist. Most working women receiving assertiveness training are trying out newly acquired assertiveness skills in an interlocking, bureaucratic work setting where self-expression often is not appreciated. In these settings there is sometimes further tension between older and younger women; the younger women, after attending assertiveness training, appear demanding and abrasive to the older, more experienced women who have been using other methods to exert and cope with authority.

THERAPIST AND GROUP VARIABLES RELATED TO ASSERTIVENESS TRAINING FAILURES

Therapist Variables and Failure

Assertiveness training for women was primarily developed by therapists with a feminist orientation; that is, they believe that women should be in charge of their own lives. Therefore, they place a high premium on assertiveness as being beneficial for women in achieving emotional and economic independence.

There has been little research exploring therapist values and treatment success and failure. One study that addressed the issue of traditional versus feminist approaches to assertiveness training (Ellis, 1977) found that both approaches were successful in facilitating assertiveness behavior. However, women with untraditional values did better in both groups, whereas women with more stable lives, possessing more traditional values, learned assertive skills more slowly and were most likely to drop out. It is possible that assertiveness training for women may be successful in meeting the needs of women more open to feminist beliefs.

Given the strong bias feminist therapists have toward assertiveness, one must expect some treatment failures among clients who remain passive and are unwilling to risk change. Many women clients coming to assertiveness training workshops are submissive and unable to take charge of their lives; they are often unclear about why they are in the group or what they want out of it. Inasmuch as one of the underpinnings of assertiveness training is allowing the client to make her own decisions, one might ask if the therapist is pressuring her unassertive client to be more assertive because she values assertiveness for all women or if the client genuinely wishes to take the risks involved in pursuing this development herself.

CASE EXAMPLE

An unassertive, somewhat depressed young wife of a lawyer is sent for assertiveness training. The husband calls to make the appointment, complaining of her wishy-washyness. "Make her more assertive, more interesting." If the therapist works with her own values, is she really acting in the client's best interest? Is the client going from one master shaper (husband) to another (feminist therapist)? In this case, the therapist might consider treatment a failure in that the wife really wanted to remain stereotypically feminine; she did not want to develop assertive skills and she continued to allow herself to be bullied by her husband. However, through treatment this client became aware of the real issues involved and decided to leave the marriage and go off with a quieter, more undemanding man. Escape was easier than pushing herself to develop behaviors that were incongruent with her personality at that point in time. Would this case be considered a treatment failure or a different form of effective assertive behavior?

Failure of Therapists to Provide Realistic Role Models

Another therapist variable hardly explored is what types of role models are therapists for the "average client"? A therapist, male or female, is capable of being self-supporting, has a prestigious job, is often self-employed, can afford to take risks, and is most often in an environment supportive of the personal traits associated with assertiveness. Many of our clients have jobs where they have bosses, are economically dependent on husbands who may expect many services, and live in communities that place less of a premium on assertive personalities. Possibly we need to match model and client more closely in order to enhance potential for change.

Failure Arising from All-Female Group Composition

Most assertiveness training is conducted in female-only groups. Generally, feminist therapists suggest that women are most comfortable beginning assertiveness training in an all-female group. However, only two out of six studies suggest superiority of such groups (Eichenbaum, 1978; Hollandsworth & Wall, 1974; Lewittes, 1976; Stebbins et al., 1977; Wall, 1977; Woolfolk & Dever, 1979). One reason women-only groups persist is that women are still more likely to seek out assertiveness training than males. They feel more comfortable being assertive in a women's group and receive group support special to women. However, feminist therapists must also begin to encourage women to try out their new behaviors in mixed groups. We run the risk of failure unless we give women the opportunity to test out their new assertive behaviors in areas where men are present during training and to persist in their own definition of what is important for them to work on.

Failing the Client by Placing the Burden of Change on the Individual

> When half the population is targeted as needing to change their behavior in order to gain fair treatment by the system, we have to ask what system are these individuals trying to fit into. (Linehan & Egan, 1979)

Linehan and Egan (1979), in their excellent critical review of assertiveness training for women, question the advisability of continuing such work as currently practiced. The present authors are in agreement with Linehan and Egan's contention that we are putting the burden of change on the individual woman instead of directing attention to methods for effecting broader societal change. However, we believe that the work with individuals must continue, as each woman is at the bottom of a causal sequence for effecting societal change. To create an environment receptive to assertive women, work must be directed toward the sources of nonreward and nonsupport. In particular, the media's role in creating an atmosphere for social change must be further studied. The popular press, on the one hand, has given broad coverage to the topic of female assertiveness and has helped women as they challenge old stereotypes, while on the other hand, the press has perpetuated equivalent stereotypes. Recently, the feminist woman has been portrayed as either out for herself or only too willing to band together with other similarly "tough" women against men. The popular press, in particular, has played on the fear in our culture of female strength as aggressive and destructive.

More education of key people in the media seems essential though this may be a difficult task with the few women in power positions in publishing feeling isolated and unsupported (Seegal, 1977). That such work is difficult is known to assertiveness trainers experienced in dealing with the press. For example, *New York Magazine* consulted with numerous assertiveness trainers about a feature story on assertiveness training for women and still chose to put on its cover a cartoon showing a woman slapping a man after attending an assertiveness training workshop (Dubrow, 1975). Assertiveness trainers need to work together to develop appropriate techniques to deal with the media and devise programs to effect attitudinal change. We will fail more women unless we can build a better societal reinforcement system.

The work that remains ahead is both demanding and important. One must not lose sight of the fact that in spite of the limitations of current assertiveness training practices and the shortcomings of our programs, women have been enrolling in assertiveness training workshops in large numbers during the past decade. What we are offering appears to have broad appeal and women, in spite of the negative portrayal of assertive women in the media and often with little encouragement from significant others and limited environmental support, are continuing to enroll in our workshops and are trying out their newly learned assertiveness skills at home, at work, and within their communities.

We are failing to take seriously the challenge of bringing to our research the real life issues that women bring to our workshops and to carefully assess and utilize some of the skills already possessed by these women. We must follow up our clients after training to study the implementation of assertiveness techniques in the natural environment and develop programs to assist women in coping effectively with new behavioral roles. Further, we must shift the assertiveness training focus from the individual woman to her family system, her colleagues in the work environment, and influential community resources so that a foundation is created for women's assertiveness to be treated equitably.

REFERENCES

Alberti, R.E., & Emmons, M.L. (1970) *Your perfect right.* San Louis Obispo, Calif. (1981): Impact.

Albin, R.W. (1981) Has feminism aided mental health? *New York Times,* June 16.

Applebaum, A. (1976) Rathus Assertiveness Schedule: Sex differences and correlation with social desirability. *Behavior Therapy,* (1977) **7,** 699.

Atkinson, M.B. (1977) The effect of complementary and noncomplementary dyadic situation and level of assertiveness on role played behaviors. *Dissertation Abstracts International,* **37,** 3591–3592.

Barry, W.A. (1970) Marriage research and conflict: An integrative review. *Psychological Bulletin,* 41–54.

Ball, P.B. The effect of group assertiveness training on selected measures of self-concept for college women. *Dissertation Abstracts International,* 1976, *37* (5-A), 2731.

Ball, P.G., & Wyman, E. (1978) Battered wives and powerlessness: what can counselors do? *Victimology: An International Journal,* (1979) **2,** 545–552.

Ballering, M.L. (1979) The effects of presenter sex and status on participants involved in the presentation on assertiveness. *Dissertation Abstracts International,* **40,** 5459.

Bellack, A.S., Hersen, M. & Lamparski, D. (1979) Role play tests for assessing social skills: Are they useful? *Journal of Consulting and Clinical Psychology,* **47,** 334–342.

Bellack, A.S., Hersen, M., & Turner, S. (1979) Relationship of role playing and knowledge of appropriate behavior to assertion in the natural environment. *Journal of Consulting and Clinical Psychology,* **47,** 670–678.

Berman, S. (1977) Bess Myerson is one tough customer. *New York Magazine,* **10,** No. 46, November 14.

Blau, J. (1978) Changes in assertiveness and marital satisfaction after participation in an assertive training group. *Dissertation Abstracts International,* **39,** (2-B).

Blechman, E. (1980) Behavior modification with women. In A. Brodsky, & R. Hare-Mustin (Eds.), *Advances in psychotherapy with women.* New York: Guildford.

Brockway, B.S. (1976) Assertive training for professional women. *Social Work,* 498–505.

Broverman, I.K., Broverman, D.M., Clarkson, F.E., Rosenkrantz, P.S., & Vogel, S.R. (1970) Sex-role stereotypes and clinical judgments of mental health. *Journal of Consulting and Clinical Psychology,* **34,** 107.

Butler, P. (1976) Assertive training: Teaching women not to discriminate against themselves. *Psychotherapy: Theory, Research and Practice,* **13,** (1), 56–60.

Chandler, T., Cook, B., & Dugovics, D. (1978) Sex differences in self-reported assertiveness. *Psychological Reports,* **43,** 395–402.

Christenson, A., & Nicol, D.C. (1980) The spouse observation checklist: Empirical analysis and critique. *American Journal of Family Therapy,* **8.**

Curran, J.P., & Gilbert, F.S. (1975) Social skills training and systematic desensitization in reducing dating anxiety. *Behavior Research and Therapy.* 13, 65–69.

Dubrow, M. (1975) Female assertiveness: How a pussycat can learn to be a panther. *New York Magazine,* July 18.

D'Zurilla, T., & Goldfried, M. (1971) Problem solving and behavior modification. *Journal of Abnormal Psychology,* **32,** 47–51.

Eichenbaum, L.A. (1978) The effects of same-sex versus mixed-sex assertion training groups on assertiveness, sex-role attitudes and locus of control beliefs of women. *Dissertation Abstracts International,* **39,** (5-B), 2493.

Eisler, R.M., Frederiksen, L.W., & Peterson, G.L. (1978) The relationship of cognitive variables to the expression of assertiveness. *Behavior Therapy,* **9,** 419–427.

Ellis, E.M. (1977) A comparative study of feminist vs. traditional group assertiveness training with unassertive women. *Dissertation Abstracts International,* **38,** (3-B), 1373.

Ellis, E.M., & Nicholas, M.P. (1979) A comparative study of feminist and traditional group assertiveness training with women. *Psychotherapy: Theory, Research and Practice,* **16,** 467–474.

Fiedler, D., & Beach, L.R. (1978) On the decision to be assertive. *Journal of Consulting and Clinical Psychology,* **46,** 537–546.

Fishbein, C. (1979) An investigation of sex-role stereotypes and assertive behavior in men and women. *Dissertation Abstracts International,* **40,** (2-B), 912.

Fodor, I.G., & Wolfe, J. (1977) Assertiveness training for mothers and daughters. In R. Alberti (Ed.), *Assertiveness, innovations, applications, issues.* San Luis Obispo, Calif.: Impact.

Fodor, I.G. (1980) The treatment of communication problems with assertiveness training. In A. Goldstein, & E. Foa (Eds.), *Handbook of behavioral interventions.* New York: Wiley.

Fodor, I.G. (1982) *Assertiveness training for dietitians and nutritionists.* Cassette Tape. American Dietetic Association.

Friedan, B. Feminism's next step. (1981) *New York Times Magazine,* July 5.

Gambrill, E.D., & Richey, C.A. (1976) It's up to you: Developing assertive social skills. Milbrae, Calif.: *Les Femmes.*

Goldfried, M.R., & D'Zurilla, T.J. (1969) A behavioral analytic model for assessing competence. In C.D. Spielberger (Ed.), *Current topics in clinical and community psychology* (Vol. 1). New York: Academic.

Gurman, A., & Klein, N.M. (1979) *Woman and behavioral marriage and family therapy: An unconscious male bias?* Paper presented at Symposium on Behavior Therapy for Women. Association for the Advancement of Behavior Therapy Annual Meeting, San Francisco.

Hall, J.R., & Black, J.D. (1979) Assertiveness, aggressiveness and attitudes toward feminism. *The Journal of Social Psychology,* **107,** 57–62.

Hartsook, J.E., Olch, D.R., & DeWolf, V.A. (1976) Personality characteristics of women's assertiveness training group participants. *Journal of Counseling Psychology,* **23,** 322–326.

Henderson, J.M. The effects of assertiveness training on self-actualization in women. Dissertation *Abstracts International*, 1976, 36 (7-B), 3 575. (1-97)

Herman, S. (1978) *Becoming assertive: A guide for nurses.* Princeton, N.J.: D. Van Nostrand.

Hersen, M., Eisler, R.M., & Miller, P.M. (1974) An experimental analysis of generalization in assertive training. *Behavior Research and Therapy,* **12,** 295–310.

Hollandsworth, J., Jr., & Wall, K. (1977) Sex differences in assertive behavior: an empirical investigation. *Journal of Counseling Psychology,* **24,** (No. 3), 217–222.

Hull, D.B., & Schroeder, H. (1979) Some interpersonal effects of assertion, nonassertion, and aggression. *Behavior Therapy,* **10,** 20–28.

Jackson, D., & Hudson, T. (1975) Physical attractiveness and assertiveness. *The Journal of Social Psychology,* **96,** 79–84.

Jakobowski-Spector, P. (1973) Facilitating the growth of women through assertive training. *The Counseling Psychologist,* **4,** 76–86.

Kiecolt, J., & McGrath, E. (1979) Social desirability responding in the measurement of assertive behavior. *Journal of Consulting and Clinical Psychology,* **47,** 640–642.

Lazarus, A.A. (1966) Behavior rehearsal vs. nondirective therapy vs. advice in effecting behavior change. *Behavior Research and Therapy,* **14,** 209–212.

Leviton, L.C. (1979) Observers' reactions to assertive behavior. *Dissertation Abstracts International,* **39,** (11-B), 5652.

Lewittes, H.J. (1976) Assertiveness training for women in mixed-sex small group discussions. *Dissertation Abstracts International,* **37,** (10-B), 5360.

Linehan, M., & Egan, K. (1979) *Assertion training for women: Square peg in a round role?* Paper presented at Symposium on Behavior Therapy for Women. Association for the Advancement of Behavior Therapy Annual Meeting, San Francisco.

Linehan, M.M., Goldfried, M.R., & Goldfried, A.P. (1979) Assertion therapy: Skill training or cognitive restructuring. *Behavior Therapy,* **10,** 372–388.

Muehlenhard, C. (1980) Dating initiation as a women's issue. *Femminist Behavior Therapist,* Fall Newsletter.

Osborn, S.M., & Harris, G.G. (1975) *Assertive training for women.* Springfield, Ill.: Thomas.

Powell, G.S. The effects of training wives in communication skills upon the marital satisfaction of both spouses. *Dissertation Abstracts International,* 1978, **38,** (8-B), 3857.

Rathus, S.A., & Nevid, J.S. (in press) Multivariate and normative data pertaining to the Rathus Assertiveness Schedule with the college population. *Behavior Therapy.*

Rich, A.R., & Schroeder, H.E. (1976) Research issues in assertiveness training. *Psychological Bulletin,* **83,** 1081–1096.

Salter, A. (1949) *Conditioned reflex therapy.* New York: Farrar, Straus & Giroux (Capricorn Books Edition, 1961).

Schwartz, R.M., & Gottman, J.M. (1976) Toward a task analysis of assertive behavior. *Journal of Consulting and Clinical Psychology,* **44,** 910–920.

Seegal, J.L. (1977) *The steamroom at the Yale Club: Women news editors and the newspaper industry.* Unpublished manuscript.

Serber, M. (1972) Teaching and nonverbal components of assertive training. *Journal of Behavior Therapy and Experimental Psychiatry,* **3,** 179–183.

Stahley, G.B. (1978) A review of select literature of spousal violence. *Victomology: An International Journal,* **2,** 591–607.

Star, B. (1978) Comparing battered and non-battered women. *Victomology: An International Journal,* **3,** 32–44.

Stebbins, C.A., Kelly, B., Tolor, A., & Power, M. (1977) Sex differences in assertiveness in college students. *The Journal of Psychology,* **95,** 309–315.

Steinmetz, S. (1978) The battered husband syndrome. *Victomology: An International Journal,* **2,** 499–509.

Steinmetz, S. (1977) *The cycle of violence.* New York: Praeger.

Stringer-Moore, D., & Jack, G.B. (1981) Assertive behavior training: *A cross-referenced annotated bibliography.* San Luis Obispo, Calif.: Impact.

Wall, K.E. (1977) Effects of all female and mixed sex assertion training groups on the assertive behavior of females. *Dissertation Abstracts International,* **38,** (12-B), 6184.

Weitz, S. (1977) *Sex roles: Biological, psychological & social foundations.* New York: Oxford.

Whitehurst, R. (1971) "Violently Jealous Husbands" Sexual Behavior, (July).

Wolfe, J.L., & Fodor, I.G. (1975) A cognitive behavioral approach to modifying assertive behavior in women. *The Counseling Psychologist,* **5,** 45–52.

Wolfe, J.L., & Fodor, I.G. (1977) A comparison of three techniques for modifying assertive behavior. *Behavior Therapy,* **8,** 467–574.

Wolpe, J. (1958) *Psychotherapy by reciprocal inhibition.* Stanford: Stanford University Press.

Woolfolk, R., & Dever, S. (1979) Perceptions of assertion: An empirical analysis. *Behavior Therapy,* **10,** 404–411.

CHAPTER 9

Failures in Rational-Emotive Therapy

ALBERT ELLIS

Failures in psychotherapy are of course common. Failures in behavior therapy (BT) and cognitive behavior therapy (CBT) may not be as common as they are in most other modes of therapy, but they certainly exist! This chapter will discuss failures in treatment in rational-emotive therapy (RET), a pioneering and popular form of CBT.

RET is a highly cognitive and philosophic school of psychological treatment; but it was also specifically designed, at its inception early in 1955, as a set of emotive-evocative and dehabituating behavioral procedures. Its theory and its practice are comprehensive and multimodal (Bard, 1980; Ellis, 1962, 1973; Ellis & Abrahms, 1978; Ellis & Grieger, 1977; Grieger & Boyd, 1980; Walen, DiGiuseppe, & Wessler, 1980; Wessler & Wessler, 1980). Its record of effective results, as tested by controlled experiments, is highly imperfect but still good (Ellis, 1983; Ellis & Whiteley, 1979). Why, then, should this unusually cognitive-emotive-behavioral therapy have its distinct share of failures? An intriguing question.

CHARACTERISTICS OF CLIENTS WHO FAILED IN RET

I could try to answer this question by citing a clinical case or two in which, in spite of my presumed competent use of RET, I dismally failed to effect any client improvement. Such cases might be very instructive. All clinical presentations, however, tend to be subjectively anecdotal rather than more objectively empirical and they almost always include no real control group. On the other hand, well controlled studies of therapy too often are analogue rather than down to earth clinical studies and, therefore, have their own serious limitations (Kazdin & Wilson, 1978). Seeking a compromise (though still imperfect) solution to this kind of research problem, I shall try a somewhat unusual procedure by employing a fairly large number (no less than 50) of my own clinical cases where RET failed and by comparing them to an equal number of other clinical cases (again my own) where it definitely appeared to succeed. These cases all saw me for individual and/or group therapy; when they were in group they also had as my associate therapist one of our Fellows at the Institute for Rational-Emotive Therapy, who assist me in group. They were rated by me (and sometimes also by my associate group therapist) as to (1) whether they succeeded or failed during the period of their being treated with RET, and (2) whether they possessed the 21 characteristics investigated in this study (listed in Table 9.1). The kind of research design used in this study clearly has its serious limitations, inasmuch as I am the only individual therapist and the main group therapist and I am the main (though not the only) evaluator of these cases. Nonetheless, this piece of research may have some real value.

To make this research even more definitive and useful, the cases of failure I shall discuss have been selected so that they only include individuals (1) who are of above average or of superior intelligence (in my judgment and that of their other group therapist); (2) who seemed really to understand RET and who were often effective (especially in group therapy) in helping others to learn and use it; (3) who in some ways made therapeutic progress and felt that they benefited by having RET but who still retained one or more serious presenting symptoms, such as severe depression, acute anxiety, overwhelming hostility, or extreme lack of self-discipline; and (4) who had at least one year of individual and/or group RET sessions, and sometimes considerably more. In important respects, then,

Table 9.1. Characteristics of Clients in Rational-Emotive Therapy (RET)

Characteristic	Number Who Failed to Respond	Number Who Responded Quite Well	Significance of χ^2 Difference
Extremely anxious	42	45	Nonsignificant
Severely neurotic or borderline	33	32	Nonsignificant
Dire need for approval or love	38	39	Nonsignificant
Overinvolved with others	10	10	Nonsignificant
Self-downing	39	49	.01
Autistic	28	8	.01
Disorganized	18	9	.02
Grandiose	11	2	.02
Often not listening to others	10	1	.01
Organicity signs	15	8	.05
Psychotic	10	1	.01
Psychopathic	11	6	Nonsignificant
Serious addictions	25	16	.01
Severely and/or often angry	36	20	.01
Severely depressed	38	26	.01
Dislikable to others	23	3	.01
Severe low frustration tolerance	33	16	.01
Stubborn, resistant, rebellious	38	12	.01
Refusal to do cognitive disputing	36	0	.01
Refusal to do activity homework assignments	34	6	.01
Refusal to generally work at therapy	34	2	.01

this group of failures consisted of fairly ideal RET clients; as did, too, the clients in the control group, who were also selected on the basis of the same four criteria but who, in addition, seemed to greatly improve, to be free of serious symptoms at the end of their RET experience, and for at least a year more remain improved.

How did the failures in this study fail? In one or more of the following ways:

1. They made initial good progress emotionally and/or behaviorally but then stopped and could not or would not advance to the level of symptom removal or achievement of greater potential that they wished to achieve through therapy.
2. They made (initial or later) good therapeutic progress but then retrogressed to a level near which, or even below which, they began therapy.
3. They made good "emotional" progress (e.g., lost much of their original feelings of anxiety, depression, hostility, or self-pity) but remained stymied behaviorally (e.g., remained self-defeatingly addicted to overeating, alcohol, or procrastination).
4. They made good behavioral progress (e.g., dieted steadily or stopped procrastinating) but relatively little cognitive and/or emotional improvement (e.g., still had severe feelings of anxiety, depression, hostility, or self-pity).

A number of characteristics of all the clients in this study was rated by me and by their other group therapists at the Institute for Rational-Emotive Therapy in New York City (at whose clinic all the clients were seen), to determine whether the clients possessed these characteristics (listed in Table 9.1). All raters had some extensive experience with the clients. When my ratings of whether a client possessed one of the 21 traits included in the study were compared to the ratings of the other therapists who also knew the clients well, an agreement of 87 percent was found. The ratings of the clients (i.e., whether they possessed the listed characteristics) were done either at the end of therapy or after they had been in therapy for a year or more and were still continuing. The characteristics rated were not carefully defined and the therapists doing the ratings were merely asked to state whether, in their opinion, the subjects had the stated characteristic. When the ratings were done, the therapists were not told what the purpose of the ratings was, nor were they told anything about the study I was doing on failures in RET.

The characteristics listed in Table 9.1 were chosen on the basis of my hunches that they might possibly be related to failure in RET. The terms "neurosis" and "psychosis," as well as similar characteristics listed in the table were given their usual (vague) meanings in this study. Those who were rated as "often not listening to others" were not deemed to be psychotic (although of those who were noted as not listening to others significantly more were probably in the psychotic than in the neurotic group). "Organicity signs" were defined as having discernible organic manifestations, such as tics, severe stuttering, peculiar eye movements, epilepsy, and the like.

When the clients were rated regarding salient characteristics included in this study, 2 × 2 tables were constructed showing the number of clients in each of these classifications who failed to respond and who responded quite well to RET; chi-squares were calculated for each set of 2 × 2 tables, to see whether significant differences were obtained for each table. Thus it was found that in the failure group, 36 (out of 50) clients were rated as often being quite angry and 14 were rated as not often being quite angry; in the "responded well to RET" group, 20 (out of 50) clients were rated as often being quite angry and 30 were rated as not often being this angry. For this 2 × 2 matrix, chi-square was calculated as being 11.1, which indicates a probability of less than .01 that a significant difference between these two distributions did not exist. The conclusion in this instance would be, therefore, that in all probability the failure clients were significantly more often rated as experiencing extreme anger than were the group of clients who responded well to RET.

Examination of Table 9.1 reveals the following:

1.   In regard to the usual diagnoses of neurotic traits, the "failure" group did not tend to differ significantly from the "responded well" group. Both groups had a remarkably equal number of individuals who were rated as being very anxious, severely neurotic or borderline, having a dire need for others' approval, and overinvolved with others. In one respect, self-downing, the "responded well" group actually included a significantly larger number of individuals (49 to 39) than the "failure" group. One reason for the similarity of both groups in these neurotic respects probably stemmed from the manner in which they were selected in the study: inasmuch as the "responded well" group (unlike many other clients who benefit from RET) was deliberately chosen to include individuals who took a year or more to complete therapy and who, therefore, were, at least at the start of therapy, highly neurotic. The reason why the "responded well" group included even more self-downing clients than the "failure" group was probably because the latter group (as will be seen below) included significantly larger numbers of autistic, grandiose, and psychotic individuals, as well as significantly larger numbers of angry individuals, many of whom tend to down others rather than to denigrate themselves and hence to not focus as much on self-downing thoughts and behaviors.

2.   Although the "failures" appeared in this study not to be rated significantly more often as neurotic than the clients who responded well to RET, they did appear more often to be rated psychotic or near-psychotic. Thus the "failures" included a significantly greater proportion of individuals who were checked off as being autistic, disorganized, grandiose, organic, and psychotic; they also included a greater proportion of individuals who were rated as being psychopathic, although this proportion did not reach statistical significance. In addition, they included a significantly greater proportion of individuals who were rated as chronically not listening to others (or to their therapist), a trait which may possibly be indicative of near-psychosis.

3.   On almost all the characteristics studied of the "failure" and the "responded well to RET" clients that included strong elements of low frustration tol-

erance, the former group consistently had a significantly greater proportion of individuals than the latter group. These characteristics included addiction to some self-defeating behavior, anger at other people, depression, possession of dislikable social traits, severe low frustration tolerance, and stubbornness and rebelliousness.

4. As might well be expected, on all the characteristics in the study that related to unwillingness to work at therapy (and which also are presumably related to low frustration tolerance), the "failure" group showed a significantly higher proportion of individuals than the "responded well to RET" group. These characteristics included refraining from disputing irrational beliefs, avoidance of carrying out activity homework assignments, and general refusal to work at therapy.

What do these findings mainly indicate? First of all, they at least partly seem to provide evidence favoring several major hypotheses or hunches with which I started when I thought about what questions to investigate about the characteristics of clients who fail to benefit appreciably from RET even though they are bright, seem to understand the principles of this kind of therapy, and spend a year or more in regular individual or group RET sessions.

Hypothesis 1.   Clients who fail in RET are more severely disturbed, and particularly more psychotic or organically ill than those who respond well to RET

As noted above, the failures did not seem to be significantly more often neurotic than those who responded well. But this may have been an artifact of the method in which both groups were selected, inasmuch as those who responded well only included individuals who stayed in therapy for a year or more (as did also the failures); and RET is a method of therapy that less neurotic individuals often respond to quite quickly—in 20 sessions or less of either group or individual therapy. My impression, from long-term clinical experience with RET, is that when clients who respond well to it are picked at random, and include those who respond rather quickly as well as those who do so after a year or more of therapy, the latter group is significantly less disturbed than the former group and that, therefore, Hypothesis 1 tends to have some evidence to back it. This impression, however, could well instigate some more careful empirical study before it is considered to be substantiated.

In regard to the part of the hypothesis concerning psychotic and organically ill clients, the present study shows some clearcut evidence that such individuals indeed wind up more frequently in the "failure" than in the "respond well to RET" group and that, therefore, there may be some validity to the notion that intensive and prolonged RET (like various other kinds of psychotherapy) works better with neurotic than with psychotic clients. This would hardly be a surprising conclusion.

Hypothesis 2.   Clients with severe low frustration tolerance tend to fail in RET more frequently than those with higher frustration tolerance

This hunch was distinctly borne out by the data of the study, in that clients in the "failure" category significantly more often displayed such characteristics as some kind of serious addiction, frequent eruptions of anger and hostility, severe depression, personal dislikability to others, stubbornness and rebelliousness, and severe general low frustration tolerance. It may be guessed that low frustration tolerance would interfere with using RET in a therapeutic situation in several ways:

1. It would tend to focus clients on the necessity for changing others and the external world conditions rather than on changing themselves.
2. It would create feelings, such as those of anger, that would notably distract them from using RET philosophies and procedures to change themselves.
3. Although RET (unlike classical behavior therapy) helps clients gain a good deal of insight to help themselves change their basic beliefs, like classical behavior therapy it does not hold that this kind of insight enables clients "automatically" to modify their beliefs and behaviors; instead, it shows them that they had better rely, mainly, on their own persistent *activity* (including cognitive and behavioral) to modify their self-defeating responses.

Clients with low frustration tolerance, therefore, who believe that conditions of life are too hard and that they must not be that hard, are less likely to work at changing themselves (or, for that matter, at changing external conditions) than those with higher frustration tolerance.

Hypothesis 3.   Clients who not only have low frustration tolerance in general but who have it specifically in regard to working at therapy will tend to fail in RET more frequently than those who have a hard-working attitude toward therapy

The data of this study consistently supported this hypothesis, inasmuch as the three characteristics that were investigated that related to clients' attitudes toward and work at therapy all turned up data favoring it. Thus failures in RET were significantly more often found to avoid disputing their irrational beliefs, to fail to do their activity homework assignments, and to refuse to work at other aspects of rational-emotive therapy. It would have been surprising if this had not been found; the fact that it was so consistently found may be exaggerated because the raters of how well or poorly all the clients in the study did at working at therapy may well have been contaminated by their knowledge that those in the "failure" group did fail whereas those in the "responded to RET" group did not. This particular finding, therefore, had better be viewed more skeptically than some of the other findings of the study.

DISCUSSION OF THE RESULTS

RET is a form of psychotherapy that specifically includes the use of a number of cognitive, emotive, and behavioral procedures. Cognitively, it stresses the acceptance by clients of responsibility for largely creating their own crooked thinking and their inappropriate feelings, and the consequent understanding by these clients of their own irrational beliefs (especially their use of absolutistic shoulds, oughts, and musts) and their employment of the disputing of these irrationalities and the use of other cognitive methods to allay or distract themselves from irrationality. In its cognitive aspects, RET also emphasizes the persistent use of reason, logic, and the scientific method to uproot clients' irrational beliefs. Consequently, it ideally requires intelligence, concentration, and high-level, consistent cognitive self-disputation and self-persuasion. These therapeutic behaviors would tend to be disrupted or blocked by extreme disturbance, by lack of organization, by grandiosity, by organic disruption, and by refusal to do RET-type disputing of irrational ideas. All these characteristics proved to be present in significantly more failures than in those clients who responded favorably to RET.

RET also, to be quite successful, involves clients' forcefully and emotively changing their beliefs and actions, and their being stubbornly determined to accept responsibility for their own inappropriate feelings and to vigorously work at changing these feelings (Ellis & Abrahms, 1978; Ellis & Whiteley, 1979). But the failure clients in this study were significantly more angry than those who responded well to RET; more of them were severely depressed and inactive, they were more often grandiose, and they were more frequently stubbornly resistant and rebellious. All these characteristics would presumably tend to interfere with the kind of emotive processes and changes that RET espouses.

RET strongly advocates that clients, in order to improve, do in vivo activity homework assignments, deliberately force themselves to engage in many painful activities until they become familiar and unpainful, and notably work and practice its multimodal techniques. But the group of clients who signally failed in this study showed abysmally low frustration tolerance, had serious behavioral addictions, led disorganized lives, refrained from doing their activity homework assignments, were more frequently psychotic, and generally refused to work at therapy. All these characteristics, which were found significantly more frequently than were found in the clients who responded quite well to RET, would tend to interfere with the behavioral methods of RET.

This brings us to a fascinating question: Inasmuch as the failures more often tended to be individuals who could be said to have inbuilt resistances to RET (and, very likely, to many or most other forms of psychotherapy), and inasmuch as their low frustration tolerance and their refusal to work at changing themselves both in their regular existences and in the course of therapy seem to often accompany their extreme states of disturbance (particularly their tendencies to be exceptionally angry, autistic, depressed, disorganized, grandiose, organically ill, and psychotic) does this reveal a kind of "Catch-22" regarding which clients require and which actually make the best use of psychotherapy. Namely, is there a strong tendency for the clients who are most disturbed and who could most use therapy to be precisely those kinds of individuals whose severe disturbances will interfere most with their actually benefiting from psychological treatment? A good deal of prior research and clinical findings tend to support this hypothesis (Garfield & Bergin, 1978) and the findings of the present study appear to confirm it once again.

If this proposition is indeed in part true, it need not engender a feeling of hopelessness in clients and therapists. As I have noted elsewhere, the strong predispositions of humans to think irrationally and to be emotionally disturbed is probably largely biological as well as environmental; but this does not mean that biological tendencies to think, emote, and act in dysfunctional ways cannot be overcome (Ellis, 1976, 1981). Similarly, if severe emotional disturbance and resistance to therapeutic change are significantly correlated, this again does not mean that seriously disturbed individuals have to continue to resist improvement, nor that they cannot change. It merely means that the problem of helping people to modify themselves is more complicated and difficult than many of us have previously thought it to be and, therefore, we require therapy procedures that are not only "effective" (i.e., bring about improved results with groups of disturbed clients) but also "efficient" (i.e., help more clients more extensively, pervasively, and preventively (Ellis, 1980a).

As far as RET and CBT are concerned, this study would tend to show that there are clients with certain characteristics who are significantly more likely to resist improvement than other types of clients. In general, neurotic clients can and do make good progress as compared to those who are autistic, depressed, disorganized, grandiose, organically ill, or psychotic. In addition, clients with abysmally low frustration tolerance or what I have elsewhere called discomfort anxiety (Ellis, 1979, 1980b), resist treatment more often than those who have higher frustration tolerance. Finally, as would be expected, clients who refuse to work hard and persistently at the therapeutic process more often signally fail at therapy than those who do the work and practice that RET particularly calls for. If these findings prove to be supported by other data than that found in this highly challengeable study, the task of RET theorists and practitioners (and perhaps of all therapists) is to keep working to discover more efficient procedures and better ways of motivating "D.C.'s" (difficult customers) to use these procedures.

COMMENTS ON FAILURES IN RET

The previous discussion has dealt mainly with failure in RET as revealed by the specific study discussed in this chapter. Several other important questions of a more general nature may be raised and I shall now attempt to answer some of these.

First, in what way is failure to benefit from RET similar and different from failure to respond to other systems of psychotherapy: for example, psychoanalysis, behavior therapy, and client-centered therapy? Regarding similarities, I would hypothesize that a large minority of all psychotherapy clients—I would guess from 20 to 30 percent—are so severely, so organically, or so psychotically disturbed that they will benefit minimally, and often hardly at all, from any of today's modes of psychotherapy, including RET. This does not necessarily mean that these kinds of clients cannot, under any conditions, appreciably change through psychotherapeutic contact, but mainly that their changing themselves is so difficult and requires such a considerable amount of persistent effort on their (and their therapists') part that they, therefore, will not take this effort to modify their thoughts, feelings, and behaviors.

I would guess that RET and classical behavior therapy are most similar in this respect, inasmuch as both these forms of psychological treatment strive to help clients make a profound philosophical-behavioral change, to surrender their disturbed symptoms, and (presumably) to maintain this relatively symptom-free condition. The exceptionally disturbed, and especially the psychotic and near-psychotic, clients referred to in the last paragraph may tend to be unable or unwilling to make this kind of change and, therefore, will "resist" RET and behavior therapy treatment. It is interesting to note that Wolpe (1973) has consistently held that behavior therapy in general, and systematic desensitization in particular, are not likely to be effective with psychotics.

Certain other kinds of therapies, however, whether or not their adherents design them this way, are easily construed by clients (and by therapists) to help clients "feel better" rather than "get better." Client-centered therapy, encounter groups, and cathartic therapies, for example, seem notable in this respect. Clients in these types of therapy, therefore, may really have different goals than clients in RET and classical behavior therapy, and may succeed at attaining these goals even when they are exceptionally disturbed and in the category of individuals who frequently do not benefit from RET and classical behavior therapy. It may also be hypothesized that some highly resistant clients may be more benefited by certain nonRET and nonBT forms of treatment in that, by these therapies, they at least feel better *with* their unchanging symptoms whereas they would not feel as well with these same remaining symptoms if they experienced RET or BT.

It may also be hypothesized that individuals who benefit most from RET tend to be reasonably educated and intelligent, and that those with less advantages in this respect may benefit more from certain other therapies, such as BT or cathartic treatment. This, however, would mainly be true of the elegant form of RET, which includes teaching clients how to use the scientific method and to do high-level cognitive disputing of their irrational beliefs. Lower-level RET, which teaches them how to use coping statements, would probably be as effective (or even more so) with less educated and less intelligent clients than would various kinds of nonRET treatments, including classical BT.

What are the most common "mistakes" in practicing RET that probably lead to failures? These have been discussed in detail in several books and articles (Ellis & Whiteley, 1979; Walen, DiGiuseppe, & Wessler, 1980; Wessler & Ellis, 1980; Wessler & Wessler, 1980), so I shall briefly summarize some of them as follows.

1. RET therapists sometimes teach the principles of RET to clients too rapidly and too abruptly, thereby interfering with their understanding and using these principles.

2. Therapists are too namby-pamby, or unforceful in encouraging RET clients to surrender their irrational thinking and behavioral dysfunctions.

3. Therapists shuttle back and forth from one symptom (e.g., self-downing) to another (e.g., anger), and fail to help clients zero in effectively on one at a time before they confuse and confound it with the second symptom.

4. Therapists deal only or mainly with primary symptoms (e.g., fear of elevators) rather than with secondary symptoms as well (e.g., fear of having the painful fear of elevators).

5. Therapists not only fail to relate warmly or intimately to clients (which is quite allowable in RET) but also are negative, impatient, and hostile to clients; they sometimes try to teach unconditional self-acceptance to clients but fail to unconditionally accept these clients themselves.

6. Therapists have significant degrees of low frustration tolerance, and do not strongly persist in using RET with clients but instead discourage themselves with difficult clients, give up too easily, and act impatiently.

7. RET therapists are not too bright or not too good at disputing irrational beliefs themselves and, therefore, are not too helpful to clients in showing them how to do RET disputation.

8. Therapists concentrate almost exclusively on clients' self-downing characteristics and the irrational beliefs that lie behind these characteristics, and consequently ignore their low frustration tolerance or discomfort anxiety, which may be equally or almost as important in their disturbances.

9. Therapists concentrate heavily on their own hypotheses about clients and their irrational beliefs, and consequently do not listen adequately to these clients and sometimes foist on them problems and solutions that they could well live without.

10. Therapists are too simplistic and focus mainly on highly obvious symptoms and the irrationalities that lie behind them, rather than going on to deal with more subtle symptoms and the basic and often more complicated irrationalities that are subsumed under them (Ellis, 1980c).

11. Therapists attempt to help clients feel calm, serene, or indifferent when they are plagued by problems and losses, instead of helping them feel appropriately, and often deeply, sorrowful, regretful, frustrated, or annoyed about these difficulties.

12. Therapists only acknowledge clients' irrational cognitions that supposedly cause their emotional and behavioral disturbances, and fail to look at the activating events and experiences that partially lead to these thoughts, and the important interactions between the thoughts and the experiences or events.

13. RET therapists too heavily focus on the important cognitive aspects of rational-emotive therapy and partially or mainly neglect the highly important emotive and behavioral methods that are an integral part of RET.

Are there any therapist variables that can impede or enhance success by RET? Some of the main therapist variables that tend to impede its success have just been listed. Some of the important variables that tend to enhance RET success probably include the following.

A high degree of intelligence by the therapist.

A vital interest by the therapist not only in helping clients change but in doing so through a multiplicity of methods, especially including those that deal with the disputing of irrational beliefs and with problem solving.

The sincere and vigorous use by the therapist of RET philosophy and methods in his or her own life, and the conquering of some of his or her own disturbances by this use.

A high energy level on the part of the therapist and the determination to use this energy to vigorously and forcefully attack clients' irrational ideas and self-defeating behaviors and to teach these clients how to internalize and use this kind of attacking themselves.

Conviction by the therapist that the scientific method is not only good for understanding human processes and for research into psychotherapy, but that it also has immense usefulness when specifically applied to the personal problems of disturbed individuals.

What are some of the reasons for premature termination (dropouts) in RET and for serious relapses on the part of clients who have previously made significant gains? A number of such reasons seem to exist, including these.

1. Because it is simple and offers clients something of a revolutionary approach to understanding and minimizing their disturbances, RET often helps bring about unusually fast results in the elimination of certain symptoms such as fear of social disapproval, sexual inadequacy, and feelings of intense hostility. When it works "too well" in these respects, clients falsely think they are completely "cured" in some instances and break off therapy after relatively few sessions, before they have worked through their problems in a thoroughgoing manner.

2. RET requires a considerable amount of work and effort by clients who

want to make a profound philosophic and behavioral change. Some clients, especially those with abysmally low frustration tolerance (and who want magical help), either drop out fairly quickly or remain in therapy but refuse to do the required work and, therefore, do not make too significant gains or else temporarily change and then fall back to previous disturbed levels of behavior.

3.   Therapists make various errors that encourage clients to drop out of therapy or to relapse after making initial gains (such as the errors in the thirteen points listed above).

4.   As noted previously in this paper, strong biological predispositions toward severe disturbance and toward refusing to work at giving up such disturbance may encourage some individuals to quit RET quickly or prematurely and to first make progress and then retrogress.

5.   Various situational factors occur (as they do in other forms of therapy) to encourage premature dropouts. Thus a woman who comes to therapy because she cannot relate adequately to men may accidentally, soon after therapy has begun, meet an almost ideal man to whom she can easily relate. Or she may use the RET techniques she has learned in the first few sessions to do better than she usually does with men, and may thereby get into an intimate relationship; and, her main therapeutic goal being quickly achieved, drop therapy before she has benefited very much from it.

6.   While participating in RET therapy, clients may for various reasons start to devoutly believe in a different system of psychotherapy or of philosophy—such as psychoanalysis, Erhard Seminar Training, (EST) or some orthodox religion—which is antithetical to some of the principles of RET and that leads them to drop RET or to surrender some of the gains that they have previously made with it.

In conclusion, it seems fairly obvious, from the results of the study of RET failures included in this chapter and from extensive clinical observation, that RET often fails for reasons similar to those why all other forms of psychotherapy frequently fail, and that it sometimes succeeds for reasons, including situational reasons, similar to those that lead to successes in other forms of psychological treatment. In many respects, however, RET differs significantly from most other kinds of therapy and also from general cognitive behavior therapy with which it is closely identified (Ellis, 1980c; Ellis & Whiteley, 1979). Some important aspects of its failures and successes, therefore, seem to be indigenous to its specific theory and practice, as has been pointed out in the above discussion. Considerably more research in regard to its failures, however, had better be done so that its efficacy and its efficiency can be appreciably improved.

REFERENCES

Bard, J. A. (1980) *Rational emotive therapy in practice.* Champaign, Ill.: Research Press.

Ellis, A. (1962) *Reason and emotion in psychotherapy.* Secaucus, N.J.: Lyle Stuart and Citadel Press.

Ellis, A. (1973) *Humanistic psychotherapy: The rational-emotive approach.* New York: Crown and McGraw-Hill Paperbacks.

Ellis, A. (1976) The biological basis of human irrationality. *Journal of Individual Psychology,* **32,** 145–168.

Ellis, A. (1979) Discomfort anxiety: A new cognitive-behavioral construct. Part 1. *Rational Living,* **14,** No. 2, 2–8.

Ellis, A. (1980a) Discomfort anxiety: A new cognitive-behavioral construct. Part 2. *Rational Living,* **15,** No. 1, 25–30.

Ellis, A. (1980b) The value of efficiency in psychotherapy. *Psychotherapy,* **17,** 414–419.

Ellis, A. (1980c) Rational-emotive therapy and cognitive behavior therapy: Similarities and differences. *Cognitive Therapy and Research,* **4,** 325–340.

Ellis, A. (1983) *Rational-emotive therapy and cognitive behavior therapy.* New York: Springer.

Ellis, A., & Abrahms, E. (1978) *Brief psychotherapy in medical and health practice.* New York: Springer.

Ellis, A., & Grieger, R. (Eds.) (1977) *Handbook of rational-emotive therapy.* New York: Springer.

Ellis, A., & Whiteley, J. M. (Eds.) (1979) *Theoretical and empirical foundations of rational-emotive therapy.* Monterey, Calif.: Brooks/Cole.

Garfield, S. L., & Bergin, A. E. (Eds.) (1978) *Handbook of psychotherapy and behavior change* (2nd ed.). New York: Wiley.

Grieger, R., & Boyd, J. (1980) *Rational emotive therapy: A skills based approach.* New York: Van Nostrand Reinhold.

Kazdin, A.E., & Wilson, G. T. (1978) *Evaluation of behavior therapy: Issues, evidence and research strategies.* Cambridge, Mass.: Ballinger.

Walen, S. R., DiGiuseppe, R., & Wessler, R. L. (1980) *A practitioner's guide to rational-emotive therapy.* NewYork:Oxford.

Wessler, R. A., & Wessler, R. L. (1980) *The principles and practice of rational-emotive therapy.* San Francisco: Jossey-Bass.

Wessler, R. L., & Ellis, A. (1980) Supervision in rational-emotive therapy. In A. K. Hess (Ed.), *Psychotherapy supervision.* New York: Wiley.

Wolpe, J. (1973) *The practice of behavior therapy.* New York: Pergamon.

CHAPTER 10

Failures in Self-Control

LIZETTE PETERSON

Over a decade ago, Paul (1967) argued that psychologists must cease to ask the simplistic question, "Does psychotherapy work?" and begin to investigate the more complicated question of, "Which therapeutic interventions applied by which therapists to which patients under which circumstances are likely to lead to which results?" The 1970s brought increasing interest in the transfer of control from the therapist to the client, with literally hundreds of attempts to train behavioral self-control in individual therapy (e.g., Kanfer & Grimm, 1977), in groups (e.g., Stuart, 1977), in workshops (e.g., Dixon, Heppner, Petersen, & Ronning, 1979), and with self-help manuals (e.g., Glasgow & Rosen, 1978). Recently, Menges and Dobroski (1977, p. 172) suggested that the challenge to investigators of self-control phenomena should be to determine, "Which components of which treatments . . .for which students planning to modify which target behaviors" result in effective treatment. If we add to this question, "With what therapist contact for what immediate and long-term effects for what reason?" this query will allow analysis not only of the strengths of behavioral self-control technology and theory, but also of the inadequacies of current self-control strategies.

With the intensive focus given to self-control processes in the last several years, the elementary question, "Does self-control work?" would seem to have been answered with a resounding, "Yes!" However, behavioral research suffers from a selection bias both in publication (Homer & Peterson, 1980) and in the conclusions drawn from published and unpublished work (Richards, 1980). Successful uses of a procedure are reported at a much higher rate than nonsuccessful uses, and many conclusions are influenced more by the researcher's optimism than they are by empirical data. Investigators of self-control procedures might do well to answer the above question on efficacy with a resounding, "Sometimes!" This chapter, rather than utilizing the traditional tack of examining cases in which a program is successful, will analyze cases in which self-control procedures have not yielded the desired results. Elucidation of possible causes for failure in

The help of Andrew Homer and William McReynolds on previous drafts of this chapter was much appreciated, and special gratitude must be expressed to C. Steven Richards for his generous and supportive help at every stage of manuscript preparation.

self-control may yield clearer answers to questions concerning effective treatment than would examination of success. It may be easier to pinpoint why a procedure fails than to determine why it succeeds, and failures in a procedure can help to define the parameters of effective procedural use (Goldfried, 1980)—which behaviors, which subjects, with what maintenance. Furthermore, examination of failures may insure future quality of self-control programs by pointing out premature acceptance of packaged treatments and the necessity for further refinement (Barlow, 1980). Failures in self-control, perhaps more than successes, can point the way toward future research questions that must be answered, as well as reminding the clinician of the importance of adhering to occasionally time-consuming techniques established as successful in past research.

This chapter will outline some sources of failure in self-control, using the above restatement of Menges and Dobroski's (1977) question as a base. Specifically, this chapter will analyze "which components" of self-control may be the source of failure, including self-evaluation, self-monitoring, and self-contracting (Kanfer & Karoly, 1972), "which treatments" may be unsuccessful, focusing especially on the use of positive and negative consequences, "which students" and which subject characteristics may predict failure, and "which target behaviors" may be most difficult to alter. Questions of "with what therapist contact" will examine the efficacy of therapist-directed, therapist-administered, self-directed, and self-administered change procedures. The query "for what immediate and long-term effects" will be examined to identify potential sources of failures in maintenance of self-control and finally "for what reason" will be considered to examine potential reasons for failure that may lie in the philosophical rationale behind the selection of self-control strategies. This discussion will rely on examples from clinical practice of the author and several colleagues (names have been changed to protect the failing therapist). In addition, some of the relatively infrequent accounts of self-control failure in the published research literature will be reviewed, and the discussion will attempt to point out alternative strategies and additional research needed to overcome failures in self-control.

TREATMENT COMPONENT FAILURES

Failures of Self-Evaluation

Many processes are involved in self-evaluation. This section will focus on problems in identifying the problem behavior, selecting an appropriate index of the problem behavior, and establishing a reasonable criterion for behavior. Assessments that are too abbreviated and shallow may sometimes result in incorrect identification of the problem response class (McReynolds, 1980). For example, Mary originally requested help in a smoking cessation program. Although she was initially successful in eliminating smoking, she quickly gained nearly 20 pounds and this weight gain remained relatively resistant to weight reduction attempts. Moreover, Mary reported increased feelings of tension and depression.

A more complete analysis revealed that Mary had very few resources for dealing with stress and that her heavy smoking had served as a time for relaxation and calming self-instruction. Her request to quit smoking had come at a time when smoking was increasing, due to increased life stress. She found it very difficult to take time out for relaxation and self-instruction per se but had been able to do so in the context of taking a cigarette break or having a snack, a not uncommon finding (Marlatt & Gordon, 1980). Correct assessment of Mary's problem might have avoided failure by identifying the designated behavior as an increase in coping and self-instruction ability, accompanied by a concomittant or subsequent decrease in smoking. Recognition of the "take-a-break" pattern Mary had established for self-instruction would have enabled the therapist to anticipate and program more adaptive substitute responses.

Other researchers note similar examples of inadequate assessment resulting in failures in self-control due to mislabeling of the problem behavior. Some individuals receiving problem-solving skills may instead require assistance in limiting available options (Dixon et al., 1979). Similarly, Stunkard (1977) and Fisher, Levenkron, Lowe, Loro, and Greer (in press) argued that failures in maintained weight control may be due to the misconception of eating in the obese. These investigators suggest that failures occur if treatment relies on substituting the eating patterns of normal individuals, rather than on the maintenance of what may be a continued abnormal pattern of eating in these susceptible individuals. Correct labeling of the problem response should always be examined when self-control fails.

It is also possible to correctly label the response class, but to select an incorrect index of the problem behavior. For example, training individuals attempting to lose weight to eat with small bites, put the utensils down between bites, eat in a prescribed place, and so on, may be inadequate in some cases (e.g., Lansky, 1981). If between-meal eating increases in proportion to the food decrease noted at mealtime, this form of self-control will be unsuccessful. As will be seen later when self-monitoring is discussed, adding "bite counting" or calorie counting to the above program will not necessarily correct the problem. Complete indexing might include amount eaten, times eating takes place during the day, food groups selected, and so on, as well as stimulus properties of the eating environment. The more elaborate the indexing required, however, the less chance that subjects will employ the technique (Richards, 1980). Thus the indexing must be complete enough to have an impact on ongoing responding and parsimonious enough to be used.

Other indexing problems have been noted in various areas of self-control. Failure to alleviate problems caused by negative self-statements, for example, is likely to result if only the number of negative self-statements are monitored. Heppner (1978) noted that focusing on decreasing negative self-statements without increasing the rate of positive self-statements is unlikely to produce beneficial results. McFall (1978) reported similar problems when indexing smoking behavior; cigarettes smoked, number of drags, depth of inhalation, and so on, all provide relevant dimensions. Again, complete and functional assessment with increased sensitivity to early effects of self-control procedures would seem to be indicated, with accompanying flexibility for reindexing a response if necessary.

Even optimal labeling and indexing of a problem behavior is likely to result in perceived failure in subjects whose criterion for appropriate behavior is unreasonable (Kanfer, 1977). For example, Peggy sought out assertion training because she felt she was too frequently hurt by friends and coworkers, and she wished to be able to avoid interpersonally upsetting encounters. Peggy did show many signs of being too passive and responded well to training in self-instruction and self-reinforcement, as well as improving in her overt ability to role-play assertive responses. However, she remained discontent with the amount of interpersonal friction in her life and although she handled many difficult situations well, continued to complain about interacting with others. Later in therapy it became apparent that Peggy truly wished to have a life entirely devoid of any interpersonal conflict and she was unmotivated to change her attitude toward or her sensitivity to others. She dropped out of therapy with the firm (and assertive) conviction that it had failed to have an impact on her problems.

Mahoney (1980) also noted the dangers of clients who set unreasonable criteria, anticipating that one should never gain weight, argue with one's spouse, or experience depression. Clear initial agreement on a reasonable criterion and on willingness to react flexibly to environmental demands may result in fewer failures of this kind (Fisher et al., 1982).

Failures in Self-Monitoring

Accurate monitoring not only of the designated behavior but also of the antecedents and consequences of the behavior may be required to avoid failure in this area. Difficulty in recording the occurrence of the problem behavior heads this list. Individuals who deliberately falsify their records have (not unexpectedly) been shown to fail more often in implementing self-change than accurate recorders (Worthington, 1979). Inasmuch as self-monitoring alone has been shown to promote positive change (Kanfer, 1977), individuals who attempt but fail to keep accurate records may also fail at self-control. Self-monitoring seems to be most useful to individuals who are not already knowledgeable about their behavior (Richards, McReynolds, Holt, & Sexton, 1976). Occasionally such failure is the result of inadequate training (Kanfer & Grimm, 1977; McFall, 1977) or of difficulty in tabulating the data (McReynolds, 1980). The use of bulky charts, difficult to follow graphs, and time-consuming longhand explanations may produce failures in self-monitoring. The degree of intrusiveness of monitoring may also contribute to failure. For example, Karoly (1980) noted that a teen-ager in high school who is attempting to maintain a low social profile is unlikely to use a frequency counting device, even though it is quick and easy to employ. Similarly, asking a busy teacher to write out negative self-statements in longhand or asking an angry office worker to graph the number of aggressive responses emitted during the busiest time of day is likely to result in quick extinction, as time-consuming monitoring leads to decreased compliance (McFall, 1977) and competition from concurrent responses leads to decreased accuracy (Epstein, Webster, & Miller, 1975). Some researchers have even noted that such requests for monitoring may be hazardous to the therapist's health (Anonymous, 1980).

The consequences that accompany the response may also influence accuracy of monitoring, with better accuracy for behaviors that are followed by positive rather than negative consequences (Lipinski, Black, Nelson, & Ciminero, 1975). Even failing to point out the importance of accurate self-monitoring can lead to decreased accuracy (Nelson, Lipinski, & Black, 1976). Watson and Tharp (1977) describe numerous methods to prevent failures in self monitoring, including (1) using specifically defined categories of behaviors, (2) recording on a device always present during the occurrence of the response, (3) employing a simple system when possible, (4) avoiding the use of punishment, and (5) utilizing rewards. They suggest placing monitoring devices in any location that will promote recording: on the refrigerator, next to the bed, or on the television set, and they advocate using others to prompt self-monitoring. Finally, overrehearsing self-recording is encouraged as a method to circumvent possible forgetting.

As has been acknowledged, recording the problem behavior is only one facet of accurate self-monitoring. Monitoring antecedents and consequences is subject to all of the problems previously discussed for the designated variable. Mislabeling of antecedents or consequences may result in failure, and as Mahoney (1977) noted, it is easy to mislabel antecendents and consequences. Often we assume that because one variable is strongly correlated with the specified response, it is causally related to that response. A functional rather than a correlational analysis may be required to determine the relationship of the specified response to such accompanying variables. Covert, automatic self-statements may be the most difficult antecedents and consequences to correctly identify, as the subject may not even be aware that they are present (Meichenbaum, 1973).

Even when the antecedents and consequences of behavior are correctly identified and indexed, they remain subject to many of the above-mentioned problems of recording. Accurate monitoring of these variables is important to the next component of self-change, the self-contract. The self-contract requires both the accurate identification and recording of antecedents and consequences as well as pre-programmed changes in the observed antecedents and consequences.

Failures in Self-Contracting

Kanfer and Karoly (1972) pointed out that one is likely to successfully contract for self-change when suffering aversive effects from or when satiated with the un-desired response, when social approval for intention statements is likely, and when environmental cues signaling problems with current behavior patterns are present. Similarly, failure to self-contract may be the result of social disapproval for the intention statements, difficulty of execution of the desired response, or low pay-off of the desired response. Failure to self-contract may also occur when the client has a history of unsuccessful attempts at self-control or when strong punishment is attached to the failure to execute the self-contract.

A relatively complete understanding of the environment in which the subject lives is necessary to understand failures to effectively self-contract (McReynolds, 1980). For example, family members may give vocal approval to a mother's self-intention statements, but may covertly indicate that they disapprove of such radical changes. Changes in the family system may be called for in such a case. For example, Ellen had resolved to complete her college degree and her family had warmly applauded her decision. However, when she attempted to program time for study behavior, she was punished by comments from her husband and children that suggested that the housecleaning, laundry, and meals were suffering from her neglect. Family members in such cases may need to alter their behavior either by helping out with family chores or by altering their requirements for housecleaning and meals, if Ellen and those like her are to succeed at their self-imposed study behavior.

In addition, unskilled clients may view the desired response pattern as too difficult; at times, simple information about the training requirements and difficulties that others have encountered may remove this block to self-contracting. It may be necessary to remove the threat of past failures or of current unreinforced attempts at change before a contract to implement self-control can be formed. An acknowledgement of the intermittent problems in change, in addition to a positive expectation for success, may be most likely to facilitate adaptive intention statements (Mahoney, 1980; Marlatt & Gordon, 1980).

In formulating a self-contract in an individual who is ready to do so, a variety of factors must be considered to avoid contract failure. The contract may be less successful if it is begun during a time of stress. McReynolds (1980) for example, notes that many clients planning weight-loss programs do well to wait until personal life stresses are behind them and the clients can devote themselves totally to the contract. Ongoing demands and problems that also demand self-control from the client can serve to weaken the self-contract (e.g., Leventhal & Cleary, 1980).

In the same vein, it is important to select reinforcers that are under the client's control (Karoly, 1980). Clinicians report a host of case history failures due to subjects relying on reinforcers that repeatedly failed to be dispensed (the examples include a dinner date with a husband who had to go out of town frequently, a trip to the toy store that was repeatedly cancelled "until we get downtown," a new dress that could not be located in the small town where the client lived, and a grade of D in spite of greatly improved study habits).

Not only must the client have control over the designated reinforcer to use it successfully, but the reinforcer must be more compelling than competing reinforcers located both within (e.g., hunger) and without (e.g., peer approval) the individual attempting self-control (Kanfer, 1977). Many of these competing reinforcers are naturally occuring positive consequences of the maladaptive response. In other cases, failures to self-control are due to alternative reinforcers that are deliberately programmed by others, such as the wife who continued to chain smoke and offer the shakily abstinent husband cigarettes or the husband who rewarded his obese but dieting wife with a trip to an ice-cream store (McReynolds, 1980).

In some cases, failure may result because there simply is not a manipulable reinforcer as compelling as the naturally occurring reinforcer for the maladaptive response. A case in point involved an obese client who claimed that nothing was as reinforcing as food. Her reinforcer survey confirmed this report. She was willing to eat alone in an unstimulating environment, forego seeing friends, going out at night, and other pleasures. She simply could not force herself to quit buying and eating sweets; there were no contingencies strong enough to warrant the behavioral change, according to this client. She would apply both the positive and negative contingencies faithfully; they simply failed to control her behavior. This failure finally turned around in the winter when the electricity failed, providing a new stimulus situation. When the consequence of no-hot-water-in-shower was applied to days during which the dieting contract had not been kept, a slow but steady loss of weight resulted, and was maintained. However, as will be seen later, it would be advisable to attempt to switch stimulus control as soon as possible to more reinforcing consequences when employing this kind of program.

It is important to note that the efficacy of the reinforcement process depends a great deal on the meaning behind the occurrence of reward (Coates & Thoresen, 1979). True self-reward may be dependent on the subject's viewing the achievement as laudable rather than simply attaining an arbitrarily set criterion (Kanfer, 1977). Programming self-attribution for change may avoid both failures in immediate and long-term impact of self-control.

Finally, the actual rather than anticipated effects of naturally occurring consequences for desired behavior must be gauged to avoid failure. For example, scholastic gains may be accompanied by increased parental expectations and demands, and conquering a small animal phobia may mean more "roughing it" with the family. A poignant example of failure due to unassessed naturally occurring consequences was seen in the unanticipated weight gain on the part of several attractive, young, previously obese women who had to that point been successful in their self-control programs. Additional analysis revealed that the role change from being viewed as a sisterly, unattractive, matronly individual to being regarded as an attractive, young, and sexually stimulating woman was more than these women had bargained for. This consequence, which might have appeared to be an additional bonus for weight control, actually functioned to punish adaptive responding. Perhaps if the subjects had been prepared for such a change in roles, this consequence could have functioned to support weight loss, or the disruptive nature of the change could have been minimized.

NEGATIVE AND POSITIVE CONTINGENCY FAILURES

This section will not employ an especially broad conceptualization of the question of "which treatments"; instead it will deal solely with the use of negative and positive contingencies in treatment. There is, unfortunately, not enough comparative research with clear results to warrant statements about the overall differential efficacy of specific self-control treatment techniques. In fact, research in self-control might continue to benefit from comparative research. Rather than exposing a single identified technology to repeated investigation, researchers in the area of self-control would do well to look at comparative efficacy of theoretically different methods of inducing self-change (Goldfried, 1980; Hersen, 1981). However, this presentation of differences in contingency control can serve to illustrate cases in which failure of self-control is due to selection of an inadequate treatment, and it may suggest means of avoiding such failure or of recognizing early signs of treatment inadequacy.

Negative Contingencies

As has already been noted, self-monitoring is less effective when a negative consequence follows the behavior (Lipinski et al., 1975). Furthermore, the rate at which individuals actually administer the contingency and the rate at which they drop out of treatment is increased by the use of negative contingencies (Kanfer, 1977). Some clinicians report that side effects from the use of self-punishment are similar to side effects of externally imposed punishment, with resultant hostility and avoidance. Others report that some forms of self-punishment, such as slapping one's wrist with a rubber band, are trivial and have little influence on many subjects (e.g., Mahoney, 1974). In general, even when self-punishment procedures are immediately successful, unless the behavior change is reinforced and comes under its own contingency control, it may be unreasonable to expect behavior to continue to be maintained in the long run by self-punishment. Finally, self-punishment may be contraindicated in situations in which the client is highly stressed, angry, or depressed, both because of motivational problems in administration and because of the negative affect that may result (Glasgow & Rosen, 1980). In general, failures in self-control due to negative contingencies may be avoided by the judicious selection of negative reinforcers only when there is a clear advantage over positive reinforcers (Homer & Peterson, 1980), by ensuring the effectiveness of the negative consequence, and by using concommitant reinforcement for adaptive behavior.

An example of a case where the latter points were not initially followed may serve as an illustration. The client, Jack, wished to cut down his rate of smoking. As part of his response-cost program, he smoked only in the tool shed, in order to reduce the number of "positive" events that were paired with smoking. He also contingently applied negative self-statements concerning the health hazards of smoking. Jack's self-monitoring records indicated a slight decrease, followed by a large and maintained increase in number of cigarettes smoked. Interviews with Jack revealed that after he had become accustomed to the tool shed it had ceased to be a punishing experience. Indeed, with his chaotic and demanding family life, the escape to the tool shed (dark and dirty though it was) had become a positive experience. In addition, even the "negative" self-statements concerning the health hazards of smoking may not have resulted in a punishing contingency. The guilt-ridden client reported feeling as though perhaps he "deserved" such health hazards and reported a curious satisfaction following the application of the negative self-statements. The switch from ineffective negative contingencies to positive contingencies for resisting urges to smoke was highly successful with this client, and had positive side effects in the form of increased self-confidence and self-esteem.

This discussion should not be interpreted to indicate that negative consequences should be totally avoided in self-control programs. However, awareness of unforeseen changes in the client's motivation for therapy or the power of the negative stimulus, as well as monitoring side effects and long-term effects of the negative consequence, may be necessary to avoid failures. As will be seen in the next section, even the use of positive consequences can lead to failures of self-control under some circumstances.

Positive Contingencies

Failures with positive as well as negative contingencies can be the result of inadequate determination of the consequence's stimulus properties (Homer & Peterson, 1980). As has been noted earlier, the consequence must be more compelling than competing reinforcers. It must be under the client's own control and to ensure maintenance, it must not be susceptible to satiation or it must give way to other, more naturally occurring reinforcers.

The consequences for success at adaptive responding should be even more positive than the consequences for mere attempts at adaptive responding. For example, failure in self-control may occur if self-reinforcement and reinforcement of others requires that the patient experience difficulty in attaining the designated behavior and fails to occur if the response is easily accomplished. This traps the client into a pattern of incomplete adaptive behavior, by reinforcing only a chain of maladaptive behavior followed by adaptive behavior. For example, Shelly was initially extremely uncomfortable in unstructured interpersonal situations like parties. As long as she experienced some tension, was apprehensive, and then bravely conquered these feelings, she received praise from her husband and herself. But when she managed to attend a dinner party without the typical precursors of anxiety and self-doubt, she noted that she felt let down and unsatisfied. Coping with anxiety, not nonanxious behavior, had inadvertently been reinforced. Additional structure to insure reinforcement of the final designated behavior was necessary to avoid failure in this case.

Occasionally, failure in self-control may be due to the communicative function of the positive stimulus. Kirschenbaum and his associates (Kirschenbaum & Karoly, 1977; Tomarken & Kirschenbaum, in 1982) have investigated causes of self-regulatory failure; they report an interesting interaction between type of stimulus considered and type of task. On high mastery academic tasks in which subjects perceived themselves as skilled, monitoring their own number of successes led to failure in self-regulation more often than monitoring the number of nonsuccessful problem solutions (Kirschenbaum & Karoly, 1977; Masters & Santrock, 1976; Wade, 1974). However, under low mastery academic tasks where subjects were not yet skilled, positive self-monitoring resulted in fewer failures than negative self-monitoring (Ewart, 1978; Gottman & McFall, 1972). Moreover, in cases where monitoring successful behavior is less effective than monitoring failures, subjects do not appear to use self-reward or experience positive affect upon positive self-monitoring (Tomarken & Kirschenbaum, in 1982). Future research may help to predict which type of monitoring is to be preferred under what circumstances.

Another commonly reported area of self-control failure induced by positive contingencies may be found when the positive contingencies are superfluous. Many clients report that overt self-reinforcement seems artificial (Richards, 1981), some researchers argue it can be embarrassing (Coates & Thoresen, 1979), and subjects may fail to utilize overt self-control (McReynolds, 1973). Cesa (1974) and Richards et al. (1976) reported that self-reinforcement did not add to the effectiveness of a study skills package, and the addition of self-reinforcement appeared to result in more failures to follow through with the program. Similarly, Barrera and Rosen (1977) found that adding a self-reward component to a self-desensitization program resulted in increased failures to follow through. It should be noted that in none of the cases in this section is "self-reinforcement" an accurate label. Inasmuch as reinforcement by definition increases the specified behavior, failures in self-control due to the misapplication of positive contingencies cannot properly be termed "reinforcement." Perhaps this functional definition must be utilized when planning and incorporating positive contingencies into self-control programs.

SUBJECT CHARACTERISTICS AND SELF-CONTROL FAILURE

There is a variety of differences between subjects that may be predictive of failure in self-control. Perhaps if attention were focused not on which subjects would ultimately succeed but on which would ultimately fail, programs could use a branching strategy where incipient failures would receive more or different instructions (Mitchell, Hall, & Piatowski, 1975).

A variety of subject characteristics and behaviors may be useful in predicting self-control failures. For example, Kirschenbaum, Humphrey, and Malett (1981) noted that subjects with lower GPAs expected more and ultimately did less in a study improvement program than subjects with higher grades. These authors suggest that low GPA students may be more likely to emit intention statements, experience self and other directed reinforcement for the intention statements alone, and thus fail to actually change their study behavior. In contrast, McFall and Hammen (1971) discovered that clients who reported being highly motivated to stop smoking were more likely to actually stop than subjects not reporting these high levels of motivation (unfortunately, these subjects were no more likely to *maintain* their abstinence than subjects with less motivation). Marston and McFall (1971) reported that those subjects most likely to fail in a smoking cessation program showed a different early pattern of smoking, experiencing a brief drop and then a rise in smoking following treatment, as opposed to a continuous decrease experienced by successful subjects. In addition, Marston and McFall (1971) examined 18 "background variables" of the subjects to ascertain their role in self-control failure. Although only "years of smoking" correlated with baserate, GPA was correlated with immediate program success (lower grades = more failures) and smoking in the subjects' mothers, and subject gender were correlated with long-term success. Men whose mothers did not smoke were ultimately more likely to fail (unfortunately, these two factors were confounded—women were more likely to have mothers who smoked). None of the other background variables predicted treatment success or failure.

In general, failure in self-control may be negatively correlated with early attempts at success in treatment. Pomerleau and Pomerleau (1977) found that individuals who did not complete early assignments were less likely to succeed than those who did, and Bellack, Glanz, and Simon (1976) noted that poor performance in a self-reinforcement task was typical of unsuccessful subjects. Several investigators have reported that subjects with poor self-monitoring performance are more likely to fail to control their own behavior (e.g. Jeffrey, Vender, & Wing, 1978; Stuart, 1967).

Observation of naturally occurring successes and failures also may highlight relevant subject characteristics for self-control programs. For example, Leon and Chamberlain (1973) noted that subjects who failed to maintain their weight loss one year after treatment ate high-caloric snacks that were not cued by hunger in a variety of situations. Perri, Richards, and Schultheis (1977) determined that success in smoking reduction was related to the use of multiple techniques, self-reinforcement, and problem solving. Doerfler and Richards (1981) observed that individuals who failed to successfully cope with depression made fewer dramatic changes in their social environment and seemed to have less confidence in positive self-instruction than did successful persons. Similarly, Heffernan and Richards (1981) reported that subjects who were successful at controlling their study behavior utilized more techniques, more self-reward, more self-monitoring, and more stimulus control in the form of schedule planning and isolation from distraction. Finally, Perri and Richards (1977) interviewed successful and unsuccessful subjects who had attempted to control their overeating, smoking, studying, or dating. Their results suggested that using more techniques for longer periods of time and using self-reinforcement successfully avoided failure for most of these subjects. Different behavior problems required different techniques for resolution, however. There were not significant relationships between subjects' internal–external locus of control and their success at self-control procedures.

There have been some suggestions that variables such as external–internal control or susceptibility to somatic stress may influence one's ability to induce self-control, but there are few demonstrations of such effects (Kanfer, 1977). A unique area that appears to confirm the role of dispositional variables is found in research analyzing self-control in medical settings. This research has most often examined coping styles characterized by active or avoiding responses. Individuals labeled as sensitizers or vigilants are thought to be characterized by intellectualization and active attention toward the stressor; they deal with stress by seeking out information, familiarizing themselves with the procedures involved, and by attempting to mitigate their responses to it. Repressors or avoiders deny or avoid stressful stimuli and typically fail to prepare for or actively deal with stressful events (e.g., Epstein & Fenz, 1967). In one study using such a dichotomy of actual responding, Cohen and Lazarus (1973) suggested that vigilant copers experienced slower recovery, more post-operative days in the hospital, and a higher rate of complications, whereas individuals characterized as avoiders recovered much more quickly and easily. Later research suggested that preoperative preparation had a negative impact on repressor subjects, a positive impact on neutral (neither repressor nor sensitizer) subjects, and no influence on sensitizer subjects (Andrew, 1970; DeLong, 1971). In summary, avoiding or repressing stress may be an effective coping strategy for some patients and in such cases, it would appear that self-control failures may be produced by typical psychological preparation (e.g., Shipley, Butt, Horwitz, & Farbry, 1978). The extent to which characteristic modes of responding may influence attempts at self-control in other areas remains unclear at this time. Further data on these and other subject characteristics may lead to increased individualization and treatment matching, and thus to fewer self-control failures in a variety of problem areas.

DESIGNATED BEHAVIOR AND FAILURE

Self-control treatments have, on at least one occasion, demonstrated immediate or long-term success with each of the designated behaviors described to this point. In other words, self-control procedures show a wide range of limited successes. A review of the other side of the coin, the differential failure rates with the myriad behaviors that have been selected as appropriate for self-control technology is out of the scope of this chapter. Furthermore, most clinicians would argue that failure should not be ascribed to the designated behavior itself but rather to an inappropriate matching of the behavior and treatment modality. However, it will be argued here that certain general properties of behavior may make specific responses more or less susceptible to self-control procedures.

First, the degree to which the current technology rests upon an accurate theoretical conceptualization of the behavioral problem will influence the degree of self-control success (Leventhal & Cleary, 1980; McFall, 1980). For example, recent discussion concerning reasons for failure in smoking cessation has suggested that an accurate theory concerning the maintenance of smoking behavior has not been forthcoming (McFall, 1978), and other researchers have argued that current conceptualizations of "physiological" as opposed to "psychological" addiction are not useful in the treatment of drug addiction (Peele, 1980). The circularity of such arguments is, of course, inevitable—the conceptualization is inadequate because it fails to produce a treatment technology that can maintain success, and the failure which is observed then is subscribed to the lack of conceptualization. It should be noted that the success of a technology does not necessarily demonstrate the accuracy of the conceptualization behind the technology. Aspirin cures headaches, yet headaches are not due to lack of aspirin. However, repeated failure of attempts to employ a variety of technologies to a problem does suggest to many investigators the need for new conceptualizations.

Interestingly, this seems particularly to be the case for specific behaviors that have already been the focal point of several previous theoretical explications. For example, Leventhal and Cleary (1980) provide a comprehensive review of the many theoretical models of smoking maintenance. They describe models of intervention in which smoking is regarded as an operant behavior susceptible to reinforcement, self-monitoring, and contingency contracting, or as a sign for the need for dynamic psychotherapy. Intervention models used by physicians, clinics, hypnotists, and those relying on sensory deprivation are then described. The public health model or mass communications model which deals with media attitude change, both leading toward and away from smoking is also discussed. When describing theories of smoking, Leventhal and Cleary (1980) note a variety of theories of stages or ontogeny of smoking, as well as pharmacological theories of smoking emphasizing fixed effects, nicotine regulation, and multiple regulation. They then review studies that fail to support the theories that have been proposed, and note that failure of intervention may be largely due to failure of the conceptualization of smoking. Finally, Leventhal and Cleary make the case for a new conceptualization of smoking which emphasizes the need for prevention in early stages of becoming a smoker. This model combines stage theories and pharmacological conceptualizations with intervention ideas from behavior therapy. The resulting model may contribute greatly toward successful intervention, or may serve as a springboard for other conceptualizations. It should be noted, in contrast, that there are those who cry "enough" and urge researchers to spend more time attempting intervention and less time attempting theoretical explanations (Richards, 1981). Future research may yield empirical validation either to atheoretical approaches or to approaches that demand adequate theoretical conceptualization of intervention.

A second generalization may be made that can be equally controversial. Although there are undoubtedly exceptions, it would seem to be true that self-control procedures with a target of increasing a deficit behavior such as appropriate child-rearing behaviors (e.g., Christensen, 1976), assertive responding (e.g., Richey, 1978), and effective study skills (Richards, 1976) more often result in more immediate and maintained change than do programs with a target of behavioral excesses such as smoking (McFall, 1978), obesity (Stunkard, 1977), and alcoholism (Miller, 1977). The problem of inadequate conceptualization may still be valid here but, in addition, the ecological role of the behavior used as a target would seem to be important. Again, in general, the presence of the previously deficit behaviors might be expected to be continually (although intermittently) rewarded not only by the subject, but also by the environment in terms of fewer fights with siblings, rewards for competency in interpersonal interactions, and better grades. On the other hand, reinforcing the absence of a behavior is more difficult. The environmental rewards for abstaining from previous behavioral excesses may be absent ("I don't have lung cancer again today") or at least hard to detect ("This lack of a hangover sure feels great").

Furthermore, the immediately reinforcing and compelling nature of the maladaptive response is always available, in many cases being modeled by numerous others in the subject's immediate vicinity. For example, Al had quit smoking over the Christmas break. Although he felt proud of the change, he didn't notice any of the hoped for physical changes. He still puffed when he walked upstairs and coughed when he came in out of the cold (in fact, some physical changes were probably taking place, but so slowly as to be imperceptible). When Al went back to work in January, he rode in a car pool with four other smokers and he returned to his office where both secretaries chain-smoked in the desks next to his. There were also innumeral environmental cues for smoking such as the coffee cup previously paired with smoking, the water cooler where he could chat and have a smoke, the telephone bringing angry complaints accompanied by hurriedly lighting up, and the cigarettes and lighter in his desk. The reinforcing nature of the cigarette seemed all around him, whereas the benefits for abstinence seemed very far away indeed. Recalling the previous discussion on the dangers of competing reinforcers and the need for adequate recognition and control over relevant variables, it does seem appropriate to expect that the reduction of "appetitive" responses will, in general, be more resistant to self-control procedures than will the establishment of deficit behaviors.

Finally, the manner in which the subject defines the designated response will partially determine the efficacy of self-control techniques (Perri & Richards, 1977). Motivation to change, the degree to which the subject identifies with the behavior (as a smoker, a lousy student, an overeater, etc.), the perceived rewards (and punishments!) for altering the behavior, and the past history of controlling that particular behavior will all be likely to contribute to self-control success or failure.

LEVEL OF THERAPIST CONTACT AND FAILURE

An apparent paradox is found in early research in self-control; a great deal of therapist time and effort was required to ensure that the clients, not the therapist, would be able to institute behavioral change themselves. The paradox is more apparent than real; the goal of many therapist-directed programs was to teach clients to become their own therapists, to transfer the change procedures familiar to the therapist to the client (Richards & Perri, 1978). The amount of therapist contact necessary to successfully effect such a transfer is not clear at this time.

There are a variety of factors to consider when planning optimal therapist contact. Cost/benefit considerations may be the most obvious; the less therapist time required, the more clients can be served at lower cost. Similarly, if less therapist contact is required, less travel time for the client and less agency time for scheduling and record keeping is required. In contrast, if diminished time allotted to a client results in an increase in self-control failures, self-administered treatments might in the long run be more costly than therapist-directed change. In addition, some investigators have suggested that clients who self-administer treatment programs may in some cases experience an intensification rather than improvement in the behavior problem, and in self-administered programs, no one else is available to provide alternative treatment or referral (Glasgow & Rosen, 1980). Reduction in motivation may also occur with self-administered treatment which may preclude the client's seeking out therapist-directed assistance (Meyers, Cuvillier, Stalgaitis, & Cooke, 1980). Finally, failure to effect self-control may lead to less self-confidence and may limit other attempts at self-change (Kanfer & Karoly, 1972).

There are relatively few studies that have examined differing levels of therapist contact. The latest review of manuals used to self-administer self-help procedures (Glasgow & Rosen, 1978) noted, for example, that only 27 percent of studies using self-help manuals examined self-administration of the program, 41 percent utilized minimal therapist contact, 56 percent utilized therapist-administered contact, and therapist-directed behavior was often compared with these forms of therapy. Furthermore, the studies that have compared differing types of therapist contact have reported contradictory results. Some studies have reported that self-administration of desensitization results in continued improvement not seen in therapist-directed desensitization subjects (Rosen, 1976), whereas others have noted a very high (50 percent) dropout rate in self-administered treatment subjects (e.g., Marshall, Presse, & Andrews, 1976; Rosen, Glasgow, & Barrera, 1977). Similarly, Hagen (1974) noted that self-administered weight control treatment was as effective as both minimal and traditional therapist contact but later research using the same manual suggested that self-administered treatment was much less effective than therapist-administered treatment (Stunkard & Mahoney, 1976). Many researchers have reported failures of bibliotherapy approaches for alcohol abstinence (Glasgow & Rosen, 1978) but others report bibliotherapy to be as effective as 10 sessions of therapist-directed behavioral self-control and relaxation training (Miller & Taylor, 1980). Some problems such as agoraphobia contraindicate complete self-administration of treatment (Sutherland, Amit, & Weiner, 1977), and there is little research to suggest that self-administered therapy can effectively reduce smoking or sexual problems or can train assertive, socially appropriate, or general self-control behaviors (Glasgow & Rosen, 1978). Present data suggest that complete self-administration increases the likelihood of failures in self-control in several areas.

In contrast, there is a growing body of literature to suggest that minimal therapist contact can avoid self-control failures. Numerous studies have shown that with minimal therapist contact clients can successfully utilize desensitization procedures (e.g., Baker, Cohen, & Saunders, 1973; Cotter, 1970; Donner & Guerny, 1969; Morris & Thomas, 1973). Agoraphobic women using a self-help manual required half the therapist contact usually required and still met with successful results (Mathews, Teasdale, Munby, Johnston, & Shaw, 1977). Similar findings have resulted with sexual therapy (Kass & Stauss, 1975; Lowe & Mikulas, 1975) and weight control (Hanson, Borden, Hall, & Hall, 1976). At times, therapist contact of just six minutes per week can make a large difference in avoiding failures of self-control (Zeiss, in press). In general, the optimal cost-benefit solution may be reached by providing minimal therapist contact and then increasing therapist contact if individualization is needed (Mitchell et al., 1975) or if failure seems likely. Similarly, the frequency of therapist contact can be decreased, if self-control progresses successfully, to facilitate generalization (e.g., Richards et al., 1976). Other techniques that may avoid failure include the use of a buddy system to prompt continued self-control (Karol & Richards, 1981) and the involvement of spouse support (Brownell, Heckerman, Westlake, Hayes, & Monti, in press). In general, the greatest maintenance can be expected for subjects who largely self-direct therapy, whereas greater generalization can be anticipated from therapist-directed self-control programs (Glasgow & Rosen, 1978). Thus in the words of one knowledgable researcher, "the therapist needs to strike a sagacious compromise between the quixotic ideals of perfection (endless treatment) and the exigencies of reality (no treatment)" (Richards, 1980).

FAILURES IN MAINTENANCE

Perhaps the most ubiquitous source of failure in self-control research is time (Richards, 1978). Successful treatment strategies are reported, only to be labeled as failures upon subsequent follow-up (e.g., Davidson & Denney, 1976; McFall, 1977; Richards & Perri, 1978; Stunkard, 1977). This problem is not limited to self-control procedures. Inasmuch as many of the previously described sources of failure include mention of maintenance problems, this discussion will be short-lived, as are many of the treatment effects to be described.

Specifically, this section will describe some recent attempts to program self-control maintenance. Richards et al. (1976) completed one of the better known attempts to foster generalization in self-control. Their study utilized study skills plus self-control strategies, and compared faded therapist contact over a six-week period with steady therapist contact. Fading therapist contact resulted in substantially less self-control failure than did the more traditional, continued therapist contact. In a subsequent study, Richards and Perri (1978) utilized fading of study skills and self-control training over a briefer period of three weeks, in comparison with no fading, and also examined a second maintenance strategy—a variant of D'Zurilla and Goldfried's (1971) problem-solving skills. Subjects receiving the latter maintenance strategy were given intensive training in orienting themselves to the problem, generating alternatives, making decisions, and verifying results. Findings indicated that the brief fading procedure was as prone to self-control failure as was the continuous treatment modality. However, the problem solving treatments significantly retarded failure, resulting in substantially more maintenance in study skills as indexed by GPA at 12-week and 1-year follow-up points.

Other investigations of self-control maintenance have utilized continued intermittent contact with therapeutic tools and agents (Best, Bass, & Owen, 1977; Elliott & Denney, 1978). For example, Cohen, Gelfand, Dodd, Jensen, and Turner (1980) found that subjects who continued self-monitoring following the end of the program experienced substantially better maintenance of weight loss. Similarly, Karol and Richards (1981) prolonged therapeutic contact by asking individuals in a smoking reduction program to make supportive phone calls to one another for three weeks following the end of treatment. Such supportive intervention involved training the group members to behave as therapists using role play and homework contracts. Modest improvements in maintenance were observed at an 8-month follow-up. Similar booster treatment effects were obtained in a nail biting reduction program (Spevak & Richards, 1980), with maintenance bibliotherapy and bibliotherapy plus phone call booster resulting in improved self-control even at a 10-month follow-up. Extending control to other agents who may persistently prompt self-control (e.g., Brownell et al., in press) also promises to reduce self-control failure.

Fisher et al. (1982) note that the maintenance of self-control responses is constantly threatened by fluctuations in the potential reinforcers and punishers in the environment. Their self-initiated self-control model utilizes properties similar to the problem-solving strategy described above, and attempts to generate individualized self-control strategies that have one's own problem behaviors as targets. The ability to generate alternative strategies might result in increased flexibility in self-change and thus decreased failure to maintain self-control. Long-term follow-up for the use of this self-initiated control model is not available, and 6- and 8-month follow-ups of smoking and weight reduction, respectively, do not overwhelmingly support maintenance of self-initiated self-control at this time. However, this research does show some promise in the self-initiated treatment modality.

Another approach to prevention of maintenance failure has been advanced by Marlatt and Gordon (1980). This approach is directed towards occasions on which relapse occurs. Marlatt and Gordon suggest training a variety of coping responses to be used in high-risk situations, both to increase chances of immediate success and impressions of self-efficacy in avoiding relapse. In addition, a set of backup skills are trained in case a minor relapse should take place. Backup skills may insure that self-control is reattained quickly. Finally, balancing lifestyle demands and acceptable rewards may assist in subjects' maintenance of self-imposed changes.

Future research should continue to attempt to train maintenance skills. In addition, research must continue to gather long-term follow-up data, *especially* when such data are disappointing. It is only by such work, possibly utilizing increased individual therapeutic flexibility and continued environmental prompts, that self-control failure can be avoided where it counts—in the long run.

PHILOSOPHICAL FAILURES

When is successful self-control not successful? When it fails to provide what the individual hoped to gain by controlling his or her own behavior. To some extent, the points to follow may be related to previously described problems. For example, establishing a reasonable criteria for behavior, the subject's own perception of the problem behavior, and the fluctuations in the value of the behavior all stem from the subject's philosophy of self-change. However, the question posed in the introduction to this chapter inquired about the reason behind the quest for self-control and this "what for" issue is separable from the "why" and "how" questions discussed previously.

Mahoney (1980) cogently argues for a more complete assessment of the goals of self-change prior to embarking on a self-improvement project. In a society seemingly obsessed with self and with self-improvement, in which therapeutic technologies are becoming increasingly commercial (Barlow, 1980), sometimes making exaggerated claims for successful outcome with minimal labor (Glasgow & Rosen, 1978), individuals are often urged to utilize the right program for the right behavior problem—for the *wrong* reason. Mahoney (1980) notes that individuals attempting self-change form a continuum, ranging from individuals with a sound sense of self-worth who wish simply to change a problematic behavior to persons "who seem to be dominated by a deep sense of unworthiness, inadequacy, and sometimes even self contempt" whose "efforts at self-change are often both desperate and ambivalent" (p. 127). These individuals often attempt to parlay a change in one or more problem behaviors into a change in self-identity or self-worth. Rather than attacking this negative self-perception directly, these individuals will attempt to alter what they identify as the source of their negative evaluation, attacking appearance via weight control and exercise, acquiring interpersonal and academic skills, or removing emotional crutches such as drinking or smoking. However, such approaches rarely result in a more acceptable self and the disappointment that accompanies self-rejection in spite of weight loss, new skills, or sought after abstinence typifies this failure in self-control.

LaGesse (1981) reported on Professor Fred McKinney who is doing a 40-year follow-up of past clients. Dr. McKinney described the example of a man who wrote a long, beautifully articulated letter to his therapist. The letter described in excellent prose the student's feelings of failure and self-rejection, and absolved the therapist from blame. This conclusion stood in stark contrast to the student's evident success with the inability to write well, the problem for which the student had sought help.

Perhaps "what for" should be the initial question pursued prior to embarking on a program to institute self-control. The therapeutic benefit anticipated from the procedure must be worthy of the cost the person may incur (Gilbert, 1978), and the primary goal of the project should be an end itself, rather than an indirect method aimed at redefining self (Mahoney, 1980). In the clear articulation of the answer to the question "what for" may lie a source of problem assessment and motivation, and a delineation of reinforcer power for the individuals choosing to control their own behavior.

SUMMARY AND CONCLUSIONS

There are undoubtedly still other sources of self-control failure that have not been examined here. If failure is regarded as the absolute or inevitable outcome of self-control procedures, then most clinicians in this field might choose to quit what they are doing altogether or at least find definitive ways to ascertain early in treatment who will fail, so that they may refer that person on to another therapist! Fortunately, failure can be viewed in quite another light. From failures in self-control, we can learn a great deal about success in self-control (Richards, 1980).

Failure in individual attempts at self-control, for example, may simply function as feedback: the monitoring system used is too complex, too intrusive, or too costly. The problem behavior has been incorrectly identified or the criterion for behavior is too high. Similarly, a failure in stimulus control may simply provide a cue for the use of available, more potent consequences for desirable behaviors.

Repeated failure across subjects to have an impact on a specific problem area may indicate a failure of the current conceptual model of that response pattern. This failure should serve as a spur toward more accurate theoretical representations of the behavior, and/or additional technologies to compete with the stimulus control of undesirable behaviors.

Failure to produce a treatment that can be entirely self-administered may cue additional research in individualizing and strengthening the self-administered program, and in assessing the optimal amount of therapist contact necessary for success. Similarly, short-term success followed by long-term relapse may call for increasing the use of maintenance providing skills within the client, such as self-monitoring, problem solving, and self-initiated change, as well as providing continued intermittent therapeutic intervention in the form of faded therapist contact and repeated environmental prompts.

These suggestions are not meant to minimize the discouraging and frustrating nature of attempts to provide self-control that ultimately fail. However, researchers who investigate self-control techniques with the expectation of demonstrated maintained success may be giving the wrong answer to the question "what for." An adaptive philosophical approach to the problem of self-control research may be to regard failures as challenges to current technology and as questions to be answered by future research. Although progress in self-control interventions may have been disappointing, this is no time to abandon the effort. Researchers and therapists must continue to move forward together, even when that movement is slow and unsteady, toward the goal of eventual success. If this goal is discarded, we must admit that self-control will always fail. If self-control always fails, it will be because clients can never learn to be their own therapists. If clients cannot be their own therapists, they will need to be in therapy forever. And if they will need to be in therapy forever, therapy will forever fail.

REFERENCES

Andrew, J. (1970) Recovery from surgery, with and without preparatory instruction for three coping styles. *Journal of Personality and Social Psychology,* **15,** 223–226.

Anonymous (1980) Personal Communication.

Baker, B. L., Cohen, D. C., & Saunders, J. T. (1973) Self-directed desensitization for acrophobia. *Behaviour Research and Therapy,* **11,** 79–89.

Barlow, D. (1980) Behavior therapy: The next decade. *Behavior Therapy,* **11,** 315–328.

Barrera, M., Jr., & Glasgow, R. E. (1976) Design and evaluation of a personalized instruction course in behavioral self-control. *Teaching of Psychology,* **3,** 81–83.

Barrera, M., Jr., & Rosen, G. M. (1977) Detrimental effects of a self-reward contracting program on subjects' involvement in self-administered desensitization. *Journal of Consulting and Clinical Psychology,* **45,** 1180–1181.

Bellack, A. S., Glanz, L., & Simon, R. (1976) Self-reinforcement style and covert imagery in the treatment of obesity. *Journal of Consulting and Clinical Psychology,* **44,** 490–491.

Best, J. A., Bass, R., & Owen, L. E. (1977) Mode of service delivery in a smoking cessation program for public health. *Canadian Journal of Public Health,* **68,** 469–473.

Brownell, K. D., Heckerman, C. L., Westlake, R. V., Hayes, C. S., & Monti, P. M. (in press) The effect of couples training and partner cooperativeness in the behavioral treatment of obesity. *Behaviour Research and Therapy.*

Cesa, T. A. (1974) *Self-monitoring and self-reinforcement applied to junior college study behavior.* Unpublished master's thesis, University of the Pacific.

Christensen, A. (1976) Cost effectiveness in behavioral family therapy (Doctoral dissertation, University of Oregon). *Dissertation Abstracts International,* **37,** 3066–B (University Microfilms No. 75–27, 634)

Coates, T. J., & Thoresen, C. E. (1979) Behavioral self-control and educational practice or do we really need self-control? In D. Berlinger (Ed.), *Review of Research in Education.* Stasca, Ill.: Praeger.

Cohen, E. A., Gelfand, D. M., Dodd, D. K., Jensen, J., & Turner, C. (1980) Self-control practices associated with weight loss maintenance in children and adolescents. *Behavior Therapy,* **11,** 26–37.

Cohen, F., & Lazarus, R. S. (1973) Active coping processes, coping dispositions, and recovery from surgery. *Psychosomatic Medicine,* **35,** 375–389.

Colletti, G., & Kopel, S. A. (1979) Maintaining behavior change: An investigation of three maintenance strategies and the relationship of self-attribution to the long-term reduction of cigarette smoking. *Journal of Consulting and Clinical Psychology,* **47,** 614–617.

Cotter, S. B. (1970) Sex differences and generalization of anxiety reduction with automated desensitization and minimal therapist interaction. *Behaviour Research and Therapy,* **8,** 273–285.

Davidson, A., & Denney, D. R. (1976) Covert sensitization and information in the reduction of nailbiting. *Behavior Therapy,* **7,** 512–518.

DeLong, D. R. (1971) *Individual differences in patterns of anxiety arousal, stress-relevant information and recovery from surgery.* Unpublished doctoral dissertation, University of California, Los Angeles.

Dixon, D. N., Heppner, P. P., Petersen, C. H., & Ronning, R. R. (1979) Problem-solving workshop training. *Journal of Counseling Psychology,* **26,** 133–139.

Doerfler, L. A., & Richards, C. S. (1981) Self-initiated attempts to cope with depression. *Cognitive Therapy and Research,* **5,** 367–371.

Donner, L., & Guerny, B. E., Jr. (1969) Automated group desensitization for test anxiety. *Behaviour Research and Therapy,* **7,** 1–13.

D'Zurilla, T. J., & Goldfried, M. R. (1971) Problem solving and behavior modification. *Journal of Abnormal Psychology,* **78,** 107–126.

Elliott, C. H., & Denney, D. R. (1978) A multiple component treatment approach to smoking. *Journal of Consulting and Clinical Psychology,* **46,** 1330–1339.

Epstein, L. H., Webster, J. S., & Miller, P. M. (1975) Accuracy and controlling effects of self-monitoring as a function of concurrent responding and reinforcement. *Behavior Therapy,* **6,** 654–666.

Epstein, S., & Fenz, W. D. (1967) The detection of areas of emotional stress through variations in perceptual threshold and physiological arousal. *Journal of Experimental Research in Personality,* **2,** 191–199.

Ewart, C. K. (1978) Self-observation in natural environments: Reactive effects of behavior desirability and goal-setting. *Cognitive Therapy and Research,* **2,** 39–56.

Fisher, L. B., Levenkron, J. C., Lowe, M. R., Loro, A. D., & Greer, L. (1982) Self-initiated self-control in risk reduction. In R. Stuart (Ed.), *Adherence, generalization, and maintenance in behavioral medicine.* New York: Brunner/Mazel.

Gilbert, T. F. (1978) *Human competence: Engineering worthy performance.* New York: McGraw-Hill.

Glasgow, R. E., & Rosen, G. M. (1978) Behavioral bibliotherapy: A review of self-help behavior therapy manuals. *Psychological Bulletin,* **85,** 1–23.

Glasgow, R. E., & Rosen, G. M. (1980) Self-help behavior therapy manuals: Recent developments and clinical usage. *Clinical Behavior Therapy Review,* **1,** No. (1), 1–20.

Goldfried, M. R. (1980) Toward the delineation of therapeutic change principles. *American Psychologist,* **35,** 991–999.

Gottman, J. M., & McFall, R. M. (1972) Self-monitoring effects in a program for potential high school dropouts: A time series analysis. *Journal of Consulting and Clinical Psychology,* **39,** 273–281.

Hagen, R. L. (1974) Group therapy vs. bibliotherapy in weight reduction. *Behavior Therapy,* **5,** 222–234.

Hanson, R. W., Borden, B. L., Hall, S. M., & Hall, R. E. (1976) Use of programmed instruction in teaching self-management skills to overweight adults. *Behavior Therapy,* **7,** 366–373.

Heffernan, T., & Richards, C. S. (1981) Self-control of study behavior: Identification and evaluation of natural methods. *Journal of Counseling Psychology, 28,* 361–364.

Heppner, P. P. (1978) The clinical alteration of covert thoughts: A critical review. *Behavior Therapy,* **9,** 717–734.

Hersen, M. (1981) Complex problems require complex solutions. *Behavior Therapy,* **12,** 15–29.

Homer, A. L., & Peterson, L. (1980) Differential reinforcement of other behavior: A preferred response elimination procedure. *Behavior Therapy,* **11,** 449–471.

Jeffrey, R. W., Vender, M., & Wing, R. R. (1978) Weight loss and behavior change one year after behavioral treatment for obesity. *Journal of Consulting and Clinical Psychology,* **46,** 368–369.

Kanfer, F. H. (1977) The many faces of self-control or behavior modification changes its focus. In R. B. Stuart (Ed.), *Behavioral self-management.* New York: Brunner/Mazel.

Kanfer, F. H., & Grimm, L. E. (1977) Behavioral analysis: Selecting target behaviors in the interview. *Behavior Modification,* **1,** 7–28.

Kanfer, F. H., & Karoly, P. (1972) Self-control: A behavioristic excursion into the lion's den. *Behavior Therapy,* **3,** 398–416.

Karol, R. L., & Richards, C. S. (1981) *Cognitive maintenance strategies for smoking reduction. JSAS Catalog of Selected Documents in Psychology*, *11*, 15. (ms. no. 2204).

Karoly, P. (1980) Self-management problems in children. In E. J. Mash, & L. E. Terdal (Eds.), *Behavioral assessment of childhood disorders.* New York: Guildord.

Kass, D. J., & Stauss, F. (1975) *Sex therapy at home.* New York: Simon & Schuster.

Kirschenbaum, D. S., Humphrey, L. L., & Malett, S. D. (1981) Specificity of planning in adult self-control: An applied investigation. *Journal of Personality and Social Psychology, 40*, 941–950.

Kirschenbaum, D. S., & Karoly, P. (1977) When self-regulation fails: Tests of some preliminary hypotheses. *Journal of Consulting and Clinical Psychology,* **45,** 1116–1125.

LaGesse, D. (1981) At peace with his time. *Columbia Daily Tribune,* Sunday, January 4, pp. 37–39.

Lansky, D. (1981) A methodological analysis of research on adherance and weight loss: Reply to Brownell and Stunkard (1978). *Behavior Therapy,* **12,** 144–149.

Leon, G. R., & Chamberlain, K. (1973) Emotional arousal, eating patterns, and body image as differential factors associated with varying success in maintaining weight loss. *Journal of Consulting and Clinical Psychology,* **40,** 474–480.

Leventhal, H., & Cleary, P. D. (1980) The smoking problem: A review of research and theory in behavioral risk modification. *Psychological Bulletin,* **88,** 370–405.

Lipinski, D. P., Black, J. L., Nelson, R. O., & Ciminero, A. R. (1975) The influence of motivational variables on the reactivity and reliability of self-recording. *Journal of Consulting and Clinical Psychology,* **43,** 637–646.

Lowe, J. C., & Mikulas, W. L. (1975) Use of written material in learning self-control of premature ejaculation. *Psychological Reports,* **37,** 295–298.

Mahoney, M. J. (1974) *Cognition and behavior modification.* Cambridge, Mass.: Ballinger.

Mahoney, M. J. (1977) Some applied issues in self-monitoring. In J. D. Cone, & R. P. Hawkins (Eds.), *Behavioral assessment: New directions in clinical psychology.* New York: Brunner/Mazel.

Mahoney, M. J. (1980) The perils of self-improvement. *Self,* **2,** 126–130.

Marlatt, G. A., & Gordon, J. R. (1980) Determinants of relapse: Implications for the maintenance of behavior change. In P. O. Davidson, & S. M. Davidson (Eds.), *Behaviour medicine: Changing health lifestyles.* New York: Brunner/Mazel.

Marshall, W. L., Presse, L., & Andrews, W. R. (1976) A self-administered program for public speaking anxiety. *Behaviour Research and Therapy,* **14,** 33–40.

Marston, A. R., & McFall, R. M. (1971) Comparison of behavior modification approaches to smoking reduction. *Journal of Consulting and Clinical Psychology,* **36,** 153–162.

Masters, M. J., & Santrock, J. W. (1976) Studies in the self-regulation of behavior: Effects of contingent cognitive and affective events. *Developmental Psychology,* **12,** 334–348.

Mathews, A., Teasdale, J., Munby, M., Johnston, D., & Shaw, P. (1977) A home-based treatment program for agoraphobia. *Behavior Therapy,* **8,** 915–924.

McFall, R. M. (1977) Parameters of self-monitoring. In R. B. Stuart (Ed.), *Behavioral self-management.* New York: Brunner/Mazel.

McFall, R. M. (1978) Smoking-cessation research. *Journal of Consulting and Clinical Psychology,* **46,** 703–712.

McFall, R. M. (1980) Personal communication, November 17.

McFall, R. M., & Hammen, C. L. (1971) Motivation, structure, and self-monitoring: Role of nonspecific factors in smoking reduction. *Journal of Consulting and Clinical Psychology,* **37,** 80–86.

McReynolds, W. T. (1973) Self-control, study skills development and counseling approaches to the improvement of study behavior. *Behaviour Research and Therapy,* **11,** 233–235.

McReynolds, W. T. (1980) Personal communication, October 10.

Meichenbaum, D. (1973) Cognitive factors in behavior modification: Modifying what clients say to themselves. In C. M. Franks, & G. T. Wilson (Eds.), *Annual review of behavior therapy and practice* (Vol. 1). New York: Brunner/Mazel.

Menges, R. J., & Dobroski, B. J. (1977) Behavioral self-modification in instructional settings: A review. *Teaching of Psychology,* **14,** 168–173.

Meyers, A. W., Cuvillier, C., Stalgaitis, S., & Cooke, C. J. (1980) An evaluation of self-help treatment programs for weight loss. *The Behavior Therapist,* **3,** 25–26.

Miller, W. R. (1977) Behavioral self-control training in the treatment of problem drinkers. In R. B. Stuart (Ed.), *Behavioral self-management* New York: Brunner/Mazel.

Miller, W. R., & Taylor, C. A. (1980) Relative effectiveness of bibliotherapy, individual and group self-control training in the treatment of problem drinkers. *Addictive Behaviors,* **5,** 13–24.

Mitchell, K. R., Hall, R. F., & Piatowski, O. E. (1975) A group program for the treatment of failing college students. *Behavior Therapy,* **6,** 324–336.

Morris, L. M., & Thomas, C. R. (1973) Treatment of phobias by a self-administered desensitization technique. *Journal of Behavior Therapy and Experimental Psychiatry,* **4,** 397–399.

Nelson, R. O., Lipinski, D. P., & Black, J. L. (1976) The relative reactivity of external observations and self-monitoring. *Behavior Therapy,* **7,** 314–321.

Paul, G. L. (1967) Strategy of outcome research in psychotherapy. *Journal of Consulting Psychology,* **31,** 109–118.

Peele, S. (1980) Addiction to an experience. *American Psychologist,* **35,** 1047–1048.

Perri, M. G., & Richards, C. S. (1977) An investigation of naturally occurring episodes of self-controlled behaviors. *Journal of Counseling Psychology,* **24,** 178–183.

Perri, M. G., Richards, C. S., & Schultheis, K. R. (1977) Behavioral self-control and smoking reduction: A study of self-initiated attempts to reduce smoking. *Behavior Therapy,* **8,** 360–365.

Pomerleau, O. F., & Pomerleau, C. S. (1977) *Break the smoking habit: A behavioral program for giving up cigarettes.* Champaign, Ill.: Research Press.

Richards, C. S. (1976) Improving study behaviors through self-control techniques. In J.

D. Krumboltz, & C. E. Thoresen (Eds.), *Counseling techniques*. New York: Holt, Rinehart & Winston.

Richards, C. S. (1978) When self-control fails: A case study of the maintenance problem in self-control treatment programs. *Cognitive Therapy and Research,* **2,** 397–401.

Richards, C. S. (1980) Personal communication, October 24.

Richards, C. S. (1981) Improving college students' study behaviors through self-control techniques: A brief review. *Behavioral Counseling Quarterly*, *1*, 159–175.

Richards, C. S., & Perri, M. G. (1978) Do self-control treatments last? An evaluation of behavioral problem solving and faded counselor contact as treatment maintenance strategies. *Journal of Counseling Psychology,* **25,** 376–383.

Richards, C. S., Perri, M. G., & Gortney, C. (1976) Increasing the maintenance of self-control treatments through faded counselor contact and high information feedback. *Journal of Counseling Psychology,* **23,** 405–406.

Richards, C. S., McReynolds, W. T., Holt, S., & Sexton, T. (1976) Effects of information feedback and self-administered consequences on self-monitoring study behavior. *Journal of Counseling Psychology,* **23,** 316–321.

Richey, C. A. (1978) *Relative effectiveness of a group training program to increase social interaction skills among shy women.* Unpublished manuscript, University of Washington, Seattle. (Cited in Glasgow, R. E., & Rosen, G. M. Self-help behavior therapy manuals: Recent developments and clinical useage, *Clinical Behavior Therapy Review,* 1979, **1,** No. (1), 1–20.)

Rosen, G. M. (1976) *Don't be afraid: A program for overcoming your fears and phobias.* Englewood Cliffs, N. J.: Prentice-Hall.

Rosen, G. M., Glasgow, R. E., & Barrera, M., Jr. (1977) A two-year follow-up on systematic desensitization with data pertaining to the external validity of laboratory fear assessment. *Journal of Consulting and Clinical Psychology,* **45,** 1188–1189.

Shipley, R., Butt, J., Horwitz, B., & Farbry, J. (1978) Preparation for a stressful medical procedure: Effect of amount of stimulus pre-exposure and coping style. *Journal of Consulting and Clinical Psychology,* **46,** 499–507.

Spevak, P. A., & Richards, C. S. (1980) Enhancing the durability of treatment effects: Maintenance strategies in the treatment of nail biting. *Cognitive Therapy and Research,* **4,** 251–258.

Stuart, R. B. (1967) Behavioral control of over-eating. *Behaviour Research and Therapy,* **5,** 357–365.

Stuart, R. B. (1977) Self-help group approach to self-management. In R. B. Stuart (Ed.), *Behavioral self-management.* New York: Brunner/Mazel.

Stunkard, A. J. (1977) Behavioral treatments of obesity: Failure to maintain weight loss. In R. B. Stuart (Ed.), *Behavioral self-management.* New York: Brunner/Mazel.

Stunkard, A. J., & Mahoney, M. J. (1976) Behavioral treatment of the eating disorders. In H. Leitenberg (Ed.), *Handbook of behavior modification.* New York: Appleton-Century-Crofts.

Sutherland, E. A., Amit, Z., & Weiner, A. (1977) *Phobia free: How to fight your fears.* New York: Jove.

Tomarken, A. J., & Kirschenbaum, D. S. (1982) Self-regulatory failure: Accentuate the positive? *Journal of Personality and Social Psychology.*, *43*, 584–597.

Wade, T. C. (1974) Relative effects on performance and motivation of self-monitoring correct and incorrect responses. *Journal of Experimental Psychology,* **77,** 245–248.

Watson, D. L., & Tharp, R. G. (1977) *Self directed behavior: Self-modification for personal adjustment* (2nd ed.). Monterey, Calif.: Brooks/Cole.

Worthington, E. L. (1979) Behavioral self-control and the contract problem. *Teaching of Psychology,* **6,** 91–94.

Zeiss, R. A. (in press) Self-directed treatment for premature ejaculation. *Journal of Consulting and Clinical Psychology.*

CHAPTER 11

Behavioral Treatment of Depression: Examining Treatment Failures

ANTONETTE M. ZEISS
STANTON L. JONES

Depression can be described as a clinical syndrome, with depressed clients exhibiting various combinations of the class of behaviors termed "symptoms" of depression. Though classification schemes for grouping these depressive behaviors have varied widely (e.g., Beck, 1967; Feighner, Robins, Guze, Woodruff, Winokur, & Munoz, 1972; Grinker, Miller, Sabshin, Nunn, & Nunnally, 1961; Lewinsohn, Biglan, & Zeiss, 1976; Spitzer, Endicott, & Robins, 1978), there has been remarkable agreement about the behaviors that characterize depressed clients. These include, but are not limited to, dysphoria, anhedonia, disruptions in interpersonal functioning (including social withdrawal and ineffective social behavior such as whining and complaining), extremely negative self-evaluations (including self-depreciation, guilt, and feelings of helplessness), disruptions in normal cognitive functioning (such as inability to concentrate or make decisions, negative expectations, and interference with normal memory and thought), and somatic symptoms (including fatigue, sleep disturbance, loss of libido and appetite, gastrointestinal disturbances, and reports of excessive pain).

In order to discuss failures in the behavioral treatment of depression, certain foundational issues must be briefly addressed. The first is the behavioral model of depression, the second is the question of what constitutes a "behavioral treatment" of depression, and the final issue is the need to define what is meant by the term "failure."

BEHAVIORAL MODEL OF DEPRESSION

There are almost as many behavioral models of depression as there are researchers in the area. Rather than adding yet another theory or model to the literature, we follow Lewinsohn et al. (1976) in viewing decreased or low levels of response-contingent positive reinforcement as the primary etiological factor behind clinical depression. This model has maximum flexibility, in that it focuses upon

197

the common endpoint of a multitude of causal factors that relate to clinical depression rather than upon a particular deficit or process that is supposed to characterize all depressed persons. It is critical to emphasize that the Lewinsohnian model is not a narrow "social skills" model, but rather affords maximum flexibility by suggesting that *any* problematic behavior or behavior pattern that decreases the relative or absolute amount of response-contingent positive reinforcement received by an individual can lead to clinical depression.

In explaining this model of depression to our clients, we might say,

> You are depressed because you are not getting the satisfactions you want out of life. Now there may be any number of things causing this—you might be wanting too much, you might not have the skills to get what you want, something might be preventing you from enjoying what satisfactions you do obtain, or maybe some of the things you want are not possible. Whatever is keeping you from getting the life satisfactions that could eliminate your depression will be the target of our treatment.

BEHAVIORAL TREATMENT OF DEPRESSION

Behavioral treatment(s) of depression might be delineated either by the specific techniques used in the process of therapy or by the process by which therapy progresses. From the latter perspective, it generally holds that behavioral treatment typically begins with a thorough assessment of the presenting complaint itself and the spectrum of possible factors functionally related to the presenting depression. The behavior therapist would then utilize any of a variety of techniques within the context of the ongoing therapeutic process to *directly* and *measureably* change the problem behaviors specified by the assessment. Therapy would typically involve specifically delineated behavior changes, accomplished in part through the use of homework assignments.

It should be emphasized that in clinical practice the behavior therapist tailors his or her treatment approach to address the specific needs of the client. Although behavioral researchers often experimentally evaluate carefully defined and somewhat restrictive technique packages (e.g., Zeiss, Lewinsohn, & Muñoz, 1979), in clinical practice the behavioral clinician approaches the client with a variety of techniques chosen for their suitability for the client (e.g., Lewinsohn et al., 1976, McLean, 1976).

One can also define behavioral approaches to the treatment of depression by the specific techniques available to the therapist. Without referencing each technique, the spectrum of behavioral techniques utilized for depression includes assertiveness training, relaxation training, systematic desensitization, pleasant events planning, contingency management, social skills training, problem-solving training, self-management training, communications training, rational restructuring, and cognitive self-control techniques such as self-monitoring of thoughts, thought-stopping, and positive thought rehearsal.

Recently, Lewinsohn and his colleagues have been developing a treatment format for depression that is built around a 12-session, learning oriented treatment course. Participants in the group are screened to ensure that they are primarily depressed (rather than being better construed as having other problems). Participants then attend group sessions in which all of the treatments listed above are described and tried by all members of the group. Participants also read about these treatment modalities in a depression self-help book, *Control Your Depression* (Lewinsohn, Muñoz, Youngren, & Zeiss, 1978). The philosophy of the group is that, although no group member is likely to need *all* of the treatment ideas, each group member will be able to discover *some* ideas that are effective for their particular case. At the end of the group, each participant designs an individual maintenance program, incorporating the most useful material. Experiences with such groups in several locations with diverse leaders suggests this may be a particularly effective means of delivering treatment to depressed adults (Brown & Lewinsohn, in press; Muñoz, 1980; Youngren, 1980; Zeiss, 1980).

WAYS TO FAIL

There are many cases which might be construed by their therapists to be "failures." The following typology of failures has some intuitive appeal and will be followed here.

The first failures occur when clients drop out of therapy after a brief exposure. For example, a client comes for a long enough period to complete intake, gather some information about the proposed therapy, and perhaps even cooperate with the initial stages of treatment, but then chooses not to return. This type of failure is usually termed a "dropout."

Other clients may remain in therapy long enough for the planned interventions to be implemented, but the client passively resists change by not completing agreed upon assignments and instead treats therapy as a weekly chat or gripe session. These clients might be termed "noncooperators."

A different kind of failure occurs when a client actively participates in the prescribed therapeutic regimen of behavior change, but fails to derive any obvious benefit. This type of failure might be called a "nonresponder."

Finally, for some clients, therapy seems to have its intended impact. These clients might be judged to be clinically improved or even "cured" at treatment termination, only to be found to have regressed toward their pretreatment status after termination. Such failures might be called "relapsers."

Our plan for the balance of this chapter is to examine the empirical literature for any light that it might shed on the questions of who is most likely to fail and why, to share some case examples of failures from our clinical work, and to close with some speculations regarding the causes of failure, some suggestions for research in this area, and some important questions that we feel should be addressed on both conceptual and empirical levels.

Empirical Data on Treatment Failures

Detailed analyses of treatment failures have not been popular in the empirical treatment literature. Well controlled studies of the effectiveness of behavioral treatment of depression have not been as common as might have been supposed (Kovacs, 1979; Whitehead, 1979), and when well controlled studies have appeared, they have rarely included analyses of failures. Single case studies reporting failures have not been published, and published reports of group comparison studies have focused upon the indicators of degree of success. Rarely have differences between treatment successes and failures been examined. Those studies that have been exceptions to this rule will be examined below.

The researchers with the Depression Research Unit of Yale University have conducted several controlled comparisons of Interpersonal Psychotherapy (IPT) and pharmacotherapy (amitriptyline) both singly and as a combined treatment. The data from these studies have been analyzed in an attempt to delineate predictors of treatment responsiveness. IPT is a short-term psychotherapy that focuses upon "the client's depression in the context of current interpersonal relationships" (Zuckerman, Prusoff, Weissman, & Padias, 1980). It is not a behavioral approach per se, but *resembles* a behavioral approach in its focus upon the client's environmental context as a key factor in the presenting depression. Thus we will examine their results in the hope that this similarity might generate hypotheses relevant to failures in behavioral treatment.

Based upon earlier research, Weissman, Prusoff, and Klerman (1978) and Zuckerman et al. (1980) examined the utility of the Neuroticism Scale of the Maudsley Personality Inventory (MPI-N; Eysenck, 1959) in predicting outcome from their treatment programs (collapsing across treatment modalities in each case). Weissman et al. (1978) administered the MPI to 150 patients in their treatment program approximately one month after intake, and then collected clinical status ratings at termination (eight months after intake) and at follow-up (20 months and 48 months after intake). The clinical status ratings were a 3-point rating of the client as either "asymptomatic, moderate, or chronic" in terms of their depressive symptomatology. Although Weissman et al. asserted that MPI-N scores "were predictive of treatment outcome" (p.799), they presented only a single histogram without accompanying statistical tests to support their conclusion. This is particularly disappointing given the large sample size of the study, which would have allowed sophisticated multivariate analyses to have been performed. Such an analysis would have presupposed a more sophisticated methodology for assessing posttreatment clinical status.

In any case, the reported relationship between MPI-N scores and posttreatment depressive symptomatology was not replicated in their other study (Zuckerman et al., 1980). In this study, MPI-N scores were gathered at intake rather than after a month's treatment, thus avoiding potential biases introduced by quick treatment responders, and clinical ratings were gathered on well validated measures at follow-up, rather than on a 3-point scale. The authors found MPI-N scores to be unrelated to posttreatment depressive symptomatology. MPI-N scores were significantly related to the clients' posttreatment "Social Adjustment Self-Report Scale" scores, but this measure had no apparent relationship to clinical status. Thus MPI-N scores appear to have no real utility for predicting or explaining success from treatment.

Prusoff, Weissman, Klerman, and Rousaville (1980) examined the utility of differential diagnosis according to the Research Diagnostic Criteria (Spitzer et al., 1978) as a predictor of outcome for the same 81 patients studied by Zuckerman et al. (1980). In terms of patient responsiveness to IPT, the authors concluded that an RDC diagnosis of endogenous depression was a predictor of poor response to IPT alone, whereas patients classified as nonendogenous were superior responders to IPT alone. In the RDC system, endogeneity is rated as a dichotomous diagnostic judgment which is independent of the judgment of the depression as "situational" or reactive in nature (Spitzer et al., 1978). Patients diagnosed as situationally depressed responded well to any active treatment (including IPT alone), whereas those diagnosed as nonsituationally depressed responded poorly to IPT alone.

These results must be viewed as more tentative than was suggested by Prusoff et al. (1980) as there were several major weaknesses of the study. The most important of these was the failure to control for a vastly inflated Type I error rate caused by their liberal usage of statistical analyses; a more conservative approach would have involved the use of multivariate analysis of covariance (MANCOVA), especially given the five strongly correlated dependent variables examined in their study.

McLean and Hakstian (1979) reported an impressively designed and executed group comparison treatment outcome study comparing behavioral treatment of depressed clients with traditional insight oriented psychotherapy, pharmacotherapy, and relaxation training (a placebo group). Their results showed the behavioral treatment to be superior to the other forms of treatment at termination and marginally superior at 3-month follow-up. As discussed by Kovacs (1979), a problem with this study is its reliance upon derived self-rated symptom scales as the predominant measures of outcome; inclusion of one of the more well validated clinical ratings scales (e.g., the Grinker or the Hamilton) would have strengthened the study. Perhaps more important, the authors' inclusion of dropouts in the group analysis, in spite of the differential dropout rates across groups, introduced possibly significant biases into the results. The behavior therapy group, which was superior at termination, also had significantly fewer dropouts. This may be taken as additional evidence of the superiority of this group. However, its apparent superiority may have been an artifact, inasmuch as fewer scores of dropouts (who presumably would have been unimproved) were added to the outcome ratings for the behavioral treatment group.

Two analytical procedures in their study provided some information about differential responsiveness to treatment. First, the authors used multivariate cluster analysis techniques on pretreatment data to group the clients in the study into four relatively homogeneous groups. In analyzing the results of their treatment interventions, the authors used a 4 × 4 (treatment by clusters) MANCOVA to analyze the outcome at treatment termination and at 3-month follow-up. For the analysis of the data at termination, the main effect for treatment was significant, although there was no suggestion of cluster membership affecting outcome or interacting with type of treatment in any way. At three-month follow-up, however, the main effects for treatment had shrunk to marginal significance. Although the authors conducted further analyses on the treatment effect, they conducted no other analyses of the cluster effect. Given the extreme statistical conservatism of the techniques used, this failure to analyze further was unfortunate, as it might have suggested patterns of differential cluster responsiveness across treatment modalities. In summary, it appears that cluster assignments affected follow-up outcome, but we have no hint of the nature of this effect.

In addition, McLean and Hakstian (1979) performed a multivariate comparison of high and low treatment responders (apparently combining our typologies of dropouts, noncooperators, and nonresponders into the latter group) across all treatments. Although they produced a discriminant function that significantly differentiated between the two groups, none of the univariate comparisons or variables in the equation between the high and low responders reached statistical significance. Thus although the two groups could be differentiated, the overall power of the discriminant function was not great (only a 68 percent "hit" rate) and no unequivocal statements about group differences on single variables could be made. The three strongest single variables indicated that high responders tended to have had more stressful life events happen to them in the six months prior to treatment and yet tended to be more satisfied with work, home, and marriage and more socially active than low responders (all data gathered at intake). The other seven variables in the discriminant function were all in the direction of suggesting more depression at admission for low responders. These results paralleled those of Prusoff et al. (1980) in suggesting that clients that would be classified as "endogenous" or "lifestyle depressives" respond less well to *any* treatment than those classified as "reactive" or "situational." These results are not specific to behavioral treatment.

Brown and Lewinsohn (in press) report somewhat different findings. They conducted an experimental investigation of the relative efficacy of the depression treatment groups described earlier, bibliotherapy (with the same book used in the group) with minimal therapist contact, and individual therapy also using the same book as a focus for treatment. Compared to delayed treatment controls, all treatment formats were significantly effective, with little difference across treatment conditions. Those who showed least response to therapy were compared to the best responders; low responders seem to be a combination of what we are calling noncooperators and nonresponders. Low responders reported a significantly earlier age of onset for the current depressive episode, significantly greater life stress prior to treatment (particularly with regard to the area of children), and significantly lower general life satisfaction (particularly in the area of friendship).

Thus Brown and Lewinsohn (in press) and McLean and Hakstian (1979) all found that low responders had low life satisfaction in general. However, Brown and Lewinsohn's (in press) finding of higher prior stress for low responders is the opposite of the pattern found by McLean and Hakstian (1979) and Prusoff et al. (1980), who found that situational or reactive depression was related to better response to treatment. Inasmuch as the studies differ on many variables (type of treatment, sample, assessment procedures, areas of life stress sampled, etc.), only further research will be able to clarify this discrepancy.

Zeiss, Lewinsohn, and Muñoz (1979) reported on the effects of three behavioral treatment modalities for depression. An interpersonal treatment modality covered three aspects of interpersonal behavior: assertion, interpersonal style of expressive behavior, and social activity. A pleasant events modality was designed to increase patients' frequency of pleasant activities and their enjoyment of potentially pleasant activities. A cognitive treatment modality was designed to facilitate changing the patients' thoughts about and general view of reality. Several elements, as follows, were common to all three modalities. Treatment of depression was brief and intensive; patients were seen in individual sessions for 12 sessions in a one-month period. Patients were expected to work, on their own, on material presented in therapy in addition to coming to sessions three times weekly, on the average. The treatment framework was designed to be structured but not rigid. Therapists were provided with outlines covering the material to be presented in each session, but they were free to take extra time on those parts that were most difficult for a particular patient. There was also time for getting to know the patient and time for the patient to discuss other issues. Each client received one of the three kinds of behaviorally oriented treatment; the three treatment modalities were equally successful and led to significant improvement as compared to delayed treatment controls. However, not all clients benefited from treatment.

Although Zeiss et al. (1979) did not report any analyses of treatment failures versus successes, subsequent analysis of the data from the sample used in that study suggests some additional hypotheses with regard to treatment success and failure. In order to look at the determinants of success versus failure in the Zeiss et al. (1979) sample, three groups were established, as shown in Table 11.1. One group, dropouts, was composed of 16 clients who left therapy after three or fewer sessions. Those who completed treatment and posttreatment assessment were divided into those who could be considered treatment successes, those who were treatment failures, and those who had ambiguous outcomes. Two independent judges examined pretreatment to posttreatment ratings in order to sort subjects into these three categories; 92 percent agreement in categorization was achieved. All disagreements were one category apart (i.e., rated ambiguous by one judge and a treatment success by the second, or ambiguous by one and a treatment failure by the other). Ambiguous subjects were dropped from further consideration. Thus the final three established groups were dropouts, ($n = 16$) treatment failures, ($n = 20$) and treatment successes, ($n = 21$). Each treatment modality was represented approximately equally in each category.

Discriminant function analysis was used to determine whether sets of variables could be identified that would statistically distinguish between these groups. Only

Table 11.1.   Variables Discriminating Depression, Treatment, Dropouts, Failures, and Successes

Pretreatment Variable	Group Means			Rotated Standardized Discriminant Function Coefficient	
	Dropouts	Failures	Successes	Function 1	Function 2
Marital status[a]	1.88	1.35	1.71	.776	−.013
Age	29.12	39.75	32.91	.437	−.010
MMPI Hy	67.75	66.95	73.14	−.405	.669
Sex[b]	1.50	1.75	1.86	.416	.666
MMPI Pt	79.56	79.90	82.76	.311	.552
MMPI D	89.81	89.90	88.19	.445	−.534

[a]1 = currently married, 2 = currently single.
[b]1 = male, 2 = female.

pretreatment variables were examined, inasmuch as the most interesting issue seemed to be whether client differences at intake could be used to predict the eventual course of their experience in behavior therapy. A step-wise procedure was followed using the Wilks lambda group discrimination method; rotation of the obtained discriminant function axes was employed to improve interpretability of the axes. Variables available for entry into the discriminant functions were client, sex, age, and marital status, T scores on MMPI Hs, MMPI D, MMPI Hy, MMPI Pt, MMPI Sc, and mean scores on Grinker factors 1, 2, 3, 5, and Endogeneity–Reactivity (Grinker et al., 1961). Two discriminant functions were extracted; each significantly discriminated between groups: $\chi^2 = 29.57$, $p < .003$ for the first function and $\chi^2 = 11.38$, $p < .04$ for the second. Table 11.2 shows the classification accuracy using the predicted group memberships based on the discriminant functions. The overall correct classification rate was 59.65 percent, where 33 percent would be the percentage of correct classification obtained by chance. Chi square analysis indicated the obtained pattern of correct classification was statistically significant ($\chi^2 = 24.11$, $p < .001$).

Interpretation of the discriminant functions, however, is not entirely simple. Differences between the three groups on sex, age, and marital status were significant looking at the univariate F ratios ($F = 3.11$, $p < .05$; $F = 3.05$, $p < .05$;

Table 11.2.   Classification Results Using Discriminant Functions

Actual Group Membership	Predicted Group Membership		
	Dropout	Failure	Success
Dropout (n = 16)	10 62.5%	0 0.0%	6 37.5%
Failure (n = 20)	4 20.0%	13 65.0%	3 15.0%
Success (n = 21)	2 9.5%	8 38.1%	11 52.4%

$F = 6.83, p < .002$, respectively). The MMPI variables did not significantly discriminate between groups using the univariate analyses of variance.

Dropouts appeared to be more likely to be single, younger, and male than treatment successes or failures. They were somewhat lower on MMPI Hy than treatment successes, but similar to failures, indicating lack of denial and greater "psychological mindedness" relative to successes. Dropouts were also lower than successes on the MMPI Pt scale at pretreatment, but did not differ from failures. Dropouts, like failures, were slightly higher on MMPI D than treatment successes. Thus dropouts were characterized by a little less anxiety and a little more depression. The most typical dropout, in this analysis, would be an unmarried male in his late twenties who is primarily depressed, with low anxiety relative to other depressed clients, and little denial of psychological problems.

Treatment failures were more likely to be married and older than clients in the other two groups. They were more likely to be female than dropouts, but less likely than successes. They were low on MMPI Hy and Pt and high on MMPI D relative to successes. They were quite similar to dropouts on these variables. The most typical treatment failure, in this analysis, was harder to characterize. The client was equally likely to be male or female, but was relatively older than other clients and probably married. The client was primarily depressed, with low anxiety relative to other depressed clients, and little denial of psychological problems.

Treatment successes were in the middle on age and marital status. They were younger than failures and older than dropouts; more likely to be married than dropouts, but less likely than failures. They were more likely to be female than were clients in the dropout or failure groups. They were high on MMPI Hy relative to the other groups, indicating greater denial of psychological problems. They were high on MMPI Pt and low on MMPI D, relative to the other two groups. The most typical treatment success, in this analysis, was a female in her early thirties who was most likely unmarried. Although showing significantly elevated depression, she was less depressed than other clients. She was more anxious and more denying of psychological problems.

In these analyses, other MMPI variables did not contribute to the discriminant functions, nor did any Grinker variables. Most notably, endogeneity–reactivity failed to contribute to statistical differentiation between dropping out, failing, or succeeding in behavioral therapy for depression in this client sample.

The goal of looking for prognostic indices of failure among client characteristics and of looking for interactions between types of treatments and client characteristics should be to help generate hypotheses for how treatment of persons likely to fail in therapy could be improved. To make an increased likelihood of failure, based upon a prognostic sign, a criterion for excluding a depressed individual from treatment would be unfortunate and possibly unethical. It is hoped that in the future such a sign would lead to a change to a more effective strategy suggested by the empirical literature.

In summary, there is currently no solid evidence of client characteristics by treatment interactions to suggest that some clients would benefit from one treatment more than any other. The specific empirical findings concerning predictors of failure have not been crossreplicated, nor have consistent findings emerged from studies using varying methodology to explore similar hypotheses. Some important areas have not been studied at all. The empirical literature can be summarized as follows.

1.   *Dropouts.*   Only the reanalysis of the Zeiss et al. (1979) data, which was conducted for this review, directly addresses the issue of who is likely to drop out of behavioral therapy for depression. Dropouts were characterized as young, unmarried, and male, with little denial or anxiety but considerable depression. This suggests that in the absence of social support it is hard for depressed clients, especially if male, to make a real commitment to therapy. The relatively low anxiety may mean that there is less pressure to improve and the more passive, indecisive depressive qualities predominate. Further speculation seems unwarranted until these findings have been replicated.

2.   *Noncooperators.*   No studies have reported data on noncooperation in behavioral treatment and its relationship to success versus failure in therapy. To our knowledge, no researchers have even systematically collected data on the degree of cooperation (attending sessions, completing homework assignments, doing assigned readings, etc.) obtained from their clients. An unknown proportion of the clients who have been included in "less improved" or "failure" groups in other empirical studies must have been noncooperators, whereas the rest were what we have called nonresponders. Lumping these groups together may obscure real differences in the characteristics of clients of each type and may reduce the interpretability of findings regarding treatment failures. In future research, data should be collected to allow these groups to be considered separately.

3.   *Nonresponders.*   The problem just cited, that is, failure in prior research to differentiate between noncooperators and nonresponders, diminishes the interpretability of findings in studies that have looked at more and less improved clients after therapy. The other problem in this area is the inconsistency of results. In almost all studies cited, some differences have been found to exist, yet these differences do not seem to be replicated by different groups of researchers (e.g., McLean & Hakstian, 1979 as compared to Brown & Lewinsohn, in press), or even by the same research group (e.g. Weissman, Prusoff, & Klerman, 1978 as compared to Zuckerman et al., 1980). There are undoubtedly numerous reasons for such failures to replicate. Behavioral therapy for depression involves a diverse set of strategies, which may be utilized to differing degrees in different studies. Outcome measures vary, as do pretherapy measures of stress, adjustment, demographic status, and so on. Qualities of the therapists offering treatment may vary, and have not been investigated as yet. Finally, the proportion of noncooperators as compared to nonresponders probably varies from study to study; this variation may eventually be found to account for some of the variability in outcomes.

4.   *Relapsers.*   No data have been published relevant to the issue of who relapses after initially successful behavioral treatment. McLean and Hakstian

(1979) found that the initial superiority of behavioral treatment over insight oriented psychotherapy, pharmacotherapy, and relaxation (placebo) therapy was diminished at follow-up. This seemed to be due to a lack of maintenance rather than delayed improvement in the other conditions. This suggests that relapse may be an important problem after behavioral treatment for depression, and that the comparison of those who relapse and those who do not is an important direction for future research.

CASE EXAMPLES

Four case examples of treatment failures from the previously described group treatment course will be discussed to highlight some recurrent themes we have observed in client "failures." Each case will exemplify one of the four failure categories: dropouts, noncooperators, nonresponders, and relapsers.

CRAIG N.: A TREATMENT DROPOUT

Craig N. was a tall, slender 35-year-old Caucasian male who was vague and unsure during the intake interview. He was hesitant to describe himself as "depressed" but complained of a pervasive lack of energy, lack of enjoyment of life, and an inability to concentrate, make decisions, or get things accomplished. His Beck Depression Inventory (BDI) score at intake was 23, and he met RDC criteria for major depressive disorders. Craig was married, but reported deriving little satisfaction from his relationship with his spouse. He reported that the previous few years had been difficult ones during which he had been building a lawn maintenance business by working at least 50 hours per week. In the months prior to coming in for treatment, Craig had found it increasingly difficult to get out of bed or to get work done while he was on the job, and he reported that he was working only a few hours a day.

The treatment group was composed of seven women and two men. During the first group meeting, which was focused upon personal introductions and a videotaped presentation of an overview of the treatment to come, Craig remained relatively quiet, sharing and participating little. In the second session, which was devoted to a general introduction of self-change and problem-solving skills, Craig began freely and inappropriately offering advice to the other group members as they began defining the problems they faced. When the focus of the group turned to him, he stated that his problem was a "lack of motivation," and resisted attempts to seek more specific problem definitions. He became especially defensive when a question about better ways to handle his life implied that he was behaving maladaptively; he retreated further into his stance that his problem was motivation.

Craig never returned for another session. He called one of the therapists and stated that they had helped him define his problem, that he felt better already, and that he was back to work at "full steam." Because our data on this client are so limited, we have little upon which to speculate about the causes of this dropout. It seemed Craig placed a high priority upon exercising complete control over his life, accepting advice or help as little as possible. To accept advice may have seemed to Craig the equivalent of admitting that he was weak or helpless. This may have been a factor in his domineering behavior toward group members. His definition of his problem as a lack of motivation can be viewed as a mysterious (and thus safe) complaint with few or no implications for change in his self-perceptions or behavior.

Another possibility is that the theme of the group may have aggravated some of Craig's difficulties. The group is designed to foster the idea that people can gain control over their feelings by learning the relationship between, what they do and how they feel. Members are encouraged to take a problem-solving approach towards the obstacles they encounter towards experiencing life satisfaction (or, phrased more precisely in the mind of the therapist, towards obtaining a higher frequency of response contingent positive reinforcement). The idea that one can be an effective problem solver and thereby take control of one's life seems to be a novel and important message for many depressed clients, especially women, who have had stronger training in being passive and dependent. However, for many it may not be a novel message at all. Craig seemed to have worked hard all his life at controlling his life, at work, with friends, at home, and emotionally. Telling him that the way out of his current difficulties was to do more of the same may have been unconvincing and may have led to his dropping out of the group.

MARTIN R.: A DROPOUT/NONCOOPERATOR

Martin R. was a 47-year-old Caucasian plumber who sought treatment for depression. He was an extremely quiet person with obviously poor assertive and social skills (slow halting speech, poor eye contact, and anxious nonverbal behavior). He appeared motivated for treatment and to be a good candidate for the group treatment program. His Beck score was 12 and he met RDC criteria for minor depressive disorder.

Inasmuch as the therapists viewed his depression to be related to his interpersonal isolation within his family, with friends, and at work, two particular segments of the group program, relaxation training and assertiveness and social skills training, were seen as possessing special potential value. His progress in the group as treatment continued was, however, poor. He rarely completed assignments; he claimed to have read the assigned chapters when questioned, but showed little sign he had read them. When the focus of the group came to assertiveness and social skill towards the end of treatment, the therapists tried during the first assertiveness session to motivate Martin and help him to express himself more freely. Martin missed the next session, claiming to be sick, and never returned to treatment despite our encouragement to do so.

Several factors seem to have been involved in this treatment failure. First, the extreme nature of his social skill deficits made it difficult for us to ascertain his progress in treatment. He would frequently smile and nod in apparent agreement at important points made in the group sessions, though we later determined that he had understood little of the content of the group. Because of his passive unassertive manner, the therapists did not pick up that the material being presented in the group was difficult for him to understand and retain.

Also, the client seemed to have felt little hope of change for himself. He saw himself as extremely limited. The prospect of change and its subsequent effects upon his social life, especially with his family, seemed frightening (based on what little he did report in group about his concerns). This observation raises the issue that even with effective techniques, behavior therapists must deal effectively with *preparing* a client for change, possibly by exploring with the client ways his or her life might change and ways that he or she could cope with those changes.

BETTY J.: A NONRESPONDER

Betty J. was a 50-year-old Caucasian client, but she appeared considerably older. Her gray hair, lined face, and stooped posture all contributed to her aged appearance. Her pregroup Beck Depression Inventory score was 29, indicating considerable depression; her RDC diagnosis was major depressive disorder. She reported sleeping at least 14 hours a day and being tired and listless when awake. She reported feeling sad and anxious, but was not tearful or visibly agitated. Betty's husband was a strikingly successful professional man who devoted considerable time and energy to his work. However, he was also quite solicitous of Betty, coming home for lunch with her daily and expressing considerable concern for her welfare. Their two children were grown and away from home; Betty seemed to be on good terms with the children and to support their development of independence. Betty's depressive pattern was long standing. She reported that her mother had "bouts of depression," and Betty assumed that she carried a genetic predisposition for depression. No pattern of manic-depression cycles was identifiable in either mother or daughter. Betty and her mother had tried numerous antidepressant medication, with little or no success. Betty had entered psychotherapy briefly once before, but left because she felt the therapist dwelt too much on the past.

Betty entered a depression treatment group and quickly began improving. She enjoyed collecting self-monitoring data and was far more conscientious in carrying out assignments than other group members. In the group she was lively, laughing, sensitive to others' needs; she looked far younger and more relaxed. Midway through the group, the participants were instructed to bring in a chart showing the course of their daily mood from the start of the group to that point. Betty brought in a very encouraging chart; her mood showed a steady, gradual uphill climb and in the prior week her average daily mood was around 8, on a scale from 1 (totally miserable) to 10 (wonderful). But her presentation in the group was far from encouraging. She was listless, subdued, and seemingly out of contact with the group. She said that looking at the chart had deeply distressed her, because such progress could only remind her of how ephemeral happiness was and how doubly sad, by contrast, her "ordinary" existence (depression) would seem. In addition, she reported that her husband, who had helped her compile the chart, had commented that such rapid change must be ill advised and could never be sustained. He also had mentioned that he felt rather useless since she was in the group, and indicated that he wanted to contact us so that he could learn how to act in order to be more helpful to her. However, he never followed up on this suggestion.

From that point on, Betty went through the motions in the group. She came to most, but not all, sessions. She kept records, but failed to actively try the suggested techniques. She expressed deepening pessimism that things could ever change for her. At the end of the group her Beck Depression Inventory score was lower than before (19), but still indicated depression. After the group, Betty asked to be accepted as an individual client. Subsequent sessions with Betty, and with Betty and her husband jointly, shed some light on possible reasons for therapeutic failure in the group.

Betty had been, as far as we could learn, an attractive, energetic, capable young woman. She was romantically involved with a man she found exciting and she was beginning to develop her own career. She dropped both to marry her husband, for reasons she had trouble describing. The closest she could come was to say that she knew he desperately needed her. By his report, as well as her own, her husband had been interpersonally isolated in his youth and had expected to live only through his work. Somehow in Betty he found a person who might care for him and help him achieve intimacy and a "normal life." They married, she left her work, and soon they had two children. Betty began experiencing periods of depression and anxiety, which she attributed to her constitutional vulnerability. With the children in junior high school, she returned to college to develop a second career. During that time she felt stressed, burdened, fatigued—but never depressed. During her last year, her husband accepted a job thousands of miles away and Betty went with him. In the new community she had no contacts and there were few jobs in her field; she gave up after a discouraging period of failing to find work. Her husband encouraged this, arguing that, with the children grown, she should stay free to accompany him on his business travels. She again began experiencing depression, again attributing it to physiological factors. Her depression prevented her from ever actually traveling with her husband, which they both said they regretted.

Betty and her husband were both committed to the view that he was a thoughtful loving husband who longed to see his wife happy and active. Her problems, they felt, were hers alone, and they refused to continue conjoint therapy after two information gathering sessions. Betty was seen individually for a while, with a predictable outcome. Various behavioral strategies were tried; the initial impact was positive. Betty was glad to try any technique as long as it was individually oriented. As she got involved and developed skills her mood would improve. Her husband would then become more solicitous, urge her not to improve too rapidly, and tactfully express his own feelings of uselessness. Betty would then express pessimism, cease using the technique, and again become depressed. This pattern appeared intensely clear to the therapist, who hoped that eventually Betty and her husband would begin to share this interpretation and agree to enter conjoint therapy designed to change the structure of their relationship. However, this was not to be; after many cycles, Betty's attributions were unchanged. Rather than perpetuate the pattern, individual therapy was terminated.

This case, as presented, seems to suggest that one condition in which behavior therapy might fail is when there are other potent environmental influences working against success. However, other possible interpretations exist. For example, neither Betty nor her mother was ever placed on lithium, so its potential effect is unknown. Betty may have accurately believed there to be familial predisposition to unipolar recurring depressive episodes, which might have responded to lithium. The pattern of her husband's responses to improvement may have existed primarily in the therapist's construct system rather than in the situation. Or the pattern may have been accurately observed, but lacked the causal power attributed to it by the therapist.

Another issue that could be raised in regard to this case is the issue of whether this should be considered a therapeutic failure or a maintenance failure. It is true that in a therapy outcome study, this would look like a failure to respond to therapy, inasmuch as preassessment to postassessment had not resulted in a clinically significant decline in depression. Betty did respond to treatment each time an intervention occurred; however, her response failed to maintain itself even until the end of therapy. It's not clear whether this is most usefully construed as demonstrating the inefficacy of the treatment techniques or the need for additional intervention to guard against rapid relapse. Stated more simply, were we doing the *wrong* things, or were we just *not* doing *enough?*

DONNA N.: A RELAPSE

Donna N. was a slender, attractive Caucasian woman in her early twenties. Her eyes were moist with tears and looked dark and puffy from crying. Donna's Beck Depression Inventory score was 19 prior to treatment; her RDC diagnosis was minor depressive disorder. She described herself as lacking confidence, feeling worthless, and behaving in a passive dependent style with her boyfriend, female friends, and family. An early marriage had quickly ended when her husband became physically and verbally abusive. Donna was contemplating marriage to her boyfriend, with whom she lived, but was unable to make a decision.

In the depression treatment group, Donna at first was silent, although attentive. After a few sessions, she began to interact, at first offering support to others and gradually describing her own problems. She sometimes failed to keep careful written records, but claimed to be keeping track of her moods and trying the techniques suggested. When the group reached the section on interpersonal skills, Donna willingly became an active participant. She described considerable difficulty in asserting herself with her boyfriend and their two house-mates. The group spent considerable time role-playing assertive responses and also discussing her concerns about the consequences of being more assertive. Her mood began to improve dramatically around this time. Improved mood and increased skills led to other changes; Donna came to group with an eager face and happy eyes. People responded to her differently, and she developed skills in friendship and social intimacy. She changed jobs and began to perceive herself as competent and able to handle challenges. Throughout the rest of the group she was enthusiastic about the changes she was making, and at the end of the group her Beck Depression Inventory score was 2. At one-month fol-low-up Donna scored 2 again, and she mentioned that she and her boyfriend had decided to get married.

Donna called from the East Coast after four months; she had married and the couple had moved to be closer to his friends and family. Donna was planning a trip back to the Southwest around our scheduled six-month follow-up time and asked that we meet while she was there, which was done. At the follow-up, her Beck Depression Inventory score was 12 and she appeared sad and worried. She talked very little at first, as in the beginning of the group.

Donna was uncertain about what had caused her to become depressed again. She claimed to be happy with her marriage, but expressed some discontent about the decision to move to the East. She felt it had been forced upon her, and couldn't explain why she had gone along with it. For her, the East Coast was associated with her early unhappy marriage and the beginning of her prior depression. She felt far away from the environmental conditions associated with self-confidence, energy, and happiness. She was unsure of how to overcome the expectations of her husband's friends and family that she would be depressed, as she was when they first knew her. She expressed the desire to leave her husband and return to the Southwest on her own, while simultaneously feeling she needed and wanted to stay with her husband and make the marriage work. She felt depressed by her life circumstances and by her indecision about what she wanted.

This case also raises issues. On the one hand, the maintenance failure could be attributed to the return to an environment associated with depression. In the group, Donna had not practiced skills for dealing with the specific issues she en-countered when she moved, so she could not be expected to deal effectively with her new life circumstances. On the other hand, the skills she did learn would seem to be relevant to her new situation, and the generalization required not terribly complex. She could, perhaps, have been more assertive about insisting that the couple remain where she would be happier, used her interpersonal skills more effectively to alter the expectations of old friends and family, and used her new job confidence to pursue a similar career on the East Coast. It is not clear why these steps were not taken. How specific does skill training need to be? What ex-pectations for generalization of skills are realistic? What timing for follow-up ses-sions might have provided optimal reinforcement of developing skills? Answers to these questions would seem to provide practical guidelines for structuring ther-apy to enhance maintenance.

DISCUSSION

Some of the available empirical evidence suggests that those who can be characterized as exhibiting a "situational" (Spitzer, et al., 1978) or reactive depression may be expected to respond better to treatment in general, and to behavioral treatment specifically, than those who might be described as an endogenous or "lifestyle" depressive, although some data contradict this finding (Brown & Lewinsohn, in press). The finding that reactive depressives may respond better makes intuitive sense from the broad behavioral perspective discussed earlier. Persons experiencing situational depression might be viewed as having developed and maintained functional behavior patterns through most of their lives, with their depressive episode resulting from some major disruption of their lives and consequent decreased life satisfaction. Treatment for these individuals involves the development of new behavior for handling the current problems and the reestablishment of intact behavior patterns which had previously served to maintain normal effective functioning.

Nonsituationally depressed individuals, on the other hand, might be better characterized as exhibiting deficits in basic behavioral capabilities necessary for normal affective experience. Additionally, they may have developed cognitive patterns that predispose them to depression. The clinician dealing with such an individual is thus facing a more Herculean task than with the situationally depressed client. Much more drastic development of skills and radical change of cognitive patterns will be involved; such fundamental change is a difficult process for both client and therapist.

Frequently, behavioral clinicians see clients who cannot be readily categorized as either prototypically endogenous or reactive depressives. We would suggest as the general principle underlying the previous few paragraphs is that *the more extreme the deficits and maladaptive behavior patterns exhibited by the client seeking help* (either in *breadth* or in *depth*), *the greater the chances of failure with that client.*

One possible reason for this may be that behavioral skill training procedures (whether social skill training, increasing pleasant events, or self-management skill training) may not have their principle effect in directly remediating the specific skill deficit. Rather, these procedures may have a greater or equal effect on the client's expectancy of personal effectiveness (cf., Zeiss et al., 1979). In other words, a particular skill training procedure may have its beneficial effect in reducing depression mainly through increasing the client's expectation that he or she can act in a skilled manner rather than in drastically affecting skill level. Clients who have previously been skilled may be more easily helped to regain confidence, overcome depression, and begin functioning well again. Clients with more severe, long-standing difficulties may need more evidence of their own skill than standard, time-limited behavioral therapies can provide.

A related suggestion for why clients with more severe deficits do more poorly in behavioral treatment is that clients often expect beneficial change within a reasonable period of time following treatment initiation. A client requiring much more extensive training before he or she can expect to receive satisfying returns from the environment may grow discouraged with the lack of perceptible change in his or her status. The client also may attempt to prematurely test out skills before they have reached a truly effective level. For example, a withdrawn woman trained in how to meet and open conversations with men may try out her new skills expecting to revolutionize her relationships and find instead that the conversation flounders after an initially smooth opening.

Another major source of failure that we have seen clinically, and that was seen in some of the case examples, has been client entrenchment in potent and dysfunctional environmental systems. The client's environment may be unresponsive to "therapeutic" change on the part of the client, as in the case of an individual who moves into a community with few people who share interests in common with the client or the case of a person "locked" into an unsatisfying profession with little chance of meaningful change. Alternatively, the social system may be genuinely resistive or antagonistic to change on the part of the client. Spouses who gain from the client's depression in some way, or who fear change in accustomed relationship patterns, can exert tremendous resistance to change by precipitating crises, undermining therapist suggestions, sabotaging assignments, and so on. Finally, the client's social system may not be unsupportive of change, but rather may be overly supportive and responsive to the client's depressive symptomatology. Spouses may be very desirous of change, but seemingly incapable of not reinforcing depressive ploys for sympathy or special consideration. In sum, any environmental or social system that supports depressive symptomatology or resists constructive change can render useless the most seemingly useful of therapeutic strategies. Doerfler and Richards (in press) have found that people who successfully coped with depression on their own (i.e., without entering therapy) often did so by changing their social environment. Of the subjects in this study who had tried coping strategies but found them to be unsuccessful, very few had made changes in their social environment.

The issue of environmental systems supporting depressive symptomatology brings up the issue of motivation for treatment. This issue is a highly charged one. "Lack of motivation" for treatment is a frequently cited reason for failure in therapy; many feel it is an excuse for poor therapeutic procedure. Yet in our experience there are clients who are simply unmotivated for change. Although not totally endorsing a rationalistic model for client cognitive processes, we might hypothesize that all clients conduct some form of a cost-benefit analysis of coming into treatment. If the aversive consequences of remaining depressed do not outweigh the uncertainties and aversive elements of going through behavioral treatment, the client will not stay in therapy. There is a tremendous need for increased study of how we might better prepare and motivate clients for entering and staying in therapy. Elements of such a process might include increasing the client's perceptions of the aversiveness of a depressive lifestyle, and presenting therapy as a slow and careful process where change on the part of the client is a totally voluntary and negotiated process.

Future Directions

We would like to close this chapter with a standard call for continued research in this important area. Methodologically, there is a tremendous need for researchers to generate data archives from large sample group comparison studies so that complex multivariate techniques might be used to answer the important questions in this area. The methods used by McLean and Hakstian (1979) are a fine model in this area.

Many questions remain to be asked. We reiterate the following, which have been suggested by our empirical review and presentation of clinical case examples:

1. Future research should carefully delineate not just response or lack of response, but the type of failure. Did the client drop out, stay but fail to actively participate, actively participate but fail to benefit, or benefit from therapy but fail to maintain gains? Characteristics of each type of failure should be examined.

2. Greater overlap in measurement procedures should be encouraged. As consistent findings begin to emerge, conceptual replication using varying methodology is helpful, but at the present stage of knowledge, the diversity of measurement used greatly complicates comparison of studies.

3. The characteristics of various behavioral depression treatment programs need to be more thoroughly described in studies of treatment outcome. Characteristics of different behavioral treatment programs should be examined to determine their interaction with client characteristics in determining treatment outcome.

4. What alterations in the treatment process could be made to cause potential "failures" to become successes? Do we need to revise techniques or radically change approaches to bring this about?

5. A final area of potentially great interest is the study of how clients perceive what therapists construe as failure. For example, dropouts often say they are leaving therapy because they have developed the confidence to pursue their goals independently. Research to examine the positive versus negative qualities of treatment failures as perceived by the clients themselves could be useful. In addition, interviewing clients regarding what they identify as the reasons for dropping out, failing to actively participate in therapy, failing to respond to therapy, and/or failing to maintain benefits could generate new and exciting directions for future empirical work.

REFERENCES

Beck, A. T. (1967) *Depression: Clinical, experimental, and theoretical aspects.* New York: Hoeber.

Brown, R. A., & Lewinsohn, P. M. (in press) A psychoeducational approach to the treatment of depression: Comparison of group, individual, and minimal contact procedures. *Journal of Consulting and Clinical Psychology.*

Doerfler, L. A., & Richards, C. S. (in press) Self-initiated attempts to cope with depression. *Cognitive Therapy and Research.*

Eysenck, H. J. (1959) *The manual of the Maudsley Personality Inventory.* London: University of London.

Feighner, J. P., Robins, E., Guze, S. B., Woodruff, R. A., Winokur, G., & Munoz, R. (1972) Diagnostic criteria for use in psychiatric research. *Archives of General Psychiatry,* **26,** 57–63.

Grinker, R. R., Miller, I., Sabshin, M., Nunn, R., & Nunnally, J. C. (1961) *The phenomena of depressions.* New York: Hoeber.

Hamilton, M. (1976) Clinical evaluation of depression: Clinical criteria and rating scales including a Guttman scale. In D. M. Gallant, & G. M. Simpson (Eds.), *Depression: behavioral, biochemical, diagnostic and treatment concepts.* New York: Spectrum.

Kovacs, M. (1979) Treating depressive disorders: The efficacy of behavior and cognitive therapies. *Behavior Modification,* **3,** 496–517.

Lewinsohn, P. M., Biglan, A., & Zeiss, A. M. (1976) Behavioral treatment of depression. In P. O. Davidson (Ed.), *The behavioral management of anxiety, depression, and pain.* New York: Brunner/Mazel.

Lewinsohn, P. M., Muñoz, R. F., Youngren, M. A., and Zeiss, A. M. (1978) *Control your depression.* Englewood Cliffs, N.J.: Prentice-Hall.

McLean, P. D. (1976) Therapeutic decision-making in the behavioral management of depression. In P. O. Davison (Ed.), *Behavioral management of anxiety, depression and pain.* New York: Brunner/Mazel.

McLean, P. D., & Hakstian, A. R. (1979) Clinical depression: Comparative efficacy of outpatient treatments. *Journal of Consulting and Clinical Psychology,* **47,** 818–836.

Muñoz, R. F. (1980) Personal communication.

Prusoff, B. A., Weissman, M. M., Klerman, G. L., & Rousaville, B. J. (1980) Research diagnostic criteria subtypes of depression. *Archives of General Psychiatry,* **37,** 796–801.

Spitzer, R. L., Endicott, J., & Robins, E. (1978) Research diagnostic criteria. *Archives of General Psychiatry,* **35,** 773–782.

Weissman, M. M., Prusoff, B. A., & Klerman, G. L. (1978) Personality and the prediction of long-term outcome of depression. *American Journal of Psychiatry,* **135,** 797–800.

Whitehead, A. (1979) Psychological treatment of depression: A review. *Behaviour Research and Therapy,* **17,** 495–509.

Youngren, M. A. (1980) Personal communication.

Zeiss, A. M. (1980) Unpublished data.

Zeiss, A. M., Lewinsohn, P. M., & Muñoz, R. (1979) Nonspecific improvement effects in depression using interpersonal skills training, pleasant activity schedules, or cognitive training. *Journal of Consulting and Clinical Psychology,* **47,** 427–439.

Zuckerman, D. M., Prusoff, B. A., Weissman, M. M., Padias, N. S. (1980) Personality as a predictor of psychotherapy and pharmacotherapy outcome for depressed outpatients. *Journal of Consulting and Clinical Psychology,* **48,** 730–735.

CHAPTER 12

Failures in Treating
Depression by
Cognitive Behavior Therapy

A. JOHN RUSH
BRIAN F. SHAW

Treatment failures are perhaps the most instructive of all experiences for psycho-therapists. The lessons gleaned from each failure have implications for improved patient selection, refinements and innovations in psychotherapeutic techniques, differential diagnosis of the disorders themselves (i.e., some types of depression may be unresponsive to psychotherapy), improving compliance with homework, improving strategies to deal with countertherapeutic social system forces, and for identification of patients who show only short-term as opposed to long-term gains.

This chapter will review the major reasons for treatment failure in the cognitive and behavioral treatment for depression; it will illustrate these points with case examples. Before proceeding, a word about post hoc analyses of the thera-peutic process and therapist characteristics is in order. Although we will focus on failures with cognitive therapy, those readers who are unfamiliar with the ther-apy are advised to refer to Beck, Rush, Shaw, and Emery (1979) for details of the approach and a review of outcome studies. Cognitive therapy does appear to be effective for a subgroup of depressed patients with regard to (1) reduction of depressive symptomatology, and possibly (2) prophylaxis or prevention of sub-sequent episodes (Kovacs, Rush, Beck, & Hollon, 1980).

With regard to therapist characteristics, the authors searched their files for cases that would be grouped in a category of failures and that illustrated a general subcategory of patients who are difficult to treat with cognitive behavioral thera-py. The authors are experienced cognitive therapists but, nevertheless, it is always difficult to tell whether therapy failed because of therapist characteristics, patient characteristics, therapeutic methods, or combinations of all three. Whereas a chapter of this type focuses on patient characteristics, in many cases it may be far more reasonable to attribute failure to combinations of the above three factors (Shaw, 1981). Clinically, it is more difficult to observe these combinations and thus we are left with our biased emphasis on the patient. Again, the hope is that the reader will bear this oversimplified approach in mind.

We have previously suggested that cognitive therapy alone will not be effective in psychotic depressions (those with hallucinations or delusions), severe endogenous depressions, schizoaffective disorders, and borderline patients (Beck et al., 1979). Inasmuch as cognitive therapy requires that patients reality-test or objectively assess their thinking pattern against real life experiences, patients with an impaired ability to tell fantasy from reality (i.e., those who are psychotic) are poor candidates for this therapy alone. Endogenous or melancholic depressions (Spitzer et al., 1978; APA, 1980) are those that lack a capacity for enjoyment or pleasure and who suffer from a pervasive mood that is unreactive to environmental events. This group, we believe, has an affective disorder that derives mainly from a central nervous system dysfunction that colors one's thinking. Cognitive change techniques alone may result in only partial or transient symptom relief in this group. Borderline patients have impulse control problems and micropsychotic episodes (APA, 1981). Cognitive therapy requires persistent diligent application of specific techniques. Borderline patients often do not have the capacity for such persistence. Furthermore, recent research suggests that quite a number of these borderline patients also evidence biological dysfunctions similar to those found in endogenous depressions (Akiskal, 1981). As noted below, such dysfunctions may relate to nonresponse to cognitive therapy.

PATIENT MOTIVATION

Perhaps the most commonly offered rationale for treatment failures in general is, "The patient isn't motivated." There is an especially great temptation to attribute "lack of motivation" to those depressed patients who fail to respond. However, this "explanation" is, in fact, both logically untenable and obfuscating. Depression, the syndrome (APA, 1980), involves by definition a reduction in energy and motivation. Thus all depressed patients are less motivated than normals to undertake most activities, including psychotherapy. In cognitive therapy, the patient is required both to attend the sessions, and to complete various homework assignments in order to obtain a therapeutic effect. These requirements are being leveled at patients, all of whom are "unmotivated." Thus "lack of motivation" explains all failures. However, those who do respond are also "unmotivated" at the outset. Therefore, lack of motivation is associated with both successes and failures (i.e., it explains nothing).

There are, of course, some patients who appear more or less difficult to engage in the treatment process. We believe this initial differential tendency to collaborate evolves out of two major forces: difficulty with trust and the pervasiveness and certainty of the negative anticipations held by the patient. Each of these issues, trust and negative anticipations, are reframed in cognitive terms and dealt with very early in treatment. Negative anticipations are elicited by the therapist and corrected with information, logical discussion, and experimental tasks (Beck et al., 1979). Trust issues are also reframed in cognitive terms. For example, the patient may believe, "If I really tell you (the therapist) how I think, you won't like me." There is often an anticipation of rejection or disappointment underlying the patient's reluctance to engage as a full collaborator with the therapist. Such patients will often begin to work in treatment and then back off, reduce compliance, and voice more hopeless and helpless notions. These notions not atypically also involve denigration of the therapist or the therapy process. Such behaviors and views may serve to protect the patient from developing an emotional personal relationship (a therapeutic alliance) and, consequently, avoid the presumed rejection and disappointment as the treatment is terminated. Again, these fears are identified, framed cognitively into "if . . ., then . . ." statements (e.g., "If I put my hopes into this treatment or the therapist and don't get better, then I'll be shattered or it means I'm incurable, etc."), and discussed logically.

More severely depressed patients are especially likely to suffer from difficulties in trust and severe negative anticipation of the future. As such, the engagement of these patients is both critical and difficult (Rush, 1980). However, by first identifying behavioral patterns that appear to represent these assumptions, by raising these assumptions in the form of questions early in treatment, and by addressing them repeatedly throughout treatment, the therapist can usually engage such "unmotivated" patients.

LACK OF SKILLS

Many have asked whether high intelligence is associated with a better outcome with cognitive therapy. The implication here is that a low intelligence will lead to failures. Although empirical outcome studies to answer this question have not yet been conducted, our clinical experience suggests that exceptional intelligence is not required. In fact, very intelligent people with an obsessive thought style are more difficult to work with. They tend to play intellectual games, report "cognitions" without much associated feeling, and will try to maneuver the therapist into a legalistic debate about some issue that is unrelated to their inner beliefs and feelings.

On the other hand, those patients with IQs in the 80 to 95 range do have difficulty in relating beliefs to cognitions in a logical manner. However, they are able to see how a series of behaviors appears to be based on a particular idea. For example, a 28-year-old depressed female with an IQ of 82 always found herself feeling irritated that everyone told her what to do and appeared unwilling to listen to her. She would "rebel" against these people by intentionally doing something that was foolish or socially inappropriate from time to time. When asked for her cognitions at these times, she simply reported, "I just felt like it." The therapist asked her if perhaps she believed that, "If I do something on my own, someone will listen to me," which she could accept. Therapy then focused on what she could do on her own (without being told) that was not simply a response to others' directions, but rather were activities that she herself preferred. She decided she'd like to try to raise houseplants and bake cookies, two new activities, which once she undertook them, led others to develop a respect for her skills and to become (at least by the patient's report) less demanding.

In this case, a detailed analysis of her cognitions and silent assumptions would have been both time-consuming, frustrating, and unrewarding. Furthermore, such a therapist–patient interaction would have replicated the problem that was already present in the patient's interpersonal relations.

Psychologically naive patients pose other problems with regard to engagement in therapy (Rush & Watkins, 1980). These patients can be more successfully engaged if (1) clearcut expectations and explanations are provided at the outset; (2) family member(s) can be informed and brought to support the therapeutic process; (3) progress is made apparent to these patients on a repeated basis; (4) negative anticipations are sought and corrected at each step in treatment. Vague and ambiguous or highly qualified responses by the therapist are especially likely to raise suspicions of therapist incompetence, anxiety, and tendencies to give up or leave treatment.

MEDICAL DISORDERS

Aside from general intelligence, which we do not feel is a critical factor in dictating success or failure, there are a number of clinical situations that can lead to failure. These include impairments in memory or concentration found in either severe depressions or early organic brain syndrome. The latter are especially likely to seek help because of low energy, sleep difficulties, sadness or apathy, and a reduced sense of self-esteem. Careful medical and psychiatric evaluation can exclude patients with these disorders.

In addition, patients will often present with minor or even major depressions (APA, 1981) that are consequences of some underlying undiagnosed medical disorder or medication. The experience at Southwestern Medical School, Affective Disorders Clinic, is that 15 to 20 percent of "depressed" outpatients have such disorders. Cognitive therapy will not work in these cases. Two brief vignettes illustrate this point:

A 35-year-old female with sadness, insomnia, self-criticism, low energy, poor concentration, weight and appetite reductions, and headaches was evaluated by both a psychiatrist and psychologist before agreeing to and participating in cognitive therapy. After 20 sessions her self-critical attitudes, according to the patient, were reduced. However, she stated, "I'm still depressed," and indeed her other symptoms were basically unchanged. A reevaluation was conducted. It was discovered that she had been taking alpha-methyl-dopa, an antihypertensive agent, that can cause depression. She had previously reported that she was taking no medications because "I've been taking these blood pressure pills for years." Her depressive symptoms disappeared completely within three weeks after the medication was stopped.

A 34-year-old nurse with multiple sclerosis that resulted in mild disabilities in motor coordination that did not preclude her continued full-time employment developed a major depressive episode (APA, 1980). She complained of apathy, loss of interest and pleasure, insomnia, low energy, suicidal thinking, and mild reductions in weight and appetite. She was chiefly preoccupied with anticipations of massive disability as her multiple sclerosis progressed. These thoughts were clearly negatively biased in that her actual disabilities were relatively mild and her illness was in relatively good control.

After 20 sessions of cognitive therapy, no relief of any of her symptoms ensued. She was then tried on two different tricyclic antidepressant medications, both of which failed. She was admitted to the hospital, where a thorough medical, neurological, and laboratory evaluation revealed severe hypothyroidism. Treatment with thyroid replacement completely relieved all of her symptoms including her negatively biased thinking. She returned to work and has remained asymptomatic for two years.

The latter case illustrates the presence of two separate medical disorders, one of which caused the depression. The therapist had initially felt that, "Anyone with multiple sclerosis would be depressed," and erroneously attributed her depressive symptoms to the stress of her neurological disease. If that diagnosis were correct, then symptomatic response should have followed cognitive therapy. Thus a failure to respond to cognitive therapy should lead the clinician to completely reevaluate the case. In addition, a thorough medical and psychiatric evaluation *prior to* beginning cognitive or behavioral treatment for depression is essential, even if the patient "knows why" he or she is depressed. Medications and medical illnesses produce mood changes and other symptoms of the depressive syndrome including cognitive symptoms such as negative views of the self, world, and future. Consequently, psychologically minded patients with an unrecognized medical illness that causes depressive symptoms can often provide themselves and the therapist with a convincing but invalid story as to why they are depressed.

UNRESPONSIVE DEPRESSIVE DISORDERS

Certain depressive disorders may not respond at all or only partially to cognitive therapy methods. Bipolar or manic depressive illness, depressed phase, psychotic depressions, and melancholic depressions (APA, 1981) are among those that clinical experience suggests will not respond. However, controlled outcome studies to document these clinical hunches are not available.

Melancholic depression is diagnosed when a major depressive episode is present according to descriptive criteria (APA, 1981) and when, in addition, there exists a loss of pleasure in all or almost all activities, lack of mood reactivity to pleasurable stimuli, and when at least three of the following are present: (1) distinct quality to the depressed mood (i.e., the mood is unlike that experienced following the death of a loved one); (2) mood is regularly worse in the morning; (3) early morning awakening; (4) marked psychomotor agitation or retardation; (5) significant anorexia or weight loss; (6) excessive or inappropriate guilt. The recognition of these melancholic depressions can be straightforward in classic inpatient cases. However, in the majority of depressions (i.e., outpatient depressions), such a diagnosis demands exceptional skill, experience, and time.

Recently, significant advances have been made in our ability to diagnose these melancholic depressions by utilizing specific laboratory measures. We will describe several of these methods briefly and then return to illustrate how they may be of value in identifying patients who may not respond well to cognitive or behavioral therapies.

The dexamethasone suppression test (DST) has been developed by Carroll and collaborators at the University of Michigan (Carroll, in press; Carroll, Curtis, & Mendels, 1976a, b). This test involves the administration of 1 mg of dexamethasone to patients in a single oral dose at midnight. The usual effect of this synthetic glucocorticoid is to suppress ACTH production by the pituitary gland which, secondarily, leads to a total suppression of cortisol production by the adrenal glands. Thus in normals, blood samples after 8, 16, and 23½ hours following dexamethasone reveal consistently low circulating cortisol levels less than 4 or 5 ug/dl at all three times). The same holds for patients with major depression without melancholic symptom features (i.e., what were loosely called neurotic depressions in the past).

However, the DST reveals "nonsuppression" or elevations in one or more of the postdexamethasone cortisol values in roughly 35 to 50 percent of melancholic outpatients and 65 to 85 percent of melancholic inpatients (Carroll et al.,). Thus DST nonsuppression is virtually pathognomonic for such melancholic depressions. Also, failure to find DST nonsuppression has no diagnostic meaning, inasmuch as both melancholic and nonmelancholic depressions can suppress normally following dexamethasone.

Does dexamethasone nonsuppression predict poor response to cognitive therapy? Do melancholic depressions fail to respond? Although empirical research cannot yet answer these questions, anecdotal case reports and inferences from the available data give us some clues. The first author has tried to treat three DST nonsuppressing, melancholic, nonpsychotic depressed outpatients with cognitive therapy. One case received 10 sessions, the second received 20 sessions, and the third received 8 sessions. All three failed to respond at all according to rating scales, therapist judgment, and patient global impression. DST nonsuppression persisted at the end of treatment. One patient finally responded completely to electroconvulsive treatment (ECT). The second responded completely to amitriptyline, and the third failed on three different antidepressants, but refused ECT.

Several reports (Carroll, Feinberg, Greden, et al, 1981; Greden, Albala, Haskett, et al, 1980; Coryell & Schlesser, 1981) also provide indirect evidence that DST nonsuppression, if it persists after partial clinical response, represents a poor prognostic sign. Subsequent suicide or rehospitalization was reported in 15 of 15 inpatients who had demonstrated sufficient clinical response to be discharged in the six months prior to this following study. All of these patients had been treated with ECT or antidepressant medication. The point here is that DST nonsuppression, should it persist over a period of time, may well relate to significant survival risk and to marked functional impairment. Thus a patient in cognitive or behavioral therapy who does not respond may well have a melancholic depression. The DST nonsuppression provides a valuable tool for identifying about 50 percent of such outpatients. We have begun to use the DST clinically as both an adjunct to diagnosis and to evaluate cognitive therapy nonresponders.

A second laboratory innovation, the sleep electroencephalogram (EEG), is now being actively explored as a diagnostic adjunct in the cognition of melancholic depressions (Kupfer, 1976; Rush, in press; Rush, Giles, Roffwarg, & Parker, in press). These depressions are characterized by a reduced time between falling asleep and the initiation of the first rapid eye movement (REM) period or dream. In addition, a marked reduction in Stage 4 sleep (deep rolling delta waves on the EEG) is noted. Finally, an increase in REM density or the number of eye movements per minute of REM sleep typifies many of these patients. The sleep EEG appears to be a bit more sensitive than the DST in detecting outpatients with melancholic depressions (Rush, el al., in press), yet nearly all DST nonsuppressors also show these typical sleep EEG changes. Therefore, a laboratory test sequence can be established: DST followed by the sleep EEG to document or assist in the recognition of melancholic depressions. An REM latency of less than 60 minutes (normal is about 90 minutes) appears to detect about 75 percent of outpatients with this type of symptomatology, whereas the DST alone detects about 40 to 50 percent of such patients.

It is also noteworthy that a sequence of 70 outpatients who were subjected to both measures (the sleep EEG and the DST) included 42 patients who showed neither laboratory abnormality. Obviously, most of these 42 were nonmelancholic. In this group, the response to antidepressant medication was lower than for those who showed either or both biological abnormalities. Perhaps these and other laboratory tests will discriminate these patients who do require antidepressants from those who would fare best with cognitive or behavioral strategies. Only further research can answer these questions. What can be stated at this point is that certain types of depression are likely to respond poorly to the exclusive use of cognitive or behavioral techniques. It is not yet clear whether some depressions do best with a combination of medication and psychotherapy. From the clinician's viewpoint, nonresponse to an adequate trial of cognitive treatment should result in a full reevaluation of the patient and the depression. In this reevaluation, laboratory tests like those above may be quite useful.

TECHNICAL PROBLEMS IN THE APPLICATION OF COGNITIVE THERAPY

A number of errors in the application of cognitive therapy can result in treatment failures. Perhaps the most common error is a failure to obtain compliance with homework assignments. In addition, a valid cognitive conceptualization of the patient and his or her problem may not be obtained. Also, less experienced therapists may attempt to pedantically rather than creatively apply published techniques. In these instances, the treatment methods may not fit particularly well with the individual patient. In applying a cognitive conceptual framework and deriving technique, it appears essential to tailor the techniques to the individual patient. The following vignette illustrates several of these technical problems.

A.K., a 23-year-old, single female graduate student was seen on three separate occasions with complaints of depression, a sense of rejection and inferiority and suicidal ideation. She was initially referred, when she began graduate school, from a psychodynamically oriented therapist who had seen her intensively for one year when she was an undergraduate. This previous therapy was described as successful, with the major gain seen as a gradual separation from the patient's domineering parents and an increased tolerance of authority figures. She was described as a person with low self-esteem and a long history of neurotic adjustment (i.e., fears, anxiety, and depression). At the time of referral, she was moderately depressed.

Therapy began with a focus on her suicidal ideation associated with a recent break-up with her boyfriend. She indicated a sense of hopelessness about future relationships, as she had been surprised by her boyfriend's sudden wish to terminate the relationship. She was more critical of her own naiveté, in not knowing that he was dissatisfied, than she was feeling rejected in the relationship. She was upset that she had "committed" herself to him and regretted their sexual involvement. She had used the frequency of their sexual relationships as a barometer of his caring for her; she repeated this reaction as a "prime example of stupidity." Furthermore, she viewed the experience as reason to call into question her own ability to know whether someone loved her or not. She was preoccupied with the notion that she was a "fool" and that she was lacking in the ability to detect whether someone else loved her or not.

The therapist was able to break through her hopelessness, with a series of questions as to whether she loved her boyfriend, and, as she began to address this issue, it became clear that her own feelings about him were mixed prior to the break-up. Following this discussion, as she considered her own mixed feelings, her reaction to his loss was partially ameliorated as compared to when she viewed herself as "made to look foolish" or "taken advantage of." In other words, it helped to take the perspective of someone who was equally in control of the relationship rather than that of a passive object or victim.

As indicated, in the early stages, the therapist's formulation was that the patient held the belief, "In order to be happy, I need to be cared for by others." One could trace her sense of insecurity to the frequent conclusion that, "No one really cares about me." It was also possible to see that her own standards of "caring" were extreme and encompassing, to the point that even minor criticisms or quarrels were taken as proof that the other person did not care.

Interestingly, there was a mix of both blaming the significant other and a disproportionate amount of self-criticism and self-blame for being stupid. From the therapist's perspective, it was essential to work toward the alteration of this basic belief. Unfortunately, this goal was not achieved despite three periods of cognitive therapy involving a total of 42 sessions (8, 21, and 14 sessions, respectively) over a period of 14 months. This period included time away from therapy—two months between the first and second period and six weeks between the second and third period.

Let us consider some of the possible reasons why cognitive therapy failed. These reasons are not necessarily exhaustive and, unfortunately, because the patient left the area and stopped contact, it is not possible to test the validity of these reasons at the present time. At least three major problems can be identified: failure to agree on central therapy goals, failure to sustain the patient in discussions of emotional importance, and failure to complete assigned homework in a consistent manner, the most important goal being a delay in entering other relationships.

The first issue concerns the therapy goals. From the beginning this was a difficulty that was only partly solved despite identification and a concerted effort to change. As indicated, the primary precipitant for the initial depressive episode was a break-up with her boyfriend. The therapist's initial interventions were effective, producing a cognitive and affective shift to a sense of greater control and diminished self-blame. The patient's hopelessness and suicidal ideation abated, and she vowed to consider her own views and needs before pursuing any other relationships. The negative cognitive triad (Beck, 1967) was evident, however, in that she reported constantly questioning whether others could love her, given her lack of physical attractiveness (i.e., too tall, thinning hair) and her aggressiveness in academics (e.g., major scholarship winner). A.K. viewed most of her daily experiences as negative, particularly the weekends when she was alone. She viewed the future as "a big question mark," given her past experience.

The therapist wanted to pursue, as a primary therapy goal, a discussion of the impact of her belief that she needed to be in a relationship in order to be happy. He proposed, for example, that she consider other activities that would help her cope with her periods of loneliness. The patient, on the other hand, saw as the main therapy goal an attempt at "self-improvement" that was directed at her lack of motivation to improve her physical appearance (e.g., by daily treatment for her hair and an exercise program) and a second problem which was a decreased interest in her academic pursuits.

The therapist followed the patient's wishes, and they began to work on the decreased interest in academics. Unfortunately, after four sessions, the patient, again, became preoccupied with her loneliness and reported that she "couldn't stand spending half of her life in libraries." Three sessions were spent vacillating between the presenting problem of her graduate studies and loneliness, with an end result that, after eight sessions, A.K. indicated that she wanted to stop therapy as it was creating too much stress in her. This difficulty is an example of a major theme that ran throughout the therapy. In the next two therapy sessions, which were considerably longer, the same difficulty arose. The therapist and patient would begin to work on an area of her life and would be interrupted with another concern. The major issues were seen as her attempt to counter her negative self-image by working on her strengths (academics, a high level of motivation for change) and her belief that these activities were trivial if she was only "destined" to spend a life alone.

The second issue that related to treatment failure was the difficulty in engaging the patient in discussions of emotional importance. In reviewing the session notes and audiotapes, it became apparent that, whenever the topic of relationships emerged, the patient would become emotional. Initially, this reaction was seen positively as an indication that important material was being discussed. Over the long term, however, the patient's emotions concerned the failure of past relationships, rather than her negative view of herself. In these past relationships she tended to see herself as a fool for entering them and it was difficult for her to experience a sense of loss for herself.

The third issue related to failure concerns the unwillingness of the patient to complete assigned homework. In the second series of therapy sessions, the therapist proposed that the patient agree to a "moratorium on relationships." One difficulty was that the patient was prone to getting into short-term relationships and, in fact, prior to her second depression, she had been involved in two such short-term affairs. The therapist could see quite clearly that her assumption was in operation and she was attempting to find the caring she believed she required. In fact, she selected partners who had a very low chance of meeting her needs; partners who were seen as reflecting her negative self-concept. A.K. was quite willing to complete homework assignments that concerned the practical issues (from her viewpoint), such as studying or physical self-improvement, but despite acknowledging the importance of gaining distance from her past relationships, she did not comply with therapeutic agreement.

As noted previously, one of the advantages of an analysis of treatment failure concerns the development of new therapeutic methods. One can certainly consider transference and countertransference issues to explain the treatment failure. These issues may be important, but the problem appeared to focus on the patient's uncertainty about what problems affected her the most. Cognitive therapy format resulted in fairly easy identification of problems, but significant difficulties in obtaining anything but the most transient of results. Notably, the patient was not depressed during this period. In fact, her depression, except during periods of suicidal ideation, fluctuated around the moderate level (because of cognitive-affective symptoms and not physiological ones).

In retrospect, it was obvious that the therapist had not made a major dent in the patient's schema of failure in relationships. Prior to involving herself with someone, she would predict failure and would point to her own past history of an inability to maintain a relationship as well as idiosyncratic self-criticisms about her appearance and "foolishness" for maintaining a good academic record. If one was to look at a cognitive schema for interpersonal relationships, it would be possible to trace A.K.'s view back to her early experience, in which she was praised contingent on her academic achievements. She is a patient for whom most cognitive therapists would predict success and yet it was quite evident that, by the end of therapy, she would continue to experience major depressions.

SOCIAL SYSTEM FORCES

A final major deterrent to therapeutic effect may consist of forces within the patient's social system. Significant others may unwittingly conceptualize the depressed patient as a helpless, negativistic, hostile person from whom nothing better can be anticipated in the future. This situation is most likely to ensue when the depression has been present for a longer period of time. Many depressed patients will overvalue the opinions and views of others. Thus in the course of cognitive therapy, behavioral or attitudinal changes hoped for by the therapist and practiced by the patient may be undercut by the fixed negative views of the patient that are held by significant others.

Several therapeutic strategies have been suggested in anecdotal reports (Rush, Shaw, & Khatami, 1979; Beck et al., 1979). Basically, if such countertherapeutic-social forces exist, it is imperative that the couple or family system members be engaged in the process of cognitive change. Often, these negativistic significant others have themselves lost hope of seeing meaningful change in the index patient. Behaviors and attitudes generated by the depression are attributed, erroneously, to the patient's character. Significant others can be employed to therapeutic benefit as assistants in obtaining compliance with homework, in practicing alternative views, themselves, of the patient's behaviors, and in modifying the reinforcement contingencies available to the patient under the therapists direction.

SUMMARY AND CONCLUSIONS

The preceding chapter has touched briefly on a number of factors that may preclude successful therapy of depression with cognitive behavioral methods. These factors include motivation, difficulties in establishing a therapist–patient collaboration, failure to recognize medical disorders that cause depressions, technical problems in conceptualizing the case or developing tailor-made techniques, failure to obtain compliance, failure to recognize or diagnose those specific depressions that do not respond to this modality, and failure to constructively deal with countertherapeutic social system forces. Further case reports of treatment failures are needed in the literature. Such reports are likely to help us better avoid future failures and refine patient selection criteria. Further research into whether specific biological measures might not detect those depressions that will not respond to cognitive therapy is also necessary.

REFERENCES

American Psychiatric Association (1980) *Diagnostic and statistical manual of mental disorders* (3rd ed.). Washington, D.C.

Beck, A.T., Rush, A.J., Shaw, B.F., & Emery, G. (1979) *Cognitive therapy of depression.* New York: Guilford.

Carroll, B.J. (in press) The dexamethasone suppression test for melancholia. *British Journal of Psychiatry.*

Carroll, B.J., Curtis, G.C., & Mendels, J. (1976a) Neuroendocrine regulation in depression. I. Limbic system-adrenocortical dysfunction. *Archives of General Psychiatry,* 1039–1044.

Carroll, B.J., Curtis, G.C., & Mendels, J. (1976b) Neuroendocrine regulation in depression. II. Discrimination of depressed from nondepressed patients. *Archives of General Psychiatry,* **33,** 1051–1057.

Carroll, B.J., Feinberg, M., Greden J.F., Tarika, J., Albala, A.A., Haskett, R.F., James, N.M.I., Kronfol, Z., Lohr, N., Steiner, M. deVigne, J.P., Young E.A. (1981). Specific laboratory test for the diagnosis of melancholia. *Archives of General Psychiatry, 38,* 15–22.

Coryell, W. & Schlesser M.A. (1981) Suicide and the dexamethas one suppression test in unipolar depression. *American Journal of Psychiatry, 138,* 1120–1121.

Greden, J.F., Albala, A.A., Haskett R.F., Carrll, B.J., Normalization of the dexamethasone suppression test: A laboratory index of recovery from depression (1980) *Biological Psychiatry, 15,* 449–458.

Kovacs, M., Rush, A.J., Beck, A.T., & Hollon, S.D. (1981). Depressed outpatients treated with cognitive therapy or pharmacotherapy. A one-year followup. *Archives of General Psychiatry, 38,* 33–39.

Kupfer, D.J. (1976) REM latency: A psychobiologic marker for primary depressive disease. *Biological Psychiatry,* **11,** 159–174.

Rush, A.J. (1980) Psychotherapy of the affective psychoses. *American Journal of Psychoanalysis,* **40,** No. 2, 99–123.

Rush, A.J. (in press) Biological markers and treatment response in affective disorders. *McLean Hospital Bulletin.*

Rush, A.J., Giles, D.E., Roffwarg, H.P., & Parker, C.R. (in press) Sleep EEG and dexamethasone suppression test findings in outpatients with unipolar major depressive disorders. *Journal of Biological Psychiatry.*

Rush, A.J., & Watkins, J.T. (1980) Cognitive therapy with psychologically naive depressed outpatients. In G. Emery, S. Hollon, & R. Bedrosian, (Eds.), *Cognitive therapy casebook.* New York: Guilford.

Shaw, B.F. (1981) Stress as an exacerbator of the depressive syndrome. In R.W.J. Neufeld (Ed.), *Psychological stress and psychopathology.* New York: McGraw-Hill.

CHAPTER 13

Failures in the Treatment
of Addictive Behaviors

R. LORRAINE COLLINS
G. ALAN MARLATT

RELAPSE AND THE ISSUE OF MAINTENANCE OF TREATMENT EFFECTS

The addictive behaviors have often been described as highly recalcitrant to treatment, thus failure in reaching treatment goals is a common experience for the clinician or researcher working with clients who have problems of addiction. This is readily documented in reviews of the literature on treatment efficacy, particularly in discussions concerning the issue of maintenance of treatment effects.

Hunt, Barnett, and Branch (1971) described a "remarkable similarity" in relapse rates over time for addictive behaviors such as heroin use, smoking, and problem drinking. The typical pattern of response to treatment shows a trend for a sharp decline in abstinence rates during the first three months after treatment. There is a gradual leveling off to a success rate of approximately 20 percent by the twelfth month after treatment. Hunt et al. suggest that this successful group may differ from relapsers in both physiological and psychological characteristics. However, attempts to assess these differentiating characteristics have not been marked by success.

We are presently pursuing attempts to study this successful group, some of whom have quit on their own. If we can learn of the techniques or experiences that contributed to their success we may be able to incorporate them in future treatment packages. For the present, reviews of the long-term efficacy of behavioral treatment for addictive behaviors often reach conclusions similar to those outlined by Hunt et al. (1971). They find good short-term efficacy and inadequate long-term (greater than three months) success. The cases to be presented in this chapter cover the areas of problem drinking, smoking, and obesity, thus the findings of recent reviews of these literatures will underscore our point.

Miller and Hester (1980) have suggested a one-year posttreatment success rate of 26 percent for alcoholics. They defined success as including abstinence from alcohol use as well as showing an improvement in drinking behavior. Similarly,

Emrick's (1975) review of the literature on treatment of alcoholics using a variety of psychological approaches found that "differences in treatment methods did not significantly affect long-term outcome" (p. 88). In assessing data for follow-ups of six months or longer, Emrick reported an average abstinence rate of 15.9 percent for those receiving no treatment or minimal treatment, and 24.5 percent for those receiving more than minimal treatment. This difference was not significant. Treatment had some added impact in producing improvement via reductions in alcohol consumption. Even given the methodological limitations in some of the studies included in Emrick's sample, an abstinence rate of approximately 25 percent for those receiving treatment conforms to the trend reported by Hunt et al. (1971).

In a review of smoking treatment studies, Leventhal and Cleary (1980) found "an impressive decrease in smoking during treatment" (p. 374), a relatively high rate of attrition, and poor maintenance within the first six months of follow-up, continuing to a 16 to 25 percent success rate at 12 months. These success rates were similar across different modes of treatment. Similarly, recent reviews of behavioral treatment of obesity (Stunkard & Penick, 1979; Wilson, & Brownell, 1980) have concluded that long-term maintenance is poor. Stunkard and Penick's (1979) review of follow-up studies found that, although behavioral treatment consistently produced greater short-term weight loss than alternative treatments, these weight losses were not maintained. They attribute this lack of long-term efficacy to a lack of focus on maintenance strategies. Wilson and Brownell's (1980) review of controlled comparisons of long-term (one year or greater) weight loss also reported either poor maintenance (where weight loss is regained) or maintenance of posttreatment weight loss without additional loss during follow-up. Even when weight loss continues to occur, the magnitude of the loss is often not seen as being clinically significant.

We hope that this brief discussion has underscored the issue of limited long-term efficacy in the behavioral treatment of problems of addiction. The patterns described in reviews of controlled comparisons of treatment efficacy are also found in individual cases seen in clinical practice. We would now like to present a model of relapse prevention that seeks to describe the process of relapse as well as suggesting interventions for lessening the likelihood of the occurrence of a relapse. Finally, we will present three cases that illustrate failure in the treatment of problems of addiction due to early relapses. Our analysis of these cases suggests strategies for transforming these clinical failures into successes.

THE RELAPSE PREVENTION MODEL

Marlatt and Gordon (1980) have developed a model of relapse prevention that addresses many of the issues outlined in our discussion of maintenance. The model includes an examination of the process of relapse as well as recommendations for interventions at different points along the chain of events leading to a relapse episode.

The development of the model began with the examination of the situational determinants of relapse and the individual's cognitive reaction to both the initial relapse episode and subsequent use of the addictive substance. Detailed accounts of relapse episodes were obtained from individuals in treatment for excessive alcohol use, smoking, and heroin addiction. These were content analyzed and placed in categories defined by the nature of the precipitant of the relapse. It was found that the interpersonal and situational determinants of relapse were similar across addictive behaviors, suggesting that both the occurrence and treatment of relapse shared commonalities. Thus the relapse prevention model can be applied to a variety of addictive behaviors.

The cognitive-behavioral model of the relapse process is presented in Figure 13.1. It assumes that the individual has voluntarily made a choice to abstain from, or to control the use of, an addicting substance. Having made that choice, the individual is often faced with "high-risk" situations which pose a threat or challenge to his or her sense of control. Maintenance of the choice to abstain while in a high-risk situation leads to an increased sense of control and self-efficacy (Bandura, 1977), and a decreased probability of relapse. The lack of a response for coping with a high-risk situation initiates a chain of events in which a decreased sense of self-efficacy leads to initial use of the substance. Initial consumption is even more likely to occur if the individual has positive expectations for the effects of the substance. For example, the problem drinker who feels that having a drink will help him or her to cope with feelings of anger or frustration is more likely to begin drinking when he or she experiences these emotions than one who believes that alcohol will exacerbate these emotions.

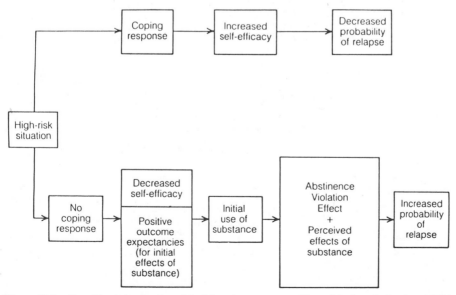

Figure 13.1.   Cognitive-behavioral model of the relapse process. (From Marlatt, & Gordon, 1980.)

Initial use of the substance following a period of abstinence may lead to a cognitive reaction to transgressing self-imposed limits on substance usage called the abstinence violation effect (AVE). The AVE is composed of two elements: cognitive dissonance and a personal attribution effect. The cognitive dissonance component involves a conflict between the individual's self-image as an abstainer (or moderate consumer of the substance) and the behavior of consuming beyond these self-imposed limits. The cause of the infraction is usually attributed to a personal weakness (e.g., lack of willpower, a disease process) or failure. Having failed once there is an expectation of continued failure. If the initial effects of the substance conform to the individual's positive expectations, the likelihood of continued use is even stronger.

Marlatt and Gordon (1980) also describe a series of cognitive and behavioral interventions that can be instituted to counteract the different components leading to a full-blown relapse.

As presented in Figure 13.2, these interventions serve to either prevent the occurrence of a relapse or to lessen the impact of a particular relapse episode. An important first step in preventing a relapse is training in the recognition and monitoring of the emotional and environmental antecedents of substance use in high-risk situations. Even before being faced with a high-risk situation the individual may initiate the process of relapse by making "apparently irrelevant deci-

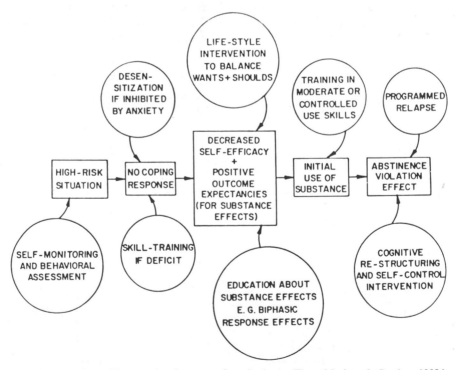

Figure 13.2.   Points of intervention for prevention of relapse. (From Marlatt, & Gordon, 1980.)

sions" (AIDS) that lead to high-risk situations. For example, the obese individual who loves pastries may for no apparent reason decide to take a route home which goes by his or her favorite bakery. Once the high-risk situation of smelling and seeing his or her favorite pastries has occurred, it becomes extremely difficult to resist surpassing self-imposed caloric limits. In such situations individuals set themselves up for a relapse by making decisions not directly related to consuming the addictive substance which place them at high risk. The tendency to make such decisions can be monitored and strategies for preventing AIDs from culminating in a relapse can be applied. This may involve teaching individuals to recognize and think through decisions that may place them at high risk and to generate alternatives to following through on an AID.

For the individual who does not possess the responses needed to cope with a particular high-risk situation, skill-training can provide a number of coping strategies. As presented in a study by Chaney, O'Leary, and Marlatt (1978), skill-training involves assessment of high-risk situations salient to the individual, followed by presentation of these situations in a format where coping strategies can be formulated. Techniques such as modeling, role-playing, and behavioral rehearsal are used to both generate and practice effective ways of handling high-risk situations. Once learned, these strategies can be implemented when necessary.

Some individuals already possess the coping response but its performance is inhibited by feelings of anxiety. Anxiety reduction techniques such as systematic desensitization can be used to lessen such anxiety, thus increasing the likelihood that the individual will effectively cope with high-risk situations. Education about the long-term negative effects of a substance may serve to counteract the initial positive effects, or to dampen positive expectations concerning its effects.

For the individual with low self-efficacy expectations both the structuring of success experiences and the development of a balanced lifestyle can be highly effective interventions. A balanced lifestyle is one in which external demands that are a source of stress (shoulds) are symmetrical with internal needs that provide pleasure (wants). If consumption of the addicting substance serves as a means of coping with lifestyle stresses, then a balance between wants and shoulds is likely to remove a powerful precipitant of relapses.

Both cognitive and behavioral interventions can be used to counter the components of the abstinence violation effect. One such intervention is the "programmed relapse" in which the individual experiences a relapse at a predetermined time under the supervision of the therapist. The therapist is available to provide some measure of control of consumption and to aid the client in processing reactions to usage of the substance. Misconceptions and faulty cognitions can be questioned and refuted while actually being experienced and behavioral alternatives can be generated and applied in vivo. A programmed relapse may be particularly useful with individuals who believe that internal factors dictate that any use of the substance inevitably leads to complete readdiction. Consumption of the addicting substance under controlled circumstances can undermine these beliefs when it is seen that no untoward consequences occur and that consumption can be externally mediated, time limited, and situation specific. The use of pharmacologically inert placebo substances such as near beer or mixed drinks such as those employed in research with the balanced placebo design in alcohol (cf., Marlatt & Roshenow, 1980), or foods in which the caloric content is disguised (cf., Ruderman & Wilson, 1979) can also serve to undermine beliefs concerning the effects of a particular substance. Interventions such as cognitive restructuring or rehearsal in imagination can also counter faulty cognitions concerning the use and effect of addictive substances.

PROBLEM DRINKING: A CASE STUDY

Liane is a 30-year-old single female who came to A.M.'s attention following the presentation of a lecture on alcoholism (Marlatt, 1978). She was a senior undergraduate majoring in psychology. She had become concerned about her drinking because it was interfering with her studies and she was doing poorly on her exams. Liane lived alone in a self-contained apartment in her parent's home. She did not have a steady boyfriend and spent much of her time either alone or with her parents with whom she often did not get along. She did not feel comfortable relating to other people unless she had been drinking. Her drinking history revealed that for the months prior to seeking treatment she used alcohol as a means of coping with negative emotional states related to her situation.

Treatment began with a two-week daily self-monitoring report of alcohol intake. The report revealed that Liane was consuming almost a quart of vodka each day. Drinking usually occurred in the evening while she sat alone watching television in her apartment. On other occasions she also consumed a variety of tranquilizers and barbituates. After this self-monitoring phase, Liane agreed to be hospitalized for medical supervision of her detoxification from alcohol and the other drugs she had been consuming. Hospitalization lasted for approximately one week. Before leaving the hospital Liane committed herself to complete abstinence from alcohol for a period of at least one year. It was agreed that her therapist would provide "supportive therapy" during this period. This support consisted of encouragement to maintain abstinence and discussion of issues of dependency and control in her relationship with her parents. Sessions were not regularly scheduled but were instituted as needed by Liane.

This arrangement was quite successful initially. For approximately the first two months following detoxification Liane perceived herself as being in control by not drinking and reported no difficulties related to urges or temptations to consume alcohol. However, 58 days following detoxification Liane consumed her first alcoholic beverage. She had gone to lunch with a neighborhood acquaintance whom she did not know well and whom she admired. At the beginning of lunch a waitress had appeared and asked for cocktail orders. Liane was unprepared for this occurrence and following on the example provided by her friend she also ordered and consumed a mixed drink. This situation was repeated approximately three weeks later when she again went out to lunch with the same friend and ordered and consumed a mixed drink. On both of these occasions Liane found drinking an unpleasant experience leading to feelings of lowered self-esteem, guilt, and remorse.

Three days after the second luncheon Liane found herself in a situation that in the past had led to drinking. It was a Saturday night and she was at home alone feeling melancholy and anxious and had nothing to do. While searching for a pharmacological agent to help relieve these feelings she found some alcohol and pills and consumed them. She became intoxicated and awoke with a hangover. This was an important occurrence in the series of events leading to a resumption of her pretreatment consumption patterns. Liane gradually resumed social drinking which sometimes led to intoxication. Once classes resumed she returned to her pattern of daily drinking. It had taken only two months for Liane to break her commitment to abstinence and even with therapeutic support she resumed daily drinking approximately four months following detoxification. In the judgment of both Liane and her therapist she was a treatment failure.

Factors Contributing to the Relapse

There are a number of factors that can be seen as contributing to Liane's relapse. The first drink following detoxification occurred in a high-risk situation for which she had no coping strategy. Liane was out with an acquaintance whom she did not know well and who did not know about her drinking problem. She also had positive expectations for the effects of alcohol. Liane had often felt that she could not relate well to others without drinking and she wanted to make a good impression on her friend, thus having a drink may have been seen as an indication of poise and as a social lubricant. There was also the element of surprise. Liane was not prepared for the encounter with the cocktail waitress and had no alternatives to modeling her friend's behavior and also ordering a drink. During both her first and second drinks Liane experienced a strong abstinence violation effect (AVE) involving both physical symptoms and emotions such as guilt, remorse, and lowered self-esteem.

Liane's first intoxication experience also occurred in a high-risk situation similar to those that had contributed to the initial development of her drinking problem. She was at home alone, feeling sad and anxious. This type of situation is often a difficult one for persons who abuse alcohol. Our categorization of relapse episodes (Marlatt & Gordon, 1980) suggests that for alcoholics, 38 percent of relapses occurred in negative emotional states such as frustration, anger, or anxiety. Liane possessed no skills for coping with these negative emotions and no alternatives to drinking or drug use as a means of coping with the situation. Lastly, she possessed strong positive expectations for the effects of alcohol as a means of relieving feelings of sadness and anxiety. The relapse prevention model suggests that the combination of these factors provided a potent precipitant for a full-blown relapse.

Alternative Interventions for Preventing Relapse

The relapse prevention model suggests a number of interventions that may have improved on the limited success seen in this case. One of the first interventions would be skill training for both monitoring and coping with the high-risk situations in which Liane's drinking occurred. Liane seemed to have particular difficulty coping with negative emotions such as sadness and boredom, and in handling indirect social pressure situations such as the modeling provided by her friend. One strategy for handling negative emotions is to construct a list of alternative activities that the client finds pleasurable. When feelings of sadness occur the client can refer to the list and choose an activity likely to provide enjoyment. Thus Liane could have made plans to be out of the house on a Saturday night, or taken a sensuous bubble bath, read, cooked, or taken a drive. For handling the negative effects of anxiety, training in anxiety reduction techniques such as meditation or relaxation may have provided effective alternatives to the anticipated anxiety reducing effects of alcohol consumption.

Training in social skills and/or assertiveness would have provided Liane with strategies for handling her other major high-risk situation, social pressure. Liane seemed to lack the self-confidence for expressing her opinions and needs. The learning of techniques for handling social situations with the public, friends, or even her parents, would have been a good initial step in the development of a more fulfilling social life. Inasmuch as Liane tended to model the drinking behavior of her friends, providing information about the modeling effect (Collins & Marlatt 1981) may have also provided a strategy for lessening conformity in drinking-related social pressure situations.

Positive expectations concerning the effects of alcohol can often be countered by education about the biphasic effects of alcohol. Recent research has indicated that the initial stimulating effects of alcohol are followed by delayed depressant effects. Liane seemed to consume alcohol for its stimulant effects, therefore, knowledge about the physiological effects of alcohol may have prevented drinking to intoxication. If she did choose to drink, training in moderate consumption to maintain low blood alcohol levels while experiencing stimulant effects would have been a viable treatment strategy.

As with other cases of relapse, Liane experienced strong abstinence violation effects. Cognitive restructuring techniques to help the client view a slip as externally mediated and situation specific are likely to have lessened feelings of guilt and remorse that contributed to subsequent excessive consumption of alcohol.

SMOKING: A CASE STUDY

Jim B. is a 42-year-old married male who came for help with his "addiction problems". He said during the initial visit that he wanted to make some important changes in his lifestyle so as to avoid the possibility that he might die of an early heart attack—his father and grandfather both died of cardiovascular disorders prior to the age of 50. In describing his current lifestyle, Mr. B. said that he was a heavy smoker, frequently drank excessively in an attempt to deal with stress, was overweight, and did not engage in any regular program of exercise. He described himself as a "workaholic", putting in long 10-hour workdays (often working both evenings and weekends) as the manager of an import-export business, rarely taking vacations or time off for himself. After discussion of various treatment goals, it was decided to begin treatment by focusing on his smoking.

Mr. B's smoking history revealed that he started smoking as a teenager and had never stopped smoking on a daily basis since then. His current daily smoking rate was approximately 30 cigarettes a day (20 per day on weekends). Smoking was his primary means of coping with the work stress during the day whereas drinking became the main coping agent in the evening. He described a strong fear of failure in becoming involved in another smoking treatment program. He had attempted to quit on two previous occasions by attending professional treatment programs such as Smokenders and the Schick Center for the Control of Smoking. Neither program was successful in that he was unable to quit smoking for longer than a 24-hour period. Because of these prior failure experiences, he felt a lack of confidence (low self-efficacy) concerning his ability to quit smoking in the present program. Despite these reservations, he agreed to set a quit date two weeks following the initial visit.

During the two weeks prior to the quit date Mr. B. was asked to cut back on his daily cigarette consumption by one third (during the first week) and to switch to a low-nicotine brand (second week), in order to taper him off his high daily doses of nicotine. This strategy seemed particularly important in his case, inasmuch as he expressed considerable anxiety about the possibility of experiencing severe physical withdrawal symptoms upon cessation.

Mr. B. was asked if it were possible for him to take a few days off from the office at the time of his quit date. He insisted that it would not be possible for him to do so because of pressing work demands. He was seen on the scheduled quit date, a Monday afternoon in January. In order to increase the cost demands of returning to smoking, a contingency contract was prepared for Mr. B. to sign on the day of his quitting (he had previously agreed to this procedure). The contract, intended to cover the first three weeks of abstinence, called for a fine of $50.00 for each cigarette smoked during this period. The money was to be sent to a social or political organization which Mr. B. particularly disliked (he chose the Ku Klux Klan). At the time of our meeting on the quit date, Mr. B. signed the contract and destroyed his remaining cigarettes. He also had prepared a list of behaviors he could use as alternatives to smoking during the first week (e.g., sipping ice water, mints, toothpicks, etc.). As he left the session, he seemed tense and ill at ease.

His tension was a sign of what was to come. Although he was able to get through that evening without smoking (he went to bed early), he smoked his first cigarette at 4:00 PM the next day. He was reluctant to return to therapy because of this "failure" experience, but was convinced to do so as soon as possible so that he could discuss what happened and make new plans. He came in a day later, reluctantly. As it turned out, this was to be his last session.

On the day of his relapse, Mr. B. went to the office at his usual time, 6:30 AM. ("I have to get there that early in order to telephone clients on the East Coast before they go out for lunch," he said.) By noon, he was feeling tense and complained of a number of stressful work pressures. His craving for a cigarette increased as the afternoon wore on, and he described himself as tense and irritable. He attributed these unpleasant feelings to physical withdrawal symptoms. He described feeling that it was like having a balloon inside that kept getting larger in size, as though someone was blowing it up. "I was afraid that if I didn't do something to relieve the pressure, the balloon would . . .burst!" He explained this further by saying that he was afraid the pressure would continue to mount until he "would lose control" or "go out of my mind." By late afternoon, he could stand it no longer. On his way out of the office, he "sneaked" a cigarette from his secretary's pack. Once in his car, he could hardly wait to light it up. "I inhaled practically the entire cigarette in one huge drag", he said sadly. "I just had to do something to make the pain go away." An attempt was made to convince Mr. B. that a single failure experience did not mean that it was impossible for him to quit in the long run, and that another approach could be tried at the next session. These arguments failed to have an effect. He canceled his next session and has not been heard from since.

Factors Contributing to the Relapse

Due to his previous failure experiences, Mr. B. began treatment with a lack of confidence in his ability to successfully quit smoking. This attitude is likely to have provided a mental set, or self-fulfilling prophecy of failure, that was substantiated by the experience of the first slip. His strong fear of failure also made it difficult for him to try alternative treatment strategies.

The timing and location of Mr. B.'s initial attempts to quit smoking were poor. His lifestyle and work situation were filled with stress and tension that his "addictive problems" served to alleviate. Inasmuch as smoking was his primary coping response for work-related stress, choosing to spend his first quit date at work placed him in a high-risk situation. Possessing no alternative strategies for effectively coping with this stress, he returned to his usual coping response, smoking.

Mr. B. also experienced strong urges to smoke. These cravings made having a cigarette seem very positive whereas the anticipation and experience of unpleasant withdrawal symptoms made abstinence aversive. The lack of strategies for coping with these cravings and urges is also likely to have facilitated the return to smoking.

Alternative Interventions for Preventing Relapse

Were Mr. B. to be seen again there are a number of things that could be done differently. First, more time should have been spent exploring his fear of failure and the anticipated agonies of withdrawal. These fears could have been lessened by stressing the fact that quitting is like learning a new skill, such as learning to ride a bicycle. Most people do not expect perfect performance the first time they attempt to ride a bicycle. Rather they know that it often takes a spill or two before they learn to maintain their balance and ride without falling. Thus each "slip" can provide a valuable learning experience (learning what to do differently the next time) instead of fulfilling the client's fear of failure.

A contingency contract or fine for smoking should not have been used in this case because it tends to emphasize the need for total abstinence and reinforces the "punishment" aspects of the failure (e.g., having to pay a fine). Instead, some attempt should have been made to intervene in Mr. B's workaholic lifestyle *before* he attempted to quit smoking. The teaching of relaxation skills, reordering of his work day to introduce more breaks or "self-time" periods, or encouragement to engage in regular exercise and other leisure activities would have created a more balanced lifestyle. Even with a more balanced lifestyle, Mr. B. should have chosen a quit date that did not coincide with the first day of a stressful work week. Quitting during a vacation or over a long weekend would maximize the probability of even short-term success.

There are a number of cognitive techniques that could be used to help Mr. B. cope with his withdrawal symptoms and urges. Specifically he could be taught to see these urges as having a limited time-course or duration, and not as continuing indefinitely. One useful approach is to provide the client with the expectation that an urge or craving (like any response) will increase in intensity until it reaches a peak or plateau. After this period of maximum discomfort however, the urge will eventually subside as long as one does not "give in" and begin smoking. Subsequent urges will have shorter durations, until eventually the urges and discomfort subside, often within a few days following cessation. He could also learn to externalize the urge (e.g., to say, "I am experiencing an urge and it will eventually pass"), rather than to identify with it in a personal manner (e.g., "I crave a cigarette and if I have one I will immediately feel better"). Personal identification with the urge tends to enhance positive expectations about the effects of the substance, thus facilitating its continued use.

Following these first weeks of treatment, with the emphasis on coping with urges and physical withdrawal symptoms, the next phase of treatment would be to prepare the client for handling high-risk situations, as specified in our relapse-prevention model. Further work to modify an imbalanced lifestyle and to reduce the stress generated by a workaholic approach to the job is also likely to have enhanced the maintenance of treatment effects.

Obesity: A Case Study

Mrs. S. is a 41-year-old married female who came to treatment for help with losing weight. She is a housewife and mother of three children ranging in age from 11 to 19 years. She described her family life as being relatively happy. She related a history of weight gain beginning after her first pregnancy at age 22. Until that time she had no weight problem and weighed approximately 125 pounds, relatively close to the ideal weight for her height of 5 ft. 4 in. Her weight continued to increase after each of her three pregnancies, as she stated, "I just never seemed to get back to normal between babies". After reaching 169 pounds 10 years ago she became involved in formal weight control programs including hypnosis, fad diets, exercise, and Overeaters Anonymous. During this time she experienced variable patterns of success in which she lost significant (up to 20 pounds) amounts of weight which she then gradually regained. For the most part she found it easy to lose weight during the initial weeks on each new program. However, when the rate of weight loss began to decrease she felt less motivated and soon the weight would be regained. Her most successful weight loss had been 20 pounds and occurred approximately six years previously when she and a friend had gone on a diet and taken an exercise class together. However, after three months her friend had moved and Mrs. S. found it difficult to continue alone. She was able to maintain the 20 pounds weight loss for almost eight months.

Mrs. S. described herself as someone who had trouble controling her food intake because of her constant exposure to food while preparing meals for her family. She served as her family's "short order cook" preparing meals at various times each day to suit the busy schedules of her husband and three children. She often found herself eating while preparing meals and snacks and/or eating food left at the end of meals. Inasmuch as she was the only member of her family who had a weight problem, she was surrounded by high calorie foods that were bought for other members of the family. Her family was somewhat supportive of her efforts to lose weight but she felt they should not have to sacrifice their favorite foods in order to accommodate her diet. She also felt that they had lost faith in her ability to lose weight having seen her limited success over the past 10 years.

Mrs. S. began her weight control program weighing 173 pounds. She set her goal weight at 130 pounds, an anticipated loss of 43 pounds. After one week of self-monitoring of her normal food intake, Mrs. S. was placed on a behavioral treatment program that included caloric restriction (1100 calories per day), self-monitoring of food intake, stimulus control, and information about nutrition and exercise. During the 10 weeks of treatment Mrs. S. was taught the behavioral techniques mentioned and was provided with strategies relevant to her particular situation. For example, she came to realize that each member of her family could prepare his or her own snacks and that desires for high calorie treats such as candy or ice cream could be met outside the home. She also began an exercise program of weekly swimming at the local YWCA and was encouraged to take daily walks.

Mrs. S. was quite successful at losing weight during the first 10 weeks of treatment. Initially, she was frustrated with the gradual weight loss resulting from a behavioral weight control program. However, she soon became pleased with her successes at learning new eating habits and with her cummulative weight loss. At the end of the 10 treatment sessions Mrs. S. had lost approximately 18 pounds, an average loss of 1.8 pounds per week. Weekly sessions were discontinued after

Mrs. S. decided that she had mastered the techniques. She felt confident that she could successfully lose the remaining 25 pounds to her goal. In fact, she promised to return "in a bikini". Mrs. S. was encouraged to contact the therapist when necessary but no sessions were scheduled beyond a follow-up meeting in four months.

Mrs. S. was contacted by telephone at one-month intervals. On each occasion she reported continued success with her weight loss program. However, she did not come in for her scheduled appointment four months after treatment. When contacted, Mrs. S. confessed to having regained seven of the 18 pounds lost during treatment. She had "felt ashamed" to report this to the therapist during previous telephone contacts. She reported that one month following the end of treatment she had regained two pounds and could feel herself falling into her old patterns of behavior. She returned to catering to her family's food needs. Increased contact with food led to increased urges to consume favorites which, in turn, led to violations of her caloric limits. She was frustrated that having made a commitment to avoid fattening foods such as desserts and ice cream, she often acted on urges to eat them. As she came closer to her scheduled four-month visit her goal seemed to slip away and she "lost heart". She was now reconciled to remaining overweight and felt badly about "having spent all that money on treatment and blowing it".

Factors Contributing to the Relapse

Mrs. S. lacked a good social support system for her weight control efforts. Her family was minimally supportive and she did not have any close friends with whom she could share her problems and triumphs. After the first 10 weeks of treatment she also lost regular contact with the therapist, who had previously served as her main external source of support.

Some of the reason for this lack of alternative social support was the fact that Mrs. S.'s lifestyle was unidimensional. She focused most of her attention and energy on the needs of her family, even when it meant denial of her own needs. This exclusive focus made it difficult for her to ask that her family accept responsibility for some of their own food needs. Thus it became easy to return to traditional patterns in which she bought and prepared food even though exposure to these food cues provided irresistable temptations and urges to consume. A paucity of alternative social and recreational activities aided in maintaining this focus on family and food.

Negative cognitions also contributed to Mrs. S.'s lack of success. Due to her previous failures she initially possessed limited confidence in her ability to lose weight. This attitude was reinforced by her family's negative expectations concerning weight loss. When she began to lose weight, Mrs. S. shifted from expectations of failure to unrealistically positive expectations concerning the potential for long-term success. Her promise to "return in a bikini" in four months is a good example of this expectation. Mrs. S. also experienced a strong abstinence violation effect after she began to regain weight. Her experiences of guilt and shame as well as self-attribution of the causes of the relapse made it difficult for her to see any possibility for change. She soon became reconciled to her state and ceased her efforts to lose weight.

Alternative Interventions for Preventing Relapse

The fact that Mrs. S.'s most successful attempts to lose weight occurred with the support of a friend suggests that external sources of social support may have been important in maintaining her motivation to lose weight. If such is the case, some attempt should have been made to provide Mrs. S. with a strong social support system. Were family members and friends not immediately available, regularly scheduled contact with the therapist should either have been maintained until the goal weight was reached or should have been curtailed gradually while Mrs. S. was encouraged to develop her own social supports. Ideally, it would have been best to include the family in treatment because responsibility for their food needs was a major precipitant of Mrs. S.'s relapses.

Mrs. S.'s focus on her family provided few opportunities for "self-time," that is, time to focus on activities that she found reinforcing and pleasurable. Strategies for balancing the "shoulds" of her responsibility to her family and to her own needs and interests may have made it easier to view her weight control efforts as being of the highest priority. Instead Mrs. S. seemed to give weight control a low priority.

Though Mrs. S. initially described problems related to the stimulus control of food, a behavioral treatment program may have been too limited in scope. Mrs. S. possessed a number of negative cognitions concerning her potential for success which contributed to her relapse. She can be said to subscribe to the irrational idea that past influences determine present feelings and behaviors, particularly in relation to her family. Once she had experienced her first slip, the abstinence violation effect added to her negative self-evaluation. The AVE and other negative cognitions should have been addressed using cognitive restructuring techniques. Teaching Mrs. S. to question her negative cognitions about herself, to distance herself from overeating behaviors, or to label herself positively would have lessened the contributions of negative cognitions to her relapse.

Inasmuch as abstinence from food is not a viable treatment goal for the obese client, individuals like Mrs. S. who are highly responsive to food cues should be prepared for the possibility that a slip or relapse may occur. This can be accomplished via discussion of the cognitive and behavioral precipitants and sequela of past slips. Preparing strategies for handling slips before they occur may not only lessen the severity and duration of future slips but may also lessen some of the impact of the abstinence violation effect. The individual who can anticipate and prepare for a slip is likely to feel less guilt or remorse inasmuch as the slip can be seen as a natural occurrence in the progress of treatment. This attitude will decrease the likelihood that a slip will inevitably lead to a full-blown relapse. In Mrs. S.'s case, preparation for the occurrence of a slip may have lessened expectations for an easy and trouble-free weight loss program.

In applications of the relapse prevention model to obesity (Rosenthal & Marx, 1980), an important component of treatment is training in the assessment and handling of high-risk situations. This training usually involves presenting the client with information concerning frequent high-risk situations, learning how to label and monitor one's own high-risk situation, and the discussion of alternative strategies for handling these situations. Role-playing, modeling, or guided imagery can be used to both develop and practice these skills. Given that Mrs. S. described high-risk situations related to the viewing and/or preparation of food, training in how to handle these situations could have been effective in reducing the likelihood of a relapse.

SUMMARY AND CONCLUSIONS

The cases presented are typical of those seen in our clinical practice and are likely to be representative of those seen by behavioral clinicians working with problems of addiction. We have described a number of interpersonal and environmental factors that can contribute to the failure to achieve or maintain treatment goals. Many of these were highlighted in the cases presented. Although there were many differences between these cases, these differences do not seem to be due to the type of addiction being treated but rather to the constellation of events that triggered and maintained use of the addictive substance. Despite individual variability, these cases highlight similar issues concerning our implementation of behavioral approaches to treatment. One common error seems to be use of the "shotgun approach" in which a variety of treatment techniques are applied without a detailed analysis of the relevance of that particular technique for that individual. A related problem is the fact that maintenance issues are either separated from treatment issues or are often not addressed.

The relapse prevention approach seeks to remedy both of these shortcomings by providing a broad cognitive-behavioral model of the factors that commonly contribute to treatment failure in the form of a relapse. It suggests that by understanding the process of relapse we can better anticipate its occurrence and can develop more efficacious treatment programs. By providing the clinician with a conceptual framework that encourages the incorporation of strategies for maintenance into the initial phases of treatment, it encourages looking beyond achievement of limited treatment goals defined by initial cessation of the use of the addictive substance.

Working to anticipate and prevent relapses before they occur is likely to both decrease the calamitous nature of their occurrence and facilitate recovery. Instead of being a failure experience, slips and relapses can become a natural occurrence in the long-term treatment of addictions that provide new opportunities for learning. Application of the relapse prevention model to problems of addiction in individual cases (Collins & Carlin, in press) and in groups (Rosenthal & Marx, 1980) have indicated some success in the enhancement of maintenance of treatment effects. We hope that continued application of the relapse prevention model will produce a greater degree of future success in the treatment of addictive behaviors.

REFERENCES

Bandura, A. (1977) Self-efficacy: Toward a unifying theory of behavior change. *Psychological Review,* **84,** 191–215.

Chaney, E.F., O'Leary, M.R., & Marlatt, G.A. (1978) Skill-training with alcoholics. *Journal of Consulting and Clinical Psychology,* **46,** 1092–1104.

Collins, R.L., & Carlin, A.S. (in press) Case study: The cognitive-behavioral treatment of a multiple drug abuser. *Psychotherapy: Theory, Research and Practice.*

Collins, R.L., & Marlatt, G.A. (1981) Social modeling as a determinant of drinking behavior: Implications for prevention and treatment. *Addictive Behaviors*, 6, 233–239.

Emrick, C.D. (1975) A review of psychologically oriented treatment of alcoholism. *Journal of Studies on Alcohol,* **36,** 88–108.

Hunt, W.A., Barnett, L.W., & Branch, L.G. (1971) Relapse rates in addiction programs. *Journal of Clinical Psychology,* **27,** 455–456.

Leventhal, H., & Cleary, P.D. (1980) The smoking problem: A review of the research and theory in behavioral risk modification. *Psychological Bulletin,* **88,** 370–405.

Marlatt, G.A. (1978) Craving for alcohol, loss of control and relapse: A cognitive-behavioral analysis. In P.E. Nathan, G.A. Marlatt, & T. Loberg (Eds.), *Alcoholism: New directions in behavioral research and treatment.* New York: Plenum.

Marlatt, G.A., & Gordon, J.R. (1980) Determinants of relapse: Implications for the maintenance of behavior change. In P.O. Davidson, & S.M. Davidson (Eds.), *Behavioral medicine: Changing health lifestyles.* New York: Brunner/Mazel.

Marlatt, G.A., & Roshenow, D.J. (1980) Cognitive processes in alcohol use: Expectancy and the balanced placebo design. In N.K. Mello (Ed.), *Advances in substance abuse: Behavioral and biological research.* Greenwich, Conn.: JAI Press.

Miller, W.R., & Hester, R.K. (1980) Treating the problem drinker: Modern approaches. In W.R. Miller (Ed.), *The addictive behaviors.* Oxford: Pergamon.

Rosenthal, B.S., & Marx, R.D. (1980) *A comparison of standard behavioral and relapse prevention weight reduction programs.* Unpublished manuscript, University of Minnesota.

Ruderman, A.J., & Wilson, G.T. (1979) Weight, restraint, cognitions, and counter-regulation. *Behaviour Research and Therapy,* **17,** 581–590.

Stunkard, A.J., & Penick, S.B. (1979) Behavior modification in the treatment of obesity: The problem of maintaining weight loss. *Archives of General Psychiatry,* **36,** 801–806.

Wilson, G.T., & Brownell, K.D. (1980) Behaviour therapy for obesity: An evaluation of treatment outcome. *Advances in Behaviour Research and Therapy,* **3,** 49–86.

CHAPTER 14

Controlled Drinking

MICHAEL PERTSCHUK

THE CONTROVERSY

A dramatic change in the study and treatment of alcoholism began 20 years ago with Davies's (1962) article reporting normal drinking among previously treated alcoholics. In routine follow-up, 7 percent were found to have been drinking normally for periods of up to 11 years. Similar observations had been made previously but Davies was the first to draw the attention of the alcohol treatment community. There followed a flurry of articles countering Davies (Fox, 1963; Lemere, 1963; Tiebout, 1963; Zwerling, 1963) but these did little to dampen the interest of other researchers. Depending on one's biases, the cat was out of the bag or Pandora's box had been opened.

Pattison (1966), in reanalyzing outcome literature to that time and in his own study (Pattison, Headley, Gleser, & Gottschalk, 1968), confirmed that a significant minority of alcoholics did resume moderate alcohol intake. Pokorny, Miller, and Cleveland (1968) found that 25 percent of alcoholic patients on follow-up were drinking normally for as long as a year. Similar results continue to be reported in the more recent literature. Bromet and Moos (1979) at six to eight-months follow-up observed that 22 percent of lower socioeconomic alcoholics and 29 percent of higher socioeconomic alcoholics were drinking moderately. Saunders and Kershaw (1979), investigating recovered alcoholics in a community-wide study, found 12 of 19 former alcoholics to be drinking moderately. The largest and most controversial study in this area was the Rand Report (Armor, Polich, and Stambul, 1976). The authors surveyed patients treated at federally sponsored alcohol treatment centers. Some 11,500 clients were assessed; 21 percent were successfully contacted for six-month follow-up and 62 percent of a designated subsample were contacted at 18 months. Normal drinking was observed in 12 percent of the six-month and 22 percent of the 18-month follow-up clients. The Rand Report, the findings about return to normal drinking, and the reaction of the members of the alcohol treatment community received considerable media attention. The authors were accused of recklessness and irresponsibility. The report was characterized by one official of the National Council on Alcoholism as "a slanted polemic advocating a return to normal drinking as a goal" (cited by Hodgson, 1979).

Anyone paging through the dry prose of the Rand Report would know that it is no polemic. The emotional greeting of this and other accounts of return to normal drinking can be traced to the immediate implications of this finding and to certain realities of the alcohol treatment "culture." If some alcoholics do resume normal drinking then loss of control over alcohol intake may be reversible. The goal of lifelong abstinence, therefore, might not be appropriate for all alcoholics. These possibilities run directly counter to Jellinek's (1960) highly influential conceptualization of what he defined as gamma alcoholism, according to which loss of control over alcohol intake is irreversible. Alcoholics Anonymous doctrine is similarly based on the idea of irreversible loss of control, "First we were smitten by an insane urge that condemned us to go on drinking and then by an allergy of the body that insured we would ultimately destroy ourselves in the process" (Alcoholics Anonymous, 1953, p. 22). As a number of alcoholism counselors and therapists come from the AA tradition and owe their rehabilitation to it, they have been, not surprisingly, less than cordial to alternative views.

Although much of the controversy over the nature of alcoholism derives from outcome data, the traditional concepts of alcoholism have also been challenged by direct observation of drinking behavior. Mello and Mendelson, in a series of pioneering studies, made alcohol available to alcoholics in laboratory settings. It was observed that alcoholics regulated their drinking according to a number of variables including the amount of work required to earn drinks (Mello & Mendelson, 1972), social circumstances of imbibing (Mendelson & Mello, 1966), and blood alcohol level (Mello & Mendelson, 1971). Gottheil, Thornton, Skolada, and Alterman (1979) similarly observed that when alcoholics were given choices of drinking or abstaining at fixed intervals during the day, few drank all the alcohol available and most regulated their intake considerably below the maximum quantity permitted. Such findings suggest that if there is a loss of control in alcoholism, it is relative and not an all or none phenomenon.

CONTROLLED DRINKING TREATMENT

The weight of evidence has been enough to convince some that there are alternatives to lifelong abstinence for the alcoholic. If loss of control is not absolute and some alcoholics resume normal drinking, then conceivably a larger number of alcoholics could be taught to improve their control and learn some approximation of normal drinking. The evidence, however, by no means compels this conclusion. The previously cited outcome data are all derived from abstinence oriented programs. It is probable that resumption of normal drinking had more to do with the course of the illness than treatment effects, a possibility suggested by the findings of similar frequencies of moderate drinking among patients receiving traditional, minimal (Oxford, Oppenheimer, & Edwards, 1976), or no treatment (Armor et al., 1976). The 10 to 20 percent of alcoholics returning to moderate intake could represent a separate, perhaps even physiologically distinct subset in which case their resumption of drinking would have no significance for the balance of the alcoholic population. A failure to find a total absence of control among alcoholics does not preclude the possibility of a relative impairment in the control mechanisms. Ludwig et al. (1978), in a study showing somewhat poorer ability among alcoholics to maintain a fixed blood alcohol level, postulated just such a relative impairment, perhaps physiologically derived. To the extent such a physiological partial impairment exists, it would impede or possibly preclude efforts at controlled drinking.

It has been clear enough that abstinence oriented treatment programs have not helped a substantial segment of the alcoholic population. The prospect of life-long abstinence may deter many from even seeking treatment. Therefore, notwithstanding the above outlined concerns, the potential of controlled drinking as a treatment goal has been sufficiently attractive to encourage research.

Lovibond and Caddy (1970) published one of the first reports on controlled drinking. Outpatient alcoholics were initially taught to discriminate different blood alcohol levels. In subsequent practice drinking sessions, painful electric shocks were administered to the face when drinking occurred with blood alcohol in excess of a predetermined value. In addition, patients were given general supportive counseling and training in self-regulation. By patient self-report, 85 percent were improved at 12 months and 59 percent at 24 months after treatment. In a later replication, Caddy and Lovibond (1976) observed a 76 percent improvement rate at 12-month follow-up. They also found that although training in self-regulation was slightly less effective than self-regulation combined with aversive conditioning, aversive conditioning alone led to considerably poorer outcome with 50 percent improved at 12 months.

Sobell and Sobell (1973, 1976) implemented a behavioral program for controlled drinking involving the administration of electric shock for inappropriate drinking behavior. Inappropriate behavior was defined as ordering a straight beverage, gulping, pacing drinks too rapidly, or ordering more than three drinks per session. Subjects were also confronted with a videotape replay of their behavior while intoxicated, and were given instructions in behavioral self-management. In contrast to the largely self-referred outpatients in the Lovibond and Caddy studies, those in the Sobell investigation were chronic alcoholic inpatients with significant psychosocial deficits. Outcome assessed as percentage of days "functioning well" (i.e., days abstinent or drinking in a controlled manner) revealed that at six-month follow-up, the behaviorally treated patients were functioning well on 85 percent of days as compared to 45 percent for traditionally treated controls. For the second posttreatment year, these figures were 85 and 42 percent, respectively. Caddy, Addington, and Perkins, (1978) in cooperation with the Sobells, performed an independent follow-up of these patients during the third posttreatment year. Controlled drinking patients were functioning well on 95 percent of days compared to 75 percent for traditionally treated patients. The meaning of these last figures is open to question, however, as 35 percent of the controlled drinking and 30 percent of the traditional treatment groups were not included in follow-up for a variety of reasons including incarceration and refusal to cooperate.

Pomerleau, Pertschuk, Adkins, and Brady (1978) conducted an outpatient program for "middle-income problem drinkers," that is, middle-class, largely socially intact individuals consuming an average of four ounces of absolute alcohol daily. Treatment included training in self-management techniques and the use of a prepaid commitment fee that was refunded for program compliance. At nine-month follow-up, 72 percent of behaviorally treated patients and 50 percent of a traditionally treated control group were rated as improved (abstinent or reduced intake). This was not a significant difference; however, the behaviorally treated group did have significantly fewer dropouts.

Miller, in a series of investigations has examined various strategies of intervention for controlled drinking. In one study (Miller, 1978), aversive conditioning, behavioral self-control training, and a combination of self-monitoring and aversive conditioning were compared. In the aversive condition, patients self-monitored intake and, during sessions conducted in a simulated bar, self-administered shock after picking up and sniffing their favorite beverage. Behavioral self-control training was directed toward identifying problem-drinking situations, altering them, reducing intake, and developing alternative coping strategies. The combination treatment included both self-control training and a replication of the Lovibond and Caddy (1970) procedure. At 12-month follow-up, all groups were performing comparably with about 60 percent categorized as abstinent or controlled drinking. In a second study (Miller and Taylor, 1980), four treatments were compared, bibliotherapy (use of a self-help manual), individual self-control training, individual self-control combined with relaxation training, and group behavioral self-control with relaxation training. Outcome at 12-month follow-up as percentage abstinent or drinking moderately was 33, 27, 38, and 60 percent, respectively. There have been other investigations, a number of which have been summarized in a review by Lloyd and Salzberg (1975).

These are studies reported as controlled drinking successes. To my knowledge there has been only one study recorded as a controlled drinking failure. Ewing and Rouse (1976) followed up 14 patients treated 27 to 55 months previously in a controlled drinking program. Treatment consisted of training in recognizing blood alcohol level, electric shock for drinking over a predetermined level and informal instruction in self-management. Categorizing patients according to their poorest functioning during any part of their follow-up, the authors reported that all 14 were treatment failures as all had experienced at least one episode of excessive drinking.

ASSESSMENT OF CONTROLLED DRINKING

The ultimate purpose of outcome studies is to demonstrate to the practitioner and public that a particular treatment is both safe and effective. The initial outcry over controlled drinking was that it was not safe. The fear was expressed that numbers of alcoholics, deluded into believing that they could drink, would drink and do themselves and society irreparable harm. There is no evidence to support the contention that controlled drinking is not safe. It has occurred without apparent detriment in treatments where it was not officially sanctioned. The increased publicity about controlled drinking has not had any notable impact on mortality or morbidity associated with alcoholism. Hingson, Scotch, and Goldman (1977) surveyed patients and staff at six alcoholism treatment centers, homeless men at a hostel, and a random sample of the general public concerning the Rand Report. They found that the report had minimal effect on attitudes and even less on behavior. Only one study, that of Ewing and Rouse (1976), implied major risk from controlled drinking. In their study, all 14 patients participating in a controlled drinking program were reported as treatment failures. If all controlled drinking programs were equally ineffective, then alcoholics receiving such treatment would be courting disaster as inevitably they would all relapse. In examining this study, it is evident that almost absurdly stringent criteria were employed. Any single episode of what was called "uncontrolled" drinking over a period of years was sufficient to categorize a patient as a treatment failure. By such criteria, virtually all therapeutic interventions for addictive and psychiatric disorders would be dismissed as ineffective or dangerous. Contrary to this study, it has been observed that approximately equivalent numbers of alcoholics demonstrate stable patterns of abstinence or controlled drinking over extended periods (Gottheil et al., 1979; Polich, Armor, & Braiker, 1980). Clearly there is a subset of alcoholics with alcohol-related health problems for whom any further drinking, even on a controlled basis, would be dangerous; however, virtually all controlled drinking programs described in the literature specifically exclude such individuals.

The effectiveness of controlled drinking is much more difficult to determine. Effectiveness may depend on the population treated, how treatment is instituted, and the match between treatment and population.

Population Variables

Population variables in controlled drinking have received some attention. Health is one such variable and as discussed above has been dealt with by excluding medically compromised alcoholics from treatment. The most extensively investigated variable has been the severity of alcohol abuse. Saunders and Kershaw (1979), in a previously cited community study, found that resumption of social drinking was more likely to occur among alcoholics with a briefer duration of illness. Abstinence was the more likely outcome for the chronic patients. Popham and Schmidt (1976), in the context of a traditional therapeutic program with controlled drinking as a stated aim, found that the best predictor of achieving controlled drinking was the pretreatment level of alcohol intake. Patients with a less severe alcohol problem were more likely to maintain a controlled drinking pattern. Orford, Oppenheimer, and Edwards (1976), analyzing two year posttreatment data, found that patients reporting controlled drinking had been less symptomatic at intake with psychological rather than physical dependence on alcohol. Those maintaining abstinence were more likely to have been physiologically dependent on alcohol. Miller and Joyce (1979) examined three-month follow-up data from 141 participants in controlled drinking programs. They observed that compared to successful abstainers, controlled drinkers had less severe drinking problems, less family history of alcoholism, and somewhat higher incomes.

To the extent that controlled drinking succeeds, it appears to succeed with individuals with less severe alcohol problems in terms of duration of illness, symptomatology, and physical dependence. The Sobell study is the exception to this trend as controlled drinking was found to be more effective than abstinence oriented traditional treatment with severe chronic alcoholics. The Sobell program, however, was considerably different from those showing poorer outcome with the more severely ill. The program was more intensive and involved aversive conditioning, active training in appropriate drinking, and confrontational techniques.

Treatment Variables

It is difficult to assess the relative merits of different controlled drinking approaches. No truly large-scale comparison has been performed with the subject variables held constant. Further, there has been little consistency in the definition of treatment modalities, making crossstudy comparisons difficult. Caddy and Lovibond (1976) found aversive conditioning by itself less effective than training in self-regulation; Miller (1978) did not observe such a difference. Aversive and/or self-management outpatient programs conducted with self-referred, largely middle-class patients appear to result in 60 to 80 percent of the patients reporting some form of controlled drinking at one-year follow-up. The differences between these approaches or variations on them have been insufficient to clearly recommend one over another. Outcome with the more intensive inpatient therapy conducted by the Sobells cannot be compared with the results from the outpatient programs because of the vastly different populations studied. This difference in treatment and population does raise an interesting issue regarding treatment–population match.

Treatment–Population Match

Less severely ill, largely self-referred alcohol abusers have received outpatient self-management or aversive conditioning therapies; hardcore alcoholics have been treated in intensive inpatient multicomponent therapies. It would seem likely that outcome in controlled drinking programs could be influenced by this match. Dr. Pomerleau and I were interested in pursuing this matter and attempted to find out how nonmiddle-class and nonself-referred patients would fare at a self-management oriented control drinking program modeled after the Pomerleau et al. (1978) program. The two groups studied were patients attending Veterans Administration Alcohol Clinic and clients from the state Driving While Intoxicated (DWI) program. The former group consisted largely of chronic alcoholics with no medical contraindications to moderate drinking; the DWI clients were not self-referred but mandated into treatment under threat of driver's license revocation. The VA and DWI programs met weekly for 12 weeks. Breath alcohol was measured at each session for each patient. Participants were given drinking logs to use during the week in which they recorded occurrence and circumstances of drinking along with degree of craving and amount of alcohol consumed. These records were used in group sessions to discuss problems in drinking patterns. Dysfunctional use of alcohol was analyzed and alternative coping strategies explored. Standard instruction was given in appropriate drinking behavior. Participants were advised to sip rather than gulp drinks, pace their drinking, and to choose more dilute beverages. No drinking actually occurred within these sessions. Emphasis was placed on expanding activity repertoires to avoid the use of alcohol as a way of passing time. Participants designated monitors to corroborate their participation in new nondrinking activities. Relaxation training was provided with encouragement to use relaxation exercises as an alternative method to cope with stress and alcohol cravings. VA patients were paid for their compliance as evidenced by attending sessions sober, keeping records, and participating in designated alternative activities. DWI patients were similarly paid except that their payments represented refunds of their own money deposited at the initiation of treatment. The programs were strikingly unsuccessful with multiple dropouts among the VA patients and minimal behavior change for the DWIs.

The failure of these pilot programs could be ascribed to the controlled drinking orientation but when similarly designed programs were attempted with an abstinence goal, the results were no better. The problem with the treatment, most likely, was related to methodology rather than to goal. Our approach relied heavily on verbal and written communication skills that the VA chronic alcoholic population typically lacked. This group also had extremely limited behavioral repertoires with minimal resources for the acquisition of new behaviors. Verbally encouraging the VA patients to engage in an activity as an alternative to drinking was a futile effort as most of the patients had no alternative interests. For this approach to have succeeded at all, treatment staff would have had to actively train patients in new activities. All the methods employed in this treatment required active patient participation. Records had to be kept, and behaviors observed and changed. The programs were thus particularly vulnerable to noncompliance. The DWIs who were there because they had to be, not because they wanted to be, effectively sabotaged treatment by following through on treatment tasks only minimally or not at all.

CASE STUDIES

Assessing controlled drinking on a study-by-study or program-by-program basis reveals that it can be moderately successful or a total failure depending on treatment methods used, population treated, and the match between treatment and patient. Although such analysis is clearly valuable, it provides little in the way of a guide to managing controlled drinking patients. For the balance of this chapter, we will switch the level of analysis from the study to the individual. Holding treatment factors relatively constant, we will explore issues in controlled drinking treatment on a case-by-case basis. In this way it may be possible to give the potential therapist a better idea of some of the factors involved in managing patients attempting controlled drinking. As the premise of this book is that much can be learned from treatment failures, we will center the discussion on instances where treatment outcome fell short of expectations. Unfortunately, we have no shortage of these instances to report. We will further limit our focus to a self-management outpatient approach which is one that is technically relatively easy to implement and with which we have had experience over a period of years. At the Center for Behavioral Medicine of the University of Pennsylvania, we had a formal controlled drinking program from 1973 to 1977 and since then have seen occasional patients seeking controlled drinking on an individual basis. The patients treated were primarily self-referred, middle- to upper middle-class with alcohol intake at a level sufficient to interfere with vocational and/or family functioning but generally not at a level to produce physical dependence. Treatment included self-monitoring of drinking behavior, alteration of dysfunctional drinking patterns, gradual reduction of intake with weekly drinking quota goals, relaxation training, and development of alternative activities to drinking. Most patients were seen in small groups, some were treated individually. Treatment was for 12 weeks, with five follow-up sessions scheduled at increasing intervals, the last occurring about a year after the start of treatment. Additionally, an attempt was made to contact patients by phone two years after therapy. A $300 deposit was paid by patients at the start of treatment and was refunded for attending sessions sober as determined by Breathalyzer, keeping drinking records, engaging in alternative activities to drinking, and attending follow-up.

Motivation

In reviewing our experience with controlled drinking, several factors appeared to have been important in determining the process of therapy and ultimate outcome. Motivation, as in most therapies, was crucial in controlled drinking. One of the selling points of controlled drinking has been its potentially greater appeal for the individual considering therapy. The prospective patient might be totally discouraged by the probability of lifelong abstinence but would be willing to try to moderate his or her intake. A motivational conflict develops when the would-be patient mistakes the more desirable outcome for an easy way out of an alcohol problem. This was observed on more than one occasion. Mr. A.B. illustrates the process.

CASE 1

Mr. A.B., 50 years old, was married with four children and ran a successful family business. His drinking began in college where he was one of a heavily drinking social group. His drinking continued after college on a daily basis at a level sufficient to make him "high" in the evenings but not to the point of interfering with work. At the time of his initial consultation he was drinking an average of one third to one half a fifth of gin and one bottle of wine daily. Aside from one or two drinks at lunch, most alcohol was consumed between his return home from work and bedtime. On weekends, he supplemented this intake with six to eight beers during the day. He stated that he enjoyed drinking, both the taste of the alcohol and the way it made him feel. He did not believe that his work was suffering because of his alcohol intake but that his family life was. His usual pattern was to become somewhat somnolent over dinner, staying awake just long enough afterwards to have one or two more drinks. He was too sleepy to interact with his wife either verbally or sexually. He acknowledged that this was a problem but also admitted that his major reason for seeking treatment was that his wife had threatened to leave him if he did not change. During the year prior to entering treatment, he had maintained abstinence on his own for three months but found that he was irritable much of the time and resented not drinking. He subsequently purchased *"How to Control Your Drinking"* (Miller & Munoz, 1976) and tried to control his drinking on his own but without success.

During the first week of our treatment, self-monitoring revealed his consumption to be 6.5 ounces absolute alcohol per day, seven out of seven days. Initial therapy was directed toward reducing his intake by eliminating what he felt were the least crucial drinks of the day which he identified as those at lunch. Subsequently, we examined alternative activities in the early evening so as to postpone his first drink. Tennis, gardening, and playing with his children were the activities agreed upon. Mr. A.B. missed his third appointment, did not self-monitor during the intervening week, nor did he consistently implement the alternative activities. He came for an additional two weeks and kept the next appointment but did not return. During treatment, his intake dropped as low as 2.2 ounces absolute alcohol per day. At this level he found that his wife was happier but that he felt more irritable. His wife was seen at her own request, two months after the patient's last visit. She indicated that he had resumed his previous drinking pattern. Although she was quite upset about this, she did not anticipate separation or divorce and was prepared to ride out the problem, hoping it eventually would be resolved.

Discussion

Mr. A.B., at one point in his treatment, said that it was as if someone had placed all the good things he had in his life, his wife, children, and financial success, on one side of a scale and alcohol on the other, and the alcohol outweighed the rest. His motivation for treatment was essentially his wife's concern. He readily admitted that were it not for her he would have been very satisfied with the status quo. His wife, evidently, was not sufficiently desperate to make good on her original threat and the patient returned to his previous pattern. Motivation was probably not the only problem with this patient. Marital and personality factors almost certainly played a role in his continued drinking; however, the patient clearly felt uncomfortable altering his drinking behavior and saw no reasons of his own to tolerate this discomfort. Mr. A.B. sought controlled drinking as an easy way out of his predicament. As controlled drinking programs go, ours was relatively benign with no aversive procedures, yet it still required considerable efforts in self-monitoring and behavior change. Motivational problems and patient dropout are by no means unique to controlled drinking, but they may be especially evident in controlled drinking programs when the demands of treatment and unrealistic patient expectations clash.

Psychopathology

Alcohol abuse can occur in the context of nonalcohol-related psychopathology. The nature and extent of psychopathology can markedly influence the course of therapy. Two patients treated in our group program suffered from clinical depression. The first patient responded well to antidepressant medication and the depression did not interfere with treatment. At two-year follow-up, he was maintaining a controlled drinking status. A second patient's depression was less easily managed, recurred episodically, and when present, undermined his control over intake. At two-year follow-up, he continued to drink in excess of what he felt was appropriate. Alcohol appeared to be a way this patient dealt with depressions when antidepressant medication failed to help. A third patient, treated individually, illustrates the difficulties pre-existing psychopathology can create in treatment.

CASE 2

At the time of initial consultation, Ms. C.D. was a 38-year-old divorcee, living with her eight-year-old daughter. She was unemployed and was supported by her former husband. She had been in psychotherapy in one form or another since age 26. She acknowledged chronic depression which was frequently associated with suicidal thoughts. Between ages 26 and 38, she had been hospitalized three times for suicide attempts by drug overdose. She began drinking heavily approximately one year prior to entering our program. Intake for the immediate preceding two months averaged one fifth of scotch per day, seven out of seven days. She described drinking at a steady rate throughout her waking hours.

The initial intervention was outpatient detoxification with gradual tapering of intake so that by the end of the second week of treatment, she had achieved abstinence. She remained abstinent for six weeks. As had been agreed upon at the initiation of treatment, drinking was subsequently reintroduced on a limited basis. The patient was able to restrict her intake to one or two glasses of wine at meals several times a week. She was encouraged to resume her previously abandoned art interests as an alternative activity to drinking. Her situation remained stable for approximately one year during which time she was in psychotherapy. Low-grade depression and suicidal ideation remained a problem although she was functioning at a considerably improved level. Major difficulties began again when she became involved in several relationships that she had trouble managing. Alcohol intake increased with episodes of drunkenness apparently in response to conflicts in these affairs. During one such instance, she again threatened suicide and was hospitalized briefly. Abstinence was recommended following discharge which she was able to maintain for approximately one month. Depression and suicidal thoughts continued and she resumed drinking. The last contact with this patient occurred approximately 18 months after the start of treatment when she took another drug overdose. She was treated medically and referred for long-term psychiatric hospitalization.

Discussion

Ms. C.D. obviously had major emotional problems. She was diagnosed as having a borderline personality disorder. Characteristic of people with this diagnosis is impulsive, acting-out behavior. For Ms. C.D., alcohol was one way of acting out. The existence of a diagnosable psychiatric disorder is not necessarily a contraindication to controlled drinking. An important consideration is the function alcohol abuse plays in the psychopathology. For patients with affective or anxiety disorders, successfully managed by psychotherapy and/or pharmacotherapy, controlled drinking may be an achievable goal. Alternatively, patients who use alcohol as a way of expressing their underlying personality and social conflicts would appear to be a greater risk for treatment failure. For these patients, abstinence may have the advantage over controlled drinking as being simpler and more clear-cut. If the patient can define alcohol as totally off limits then it cannot be used as a way of detouring internal conflict. It is doubtful, however, if patients with the degree of emotional disturbance demonstrated by Ms. C.D. would stabilize under any condition for an extended period.

Social Context

We observed the social context of alcohol abuse to be a frequent issue among the controlled drinking patients. Many of these patients had managed to separate their alcohol from their work but virtually all had incurred family problems in the course of drinking. Spouses were almost always brought into treatment, at least to a limited extent. Some contact was necessary as most spouses did not have experience with this treatment orientation and required education as to what constituted controlled drinking and how the program worked. Even with such explanation, it was not uncommon to hear spouses voice concern over any drinking behavior, appropriate or otherwise. In some instances, the significance of the family situation went beyond treatment and appeared to be basic to the alcohol problem itself.

CASE 3

Mr. E.F. was a 43-year-old nurse who presented to therapy with a history of episodic alcohol abuse. He gave a history of continuous consumption of beer and bourbon over a period of two to three weeks during an alcohol binge. These episodes were described as having had occurred several times a year over the previous five years. At the time of his initial consultation, he stated that his intake was restricted to one or two cans of beer, three or four times per week. He was seeking help to maintain this level of intake.

During the first week of treatment his consumption averaged .85 ounces of alcohol per day on five out of seven days. Early in treatment, it became evident from his conversation that the patient had significant marital difficulties. He described frequent arguments and it was decided to bring the wife into therapy for at least a few sessions. It was apparent from their interaction in treatment that indeed there were major difficulties. The patient clearly felt one down in the relationship. The wife tended to infantize him emphasizing his inability to function when intoxicated. She had a better paying job than the patient and made most of the decisions in the marriage. She presented herself as by far the more competent of the two. Although the patient was frustrated with the situation, he responded only with ineffective protests. It seemed likely that although there may have been additional reasons for the patient's alcohol abuse, his marital problems were an important contributing factor. When intoxicated, he would become abusive, particularly towards his wife, and had destroyed furniture and verbally threatened her during the course of drinking binges.

In therapy, we continued to monitor his intake and simultaneously worked toward improving the marital relationship. The probable connection between their problems as a couple and drinking was discussed. Assignments were given directed towards joint decision making. After three couple sessions, the wife began predicting the onset of an alcohol binge which materialized two weeks later. During this episode, the patient struck his wife, resulting in the wife's leaving. Subsequently, the couple separated and the patient decided to try abstinence. He was seen over an additional three weeks during which he remained abstinent. Subsequently, he terminated therapy.

Discussion

As with psychopathology, difficult family situations did not appear to be absolute contraindications to controlled drinking. Patients going through divorce or with chronic marital problems were able to moderate alcohol intake. The critical issue appeared to be the role drinking played in the marital-social setting. When alcohol serves as a weapon within a social interaction it may be particularly difficult to control intake. Abstinence in such instances would have the advantage of totally removing the possibility of misusing alcohol in social conflict.

Degrees of Control

Motivation, psychopathology, and social-marital problems are factors that influence any alcohol treatment, although, as we have tried to point out, each may have an impact on controlled drinking therapies in special ways. A variable of unique significance to controlled drinking is the ability of the individual to exercise control over alcohol intake. The outcome statistics in virtually all controlled drinking studies indicate there are considerable individual differences in this ability. Viewed on a case-by-case basis, we observed a tremendous range of control from nonexistent to excellent with many levels inbetween. The next three case vignettes illustrate some of these different levels.

CASE 4

Mr. G.H., when first seen, was a 37-year-old lawyer. He had recently separated from his wife because of his drinking. Much to the distress of his employer, he had appeared intoxicated at work on several occasions and was in immediate danger of losing his position if he did not modify his drinking. He was very interested in controlled drinking as he feared the prospect of lifelong abstinence. His drinking difficulties had gradually increased over a period of two years following his graduation from evening law school. His intake at initiation of treatment was 4.5 ounces of absolute alcohol daily; he was drinking seven out of seven days. His problem with alcohol was especially destructive as his tolerance was fairly low and he was prone to boisterous and generally obnoxious behavior while intoxicated.

Intake during the second week of treatment dropped slightly to an average 4.0 ounces, but only because he was abstinent for one day; drinking on drinking days remained the same. Alcohol consumption during working hours was pinpointed initially for control. Alternative lunch arrangements were considered, for example, eating in the office where no alcohol was available rather than going out and possibly drinking. The third week of treatment, he came to the session with a BAC in excess of .10 mg percent. He was grossly intoxicated and was sent home with the friend who had brought him in. The following week there was no change in drinking pattern and he was on the verge of losing his job. Therapeutic goals were discussed with him. It was explained that controlled drinking did not seem possible and that abstinence would be the only workable alternative. He agreed to this and we shifted to an abstinence goal. He was able to avoid alcohol on all but two occasions on the following two weeks, however he subsequently resumed his previous pattern of intake and dropped out of treatment.

Discussion

This patient was unable to exercise any degree of control over alcohol. He could reduce his weekly average intake only by remaining abstinent on one or more days. When he drank, he consistently drank to the point of intoxication. The treatment staff, after one month's experience with him, had no doubt that abstinence was the only feasible goal for this patient. In assessing the appropriateness of treatment, problems with loss of control do not always present in such a clear manner.

CASE 5

When initially seen, Mr. I.J. was 29 years of age and married. He was self-employed as a master plumber. He had always been a heavy social drinker, but over a period of three to four years his consumption had increased to a point where it was a major source of disagreement with his wife. He also acknowledged that his drinking was reducing his effectiveness at work as he frequently drank on the job. At the start of treatment, his intake averaged 10 ounces absolute alcohol per day. Most of this was consumed as bourbon or beer, His pattern was to have several beers with lunch and to stop off at a bar after quitting work or alternatively to drink at home. It was evident from his drinking logs that his range of activities was limited to working for pay on weekdays and working for himself, refurbishing a boathouse, on weekends.

Treatment was begun with the immediate goals of restricting daytime and early evening drinking and expanding his repertoire of activities. He worked on changing his lunchtime routine, specifically seeking out places where alcohol was not served. He was counseled on ways of pacing and generally slowing his alcohol intake when drinking at bars. Mr. I.J. had previously enjoyed deep sea fishing and he was encouraged to resume this hobby. The patient followed up on these suggestions with moderate improvement. His wife participated in several sessions and specifically arranged to investigate ways of improving their relationship. A contract was established whereby the patient's wife agreed to be less critical in exchange for a specified limit to drinking in the home. By the end of the seventh week he was drinking on an average of 3.7 ounces absolute alcohol per day on seven out of seven days. His intake level did not change appreciably from this for the duration of the program and into follow-up. Eighteen months after treatment Mr. I.J. contacted the Center, informing us that he had been drinking very heavily, had struck his wife in an argument and was now separated. He requested a prescription for Antabuse and a referral to an abstinence oriented program.

Discussion

It is difficult to categorize Mr. I.J. as a treatment success or failure. Numerically, he was much improved by the end of treatment, cutting his intake by two thirds. Yet, 25 ounces of absolute alcohol per week is without doubt in excess of desirable levels. He continued to drink on the job and was still plagued by marital difficulties related to alcohol. He would have been better off abstinent although it is by no means clear that he would have adhered to this goal. Follow-up information after he initiated abstinence is not available. This "inbetween" patient may be the most difficult to manage; he does not function so badly as to absolutely require abstinence, but his control remains limited to a degree where drinking continues to be a problem. It may be, as it was for Mr. I.J., that the final decision in these cases has to rest with the patient.

Not all patients who do well initially manage indefinitely without difficulty.

Whether relapsing patients are considered a success or failure depends on one's orientation.

CASE 6

Mr. K.L., a 47-year-old married salesman, was seen at his own request for problem drinking. He described a very gradual increase in alcohol consumption over a period of 8 to 10 years. He believed that this was associated, especially in recent years, with a decrease in his level of alcohol tolerance. He felt that he was groggy most evenings after his usual several drinks and often felt hung over in the mornings. He noticed that his wife was also getting annoyed with his dozing off after dinner. He denied drinking during the day except at business luncheons, three or four times a month which was not a problem. At intake he was drinking five out of seven days for a total of 20 ounces absolute alcohol over the week.

As most of his drinking occurred between his return home from work and dinner, we encouraged him to consider some alternative routines on his coming home. He hit upon walking his dog for one half hour before dinner and moving the dinner hour one half hour earlier. This appeared to work extremely well. He was also counseled in several techniques to slow his rate of consumption, for example, sipping and pouring more dilute drinks. By the end of treatment, Mr. K.L. was drinking on three of seven days and limited his intake to three ounces or less on days when drinking occurred. He was followed up over the next two years with periodic contacts. On two occasions, he consulted the Center staff because of a return to excessive drinking, both times in response to job stress. These relapses lasted approximately two weeks each, were marked by a return to pretreatment levels and were dealt with by reinforcing previously learned techniques.

Discussion

According to the Ewing and Rouse standards, this patient would be considered a failure, he relapsed twice in two years. We counted him as a treatment success. His consumption was reduced to a level at which he felt comfortable and for almost 100 out of 104 weeks, he was functioning well. Relapse represented inconvenience and disappointment, but not disaster as he fairly quickly regained control with no lasting consequences. In this case, the control achieved was not absolute but was sufficient to maintain a normal lifestyle under most circumstances.

SUMMARY AND CONCLUSIONS

Treatment failures along with successes have begun to define the strengths and weaknesses of controlled drinking. The approach has not been the monster let loose upon the world that some from AA predicted nor has it been any panacea. Compared with abstinence, controlled drinking is at least as subject to the influence of nontreatment specific patient factors. Because of the broader appeal of controlled drinking, there is a probability of attracting would-be patients who are looking for an easy way out rather than an active treatment. They are not likely to succeed. Because controlled drinking demands a continuous series of choices concerning circumstance and quantity of alcohol consumption, the approach may be more vulnerable to judgment impaired by underlying psychopathology or severe social pressure. Outcome in controlled drinking has depended to a great extent on the match between therapeutic technique and treatment population.

The principal behavioral strategies employed over the last decade have been: (1) retraining, exemplified by the Sobell work involving active practice in appropriate drinking behavior and aversive conditioning for inappropriate patterns; (2) aversive conditioning alone, emphasizing elimination of destructive drinking patterns; and (3) self-control techniques, relying on self-monitoring, recognition of dysfunctional patterns, and counseling for more desirable drinking behavior. Retraining has been used successfully with chronic alcoholics but is a very time- and staff-intensive approach. Given the cost involved, it is not surprising that there has been no great rush to replicate the Sobell study. Aversive conditioning and behavioral self-control seem to work for roughly the same middle-class, less seriously impaired population. If these approaches are indeed comparable, self-control would have the edge because of its greater acceptability and ease of implementation.

After a decade of research, the final word on controlled drinking is not yet in. Investigation of alternative behavioral methodologies (e.g., behavioral couples therapy, cognitive therapy) might indicate additional populations for whom the approach would have some validity. At this moment, experience suggests that controlled drinking is workable but for only a limited population. Unless the therapist has extensive resources for equipment, time, and personnel, controlled drinking is not the goal of choice for chronic alcoholics or patients with physical alcohol dependence. The best candidates for controlled drinking are those individuals who have a history of normal drinking at some point in their lives and are neither physically dependent on alcohol nor drinking sufficient quantities to severely impair functioning. It could be argued, with some logic, that the population so defined is not actually alcoholic. In this sense, the naysayers may have been right all along. Nonetheless, there are people fitting this description who need to alter their drinking patterns. Controlled drinking remains a reasonable alternative for this group.

REFERENCES

Alcoholics Anonymous (1953) *Twelve steps and twelve traditions.* New York: Alcoholics Anonymous World Services.

Armor, D.J., Polich, J.M., & Stambul, H.B. (Eds.) (1976) *Alcoholism and treatment,* Santa Monica Calif.: Rand.

Bromet, E.J., & Moos, R. (1979) Prognosis of alcoholic patients: Comparisons of abstainers and moderate drinkers, *British Journal of Addiction,* 74, 183–188.

Caddy, G.R. (1981) Personal communication.

Caddy, G.R., Addington, H.J., & Perkins, D. (1978) Individualized behavior therapy for alcoholics: A third year independent double-blind follow-up. *Behavior Research and Therapy,* 16, 345–362.

Caddy, G.R., & Lovibond, S.H. (1976) Self-regulation and discriminated aversive conditioning in the modification of alcoholics' drinking behavior. *Behavior Therapy,* 7, 223–230.

Davies, D.L. (1962) Normal drinking in recovered alcohol addicts. *Quarterly Journal of Studies on Alcohol,* 23, 94–104.

Ewing, J., & Rouse, B. (1976) Failure of an experimental treatment program to inculcate controlled drinking in alcoholics. *British Journal of Addiction,* 71, 123–134.

Fox, R. (1963) Comments on normal drinking in recovered alcoholic addicts. *Quarterly Journal of Studies on Alcohol,* 24, 117.

Gottheil, E., Thornton, C.C., Skolada, T.E., & Alterman, A.I. (1979) Follow-up study of alcoholics at 6, 12, and 24 months. *Currents in Alcoholism,* 6, 91–109.

Hingson, R., Scotch, N., & Goldman, E. (1977) Impact of the "Rand Report" on alcoholics, treatment personnel and Boston residents. *Journal of Studies on Alcohol,* 38, 2065–2074.

Hodgson, R. (1979) Much ado about nothing much: Alcoholism treatment and the Rand Report. *British Journal of Addiction,* 74, 227–234.

Jellinek, E.M. (1960) *The disease concept of alcoholism.* New Brunswick, N.J.: Hillhouse.

Lemere, F. (1963) Comments on normal drinking in recovered alcohol addicts. *Quarterly Journal of Studies on Alcohol,* 24, 727–728.

Lloyd, R.W., & Salzberg, H.C. (1975) Controlled social drinking: An alternative to abstinence as a treatment goal for some alcohol abusers. *Psychological Bulletin,* 82, 815–842.

Lovibond, S.H., & Caddy, G. (1970) Discriminated aversive control in the moderation of alcoholics' drinking behavior. *Behavior Therapy,* 1, 437–444.

Ludwig, A.M., Bendfeldt, F., Wikler, A., & Cain, R.B. (1978) 'Loss of Control' in alcoholics. *Archives of General Psychiatry,* 35, 370–373.

Mello, N.K., & Mendelson, J.H. (1971) A quantitative analysis of drinking patterns in alcoholics. *Archives of General Psychiatry,* 25, 527–539.

Mello, N.K., & Mendelson, J.H. (1972) Drinking patterns during work-contingent and non-contingent alcohol acquisition. *Psychosomatic Medicine,* 34, 139–164.

Mendelson, J.H., & Mello, N.K. (1966) Experimental analysis of drinking behavior of chronic alcoholics. *Annals of the New York Academy of Science,* 133, 826–845.

Miller, W.R. (1978) Behavioral treatment of problem drinkers: A comparative outcome study of three controlled drinking therapies. *Journal of Consulting and Clinical Psychology,* 46, 74–86.

Miller, W.R., & Joyce, M.A. (1979) Prediction of abstinence, controlled drinking, and heavy drinking outcomes following behavioral self control training. *Journal of Consulting and Clinical Psychology,* 47, 773–775.

Miller, W.R., & Munoz, R.F. (1976) *How to control your drinking.* Englewood Cliffs, N.J.: Prentice-Hall.

Miller, W.R., & Taylor, C.A. (1980) Relative effectiveness of bibliotherapy, individual and group self-control training in the treatment of problem drinkers. *Addictive Behaviors,* **5,** 13–24.

Orford, J., Oppenheimer, E., & Edwards, G. (1976) Abstinence or control: The outcome for excessive drinkers two years after consultation. *Behavior Research and Therapy,* **14,** 409–418.

Pattison, E.M. (1966) A critique of alcoholism treatment concepts with special reference to abstinence. *Quarterly Journal of Studies on Alcohol,* **27,** 49–71.

Pattison, E.M., Headley, E.B., Gleser, G.C., & Gottschalk, L.A. (1968) Abstinence and normal drinking: An assessment of changes in drinking patterns in alcoholics after treatment. *Quarterly Journal of Studies on Alcohol,* **29,** 610–633.

Pokorny, A.D., Miller, B.A., & Cleveland, S.E. (1968) Response to treatment of alcoholism: A follow-up study. *Quarterly Journal of Studies on Alcohol,* **29,** 364–381.

Polich, J.M., Armor, D.J., & Braiker, H.B. (1980) Patterns of alcoholism over four years. *Journal of Studies on Alcohol,* **41,** 397–415.

Pomerleau, O., Pertschuk M., Adkins, D., & Brady, J.P. (1978) A comparison of behavioral and traditional treatment for middle-income problem drinkers. *Journal of Behavioral Medicine,* **1,** 187–200.

Popham, R.E., & Schmidt, W. (1976) Some factors affecting the likelihood of moderate drinking by treated alcoholics. *Journal of Studies on Alcohol,* **37,** 868–882.

Saunders, W.M., & Kershaw, P.W. (1979) Spontaneous remission from alcoholism—a community study. *British Journal of Addiction,* **74,** 251–265.

Sobell, M.B., & Sobell, L.C. (1973) Individualized behavior therapy for alcoholics. *Behavior Therapy,* **4,** 49–72.

Sobell, M.B., & Sobell, L.C. (1976) Second year treatment outcome of alcoholics treated by individualized behavior therapy: Results. *Behavior Research and Therapy,* **14,** 195–215.

Tiebout, H.M. (1963) Comments on normal drinking in recovered alcohol addicts. *Quarterly Journal of Studies on Alcohol,* **24,** 109–111.

Zwerling, I. (1963) Comments on normal drinking in recovered alcohol addicts. *Quarterly Journal of Studies on Alcohol,* **24,** 117–118.

CHAPTER 15

Failures in Behavior Therapy for Obesity: Causes, Correlates, and Consequences

PATRICIA M. DUBBERT
G. TERENCE WILSON

A consideration of therapeutic failures in the treatment of obesity inevitably brings to mind Stunkard's (1958) unrelentingly pessimistic conclusion about treatments for obesity prior to the development of behavior therapy: "Most obese persons will not stay in treatment for obesity. Of those who stay in treatment most will not lose weight and of those who do lose weight, most will regain it" (p. 79). Stunkard (1972) subsequently went on to revise this conclusion, suggesting that behavioral treatment appeared to be effective for cases of mild to moderate obesity. Yet in most behavioral programs for the treatment of obesity, some individuals lose a significant amount of weight, others lose very little, and a few lose nothing or even gain weight. There is also considerable variability in weight change during the first few months after treatment ends, as some clients continue to lose, some just maintain the losses they achieved during the treatment phase, and others quickly regain weight. Such variability has been one of the more persistent and unsettling findings of research in the behavioral treatment of obesity, and it may well be an indication that the critical variables controlling weight loss have yet to be identified, or that behavioral approaches are effective for only a certain subset of obese individuals. This chapter is concerned with one side of the continuum of variability in response to behavioral treatment of obesity—that of treatment failure.

Any serious attempt to analyze treatment failure in behavioral weight control programs must be based upon the operational specification of treatment outcome criteria and acceptable definitions of therapeutic success and failure. We propose the following framework within which treatment failures can be critically considered:

1. Meeting of predetermined admission criteria for the program in question.
2. Completion of the treatment program.
3. Adherence to the requirements of the treatment program.

4.   Loss of weight and/or registering of other related forms of improvement (e.g., enhanced cardiovascular functioning).

5.   Maintenance of treatment-produced improvement over time (i.e., relapse).

This conceptual framework is deliberately broad in nature. It might be objected that the first stage cannot be viewed as a form of treatment failure inasmuch as no treatment is actually received, yet, different selection criteria at this crucial entry point into treatment might affect outcome and determine the extent to which findings may be generalized. As we shall point out, the overwhelming majority of controlled behavioral treatment studies have consistently focused on a relatively limited range of obese individuals. The second and third stages of the framework are self-explanatory and refer to the vitally important processes of attrition and adherence respectively. The fourth stage emphasizes multiple measures of treatment outcome (Rogers, Mahoney, Mahoney, Straw & Kenigsberg, 1980). Finally, the fifth stage recognizes the now well established finding that improvement at the end of treatment is not necessarily maintained unless explicit efforts are made to prevent relapse.

The remainder of this chapter organizes the information from existing research studies and clinical trials on behavioral treatment failures within our proposed framework. In addition, we summarize the results of a fine-grained analysis of treatment failure at each stage of a comprehensive cognitive-behavioral treatment program conducted at Rutgers University (Dubbert, 1982; Dubbert, Wilson, Augusto, Langenbucher, & McGee, 1981) in order to provide an in-depth illustration of behavioral treatment failures.

RECRUITMENT AND SCREENING: FAILURE AT TREATMENT ENTRY

Virtually all behavioral studies of obesity have employed specific recruitment procedures and subject selection criteria, usually involving advertising the program and contacting physicians and other appropriate treatment facilities. Although it has been asserted that individuals who are recruited for studies through advertising their availability (so-called "volunteers") are not "real patients" and present fewer therapeutic difficulties than clients who initiate contact with therapists themselves (e.g., Gurman, 1978; Marks, 1978), contrasting "volunteers" with "real patients" is a false dichotomy that obscures evaluation of treatment efficacy (see Kazdin & Wilson, 1978; Rachman & Wilson, 1980; for a critical reanalysis of this argument). The important issues that determine outcome are the type, severity, duration, and complexity of the individual's problem rather than his or her arbitrarily defined status as a "volunteer." Foreyt, Goodrick, and Gotto (1981) compared studies that included patients referred by health professionals to those that recruited subjects through advertising the program and concluded: "There appears to be no relationship between mode of referral and either treatment success or percent lost to follow-up." At this time, then, there is no logical nor empirical basis for presupposing that recruitment or referral mode will influence who is likely to succeed or fail in behavioral weight control programs.

Among the typical subject selection criteria are the following: a minimum of 15 lbs. (6.8 kg) and/or 10 percent overweight based on the 1959 Metropolitan Life Insurance Company norms (U.S. Department of Health, Education, and Welfare, 1967); permission from a physician to participate in a weight loss program and an absence of medical disorders that would contraindicate weight loss; no medication regimen that would affect water retention, metabolism, or appetite; no concurrent involvement in any other weight reduction program or psychotherapy; no plans to become pregnant during the time span of the program; a willingness to make a commitment to the program, which might include a money deposit refundable contingent upon attendance, adherence to therapeutic instructions, behavior change, or weight loss itself.

Procedures followed in the Rutgers Weight Control Program (Dubbert 1982) were similar to the recruiting and selection policies adopted in other behavioral outcome studies, with the important exception that only those individuals who had spouses willing to participate in treatment were selected. Survivors of initial telephone interviews were sent applications, and appointments for the pretreatment assessment were scheduled when the completed application had been returned to the program office. About one of every five respondents failed to return application forms within the three-week deadline. Otherwise, research requirements were responsible for most rejections: 30 percent of the applicants were denied entrance because they were single or their spouse was not able or willing to participate in treatment. One would be tempted to conclude that excluding these individuals would inflate the success of therapy outcome. Yet Brownell, Heckerman, Westlake, Hayes, and Monti (1978) found that in the absence of formal spouse training, obese subjects with spouses who had expressed a willingness to cooperate in treatment fared no better in terms of weight loss than their obese counterparts with uncooperative spouses. Ten percent of the applicants were excluded because of significant medical problems other than obesity. Another 5 percent of the potential participants were screened out because they were less than 15 percent overweight or more than 100 percent overweight.

The resulting client population was remarkably similar to those recruited for other behavioral weight control research programs. Wilson and Brownell's (1980) review of outcome studies showed that women were four times more likely to have been participants than men, the average age was 40 years, and the typical subject weighed 200 pounds and was roughly 50 percent overweight. Foreyt et al. (in press) in their analysis of much of the same literature arrived at virtually identical conclusions. The subject sample in the Rutgers Weight Control Program was 77 percent female, had an average age of 43.4 years, and started treatment at an average weight of 197 pounds.

ATTRITION: FAILURE TO COMPLETE TREATMENT

Interpreting results from clinical outcome studies is complicated by differing dropout rates. It is commonly assumed that the least successful participants are likely to discontinue treatment, so results based on treatment "survivors" may be biased. Consequently, investigators who are sufficiently skilled to discourage attrition, or who are sufficiently aggressive to assemble most subjects for periodic assessments may retain the least successful subjects and, therefore, show smaller average weight losses. However, very little is actually known about attrition and about the performance of persons who leave treatment prematurely.

Traditional medical treatment has high attrition, sometimes reaching 80 percent (Stunkard, 1978). One hallmark of behavior therapy is lowered attrition (Stunkard & Mahoney, 1976). In the first systematic analysis of attrition rates within behavioral programs, Wilson and Brownell (1980) reported a mean attrition rate of 13.5 percent for controlled studies with a follow-up of at least one year. As might be expected, attrition increased during follow-up in almost all cases. Attrition in uncontrolled studies was similar: typically less than 20 percent during initial treatment, but great variability during follow-up. Thus attrition in behavior therapy studies is far lower than in traditional treatments or in the other most widely used programs, self-help groups (Stunkard & Brownell, 1979). This is significant, for treatment cannot be effective if subjects do not participate. However, the variability in attrition among the behavior therapy studies is noteworthy, and it is important to search for the factors that are responsible for these differences.

One possible factor is the presence or absence of a deposit-refund contingency. In the Wilson and Brownell (1980) analysis, for instance, 10 of the 17 controlled studies included a deposit that was refundable contingent upon attendance. The average attrition for the studies with a deposit was 9.5 percent, compared to average attrition of 19.3 percent for the studies not requiring a deposit. In the only direct test of this contingency, Hagen, Foreyt, and Durham (1976) found that subjects with the $20.00 deposit showed significantly lower attrition than those without a deposit.

Wilson and Brownell (1980) also queried too unyielding a commitment to the notion of gradual weight loss in behavioral programs, pointing out that many clients drop out of treatment because weight loss is too slow, too little, or too variable. In a recent study by Clausen, Silfen, Coombs, Ayers, and Altschul (1980), subjects in a behavioral weight control program that followed dietary regimens with severe caloric deficits (400 to 600 kcal) showed significantly lower attrition rates and lost more weight than subjects on 1200 kcal diets and those who failed to diet. Confirming Wilson and Brownell's (1980) speculations about combining behavior therapy with drugs or specialized diets, Clausen et al. (1980) concluded that "behavior modification treatments without a more severe caloric deficit usually will not provide sufficient weight loss to reinforce the behavioral aspect of the program, and hence, motivate subjects to remain in the program" (p. 255).

In the Rutgers Weight Control Program, 10 (16 percent) of the participants failed to complete the attendance requirement of at least 12 treatment sessions. Two others (both females) were excluded because their spouses failed to attend. Attrition was greater for females (21 percent) than for males (7 percent). No significant differences were found between the dropouts and those who successfully finished treatment on such subject variables as pretreatment weight and percentage of body fat, age, reported age of obesity onset, current weight loss goal, binge scale score, or marital adjustment score. There were also no differences between dropouts and finishers for weight loss during the first four weeks of treatment. Thus none of the measures available to us during the pretreatment assessments or during the first month of treatment predicted retention. Retention was also examined with respect to the different treatment conditions and the four primary therapists. Dropouts were about evenly split between the two spouse involvement and two goal-setting conditions. One of the four therapists lost four clients, two lost three, and the other lost two clients. These frequencies suggest that attrition was not related to type of treatment or to individual therapists.

Eleven (91.7 percent) of the dropouts were able to lose at least five pounds at some point before they left treatment; six (50 percent) lost 10 pounds or more; two (16.7 percent) lost more than 15 pounds, and one (8.3 percent) lost more than 25 pounds. At the time of the posttreatment assessment, seven of the dropouts were weighed and four others were contacted by phone. All but two of the dropouts still weighed less than when they entered treatment, with an average weight loss since the pretreatment assessment of 10.3 pounds. Although this compares favorably with the average weight loss of those who complete many behavioral weight reduction programs, it was considerably less than the average loss of more than 17 pounds achieved by participants in our program who completed treatment. At the time of the three-month follow-up, six dropouts were weighed and three were contacted by phone or mail. Weight change during the three months since the last contact had been extremely variable, ranging from a gain of 11.25 pounds to a loss of 13.0 pounds. All but two of the dropouts still weighed less than at the pretreatment assessment.

NONCOMPLIANCE: FAILURE TO ADHERE TO TREATMENT PROCEDURES

Few weight reduction studies have measured the extent to which patients follow therapeutic instructions. This omission has serious consequences for both theoretical and clinical reasons and it critically affects the analysis of treatment failure. On the one hand, even powerful interventions may be ineffective if clients fail to use them. On the other hand, the relationship between failure to reduce and adherence failure has yet to be clarified. Wooley, Wooley, and Dyrenforth (1979) have argued convincingly that it is naive for weight control therapists to assume that failure to lose indicates the client is not following the therapeutic program. Behavior change and weight change represent only two components of a complex chain that involves therapeutic instructions, eating and exercise behaviors, energy balance, and weight change.

The failure of a program to produce weight change could result from an interruption at any place in the chain. If patients do not comply with program guidelines, eating and exercise behaviors may not change. Weight may change, however, perhaps from the use of nonprogram procedures (e.g., crash diets). There is also the possibility that specified eating and/or exercise behaviors may not be associated with the balance between energy intake and energy expenditure: for example, slowing the rate of eating may not decrease food consumption. Even if food intake decreases, changes in energy expenditure may offset this effect. Finally, metabolic factors may obscure the relationship between energy balance and weight change (Bray, 1976; Brownell, & Stunkard, 1980; Wooley et al., 1979).

The relationship between weight loss and adherence to behavioral treatment prescriptions is still unclear (e.g., Brownell & Stunkard, 1978; Johnson, Wildman, & O'Brien, 1980; Lansky, 1981). The Rutgers Program was designed to circumvent some of the commonly cited problems of inducing and assessing adherence to treatment prescriptions. The complexity of a therapeutic intervention is negatively correlated with adherence (Dunbar & Stunkard, 1979), and the more comprehensible the treatment, the greater the adherence. With these two considerations in mind, the Rutgers program included highly specific, unambiguous behavior change prescriptions that as far as possible were limited to those techniques that appear to be essential for successful weight reduction. Several recent studies provide support for the key role of a goal-setting component in treatment programs (Bandura & Simon, 1977; Chapman & Jeffrey, 1979; Loro, Fisher, & Kevenkron, 1979). According to social learning theory (Bandura, 1977), goals that are explicitly defined, set at a level which is challenging but attainable, and immediate (as opposed to set in the distant future) are most likely to mobilize effort in the here and now. Bandura and Simon (1977), for example, showed that proximal (daily) goal-setting produced greater change in eating behavior and weight of obese persons than distal (weekly) goals or self-monitoring alone. The Rutgers Program emphasized self-evaluation of progress towards weekly or daily caloric and aerobic exercise goals, with problem-solving sessions for overcoming difficulties clients encountered in carrying out these self-regulatory activities.

All participants in the Rutgers study were assigned to a single primary therapist for the duration of treatment. Available evidence suggests that contact with the same therapist at each appointment facilitates adherence (Franks & Wilson, 1979). Self-monitoring adherence was checked twice each week for the first eight weeks of treatment and on a weekly basis thereafter. Several types of data were gathered that bear on adherence to treatment prescriptions, but for present purposes, adherence was simply defined as number of days of recording estimated caloric intake and output and aerobic exercise.

Adherence to calorie record-keeping by the Rutgers clients was generally satisfactory. Analysis of the calorie records turned in by participants showed an overall average of 5.3 days of food calorie recording per week and 4.4 days of exercise calorie recording per week during the first 16 weeks of treatment. Of course, the accuracy of these self-recordings of caloric intake and output is unknown. Self-monitoring can be reactive even if accuracy is poor (McFall, 1977). Furthermore, failure in weight reduction was significantly associated with failure in adherence to calorie record-keeping. Failure to submit weekly calorie records during the initial weeks of treatment was more frequent among those who failed to lose weight (defined as at least 10 pounds). Only 15 percent of those who lost 10 pounds or more during treatment failed to complete calorie records during the first four weeks of treatment, whereas 50 percent of those who failed to lose had missed at least one week of self-monitoring during the first four weeks.

Determinants of Adherence Failure

To the best of our knowledge, no systematic attempt has been made to analyze the determinants of adherence to treatment prescriptions and to identify the reasons why some individuals fail to adhere although, as we describe below, recent analyses of reasons for relapse following successful weight loss have been reported. In a clinical report, Sjoberg and Persson (1979) described the cognitions and feelings of nine overweight individuals treated at a weight reduction clinic in Sweden. Interviews at various points during and following treatment led Sjoberg and Persson to conclude that "in the majority of cases, breakdowns occurred under mood pressure due to strong emotional stress, and were preceded by distorted reasoning." None of Sjoberg and Persson's patients who was successful in losing significant amounts of weight reported feelings of guilt or self-blame or negative self-statements about current or future ability to lose weight during the dieting process.

   In an initial study of failures in adherence to program prescriptions during the Rutgers Program, beginning with the fifth week of the program, subjects who failed to self-record food calorie intake for more than two days in a week or who gained three pounds or more between treatment sessions were interviewed by their therapists to determine the circumstances under which adherence failure had occurred. (In all cases the interview was triggered by a failure to self-monitor calories). This interview consisted of questions adapted from the interview format used by Marlatt and Gordon (1979). Twenty-eight subjects were interviewed in this manner at the time of their initial adherence failure, including 10 of the 16 who subsequently failed to lose at least 10 pounds during the treatment program. (Of the remaining six who failed to lose, five had already dropped out of treatment). Notably, 43 percent of the subjects had already resumed self-monitoring by the time they were interviewed, and only one subject never resumed self-monitoring at all after the initial two-day lapse.

   The adherence failure interviews were analyzed via a classification system also developed by Marlatt and Gordon (1979) for examination of relapse determinants and processes among alcohol abusers and smokers. In this system, the adherence failure is categorized, first, as "intrapersonal" or "interpersonal," depending upon the salience of other people in causing the slip. Within each of these two major categories are subcategories that occur within either one: coping with negative emotional states (e.g., frustration, anger, and depression); coping with negative physical states (e.g., pain, illness, and fatigue); enhancement of positive emotional states (e.g., celebrations and travel); testing personal control; giving in to temptation and urges; reaction to social pressure. Subjects in the Rutgers program reported that 48 percent of the adherence failures had occurred in intrapersonal situations, and 52 percent in situations classified as interpersonal. The frequencies for these major categories were identical to those reported by Rosenthal, Marx, and Adams (1979) for posttreatment relapses by dieters as shown in Table 15.1.

Table 15.1. Adherence Failure Situations During Treatment and Maintenance

Situation	Rutgers Program		Rosenthal, Marx, & Adams (1979)
	Treatment (%)	Follow-Up (%)	Follow-Up (%)
Intrapersonal determinants	48[a]	43[b]	48[c]
Negative emotional states	21	43	32
Negative physical states	10	—	5
Positive emotional states	8	—	11
Testing personal control	6	—	—
Urges and temptations	3	—	—
Interpersonal determinants	52	57	52
Interpersonal conflict	3	—	10
Indirect social pressure	14	14	10
Positive emotional states	36	43	32

[a] $n = 28$.
[b] $n = 7$.
[c] $n = 28$.

MINIMAL WEIGHT LOSS (OR WEIGHT GAIN): FAILURE TO IMPROVE DURING TREATMENT

What constitutes therapeutic success or failure in the treatment of obesity would seem to be obvious—weight loss. Indeed, the availability of a handy hard measure of treatment outcome initially attracted the attention of behavioral researchers to the modification of obesity. It is now generally accepted, however, that evaluation of treatment outcome must necessarily be broader in scope and include multiple measures of psychological and physiological functioning (Rogers et al., 1980; Wilson, 1978). Weight loss remains a crucial element of evaluating the treatment of obesity, but even with this easily obtained objective measure, there is no consensus about what exactly is treatment success or failure.

In the studies reviewed by Wilson and Brownell (1980), the mean weight loss at the end of treatments that averaged 10 weeks was approximately 11 pounds.

By and large, this is consistent with the explicit goals of many behavioral treatment programs, namely, a weekly weight loss of 1 to 2 pounds. Whether this sort of weight loss should be defined as success or failure will depend on a number of different variables. (Of course, it was originally assumed that clients would continue to lose weight after the termination of the formal treatment program as they implemented the self-control strategies that they had presumably acquired. This hope has not been realized, as we indicate in the following section on maintenance of weight loss).

Whereas obesity (30 percent or more above "ideal" bodyweight) is generally considered a serious health risk (Bray, 1978), current research indicates that the link between obesity and health is complex and not one of simple cause and effect. There is convincing evidence that slight to mild obesity (10 to 30 percent overweight) is not linked to mortality or morbidity. Slightly to mildly obese individuals, in fact, may live longer than normal weight or slightly underweight individuals. However, individuals greater than 40 percent over their ideal body weight incur a health risk (Hanna, Loro, and Power, 1981). As these authors point out, failure to differentiate "relative overweightness may obscure important differences among individuals of varying degrees of body weight. It also hinders an examination of the relationships between risk factors and degrees of overweight." Although many of the adverse effects of obesity on cardiovascular risk may be mediated through other risk factors, the Framingham research has indicated that every 10 percent increase in relative weight is associated with notable increases in blood pressure, serum cholesterol, fasting blood sugar, and uric acid; weight losses are associated with equivalent decrements in these risk indicators (Van Itallie, 1979).

Inasmuch as it is body fat rather than body weight that is the target of obesity treatment programs, direct measures of body fat have been advocated. Rogers et al. (1980) found that bodyweight was a relatively poor predictor of cardiovascular health risk indices, but estimates of body fat were strongly correlated with maximum aerobic capacity, a major index of cardiovascular health. Thus if improved physical health is the primary goal of treatment, weight loss would not necessarily represent therapeutic success. Taking body fat into account in evaluating treatment outcome might affect the results in important ways, as indicated by the findings of the Rutgers Program discussed below.

Although weight reduction has been associated with health benefits, it is our strong clinical impression that the women who consistently comprise the majority of subjects or clients in our studies are motivated primarily by cosmetic reasons. The cosmetic changes resulting from a loss of about one pound per week will depend on the initial degree of overweight and the length of the program. For the Rutgers clients, an average loss of 15.7 pounds in 19 weeks was associated with decreases of more than three inches in waist and hip girths, which was reported by many clients to represent two or more clothing sizes. (It should be noted that the girth changes were probably enhanced by the emphasis on walking and other forms of exercise.)

Rosenthal (in press) makes an important point in observing that classifying clients as treatment successes or failures on the basis of weight loss or body fat reductions as described above reflects the therapists' view of outcome, which may not necessarily "correspond with the dieter's own perception of success or failure. To date, no reported studies have asked dieters to assess their own levels of success. Yet it is highly likely that individuals differ considerably in their subjective assessments of success and failure." One month after treatment ended, the Rutgers clients were asked to rate their satisfaction with the weight loss and eating and exercise behavior changes they had accomplished. On a 9-point scale, with 1 representing "not at all," 5 representing "moderately," and 9 representing "very satisfied," the mean ratings were as follows: for weight loss, 5.7; for eating behavior change, 5.8; for exercise behavior change, 6.3. Thus, on average, clients were at least "moderately" satisfied with the changes they had achieved. Moreover, satisfaction ratings for eating and exercise behavior change (but *not* for weight loss) proved to be significant predictors of continued weight loss at the six-month follow-up.

Behavioral performance and psychological factors also need to be entered into any equation of therapeutic failure. Adherence to program prescriptions may relate only loosely to actual weight loss as described above. Behaviorally speaking, a client who adheres consistently to treatment instructions, namely, displays behavior change, cannot be said to be a treatment failure. The client's emotional well-being must also be considered. It is possible to lose weight and feel irritable, deprived, and depressed (Stunkard & Rush, 1974). Such emotional side-effects of weight loss would compromise an overall evaluation of therapeutic success. Happily, the available evidence consistently shows that the psychological concomitants of gradual weight loss in behavioral treatment programs have been positive (Wilson & Brownell, 1980). Considering possible biological boundaries of weight control (e.g., Wooley, et al., 1979), if relatively minimal weight loss following treatment is accompanied by positive psychological change such as less guilt, greater self-acceptance, and improved self-esteem, this picture should not easily be dismissed as treatment failure.

Who Succeeds and Who Fails? Predicting Treatment Outcome

Despite attempts by numerous investigators to demonstrate a relationship between demographic, personality, and behavioral variables and success or failure in weight reduction, reviewers are in agreement that the evidence for predictive utility of any of these variables is still inconsistent or equivocal (Cooke & Meyers, 1980; Stunkard, 1978; Weiss, 1977). In our analysis of the findings from the Rutgers Program, inasmuch as there were no significant effects of the spouse involvement or goal-setting experimental treatment manipulations on weight losses by the posttreatment assessment, we used the entire subject population to examine correlations between observed weight losses during treatment and measures that have been reported to be associated with outcome by previous researchers. We also examined differences between our extreme cases of arbitrarily defined "success" and "failure." The failure group included 16 clients (26 percent of all the cases) who lost less than 10 pounds. The success group included 15 clients (24 percent of the cases) who lost 20 pounds or more during that same period of time.

Body Composition

Jeffery, Wing, & Stunkard (1978) found that the most consistent predictor of weight loss by clients in the Stanford program was absolute body weight prior to treatment. A second measure that has been a consistent predictor of weight reduction in both behavioral and nonbehavioral treatment programs is percentage overweight (Stunkard, 1978). Finally, Sjostrom (1980) found that over 80 percent of the variance in weight reduction was accounted for by pretreatment measures of fat cell number and metabolic rate.

The best predictor of total weight loss during treatment for clients in the Rutgers program was the pretreatment estimate of percent body fat, derived from measures of skinfold thickness at four body sites ($r = -.37, p < .01$). In light of Sjostrom's (1980) findings, this is not surprising, inasmuch as individuals with a very high percentage of body fat are more likely to have an increased number of fat cells and because basal metabolic rate of fat tissue is lower than that of lean body tissue (Katch & McArdle, 1977). Estimated percentage of body fat was not significantly correlated with subjects' initial weight, a finding also reported by Rogers et al. (1980); and after percentage of fat was statistically controlled, initial weight did not significantly increase the explained variance in weight loss. Without data about percentage of fat, though, initial weight would have been a more interesting predictor of total weight loss by the Rutgers subjects ($r = .26$, $p < .05$), explaining the same amount of variance in weight loss as Jeffery et al. (1978) had reported.

Weight Loss Early in Treatment

Jeffery et al. (1978) found that weight losses early in treatment predicted later success. Our findings were very similar. Weight losses during the first two weeks of treatment were correlated .41 ($p < .01$) with total loss during the entire 19 weeks of treatment. By Week 4 of the Rutgers program, mean weight losses were significantly different for the extreme weight loss failure and success cases. Subjects who failed to lose at least 10 pounds total had lost only 2.5 pounds by the end of Week 4, whereas those who would go on to lose 20 pounds or more had already lost 9 pounds by this time.

Social Support

Several analyses have suggested that family support might influence weight control (e.g., Brownell et al., 1978; Pearce, LeBow, & Orchard, 1981; Rosenthal, Allen, & Winter, 1980). Jeffery et al., (1978) reported a correlation of .22 ($p < .05$) between weight loss during treatment and a measure of social support. In the Rutgers program, we examined spouses' weight status and two measures of spouse support as potential predictors of outcome at posttreatment. Both participant and spouse scores on the Marital Adjustment Test (Locke & Wallace, 1959) failed to correlate significantly with weight loss during treatment. However, some suggestive findings did emerge when we examined the extreme cases. At pretreatment, all subjects were asked to give their reasons for desiring to lose weight. On this checklist, those who failed to lose at least 10 pounds were not more or less likely than other participants to check concern about health or cosmetic appearance as motivating factors. They were, however, significantly less likely to check the item referring to concern about their spouse's reactions to their being overweight. Also, contrary to our expectations, the marital adjustment scores of those who lost less than 10 pounds were significantly *higher* than those of clients who lost 20 pounds or more. These unexpected observations led us to wonder whether those who had failed to lose might have spouses who were themselves more overweight and, therefore, more accepting of the subject remaining obese or more likely to model eating and exercise habits that maintain obesity. The available data provide some support for this hypothesis. Spouses of those who failed to lose at least 10 pounds averaged 31.2 percent overweight, whereas spouses of those who lost most successfully averaged only 19.4 percent overweight.

Sex of Subject

Males have been found to lose weight more rapidly than females in some studies (e.g., O'Neill, Currey, Hirsch, Riddle, Taylor, Malcolm, & Sexauer, 1979), but the evidence for sex differences in weight loss is difficult to interpret for a number of reasons (Weiss, 1977). In most studies, the number of male subjects is small, and those males who participate have been split among the treatment and control conditions. Another confounding factor is that the males usually are heavier than the females in a study population, and heavier clients typically lose more weight (Jeffery, et al., 1978).

In the Rutgers program, the 14 males were about 32 pounds heavier (average weight 222.9) than the females (average pretreatment weight 190.6 pounds). As predicted, the males were observed to lose at a faster pace throughout the treatment phase. At the end of treatment, males had lost 18.1 pounds, or about 0.95 pounds per week, whereas females lost a total of 15.0 pounds, at an average rate of 0.79 pounds per week. This was in spite of the fact that the self-reported average daily caloric intake for males (1333 calories per day) was considerably greater than the intake reported by females (1097 per day). However, the effect of sex of subject was not significant after percentage of body fat, initial weight, and age had been statistically controlled. Examination of the extreme cases also indicated that gender was not in itself a useful predictor of treatment outcome.

Age

Weiss (1977) and Cooke and Meyers (1980) concluded from their reviews that there is little evidence linking clients' age with ease of losing weight. Yet in our subject population age was a significant univariate predictor of total weight loss during treatment ($r = -.42, p < .01$). Older clients did not lose weight as readily as the younger individuals. However, as with gender, the relationship of age to weight loss was complicated by strong intercorrelations with initial weight and percentage of body fat. When the effects of these two variables were statistically controlled, the age was no longer a significant predictor.

Inasmuch as our average client was a middle-aged female, we wondered if the hormonal changes associated with menopause might be related to failure to reduce. Fifteen (31 percent) of our female clients reported they were postmenopausal, and 11 of these fell into our groups of "extreme cases." However, our observations provided no support for an hypothesis that it will be more difficult for women to lose weight after menopause. Only 4 of 13 women who failed to lose at least 10 pounds had reached menopause, whereas 7 of 10 who succeeded in losing 20 pounds or more were postmenopausal.

Age of Obesity Onset

Age of obesity onset has been believed to be a potential predictor of response to treatment primarily because of an hypothesized relationship between the age at which the individual first stored excessive body fat and adipose cellularity (Sjostrom, 1980). In behavioral research, the association between age of onset of obesity and weight loss or failure to reduce has been inconsistent (Cooke & Meyers, 1980; Weiss, 1977). For clients in the Rutgers program, the onset age was significantly and negatively correlated with pretreatment initial weight ($r = -.35, p < .01$), indicating that clients who had been overweight since childhood were the heaviest in our group. However, we found no significant correlation between the obesity onset age and weight loss during treatment. Among the extreme cases, the proportions of clients who reported onset of obesity before age 10 were nearly identical for both the extreme failures and successes in weight reduction.

Dieting and Weight Loss History

Several types of evidence suggest that dieting and weight loss history might predict success in a new weight reduction effort. Research on the physiological changes associated with dieting indicate that one adaptation to caloric intake restriction is a drop in metabolic rate, which serves to lower the demand for energy and, therefore, reduces the impact of the energy intake deficit. Each time the individual begins a new diet, this adaptation to the restricted caloric intake may occur more rapidly, making it more difficult to lose (Wooley, et al., 1979).

Subjects in the Rutgers program reported dieting for an average of more than 18 years before beginning the program, or nearly all their adult lives. The problem of maintenance was strikingly highlighted by the participants' responses concerning previous maximal weight losses. Our subjects claimed average previous maximum weight losses averaging 33 pounds, but reported that these previous losses had been maintained for an average of less than two years. None of the measures of dieting and weight loss history proved to be useful predictors of successful reduction or failure to lose in our program. Nor were Binge Scale (Hawkins & Clement, 1980) scores correlated with weight loss.

Other Predictor Variables

For the Rutgers program population, a combination of the best six predictor measures available early in treatment (pretreatment percentage of body fat, initial weight, age, spouse percentage overweight, reported caloric intake during Week 2, and weight lost during the first three weeks) accounted for 59 percent of the variance in total weight loss through the 19-week program. Jeffery et al. (1978) had found that a combination of six subject characteristic variables accounted for about 25 percent of the variance in outcome for clients in their program. To the clinician, the reduction in unexplained variance we are reporting is not particularly encouraging, for the predictor variables we used are, like Jeffery et al.'s (1978) subject characteristics, probably not susceptible to treatment manipulation. Thus the question of whether individuals who are likely to fail to reduce can be identified prior to treatment or during the early weeks of treatment is all the more relevant. Unfortunately, a discriminant function analysis using the best predictor variables correctly classified only 4 of the 16 extreme cases who failed to lose at least 10 pounds during the treatment phase.

Identification of High Risk Clients

At the present time, early identification of clients with characteristics associated with failure to reduce is probably our best bet. For the clients in the Rutgers program, the following were the indicators:

1. *High percentage of body fat.*   Fifty-six percent of the extreme failure cases had a percentage of body fat estimated at 45 percent or greater; as compared with only 28 percent of those who lost 10 pounds or more.

2. *Older age.*   Forty-four percent of the clients who failed to reduce by at least 10 pounds, but only 24 percent of those who lost more than 10 pounds, were over age 50 when they began the program.

3. *High pretreatment marital satisfaction and/or obese spouse.*   Ninety-three percent of the treatment failures had either an exceptionally high Locke–Wallace scores (120 or greater) *or* an obese spouse *or both* factors operating; only 39 percent of those who lost more than 10 pounds had either or both. Of course, it is not possible to say to what extent the relationships among successful weight reduction and marital satisfaction or an obese spouse may represent a more general phenomenon which would also apply to significant social relationships of unmarried weight control clients.

4. *Minimal weight loss during the first weeks of treatment.*   Of those who eventually failed to lose, 50 percent either lost less than two pounds or gained weight during the first three weeks of treatment. Only 20 percent of those who lost successfully had such a slow start.

5. *Adherence failure during first month of treatment.*   Half of those who achieved only minimal weight losses failed to self-monitor calories at least one week during the first month, whereas only 15 percent of those who lost 10 pounds or more failed to self-monitor during the first month.

Clients with one or more of the above characteristics may be considered at higher risk for continued successful treatment. Some of these higher risk clients will be able to reduce successfully; however, reassessment of their motivation to continue may be appropriate after the first three or four weeks of treatment. At this time, the economic, emotional, and potential health risk costs associated with continued attempts to reduce can be weighed against the potential benefits from weight reduction that could be realistically expected.

RELAPSE: THE FAILURE TO MAINTAIN WEIGHT LOSS

Most obese people can lose weight—indeed, have lost weight on many occasions—but cannot successfully maintain this weight loss over time. Wilson and Brownell (1980) summarized the evidence as follows:

1.   In general, behavioral treatments have produced weight losses that were maintained at the one-year follow-up.
2.   Most subjects do not continue to lose weight after the end of the treatment.
3.   Maintenance beyond one year is far less satisfactory.
4.   Some behavioral methods are more effective than others in facilitating long-term maintenance.

The specifics of the program that is used do appear to influence who succeeds and who fails although the evidence on this point is far from consistent.

As in the case of immediate treatment success or failure discussed above, quantifying relapse following the end of formal treatment raises a number of conceptual and definitional problems. Different investigators have used different definitions of successful maintenance over time. In the Rutgers program we used a weight gain of five or more pounds between posttreatment and the three-month follow-up as our criterion of relapse, as explained below.

Two major experimental methodologies have been employed to study the processes and determinants of relapse in weight reduction programs—correlational and experimental analysis. The more common approach is a correlational one in which there is a retrospective attempt to identify the correlates of maintenance and relapse, respectively. Leon and Chamberlain (1973) reported that those individuals who failed to maintain weight loss were more likely to eat in response to emotional states than their counterparts who did not relapse. Chapman and Jeffrey (1979) found that weight loss during follow-up was related to reported continued adherence to the standard-setting and self-reward techniques emphasized during treatment; Levitz, Jordan, LeBow, and Coopersmith (1980) likewise reported that successful maintenance was related to weight reduction strategies promoted during treatment, such as daily or weekly weighing, record-keeping, and exercise. In contrast to Stunkard and Penick's (1979) dismal finding that those who lost the most weight during treatment also regained the most during the follow-up, Levitz et al. (1980) found that subjects who were heavier initially were successful maintainers. Involvement of spouses in the treatment effort has been associated with continued losses or more successful maintenance after treatment ended in some studies (e.g., Brownell et al., 1978; Pearce et al., 1981), but not all studies (e.g., Brownell & Stunkard, 1981).

A study of the correlates of successful maintenance of weight loss by Stuart and Guire (1978) is particularly informative because it entailed a long-term follow-up of a large number of obese individuals who had lost substantial amounts of weight. Stuart and Guire (1978) collected long-term maintenance data from 721 members of Weight Watchers classes 15 months after they had reached their goal weights. Those members who had maintained their goal weight, as opposed to those who had regained weight, shared several characteristics. Among the correlates of successful maintenance were lower initial weights; continued attendance at classes with the same lecturers; improved self-concepts; the perception of being overweight when roughly three pounds above goal weight; the use of techniques learned during the period of weight loss; and a greater number of lifestyle changes supporting weight control. Scores on the Restrained Eating Scale (Herman, 1978) failed to differentiate between the groups.

The finding that a perception of being overweight after gaining a few pounds was strongly associated with long-term success is particularly intriguing in view of a social learning analysis of maintenance strategies. According to this approach, clients have to learn to monitor their problem behaviors and to reinstate self-corrective procedures at the first signs of the erosion of treatment-produced improvement. An example of this type of maintenance strategy is described by Bandura and Simon (1977) where clients monitored their weight and used a specific weight level as a cue to reinstate self-regulatory strategies for controlling weight gain. Successful maintenance of therapeutic change also involves arranging the incentives that sustain the reinstatement of self-regulatory measures. Booster sessions may be too little too late to shape up deteriorating self-regulatory capacities, as they apparently do not reduce relapse rates (see Foreyt et al., 1981; Wilson & Brownell, 1980).

Gormally (1980) selected 38 participants who had lost a minimum of 15 pounds from a treatment program that included 112 moderately overweight women and lasted 16 weeks. At a seven-month follow-up, of these 38 treatment successes, 16 were identified as successful maintainers and 12 as failures (relapses). The failures had regained more than 50 percent of their weight loss at posttreatment.

Based on detailed interviews with these two groups of participants, Gormally identified four dimensions along which they seemed to have differed. First, those who maintained weight loss continued to monitor bodyweight or eating habits. Those who relapsed ceased to monitor when they stopped restricting caloric intake.

Second, over 50 percent of those who maintained weight loss reported regular and vigorous planned exercise, and nearly two thirds of those who relapsed reported little or no exercise.

Third, the ability of those who maintained their weight loss to cope constructively with difficult or high-risk situations for excessive eating seemed to set them apart from those who relapsed. Most (82 percent) of those who relapsed responded to emotional states (depression, stress) by eating whereas none of their counterparts who maintained weight loss reported such behavior. In line with our own clinical experience, Gormally found that unexpected, unpredictable, and stressful life events were significantly associated with relapse.

Fourth, those who failed to maintain weight loss gave evidence of maladaptive cognitions concerning their efforts at weight control.

Rosenthal et al. (1979) interviewed 28 former participants of a nine-week behavioral weight reduction program 60 days after the end of treatment. The interview was adapted from Marlatt and Gordon's (1979) research as indicated earlier in this chapter.

At the outset, the limitations of this analysis of relapse must be mentioned. A follow-up of only 60 days does not come to grips with the real problem of long-term maintenance and the subject sample was relatively small. Nonetheless, the findings from this innovative analysis are suggestive. All 28 subjects had experienced one or more "slip," or failure to use any weight control method for a 24-hour period. As summarized in Table 15.1, intrapersonal factors accounted for 48 percent and interpersonal influences for 52 percent of the initial slips. "Relapse" was defined as a regain of $\geq$ 5 pounds since posttreatment. Subjects who did not relapse reported a 73 percent adherence rate to a critical dietary habit that they had identified as especially helpful in their weight control efforts. Only 46 percent of those who relapsed reported adherence to a critical dietary habit. Whereas 89 percent of subjects who maintained weight loss reported relying upon record keeping and calorie counting as primary means of controlling weight regain posttreatment, only 53 percent of the subjects who regained $\geq$ 5 pounds reported utilizing this method.

The three-month follow-up data from the Rutgers Program provide support for Bandura's (1969) observation that the variables controlling generalization and maintenance might not be the same as those controlling outcome during the initial induction phase of treatment. For the 50 subjects who completed treatment, weight changes from the final treatment session (Week 19) to the three-month follow-up (Week 32) varied from a loss of 11.25 pounds to a gain of 16.75 pounds. Thirty-one (63 percent) were still within five pounds of their weight at the final treatment session.

The variables predicting weight change during follow-up were different from those associated with weight loss during the treatment phase. Initial (pretreatment) weight was not significantly correlated with outcome during the initial follow-up. Percentage of body fat, which was significantly and negatively associated with weight loss during treatment, was significantly and positively correlated with weight change during the follow-up. The reason for this may be that a number of subjects with a relatively low percentage of body fat had already reached their weight loss goals at the end of treatment and did not reduce further, whereas a few high percentage of fat subjects continued to reduce successfully after treatment ended. Although a potential relationship between measures of marital satisfaction and outcome became apparent only when the extreme success and failure cases were compared at the end of treatment, spouse and participant marital satisfaction scores emerged as the best predictors of weight change during follow-up. Spouses' marital adjustment test scores obtained months earlier correlated .45 ($p < .01$) with weight change during maintenance, and participants' own pretreatment marital adjustment scores correlated .34 ($p < .05$) with their success during the initial follow-up. Perceived spouse cooperativeness, a score representing the number of cooperative behaviors participants reported their spouses performed during the weight reduction effort, was also significantly correlated with continued weight loss (Dubbert et al., 1981). There were, however, no significant differences in total weight loss between subjects whose spouses were involved in the program (couples treatment) and those whose spouses attended assessment sessions only (individual treatment). These results suggest that, although spouse support operated as predicted to help maintain the participants' weight control efforts after treatment ended, our attempts to manipulate cooperativeness by involving spouses in the treatment sessions were not effective.

Seven of the nine Rutgers program subjects who had regained five pounds or more between the final treatment session and the three-month follow-up assessment were interviewed about the circumstances surrounding relapse. By the three-month follow-up these subjects had regained an average of 48 percent (range = 18 to 100 percent) of their total weight loss. Analysis of the reasons subjects reported for failure to maintain their treatment-produced weight losses indicated that intrapersonal factors (reactions to unexpected bereavement) were associated with relapse in three of our subjects and positive interpersonal factors in four others.

The four clients whose relapse situations were classified as interpersonal in nature said they gave up weight control efforts while enjoying summer vacation. It is not clear how the determinants of relapse for our clients differed, if indeed they did, from the types of situations that triggered adherence failure (or possibly dropping out) during the treatment phase (see Table 15.1). One interesting difference was that most subjects who were interviewed because of adherence failures during treatment had already resumed calorie recording by the time they met with the therapist a week or so later. Despite the recommendation of the five-pound regain as a cue for resuming calorie recording, none of the relapsers had, in fact, reinstated self-monitoring when they were seen at the three-month follow-up.

Experimental Analyses

Correlates of success and failure in the attempt to maintain treatment-produced weight loss do not necessarily enlighten us about the cause of relapse. Causal analyses of failure to maintain weight loss go beyond correlational studies and experimentally manipulate factors that are presumed to determine relapse. To date, little research has been completed along these lines.

Rosenthal (in press) has reported an experimental analysis of factors associated with relapse in the behavioral treatment of obesity. Following her finding that approximately two thirds of the initial slips clients in weight reduction programs experience can be attributed to either negative emotional states or specifical social situations (Rosenthal et al., 1979; see Table 15.1), she compared a "standard" behavioral treatment program to one that included strategies designed to help clients cope effectively with the emotional and social factors she and her colleagues had identified.

The "standard" treatment program included record keeping, stimulus control procedures, methods for slowing down eating rate, satiation and hunger control techniques, use of rewards, chaining procedures, methods of obtaining social support, and assertiveness training. The "relapse prevention" program was derived from Marlatt and Gordon's (1979) conceptual model of the relapse process. Briefly, this program tried to teach subjects to recognize high-risk situations such as negative emotions and positive interpersonal occasions and to cope constructively with them rather than eating. Among the methods used were behavior rehearsal and other cognitive strategies designed to enhance subjects' sense of self-efficacy as described by Bandura (1977). An especially important component of this relapse prevention approach is the focus on what Marlatt and Gordon (1979) have called the "abstinence violation effect," (AVE) which is defined as the cognitive and emotional reactions to an initial slip following a period of controlled substance use or abstinence. As Rosenthal describes it, the AVE was explained to participants who then discussed diet-related experiences within this framework. For example, they were told, "You can expect to feel guilty and disappointed with yourself after you overeat, but these feelings do *not* mean that you are a failure at dieting. If you wait and do not overeat further, these feelings will pass." Group members' experiences with such phenomena were then solicited and discussed. Participants were given specific suggestions and techniques for handling the reactions that make up the AVE. They were encouraged to view a slip as an opportunity to examine remaining difficulties and practice new coping strategies.

Forty-three overweight subjects who completed the nine-week treatment programs participated in interviews similar to those used by Rosenthal et al. (1979) roughly 60 days after the end of treatment. Whereas the two groups did not differ at posttreatment, the "relapse prevention" group had lost more weight (13.9 pounds) than the "standard" group (8.7 pounds) at follow-up. Also, twice as many subjects in the standard condition regained weight during the 60-day posttreatment interval. Rosenthal interprets these findings and subjects' reports of their cognitive and affective reactions to initial "slips" as supportive of Marlatt and Gordon's (1979) model of the causes for failure to maintain treatment-produced weight loss. However, there are several reasons for viewing these findings with considerable caution.

First, it must be reemphasized that 60 days is far too short a follow-up period to permit satisfactory analysis of failure to maintain weight loss. Second, the actual weight losses at follow-up were unimpressive, with the two groups differing by a mere five pounds. Third, and most important, is the failure to replicate these results. Collins, Wilson, and Rothblum (1980) compared a cognitive behavioral treatment that included a relapse prevention component similar to that described by Rosenthal (in press) with a "standard" behavioral program and failed to show a significant difference at either 7- or 12-month follow-ups although the weight loss data were in the same direction as Rosenthal's. Despite this disappointing failure to replicate (no rarity in the treatment of obesity, alas!), it can be said at this point that Marlatt's model provides a heuristic and testable framework for studying failure to maintain weight loss and for developing more effective methods to combat relapse. Indeed, Gormally's (1980) results summarized in the previous section on correlates of treatment failure are encouragingly consistent with the predictions from the model.

WHEN BEHAVIORAL TREATMENT FAILS

Failure following participation in behavioral treatment may have psychological or physiological consequences for the individual client. There is evidence showing that the typical pattern of failure to achieve weight loss—repeated periods of severe caloric restriction and weight loss followed by overeating and weight gain may have the result that recovery of metabolic rate to prerestriction levels takes longer and that metabolic rate falls more rapidly with return to caloric restriction than it did originally. Exercise, an increasingly important component of behavioral treatment programs, may help to reverse this metabolic effect. Furthermore, relatively brief periods of severe caloric restriction may be interspersed with less extreme alterations in eating pattern in order to circumvent unhelpful accomodations of the obese person's metabolism (Wooley et al., 1979). The results from the Clausen et al. (1980) study referred to earlier in this chapter encourage future investigation of alternation of different caloric diets.

In a comprehensive behavioral weight control program emphasizing gradual weight loss through caloric intake restriction and increased exercise to expend calories, the health risks incurred by the weight loss effort itself are probably minimal. Even without formal nutrition counseling, the nutrient intakes recorded by behavioral weight control program participants have been found to indicate consumption of a fairly nutritious diet not very different from pretreatment diet except for a reduction in amounts eaten (Brightwell, Foster, Lee, & Naylor, 1979). There may be some increased risk involved for those who try to lose by caloric deprivation alone without increased exercise. In one study, clients who did so showed a decrease in the high density lipoproteins believed to be associated with lower cardiovascular risk (Weltman, Matter, & Stamford, 1980). Yet clients who begin to exercise may successfully reduce their cardiovascular risk through favorable changes in the ratio of high density and low density lipoproteins even if they do not restrict caloric intake sufficiently to lose much weight (Lewis, Haskell, Wood, Mannogian, Bailey, & Pereira, 1976; Weltman et al., 1980).

Some of the psychological effects of failure (dropping out of treatment, inability to lose weight, or relatively rapid regaining of weight that was lost in treatment) have already been touched upon in the discussion of Marlatt and Gordon's (1979) cognitive-behavioral model of the relapse process. The unsuccessful participant may feel guilty or depressed, develop a sense of helplessness or hopelessness about controlling his or her weight, engage in self-blame, and experience a diminished sense of self-efficacy. To the extent that treatment failures suffer these emotional reactions they are less likely to succeed in subsequent weight control efforts. Yet it is clear that failure to lose weight in one sort of treatment does little to deter a great number of obese people from trying the same program at later times or shopping around for alternative forms of treatment. In our research and practice we inevitably find that our clients have been veterans of other weight reduction approaches, including different diets, drugs, hypnosis, commercial programs such as Weight Watchers, Lean Line, and so on. For example, in the Rutgers program all but three of the participants stated that they have been involved in previous treatment programs of one form or another without lasting success. We are also aware that some of our own treatment failures have sought other means of help for their weight problems.

It is clear that many of these obese individuals who seek behavioral treatment following previous failures can be helped to lose weight and even to maintain this weight loss. In the Rutgers program, as noted above, none of the measures of previous dieting or unsuccessful weight loss history correlated significantly with weight loss at posttreatment. We can conclude, therefore, that treatment failure in either behavioral or nonbehavioral programs does not doom the person who would be slimmer to inevitable or recurring lack of success in subsequent behavioral programs.

How does one explain the success of a client who has previously failed repeatedly in a variety of treatment programs including those that seem to incorporate some of the features of a behavioral approach (e.g., a commercial program such as Lean Line)? One reason may be that the behavioral program in which the client finally succeeds is simply more effective than previous methods. Although the literature does not provide definitive evidence on what are the most effective treatment strategies, there is a sound clinical basis for believing that a thorough assessment of the psychosocial conditions that prompt faulty eating or lack of exercise is critically important and that intervention should be multifaceted with explicit maintenance strategies that directly address the potential problem of failure. Some clients probably connect better with particular therapists (the nature of this largely adventitious matching being well beyond our knowledge at this time) and the therapeutic relationship can make a difference in terms of enhancing compliance. Lastly, it is our admittedly unsupported view that, for whatever reasons, some clients finally become more motivated to succeed and make whatever program they are in work. We customarily ask new clients what they feel will be different this time. Why do they think they might succeed this time? Aside from comments about promising sounding elements of our treatment program, clients' answers also often include statements about being "more motivated" this time, or that the decision to seek therapy is really their own, whereas in the past they had felt pressured into seeking treatment by family or friends. Of course, these assertions of motivation and commitment do not always translate into therapeutic success, but they warrant more systematic exploration in future research.

Despite the best efforts of competent therapists using the most effective methods, obesity often remains refractory to change. All too often, weight loss does not occur, is minimal, or too variable. In view of this well established finding, we strongly endorse Wooley et al.'s (1979) recommendation that we should "define more broadly the goals of treatment so as to deal with the severe problems in self-esteem stemming from social prejudice and repeated failure" (p. 21). To consider seriously the possibility of failure to achieve lasting weight control is not only humane but very sensible. It would seem to be demanded by the client-centered goals of behavior therapy and the specific assumptions of the cognitive-behavioral model of maintenance that has been described above.

The sense of this discussion is succinctly summarized by Wooley et al. in the following excerpt, sounding a theme on which we conclude this chapter:

> It would seem to be consistent with the philosophy and tradition of behavior therapies to acquaint patients with the facts about obesity, including the lack of evidence that the obese eat more than others, the effects of dieting on metabolism, and the modest outcomes of most treatment, and to engage them in a process of goal-setting based on these facts. Although therapists tend to be reluctant to discourage patients, the facts of their own experience will have discouraged them or given them hope. If the experience of dieting has been one of constant failure, despite enormous effort, they will be relieved to have their experience confirmed and understood, and some may be better able to withstand the difficulties knowing that they are not exclusively attributable to their own failings. Some may choose to give up dieting and work on minimizing the negative consequences of being obese. Others will recognize that weight loss is, in fact, relatively easy for them and worth the effort. It has been our experience that few patients embrace these pieces of information as "rationalizations": the concept of rationalization, of course, implies a self-serving denial of the "truth," which in the case of obesity is not known. (p. 20)

REFERENCES

Bandura, A. (1969) *Principles of behavior modification.* New York: Holt, Rinehart & Winston.

Bandura, A. (1977) *Social learning theory.* Englewood Cliffs, N.J.: Prentice-Hall.

Bandura, A., & Simon, K.M. (1977) The role of proximal intentions in self-regulation of refractory behavior. *Cognitive Therapy and Research,* **1,** 177–193.

Bray, G.A. (1976) *The obese patient.* Philadelphia: Saunders.

Bray, G.A. (1978) Definition, measurement and classification of the syndromes of obesity. *International Journal of Obesity,* **2,** 99–112.

Brightwell, D.R., Foster, D., Lee, S., & Naylor, C.S. (1979) Effects of behavioral and pharmacological weight loss programs on nutrient intake. *American Journal of Clinical Nutrition,* **32,** 2005–2008.

Brownell, K.D., Heckerman, C., Westlake, R.J., Hayes, S.C., & Monti, P. (1978) The effect of couples training and partner cooperativeness in the behavioral treatment of obesity. *Behaviour Research and Therapy,* **16,** 323–333.

Brownell, K.D., & Stunkard, A.J. (1978) Behavior therapy and behavior change: uncertainities in programs for weight control. *Behaviour Research and Therapy,* **16,** 301–302.

Brownell, K.D., & Stunkard, A.J. (1981) Couples training, pharmacotherapy, and behavior therapy in the treatment of obesity. *Archives of General Psychiatry,* *38,* 1224–1229.

Chapman, S.L., & Jeffrey, B. (1979) Processes in the maintenance of weight loss with behavior therapy. *Behavior Therapy,* **10,** 566–570.

Clausen, J.D., Silfen, M., Coombs, J., Ayers, W., & Altschul, A.M. (1980) Relationship of dietary regimens to success, efficiency, and cost of weight loss. *Journal of the American Dietetic Association,* **77,** 249–256.

Collins, R.L., Wilson, G.T., & Rothblum, E. (1980) *The comparative efficacy of cognitive and behavioral approaches in weight reduction.* Paper presented at Association for Advancement of Behavior Therapy, New York, November.

Cooke, C.J., & Meyers, A. (1980) Assessment of subject characteristics in the behavioral treatment of obesity. *Behavioral Assessment,* **2,** 59–70.

Dubbert, P. (1982) *Goal-setting and spouse involvement in the treatment of obesity.* Unpublished doctoral dissertation, Rutgers University.

Dubbert, P., Wilson, G.T., Augusto, F., Langenbucher, J., & McGee, D. (1981) *Cooperative behavior of involved and noninvolved spouses of weight control program participants.* Paper presented at Annual Convention of Association for Advancement of Behavior Therapy, Toronto.

Dunbar, J.M., & Stunkard, A.J. (1979) Adherence to medical regimen. In R. Levy, B. Rifkind, B. Dennis, & N. Ernst (Eds.), *Nutrition, lipids, and coronary heart disease.* New York: Raven.

Foreyt, J., Goodrick, K., & Gotto, A.M. (1981) Limitations of behavioral treatment of obesity: Review and analysis. *Journal of Behavioral Medicine.,* *4,* 159–174.

Foreyt, J.P., Scott, L.W., Mitchell, R.E., & Gotto, A.M. (1979) Plasma lipid changes in the normal population following behavioral treatment. *Journal of Consulting and Clinical Psychology,* **47,** 440–452.

Franks, C.M., & Wilson, G.T. (1979) *Annual review of behavior therapy: Theory and practice* (Vol. 7). New York: Brunner/Mazel.

Gormally, J. (1980) *Factors associated with weight loss maintenance.* Paper presented at Annual Convention of the American Psychological Association, Montreal.

Gormally, J., Rardin, D., & Black, S. (1980) Correlates of successful response to a behavioral weight control clinic. *Journal of Counseling Psychology,* **27,** No. 2, 179–191.

Gurman, A.S. (1978) Contemporary marital therapies: A critique and comparative analysis of psychodynamic, systems and behavioral approaches. In T. Paolino, & B. McCrady (Eds.), *Marriage and marital therapy from three perspectives.* New York: Brunner/Mazel.

Hagen, R.L., Foreyt, J.P., & Durham, T.W. (1976) The dropout problem: Reducing attrition in obesity research. *Behavior Therapy,* **7,** 463–471.

Hanna, C.F., Loro, A.D., & Power, D. (1981) Differences in the degree of overweight: A note on its importance. *Addictive Behaviors,* 6, 61–62.

Harris, M.B., Sutton, M., Kaufman, E.M., & Carmichael, C.W. (1980) Correlates of success and retention in a multi-faceted, long-term behavior modification program for obese adolescent girls. *Addictive Behaviors,* **5,** 25–34.

Hawkins, R.C., & Clement, P.F. (1980) Development and construct validation of a self-report measure of binge eating tendencies. *Addictive Behaviors,* **5,** 219–226.

Herman, P. (1978) Restrained eating. *The Psychiatric Clinics of North America,* **1,** 593–607.

Jeffrey, R.W., Wing, R.R., & Stunkard, A.J. (1978) Behavioral treatment of obesity: The state of the art. *Behavior Therapy,* **9,** 189–199.

Johnson, W.G., Wildman, H.E., & O'Brien, T. (1980) The assessment of program adherence: The Achilles heel of behavioral weight reduction? *Behavioral Assessment,* **2,** 297–302.

Katch, F.I., & McArdle, W.D. (1977) *Nutrition, weight control, and exercise.* Boston: Houghton Mifflin.

Kazdin, A.E., & Wilson, G.T. (1978) *Evaluation of behavior therapy.* Cambridge: Ballinger.

Lansky, D. (1981) A methodological analysis of research on adherence and weight loss: Reply to Brownell and Stunkard (1978). *Behavior Therapy,* **12,** 144–149.

Leon, G.R., & Chamberlain, K. (1973) Comparison of daily eating habits and emotional states of overweight persons successful or unsuccessful in maintaining a weight loss. *Journal of Consulting and Clinical Psychology,* **41,** 108–115.

Levitz, L.S., Jordan, H.A., LeBow, M.D., & Coopersmith, M.L. (1980). Weight loss five years after behavioral treatment. Paper presented at the American Psychological Association meeting, Montreal.

Lewis, S., Haskell, W.I., Wood, P.D., Mannogian, N., Bailey, J.E., & Pereira, M. (1976) Effects of physical activity on weight reduction in obese middle-aged women. *American Journal of Clinical Nutrition,* **29,** 151–156.

Locke, H.J., & Wallace, K.M. (1959) Short marital adjustment and prediction tests: Their reliability and validity. *Marriage and Family Living,* **21,** 251–255.

Loro, A.D., Jr., Fisher, E.B., Jr., & Levenkron, J.C. (1979) Comparison of established and innovative weight-reduction treatment procedures. *Journal of Applied Behavior Analysis,* **12,** 141–155.

Mahoney, M.J., & Mahoney, K. (1976) *Permanent weight control.* New York: W.W. Norton.

Marks, I. (1978) Behavioral psychotherapy of adult neurosis. In S.L. Garfield, & A.E. Bergin (Eds.), *Handbook of psychotherapy and behavior change* (2nd Ed.). New York: Wiley.

Marlatt, G.A., & Gordon, J.R. (1979) Determinants of Relapse: Implications for the maintenance of behavior change. In P. Davidson, & S. Davidson (Eds.), *Behavioral medicine: Changing health lifestyles.* New York: Brunner/Mazel.

McFall, R.M. (1979) Parameters of self-monitoring. In R.B. Stuart (Ed.), *Behavioral self-management*. New York: Brunner/Mazel.

O'Neil, P.M., Currey, H.S., Hirsch, A.A., Riddle, F.E., Taylor, C.I., Malcolm, R.J., & Sexauer, J.D. (1979) Effects of sex of subject and spouse involvement on weight loss in a behavioral treatment program: A retrospective investigation. *Addictive Behavior,* **4,** 167–178.

Pearce, J.W., LeBow, M., & Orchard, J. (1981) Role of spouse involvement in the behavioral treatment of overweight women. *Journal of Consulting and Clinical Psychology,* **49,** 236–244.

Rachman, S., & Wilson, G.T. (1980) *The effects of psychological therapy.* Oxford: Pergamon.

Rogers, T., Mahoney, M.J., Mahoney, K., Shaw, M., & Kenigsberg, M. (1980) Clinical assessment of obesity: An empirical evaluation of diverse techniques. *Behavioral Assessment,* **2,** 161–182.

Rosenthal, B.S. (in press). Relapse in weight control: Definitions, processes, and prevention strategies. In G.A. Marlatt (Ed.) *Relapse prevention.* New York: Guilford.

Rosenthal, B.S., Allen, G.J., & Winter, C. (1980) Husband involvement in the behavioral treatment of overweight women: Initial effects and long-term follow-up. *International Journal of Obesity,* 165–173.

Sjoberg, L., & Persson, L. (1979) A study of attempts by obese patients to regulate eating. *Addictive Behaviors,* *4,* 349–359.

Sjostrom, L. (1980) Fat cells and body weight. In A.J. Stunkard (Ed.), *Obesity.* Philadelphia: Saunders.

Stuart, R.B., & Guire, K. (1978) Some correlates of the maintenance of weight loss through behavior modification. *International Journal of Obesity,* **2,** 225–235.

Stunkard, A.J. (1958) The management of obesity. *New York Journal of Medicine,* **58,** 79–87.

Stunkard, A.J. (1972) New therapies for the eating disorders: Behavior modification of obesity and anorexia nervosa. *Archives of General Psychiatry,* **26,** 391–398.

Stunkard, A.J. (1978) Behavioral treatment of obesity: The current status. *International Journal of Obesity,* **2,** 237–249.

Stunkard, A.J. (1980) (Ed.), *Obesity.* Philadelphia: Saunders.

Stunkard, A.J., & Brownell, K.D. (1979) Behavior therapy and self-help programmers for obesity. In J.F. Munno (Ed.), *Treatment of obesity.* Lancaster, England: MTP Press.

Stunkard, A.J., & Mahoney, M.J. (1976) Behavioral treatment of the eating disorders. In H. Leitenberg (Ed.), *Handbook of behavior modification and behavior therapy.* Englewood Cliffs, N.J.: Prentice-Hall.

Stunkard, A.J., & Penick, S. (in press) Behavior modification in the treatment of obesity: The problem of maintaining weight loss. *Archives of General Psychiatry.*

Stunkard, A.J., & Rush, J. (1974) Dieting and depression re-examined: A critical review of reports of untoward responses during weight reduction for obesity. *Annals of Internal Medicine,* **81,** 526–533.

United States Department of Health, Education, and Welfare (1967). *Obesity and health.* Arlington, VA: United States Public Health Service.

Van Itallie, T.B. (1979) Obesity: Adverse effects on health and longevity. *American Journal of Clinical Nutrition,* **32,** 2723–2733.

Weltman, A., Matter, S., & Stanford, B.A. (1980) Caloric restriction and/or mild exercise: Effects on serum lipids and body composition. *American Journal of Clinical Nutrition,* **33,** 1002–1009.

Weiss, A.R. (1977) Characteristics of successful weight reducers: A brief review of predictor variables. *Addictive Behaviors,* **2,** 193–202.

Wilson, G.T. (1978) Methodological considerations in treatment outcome research on obesity. *Journal of Consulting and Clinical Psychology,* **46,** 687–702.

Wilson, G.T., & Brownell, K. (1980) Behavior therapy for obesity: An evaluation of treatment outcome. *Advances in Behavior Research and Therapy,* **3,** 49–86.

Wooley, S.C., Wooley, O.W., & Dyrenforth, S.R. (1979) Theoretical, practical, and social issues in behavioral treatments of obesity. *Journal of Applied Behavior Analysis,* **12,** 3–25.

CHAPTER 16

Failures in the
Treatment of Insomnia:
A Plea for Differential Diagnosis

RALPH M. TURNER
ROBERT DI TOMASSO
THOMAS GILES

Insomnia, defined as a chronic inability to initiate and maintain adequate sleep, is a common clinical complaint in outpatient settings (Bootzin & Nicassio, 1978; Sleep Disorders Classification Committee, 1979; Williams, Karacan, & Hursch, 1974). Epidemiological estimates of the incidence of insomnia range between 30 and 45 percent of the general population. Researchers have concurred that 10 to 15 percent of the general population complain of mild or occasional insomnia and an additional 10 to 15 percent suffer from severe and frequent insomnia (Kales, Bixler, Lee, Healy, & Slye, 1974; Montgomery, Perkins, & Wise, 1975; Webb, 1975). In fact, in a sample of 1,645 individuals residing in Florida, Williams, Karacan, and Hursch (1974) discovered that 45 percent of the sample reported disturbances in initiating and maintaining sleep. The alarming rise in the consumption of tranquilizers and sedative-hypnotics in the United States over the past several years seems to be an additional confirmation of the prevalence of sleep disturbance (Turner & DiTomasso, 1980).

Insomnia is classified as either primary or secondary (Williams, Karacan, & Hursch, 1974). The critical feature of primary insomnia is the predominance of the sleep disturbance symptoms in the medical and psychological profile of the patient. It usually appears in the following forms: (1) protracted latency in sleep onset; (2) night interruptions, sometimes associated with difficulty in returning to sleep; and (3) early morning awakening. Secondary insomnia includes sleep disturbances that are associated with physical illness (e.g., arthritis) or severe psychological maladjustment (e.g., depression or mania).

Treatments for primary insomnia vary widely. Physicians usually treat insomniacs with chemotherapeutic agents. The most commonly prescribed medications are sedative-hypnotics including the benzodiazepines (flurazepam, diazepam, chlordizepoxicde, nitrazepam) the piperidinedione derivatives (glutethimide, methypaylon, dipenhydramine), the barbiturates (phenobarbital and seconbarbital), methaqualone, and ethclorvyno. However, the potential physical and psychological risks associated with drug-based interventions greatly offset the resultant but transitory gains observed in patients. Some of the more serious risks associated with pharmacological treatments include the following: (1) REM sleep suppression, (2) tolerance cycles which may lead to physical and/or psychological dependency, (3) possible drug interactions with other medications, and (4) the abuse potential of sedative-hypnotics with alcohol. Psychodynamically oriented therapists, on the other hand, prescribe long-term analysis for insomniacs with the goal of helping them to work through repressed impulses and conflicts. It was the search for short-term and effective nondrug treatment alternatives that led to the development, evaluation, and application of behavioral treatment strategies. Within recent years behavioral clinicians, who operate from the scientist-practitioner perspective, have made significant contributions to both the understanding and treatment of insomnia.

Three major behavioral hypotheses have been posited to explain the causes and maintenance of primary insomnia (for a detailed review, see Turner & DiTomasso, 1980). One view suggests that excessive physiological tension is associated with sleep disturbance. This tension presumably results from either the buildup of muscular tension throughout the day or an anxious personality style. Thus, at bedtime the patient experiences a high level of arousal that is antagonistic to sleep. In support of the above hypothesis, "poor sleepers" appear to be more aroused than "good sleepers" before and during sleep on a variety of indicators (Monroe, 1967).

A second perspective is found in Bootzin's (1972) operant learning conceptualization of sleep disturbance. Based upon the stimulus control research by Brown (1965), MacIntosh (1977), and Riling (1977), proponents of this viewpoint hypothesize that the bed and bedroom serve as discriminative stimuli for sleeping. In other words, the bedroom environment can be considered to include a variety of cues that signal an opportunity for the performance of sleeping behavior. Primary insomnia might, then, be related to the tendency of some poor sleepers to perform activities in bed that vitiate the bed's cueing potential for sleep. For example, it is not uncommon for insomniacs to report that they engage in one or more of a variety of activities at bedtime (e.g., reading, writing, watching television, sewing, eating, cognitive planning, problem solving), all of which are more appropriately conducted in other parts of the person's environment and at different times. For instance, cognitive planning and problem solving are particularly disruptive behaviors in which some insomniacs engage while in bed. Many adults with overextended daily activities have little time for such reflection during the day and relegate it to the first several minutes before retiring. Such a pattern of behavior can become habitual and can encroach upon the time normally scheduled for sleeping.

The third hypothesis of primary insomnia listed by Turner and DiTomasso (1980) suggests that sleep difficulties are maintained by the patient's unsuccessful attempts to voluntarily control the sleeping process (Ascher & Efran, 1978; Ascher & Turner, 1980; Frankl, 1975; Turner & Ascher, 1979a, b). Attempts to bring about sleep presumably result in an increase in sympathetic nervous system activity that is incompatible with sleeping. The urgency to fall asleep is usually related to fears that the loss of sleep will produce a cumulative, deleterious physiological effect or that poor sleeping is indicative of a disordered personality. Thus the individual generates additional performance anxiety that, in turn, results in a vicious circle of his or her continually trying harder to fall asleep and simultaneously creating more tension which interferes with sleep.

These diverse but complementary conceptualizations of primary insomnia have spawned a number of behavioral interventions. A basic tenet of behavior therapy is that those techniques included under the label "behavioral" must be subject to empirical test and validation (Rimm & Masters, 1975). Behavioral clinicians place the highest priority upon testing the efficacy of treatments. Not surprisingly, then, a fairly substantial amount of literature about the behavioral treatment of insomnia exists. In a recent review and methodological analysis of the evidence, Turner and DiTomasso (1980) concluded that progressive relaxation therapy, other anxiety-reducing procedures, and stimulus control therapy are efficacious treatments for primary insomnia. They also suggested that although there appears to be some support for paradoxical intention at this time, further outcome data is necessary.

In their continual quest to identify potent treatment packages for selected psychological disturbances, empirical clinicians have sometimes overlooked those variables that may negatively affect the course of outcome in behavioral therapy. An exposition of those factors that contribute to "failures" in the behavioral treatment of insomnia is timely. There are undoubtedly a host of reasons why insomniacs sometimes fail to respond to a prescribed behavioral treatment regimen. In the present chapter we have categorized the several causes for "failure" into three broad categories: theoretical, empirical, and clinical issues. In the first section, we discuss possible theoretical conceptualizations of sleep functioning that may account for failures. In the second, we delineate one empirical factor that generated treatment failures in our own research. Finally, we describe those variables confronting behavior therapists in the clinical session.

The goals of this chapter are twofold: to sensitize practicing clinicians to factors that may precipitate failure in the treatment of insomnia, and to recommend some useful alternatives and strategies for dealing with these factors, where possible.

THEORETICAL ISSUES

Failure Due to Inadequate Conceptualization of Insomnia

In order to design a treatment program for the chronic primary insomniac, the clinician must first identify the factor or combination of factors that seems to be causing the sleeping difficulty. Specifically, the clinician must conduct a thorough behavioral analysis (see Wolpe, 1970, 1979) and assess the presence or absence of such contributors as performance anxiety, hyperarousal, and/or lack of stimulus control over sleeping behavior. The behavioral intervention that is subsequently selected and applied by the clinician is tailor-fitted to the needs of the particular patient (Wolpe, 1979).

We would urge caution here, however. Treating the chronic primary insomniac is not always a simple matter for the behavioral clinician. Behaviorists have been criticized for using what works with little regard for why it works. In other words, we have been short on theory. For example, though paradoxical intention, relaxation, and stimulus control techniques have been demonstrated to be effective treatment strategies for primary insomnia (e.g., Turner & Ascher, 1979a), a substantial number of theoretical questions are evidenced by empirical inconsistencies in the literature. The clinician who disregards these inconsistencies may inadvertently sabotage his or her therapy beforehand. Therefore, in the following subsection we elaborate upon some of the inconsistencies in present research and then describe an alternative theoretical framework for understanding them. We believe that this alternative explanation, the Overload/Underload Mismatch Theory of Insomnia (de la Pena, 1978), may provide important implications for the behavioral practitioner in planning therapy and, we hope, avoiding treatment failures.

Inconsistencies of Research Findings

A careful review of the existing research on insomnia seems to engender more theoretcal questions than answers. The following findings exemplify this point:

1.   Relaxation therapy for insomnia has yielded differential improvement rates across studies. Significant improvement rates vary from 35 to 75 percent with ostensibly similar populations (e.g., Bootzin, & Nicassio, 1978).

2.   Although some studies suggest that stimulus control techniques produce significantly better improvement for primary insomniacs than relaxation therapy (Bootzin & Nicassio, 1978), others, however, show no differential efficacy (e.g., Turner & Ascher, 1979a).

3.   The effects of placebo treatments vary widely across studies (e.g., Bootzin & Nicassio, 1978).

4.   The MMPI profiles of primary insomniacs differ across studies. For example, some studies show elevations on measures of anxiety and depression whereas others show elevations on the psychopathic deviant and schizophrenia scales (Beutler, Thornby, & Karacan, 1978). Interestingly, other studies show little elevations on these scales whatsoever and no differences from normal controls (Beutler, Thornby, & Karacan, 1978).

5.   Electroencephalographic (EEG) data on primary insomniacs often varies considerably both between patients and within individual patients, and considerable EEG variation occurs from night to night (de la Pena, 1978).

6.   Although there is evidence to support the hyperarousal hypothesis of in-

somnia, evidence also exists to suggest the *opposite* relationship, that is, that hypoarousal interferes with sleep (see de la Pena, 1978, for review).

The inconsistencies outlined above suggest that present behavioral formulations of chronic primary insomnia may *oversimplify* the problem. The behavioral conceptualizations of insomnia previously discussed cannot adequately explain the variability of outcomes, inconsistencies in arousal data, or differences both within and between sleeping trials with insomniacs. Thus although Bootzin (1975) reported a 57 percent significant improvement rate for his insomniac population treated with stimulus control, there is little theoretical or empirical indication from the behavioral literature as to what steps to take with the remaining failures.

That any blanket treatment package for insomnia will result in a certain percentage of treatment failures seems inevitable. The empirical inconsistencies just reviewed suggest that treatment failures may be due to complex individual differences in patient characteristics, the type of treatment intervention administered, and/or the outcome measures selected. De la Pena (1978) has attempted to reconcile these differences or explain the lack of replication in results.

Mismatch Theory and the Failure to Distinguish Between Stimulus Overload- and Underload-Induced Insomnia

de la Pena's Overload/Underload Mismatch Theory of Insomnia is quite comprehensive and attempts to explain not only the inconsistencies mentioned above but also the etiological bases of *all* forms of insomnia (e.g., sleep apnea, hypersomnia, nocturnal myoclonis, age-induced insomnia, etc.). To remain within the scope of this chapter, we will focus our attention upon that aspect of the mismatch theory that, in de la Pena's (1978) view, is most likely to cause chronic primary insomnia.

The most important hypothesis of the mismatch theory is that the central nervous system (CNS) functions homeostatically during sleep and waking to maintain information processing levels within an optimal range. Primary insomnia most often occurs when the system's general information input has been chronically and severely underloaded.

To explicate this process more fully, de la Pena assumes that the highly developed central nervous system of the adult human tends to process the sensory components of incoming stimulus configurations in a highly efficient manner. This allows the human organism to devote more conceptual or ideational attention to the environment, which may be an evolutionary consequence as well as an adaptive advantage. The general information processing level of the CNS varies proportionately to the amount of uncertainty in the stimulus environment. When the incoming stimulus configuration is novel, the CNS operates under high uncertainty and thus processes information at a high rate. After the stimulus configuration has been frequently presented, however, the amount of uncertainty as well as the resulting amount of CNS activity declines; that is, the organism habituates. According to de la Pena (1978), the cognitive or conceptual abilities of adult humans predispose them to psychological disruption through habituation to familiar environmental input. This presumably results in severe stimulus underload and creates a mismatch between the amount of information needed and that which is obtained.

When the underload mismatch is low to moderate, de la Pena hypothesizes that brain control mechanisms operate *during sleep* to increase the rate of sensory information processing. The result is that REM phasic density and intensity may increase while latency to first REM may decrease. The individual may begin to experience difficulty falling asleep in a quiet environment and may switch on a radio or a fan to increase sensory input. In addition, the duration of NREM periods, especially Stage 4, may decrease.

Individuals who have low to moderate underload deficits are hypothetically able to resolve these deficits during sleep with little or no disruption in sleep or waking functions. If the underload becomes more extreme, however, homeostasis will not be regained during sleep alone, and attempts to obtain greater sensory input will then ensue. Individuals with severe stimulus underload may become agitated, hyperactive, and restless *during the day.* They may begin to ruminate and worry over personal problems and feel increasingly anxious at bedtime. Coffee and nicotine consumption may increase along with boredom, depression, and generalized anxiety. These individuals may also begin having greater latencies to sleep, frequent awakenings during the night, less total sleep time, and/or early morning awakenings. In other words, primary insomnia obtains. Therefore, according to de la Pena, the etiology of chronic primary insomnia is usually chronic stimulus underload. Thus chronic primary insomnia serves to balance the resulting disequilibrium by increasing input.

We note in passing that de la Pena (1978) hypothesizes that insomnia obtains, although less frequently, when people are chronically *overstimulated* to a low or moderate degree. People who work in overly stimulating or frequently changing environments are particularly susceptible to this problem. Those with "less efficient nervous systems" (de la Pena, 1978) are also presumed at risk.

The notion of stimulus overload as an etiological factor in insomnia bears resemblance to the hyperarousal hypotheses (i.e., performance anxiety, autonomic arousal, circadian dysrhythmia, etc.) so well evidenced in the behavioral literature. Although both points of view predict that reduction of environmental and autonomic stimulation will cure insomnia, the mismatch theory makes the additional prediction that insomnia in overstimulated individuals can be drastically reversed by *raising* their information overload from a moderate to a severe degree. In severe stimulus overload de la Pena hypothesizes that information processing homeostatically reduces to very low levels. The individual becomes easily tired and fatigued. Also, activity becomes difficult, sleep onset latency shorter, and total sleep time increases. In other words, hypersomnia obtains and is the clinical picture of severe stimulus overload.

The major contributions of mismatch theory are: (1) the attention given to waking behavior in the study of insomnia, (2) the hypothesis that information processing is the function and etiology of insomnia, and (3) the contention that primary insomnia is most often the behavioral correlate of chronic stimulus underload. The underload component of mismatch theory seems to explain many disparate findings in previous research such as the following:

1.   Many insomniacs show a "reverse" first night effect in the sleep lab. That is, they sleep better the first night than on subsequent nights in the laboratory. This first night's sleep is also better than general sleep at home (efficient sleepers show the opposite effect). De la Pena explains this through novelty of the laboratory sleep environment. This novelty provides the chronically understimulated insomniac with an overload sensory input and thus raises information processing to a level where sleep disturbance and waking are no longer required. De la Pena (1976) found that insomniacs showing reverse first night effects had higher sensation-seeking scores, more self-rated boredom, and smoked more cigarettes that insomniacs showing normal first night effects.

2.   Insomnia, especially maintenance insomnia, tends to increase with old age. Consistent with mismatch theory, old age is associated with a decrease in most physiological parameters. This, in turn, leads to lowered sensory input and chronic understimulation.

3.   Very quiet and monotonous sleep environments seem to result in increasingly disrupted sleep. (See de la Pena, 1978 for review.) The insomnia often accompanying depression may be the central nervous system's attempt to gain stimulus input in the face of waking stimulus underload.

The hypothesis that overloaded and underloaded insomniacs have been mixed unsystematically in previous research seems to explain many of the inconsistencies mentioned previously in this chapter.

In spite of the enormous range of explanation of mismatch theory and the impressive diversity of data that de la Pena has gathered to support it, the theory in present form is unrefined and begging for further research. De la Pena uses a conglomerate of techniques to treat underload and overload insomnia, and it is unclear as to whether the entire treatment package or parts of it are necessary or sufficient. De la Pena has delineated a number of variables that can be used diagnostically to discriminate overload versus underload insomniacs (see below), but there is little indication of their relative importance or what to do with insomniacs who have both underload and overload characteristics. Similarly, there is little indication of how to discriminate low to moderate from severe overload or underload patients. To our knowledge, no outcome data on the method has been reported, and no placebo or active treatment comparisons have been made. Finally, de la Pena suggests that insomniacs can be overloaded and underloaded simultaneously. This seems particularly confusing since, as discussed below, de la Pena's treatments for the overload and underload insomniacs are diametrically opposed.

Hence the behavioral literature has an abundance of outcome data and research but no impelling theoretical conceptualization. De la Pena has the beginnings of an impelling conceptualization that requires further outcome data and research for substantiation. In light of this limitation, we would suggest a traditional behavioral analysis and behavior therapy program as the first step in the treatment of chronic primary insomnia. This approach is consistent with behavioral hypotheses as well as with many of De la Pena's speculations on chronic stimulus overload. Concomitantly, however, the clinician should attempt to assess the presence or absence of chronic stimulus underload. In de la Pena's (1976) study of 20 poor sleepers, for example, 60 percent had diastolic blood pressures of 77 mm or less. Seventy percent had experienced allergies and/or exacerbation or initiation of psychiatric somatic problems upon administration of CNS depressant medications. Seventy-five percent stated that boredom and/or depression had been a problem since early childhood. Sixty percent reported sleeping better in a moderately noisy environment than in a quiet one, and 70 percent reported that drinking a cup of coffee or tea and/or smoking a cigarette helped them to relax and fall asleep. Other indications of underload include: relatively high scores on measures of boredom, anxiety, depression, and sensation seeking (e.g., the Zuckerman Sensation-Seeking Scale); reduced latency to REM sleep and/or elevated REM intensity or density; the report of better sleep in strange environments; evidence of the reverse first night effect in the laboratory; and reduced Stage 4 sleep (De la Pena, 1978, p. 131).

If evidence of stimulus underload emerges from this assessment, the clinician has additional treatment options available. For these patients de la Pena's treatment recommendations include: (1) short-term prescription of drugs that enhance sensory flow and reactivation (e.g., antidepressants, Ritalin); (2) sleep environment stimulation such as television, radio, light, or fan; (3) high protein, low carbohydrate diet (theoretically, this prevents adrenergic alerting reactions and increases sensory flow and activation); and (4) challenging work duties and/or a variety of stimulating hobbies and interests (De la Pena, 1978, pp. 132–134).

Only further research will indicate whether mismatch theory can be useful for clinicians in treating insomnia. Turner and Ascher (1979a), after finding paradoxical intention, relaxation, and stimulus control equally effective in the treatment of insomnia, hypothesized that these techniques may have worked due to a common mechanism. According to mismatch theory, this mechanism may have been the therapeutic correction of chronic stimulus overload. If so, and if reliable means for discriminating such patients are developed, then morning exercise, reduction of afternoon and evening stimulation, and so on (De la Pena, 1978, pp. 132–134) may prove very useful in boosting the efficacy of behavioral techniques.

As is evidenced in the work of De la Pena (1978), clinicians and researchers often fall prey to what Kiesler (1971) calls the "patient uniformity myth." In other words, one common misconception is the assumption that all insomniacs are alike. There is little doubt that the patient uniformity myth could easily contribute to treatment failures. In the next section we discuss the recent work of Borkovec and his associates who have identified two subgroups of insomniacs.

Failure to Distinguish between "Pseudoinsomniacs" and Idiopathic Insomniacs

Borkovec and his colleagues (Borkovec, 1979; Borkovec, Grayson, O'Brien, & Weerts, 1978) have emphasized the importance of differentiating between two subtypes of primary insomniacs: experiential and objective. Estimates by Dement (1972) at the Stanford Sleep Clinic indicate that perhaps one half of their primary insomniac patients evidenced little objective sleep deficits according to electroencephalographic criteria (EEG). These "pseudoinsomniacs" exhibit discrepancies between self-reports about sleeping and actual EEG recordings. In other words, the experiential insomniacs complain about both long sleep onset latencies as well as interrupted sleep throughout the night. However, objective recordings obtained during sleep demonstrate that their sleep onset latencies and total amount of sleep time are closer to normal. Borkovec et al. (1979) investigated the efficacy of progressive muscle relaxation with experiential and objective insomniacs. In light of the present discussion their findings are intriguing. First, experiential insomniacs indicated that they were bothered by obsessive cognitive activity and were unlike the objective insomniacs whom Borkovec postulates are not troubled by intrusive cognitions but suffer from a "weak sleep system." Secondly, Borkovec reports that the muscle tension release component of progressive relaxation effectively reduces subjective latency to sleep onset for both subgroups of clients but shortened objective latency to sleep onset only for idiopathic insomniacs. Borkovec's work on experiential and objective insomnia clearly indicates the importance of electrophysiological measures for an adequate behavior analysis in cases of insomnia.

Theoretical Perspectives on Failure

Taken together, de la Pena's and Borkovec's theoretical models appear to explain some potential failures for the behavioral treatment strategies. For instance, although Borkovec states that progressive relaxation ameliorates the cognitive intrusions experienced by the *pseudoinsomniac,* we cannot be certain that progressive relaxation will always be sufficient to modify the *idiopathic* insomniacs weak sleep system. Thus it is conceivable that for some patients, medication may be needed to break up a disturbed sleep pattern, whereas for other clients turning on a radio or television may be helpful. Hence behavioral procedures sometimes will fail for lack of potency in affecting the client's weak sleep system. To give another example, De la Pena posits that both underloads and overloads in cognitive information processing may lead to insomnia. If this is true, then the clinician who neglects the assessment of the client's general processing load may simply exacerbate the problem. For instance, progressive relaxation aimed at reducing arousal for the underload type client would perhaps worsen the problem by reducing stimulation still further. Clearly, the major emphasis of these positions is upon accurate diagnosis and avoidance of the patient uniformity myth. In sum, not knowing what type of insomniac one is treating or assuming unitary causality is the royal road to failure.

In the next major section of this chapter, we outline a project in which we examined the implications of the mismatch hypothesis for the behavioral treatment of insomnia.

EMPIRICAL ISSUES

Empirically Derived Cause for Failure: The Mismatch of Client with Treatment

From our own initial analysis, which indicated equal effectiveness of progressive relaxation and the stimulus control interventions in the treatment of insomnia symptoms, we expected that a combined treatment package would be superior to prescribing either treatment component alone. (Turner & Ascher, 1979a; Turner & Ascher, 1979b; Ascher & Turner, 1980; Turner & DiTomasso, 1980). Our working hypothesis was that clients improved with the self-control programs because they experienced themselves as obtaining control over their sleep behavior and this experience of control was rewarding enough to promote use of the assigned technique, be it progressive relaxation or stimulus control (Turner & Ascher, 1979 a,b). It made sense that combining the procedures would give the client more tools and consequently more confidence in their own self-control and their sleep behavior (Turner & DiTomasso, 1980). However, the opposite would be predicted from De la Pena's model. A failure of treatment is expected when an arousal-reducing intervention (e.g., relaxation) is combined with an arousing instruction such as "get out of bed and do something else" (e.g., stimulus control). This is because one of the two sets of instructions would necessarily be antagonistic to the client's information processing underload or overload mismatch dysfunction and hence act to exacerbate the problem. We discussed earlier in this chapter that the mismatch hypothesis offers an explanation for individual failure with either stimulus control or progressive relaxation used alone. To reiterate, failure occurs when the high-arousal client receives an arousal-increasing program like stimulus control or the low-arousal client receives an arousal-reducing treatment such as progressive relaxation. Although the use of progressive relaxation or stimulus control alone will theoretically produce some successes and some failures due to the lack of matching client dysfunction and treatment, the combined program would almost surely lead to high rates of failure inasmuch as every client would now receive an antagonistic treatment component along with the ameliorative component.

The purpose of the present investigation, then, was to assess these differential predictions emanating from Turner and Ascher, 1979a,b) and De la Pena (1978). Of particular interest was the prediction of failure for the combined treatment package according to the mismatch hypothesis.

METHOD

Design

The study focused upon a single factor. The experimental factor consisted of four treatment conditions. The design is best described as a "recurrent institution cycle design": a quasiexperimental design where new treatment data are contrasted with data previously gathered (Campbell, & Stanley, 1963, pp. 57–61). Campbell and Stanley (1963) suggested that this type of strategy is especially useful for field research. In this type of design, variations in treatment procedures are contrasted with previously gathered data. This allows for assessment of improvements in treatment strategies in the ongoing clinical process. In this study, data previously collected from a no treatment control group, stimulus control, and progressive relaxation conditions (Turner & Ascher, 1979a) were contrasted with the new combined treatment condition. The dependent variables were the posttherapy values of Monroe's Daily Sleep Questionnaire (1967).

Subjects

Subjects were recruited through referrals from local physicians and psychologists who knew of the Temple Insomnia Clinic and referred their clients for this specific treatment.

Clients paid a fee of $25 per session. The no-treatment control subjects were provided with treatment following their waiting list period; however, they were not included in other groups in this analysis. Forty subjects were assessed in this study; the ages ranged from 23 to 62; the mean age of sample was 31 years. There were 15 men and 25 women. Mean reported latency to sleep onset was 64.5 minutes, and mean reported duration of problem was four years.

Measures
Outcome Measures

The dependent variables were clients' scores on the seven items of the revised Daily Sleep Questionnaire (Turner, & Ascher, 1979a): (1) number of minutes to sleep onset, (2) number of awakenings with difficulty returning to sleep, (3) a 1 to 7 rating scale of restedness, (4) a 1 to 7 rating scale of difficulty (with 1 being no difficulty falling asleep and 7 indicating much difficulty falling asleep), (5) number of hours of sleep, and (6) an index of current medication intake derived by counting the number of nights per week on which the client took sleep medication. Scores for every subject were averaged for the last seven days of baseline period and for the last week of the study.

Spouse-Roommate Reliability Checks

A spouse-roommate reliability check procedure was used to obtain a significant other's estimate of the client's sleep disturbance. During the initial interview, the client was asked to request his or her spouse or roommate to make a check on subject's sleep onset latency at least one night during the treatment. The spouse-roommate was instructed to record sleep onset latency when the client met the following criteria: (1) eyes closed, (2) no voluntary movement for 10 minutes, and (3) failure of the client to respond when his or her name was whispered by the spouse-roommate. The spouse-roommate received a separate questionnaire on which to record the number of minutes to client's sleep onset. Recent reports have questioned the reliability of the spouse-roommate procedure for assessing the accuracy of self-reported sleep parameters. We felt it necessary to obtain this type of information inasmuch as EEG technology was not available to us. Moreover, several psychotherapy outcome researchers have emphasized the importance of obtaining ratings of the client's problem behavior from significant others involved with the client in the community (Keisler, 1971).

Procedure

Initially, clients went through an intensive intake interview with an independent assessor describing the nature and history of the symptoms, the estimated latency to sleep onset, drug usage (including nicotine and caffeine), and general psychological status. Clients also filled out the MMPI, the Fear Survey Schedule, and the Willoughby Personality Schedule. At this time clients were given information about the program. Through a structured clinical interview and psychological testing, any volunteer demonstrating secondary insomnia (i.e., sleep difficulty seemingly due to a complication of other physical or psychological problems) was excluded from the study. Subjects were told that therapy would begin in 10 days due to the necessity of obtaining sufficient baseline information to evaluate treatment.

Clients were assigned to each of the treatments following a 10-day baseline period. Individual sessions of 30 to 45 minutes were conducted once per week for four weeks. Postdoctoral psychologists and psychiatric residents participated in the treatment administration. These therapists received 10 training sessions in behavioral techniques for insomnia from the first author. Training involved didactic lectures, videotaping, modeling, and role-play exercises. The therapists earned $10 per session for treating subjects in the study.

During the first session, clients were presented with instructions and a rationale for the treatment that they were to receive. The second, third, and fourth sessions differed according to the specific program to which the client was assigned.

Stimulus control

Clients administered this condition were instructed to comply with the following regimen: (1) go to bed only when sleepy; (2) do not read, watch TV, or eat in bed; (3) if you find yourself unable to fall asleep after 20 minutes, get out of bed, returning to bed only when sleepy, and continue this procedure throughout the night as necessary (clients who experienced disturbances of sleep were instructed to follow this procedure as necessary when awakened); (4) set your alarm and get up at the same time every morning irrespective of the amount of sleep you obtained during the night; and (5) do not nap during the day. Individuals in this condition were asked to monitor their behavior in terms of foregoing criteria. The remaining therapy sessions focused on difficulties that the client experienced with the procedure and ways to improve his or her ability to follow the instructions.

Progressive Relaxation

Clients were instructed in progressive relaxation during the first session and were told to practice relaxation for two 20-minute sessions each day, with the last practice session occurring just prior to retiring. The additional therapy sessions were utilized to further clarify instructions and/or rectify procedural problems.

Combined Treatment Package

These clients received a combination of the treatments described above.

Waiting List Controls

The no-treatment control clients were asked to forego treatment for five weeks and to serve as control subjects. These subjects were assured of receiving treatment in four weeks.

Postexperimental Session

After the final week of therapy, clients were interviewed by an independent observer. Following the postexperimental debriefing, subjects originally assigned to control treatments were given a combination of stimulus control therapy and progressive relaxation.

RESULTS AND DISCUSSION

The means and standard deviations for the Daily Sleep Questionnaire items (baseline and posttherapy periods) are presented in Table 16.1. The first step in the

Table 16.1. Means and Standard Deviations

	n	Latency	Awakenings	Rating of Restedness	Rating of Difficulty Falling Asleep	Hours of Sleep	Drug Intake
Pretherapy							
Progressive relaxation	9	64.1 (34.06)	1.56 (1.33)	4.0 (1.22)	4.1 (6.93)	5.4 (1.51)	3.33 (3.0)
Stimulus control	10	69.7 (43.01)	1.2 (.787)	4.1 (1.5)	4.2 (1.03)	5.5 (1.72)	3.4 (2.84)
Combined treatment	11	64.72 (27.19)	.73 (.786)	3.8 (1.1)	4.18 (.75)	5.8 (1.60)	3.54 (3.17)
No-treatment control	10	63.9 (19.01)	1.6 (1.35)	3.7 (.823)	3.0 (1.05)	5.5 (1.35)	3.5 (2.32)
Posttherapy							
Progressive relaxation	9	48.56 (44)	1.0 (1.0)	4.78 (1.48)	5.1 (1.27)	5.9 (1.4)	3.6 (3.5)
Stimulus control	10	48.4 (34.02)	.6 (.516)	4.1 (1.6)	4.6 (1.58)	6.2 (1.93)	2.1 (2.88)
Combined treatment	11	69.0 (46.23)	1.545 (.82)	4.55 (1.44)	4.5 (1.03)	6.18 (1.167)	3.5 (3.17)
No-treatment control	10	59.0 (23)	1.7 (1.25)	3.6 (.843)	3.1 (.876)	5.9 (.8756)	4.0 (2.5)

data analysis was to assess the equality among the groups on the baseline measures. A one-way MANOVA was nonsignificant. Prior to conducting the test to assess the differential impact of the treatments, change scores for each of the individual variables were computed. These change scores were then submitted to separate Kruskal–Wallis nonparametric analyses of variance due to unequal variances in the dependent measures. The Kruskal–Wallis test for the latency to sleep onset change score was significant, $\varphi^2 = 26.617$; $p \leq .01$. The average change in latency for the progressive relaxation group was 15.56 minutes, for stimulus control it was 21.3 minutes, for the combined treatment the average change in sleep onset latency was -4.27 minutes, and, finally, for the waiting list control the average change in sleep latency was 4.1 minutes. The Kruskal–Wallis test for changes in the number of awakenings with difficulty returning to sleep was also significant, $\varphi^2 = 8.034$, $p \leq .05$. Again progressive relaxation and stimulus control therapies produced more improvement than the combined treatment or the waiting list control condition. Importantly, the combined treatment group actually worsened during the course of therapy with regard to these two variables.

The remaining dependent variables evidenced no significant differences among groups. For the rating of restedness the finding was: $\varphi^2_{(3)} = 1.148\ p \leq .536$. For the rating of difficulty falling asleep the results were: $\varphi^2_{(3)} = 3.09\ p \leq .181$. Finally, for the number of hours of sleep obtained and the number of nights on which clients took sedative-hypnotics the results were nonsignificant, $\varphi^2_{(3)} = 1.029$, $p \leq .541$ and $\varphi^2_{(3)} = 2.0$, p $\leq .273$.

Inasmuch as we were primarily interested in the actual number of successes and failures resulting from the treatment, a clinical criterion of less than 30 minutes latency to sleep onset on the average per week was set as the demarcation of clinical success. Clients falling asleep within 30 minutes were counted as successes and those requiring greater than 30 minutes were failures. Table 16.2 presents the results for the three treatment groups. Both progressive relaxation and stimulus control produced more successes and fewer failures than the combined treatment group. In fact, there were only two successes or 18 percent success rate with the combined programs, whereas the progressive relaxation and stimulus control procedures generated improvement in at least 50 percent of the cases.

Table 16.2.   Analysis of Successes and Failures

Treatments	Progressive Relaxation	Stimulus Control	Combined
Successes	6	5	2
Failures	4	5	9

Reliability Assessment

Eighty percent of the spouses or roommates from this group provided reliability assessments for the client's self-report of latency to sleep onset ($r = .84$). The product-moment reliability estimates were not calculated for the remaining variates because the spouses and roommates were unable to independently monitor the subjects' behavior.

CONCLUSIONS

It would seem that the 82 percent failure rate of the combined treatment package supports de la Pena's (1978) prediction that treating insomniacs with antagonistic arousal-reducing and arousal-increasing procedures will lead to therapeutic failure. Consequently, the clinician must take great care in the behavioral analysis to determine the exact nature of the client's sleep dysfunction (i.e., hyper- or hypo-arousal) and plan the nondrug program accordingly. The present data also suggest that the simplistic attribution hypothesis, espoused by Turner and Ascher (1979a,b), to explain the mechanism by which behavior therapy techniques operate to reduce sleep disturbance is incorrect. Most likely these procedures operate through different mechanisms and perhaps attend to differential underarousal or overarousal dysfunctions as hypothesized by de la Pena (1978). Further studies are required to see if the 40 to 50 percent failure rates with progressive relaxation and stimulus control can be reduced by a differential diagnosis procedure and intervention strategies of the type described by de la Pena (1978).

In the final section, we address issues facing behavioral therapists in the clinical session.

CLINICAL ISSUES IN FAILURE

Behavioral clinicians probably contribute to treatment failures in at least some instances by failing to attend to important clinical factors in the therapeutic relationship and treatment planning. We have chosen to focus upon the following: (1) the quality of the therapist–patient relationship, (2) patient noncompliance with clinician instructions (e.g., homework), and (3) the failure to incorporate a maintenance component to treatment.

Therapist–Patient Relationship

How important is the therapist–patient relationship for outcome in behavior therapy for insomnia? Behavior therapists view relationship factors as necessary but not sufficient for positive outcome in therapy. The viewpoint stems solely from the belief on the part of behaviorists that "techniques" are of primary importance in producing client change. Thus behaviorists differ sharply from Rogerian oriented psychotherapists who place primary emphasis upon the "necessary and sufficient" conditions in the therapeutic relationship. Only in recent years have behavioral clinicians begun to pay attention to patient–therapist interaction in behavior therapy. DeVoge and Beck (1978) have reviewed the literature pertaining to patient–therapist interactional effects in behavior therapy and have made several points worth our considering here. First, there is evidence that placebo procedures produce positive outcome in behavioral therapy research with primary insomniacs. If placebo treatments are designed to control for nonspecific therapist factors in research, then positive outcome with such procedures would seem to suggest that therapist variables are important in behavior therapy. Secondly, however, there is also evidence available to demonstrate that automated treatments are as effective as live therapists (e.g., DeVoge & Beck, 1978). Some behaviorists would conclude that these findings argue against the importance of relationship factors. DeVoge and Beck (1978), however, downplay these findings as neglecting to consider therapist–patient characteristics and interactive patterns influencing outcome. To bolster their viewpoint they cite several studies where relationship factors were important to outcome. For instance, Reppucci and Baker (1968) showed that the efficacy of a self-help desensitization take-home package varied as a function of client characteristics. Morris and Suckerman (1974) found that therapist warmth enhanced the effects of desensitization. Likewise, Leitenberg, Argras, Barlow, and Olivear (1969) found a "friendly praising therapist plus optimistic instructions" produced significantly better outcome than a neutral therapist without instructions. These findings lead to the suggestion that although the technical aspects of the desensitization package are efficacious, the presence of a warm friendly therapist enhances its effects (DeVoge & Beck, 1978). What do these findings imply for the practicing clinician in treating insomniacs? The forming of a good working relationship with a patient is important and necessary for change. Creating a warm, trusting, safe, empathic, accepting, and understanding atmosphere sets the stage for client change. As Goldstein (1973) has noted:

> Obviously the process of behavior therapy is not one of straightforward conditioning of the patient. The therapist cannot impose conditioning or relearning on anyone, for the most potent of techniques is useless without the cooperation and motivation of the patient. (p. 220)

Noncompliance With Clinician Instruction

What we have learned over the last decade or so about patient adherence to medical advice, or what is commonly called patient compliance, has important implications for behavioral clinicians. Do our patients comply with what they are reasonably instructed to do? To our knowledge behavior therapists have generally ignored this topic in relation to behavioral interventions for clinical problems such as insomnia. Like physicians, behavioral psychotherapists often assume that patients comply with homework instructions or assignments that are designed to facilitate the treatment process and ensure eventual outcome. However, this assumption may not necessarily be justified. For example, Dunbar and Stunkard (1979) reported that whereas between 20 to 80 percent of medical patients make errors in taking prescribed medications, between 25 to 60 percent of them fail to follow treatment advice (i.e., taking medication) for the recommended period of time. Moreover, physicians also tend to underestimate the prevalence of patient noncompliance with treatment regimens (Dunbar & Stunkard, 1979). Whether these findings can be justifiably extrapolated to insomniacs and behavioral therapists are empirical questions. Research here again is called for to address these questions. Nonetheless, we suppose that insomniacs who do not comply with instructions to employ stimulus control or to practice relaxation at home are probably doomed to become treatment failures. Dunbar (1980) has recently warned that patients who are asked to change habits are at high risk for poor compliance. As behavior therapists we can probably help patients to adhere to behavioral prescriptions by ensuring that they *thoroughly* understand how to apply particular procedures (e.g., stimulus control) in vivo. Likewise, strategies for helping patients to remember to follow through with assigned homework (e.g., practice of charting the relaxation) are oftentimes necessary. Self-monitoring procedures and contingency contracting may be helpful in allowing patients to comply and, therefore, obtain maximal benefits from therapy.

Failure to Incorporate Maintenance Follow-Up

In at least some cases behavioral interventions undoubtedly fail because the therapist neglects to incorporate a follow-up maintenance aspect to the treatment package. Bernstein (1969) has provided a similar warning with respect to the treatment of smoking. Overcoming primary insomnia necessitates in most cases either the development of new habits and/or the substitution of relaxation for arousal (anxiety). For some cases it has been our experience that although at the designated end of therapy outcome is positive, relapse is inevitable. We suspect that relapse can be accounted for by "spontaneous recovery" (the reemergence of the behavior without further training) or simply by the fact that new patterns of behavior have not been strongly or permanently acquired. Thus it is crucial for behavioral clinicians to prepare patients for the possibility of a relapse. In short, clients must be prepared with respect to what to do if a slip occurs (i.e., a sleepless night). Otherwise, a slip, which most insomniacs would probably find terrifying, might precipitate the emergence of old habits and the gradual resurgence of the full-blown problem. Consequently, arranging follow-up booster sessions should be a desideratum of the therapist from the initiation of treatment. That these future sessions will be a component of the comprehensive treatment plan should be made apparent to the patient during the intake interview. In doing this the clinician needs to be sure the client understands the purpose of the booster sessions in sustaining the improvements in sleep that will be made during the intensive treatment phase.

SUMMARY

The study of treatment failures in behavior therapy is a new enterprise, and we do not have a good roadmap to guide our work at this time. We reviewed the literature for examples and explanations for failures in the self-control treatment of insomnia, but found nothing. In fact the studies, in general, did not report successes and failures but focused upon statistical significance among treatment groups (e.g., Turner & Ascher, 1979b). In the one study which did focus upon changing the clinical significance (Turner & Ascher, 1979a) of the client's sleep problem, no emphasis was given to understanding why a patient failed to improve.

Consequently, we turned to examining some promising theoretical conceptualizations of sleep disorders and their treatment. The work of both de la Pena (1978) and Borkovec (1979) suggests that failure to make an accurate differential diagnosis of "insomniac type" and selecting a therapeutic intervention accordingly is the primary cause for failure. We focused the preponderance of our attention upon de la Pena's Overload/Underload Information Processing Mismatch Conceptualization of Insomnia.

Pursuing this line of reasoning further, we conducted a quasiexperiment that examined the effect of purposely ignoring a differential diagnosis of insomniac subtype and simply providing patients with an all-inclusive therapy package. We discovered that the all-inclusive treatment package was less effective in reducing sleep disturbance to clinically significant levels than either relaxation or stimulus control alone. For the stimulus control and relaxation-only groups the improvement rates were good, but not as in some previous studies. Thus failure, perhaps, occurs when the over-aroused client receives an arousal-increasing program such as stimulus control or the under-aroused patient tries relaxation. Although the utilization of relaxation training or stimulus control alone produced some successes and some failures due to the mismatch of client dysfunction and treatment, the combined program produced a higher rate of failures. Perhaps this is because each client received a treatment component antagonistic to ameliorating their dysfunction. One plausible alternative explanation for these results is that the combination treatment subjects received inadequate training in progressive relaxation and stimulus control. The amount of time spent in therapy sessions was held constant; thus the subjects receiving either progressive relaxation or stimulus control would have more exposure to the procedure; hence they would become more proficient in using the technique. This, taken together with the quasiexperimental nature of this study, limits the generalizability of the results; however, it does suggest differential diagnosis is an important component of treatment.

In addition to these diagnostic considerations, we also pointed out that factors such as the patient–therapist relationship, the lack of patient compliance with the treatment prescription, and the failure to incorporate follow-up booster sessions all probably contribute to failure in one way or another.

As an initial study of treatment failures in the behavioral nondrug treatment of insomnia, the present ideas and findings are quite promising. Clearly, though, we have few answers.

REFERENCES

Ascher, L. M., & Efran, J. S. (1978) The use of paradoxical intention in a behavioral program for sleep onset insomnia. *Journal of Consulting and Clinical Psychology,* **46,** 547–550.

Ascher, L. M., & Turner, R. M. (1980) A comparison of two methods for the administration of paradoxical intention. *Behaviour Research and Therapy,* **18,** 121–126.

Bernstein, D. A. (1969) Modification of something behavior: An evaluative review. *Psychological Bulletin,* **71,** 418–440.

Beutler, L., Thornby, J., & Karacan, I. (1978) Psychological variables in the diagnosis of insomnia. In R. Williams, & I. Karacan (Eds.), *Sleep disorders.* New York: Wiley.

Bootzin, R. (1972) A stimulus control treatment for insomnia. *Procedures of the American Psychology Association,* 395–396.

Bootzin, R. (1975) *A comparison of stimulus control instructions and progressive relaxation training in the treatment of sleep-onset insomnia.* Unpublished manuscript, Northwestern University.

Bootzin, R., & Nicassio, P. (1978) Behavioral treatments for insomnia. In M. Hersen, R. Eisler, & P. Miller (Eds.), *Progress in behavior modification.* New York: Academic.

Borkovec, T. D. (1979) Pseudo (experimental) insomnia and idiopathic (objective) insomnia: Theoretical and therapeutic issues. *Advances in Behavior Research and Therapy,* **2,** 27–55.

Borkovec, T. D., Grayson, J., O'Brien, G. T., and Weerts, T. C. (1979) Treatment of pseudo-insomnia and idiopathic insomnia via progressive relaxation with and without muscle tension release: An electroencephalographic evaluation. *Journal of Applied Behavior Analysis,* **12,** 37–54.

Brown, J. S. (1965) Generalization and discrimination. In D. I. Mostofsky (Ed.), *Stimulus generalization.* Stanford: Stanford University Press.

Campbell, D. T., & Stanley, J. (1963) *Experimental and quasiexperimental designs for research.* Chicago: Rand McNally. de la Pena (1976) Poor sleepers: A descriptive summary of a VA sleep clinic population. *Sleep Research,* **5,** 164.

De la Pena (1978) Toward a psychophipidogic conceptualization of insomnia. In R. Williams, & I. Karacan (Eds.), *Sleep disorders: Diagnosis and treatment* New York: Wiley.

Dement, W. C. (1972) *Some must watch while some must sleep.* Stanford: Stanford Alumni Association.

DeVoge, J. T., & Beck, S. (1978) The therapist–client relationship in behavior therapy. In M. Hersen, R. M. Eisler, & P. M. Miller (Eds.), *Progress in behavior modification.* New York: Academic.

Dunbar, J., & Stunkard, A. (1979) Adherence to diet and drug regimen. In R. Levy, B. Rifkind, B. Dennis, & N. Ernst (Eds.), *Nutrition, lipids, and coronary heart disease.* New York: Raven.

Dunbar, J. (1980) Adhering to medical advice: A review. *International Journal of Mental Health,* **9,** 70–87.

Frankl, V. E. (1975) Paradoxical intention and dereflection. *Psychotherapy: Theory, Research, and Practice,* **12,** 226.

Goldstein, A. (1973) Behavior therapy. In R. Corsini (Ed.), *Current psychotherapies.* New York: Peacock.

Kales, A., Bixler, E. O., Lee, I. A., Healy, S., & Slye, E. (1974) Incidence of insomnia in the Los Angeles metropolitan area. *Sleep Research,* **4,** 139.

Kiesler, D. J. (1971) Experimental designs in psychotherapy research. In A. E. Bergen, & S. L. Garfield (Eds.), *Handbook of psychotherapy and behavior change.* New York: Wiley.

Leitenberg, H., Agras, W. S., Barlow, D. H., and Olivean, D. C. (1969) Contribution of selective positive reinforcement and therapeutic instructions to systematic desensitization therapy. *Journal of Abnormal Psychology,* **74,** 113–118.

MacIntosh, N. J. (1977) Stimulus control: Attentional factors. In W. K. Honig, & J. E. R. Staddon (Eds.), *Handbook of operant behavior.* Englewood Cliffs, N. J.: Prentice-Hall.

Marlatt, G. A. (1979) A cognitive behavioral model of the relapse process. In National Institute on Drug Abuse, Research Monograph Series, *Behavioral analysis and treatment of substance abuse.* Washington: Division of Research.

Monroe, L. J. (1967) Psychological and physiological differences between good and poor sleepers. *Journal of Abnormal Psychology,* **72,** 255.

Montgomery, I., Perkins, G., & Wise, D. (1975) A review of behavioral treatments for insomnia. *Journal of Behavior Therapy and Experimental Psychiatry,* **6,** 93.

Morris, R. J., & Suckerman, K. R. (1974) The importance of the therapeutic relationship in systematic desensitization. *Journal of Consulting and Clinical Psychology,* **42,** 147.

Reppucci, N. D., & Baker, B. L. (1968) Self-desensitization: Implications for treatment and teaching. In R. D. Rubin, & C. M. Franks (Eds.), *Advances in behavior therapy.* New York: Academic.

Riling, M. (1977) Stimulus control and inhibitory processes. In W. K. Honig, & E. R. Staddon (Eds.)

Rimm, D. C., & Masters, J. C. (1974) *Behavior therapy: Techniques and empirical findings.* New York: Academic.

Sleep Disorder Classification Committee (1979) *Diagnostic classification of sleep and arousal disorders.* New York: Raven.

Turner, R. M., & Ascher, L. M. (1979a) Controlled comparison of progressive relaxation, stimulus control, and paradoxical intention therapies for insomnia. *Journal of Consulting and Clinical Psychology,* **47,** 500.

Turner, R. M., & Ascher, L. M. (1979b) A within subject analysis of stimulus control therapy with severe sleep onset insomnia. *Behaviour Research and Therapy,* **17,** 107–112.

Turner, R. M., & DiTomasso, R. A. (1980) The behavioral treatment of insomnia: A review and methodological analyses of the evidence. *International Journal of Mental Health,* **9,** 129–148.

Webb, W. B. (1975) *Sleep: The gentle tyrant.* Englewood Cliffs, N. J.: Prentice-Hall.

Williams, R. L., Karacan, I., & Hursch, C. J. (1974) *EEG of human sleep.* New York: Wiley.

Wolpe, J. (1970) Behavior analysis of a case of hypochondriacal anxiety: Transcript of first interview. *Journal of Behavior Therapy and Experimental Psychiatry,* **1,** 217–224.

Wolpe, J. (1979) The experimental model and treatment of neurotic depression. *Behaviour Research and Therapy,* **17,** 555–565.

CHAPTER 17

Failures in the Operant Treatment of Chronic Pain

MICHAEL J. FOLLICK
ROBERT E. ZITTER
DAVID K. AHERN

Chronic pain is one of the most difficult and expensive problems in medicine and continues to provide a difficult challenge for health care professionals. A behavioral conceptualization of chronic pain, as proposed by Fordyce (1974, 1976) emphasizes the role and importance of environmental factors in chronic pain states and has dramatically advanced our understanding and treatment of the problem.

Chronic pain is defined as pain that has persisted for a period of six months or more, is usually experienced daily, is often incapacitating, and typically interferes with a person's daily functioning. Despite medical and surgical advances, it is estimated that only 30 to 40 percent of chronic pain patients obtain adequate long-term relief from pharmacological or surgical treatments (e.g., Loesser, 1974; White, 1969). Many pain experts contend that pharmacological and surgical treatments have a poor success rate because they are aimed at only a part of the chronic pain problem. They argue that pain is a much more complex phenomenon than a simple and linear relationship between the amount of organic pathology and the experience of pain as proposed by traditional "specificity theory."

Psychological and environmental variables, as well as biological factors, are involved in chronic pain states (Block, Kremer, & Gaylor 1980b; Fordyce, 1976; Melzack, 1974). A biopsychosocial model, then, can explain why procedures designed to correct the physical pathology, or block the so-called "pain pathway" have not been consistently successful. The notion that biological, psychological, and social or environmental factors interact in chronic pain states makes it easier to account for individual differences and variability in a patient's condition over time. Thus pain behavior represents a final common pathway for the presentation of a number of interacting variables. This conceptualization has led directly to the development of multidisciplinary efforts in both the study and treatment of chronic pain, and thereby represents the ideal of the behavioral medicine approach.

The behavioral model of chronic pain proposes that, in some chronic pain patients, pain behaviors occur as a result of environmental contingencies, rather than resulting from antecedent stimuli (i.e., tissue damage). There are two types of pain behaviors—respondent and operant. Respondent pain behaviors occur reflexively to antecedent stimuli arising from the site of tissue damage. Operant pain behaviors, on the other hand, are controlled directly by environmental consequences. When a behavior is systematically followed by a reinforcing consequence, the likelihood of that behavior occurring again will increase. Fordyce (1976) contends that in chronic pain states, behaviors that were originally respondent in nature can become operant in character through the process of learning. He postulates that the following sets of conditions can influence the frequency of pain behavior:

1. Positive reinforcement such as attention, sympathy and concern, compensation payments, or medications.
2. Negative reinforcement or the removal of noxious stimulation such as anxiety-invoking situations, the avoidance of work, or other unpleasant responsibilities.
3. Extinction or nonreinforcement of "well" behavior.

Pain is a private subjective experience and does not lend itself to objective measurement and control. Pain behavior, on the other hand, can be objectively measured and modified. The learning theory model of chronic pain has direct implications for the treatment of chronic pain states. In those instances where pain behaviors are operant in nature, the reinforcement for those behaviors should be withdrawn and reinforcement must be provided for activity or "well" behaviors. Pain behaviors will decrease in frequency and will ultimately be extinguished if reinforcement no longer follows those behaviors. Thus the behavioral approach does not attempt to modify pain directly, but rather to modify maladaptive *pain behaviors* and thereby alter the patient's disability. Pain behaviors such as moaning, grimacing, lying down, and the like, are the critical determinants of the Chronic Pain Syndrome and the defining characteristics of functional impairment and disability. Chronic pain patients typically spend over 30 percent of their waking hours lying down and over three hours per day in pain relief activities or devices such as home traction, hot packs, or massage (Follick, 1979). Thus *if there is no pain behavior, there is no pain problem.* Inasmuch as the goal is to modify the patient's behavior, which is believed to be in large part a function of the environment, it is necessary to involve the spouse and perhaps other family members in the retraining process. This requirement is important to ensure that the pain behavior no longer receives sustaining reinforcement and that activity or "well" behavior is appropriately reinforced.

This chapter is devoted to a discussion of the sources of failure associated with the behavioral management of chronic low back or musculoskeletal pain. We first review the assessment procedures employed and the outcome data (i.e., success or failure of the intervention). We then describe potential sources of failure in the behavioral management of chronic pain and present directions for future research and modifications of the existing treatment protocol. Our discussion is limited to what has been referred to as the operant approach to chronic pain management and does not include detailed discussions of the primarily cognitive interventions (e.g., Meichenbaum & Turk, 1976; Rybstein-Blinchik & Grzesiak, 1979). Although these "coping skills" interventions are considered cognitive-behavior therapy, their focus is primarily on the pain experience. Thus the mechanisms relating to their success or failure may be entirely different from those associated with the operant approach. Similarly, biofeedback procedures in chronic low back pain management are not reviewed in this chapter.

ASSESSMENT AND EVALUATION OF OUTCOME

Definition of Success and Failure

In order to determine success and, conversely, failure, treatment goals need to be well specified and measurable. The goals of a behaviorally oriented pain program typically include: (1) reduce the frequency of pain behaviors; (2) increase the patient's physical capabilities and activities to a level considered normal for his or her age and sex; (3) eliminate the patient's reliance on pain relieving medications; and (4) reduce the patient's utilization of medical care resources for purposes of pain relief. Considering these goals, the following questions arise:

1. Is the patient considered a success or a failure if he or she achieves only a subset of the treatment goals?
2. Should we differentiate among levels of success, based upon the magnitude of change obtained on each of the treatment goals?
3. Should we differentiate among levels of success in terms of posttreatment change and the amount of that change maintained at follow-up?

These questions represent major problems in the literature on the operant treatment of chronic pain. At the present time, no standardized set of treatment goals or outcome criteria has been set forth. This is not surprising, however, inasmuch as the Chronic Pain Syndrome has multiple determinants. Therefore, goal setting and outcome criteria must address all of the relevant factors of the pain problem. Some of the goals should be standardized and consistent across all patients, whereas others should be individualized and tailored to that particular patient's needs. The goals listed above appear to be generally accepted and useful in that they are measurable and represent the major components of the Chronic Pain Syndrome. However, the issue of what criteria define treatment success and failure remains unanswered.

Assessment of Outcome

Inasmuch as the behavioral management of chronic pain has as its goal the reduction in frequency, intensity, and duration of pain behaviors and an increase in "well" behaviors, methods of measurement have been developed to evaluate behavioral change across these dimensions. Direct observation methods have been used by several researchers (e.g., Gottlieb, Strite, Koller, Madorsky, Hockersmith, Kleeman, & Wagner, (1977); Shealy & Shealy, (1976); and Swanson, Swenson, Maruta, & McPhee, (1976). Fordyce (1976) has employed family members to independently observe patients' responses at home. Self-observation methods have also been used frequently. Some investigators have asked patients to self-monitor nonverbal behaviors by means of an hourly behavioral diary of such activities as time spent standing, walking, sitting, and engaging in other functional activities (Fordyce, 1976; Fordyce, Fowler, & Delateur, 1968; Ignelzi, Sternbach, & Timmermans, 1977; Sternbach, 1974). Other investigators have used automatic recording devices (Cairns & Pasino, 1977; Cairns, Thomas, Mooney, & Pace, 1976; Sanders, 1980; Saunders, Goldstein, & Stein, 1978) to measure patients' activities such as "up time" or walking. A more thorough review of assessment strategies can be found in Sanders (1979), and Keefe, Brown, Ziesat and Scott, (in press).

Recognizing that health care utilization is a significant parameter of the Chronic Pain Syndrome, Follick, Zitter, Kulich, and Harris (1979) have developed a health care utilization questionnaire, which consists of items such as days in the hospital, physician visits, number of surgeries, and the number of diagnostic tests and treatments received. Such information is important for evaluating the impact of the intervention on the health care system and overall cost-effectiveness.

The evaluation of treatment outcome would benefit from the development of a standardized classification scheme of pain behaviors, including verbal, nonverbal, and covert behaviors. Recommendations can be made for utilizing more direct measurements of overt behavior through the use of portable automated devices to monitor overt pain and "well behavior," and the use of videotape recordings to assess overt responses.

Despite the lack of standardized criteria and assessment measures, several researchers have published the results of their treatment programs. Prior to a detailed discussion of failures, we briefly review this literature in an attempt to determine if the behavioral management of chronic pain works and, if so, for what proportion of patients.

Review of Outcome Studies

Fordyce, Fowler, Lehmann, Delateur, Sand, and Trieschmann (1973) reported the results of the first behaviorally oriented program. Patients followed 5 to 175 weeks after treatment were reporting significantly less pain, less interference with daily activities, reduction in the use of pain medication, and a reduction in the amount of time in bed due to pain. Anderson, Cole, Gullickson, Hudgens, and Roberts (1977) found that 25 (74 percent) of the 34 patients who completed an eight-week inpatient program were leading "normal lives" without medication when followed between six months and seven years after treatment. In a long-term follow-up of the effectiveness of the same program, Roberts and Reinhardt (1980) compared the group that completed treatment to a group of 20 individuals rejected for treatment, and a group of 12 individuals accepted for treatment, but who refused to participate. Of all the comparison subjects, only one individual was leading a "normal" life without medication at long-term follow-up. Cairns et al. (1976) found that at 10-month follow-up, 75 percent of their patients reported a significant decrease in pain, with an associated increase in activity level. Fifty-eight percent reported that they no longer required narcotic pain medications and 74 percent sought no further medical advice. Reporting on the first seven successive admissions to an outpatient-based behaviorally oriented chronic pain program, Follick et al. (1979) found that the average amount of time spent lying down per day was reduced by 88 percent (4.5 hours) whereas sitting and standing or walking increased by 42 and 60 percent, respectively, as indicated by daily activity diaries. The amount of time that patients spent engaged in pain relief activities was reduced from an average of 5 hours per day to 0.2 hours per day, and all patients had stopped taking pain medication at discharge, while marital adjustment had significantly improved as measured by marital adjustment surveys. It was further noted that there was a substantial reduction in health care utilization following treatment in those patients for whom one-year follow-up was available ($11,747 in 12 months pretreatment to $60 in 12 months posttreatment). Thus these findings would suggest that, at least clinically, approximately 70 percent of patients who enter an operant based chronic pain treatment program show improvement at the end of treatment and at follow-up.

Several pain treatment programs have combined operant procedures with other therapeutic components such as group discussion, supportive psychotherapy, biofeedback, relaxation, social skills training, and marital counseling. Newman, Seres, Yospe, and Garlington (1978) demonstrated significant increases on measures of physical functioning, as well as marked reductions in analgesics and health care utilization in a group of patients with low levels of pain. These changes were maintained at an 80-week follow-up. Gottlieb et al. (1977) found that 80 percent of the 72 chronic low back pain patients treated attained normal levels of physical activity, and about the same percentage were functioning successfully in vocational activities. Khatami and Rush (1978) reported that five (83 percent) of six chronic pain outpatients showed statistically significant decreases in pain, hopelessness, depression, and analgesic medication intake when treated with a tripartite package designed to provide symptom control, stimulus control, and social system modification. Swanson, Maruta, and Swenson (1979) reported that of 200 patients with chronic pain who were treated in an inpatient program where the operant approach was the primary component, 59 percent of the patients had achieved moderate improvement as measured by activity level, pain level, use of medication, and acceptance of the need to live with pain.

In addition, 65 percent of those successfully treated maintained these gains at one-year follow-up.

Results from these multicomponent programs are consistent with those obtained by "pure" operant programs. Many patients show clinical improvement at posttreatment, which is often maintained at follow-up. Although it is not possible to determine which components are effective, the operant approach is a major aspect of most of these programs, and research demonstrating the controlling effect of contingency management procedures on overt pain behaviors supports the assumption that the operant procedures are an active component (e.g., Cairns & Pasino, 1977; Fordyce, 1976). It is interesting to note that the combined approaches obtain no greater positive results than the operant approach alone.

Despite methodological weaknesses (e.g., lack of adequate control groups and inappropriate data analytic procedures), the literature indicates that a large percentage of the patients show improvement following treatment. In fact, as noted above, approximately 70 percent of the patients who enter a primarily operant-based chronic pain treatment program show improvement at posttreatment, and most of those patients maintain improvement at follow-up. This estimate would suggest cautious optimism about the effectiveness of the treatment approach. However, there still remain approximately 30 percent of the patients who do not show changes at posttreatment, and others who relapse at maintenance. Thus it appears important to look for patient and treatment variables that may account for these therapeutic failures.

PREDICTION OF TREATMENT OUTCOME

Since not all pain patients benefit from a behaviorally oriented program, it seems worthwhile to examine closely those individuals who are considered treatment failures, and search for variables that differentiate them from patients who succeed. These variables may be useful in predicting who will benefit from a behavioral treatment program. Hopefully, such research will ultimately lead to an empirically based set of selection criteria for behavioral programs. This type of predictive research is invaluable given the high cost of inpatient programs and the deleterious effects of certain types of patients on other program participants. Treatment outcome can be greatly enhanced if we can control for a major source of failure—an inadequate selection process.

Research directed at predicting success or failure of pain treatment programs is plagued by many of the same methodological considerations that relate to treatment outcome. The treatment components, goals of therapy, and outcome measures, will all affect which variables are predictive of success. As most predictive studies use different criteria for success, as well as varying treatment components, generalization of results across studies is difficult. In addition, such research is generally conducted with small numbers of patients, thus leading to very tentative conclusions. Most studies are retrospective and it is rare to find crossvalidation studies extending prediction formulas to new patient samples. Some researchers report only anecdotal evidence regarding characteristics of treatment successes or failures. Much of the prediction literature on chronic pain has focused on personality variables as opposed to cognitive and behavioral factors that might be more relevant to the behavioral approach. The whole area of prediction in relation to behavioral pain programs is a relatively new endeavor, which probably accounts for its somewhat primitive stage of development.

Functional Versus Organic

Historically, prediction research focused first on predicting "organic" versus "functional" pain (Cox, Chapman, & Black, 1978; Gilberstadt & Jancis, 1967; Hanvik, 1951). This work was based on the assumption that these two populations were clearly separate and should be treated by distinctly different approaches. The results, unfortunately, are generally inconclusive. Chronic pain patients with identifiable organic pathology appear similar to those without physical findings on psychological tests. One consistent exception is the work of Leavitt and his associates (1978, 1979), who have developed a scale consisting of pain descriptors. This inventory appears to correlate well with independent medical evaluations of discernible organic pathology, even on crossvalidation. However, many indices of organic pathology have high error rates as will be noted later in this chapter.

The organic versus functional pain distinction is an impossible task because a determination of functional pain is a diagnosis by exclusion. Comprehensive medical evaluation is required for admission to a pain program that identifies those patients with clear physical findings necessitating medical or surgical intervention. Those patients without such findings, or for whom nothing further can be done, must find alternative avenues for coping with their pain. Some of these patients will be appropriate for a behavioral program, whereas others will not. Thus the more relevant question is which patients will most likely benefit from a behavioral approach.

Behavioral Intervention

There has been only a handful of studies examining predictive variables in behavioral pain treatment programs. Maruta, Swanson, and Swenson (1979), in an operant-based pain program, compared 35 failures and 35 successes, and found that duration of pain complaints, number of previous operations, level of baseline self-report of pain, number of days of work lost due to pain, and drug dependency were all negatively correlated with success. Failures tended to have higher scores on the Hs and the Hy MMPI scales, but not significantly so. A seven-item scale, consisting of the above variables, predicted 71 percent of the treatment successes and 80 percent of the failures. Financial compensation was not a significant factor in this study.

Financial compensation, however, has been found, in other studies, to mitigate against successful behavioral programs (Block, Kremer, & Gaylor, 1980a). Herman and Baptiste (1981), in a cognitive-behavioral outpatient-based program, also found that receiving financial compensation correlated with lower success rates. Interestingly, they reported that three patients who disclaimed financial benefits made dramatic improvement afterwards. Stated motivation to return to work was also associated with more improvement. It is interesting to note that Herman and Baptiste stated that one of the most prominent predictive variables was changed versus unchanged thought patterns with respect to pain. Although this was not a pretreatment variable, but, rather, an observation of pre-post change, this study is noteworthy in that it is one of the few to address cognitive variables.

Roberts and Reinhardt (1980) reported that medication intake, scores on the Pa and Ego Strength scales of the MMPI, spouse scores on the Hy and Hs scales of the MMPI, duration of pain complaints, and a report that working exacerbated pain were positively correlated with failure at one- to eight-year follow-up of an operant inpatient pain program. However, the unsuccessful group at follow-up consisted of only six subjects. No other studies have evaluated spouse variables as was done in this study. Given the strong influence of family reinforcement, and the finding that spouses can serve as discriminative stimuli for pain behavior (Block et al., 1980b), a closer examination of spouse characteristics should be undertaken. Finally, Green, Meagher, and Millon (in press) developed a 150-item true or false questionnaire assessing interpersonal styles. They have identified three types of patients who were found to be destructive in an inpatient behaviorally oriented pain program. With this inventory, they correctly identified 86 percent of their pain patients as problem or nonproblem patients, as independently rated by the treatment staff. There have been no reports yet correlating this measure with actual treatment outcome.

Summarizing the behavioral studies, it appears that drug dependence, more complicated medical history (e.g., number of operations and surgeries, multiple pain complaints), longer duration of pain complaints, and financial compensation are associated with poor outcome. It also appears that a higher elevation of the neurotic triad of the MMPI may correlate with poor treatment results. In addition, there is an indication that cognitive factors, as well as spouse variables influence treatment outcome and should be given further attention. It is interesting to note that at least two of these variables, neurotic MMPI triad (Blumetti & Modesti, 1975; Smith & Durksen, 1980; Strassberg, et. al. 1980; Wilkes & Rocchio, 1975) and financial compensation (Krusen & Ford, 1958) have also been predictive of failure with medical or surgical intervention.

It is hoped that through future studies of treatment failures and successes, we will be able to better predict who is likely to benefit from a behaviorally oriented treatment approach and improve our selection process. Toward this end, Brena and Koch (1975) have proposed a quantifiable classification schema consisting of two major dimensions: tissue pathology (the results of physical, neurological, radiologic, laboratory studies) and pain behavior (including measures of activity level, medication usage, scores on the MMPI, and the somatic inventory). In this system, patients who score high on tissue damage and high on pain behavior are felt to be the best surgical candidates, whereas patients who score low on tissue damage and high on pain behavior are appropriate candidates for an operant-based pain program. Duncan, Gregg, and Ghia (1978) have developed a similar classification system, including pathophysiologic, psychologic, and behavioral aspects of chronic pain. These classification systems hold promise but still need to be validated.

To date, in lieu of a systematic classification system, a clinically based screening procedure must be relied upon to select patients for a behavioral pain treatment program. Based upon the foregoing review and clinical experience, the following criteria have been developed and are used at several treatment centers. We propose that these criteria be adopted in a more uniform fashion because many pain programs use almost no screening criteria and, by the use of a more stringent selection process, may substantially improve their treatment outcome and will make data more comparable. The selection criteria that appear most appropriate at this time are the following.

Inclusion Criteria

1. Further medical or surgical intervention must be judged impractical or of no additional value; in cases where medical or surgical procedures may offer a limited probability of pain relief, *both* the patient and physician must agree that a pain rehabilitation program focusing on the restoration of functional capabilities is the preferred treatment approach.
2. There can be no contraindications to an extensive physical exercise program (e.g., unstable cardiac condition) and the patient should be medically capable of restoration of physical functioning.
3. The patient must exhibit observable and measurable pain behaviors (e.g., complaints of pain, grimacing, limping, etc.) and these behaviors must have identifiable environmental consequences that are potentially modifiable.
4. The patient's pain must be interfering with his or her life, and preventing him or her from engaging in desired physical activities (e.g., work, driving a car, attending social functions, etc.).
5. The patient should be able to identify specific goals that are observable and measurable, and that are achievable within the time constraints of the program.
6. The patient must be motivated to participate in the program, and indicate explicitly that he or she is willing to learn to live with pain.
7. The family members must be motivated and willing to change their behaviors and help the patient learn to change his or her behaviors.

Exclusion Criteria

1.   The patient should have no litigation pending related to the injury that is judged to be important in the maintenance and promotion of a continued disability.
2.   There should be no serious psychopathology; that is, the patient should not be suffering from a psychosis or an organic brain syndrome.
3.   The patient should *not* be severely addicted to pain medications. In those instances where chemical dependency is judged to be primary rather than secondary to the pain condition, the patient should be referred to a chemical dependency treatment center for detoxification.

SOURCES OF FAILURE

In this section, we review several factors that we believe contribute to poor outcome in the behavioral management of chronic pain. These factors are taken primarily from our clinical experience and from our preceding discussion. We have identified six potential sources of failure, including: misclassification, failure to alter contingencies or identify effective reinforcers, incomplete problem list, covert pain behaviors, attributional changes, and maintenance.

Misclassification

As noted earlier, the behavioral approach is not the appropriate treatment for all chronic pain patients. Patient selection is a critical component of the total treatment process. In some instances, behavioral interventions may fail, not through fault of the treatment intervention per se, but rather because it was applied to the wrong patient. It is important that behaviorists not conceptualize all pain behavior as operant. Pain behavior, in an acute context, has survival value for the individual, signaling the need for medical care. When pain behaviors are chronic, and we can identify potential maintaining contingencies, we make the *assumption* that the behaviors are operantly determined, and that survival value no longer exists. As Fordyce (1976) points out:

> Behavioral analysis has nothing whatever to say about whether there is respondent pain. This is a point of fundamental importance. Establishing what appear to be tight relationships between the occurrence of pain behaviors and what appear to be reinforcing environmental consequences does *not* by itself indicate that there are not physical findings to be found to account for the pain . . .Even in situations in which pain behavior-reinforcing consequence relationships are close and persuasive, all or part of the pain problem may in fact be the result of some organically based factor. Behavioral analysis is neither a diagnostic nor a treatment panacea. It should follow, not precede, a disease model analysis. (p. 121)

For many chronic low back pain patients, the behavioral approach is the treatment of choice in terms of decreasing their disability and returning them to a functional and satisfying way of life. However, this is not always the case. In many instances, we will be asked to see patients who have had only one or perhaps even no surgeries or aggressive medical interventions. It is not uncommon for physicians to become frustrated with these patients even during the diagnostic process, and label them as "crocks." Behaviorists must ensure that patients receive thorough medical evaluation prior to implementing treatment. This is especially important for outpatient-based programs or attempts to treat an individual outpatient. Most pain programs are located within a medical institution for precisely this reason.

In our program, we require that patients have complete and comprehensive medical evaluations prior to treatment and that the referring physician state in writing that no further medical or surgical intervention is indicated and that there are no contraindications to an extensive physical therapy program. Patients typically have fears that something has been missed or else, "Why would I still have the pain?". To implement a behavioral program, it must be assumed that nothing "has been missed," and that modification of the patient's disability by behavior change, without specific pain relief, is necessary and the treatment of choice.

CASE EXAMPLE: MRS. C.

Mrs. C. is a 38-year-old married woman with two children. She had a 14-month history of low back pain as well as leg, arm, and head pain. She had been evaluated by multiple specialists at three of the most prestigious medical centers in the Northeast, all of whom could identify no specific etiology. They were particularly puzzled by the multiple pain complaints whose locations varied from time to time. The majority of her evaluations alluded to an "hysterical personality" and the possible contribution of family and marital difficulties. Our evaluation indicated that the patient's pain behaviors were associated with specific environmental events. The patient placed numerous demands upon the spouse, at times requiring that he leave work during the day and return home to assist her. The patient indicated that she had always been bothered by the fact that her husband, who was a busy health professional, put his practice before her. In addition, the patient's pain behaviors resulted in the avoidance of family and social responsibilities which she indicated she "just could not handle." A behavioral intervention program was implemented, which included extensive physical therapy, functional goals and objectives (i.e., resumption of family responsibilities such as cooking, housework, spending time with the children, etc.), and conjoint marital therapy. The patient evidenced signs of improvement over the first couple of weeks of treatment. She began to decrease her intake of narcotic medication, increase her physical capabilities as evidenced by her physical therapy charts and graphs, and made some improvement in terms of the individualized goals and objectives that had been identified. However, after approximately three weeks of treatment, the patient indicated that she could no longer prepare food for the family, or even remain at the dinner table while they ate, because the sight and smell of food made her nauseous. Despite numerous contracting procedures, the patient was unable to attain those goals and evidenced significant weight loss and social withdrawal. Inasmuch as the patient began to evidence increasing mood disturbance, the treatment team, along with the patient and her spouse, concluded that the intervention did not appear to be working, and that an alternative approach was indicated. The patient was admitted to the hospital and again "worked up" prior to referral for psychiatric treatment. At this time, the patient received her third bone scan within the past year, which identified that she had cancer. Why it had not shown up on earlier scans is unknown, but it is interesting to note that everywhere that the patient complained of pain, there appeared a "hot spot" on the scan. The patient began chemotherapy and narcotic medications were reinstituted; unfortunately, the patient died within the following year.

In this instance, the failure of the procedure was not a function of the therapeutic intervention, but rather attributable to the fact that the patient's pain behaviors were largely respondent in nature and represented a degenerative process. The patient had a consistent fear that this was the case, and always felt that she was going to die. The patient indicated on numerous occasions that she feared she had "cancer." This case is a somewhat dramatic example of an obvious source of failure, but it serves to illustrate the importance of selection factors. Although, as in this case, there is always a certain imprecision in the evaluation process, every effort should be made to ensure that the patient does not need further medical or surgical care. It should be noted that this is only one component of the selection process and points to the need for a comprehensive and reliable classification system for chronic pain patients. Only in this manner will we be able to maximize the likelihood of matching the right treatment to the right patient.

Failure to Alter Contingencies or Identify Effective Reinforcers

The behavioral management of chronic pain is based upon the premise that pain behaviors are under the control of environmental contingencies. Spouse and professional attention and narcotic medication are hypothesized to be the most frequent and potent reinforcers of pain behavior, and if responses to the patient's behavior cannot be controlled, the intervention is likely to fail. Thus it is essential that the spouse agrees with the treatment approach, and knows *how* and *when* to modify his or her behavior. It is not uncommon for a patient's spouse to have difficulty during the extinction and the shaping processes. After all, he or she is essentially being asked to ignore signs of pain and suffering in their loved one. If the spouse does not recognize and accept that this is in the patient's best interest, it will be difficult, if not impossible, for her or him to change the behavior. This is likely to result in the patient receiving inconsistent contingencies, and effectively a shift to a partial reinforcement schedule that will ultimately make the behavior more difficult to extinguish. Similarly, members of the patient's health care network, especially his or her physician, must be included in this process.

Here we are referring not just to members of the treatment team, but also to the patient's private physician or physicians. It can ultimately become an issue of systems management.

In certain situations, the failure to reduce the frequency of pain behaviors may represent a failure to be able to control naturally occurring contingencies. Although this difficulty can be bypassed, at least in part, by placing the patient in an inpatient setting, it reappears upon discharge and can be the critically important determinant of generalization and maintenance of any behavior change that has occurred. There may be no easy way around this problem if it persists despite efforts of the treatment team to educate and influence the behavior of the spouse or "significant other." However, it may be possible to develop specific assessments and instruments to predict which spouses will manifest these difficulties. Although this problem may appear to represent inadequate behavioral assessment, in actuality, however, the problem represents the difficulty in *controlling* naturally occurring reinforcers.

Therapy must not only focus on the extinction of pain behaviors alone, but must also include the development of specific goals and objectives that are incompatible with pain behavior and disability. These activities, however, must be enjoyable and rewarding to the patient. Therapists must also be sensitive to the spouse in this regard. If the designated activities are not rewarding or pleasant to the spouse, he or she may undermine the intervention. We have observed that some spouses actually get worse as the patient gets better, and present significant obstacles to treatment. The reinforcement of activity and "well" behaviors by the treatment team, spouse, and other members of the patient's health care network, is a critical component of the treatment process. As Kazdin (1975) points out, "extinction may effectively decrease the behavior, but it does not ensure that a desirable behavior will replace the (one) that has been eliminated" (p. 187). Effective reinforcers must be identified and the treatment team must ensure that these reinforcers are consistently applied.

Incomplete Problem List

Chronic pain is generally viewed as a complex multifaceted syndrome. As such, assessment must be multidimensional, including physical pathology, specific muscle weakness, sources of inappropriate social or environmental contingenices, medication behaviors, conditioned cues, skills deficits, cognitive set, vocational deficits, marital and family interaction patterns, and psychopathology. Without such a comprehensive assessment, appropriate treatment plans cannot be developed, increasing the likelihood that the intervention will fail.

Many chronic pain patients lack important adaptive skills. An intervention that focuses primarily on extinction of pain behavior without specifying remediation of deficit skills for a particular patient (e.g., assertiveness, anxiety management, etc.) will be less successful. We have found that pain patients often have specific fears or phobias. These fears typically relate to their initial injury. For example, one patient injured by a power tool had developed a marked fear of power tools, which interfered with his returning to his former job. Another patient suffered from a fear of walking up stairs as a result of previous falls. Similarly, a young woman, injured in an auto accident, had such a pervasive fear of driving that she was unable to get behind the wheel of her car. Treatment plans in all of these cases included desensitization of the patient's specific phobia.

Similarly, many patients have sexual and marital problems. The spouse of a chronic pain patient often has unresolved hostility toward the patient, resulting from having to assume additional responsibilities or abstain from sexual activity due to the patient's incapacities. Communication patterns are frequently so disturbed that the couple only communicates "through the patient's illness." Some spouses report that they can no longer stand to live "this way." Couples sessions should entail much more than just training the spouse in principles of reinforcement. Specific marital problems that exist should be identified and addressed in conjoint marital therapy sessions. As noted in the preceding section, the spouse's participation is critical, and pinpointing his or her needs in these sessions can improve participation.

Thus a problem list, which is as broad as possible, should be developed for each patient. In our experience, a minimum of one week is needed for a complete evaluation. This allows the multidisciplinary treatment team to observe pain behaviors, interpersonal skills, patient–spouse interaction patterns, identify reinforcers, and thoroughly evaluate the patient. Following the evaluation week, the staff operationalizes each problem area and formulates specific treatment plans for each problem. This results in a program that is tailored specifically to that individual's needs, and thereby maximizes the likelihood of a successful outcome.

Covert Pain Behaviors

The primary goal in the behavioral management of chronic pain is to modify pain behaviors. Fordyce (1976) has defined pain behaviors as: (1) blanching, flushing, alterations in pulse rate and other autonomically mediated pain indicators; (2) visible and audible, although nonverbal, signals that pain is being experienced (gasps, moans, spasm, compensatory posturing, guarded movement, etc.); (3) verbal reports of pain, including completely vivid and precise descriptions of the quality, intensity, and distribution of the pain; (4) requests for ministrations or assistance because of the pain (requests for medication, for a heating pad, for a back rub, for relief from a task, or for physician contact and medical assistance); and (5) functional limitation or restricted movement reportedly because of the pain (reclining, falling because of a painful or weakened muscle, momentary or enduring interruptions of normal activity). Although he admits that this definition may be somewhat narrow, he has omitted *covert* pain behaviors. Overt pain behaviors, as mentioned earlier, are the critical determinants of the Chronic Pain Syndrome and the defining characteristics of functional impairment and disability. Thus overt pain behaviors are clearly the primary targets for behavior change. However, many chronic pain patients report covert pain behaviors in the form of thoughts or self-evaluative statements concerning physical symptoms or limitations. These self-statements are usually related to and reflect the patients' perceptions of their disability and physical limitations. Inasmuch as covert behaviors are believed to be related to and can potentially influence overt behaviors, failure to address covert pain behaviors in the context of a behavioral program may result in a failure to achieve the desired behavior change. It is possible that some of the chronic pain patients for whom a behavioral intervention was ineffective had preoccupations with their pain and disability, which persisted and maintained the patient's overt pain behaviors. It appears, at least clinically, that self-statements reflecting disability and fear of injury seriously limit the generalization of "well" behaviors. In some patients, these self-evaluative statements may change as the patient progresses in physical therapy and attains the goals established within the context of the program, and lead to an enhanced sense of self-efficacy. In other patients, however, these covert pain behaviors may require specific intervention.

CASE EXAMPLE: MS. Z.

Ms. Z is a 29-year-old female with a 2½-year history of low back and leg pain following an accident where she fell to the floor after the chair she was sitting on collapsed. Despite multiple treatments, her pain and disability persisted and restricted her progress toward obtaining her PhD, influenced her ability to lecture, affected her attendance at work, decreased the quantity and quality of social and interpersonal interactions, and prohibited her from engaging in athletic pursuits. She also evidenced marked emotional distress and stated that her pain problem was a significant contributing factor to marital discord and her subsequent divorce. She reported frequently experiencing anxiety or "panic attacks" in anticipation of pain, and engaged in complex avoidance response patterns in situations which signalled pain or anxiety (e.g., waiting in grocery store lines, driving a car, etc.). She was admitted to the chronic pain unit and a structured program was established, including both physical therapy and specific activity goals. Although Ms. Z. demonstrated good progress in physical therapy, approximately halfway through the program she began to develop difficulties and was unable to attain some of her specific activity goals. Upon further inquiry, it was noted that she was engaging in covert pain behaviors prior to undertaking a specific activity. We hypothesized that these covert pain behaviors were related to her avoidance of those activities and her difficulty in achieving her specific goals. As a result, we asked her to monitor her covert pain behavior and found that in the course of a day there were 46 discrete and identifiable situations in which the patient made self-statements that reflected concerns over her physical limitations, general health, interpretation of physical symptoms, such as aches and pains, or fear of further injury. We determined that the specific activities that she was having difficulty achieving had specific self-statements associated with them. Therefore, we established alternative self-statements to counteract the covert pain behaviors. The patient was instructed to rehearse the adaptive self-statements on a daily basis and just prior to engaging in a specific activity. When she successfully completed a particular goal, she was asked to examine her previous self-statements which reflected fear and limitations. Using this positive self-statement procedure, along with relaxation exercises, the patient was able to successfully overcome her fears, modify her covert pain behaviors, and ultimately achieve the specific goals and activities that she was formerly unable to accomplish.

A broader definition of pain behavior is needed: one that includes overt, covert, and physiological components (cf. Keefe et. al. in press; Sanders 1979). In addition, specific procedures for the assessment of covert pain behaviors are needed. And lastly, to increase therapeutic effectiveness, behavioral treatment procedures may need to include components designed to specifically modify covert pain behaviors.

Attributional Changes

When a patient initially presents to a pain clinic, he or she usually possesses a disease model orientation. There is a belief that some previously undetected cause of the pain will be uncovered and that some new treatment will be received that will remove the pain and suffering. It is extremely rare that a patient presents with an understanding of the behavioral or rehabilitation model. However, it is absolutely critical that the patient's goals and expectations be consistent with that of the treatment program, or the intervention will be doomed to failure because the patient does not want his or her behavior modified, but rather, wants pain relief. Furthermore, many patients are caught up in the functional versus organic "trap." This is usually a result of their physician's frustration at being either unable to identify the physiological source of the patient's pain or being unable to modify or eliminate the patient's pain complaints and behavior. This places patients in an extremely difficult position because they have essentially been told that their pain is "all in their heads." Inasmuch as pain is a private and subjective experience, the validity of a patient's pain is manifested by his or her pain behavior and disability. If the pain behavior and disability changes, in the absence of any specific intervention designed to alter the underlying physiological mechanisms, it is difficult for the patient to reconcile that this does not indicate, at least on the surface, that their pain was, in fact, not "real." One of our patients, after emerging from a crisis during treatment, reported that she feared that if she got better and reported a reduction in her pain, it proved that her pain was not real and was "all in her head." Thus the first and absolutely essential phase of a behavioral intervention with this population is to confront the patient with the fact that pain relief may not be possible, but he or she may be able to increase his or her functional capacity and thereby control the impact that pain has on his or her life. The behavioral approach has no bearing on whether the pain is "real" or "unreal." We indicate to all our patients that it is a "given" that their pain is real. However, we attempt to clarify with them which elements of their pain and dysfunction are modifiable and to what degree.

Patients must ultimately come to recognize that the "pain" is only one of their problems. They may also be experiencing medication dependence, marital and sexual dysfunction, depression, emotional distress, vocational difficulties, financial difficulties, as well as specific functional limitations and impairments. Although we may be unable to modify the pain per se, it is possible to modify the other problems that have developed as a consequence of their chronic and long-standing pain problem. We do this in the form of a "therapeutic challenge" (Follick et al., in press). This challenge is designed to help the patient realize that if he or she is going to return to a normal and satisfying way of life, he or she must take the responsibility for these changes. It is accomplished by challenging the patient's irrational cognitions directly—for example, "I should not have pain," or, "Once you eliminate my pain, all of my other problems will be automatically resolved." The patient who expects total pain relief or believes that health care professionals should provide that total relief, will engage in a relentless search for the "magic treatment" that will eliminate the pain. If patients come to expect that total relief may not be possible, and assume the responsibility of learning to control the influence of pain on their lives, they will no longer search for someone who can provide a cure, but will engage in that process themselves. It is our experience that, if a patient does not accept the major premises, goals, and objectives of a behavioral or rehabilitative model, then treatment should not be undertaken. Failure to "buy" the treatment approach and alter their goals and expectations may account for many of the dropouts, patients who reject treatment, and a large percentage of those patients who do not benefit from a behavioral intervention.

Failure to adopt the conceptual basis and goals of a behavioral intervention may not only result in failure to achieve behavior change during the course of treatment, but it may also account for failure of some patients to maintain behavior change. Thus although they may appear to be successes immediately posttreatment, in the long run they are ultimately failures. As Roberts (1981) points out:

> Patients leaving the program may be functioning at fully normal levels for age and sex, having entered treatment totally or almost totally incapacitated, and still report that they have gained no benefits from treatment even though they have collected and graphed the data which contradicts this feeling. (p. 186)

We argue that, in this subgroup of patients, it is likely that the patient has never fully accepted or agreed with the underlying conceptual model and goals of the program. The patient reports having gained no benefits from treatment, because the treatment has not provided him or her with what he or she wants. This problem may also be the essential determinant in the patient's seeking further treatment and continual use of health care resources for purposes of pain relief.

CASE EXAMPLE: MRS. T.

Mrs. T. is a 39-year-old woman with a three-year history of low back pain and sciatica. At the time of her evaluation, she evidenced some degree of emotional distress because of her inability to continue employment, perform housework, and engage in a variety of previously enjoyed activities with her husband (e.g., driving long distances, attending movies and sports activities). Marital difficulties were denied, although the husband reported that he was distressed by his wife's disability, and was especially interested in having her increase her physical activity level. Financial difficulties were present, and stemmed mainly from the loss of Mrs. T.'s income, and could potentially be eliminated by her return to work. The staff and the patient identified her pain behaviors to include: verbal complaints, constant shifting in her seat while sitting, facial grimacing with moans and groans, a limp favoring the right leg, avoidance of physical activities, lying down, holding her back, use of pain medications, and the daily use of a corset.

The following exercise goals were established for, and achieved by, the patient over the course of treatment:

Exercise	Starting Level	Goal Level
Pelvic tilt	5 repetitions	20 repetitions
Leg lifts	3 repetitions	20 repetitions
Knee bends	3 repetitions	20 repetitions
Hip abduction	3 repetitions	20 repetitions
Sit-ups	2 repetitions	19 repetitions
Shoulder flexion	4 repetitions (with ½ kg.)	21 repetitions (with 1 kg.)
Shoulder abduction	4 repetitions (with ½ kg.)	21 repetitions (with 1 kg.)
Bicycling	1 minute	18 minutes
Walking	1 minute	19 minutes

Although Mrs. T. was able to achieve the above exercise goals, the execution and form of her exercises remained remarkably poor. In addition, although she was able to eliminate her medication, use of a corset, reduce her limp, drive long distances again, go shopping, and do the clothes washing, she persisted in the display of certain pain behaviors (i.e., grimacing, verbal complaints, and moaning). Furthermore, despite urging by the treatment staff, Mrs. T. failed to develop a repertoire of self-directed activities, and had to be prodded to perform at all stages of the program. That is, the activity level increases that she evidenced were those that were required by her treatment contract. She developed no activity goals on her own and, therefore, received limited social support and reinforcement outside of her family network. Her resistance to participation in the hospital volunteer program as an intermediate step toward return to work further illustrates that she was not ready to make a further or complete change in her activity level. Her stated reason for not wanting to participate in the volunteer program was "their" fear that she would reinjure herself. Although Mrs. T. was able to meet the exercise and activity goals required within the structure of her program, she is most appropriately viewed as a treatment failure. She resisted attempts to alter many of her pain behaviors and evidenced behavior throughout the program that suggested that she was still seeking pain relief. Although Mrs. T. and her husband were content with certain aspects of her progress, they were frustrated with the fact that her "pain was not eliminated." When they returned for their first fol-low-up appointment, they indicated that they would like to search for additional methods to eliminate her pain.

This case example is included to illustrate how a patient can make changes in pain behavior, yet still be considered a treatment failure. It has been our experi-ence that not only must patients be "challenged" prior to intervention to ensure that they share the conceptual approach and goals of the program, but that they must be repeatedly rechallenged in this regard. Some conjoint marital sessions should also be devoted to this issue as it relates to both the patient and the spouse. A failure to address the attributional changes or cognitive restructuring compo-nent of the intervention can, in our opinion, be the most frequent source of thera-peutic failure.

Maintenance

Important to any behavior change program is the long-term maintenance of be-havior change. Although short-term modification of pain behavior does demon-strate that pain behaviors can be under the control of environmental contingen-cies, it may have little impact on the patient's ultimate health care utilization if the behavior change does not persist. Considering the treatment of addictive be-havior (e.g., obesity, smoking, and alcohol abuse), one often finds a strong treat-ment effect followed by high recidivism at one-year follow-up. Follow-up studies of behavioral pain programs, although limited by methodological difficulties, are encouraging in terms of long-term efficacy (Fordyce & Steger, 1979). Nonethe-less, there are a number of chronic pain patients who evidence dramatic changes over the course of treatment, but fail to maintain these changes.

Several of the previously discussed sources of failure may also contribute to long-term failure of the intervention. An inability to modify covert pain behaviors or produce the necessary attributional changes or cognitive restructuring are two important factors. Although some of the factors contributing to long-term failure may be the same as those related to direct failure of treatment, there appear to be additional factors that need to be identified and addressed.

Most behavioral programs use an inpatient approach that has inherent limita-tions to long-term maintenance. The most obvious is that the extinction of previ-ously conditioned stimuli has not occurred, and there has been no opportunity for the generalization of new behaviors. Most inpatient programs recorded in the literature have little or no systematic maintenance phase to enable the pain patient and his or her family to practice their new skills and facilitate generalization of treatment effects to the natural environment. Although having other disadvan-tages, this problem is bypassed by the outpatient approach. Independent of whether the intervention is inpatient- or outpatient-based, the need for a structured and specific follow-up component exists. It has been our experience that patients frequently experience a setback (e.g., recurrence of symptoms or disability) within six months after completion of the program. Consequently, we have developed a structured follow-up component to deal with these occurrences and facilitate the maintenance of treatment gains. During the follow-up component, both physical therapy and conjoint sessions are arranged, with a gradual tapering in their frequency. The patient is encouraged to examine the role of emotional factors in the setback, and is assisted in mobilizing his or her acquired coping skills. Counseling and emotional support are provided during this time, and if the patient suffers a loss in physical functioning, he or she is asked to construct a set of exercise graphs to assist them in getting back to their prior level of functioning.

Although certain factors that contribute to a failure to maintain treatment gains can be identified and potentially addressed within the context of the treatment process, there are other variables beyond the control of either the therapist or the patient that can have a devastating effect on maintenance. Workmens' compensation and employers' hiring practices are two important examples. If a patient who is plagued by financial difficulties is unable to obtain gainful employment, he or she will be forced to remain in the "sick role" in order to continue receiving compensation or disability payments.

CASE EXAMPLE: MR. W.

Mr. W. is a 44-year-old male with an eight-year history of chronic low back pain and sciatica. Mr. W. had suffered three work-related injuries, the last of which was two years prior to entering treatment when he slipped on a wet floor and reinjured his back. Mr. W. had undergone three surgical procedures including two laminectomies and a fusion. At the time of treatment, he was taking eight Percodan per day and evidenced significant disability and emotional distress. Mr. W. was able to ambulate only with assistance, and displayed a pronounced leg shake upon weight bearing. He had numerous pain behaviors, including facial grimacing, verbal complaints, difficulty ambulating, difficulty sitting, and spent almost his entire day lying down. Over the course of treatment, Mr. W. made dramatic changes, including an elimination of all pain behaviors, completed an extensive physical exercise program, ambulated normally without a cane, returned to driving a car, returned to full and normal responsibilities within his family system, and returned to school to complete his associate's degree. However, six months later, after he completed school, Mr. W. began to search for full-time employment. He wanted to get off disability and return to work so that he and his wife could again afford to own their own house. Despite a long and arduous search, with assistance from Vocational Rehabilitation and various employment services, Mr. W. was unable to acquire a job because of his past history of three work-related injuries. He was routinely rejected because he was a "bad risk." Following approximately six months of repeated rejection, Mr. W. evidenced significant emotional distress and multiple setbacks. He was essentially forced to remain in the "sick role" in order to continue to receive his disability payments. Although at one level Mr. W. can be considered a long-term treatment failure, a number of treatment gains persisted. He remained medication-free, continued to drive and function within a social context, maintained improvements in his family relations, and, perhaps most importantly, his physician, while continuing to maintain contact and supervision, did not rehospitalize the patient or attempt further surgical intervention.

The above case example illustrates the impact of patients' histories, in spite of documented rehabilitation efforts, on employers' hiring practices. Such uncontrollable factors may contribute to failure at maintenance.

SUMMARY AND CONCLUSIONS

This chapter has focused on factors related to failure in the operant management of chronic pain. A review of the outcome literature indicates that operant programs are effective for a majority of patients who enter treatment, and this is recognized as no small feat, because these patients have a history of multiple treatment failures. However, a significant percentage of these patients fail to show improvement. We have reviewed the literature in regard to characteristics of patients who are considered treatment failures and have identified from our clinical experience a number of factors that we believe are related to poor outcome. However, it should be noted that these factors are proposed as suggestive and worthy of further study. It is our conviction that the study of treatment failures in the behavioral management of chronic pain may assist in the development of a more effective therapeutic intervention, improve the selection process, and ultimately make the programs more cost-effective. In addition to studying patients who fail in treatment, it may also be useful to examine patients with low back pain problems who are functional in spite of pain, and who have not received any systematic treatment. This group of patients, who do well on their own, may provide us with valuable insights that could potentially lead to refinements in our treatment protocols (cf. Turk, Sobel, Follick, & Youkilis, 1980). Furthermore, it may also be productive to examine patients who drop out of treatment to determine why and, in addition to searching for factors that lead to failure during treatment, we must also search for factors that lead to a failure to maintain treatment gains.

In order to systematically examine treatment failures and successes, we need to further develop our outcome measures. A taxonomy of pain behaviors would be a major step towards developing a standardized set of criteria of success and failure, and videotape procedures may be helpful in terms of identifying overt pain behaviors, and documenting therapeutic effectiveness. In addition, assessment strategies need to be refined, especially in regard to covert pain behaviors. Perhaps most importantly, there is urgent need for a quantifiable classification scheme, such as proposed by Brena and Koch (1975), that will lead to refinements in our selection process.

REFERENCES

Anderson, T.P., Cole, T.M., Gullickson, G., Hudgens, A., & Roberts, A.H. (1977) Behavior modification of chronic pain: A treatment program by a multidisciplinary team. *Clinical Orthopedics and Related Research,* **129,** 96–100.

Block, A.R., Kremer, E., & Gaylor, M. (1980 a) Behavioral treatment of chronic pain: Variables affecting treatment efficacy. *Pain.* , 9, 235–242.

Block, A.R., Kremer, E., & Gaylor, M. (1980 b) Behavioral treatment of chronic pain: the spouse as the discriminative cue for pain behavior. *Pain.* , 9, 243–252.

Blumetti, A.E., & Modesti, M.M. (1975) Psychological predicators of success or failure of surgical intervention for intractable back pain. In J. Bonica, & D. Able-Fessard (Eds.), *Advances in pain research and therapy.* New York: Raven.

Brena, S.F., & Koch, D.L. (1975) A "pain estimate" model for quantification and classification of chronic pain. *Anesthesiology Review,* February, 8–13.

Cairns, D., & Pasino, J.A. (1977) Comparison of verbal reinforcement and feedback in the operant treatment of disability due to chronic low back pain. *Behavior Therapy,* **8,** 621–630.

Cairns, D., Thomas, L., Mooney, T.L., & Pace, J.B. (1976) A comprehensive treatment approach to chronic low back pain. *Pain,* **2,** 301–308.

Cox, G.B., Chapman, C.R., & Black, R.G. (1978) The MMPI and chronic pain: The diagnosis of psychogenic pain. *Journal of Behavioral Medicine,* **1,** 437–443.

Duncan, G.H., Gregg, J.M., & Ghia, J.N. (1978) The pain profile: A computerized system for assessment of chronic pain. *Pain,* **5,** 275–284

Follick, M.J. (1979) *An outpatient based behaviorally oriented approach to the management of chronic pain.* Paper presented at the Annual Meeting of the American Psychological Association, New York.

Follick, M.J., Zitter, R.E., & Kulich, R.J. (in press) Outpatient management of chronic pain. In T.J. Coates (Ed.), *Behavioral medicine: A practical handbook.* Research Press.

Follick, M.J., Zitter, R.E., Kulich, R.J., & Harris, R. (1979) *An outpatient based, behaviorally oriented, multidisciplinary approach to the treatment of chronic pain.* Paper presented at the Annual Meeting of the Association for the Advancement of Behavior Therapy, San Francisco.

Fordyce, W.E. (1974) Chronic pain as learned behavior. In J.J. Bonica (Ed.), *Advances in neurology* (Vol. 4). New York: Raven.

Fordyce, W.E. (1976) *Behavioral methods for chronic pain and illness.* St. Louis: Mosby.

Fordyce, W.E., Fowler, R., & Delateur, D. (1968) An application of behavior modification technique to a problem of chronic pain. *Behavior Research and Therapy,* **6,** 105–107.

Fordyce, W.E., Fowler, R.S., Lehman, J.F., Delateur, B.J., Sand, P.L., & Trieschmann, R.B. (1973) Operant conditioning in the treatment of chronic pain. *Archives of Physical Medicine and Rehabilitation,* **54,** 399–408.

Fordyce, W.E., & Steger, J.C. Chronic Pain. (1979) In O.F. Pomerleau, & J.P. Brady (Eds.), *Behavioral medicine: Theory and practice.* Baltimore: Williams & Wilkins.

Gilberstadt, H., & Jancis, M. (1967) "Organic" versus "functional" diagnosis from one-three MMPI profiles. *Journal of Clinical Psychology,* **23,** 480–483.

Gottlieb, H., Strite, L.C., Koller, R., Madorsky, A., Hockersmith, V., Kleeman, M., & Wagner, J. (1977) Comprehensive rehabilitation of patients having chronic low back pain. *Archives of Physical Medicine and Rehabilitation,* **58,** 101–108.

Greene, C.J., Meagher, R.B., & Millon, T. (in press) Patients' social responses in a pain program: Uses of the MBHI.

Hanvik, L.J. (1949) Some psychological dimensions of low back pain. *Doctoral dissertation,* University of Minnesota.

Herman, E., & Baptiste, S. (1981) Pain control: Mastery through group experience. *Pain,* **10,** 79–86.

Ignelzi, R.A., Sternbach, R.A., & Timmermans, G. (1977) The pain ward follow-up analyses. *Pain,* **3,** 277–280.

Kazdin, A.E. (1975) *Behavior modification in applied settings.* Homewood, Ill.: Dorsey.

Keefe, F.J., Brown, C.J., Ziesat, H., & Scott, D. (in press) Behavioral assessment of chronic pain. In F.S. Keefe, & J. Blumenthal (Eds.), *Assessment strategies in behavioral medicine.* Grune and Stratton.

Khatami, M., & Rush, A.J. (1978) A pilot study of the treatment of outpatients with chronic pain: Symptom control, stimulus control and social system intervention. *Pain,* **5,** 163–172.

Kremer, E., Block, A., Morgan, C., & Gaylor, M. (1979) Behavioral approaches in pain management: Social communication skills and pain relief. In D. Osborne, & D. Esier (Eds.), *Psychology and medicine.* New York: Academic.

Krusen, E.M., & Ford, D.E. (1958) Compensation factor in low back injuries. *American Medical Association,* **156,** 1128–1133.

Leavitt, F., Garron, D.C., D'Angelo, C.M., & McNeill, T.W. (1979) Low back pain in patients with and without demonstrable organic disease. *Pain,* **6,** 191–200.

Loesser, J.D. (1974) Dorsal rhizotomy: Indications and results. In J.J. Bonica (Ed.), *Advances in neurology* (Vol. 4). New York: Raven.

Maruta, T., Swanson, D.W., & Swenson, W.M. (1979) Chronic pain: Which patients may a pain-management program help? *Pain,* **7,** 321–329.

Melzack, R. (1974) Psychological concepts and methods for the control of pain. In J.J. Bonica (Ed.), *Advances in neurology (Vol. 4).* New York: Raven.

Miechenbaum, D.H., & Turk, D.C. (1976) The cognitive-behavioral management of anxiety, anger, and pain. In P.O. Davidson (Ed.), *The behavioral management of anxiety, depression, and pain.* New York: Brunner/Mazel.

Newman, R.I., Seres, J.L., Yospe, L.P., & Garlington, B. (1978) Multidisciplinary treatment of chronic pain: Long-term follow-up of low back pain patients. *Pain,* **4,** 283–292.

Roberts, A.H. (1981) The behavioral treatment of chronic pain. In J.M. Ferguson, & C.B. Taylor (Eds.), *The comprehensive handbook of behavioral medicine (Vol. 2).* New York: Spectrum.

Roberts, A.H. and Reinhardt L. (1980) The Behavioral Management of Chronic Pain: Long Term follow-up with comparison groups. *Pain*, 8, 151–162.

Rybstein-Blinchik, E., & Grzesiak, R.C. (1979) Reinterpretative cognitive strategies in chronic pain management. *Archives of Physical Medicine and Rehabilitation,* **60,** 609–612.

Sanders, S.H. (1979) The behavioral assessment and treatment of clinical pain: Appraisal of current status. In M. Hersen, R. Eisler, & P. Miller (Eds.), *Progress in behavior modification* (Vol. 8). New York: Academic.

Sanders, S.H. (1980) Toward a practical instrumentation system for the automatic measurement of "up-time" in chronic pain patients. *Pain,* **9,** 103–109.

Saunders, K.J., Goldstein, M.K., & Stein, G.R. (1978) Automated measurement of patient activity on a hospital rehabilitation ward. *Archives of Physical Medicine and Rehabilitation,* **59,** 255–257.

Shealy, C., & Shealy, M. (1976) Behavioral techniques in the control of pain: A case of health maintenance vs. disease treatment. In M. Weisenberg, & B. Tursky (Eds.), *Pain: New perspectives in therapy and research.* New York: Plenum.

Smith, W.L., & Durksen, D.L. (1980) Personality and the relief of chronic pain: Predicting surgical outcome. In W.V. Smith, H. Kersky, & S.C. Gross (Eds.), *Pain: Meaning and Management.* New York: Spectrum.

Sternbach, R.A. (1974) *Pain patients: Traits and treatments.* New York: Academic.

Strassberg, D.S., Reimherr, F., Ward, M., Russell, S., & Cole, A. (1981) The MMPI and chronic pain. *Journal of Consulting and Clinical Psychology,* **49,** 220–226.

Swanson, D.W., Maruta, T., & Swenson, W.M. (1979) Results of behavior modification in the treatment of chronic pain. *Psychosomatic Medicine,* **41,** No. 1.

Swenson, D., Swenson, W., Maruta, T., & McPhee, M. (1976) Program for managing chronic pain: Parts I and II. Mayo Clinic Proceedings, 401–411.

Turk, D.C., & Genest, M. (1979) The regulation of pain, the application of cognitive and behavioral techniques for prevention and remediation. In P. Kendall, & S. Hollon (Eds.), *Cognitive behavioral interventions: Theory, research and procedures.* New York: Academic.

Turk, D.C., Sobel, H.J., Follick, M.J., & Youkilis, H.D. (1980) A sequential criterion analysis for assessing coping with chronic illness. *Journal of Human Stress,* **6,** No. 2, 35–40.

White, A.W. (1969) Low back pain in men receiving workmen's compensation: A follow-up study. *Canadian Medical Association Journal,* **101,** 61–67.

Wilkes, L.I., & Rocchio, T.D. (1975) Preoperative psychological tests as predictors of success of chemonucleolysis in the treatment of the low back syndrome. *Journal of Bone and Joint Surgery,* **57A,** 478–483.

CHAPTER 18

Failure of Persons
to Respond to the Token Economy

ALAN E. KAZDIN

The token economy consists of an incentive system in which a particular medium of exchange (the token) is provided for well specified behaviors. Delivery of the tokens (e.g., stars, points, tickets, checkmarks, money) is contingent upon performance. The tokens can be exchanged for a variety of other rewards, referred to as backup reinforcers. For example, in a typical program for psychiatric patients, tokens may be delivered for self-care behaviors, social interaction, attendance to and participation in activities, and behaviors incompatible with psychotic symptoms (e.g., rational speech). The tokens may be exchanged for the purchase or rental of several items from a store in the hospital, special privileges, free time, overnight passes, and so on.

The token economy has been implemented effectively in an extraordinarily wide range of settings including psychiatric hospitals, prison and detention centers, institutions for the mentally retarded, daycare centers, nursing homes, schools, the home, outpatient treatment, and other settings (Kazdin, 1977b). Very few settings devoted to treatment, rehabilitation, or education have been free from the impact of token economies. Many other settings including business and industry, the military, and the community at large have also profited from the use of token economies.

A large number of outcome studies have demonstrated the effectiveness of token economies. A few of the investigations have received special attention because of their programmatic nature, scope, and extended follow-up. Prominent examples include token economies for psychiatric patients (Paul & Lentz, 1977), predelinquents (Kirigin, Wolf, Braukmann, Fixsen, & Phillips, 1979), and disadvantaged students (Bushell, 1978).

Although token economies have led to dramatic changes in behavior, this should not imply that they are invariably effective. Token economies are complex systems with several administrative, staffing, and consultative requirements. Thus there are multiple points in the implementation of token economies where the

Completion of this chapter was facilitated by a Research Scientist Development Award (MH00353) from the National Institute of Mental Health.

program can break down and fail. Several authors have commented on the administrative and sociopolitical features of the program (e.g., staff training and morale, institutional constraints, supervision of the execution of the program) that can cause token economies to fail (e.g., Drabman & Tucker, 1974; Hall & Baker, 1973; Liberman, 1979; Walker, Hedberg, Clement, & Wright, 1981). Assuming that a program is successfully in operation, it is still possible for individual patients or clients not to respond to the contingencies. The present chapter examines the failure of persons to respond to token economies, identifies possible bases for such failures, and recommends ways in which failures can be minimized.

FAILURES TO RESPOND

Multiple Meanings of Failure

The thrust of the chapter is to discuss failures in treatment. However, "failure" is not a very useful term in evaluating the results of token economies, if any treatment modality. The term is much too general and does not describe the multiple response patterns that may be evident. In the context of a token economy, failure could refer to several different response patterns. Table 18.1 provides a summary of major types of response patterns that might be referred to as treatment failures.

The multiple meanings of failure make evaluation of the token economy difficult. In the usual case, failure refers primarily to the absence of change in performance over the course of a token economy. However, even here it is difficult to discuss failures in the general case without specifying the context of the program.

Table 18.1.   Patterns of Performance That Might Be Referred to as Failures to Respond

Client Response to the Token Economy	Explanation
No change in performance	The client fails to improve while the program is in effect.
Deterioration in performance	The client changes in a direction opposite from expected in the program; he or she becomes worse.
Only slight or small improvements	Program effects are weak; improvement is evident but it is insufficient for a clinically significant change.
Circumscribed improvements	Changes in some behaviors but not in others; some areas where improvements are not marked.
Transient change	Improvements are made but they do not last; changes when program is in effect but they are lost at follow-up or changes at the beginning of the program which attenuate over time.
Lack of response to withdrawal of the contingencies	Client behavior improves with the onset of the program but attempts to demonstrate the program is responsible for change (e.g., temporary suspension of the program) fail.

For example, in a token economy for chronic psychiatric patients most patients did not change in their bizarre and symptomatic behaviors (Mishara, 1978). However, an important consideration is that the participants were geriatric patients suffering organic brain syndromes; the predicted course of behavior change was deterioration. Improvement in symptomatic behaviors would be a measure of success. Yet, the absence of change might also mean a reduction or delay in patient deterioration. Thus whether the absence of improvement among persons who completed the program is a measure of success or failure may be arguable.

The types of failure illustrated in the table generally refer to the ways in which individual clients respond or fail to respond to the program. An exception is the final definition listed in the table in which the client may show marked improvements when the program is implemented but fails to respond when the contingencies are withdrawn. In this case, attempts to show that the token economy rather than extraneous events was responsible for change are unclear. In such circumstances, persons responsible for clinical care for the client are not likely to refer to the program as a failure. However, persons who evaluate research reports of such programs are quite likely to use such terms in referring to what was demonstrated. For present purposes, the failures of token economies are discussed in terms of the performance of individual patients or clients rather than the demonstration of overall program effects.

Overview of the Evidence

The different types of response patterns illustrated in Table 18.1 have several exemplars in the token economy literature. A selective review conveys the multiple ways in which clients may respond less than optimally to the program. As already noted, "failures" usually refer to persons who do not respond to the contingencies (Kazdin, 1973). Unresponsiveness refers to the fact that the clients do not show changes in the designated behaviors while a particular program is in effect. The fact that clients do not respond does not mean that the program or a particular form of treatment is a failure. As discussed later, persons who have not responded to a particular program often respond when the procedures are varied.

Token economies are usually implemented as a general means of managing groups of persons in treatment, rehabilitation, and educational settings. Standardized contingencies typically are implemented that are the same for all persons participating in the setting. Thus unresponsiveness of the participants refers primarily to the lack of response to a standardized treatment regimen. The failure of some persons to respond to token economies has been evident since the appearance of early programs in the field.

In the first and most influential formal token economy with adult psychiatric patients, Ayllon and Azrin (1965) reported that 18 percent ($n = 8$) of the chronic schizophrenic patients were unaffected by the procedures. These patients apparently earned some tokens for self-care but did not respond to contingencies related to job assignments in which several experiments were conducted. Subsequent programs with chronic psychiatric patients reported similar findings using other measures than job performance. For example, Atthowe and Krasner (1968) reported that 10 percent ($n = 6$) of their patients did not gain from the program as evidenced by failure to increase in activity and social interaction on the ward. In other programs for psychiatric patients some small number of patients have failed to respond to the contingencies (e.g., Allen & Magaro, 1971; Liberman, 1968; Lloyd & Garlington, 1968).

The lack of responsiveness of token reinforcement has not been restricted to psychiatric patients. Programs for the mentally retarded have also reported failures of some persons to respond to the contingencies. For example, Zimmerman, Zimmerman, and Russell (1969) reported that three of seven retarded children and adolescents were not affected by the token reinforcement system designed to develop instruction-following. One of the children responded at high levels throughout the program whereas two others failed to respond. Other programs conducted in classroom, workshop, and institutional settings and with children, adolescents, and adults have reported that a small percentage of retarded persons failed to respond (e.g., Baer, Ascione, & Casto, 1977; Hunt, Fitzhugh, & Fitzhugh, 1968; Hunt & Zimmerman, 1969; Logan, Kinsinger, Shelton, & Brown, 1971). Similarly, with delinquent youths and adult offenders token reinforcement has failed to affect behavior of a small percentage of institutionalized residents (e.g., Moran, Kass, & Munz, 1977; Tyler & Brown, 1968).

The extent to which persons fail to respond in token economies is difficult to estimate. Many programs report intervention effects on the basis of group performance over time so that information about individuals often is unavailable. However, sufficient evidence exists that some small percentage of persons are likely not to respond to an overall general program.

Deterioration of performance is infrequently reported in token economies. Certainly a difficulty is demonstrating that the person whose performance becomes worse over time does so as a direct function of the token economy. Perhaps the clearest demonstration of deterioration of performance comes from a token economy on a psychiatric ward (Boren & Colman, 1970). In this program several contingency manipulations were made, one of which included levying fines for the failure of patients to attend a general ward meeting. When patients were fined for staying in bed rather than attending the meeting, attendance consistently became *worse*. Attendance quickly improved when the response cost contingency was lifted. The investigators reported an attempt of patients to "rebel" against the punishment contingency.

Aside from the absence of change or deterioration, Table 18.1 notes that only a small improvement in performance may be viewed as a failure. Essentially change is achieved but the importance of the change can be questioned. Taken to extremes, this criterion might be viewed as an indictment of most token economies. The reason is that there is relatively little evidence that token economies (or most other treatments for that matter) achieve clinically important changes. The demonstration of marked changes either by visual inspection or statistical criteria may not reflect changes that make a difference in the person's life.

Separate problems can be identified in demonstrating a clinically important change. First, the criteria for evaluating the clinical significance of change are not well developed or agreed upon, even though some suggestions have been offered (Kazdin, 1977a; Wolf, 1978). Thus the magnitude of change required to be assured that the improvements are therapeutic is not always clear. Second, the specific measures used to reflect change are not necessarily therapeutically important. Assessment in token economies emphasizes changes in specific behaviors which may or may not reflect socially important measures. Measures such as rehospitalization and community stay of psychiatric patients, recidivism and community adjustment of delinquents, academic and achievement gains of students, and other socially relevant variables are infrequently assessed, although there are exceptions (see Kazdin, 1977b).

The failure of a program might also be evident when improvements occur for some but not all of the specified behaviors. That is, the effects of the program are circumscribed, as defined in Table 18.1. For example, Last, Ginor, Lowental, and Klein (1978) reported a token economy for chronic psychiatric patients that focused upon self-care, work habits, and social participation. Responsiveness to the program was evaluated on the magnitude and stability of performance in these separate areas. Responsiveness varied across designated areas. More persons responded to the social participation contingencies than to work or self-care contingencies. Thus responsiveness of a given patient depended in part on the area of performance that was examined. From the reported data, it is not possible to examine how many persons failed to respond in each area of the program.

Differential responsiveness across areas of performance was also reported by Baker, Hall, Hutchinson, and Bridge (1977) in a token economy for chronic schizophrenic patients. Persons who participated in a reinforcement program based upon approval, information, and contingent or noncontingent tokens improved in social behavior, the major focus of the program. However, changes were not evident in symptomatic behaviors (e.g., ratings of thought disorder, delusions, emotional disorder, and others) over the 12-month course of treatment. Thus the success of the program or responsiveness of the patients might be viewed differently depending upon the criteria used to evaluate change.

Transient changes in patient or client performance might be considered as evidence of a treatment failure. Transient changes as a possible measure of failure represent a particularly difficult criterion to invoke. Many programs are evaluated in single-case experimental designs in which the program is withdrawn at some point during its evaluation. The demonstration of a reversal of performance by withdrawing the program or continuing administration of tokens on a noncontingent basis suggests that the results will be transient when the program ultimately is withdrawn (cf. Hartmann & Atkinson, 1973). Thus for most persons the changes may be transient. The gains are usually lost with termination of the program.

Even if behaviors are not lost or reversed during experimental evaluation of the program, the gains may still prove to be transient. Relatively few programs have collected follow-up data to show that treatment effects are sustained (Kazdin, 1977b). In studies in which long-term follow-up data are gathered, it is not always clear that the effects were due to the token economy rather than to some other extraneous factors. A few experiments or quasi-experiments with psychiatric patients (Paul & Lentz, 1977), delinquents (Kirigin et al., 1979), and disadvantaged school students (Bushell, 1978) have shown that the effects of token reinforcement programs can be still evident years after the program has been terminated. However, these programs were multifaceted interventions conducted over protracted periods. The durability of the results may have depended upon several aspects of treatment beyond the basic characteristics of a token economy. Notwithstanding a few excellent demonstrations, collection of follow-up data is still the exception rather than the rule in token economies. Without follow-up data, even programs that appear very successful while in operation may have little or no long-term effects on performance.

Even while a token economy is in effect, conclusions reached about its effects are likely to vary as a function of the point in time that behavior is assessed. Persons are likely to differ in the time it takes to respond to the contingencies so that some persons who appear not to respond merely may be taking longer to respond. For example, Butler (1979) found that chronic schizophrenic patients differed greatly in the time it took for them to reach criterion levels of performance for several behaviors. Some persons responded relatively quickly (within 5 weeks), others gradually (6 to 23 weeks), and some never reached target levels. Thus conclusions about the responsiveness of individual patients might vary depending upon the point at which the program had been terminated.

As evident from the selective review, several different types of program effects have been obtained, many of which might be viewed as treatment failures. In evaluating a token economy and perhaps other treatments as well, it would be misleading to examine change on one or two measures at one or a few points in time and then to draw conclusions about the success or failure of treatment. The diversity and complexity of treatment effects make interpretation of success and failure somewhat unclear. The criteria required to evaluate outcomes of psychosocial interventions are still a matter of active discussion (cf. Kazdin & Wilson, 1978; Strupp & Hadley, 1977). Hence any treatments might be evaluated differently for the individual client depending upon which criteria are adopted.

EXPLANATIONS FOR UNRESPONSIVENESS TO TOKEN ECONOMIES

Several explanations might be proffered to account for the lack of responsiveness of some persons to token economies. The reasons vary in the extent to which they place primary responsibility on features of the program and its implementation, or characteristics of the clients. Of course, in any given case, several reasons might account for lack of responsiveness. However, for purposes of clarity it is useful to consider possible explanations separately.

Parameters of Reinforcement

Token economies are complex reinforcement systems that depend upon a number of variables for their success. A general explanation for unresponsiveness is that some facet of the program does not meet ideal conditions to alter behavior. For example, clients may not respond initially to the program because of the use of inappropriate or insufficiently powerful reinforcers. This is possible because when tokens have no actual backup value (i.e., cannot be exchanged for other rewards), behavior does not usually change (e.g., Bushell, Wrobel, & Michaelis, 1968). Indeed, even when events are administered that are usually considered to be positive reinforcers, they may function as aversive events rather than as positive consequences. For example, social praise for conduct-problem children often exacerbate rather than improve behavior (e.g., Herbert, Pinkston, Hayden, Sajwaj, Pinkston, Cordua, & Jackson, 1973). Thus failure to respond to the contingencies may reflect on the consequences that are used to "reinforce" behavior. Either the tokens or backup rewards may not serve as functional reinforcers.

A related explanation is that reinforcer delivery in some way is not optimal so that behavior does not change in response to weak contingencies. For example, for some persons, the delay between performance and token reinforcement or between token reinforcement and the exchange for backup reinforcers for a given individual may be too long to alter performance.

Another explanation of unresponsiveness is that the responses to be reinforced with tokens are not in the repertoires of the clients. Several behavioral deficits may result in unresponsiveness because the program may not adequately shape approximations of the desired behaviors. Programs typically devise contingencies that apply in a similar fashion to all members of the group (e.g., patients on a ward, students in a class). Without shaping procedures and individualized contingencies, unresponsiveness of many persons might be expected.

Unresponsiveness may also be explained by the failure of some persons to understand or to be cognizant of the relationship between their performance and reinforcement. The role of instructions that convey the reinforcement contingencies may be very important. Occasionally, reinforcement has had little or no effect on behavior in applied settings when it has been administered without instructions (Ayllon & Azrin, 1964; Herman & Tramontana, 1971). Some persons may not comprehend the instructions and hence fail to respond to the contingencies.

The above explanations are quite reasonable in many instances in which particular persons do not respond to the contingencies. And, as will be evident later, change in one of the above dimensions of the program can improve the behavior of a previously unresponsive client. On the other hand, there is a conceptual pitfall one must avoid. If one or a few persons do not respond, this is often taken as evidence for one of the above explanations, that is, that the reinforcement was not potent enough or that other features of the contingencies were somehow misapplied. The pitfall is the potential circularity when a client's unresponsiveness is taken as evidence that the contingencies are inadequate and the inadequacy of the contingency is deduced from the client's lack of response. To avoid this circularity, any aspect of the contingency that might be considered responsible for a person's unresponsiveness must be presented as a testable hypothesis that permits falsification. For example, when a client fails to respond to token reinforcement and later responds when the backup reinforcers are altered or reinforcement is administered more immediately, this suggests that a specific facet of the contingency accounted for unresponsiveness.

Integrity and Execution of Treatment

The above explanations refer to problems in the design of the reinforcement contingencies. It is quite possible that the program is well designed but that the implementation departs from what is intended. The extent to which the program is carried out as intended is referred to as the *integrity of treatment* and is an extremely important issue for treatment programs in general (Yeaton & Sechrest, 1981). Different problems may arise regarding the manner in which programs are actually implemented that may explain why some persons do not respond or respond less well than desired.

Problems of a breakdown in the integrity of treatment and the implications of responsiveness to a token economy were reported by Bassett and Blanchard (1977) who implemented a token economy in a prison setting for male adult offenders. The program relied upon token reinforcement for appropriate behaviors and response cost for inappropriate behaviors. During the course of the program, the director took a temporary leave of absence and provided supervision only on a consulting basis. Without close monitoring, the program deteriorated rapidly. Specifically, the staff withheld tokens for appropriate behaviors, increased the use of fines, and became inconsistent in the magnitude of fines that were invoked. The eventual return of the program director and careful monitoring of the contingencies returned the program to its original state. In any case, this study suggested that the adherence of the staff to the program may deteriorate unless it is continually supervised. When persons fail to respond to a program, the possibility exists that the program is not being implemented or implemented correctly. Fortunately, the administration of contingencies to particular clients in a reinforcement program can be checked to determine the plausibility of this explanation.

Client Characteristics

Another explanation for lack of responsiveness is that token economies may be likely to produce change in some clients rather than others. One would not expect the token economy or any singular procedure to be well suited to everyone. Perhaps unresponsiveness is characteristic of persons who evince specific subject and demographic characteristics.

Unfortunately, research has not suggested a clear set of characteristics that predispose one not to respond to a token economy. In token economies for psychiatric patients, most investigators have reported that degree of patient withdrawal, social isolation, and length of hospitalization are negatively correlated with improvement (Atthowe & Krasner, 1968; Ayllon & Azrin, 1968a; Butler, 1979; Fullerton, Cayner, & McLaughlin-Reidel, 1978; Steffy, 1968). On the other hand, other authors have reported that length of hospitalization is not related to responsiveness to the contingencies (Allen & Magaro, 1971) and may even be positively correlated with success in the program (Birky, Chambliss, & Wasden, 1971). Severity of symptoms (e.g., psychotic disorganization) has been positively correlated with responsiveness (Mishara, 1978). In the same vein, age has been positively associated with improvements for adult psychiatric patients in some programs (Last et al., 1978) but not in others (Allen & Magaro, 1971; Fullerton et al., 1978; Mishara, 1978). Unfortunately, the actual range of patient ages has not been provided among the alternative studies to clarify one possible basis for the discrepancy. At this point, across several adult populations including geriatric patients (Mishara, 1978), age does not seem to be a significant correlate of responsiveness to the program.

Other variables for psychiatric patients have been investigated. For example, in one token economy, IQ was positively related to responsiveness in the program. Patients with IQs over 80 performed better than those with IQs under 80 (Fullerton et al., 1978). Also, success in a token economy has been associated with staff-rated physical attractiveness (Choban, Cavior, & Bennett, 1974). Patients judged as more attractive tended to earn more tokens and showed a higher discharge rate than those judged as less attractive.

Among a prison sample, responsiveness to the token economy was related to IQ and age. Males and females who were older and males who had higher IQs were more likely to succeed in the program as defined by progress through a multilevel system prior to community employment (Moran et al., 1977). However, success in this program was even more highly associated with a history of sustained employment prior to admission and education in school.

In general, data indicate many inconsistencies in the type of persons who respond or fail to respond to token economies. The difficulty has been the heterogeneity of populations investigated and the methods of investigation. Typically, one or two client variables are examined in isolation. An improved approach might be to examine several variables and the manner in which they combine to predict responsiveness to treatment. For example, using multiple regression techniques, Mishara (1978) identified a constellation of variables including the degree of psychotic disorganization, total years of hospitalization, self-care habits, and physical condition that predicted responsiveness to a token program for geriatric psychiatric patients. Regression analyses can provide a more useful tool for predicting responsiveness than isolated correlations with one or two variables.

TECHNIQUES TO INCREASE RESPONSIVENESS TO TOKEN ECONOMIES

When a patient or client fails to respond to a particular program, caution needs to be exercised in the manner in which this is interpreted. Lack of responsiveness to a particular program does not necessarily mean that the person would not respond to the program with some minor or major variation. Considerable evidence exists that persons who do not respond initially to a program may readily respond when some alterations are made in the contingencies. An extraordinarily wide range of options are available for increasing responsiveness of persons to a token economy.

Varying Administration of Reinforcers

Several changes in the manner in which reinforcers are administered can lead to marked increases in performance. Perhaps the most obvious method is to vary the *magnitude of reinforcement.* Increases in the amount of tokens or backup events can enhance performance. For example, Ayllon, Milan, Roberts, and McKee (1979) provided prisoners with points for completion of academic tasks on programmed materials. Contingent delivery of points led to systematic improvements in math and English assignments. However, the rates of improvement systematically increased during an "enriched schedule" in which more tokens were provided for completion of the tasks. Other programs have also shown that responsiveness to token reinforcement contingencies can be increased by manipulation of the amount of tokens provided for performance (e.g., Bassett, Blanchard, & Koshland, 1975; Rickard, Melvin, Creel, & Creel, 1973).

Another procedure for improving responsiveness is to utilize *reinforcer sampling* (Ayllon & Azrin, 1968b) which consists of exposing the client to a portion of the backup reinforcer such as a part of a meal, a few minutes of social activity, or special privileges. By sampling a portion of the reinforcers on a noncontingent basis, the client is more likely to purchase the event with tokens. Thus reinforcer sampling increases utilization of the backup events in token economies which, in turn, increases token-earning behaviors. Reinforcer sampling has been utilized in several studies with psychiatric patients who fail to respond or who respond minimally to the program (Ayllon & Azrin, 1968a, b; Curran, Lentz & Paul, 1973; Sobell, Schaefer, Sobell, & Kremer, 1970).

Token economies depend upon the value of the backup events for which tokens can be exchanged. Responsiveness to the contingencies may vary greatly depending upon the rewards. Simple *variations in backup reinforcers* occasionally increase responsiveness to the contingencies. For example, Ayllon, Garber, and Pisor (1975) found that token reinforcement produced weak and transient changes in the disruptive behaviors of third-grade students. A new reinforcer was introduced for behavior. Specifically, the teacher sent a "good behavior letter" home to parents of those children who had responded well. The parents were instructed to express approval or disappointment, respectively, if the letter was or was not sent home. The contingent delivery of the letter greatly improved responsiveness to the program. Thus the initial weak effects were readily altered with modification of the consequences for behavior.

Several other procedures related to the administration of reinforcers in token economies can be used to enhance performance, although they are less well investigated than the above techniques. For example, requiring persons to *preselect the backup reinforcers* for which they will be working can enhance responsiveness. In the usual token economy, clients earn tokens and decide what to purchase when the opportunities for exchange of tokens are provided. With preselection, clients select in advance how they will spend their reinforcers. Kazdin and Geesey (1980) found that children performed at higher levels in a classroom token economy when they were required to preselect their backup reinforcers.

Another procedure for improving responsiveness is to allow persons to *earn their way off the system.* In many token programs levels are used so that a client begins at an initial level and, with consistent performance, can advance to new levels (e.g., Melin & Gotestam, 1973; Paul & Lentz, 1977). The incentive for progress is that at each level additional privileges and activities are available as reinforcers. At the final level, often persons can earn their way off direct contingencies so that reinforcers are freely available as long as high levels of performance are sustained. Although leveled programs are in wide use, little research has examined directly whether use of a leveled system can enhance performance of persons who do not respond. A study that approximated features of a leveled system was reported in a classroom setting where children had the opportunity to earn their way off the token system. If performance met prespecified standards during one period of the day, the students could earn a period of time in which the token system would not be in effect (Kazdin & Mascitelli, 1980). Children responded better to the program (i.e., evinced higher levels of attentiveness to their work) during periods when they had the opportunity to earn their way off the system. Thus earning off the system may be an added incentive that can be used to enhance responsiveness.

Manipulation of Economic Variables

The token economy is usually evaluated from the standpoint of operant conditioning principles and modifications of the program are conceived in terms of parameters of reinforcement. A token program can also be viewed as an economic system. The advantage is that several economic variables can be proposed to influence client responsiveness (cf. Fisher, Winkler, Krasner, Kagel, Battalio, & Basmann, 1978; Kagel & Winkler, 1972; Winkler, 1972).

Essentially, token-earning behaviors represent work *output;* the delivery of tokens represents *income* or *wages;* the backup events represent *expenditures;* and the accumulated tokens can be viewed as *savings.* The advantage of translating the token economy into economic terms has stemmed from demonstrations that economic variables can enhance client performance. Although the range of economic variables that can influence responsiveness to token economies has been reviewed elsewhere (Kazdin, 1977b), it is useful to highlight some of the findings.

The *amount of savings* has been shown to be an important determinant of performance in a token economy (Winkler, 1972). When savings of tokens reach a critical level, token-earning behaviors are likely to decline. When savings fall below this level, token-earning behaviors increase. Hence one economic variable that can be manipulated to increase responsiveness is the level of savings. Winkler (1973) demonstrated the influence of savings on responsiveness to a token economy for psychiatric patients. After a token economy had been in operation, a new token system was substituted in which the only medium of exchange to purchase backup events was the new token. This procedure effectively eliminated all savings the patients had previously accumulated. Token-earning behaviors increased with the new system. In separate experiments, token-earning behaviors were shown to increase when savings were low and to decrease when savings again became high. Thus performance was directly related to the extent to which savings were allowed to accrue.

Another variable is the effect of increased *costs of backup reinforcers* (i.e., inflation) on responsiveness of persons in a token economy. For example, Hung (1977) trained schizophrenic and autistic children in a three-week summer camp setting to engage in self-help routines and to ask questions spontaneously. Although training improved performance, spontaneous questions did not extend beyond the training situations, even though tokens could be earned in these other situations. The price of backup rewards was increased creating the need to earn more tokens. All three children exposed to the inflation manipulation improved rapidly in their spontaneous questions outside the training situation. Thus lack of responsiveness in nontraining situations was altered by diminishing the value of the tokens.

Several other economic variables have been shown to influence responsiveness to the token economy. Increasing the extent to which persons consume backup events by expanding the range and attractiveness of backup events, stimulation of spending through occasional sales, the use of forced spending by placing expiration dates on the tokens, increasing prices of some of the backup events, and similar procedures has been shown to increase responsiveness to token reinforcement procedures (Hersen, Eisler, Smith, & Agras, 1972; Milby, Clarke, Charles, & Willcutt, 1977; Winkler, 1971a, b, 1972).

Peer Involvement With the Contingencies

Responsiveness to token reinforcement contingencies can be enhanced by involving peers into the program. One procedure is *consequence sharing* and consists of designing a program for a particular individual and having the person share the earned consequences with others. The peers receive the reinforcing consequences that were earned by the target client. Typically, the client receives the consequences he or she has earned, and these same consequences are provided to peers. Thus there is no net loss of reinforcement for the client. Earning for oneself and for one's peers can enhance responsiveness to the contingencies.

For example, in one program, a chronic schizophrenic patient failed to respond, as evident by poor social interaction and a failure to engage in work and self-care skills (Feingold & Migler, 1972). To increase responsiveness, an arrangement was made in which other patients on the ward received the same number of tokens earned by the particular patient. The patient's job performance, self-care skills, and social behavior increased with the consequence sharing procedure. Other token programs have reported that sharing consequences with others often leads to higher levels of performance than when one earns the same consequences for oneself alone (Kazdin & Geesey, 1977; Wolf, Hanley, King, Lachowicz, & Giles, 1970).

Consequence sharing usually increases the reinforcement, prompting, and general concern of peers for the client. A more direct way of involving peers in the program is to have them administer reinforcers directly. For example, peers have been used in the Achievement Place program for predelinquents (Phillips, Phillips, Wolf, & Fixsen, 1973). A peer manager was utilized to administer or withdraw token reinforcers from peers based upon their room-cleaning behaviors. The manager assigned jobs and provided tokens or fines for performance. When the room was checked by the teaching parents, the manager earned or lost tokens based upon how well the task had been completed. The peer manager system of administering tokens led to higher levels of performance than did the ordinary token reinforcement contingencies administered by the teaching parents.

The use of consequence sharing and peer administration of consequences has been reported often in reinforcement programs in general aside from token economies (Kazdin, 1980). As a means of combating nonresponsiveness, these procedures have been infrequently studied. However, existing research suggests that involvement of peers can improve the efficacy of the contingencies.

Additional Program Variations and Treatments

Responsiveness to a token economy often is enhanced by the addition of other procedures to the program. These other procedures can range from mere variations of contingency manipulations to entirely different treatments. Of course, new procedures added to a token economy are assumed to provide a more effective procedure than the token economy or that new procedure alone. In many instances, this assumption is supported.

As an illustration of a relatively minor addition, many token economies utilize response cost or fines as part of the contingencies. Thus tokens are delivered for some behaviors (positive reinforcement) and withdrawn for other behaviors (punishment). Several programs have shown that the addition of response cost to a token reinforcement program adds to the effectiveness of the procedure. For example, Phillips et al. (1973) evaluated the individual and combined effects of token reinforcement and response cost in increasing knowledge of current events among predelinquent boys participating in a token economy. Consequences were provided for knowledge the boys demonstrated after watching television news. The combination of reinforcement and response cost was more effective than either procedure used alone. In several other programs, the addition of response cost to token reinforcement contingencies has enhanced performance (Baer et al. 1977; Walker, Hops, & Fiegenbaum, 1976). In some instances, response cost has led to behavior change among persons who previously had not responded or responded only minimally to token reinforcement (McLaughlin & Malaby, 1977).

It should be noted that the increased responsiveness appears to be due to the combination of response cost and token reinforcement, inasmuch as these procedures when used separately typically do not differ in efficacy (see Kazdin, 1977b).

Often entirely different treatment techniques are added to increase the efficacy of token economies. For example, Greenberg, Scott, Pisa and Friesen (1975) compared a token economy with a token economy combined with milieu treatment with psychiatric patients. The milieu treatment consisted of group-incentive contingencies designed to develop decision-making responsibilities and to maximize peers as a source of influence. The combined token economy–milieu procedure led to increased effectiveness (e.g., more days out of the hospital) relative to the token economy alone.

Occasionally, token economies have been combined with medication for psychiatric patients in an attempt to increase responsiveness to the contingencies. For example, McCreadie, Main, and Dunlop (1978) evaluated the effects of a token economy in altering behavior of chronic male psychiatric patients. Tokens were earned for self-care, social, and work behaviors. Introduction of antipsychotic medication (pimozide or chlorpromazine introduced in a crossover design) led to increases in token-earning behaviors. Improvements in the combined token reinforcement plus medication procedures were evident in social competence, irritability, and manifest psychosis. The results suggested that the addition of medication increased responsiveness to the contingencies.

Snyder and White (1979) reported the addition of self-instruction training to a reinforcement program for delinquent adolescents who had not responded. Training subjects to engage in self-verbalization (e.g., problem-solving skills, self-evaluation) and to apply these skills to daily activities led to reductions in truancy from class and impulsive behavior, and to increases in social and self-care behaviors. Thus the addition of self-instruction training to the reinforcement program enhanced performance. Whether self-instruction training alone would have had similar effects without the reinforcement program is not known.

General Comments

The above techniques indicate an extremely large range of conditions that can be varied to enhance responsiveness of persons to token economies. Thus when persons fail to respond to a program, this is frequently interpreted as reflecting unresolvable problems with the treatment technique. Token economies are multifaceted treatments because of the range of variables that can contribute to behavior change. The above discussion highlighted selected parameters of reinforcement, economic variables, peer influences, and the combinations of treatments. In many investigations, changes in only one of these areas has had marked effects on responsiveness and the conclusions that would be reached about a particular program or client. The fact that many variables can overcome initial unresponsiveness to the program does not mean that token economies do not "fail" in the many meanings of that term. However, the lack of responsiveness often can be readily controverted with changes in the contingencies. Treatment options such as those reviewed above need to be explored during a program if preliminary data suggest lack of responsiveness or insufficient change.

UNRESPONSIVENESS: SUMMARY AND CONCLUSIONS

Evidence suggests that patients occasionally do not respond to token reinforcement contingencies. It is difficult to discern a particular pattern, profile, or persons whose behaviors do not change. Token economies have been conducted with an extraordinarily wide range of treatment populations, age groups, and settings so programs are difficult to compare. Also, the manner in which token programs are implemented, the precise behaviors for a given population, and the rewards that are provided may vary and have implications for responsiveness of the participants.

The lack of responsiveness of some persons is difficult to evaluate for other reasons. In many token programs, patients or clients are included precisely because they have not responded to other forms of treatment. For example, Hofmeister, Scheckenbach, and Clayton (1979) utilized a token economy for chronic schizophrenic patients. The patients were selected in part because they failed to respond to a milieu program and evidenced a decline in social and adaptive behaviors. After a year of follow-up, 80 percent of the patients continued to remain in the community (i.e., no recidivism). Although it is tempting to refer to the other 20 percent as "failures" in some way, the initial selection of patients makes the percentages difficult to evaluate. Similarly, in a token economy for criminal offenders, Moran et al. (1977) reported that 35 percent of the sample were "failures" (i.e., recidivists and parole or probation violaters). This too is difficult to evaluate because the population was viewed as a high-risk group for future crime and the effects of the token program in altering the rate of recidivism that would otherwise have been evident are not known.

In general, it is difficult to evaluate lack of responsiveness of persons to a token economy. It is possible that a given percentage of persons who fail to respond to the program, by various definitions discussed earlier, might be cause for alarm or celebration. Without comparative data regarding the base rate of responsiveness of persons to alternative treatments or to no treatment, responsiveness to the token economy is difficult to evaluate.

Most program "failures" are discussed in terms of the lack of responsiveness of the patients or clients while the program is in effect. However, improving the behaviors of persons who initially have not responded to the program may not be the major issue for designing effective token economies. In fact, multiple procedures, reviewed earlier, are already available to improve responsiveness to a program while that program is in effect. The major criterion is whether the token economy can accomplish long-term treatment goals. The question for evaluating the "success" and "failure" of token economies is whether clinically important changes can be achieved that are sustained and that extend beyond the treatment setting. There is little question that the token economy is capable of achieving

--such changes (e.g., Bushell, 1978; Kirigin et al., 1979; Paul & Lentz, 1977) Whether marked, durable, and generalizable changes occur in most instances in which token economies are applied and the reasons for failures to achieve these changes await further investigation.

REFERENCES

Allen, D.J., & Magaro, P.A. (1971) Measures of change in token-economy programs. *Behaviour Research and Therapy,* **9,** 311–318.

Atthowe, J.M., Jr., & Krasner, L. (1968) Preliminary report on the application of contingent reinforcement procedures (token economy) on a "chronic" psychiatric ward. *Journal of Abnormal Psychology,* **73,** 37–43.

Ayllon, T., & Azrin, N.H. (1964) Reinforcement and instructions with mental patients. *Journal of the Experimental Analysis of Behavior,* **7,** 327–331.

Ayllon, T., & Azrin, N.H. (1965) The measurement and reinforcement of behavior of psychotics. *Journal of the Experimental Analysis of Behavior,* **8,** 356–383.

Ayllon, T., & Azrin, N.H. (1968a) Reinforcer sampling: A technique for increasing the behavior of mental patients. *Journal of Applied Behavior Analysis,* **1,** 13–20.

Ayllon, T., & Azrin, N.H. (1968b) *The token economy: A motivational system for therapy and rehabilitation.* New York: Appleton-Century-Crofts.

Ayllon, T., Garber, S., & Pisor, K. (1975) The elimination of discipline problems through a combined school–home motivation system. *Behavior Therapy,* **6,** 616–626.

Ayllon, T., Milan, M.A., Roberts, M.D., & McKee, J.M. (1979) *Correctional rehabilitation and management: A psychological approach.* New York: Wiley.

Baer, R., Ascione, F., & Casto, G. (1977) Relative efficacy of two token economy procedures for decreasing the disruptive classroom behavior of retarded children. *Journal of Abnormal Child Psychology,* **5,** 135–145.

Baker, R., Hall, J.N., Hutchinson, K., & Bridge, G. (1977) Symptom changes in chronic schizophrenic patients on a token economy: A controlled experiment. *British Journal of Psychiatry,* **131,** 381–393.

Bassett, J.E., & Blanchard, E.B. (1977) The effect of the absence of close supervision on the use of response cost in a prison token economy. *Journal of Applied Behavior Analysis,* **10,** 375–379.

Bassett, J.E., Blanchard, E.B., & Kosland, E. (1975) Applied behavior analysis in a penal setting: Targeting "free world" behaviors. *Behavior Therapy,* **6,** 639–648.

Birky, H.J., Chambliss, J.E., & Wasden, R. (1971) A comparison of residents discharged from a token economy and two traditional psychiatric programs. *Behavior Therapy,* **2,** 46–51.

Boren, J.J., & Colman, A.D. (1970) Some experiments on reinforcement principles within a psychiatric ward for delinquent soldiers. *Journal of Applied Behavior Analysis,* **3,** 29–37.

Bushell, D., Jr. (1978) An engineering approach to the elementary classroom: The Behavior Analysis Follow Through project. In A.C. Catania, & T.A. Brigham (Eds.), *Hand-*

book of applied behavior analysis: Social and instructional processes. New York: Irvington.

Bushell, D., Jr., Wrobel, P.A., & Michaelis, M.L. (1968) Applying "group" contingencies to the classroom study behavior of preschool children. *Journal of Applied Behavior Analysis,* **1,** 55–61.

Butler, R.J. (1979) An analysis of individual treatment on a token economy for chronic schizophrenic patients. *British Journal of Medical Psychology,* **52,** 235–242.

Choban, M.C., Cavior, N., & Bennett, P. (1974) *Effects of physical attractiveness of patients on outcome in a token economy.* Paper presented at the 82nd Annual Convention of the American Psychological Association, New Orleans, August.

Curran, J.P., Lentz, R.J., & Paul, G.L. (1973) Effectiveness of sampling-exposure procedures on facilities utilization by psychiatric hard-core chronic patients. *Journal of Behavior Therapy and Experimental Psychiatry,* **4,** 201–207.

Drabman, R.S., & Tucker, R.D. (1974) Why classroom token economies fail. *Journal of School Psychology,* **12,** 178–188.

Feingold, L., & Migler, B. (1972) The use of experimental dependency relationships as a motivating procedure on a token economy ward. In R.D. Rubin, H. Fensterheim, J.D. Henderson, & L.P. Ullmann (Eds.), *Advances in behavior therapy.* New York: Academic.

Fisher, E.B., Jr., Winkler, R.C., Krasner, L., Kagel, J., Battalio, R.C., & Basmann, R.L. (1978) Economic perspectives in behavior therapy: Complex interdependencies in token economies. *Behavior Therapy* (1978) **9,** 391–403.

Fullerton, D.T., Cayner, J.J., & McLaughlin-Reidel, T. (1978) Results of a token economy. *Archives of General Psychiatry,* **35,** 1451–1453.

Greenberg, D.J., Scott, S.B., Pisa, A., & Friesen, D.D. (1975) Beyond the token economy: A comparison of two contingency programs. *Journal of Consulting and Clinical Psychology,* **43,** 498–503.

Hall, J., & Baker, R. (1973) Token economy systems: Breakdown and control. *Behaviour Research and Therapy,* **11,** 253–263.

Hartmann, D.P., & Atkinson, C. (1973) Having your cake and eating it too: A note on some apparent contradictions between therapeutic achievements and design requirements in $N = 1$ studies. *Behavior Therapy,* **4,** 589–591.

Herbert, E.W., Pinkston, E.M., Hayden, M., Sajwaj, T.E., Pinkston, S., Cordua, G., & Jackson, C. (1973) Adverse effects of differential parental attention. *Journal of Applied Behavior Analysis,* **6,** 15–30.

Herman, S., & Tramontana, J. (1971) Instructions and group versus individual reinforcement in modifying disruptive group behavior. *Journal of Applied Behavior Analysis,* **4,** 113–119.

Hersen, M., Eisler, R.M., Smith, B.S., & Agras, W.S. (1972) A token reinforcement ward for young psychiatric patients. *American Journal of Psychiatry,* **129,** 142–147.

Hofmeister, J.F., Scheckenbach, A.F., & Clayton, S.H. (1979) A behavioral program for the treatment of chronic patients. *American Journal of Psychiatry,* **136,** 396–400.

Hung, D.W. (1977) Generalization of "curiosity" questioning behavior in autistic children. *Journal of Behavior Therapy and Experimental Psychiatry,* **8,** 237–245.

Hunt, J.G., Fitzhugh, L.C., & Fitzhugh, K.B. (1968) Teaching "exit-ward" patients appropriate personal appearance by using reinforcement techniques. *American Journal of Mental Deficiency,* **73,** 41–45.

Hunt, J.G., & Zimmerman, J. (1969) Stimulating productivity in a simulated sheltered workshop setting. *American Journal of Mental Deficiency,* **74,** 43–49.

Kagel, J.H., & Winkler, R.C. (1972) Behavioral economics: Areas of cooperative research between economics and applied behavior analysis. *Journal of Applied Behavior Analysis,* **5,** 335–342.

Kazdin, A.E. (1973) The failure of some patients to respond to token programs. *Journal of Behavior Therapy and Experimental Psychiatry,* **4,** 7–14.

Kazdin, A.E. (1977a) Assessing the clinical or applied significance of behavior change through social validation. *Behavior Modification,* **1,** 427–452.

Kazdin, A.E. (1977b) *The token economy: A review and evaluation.* New York: Plenum.

Kazdin, A.E. (1980) *Behavior modification in applied settings* (2nd ed.). Homewood, Ill: Dorsey.

Kazdin, A.E., & Geesey, S. (1977) Simultaneous-treatment design comparisons of the effects of earning reinforcers for one's peers versus for oneself. *Behavior Therapy,* **8,** 682–693.

Kazdin, A.E., & Geesey, S. (1980) Enhancing classroom attentiveness by preselection of back-up reinforcers in a token economy. *Behavior Modification,* **4,** 98–114.

Kazdin, A.E., & Mascitelli, S. (1980) The opportunity to earn oneself off a token system as a reinforcer for attentive behavior. *Behavior Therapy,* **11,** 68–78.

Kazdin, A.E., & Wilson, G.T. (1978) Criteria for evaluating psychotherapy. *Archives of General Psychiatry,* **35,** 407–416.

Kirigin, K.A., Wolf, M.M., Braukmann, C.J., Fixsen, D.L., & Phillips, E.L. (1979) Achievement Place: A preliminary outcome evaluation. In J.S. Stumphauzer (Ed.), *Progress in behavior therapy with delinquents.* Springfield, Ill.: Thomas.

Last, R., Ginor, M., Lowental, U., & Klein, H. (1978) A token economy in the framework of a hospital therapeutic community—practice and psychosocial implications. *Mental Health Society,* **5,** 200–214.

Liberman, R.P. (1968) A view of behavior modification projects in California. *Behaviour Research and Therapy,* **6,** 331–341.

Liberman, R.P. (1979) Social and political challenges to the development of behavioral programs in organizations. In P. Sjoden, S. Bates, & W.S. Dockens, III (Eds.), *Trends in behavior therapy.* New York: Academic.

Lloyd, K.E., & Garlington, W.K. (1968) Weekly variations in performance on a token economy psychiatric ward. *Behaviour Research and Therapy,* **6,** 407–410.

Logan, D.L., Kinsinger, J., Shelton, G., & Brown, J.M. (1971) The use of multiple reinforcers in a rehabilitation setting. *Mental Retardation,* **9,** 3–5.

McCreadie, R.G., Main, C.J., & Dunlop, R.A. (1978) Token economy, pimozide and chronic schizophrenia. *British Journal of Psychiatry,* **133,** 179–181.

McLaughlin, T.F., & Malaby, J.E. (1977) The comparative effects of token-reinforcement with and without a response cost contingency with special education children. *Educational Research Quarterly,* **2,** 34–41.

Melin, G.L., & Gotestam, K.G. (1973) A contingency management program on a drug-free unit for intravenous amphetamine addicts. *Journal of Behavior Therapy and Experimental Psychiatry,* **4,** 331–337.

Milby, J.B., Clarke, C., Charles, E., & Wilcutt, H.C. (1977) Token economy process variables: Effects of increasing and decreasing the critical range of savings. *Behavior Therapy,* **8,** 137–145.

Mishara, B.L. (1978) Geriatric patients who improve in token economy and general milieu treatment programs: A multivariate analysis. *Journal of Consulting and Clinical Psychology,* **46,** 1340–1348.

Moran, E.L., Kass, W.A., & Munz, D.C. (1977) In-program evaluation of a community correctional agency of high-risk offenders. *Corrective and Social Psychiatry,* **23,** 48–52.

Paul, G.L., & Lentz, R.J. (1977) *Psychosocial treatment of chronic mental patients: Milieu versus social-learning programs.* Cambridge, Mass.: Harvard.

Phillips, E.L., Phillips, E.A., Wolf, M.M., & Fixsen, D.L. (1973) Achievement Place: Development of the elected manager system. *Journal of Applied Behavior Analysis,* **6,** 541–561.

Rickard, H.C., Melvin, K.B., Creel, J., & Creel, L. (1973) The effects of bonus tokens upon productivity in a remedial classroom for behaviorally disturbed children. *Behavior Therapy,* **4,** 378–385.

Snyder, J.J., & White, M.J. (1979) The use of cognitive self-instruction in the treatment of behaviorally disturbed adolescents. *Behavior Therapy,* **10,** 227–235.

Sobell, L.C., Schaefer, H.H., Sobell, M.B., & Kremer, M.E. (1970) Food priming: A therapeutic tool to increase the percentage of meals bought by chronic mental patients. *Behaviour Research and Therapy,* **8,** 339–345.

Steffy, R.A. (1968) *Service applications: Psychotic adolescents and adults. Treatment of aggression.* Paper presented to American Psychological Association, San Francisco, September.

Strupp, H.H., & Hadley, S.W. (1977) A tripartite model of mental health and therapeutic outcomes. *American Psychologist,* **32,** 187–196.

Tyler, V.O., & Brown, G.D. (1968) Token reinforcement of academic performance with institutionalized delinquent boys. *Journal of Educational Psychology,* **59,** 164–168.

Walker, C.E., Hedberg, A., Clement, P.W., & Wright, L. (1981) *Clinical procedures for behavior therapy.* Englewood Cliffs, N.J.: Prentice-Hall.

Walker, H.M., Hops, H., & Fiegenbaum, E. (1976) Deviant classroom behavior as a function of combinations of social and token reinforcement and cost contingency. *Behavior Therapy,* **7,** 76–88.

Winkler, R.C. (1971a) Reinforcement schedules for individual patients in a token economy. *Behavior Therapy,* **2,** 534–537.

Winkler, R.C. (1971b) The relevance of economic theory and technology of token reinforcement systems. *Behaviour Research and Therapy,* **9,** 81–88.

Winkler, R.C. (1972) A theory of equilibrium in token economies. *Journal of Abnormal Psychology,* **79,** 169–173.

Winkler, R.C. (1973) An experimental analysis of economic balance, savings and wages in a token economy. *Behavior Therapy,* **4,** 22–40.

Wolf, M.M. (1978) Social validity: The case for subjective measurement or how applied behavior analysis is finding its heart. *Journal of Applied Behavior Analysis*, **11**, 203–214.

Wolf, M.M., Hanley, E.L., King, L.A., Lachowicz, J., & Giles, D.K. (1970) The timer-game: A variable interval contingency for the management of out-of-seat behavior. *Exceptional Children*, **37**, 113–117.

Yeaton, W.H., & Sechrest, L. (1981) Critical dimensions in the choice and maintenance of successful treatments: Strength, integrity, and effectiveness. *Journal of Consulting and Clinical Psychology.*, *49*, 156–167.

Zimmerman, E.H., Zimmerman, J., & Russell, C.D. (1969) Differential effects of token reinforcement on instruction-following behavior in retarded students instructed as a group. *Journal of Applied Behavior Analysis*, **2**, 101–112.

CHAPTER 19

Failure to Modify
Delinquent Behavior:
A Constructive Analysis

THEODORE W. LANE
JOHN D. BURCHARD

When the field of behavior modification and behavior therapy began to emerge in the mid-1960s there was considerable optimism with respect to its application towards the treatment of delinquents. Because the impulsive pursuit of external reinforcers seemed to maintain their antisocial behavior, it seemed logical that by rearranging the reinforcement contingencies delinquents could be taught a repertoire of socially acceptable skills that would enable them to adjust to the mainstream. Unfortunately, that optimism has been tarnished by 15 years of "blood, sweat, and tears" on the part of a multitude of people who have tried to modify the behavior of delinquents both in the institution and in the community. Although the verdict is not yet in, it would appear that we have achieved less success than failure.

This review will focus on the success or failure of the more traditional behavioral programs for delinquent youth. It will consist of three parts: behavioral programs in institutional settings, residential community-based settings, and nonresidential community-based settings. Each section will be followed by a discussion of ways to improve the success rate of these programs.

INSTITUTIONAL BEHAVIOR MODIFICATION PROGRAMS

With respect to institutional behavior modification programs with delinquents, most of the literature (and most of the programs that exist today) relates to programs involving a large number of residents (e.g., an entire cottage, unit, or cell block) as opposed to individual case studies.

The success or failure of institutional behavior modification programs depends upon how success or failure is defined. In this case two criteria were used: the direct effect (e.g., "Was there any desirable behavior change in response to the intervention procedure?") and the generalization effect (e.g., "Did the behavioral change persist in the noninstitutional environment?"). In reviewing the track record of institutional behavior modification programs with delinquents, it appears that the first criteria has been met with considerable success but that the second has resulted in failure.

There is considerable evidence that indicates that when contingencies are manipulated in accordance with social learning principles positive behavioral change has occurred. In a review of 20 studies involving the use of behavior modification in institutions for juvenile delinquents, Davidson and Seidman (1974) found that in each case a substantial positive change in behavior appeared to be associated with a corresponding change in reinforcement and/or punishment contingencies. Numerous subsequent demonstrations of such functional relationships have also taken place involving both delinquents and criminals (cf. Bassett, Blanchard, & Koshland, 1975; Burchard, & Harig, 1976; McNamara & Andrasik, 1977; Milan & McKee, 1976).

One of the most convincing demonstrations of the effects of contingent reinforcement in an institutional or correctional setting is provided by Hobbs and Holt (1976). The subjects were 125 adjudicated 12- to 15-year-old boys residing in the Alabama Boys Industrial School. Focusing on social behaviors, following rules and instructions, completing chores, and avoiding antisocial behaviors, the authors utilized a multiple baseline design across three different cottages to evaluate the effect of a token economy program. In this particular program paper money served as tokens that could be exchanged for commissary items, off-campus trips, passes home, and final release from the institution. In general, the results demonstrated the power of the token economy system: Each time contingencies were applied to a different cottage there was a marked improvement in specific behaviors of boys in that cottage.

Although not all institutional behavior modification programs for delinquents have been able to demonstrate success in terms of a direct short-term effect, it appears that in most cases where this has not occurred the problem has been because of an inability or unwillingness to administer the appropriate contingencies, not because the contingencies themselves were ineffective. For example, in a training school in Connecticut a project failed because of a lack of cooperation with a commissioner, a business director, and the institution staff rather than because of ineffective contingencies (Dean & Reppucci, 1974). It raises the question as to whether it would be more productive for behavior modification advocates to focus more attention on the behavior of administrators and staff rather than to focus most of their attention on the behavior of the residents.

It seems clear that behavior modification procedures can be used successfully to improve behavior within institutional settings, however, it is important to ask whether the delinquent or criminal who participates in such a program is able to make a better adjustment to the community. The question is not easily answered. There are little follow-up data that document the recidivism rates of the graduates of behavior modification programs and in those instances where such data do exist, there usually hasn't been adequate methodological safeguards (e.g., random assignment) in order to preclude nonspecific variables from being responsible for the outcome.

At least five studies have been conducted that compare the outcome of behavior modification and nonbehavior modification programs. Taken as a whole the picture is not very promising.

First, a comparison of the programmed learning–token economy program that Cohen and his associates administered at the National Training School in Washington, D.C. with the traditional institutional program suggested less recidivism at the one- and two-year follow-up periods, but equal recidivism at the end of Year three (Cohen & Filipczak, 1971). Second, a comparison of a cell block token economy program with three control groups showed that 28 percent of the token economy group had committed a criminal offense compared to 47 percent in the occupational training group, 32 percent in the state trade school group, and 37 percent in the regular Draper program group (Jenkins, Witherspoon, DeVine, DeZalera, Muller, Barton, & McKee, 1974).

Two additional studies were conducted by the California Youth Authority in the 1970s analyzing the effects of contingency contracting and token economy programs in institutional settings. In the first study, 452 youths who participated in a contingency contracting program obtained a recidivism rate that was almost 10 percent higher than that for 329 youths at a comparable "control" institution (Ferdun, Webb, Lockard, & Mahan, 1972). In the second study in which youth were randomly assigned to either a behavior modification or a transactional analysis program, 32 percent of both groups had been returned to an institution 12 months after parole release and, at 24 months, failure rates in both groups had increased to 48 percent (Jesness, 1975a).

In the final outcome study, 25 juvenile females who went through a token economy–contingency management program obtained a significantly higher recidivism rate at 12-month follow-up than 25 matched control subjects who did not (Ross & McKay, 1976).

Based upon all the studies cited above, the evidence indicates that behavior modification programs can be used to change institutional behavior but that those changes will not necessarily generalize to improved behavior back in the community. If so, the issue then is whether improved institutional behavior is all that can be obtained. Are there ways to change the behavior modification programs that occur in institutions in order to achieve better generalization and a better adjustment in the community? One area where change might be warranted involves the heavy emphasis on the development of compliance behavior through external reinforcement. Clearly, in a totally controlled restricted environment inmates or residents will clean their rooms or go to school in order to obtain rewarding privileges or material goods. But in so doing has the individual learned very much about how to solve a problem, make a difficult decision, or formulate short-term objectives? Probably not. The program administrators have made it very clear that if one does A, one will get B. And if one does it, it is doubtful that one will attribute the change to something for which one was responsible.

In essence, many behavior modification programs seem to foster dependency on contingencies that are all too unrealistic and artificial. It would seem possible to develop a program that shapes decision making, self-control, and problem solving. Rather than present the individual with a reinforcement menu for compliance behavior, individuals could be taught to develop their own day-to-day objectives and they could be afforded with opportunities to reinforce their own behaviors. Although such a cognitive form of behavior modification is more often employed in community-based programs (see Kendall & Hollon, 1979), it also has potential for behavioral programs within institutional settings.

COMMUNITY-BASED RESIDENTIAL BEHAVIOR MODIFICATION PROGRAMS

Investigations regarding behaviorally oriented, community-based residential programs have been limited largely to group home placements in general, and to teaching-family homes in particular. These studies include over 60 publications relating primarily to the process variables of the programs in addition to three outcome studies of the teaching-family model (cf. Braukmann & Fixsen, 1975; Burchard & Harig, 1976; Burchard & Lane, in press; Davidson & Seidman, 1974; Kirigin, Braukmann, Atwater, & Wolf, 1982).

In terms of process research, numerous studies have demonstrated the effectiveness of contingency management procedures in modifying a wide variety of behaviors. These demonstrations have taken place in teaching-family group homes as well as in group homes modeled after the teaching-family model. More specifically, effectively modified behaviors include classroom behaviors (Bailey, Wolf, & Phillips, 1970; Kirigin, Phillips, Timbers, Fixsen, & Wolf, 1975), interview skills (Braukmann, Maloney, Fixsen, Phillips, & Wolf, 1974), negotiation skills (Kifer, Lewis, Green, & Phillips, 1974), communication skills (Bailey, Timbers, Phillips, & Wolf, 1971; Maloney, Harper, Braukmann, Fixsen, Phillips, & Wolf, 1976), vocational skills (Ayala, Minkin, Phillips, Fixsen, & Wolf, 1973), and skills to prepare youths for encounters with police officers (Werner, Minkin, Minkin, Fixsen, Phillips, & Wolf, 1975). In addition to studies relating to youth behavior, several investigations have dealt with the behavior of teaching-parents. These include papers focusing on staff training (Maloney, Phillips, Fixsen, & Wolf, 1975), the certification of teaching-parents (Braukmann, Fixsen, Kirigin, Phillips, Phillips, & Wolf, 1975), and the training of staff in specific social behaviors that are preferred by youths (Willner, Braukmann, Kirigin, Fixsen, Phillips, & Wolf, 1977).

In terms of outcome, Kirigin, Wolf, Braukmann, Fixsen, and Phillips (1979) presented data that compared 26 youths who had participated in Achievement Place with 37 youths who had not. In one comparison, 18 Achievement Place youths were compared with 19 youths who attended an institution (Boys School). Although random assignment was not achieved for this comparison, the institutionalization rate for the Achievement Place youths during the first follow-up year (17 percent) and the second follow-up year (22 percent) was approximately one half the rate for the Boys School youth for each follow-up year (42 and 47 percent, respectively).

In a second comparison, 8 Achievement Place youths were compared with 18 control group youths who were randomly not selected into the program. Similar results were reported: The two-year rate of postselection institutionalization for the Achievement Place youths (12 and 12 percent, respectively) was less than one half that for the nonAchievement Place youths (44 and 56 percent, respectively).

Jones and his associates (Howard, 1979; Jones, 1978, 1979; Jones & Weinrott, 1977; Weinrott, 1979) have presented preliminary findings stemming from a five-year longitudinal study comparing 27 teaching-family group homes with 25 nonteaching-family comparison group homes. According to Burchard and Lane (in press), preliminary findings based on more than 300 youths in each type of group home are as follows:

1.   About 40 percent of the youths in both teaching-family and nonteaching-family samples failed to complete their programs.

2.   The grade point averages of the youths tend to stabilize during the program year in the teaching-family sample but not in the nonteaching-family sample.

3.   In terms of recidivism, there is a reduction in offense rates from preprogram to postprogram periods: 67.5 percent for the teaching-family youths and 62 percent for the nonteaching-family youths.

4.   On the basis of self-report data, there appears to have been less consumption of postprogram services by teaching-family youths than by nonteaching-family youths (e.g., training schools, institutions, parole and probation services).

5.   Community consumers tend to rate the teaching-family programs more favorably than they rate the nonteaching-family programs.

6.   The teaching-family programs cost about one third less than the nonteaching-family programs.

A final outcome study was reported by Davidson and Wolfred (1977). In this case, 42 youths who had participated in a residential program that incorporated many components of the teaching-family model were compared with 42 youths who had not. Although random assignment was not achieved, youths were matched on the basis of sex, age, grade in school, presenting problem, and date of contact with state or juvenile authorities. At nine-month follow-up the control subjects displayed a significantly higher rate of school attendance relative to the experimental subjects, whereas the experimental subjects displayed a significantly higher rate of juvenile contacts, criminal contacts, and institutional placements relative to the control subjects. In terms of precomparisons to postcomparisons for the experimental subjects, the only significant change was an increase in institutional placements.

Although each of the above outcome studies must be interpreted cautiously due to the experimental designs utilized, they have provided the clearest picture to date. Based on their review, Burchard and Lane (in press) present the following conclusions in this regard:

1.   Community-based, group home residential behavior modification programs appear more effective than institutional programs for troubled youth (Kirigin et. al., 1979).

2.   Community-based, group home residential behavior modification programs appear equally effective but less expensive than other community-based group home programs for troubled youth (Jones, 1979).

3.   Community-based, group home residential behavior modification programs appear less effective than other community-based, nongroup home residential alternatives (Davidson & Wolfred, 1977).

The published literature reviewed above suggests that through the systematic modification of reinforcement and punishment contingencies, specific behavior change can be effected and that this change results in comparatively positive long-term impact. Clinical experience, however, suggests that these results are often difficult to achieve. The remainder of this section will present and discuss some of the difficulties encountered in Vermont over the past two and one half years following its decision to implement the teaching-family model with new group homes for predelinquent and delinquent youths.

Since Vermont closed its only institution for delinquent youths two and one half years ago, six new group homes have been established, all of which involved the teaching-family model. Whereas four of these group homes were developed approximately two and one half years ago, two have been in operation for only the past six months. Additionally, an elaborate and expensive teaching-parent training center was developed to provide Vermont with a pool of trained and certified teaching-parents. Initially, however, the group homes were staffed with teaching-parents trained and certified at Boys Town. Although Vermont's experience with the teaching-family model has been somewhat limited, the following data allow for a preliminary evaluation:

1.   Compared with other group homes in Vermont which cost between $14,000 and $16,000 per youth per year, the teaching-family group homes cost between $13,000 and $15,000 per youth per year.

2.   One and one half years after the development of the first four teaching-family group homes, only one still existed.

3.   Out of the eight teaching-parent couples hired during the last two and one half years, only two are still employed today; three couples were terminated due to the closing of their respective group homes.

4.   Two thirds of the teaching-family group homes encountered community resistance (two of the teaching-family homes were established in al-

ready existing group homes which enhanced their success in this regard); of the initial four group homes, only one was established in the town where it was originally planned (in other words, 75 percent of these group homes were unable to gain entrance into the designated communities).

5.   In terms of utilization, only one of the four initial group homes consistently operated at full capacity (i.e., six youths); it is impossible to assess the utilization of the remaining two group homes inasmuch as they have only been in operation for six months.

In addition to the above data, Vermont has had experience with one other group home that closely resembles the teaching-family model. The Residential Learning Center (RLC) is a community-based group home for eight predelinquent and delinquent males in Burlington, Vermont. It was developed in 1970 after the teaching-family model for six male residents by faculty of the Psychology Department at the University of Vermont. As a "teaching-family" group home, the RLC had a tenure of only four years. During that time, three different "teaching-parent" couples were utilized (average tenure of 1.33 years per couple). One of these couples (and possibly another) was divorced stemming to some extent from their experience as "teaching-parents." Because of this less than positive experience with "teaching-parents" the RLC adopted a more typical staffing pattern where each staff member worked 40 hours per week. This change clearly had an impact on staff tenure: Three of the four current full-time staff members have been employed for over five years (average tenure = 4.1 years). This does not necessarily suggest that the current staffing pattern is preferable to the use of teaching-parents, however, inasmuch as a number of problems arise from such a pattern (e.g., interstaff communication becomes more difficult). However, it does suggest that the selection, training, and ongoing support of the teaching-parents is a critical factor in their effective utilization.

Thus Vermont's experience with the teaching-family model of group home management has not been very successful. Although these data do not allow for a controlled evaluation of the teaching-family model, they do suggest areas that deserve attention clinically and in terms of experimental investigation. Two of these areas are discussed below: community acceptance and the selection, training, and supervision or support of teaching-parents.

The issue of community acceptance is not unique to behaviorally oriented group home programs. However, it is an issue that cannot be ignored and behavioral technology can clearly be utilized in this regard. At least two problems need to be addressed: how to smoothly gain entrance into a given community, and how to effectively maintain community support once a group home has been established.

In terms of entrance into the community, Vermont has tended to use a tactic involving silence. In other words, group homes are put in place without first educating the community, speaking to neighbors, dealing with zoning problems, and so on, hoping that by the time the group home becomes public it will have established a positive track record (e.g., lack of theft in the neighborhood) and, therefore, be accepted. The problem with this approach is that it often does not work and it creates a distrust of the juvenile services system that is difficult to overcome.

In contrast to the above approach, it seems that efforts should be applied at two levels, including broad educational programs in addition to the effective utilization of teaching-parents at the local level. The selection and training of teaching-parents in this regard is obviously critical. Regardless of how effective the teaching-parents may be in terms of the implementation of behavioral programs with troubled youth, if they are unable to effectively interact with neighbors and influential community leaders they will in all probability be out of a job.

Once a group home has been established, community acceptance has to be maintained. Important relationships to be developed and maintained should include people from the immediate neighborhood, the press, social services, the courts, and the schools. Although the approach taken by the teaching-parents may need to be different in each of these areas, interpersonal skills are essential across all of them. An example from the experience of the RLC illustrates a potentially serious situation that could have been easily avoided. In 1978, a number of neighbors made complaints about the RLC to the legislature, among others. One effect of their complaints involved repeated visits to the group home by the Department of Labor and Industry, each followed by a list of fire code infractions. Following the implementation of numerous interventions (e.g., an open-house for neighbors, adding a neighbor to the Board of Directors, etc.), it became clear that the problem involved the outside appearance of the group home (e.g., too many parked cars on the lawn, poor paint job on the house, etc.). Obviously, this problem should not have occurred in the first place. However, had the group home staff maintained close positive relationships with the neighbors, they would have been more likely to express their concerns directly to the group home rather than complain to others.

In addition to poor community acceptance, it appears that Vermont's less than positive success rate with the teaching-family model has been a function of inadequate teaching-parent effectiveness. Reflecting on this experience generates two issues that are discussed below: generalization from Boys Town to other communities, and the importance of individual differences among teaching-parents.

Generalization from the institutional atmosphere at Boys Town to the clearly community-based situation in Vermont was problematical. Although there was a network of teaching-parents in Vermont from which a teaching-parent couple could obtain support and/or consultation, the situation was clearly different from Boys Town where there are numerous teaching-parents in the same community. The issue relates to the intensity and content of training required by the teaching-parents given their subsequent exit from the training site (e.g., Boys Town). This is an issue that needs to be addressed empirically; however, it seems probable that training will need to be broader and more intense for teaching-parents who will be functioning relatively independently.

Ideally, the implementation of behavioral technology should effect change regardless of the individual involved in its implementation. Recently, however, researchers have been finding that this is not the case (e.g., Alexander, Barton, Schiavo, & Parsons, 1976; Jesness, 1975b). It seems clear in Vermont, for example, that the major variable in the success or failure of a given teaching-family group home involves significant interpersonal characteristics of the teaching-parents. A more advanced technology is needed with which to select teaching-parents who will have the highest probability of success in addition to the identification of specific skills that the teaching-parents can be taught.

COMMUNITY-BASED NONRESIDENTIAL BEHAVIOR MODIFICATION PROGRAMS

Community-based nonresidential behavioral programs can be divided into the following categories: family, school, employment, probation, and mediated behavior modification programs.

Family Behavior Modification Programs

Alexander, Parsons, and their associates have published a series of studies relating to a systems-behavioral approach to family intervention (see Alexander & Barton, 1980; Burchard & Lane, in press). The intervention program is designed to modify the interaction patterns of families with delinquent adolescents so as to approximate the patterns demonstrated by families without delinquent adolescents. Their findings, as reviewed by Burchard and Lane (in press), include the following:

1.   There are specific family interaction patterns that distinguish families with delinquent youth from families without delinquent youth (Alexander, 1973).
2.   Short-term behavioral intervention can produce relevant changes in family interaction patterns across family members (Parsons & Alexander, 1973).
3.   Changes in family interaction are related to reduced recidivism rates in comparison to alternative treatments or no treatment for periods of up to 18 months (Alexander & Parsons, 1973).
4.   "Relationship" and "structuring" skills demonstrated by therapists are positively related to completion of the treatment program; further, completion of the treatment program is related to reduced recidivism, suggesting a relationship between therapist skills and recidivism (Alexander et al., 1976).
5.   Although long-term effectiveness has not been demonstrated for treated adolescents (i.e., over two years follow-up), there does seem to be an indication that siblings of treated youth demonstrate lower recidivism than sib-

lings in families receiving either alternative treatments or no treatment at three-year follow-up (Klein, Alexander, & Parsons, 1977).

Weathers and Liberman (1975) reported the use of a similar treatment program with a group of 28 families with delinquent adolescents. Unfortunately, the effectiveness of treatment was impossible to evaluate due to a dropout rate of 79 percent.

Barnard, Gant, Kuehn, Jones, and Christophersen (1980) reported the use of an intensive home-based behavioral treatment program with the families of juvenile probationers. Results indicated that the experimental youths demonstrated significantly greater reductions in the rate of reported offenses than control youths from preintervention to follow-up (i.e., 89 percent total reduction in offense rate versus 34 percent total reduction in offense rate). However, no differences were demonstrated between groups in terms of the other outcome measures (i.e., readjudications, detentions, and out-of-home placements).

Patterson and his associates at the Oregon Social Learning Project have treated over 100 families with out-of-control children between 3 and 12 years of age (cf. Burchard & Harig, 1976; Patterson, 1979; Patterson & Fleischman, 1979). The goal of their treatment program involved the reduction of reciprocally coercive behavior among all family members through a focus on family interaction and effective behavior management skills. In addition to numerous demonstrations of significant changes in family process (see Patterson & Fleischman, 1979), outcome evaluations have demonstrated significant reductions in the aversive behavior of specific children in terms of behavioral observations as well as parent ratings for up to 12 months.

According to Burchard and Lane (in press), the literature to date in terms of family-behavioral intervention suggests the following:

1.   Family-behavioral intervention can successfully produce positive changes in family interaction.

2.   Positive changes in family interaction are related to significant reductions in aversive child behavior, postintervention offense rates on the part of delinquent adolescents, and sibling recidivism in terms of reported offenses.

3.   Family-behavioral intervention appears to be more effective than client-centered family treatment, psychodynamic family treatment, traditional probation services, and no treatment in effecting significant reductions in postintervention offense rates.

4.   Differences between family-behavioral intervention and alternative interventions (or no treatment) have yet to be demonstrated in terms of measures other than reported offense rates (i.e., subsequent criminal offenses, readjudications, detentions, or out-of-home placements).

Although these conclusions are encouraging, there are several areas of concern that need to be addressed in regard to the success or failure of family-behavioral interventions with this population. First, it is clear that families are often unwilling to participate in the intervention and, if they do agree, often drop out of treatment prematurely. Although research has been performed that relates to this issue (cf. Alexander et. al., 1976; Fleischman, 1979), more work is clearly needed. An additional concern relates to the ability of these interventions to reduce the likelihood of institutionalization, detention, readjudication, or other negative outcomes in addition to their apparent effectiveness in reducing subsequent offense rates. The relevance of the treatment becomes questionable to the extent that these areas are not involved, especially given the potential for bias in the reporting of offenses by persons in the community who are often aware that a given youth is receiving treatment. The extent to which family-behavioral intervention is a "treatment of choice" for hardcore delinquents and/or older delinquent adolescents is also unclear. Most of the research to date has been performed with younger status offenders. Fortunately, data are currently being collected by Alexander and his associates in Utah relating to an evaluation of their treatment program with hardcore delinquents (e.g., murder and rape). To date, 43 families have received treatment and have demonstrated a recidivism rate of 32 to 35 percent compared to a baserate of 70 to 75 percent in Utah (Barton, 1980).

Finally, therapist skills and/or attributes are associated with the success or failure of family-behavioral intervention (Alexander et. al., 1976). This finding has been noted earlier in this chapter in relation to other behavioral interventions and will be noted again. Clearly, behavioral clinicians or researchers will have to become more attuned to these variables in their treatment and/or research in order for the field to make the advances required in the development of effective treatment programs for delinquent youth.

School Behavior Modification Programs

Filipczak and his associates have presented data relating to over 600 troubled students who have participated in the Preparation through Responsive Educational Program (PREP) (cf. Burchard & Lane, in press; Filipczak, Friedman, & Reese, 1979). The PREP program can be divided into two components: academic training in reading, English, and mathematics, social or interpersonal skills training, and family skills training for students, and training for teachers and other staff that enables them to conduct all phases of the program. Based on their review of this extensive body of research, Burchard and Lane (in press) presented the following summary:

1. Although PREP is able to effect limited to moderate changes in the academic behavior of the youth it serves, these benefits appear to largely disappear within four years.

2. There is little, if any, evidence of long-term change in nonacademic areas (including delinquency) as measured by self-report, parent-report, and official court records.

3.   There is no difference in subsequent dropout rate between PREP and nonPREP students.

Heaton, Safer, Allen, Spinnato, and Prumo (1976) reported the results of a contingency management program established in a junior high school for eighth graders. The 14 students participating in the program were compared with 32 similar students from two other junior high schools. Results indicated significant differences in favor of the students in the contingency management program for the program year in terms of leaving school, absenteeism, discipline referrals, and suspensions. Significant differences were also obtained for the reading section of the WRAT, although no differences between groups were demonstrated for the spelling or arithmetic sections of the test. No follow-up data were reported.

Stuart and his associates have reported a number of studies that have involved the use of behavioral contracts with predelinquent youth in school settings (Stuart, Jayaratne, & Tripodi, 1976; Stuart & Tripodi, 1973; Stuart, Tripodi, Jayaratne, & Camburn, 1976). One study (Stuart & Tripodi, 1973) compared the relative effectiveness of treatment prescribed to terminate in 15, 45, or 90 days. Results indicated that length of treatment was not related to outcome. In the same study, treatment subjects were compared to a post hoc untreated control group. Although significant differences were found in favor of the treatment students for attendance and grades in school, no differences were found in terms of tardiness or court contacts. Inasmuch as the control group consisted of treatment refusals, these data have to be interpreted with caution.

In subsequent reports, 87 predelinquents were compared to randomly assigned controls on various parent- and teacher-report measures as well as school grades, attendance, and subsequent court contacts (Stuart, Jayaratne, & Tripodi, 1976; Stuart, Tripodi, Jayaratne, & Camburn, 1976). In terms of parent and teacher ratings, statistically significant differences in favor of the experimental students were obtained for 50 percent of the measures (i.e., 9 out of 18 ratings). No differences were found in terms of grades, attendance, or court contacts.

Inschool behavioral delinquency programs to date have involved primarily junior high school students and have been preventive in nature. According to Burchard and Lane (in press), they suggest the following conclusions:

1.   These programs can effect short-term changes in academic performance, in-school negative behavior, and problem home behavior.

2.   There is little, if any, support relating to the long-term maintenance of these effects.

3.   There is no indication that these programs enhance the probability that students who participate in them will remain in school longer than students who do not.

4.   There is little, if any, indication that these programs reduce the probability of subsequent court contacts for students who participate in them.

Clearly, the goal of reduced crime and/or school attrition has not yet been met. These results are discouraging and raise the question of cost-effectiveness. Possibly, schools should focus on behavior management objectives with the goal of providing a positive school climate rather than delinquency prevention. Additionally, in terms of delinquency prevention, the direction to take would appear to be the provision of family-behavioral intervention. For dropouts, intervention might be best utilized through the provision of G.E.D. tutoring and job placement (see following section). To the extent that these inschool delinquency prevention programs continue, however, a change in designated behaviors seems indicated. Thus, for example, students should be involved in setting personal objectives, self-evaluation, problem solving, and other more internally controlled, cognitive activities rather than being the passive participants of externally controlled, isolated classrooms (i.e., out of the mainstream).

Employment-Related Behavior Modification Programs

Mills and Walter (1979) provided a "behavioral-employment" intervention program for 53 delinquent youth aged 14 to 17 years. These youth were considered the court's most serious offenders with from one to eight prior convictions (mean = 3.85), including a significant number of felony offenses. Intervention consisted of recruitment and behavioral training of local employers, establishment of contingency contracts between delinquents and the project director, shaping delinquents in preemployment behavior, and placing delinquents on jobs. Out of 76 referred delinquents, 23 were assigned to a control group. Unfortunately, the extent to which the group assignment was random is unclear.

Their results indicated that (1) 90.6 percent of the experimental subjects had no further arrests and were not institutionalized at follow-up of approximately one year, whereas 30.4 percent of the control subjects had no further arrests and 47.8 percent avoided institutionalization; (2) 85.7 percent of the experimental subjects who were initially in school were still in school at follow-up versus 33.3 percent of the controls; and (3) 100 percent of the experimental subjects obtained jobs and 34 percent were still on jobs at follow-up (mean tenure of 13.6 weeks), whereas 39 percent of the control subjects obtained jobs and 0 percent were still on jobs at follow-up (mean tenure of 2.7 weeks).

Odell (1974) presented data evaluating the relative effectiveness of four intervention programs, including traditional casework, intensive casework, high school equivalency diploma (G.E.D.) program plus job placement, and high school equivalency diploma program alone. Program participants included 60 high school dropouts, ages 15 years and 10 months to 16 years and 3 months, with serious and persistent patterns of juvenile offenses (mean of 10.7 prior offenses). The 60 participants were randomly assigned to one of the four intervention programs resulting in 15 subjects per group. Intervention in each group took place during a three-month period.

Results indicated that over the nine months postintervention period, the two intervention programs including G.E.D. training performed significantly better than the two casework groups in terms of enrollment in school training programs or employment, mean weekly income for those working, and recidivism (i.e., adjudicated offenses). In addition, the data indicated that a high school equivalency program coupled with a job placement program is more effective than a high school equivalency program unsupported by a job placement program.

The value of an employment-related emphasis in treatment programs for delinquents is given additional support by the 15-year follow-up data reported by Shore and Massimo (1979). Although the authors did not describe their intervention program in behavioral terms, the treatment was skills oriented and assisted the participants in becoming more proficient in the area of employment. Twenty males ranging in age between 15 and 17 years who had been suspended from school (or had dropped out of school) and had a history of antisocial behavior were randomly assigned to experimental conditions which included a treatment program and a no-treatment control group. Treatment included preemployment counseling, job placement, and employment counseling focusing on interpersonal problems.

Although the outcome data were not evaluated statistically, results clearly favored the treatment group in terms of enhanced academic achievement and employment history, and reduced subsequent arrests and institutionalizations.

Davidson and Robinson (1975) developed and evaluated a treatment program for 125 chronic male delinquents who were being considered for long-term institutional placements. On the average, participating youths were 16 years old, were functioning at the 5.3 grade level, had been on probation 2.6 years, and had committed an average of 2.95 offenses per year while on probation. Treatment consisted of working 15 hours per week in the community on various work projects in addition to 15 hours per week of individualized programmed instruction. The program utilized a contingency point system focusing on the areas of work performance, academic performance, and appropriate verbalizations. On the average it took nine weeks to complete the program.

Follow-up data were presented on 117 subjects consisting of 95 graduates of the program and 22 nongraduates. Eighteen months after the graduates had completed the program, 29 percent were in school, 35 percent were employed, and 17 percent were in correctional institutions. For the nongraduates, 0 percent were in school, 9 percent were employed, and 53 percent were in correctional institutions. The authors also reported a postprogram arrest rate of .46 per year for the 95 graduates.

These four program evaluations suggest that interventions which stress job placement and provide training in relevant job-related skills (e.g., academic skills, interpersonal skills, problem-solving skills, etc.) are effective in terms of reducing subsequent criminal behavior and of enhancing subsequent employability. These results are all the more impressive given the relative frequency and severity of the delinquency engaged in by the populations served by these programs. However, given the less than adequate research methodology utilized in the majority of these studies, further research of an evaluative outcome nature is required.

Obviously, employment-related interventions will not be successful with all delinquent youth. First of all, there are restrictions placed on who can work (e.g., age of the youth) and what type of work can be performed by a given youth as a function of the child labor laws. Given these restrictions, however, there are other issues that relate to the success or failure of work-related interventions. One of the most critical variables in this regard relates to the availability of income independent of any job offered through the intervention program. Many delinquent youths have developed quite successful means of obtaining income through both legal and illegal channels. Whether the youth with alternative means of income will participate in the employment-related intervention will depend in part on the perceived status of the potential job, the increment in income level obtainable, and the extent to which other demands are made of him or her. For example, many delinquent youths in the author's experience do not respond well to excessive external controls. Depending on the relative level of restriction of a given program, a youth may respond to controls (e.g., contingencies) by not participating in the program or by engaging in other countercontrol behaviors (cf. Mahoney, 1979).

The extent to which jobs are available in a given community also relates to the success or failure of employment-related intervention programs, especially now that funds are becoming less available with which to provide subsidized employment. This issue is related to the selection of employers to participate in the program. Although some employers are motivated to provide jobs for this population, others only hire these youths when no other youths are available for employment. Thus it seems clear that the success of a job program will depend largely on the extent to which the program has support from a group of understanding and influential local employers. This group of employers would be instrumental in developing local support for the program, locating potential job placements, and providing jobs for youth within their own businesses.

Finally, the interpersonal skills of the employer as well as the program director will undoubtedly have an impact on the relative success or failure of the program. The program director, for instance, will have to be able to effectively communicate and negotiate with both the youth participants and the employer participants, whereas the employer will have to be able to effectively train, supervise, and give feedback to the youth employee.

Probation Behavior Modification Programs

Jesness (1975b) presented the results of the Cooperative Behavior Demonstration Project which involved training and evaluating probation officers in the use of contingency contracting procedures. The project included 90 probation officers and 412 youths (mean age of 15.1 years). A triadic implementation model was utilized whereby project staff first trained 33 supervisory personnel who were, in turn, responsible for training 90 field officers from 16 probation units located in eight adjacent counties. Each probation officer received 40 hours of basic classroom training and an average of 22 hours of consultation in contingency contracting from staff throughout the duration of the project.

The outcome of the project as reviewed by Burchard and Lane (in press) included the following findings:

1.   Among the 412 total project probationers, 1,248 behavioral problems were identified and marked for change; contingency contracts were written on 22 percent of those behaviors; by the end of the project, 59 percent of the problem behaviors involving contingency contracts were in remission, whereas 43 percent of the problem behaviors not involving contingency contracts were in remission.

2.   There was no statistically significant difference between probationers who were involved in contingency contracting and project probationers who were not, in terms of six-month recidivism rates (i.e., illegal behavior recorded in the probation office files).

3.   There was a significant relationship between a probation officer's expressed regard for a client and six-month recidivism rate: Project probationers for whom officers expressed above average positive regard had lower recidivism rates (11 percent violators) than project probationers whose officers expressed below average regard (33 percent violators).

4.   There was no significant difference in the six-month recidivism rates of the first 194 experimental subjects and a control group of probationers that were not part of the project (both 18 percent violators).

Burkhart, Behles, and Stumphauzer (1976) trained nine probation officers in the use of behavior modification procedures during a six-week training program. The nine probation officers were compared with nine probation officers who did not receive training in terms of their knowledge of behavioral principles, attitudes toward behavior modification, and their behavioral competence in the use of behavioral methods. Following the training program, the only significant difference between groups related to the officers' behavioral competency in the application of behavioral methods, with the trained officers demonstrating more competence. Six-month follow-up data indicated that a majority of the trained probation officers were still utilizing the behavioral skills learned during the training program (Stumphauzer, Candelora, & Venema, 1976). Unfortunately, no data were provided with which to evaluate the impact of the training program on probationer behavior.

These data are not very encouraging. Although there is some support for the ability of behavioral contracts to effect short-term change in specific behavior, the only variable associated with reduced recidivism according to the findings of Jesness (1975b) involved the probationer officers' expressed positive regard for their clients. Further, these data point out the difficulty involved in maintaining consistent implementation of behavioral methods by probation officers. In this regard, however, it may be that probation officers with high positive regard for their clients who utilize contingency contracts in a consistent fashion may have more impact on their clients in terms of recidivism than probation officers with high positive regard who do not use contingency contracts. Given the seemingly inconsistent utilization of behavioral contracting by the probation officers in the Jesness (1975b) study, it seems fair to assume that the data are inconclusive. At any rate, it is clear that the success or failure of probation behavior modification programs is associated with the attributes of the probation officer and the extent to which the probation officer implements the procedures in a consistent fashion. Also clear is the need for additional research of an evaluative outcome nature that continues to assess variables relating to the characteristics of probation officers.

Behavior Modification Programs with Natural Mediators

Tharp and Wetzel (1969) developed a system in which a small number of consultants supervised a larger number of natural mediators who, in turn, administered contingency contracts with a still larger number of youths. Because of the lack of a control group the relative effectiveness of the program could not be determined.

O'Donnell, Lydgate, and Fo (1979) presented follow-up data on 334 youths who had participated in the Buddy System and 218 youth who had not on the basis of random assignment. The Buddy System was modeled after the Tharp and Wetzel triadic model of intervention, the one difference being the use of indigenous nonprofessionals as the natural mediators. Results indicated that (1) experimental subjects with prior offenses demonstrated a significantly lower arrest rate than control subjects with prior offenses (i.e., 56 versus 78 percent); (2) experimental subjects without prior offenses demonstrated a significantly greater arrest rate than control subjects without prior offenses (i.e., 22.5 versus 16.4 percent); and (3) experimental subjects without prior offenses who participated in the Buddy System for more than one year demonstrated a significantly greater arrest rate than experimental subjects without prior offenses who participated for only one year (i.e., 34.4 versus 18.8 percent). Thus the Buddy System is relatively effective with youth who have been arrested for major offenses in the preceding year. However, the arrest rate demonstrated by these youths is still unacceptably high (i.e., 56 percent). Further, the Buddy System is detrimental for youths without prior arrest records involving major offenses.

Summary of Community-Based, Nonresidential Behavior Modification Programs

The success or failure of these community-based, nonresidential behavior modification programs are a function of at least four variables: the characteristics of the service provider, the characteristics of the youth participant, the characteristics of the intervention program, and the interaction of the above three variables. The research literature as well as clinical experience consistently demonstrates the importance of the interpersonal skills of the service provider in the successful implementation of behavioral procedures or programs. It is apparent that behavioral researchers will need to more adequately address this area in order for the field to advance beyond its current status.

In terms of the characteristics of the youth participant, at least two variables have been identified that relate to the success or failure of the intervention program: the age of the youth, and the extent to which the youth has been involved in delinquent behavior. The only treatment approach in the literature to date which has shown merit for the younger predelinquent youth has been family-behavioral intervention. Otherwise, the younger youth and/or the youth without prior delinquent behavior is associated with program failure. Clearly, this is a discouraging finding and further research is critically needed.

The characteristics of the intervention also relate to the success or failure of behavioral treatment programs. In this regard, inschool educational programs have met without success in terms of delinquency prevention and/or rehabilitation. On the other hand, family-behavioral intervention, employment-related intervention, and mediated intervention have each demonstrated promise with some delinquent youths.

Although it is possible to isolate each of the above-mentioned variables, their interaction is critical to the success or failure of a given intervention program. Although more data are needed, it is possible to make a few suggestions in this regard based on the available literature. First, it appears that the treatment of choice for the younger, predelinquent, or status offender should involve family-behavioral intervention with a focus on the modification of inappropriate family interactions. Interventions with this population have met with failure in both school-based and mediator-based programs. Although family-behavioral intervention may be successful with older delinquent adolescents, the treatment of choice for this population seems to involve a combination of G.E.D. tutoring and job placement utilizing a triadic model of implementation. This intervention approach has been shown to be successful across a number of studies with serious juvenile offenders in terms of reduced subsequent offense rates as well as enhanced employability. Finally, a warm, humorous, and direct service provider who effectively demonstrates a high positive regard for the youth being served appears critical to the success of any intervention program for delinquent adolescents.

SUMMARY AND CONCLUSIONS

This review has focused on the success versus failure of behavior modification programs in reducing the frequency of delinquent behavior. The approach taken in this regard involved a review of the published literature with the goal of identifying variables associated with successful as well as unsuccessful outcomes in terms of delinquency prevention and/or rehabilitation. To the extent the goal has been achieved, this review will, it is hoped, provide direction to both clinicians and researchers in their respective endeavors with this population.

On the basis of this review, the effectiveness of these programs depends largely upon the setting in which they are applied, the specific behaviors that are being modified, and the characteristics of both service providers and clients. In regard to the setting in which the intervention program is implemented, there appears to be an association between success in terms of recidivism and the extent to which the program is implemented in a nonrestrictive environment. It is more difficult to teach community-adaptation skills to a person within a very restricted, artificial environment. To the extent that delinquents and criminals are locked up in institutions, the rationale for doing so should be to punish and/or to temporarily protect the community, not to rehabilitate. Very restrictive environments make rehabilitation less likely to happen. Inasmuch as there is also an association between cost and level of restrictiveness (i.e., the more restrictive the program, the higher the cost), it seems critical to expend further efforts towards the goal of developing effective community-based, nonrestrictive intervention programs.

The situation is somewhat more complex with regard to the choice of specific behaviors. However, a number of directions have been identified with which to enhance the success of intervention. For example, it appears critical in family-behavioral intervention to modify inappropriate family interaction in addition to the development of behavioral contracts. In general, specifying behaviors that will enhance the extent to which the youth demonstrates internal control will in all likelihood be associated with successful outcome.

Finally, as has been noted throughout this review, the characteristics of the service provider and client are important variables in terms of the relative success versus failure of behavioral intervention programs with delinquent youths. Fortunately, there has been a recent interest in this area and relevant data are becoming available. Clearly, however, further research is necessary before it will be possible to effectively select and/or train service providers in order to enhance to the full extent the probability of obtaining a successful outcome.

REFERENCES

Alexander, J.F. (1973) Defensive and supportive communications in normal and deviant families. *Journal of Consulting and Clinical Psychology,* **40,** 223–231.

Alexander, J.F., & Barton, C. (1980) Systems-behavioral intervention with delinquent families: Clinical, methodological, and conceptual considerations. In J.P. Vincent (Ed.), *Advances in family intervention, assessment and theory* (Vol. 1). Greenwich, Conn.: JAI Press.

Alexander, J.F., Barton, C., Schiavo, R.S., & Parsons, B.V. (1976) Systems-behavioral intervention with families of delinquents: Therapist characteristics, family behavior, and outcome. *Journal of Consulting and Clinical Psychology,* **44,** 656–664.

Alexander, J.F., & Parsons, B.V. (1973) Short-term behavioral intervention with delinquent families: Impact on family process and recidivism. *Journal of Abnormal Psychology,* **81,** 219–225.

Ayala, H.E., Minkin, N., Phillips, E.L., Fixsen, D.L., & Wolf, M.M. (1973) Achievement Place: The training and analysis of vocational behaviors. Paper presented at the meeting of the American Psychological Association.

Bailey, J.S., Wolf, M.M., & Phillips, E.L. (1970) Home-based reinforcement and the modification of pre-delinquents' classroom behavior. *Journal of Applied Behavior Analysis,* **3,** 223–233.

Bailey, J.S., Timbers, G.D., Phillips, E.L., & Wolf, M.M. (1971) Modification of articulation errors of pre-delinquents by their peers. *Journal of Applied Behavior Analysis,* **4,** 265–281.

Barnard, J.D., Gant, B.L., Kuehn, F.E., Jones, H.H., & Christophersen, E.R. (1980) *Home-based treatment of the juvenile probationer.* Manuscript submitted for publication.

Barton, C. (1980) Personal communication. University of Utah, Department of Psychology, Salt Lake City, Utah, 84112.

Bassett, J.E., Blanchard, E.B., & Koshland, E. (1975) Applied behavior analysis in a penal setting: Targeting "free world" behaviors. *Behavior Therapy,* **6,** 639–648.

Braukmann, C.J., & Fixsen, D.L. (1975) Behavior modification with delinquents. In M. Hersen, R.M. Eisler, & P.M. Miller (Eds.), *Progress in behavior modification* (Vol. 1). New York: Academic.

Braukmann, C.J., Maloney, D.M., Fixsen, D.L., Phillips, E.L., & Wolf, M.M. (1974) An analysis of a selection interview training package for predelinquents at Achievement Place. *Criminal Justice and Behavior,* **1,** 30–42.

Braukmann, C.J., Fixsen, D.L., Kirigin, K.A., Phillips, E.A., Phillips, E.L., & Wolf, M.M. (1975) Achievement Place: The training and certification of teaching-parents. In W.S. Wood (Ed.), *Issues in evaluating behavior modification.* Champaign, Ill.: Research Press.

Burchard, J.D., & Harig, P.T. (1976) Behavior modification and juvenile delinquency. In H. Leitenberg (Ed.), *Handbook of behavior modification and behavior therapy.* Englewood Cliffs, N.J.: Prentice-Hall.

Burchard, J.D., & Lane, T.W. (in press) Crime and delinquency. In A. Bellack, M. Hersen, & A. Kazdin (Eds.), *International handbook of behavior modification and therapy* (Vol. 2). New York: Plenum.

Burkhart, B.R., Behles, M.W., & Stumphauzer, J.S. (1976) Training juvenile probation officers in behavior modification: Knowledge, attitude change, or behavioral competence? *Behavior Therapy,* **7,** 47–53.

Cohen, H.L., & Filipczak, J.A. (1971) *A new learning environment.* San Francisco: Jossey-Bass.

Davidson, W.S., & Robinson, M.J. (1975) Community psychology and behavior modification: A community-based program for the prevention of delinquency. *Journal of Corrective Psychiatry and Behavior Therapy,* **21,** 1–12.

Davidson, W.S., & Seidman, E. (1974) Studies of behavior modification and juvenile delinquency: A review, methodological critique, and social perspective. *Psychological Bulletin,* **81,** 998–1011.

Davidson, W.S., & Wolfred, T.R. (1977) Evaluation of a community-based behavior modification program for prevention of delinquency: The failure of success. *Community Mental Health Journal,* **13,** 296–306.

Dean, C.W., & Reppucci, N.D. (1974) Juvenile correctional institutions. In D. Glaser (Ed.), *Handbook of criminology.* Chicago: Rand McNally.

Ferdun, G.S., Webb, M.P., Lockard, H.R., & Mahan, J. (1972) *Compensatory education 1971–1972.* Sacramento: California Youth Authority.

Filipczak, J., Friedman, R.M., & Reese, S.C., (1979) PREP: Educational programming to prevent juvenile problems. In J.S. Stumphauzer (Ed.), *Progress in behavior therapy with delinquents.* Springfield, Ill.: Thomas.

Fleischman, M.J. (1979) Using parenting salaries to control attrition and cooperation in therapy. *Behavior Therapy,* **10,** 111–116.

Heaton, R.C., Safer, D.J., Allen, R.P., Spinnato, N.C., & Prumo, F.M. (1976) A motivational environment for behaviorally deviant junior high school students. *Journal of Abnormal Child Psychology,* **4,** 263–275.

Hobbs, T.R., & Holt, N.M. (1976) The effects of token reinforcement on the behavior of delinquents in cottage settings. *Journal of Applied Behavior Analysis,* **9,** 189–198.

Howard, J.R. (1979) *Consumer evaluations of teaching family group homes for delinquents.* Paper presented at the meeting of American Psychological Association, New York.

Jenkins, W.O., Witherspoon, A.D., DeVine, M.D., DeZalera, E.K., Muller, J.B., Barton, M.C., & McKee, J.M. (1974) *The post-prison analysis of criminal behavior and longitudinal follow-up evaluation of institutional treatment.* Montgomery, Ala.: Rehabilitation Research Foundation.

Jesness, C.F. (1975a) Comparative effectiveness of behavior modification and transactional analysis programs for delinquents. *Journal of Consulting and Clinical Psychology,* **43,** 758–799.

Jesness, C.F. (1975b) *The cooperative behavior demonstration project: Submitted as the final report to the office of criminal justice planning.* Sacramento: California Youth Authority.

Jones, R.R. (1978) *First findings from the national evaluation of the teaching family model.* Paper presented at the meeting of the National Teaching Family Association, Boys Town, Nebraska, October 25–27.

Jones, R.R. (1979) *Therapeutic effects of the teaching family group home model.* Paper presented at the meeting of American Psychological Association, New York, September.

Jones, R.R., & Weinrott, N.R. (1977) *Comparability between pre-existing samples of the community-based programs for delinquent youth.* Paper presented at the meeting of the Western Psychological Association, Seattle, April.

Kendall, P.C., & Hollon, S.D. (Eds.). (1979) *Cognitive-behavioral interventions: Theory, research, and procedures.* New York: Academic.

Kifer, R.E., Lewis, M.A., Green, D.R., & Phillips, E.L. (1974) Training pre-delinquent youths and their parents to negotiate conflict situations. *Journal of Applied Behavior Analysis,* **7,** 357–364.

Kirigin, K.A., Braukmann, C.J., Atwater, J., & Wolf, M.M. (1982) An evaluation of a Teaching-Family (Achievement Place) group homes for Juvenile offenders. *Journal of Applied Behavior Analysis*, **15**, 1–76.

Kirigin, K.A., Phillips, E.L., Timbers, G.D., Fixsen, D.L., & Wolf, M.M. (1975) Achievement Place: The modification of academic behavior problems of youths in a group home setting. In B.C. Etzel, J.M. LeBlanc, & D.M. Baer (Eds.), *New developments in behavioral research: Theory, method and application.* Trenton, N.J.: Lawrence Erlbaum Associates.

Kirigin, K.A., Wolf, M.M., Braukmann, C.J., Fixsen, D.L., & Phillips, E.L. (1979)

Achievement Place: A preliminary outcome evaluation. In J.S. Stumphauzer (Ed.), *Progress in behavior therapy with delinquents.* Springfield, Ill.: Thomas.

Klein, N.C., Alexander, J.F., & Parsons, B.V. (1977) Impact of family systems intervention on recidivism and sibling delinquency: A model of primary prevention and program evaluation. *Journal of Consulting and Clinical Psychology,* **45,** 469–474.

Mahoney, M.J. (1979) Cognitive issues in the treatment of delinquency. In J.S. Stumphauzer (Ed.), *Progress in behavior therapy with delinquents.* Springfield, Ill.: Thomas.

Maloney, D.M., Phillips, E.L., Fixsen, D.L., & Wolf, M.M. (1975) Training techniques for staff in group homes for juvenile offenders: An analysis. *Criminal Justice and Behavior,* **2,** 195–216.

Maloney, D.M., Harper, T.M., Braukmann, C.J., Fixsen, D.L., Phillips, E.L., & Wolf, M.M. (1976) Teaching conversation skills to predelinquent girls. *Journal of Applied Behavior Analysis,* **9,** 371.

McNamara, J.R., & Andrasik, S. (1977) Systematic program change: Its effects on resident behavior in a forensic psychiatry institution. *Journal of Behavior Therapy and Experimental Psychiatry,* **8,** 19–23.

Milan, M.A., & McKee, J.M. (1976) The cellblock token economy: Token reinforcement procedures in a maximum security correctional institution for adult male felons. *Journal of Applied Behavior Analysis,* **9,** 254–275.

Mills, C.M., & Walter, T.L. (1979) Reducing juvenile delinquency: A behavioral-employment intervention. In J.S. Stumphauzer (Ed.), *Progress in behavior therapy with delinquents.* Springfield, Ill.: Thomas.

Odell, B.N. (1974) Accelerating entry into the opportunity structure: A sociologically-based treatment for delinquent youth. *Sociology and Social Research,* **58,** 312–317.

O'Donnell, C.R., Lydgate, T., & Fo, W.S.O. (1979) The Buddy System: Review and follow-up. *Child Behavior Therapy,* **1,** 161–169.

Parsons, B.V., & Alexander, J.F. (1973) Short-term family intervention: A therapy outcome study. *Journal of Consulting and Clinical Psychology,* **41,** 195–201.

Patterson, G.R. (1979) Treatment for children with conduct problems: A review of outcome studies. In S. Feshback, & A. Fraczek (Eds.), *Aggression and behavior change: Biological and social processes.* New York: Praeger.

Patterson, G.R., & Fleischman, M.J. (1979) Maintenance of treatment effects: Some considerations concerning family systems and follow-up data. *Behavior Therapy,* **10,** 168–185.

Ross, R.R., & McKay, H.B. (1976) A study of institutional treatment programs. *International Journal of Offender Therapy and Comparative Criminology,* **20,** 165–173.

Shore, M.F., & Massimo, J.L. (1979) Fifteen years after treatment: A follow-up study of comprehensive vocationally oriented psychotherapy. *American Journal of Orthopsychiatry,* **49,** 240–245.

Stuart, R.B., Jayaratne, S., & Tripodi, T. (1976) Changing adolescent deviant behavior through reprogramming the behavior of parents and teachers: An experimental evaluation. *Canadian Journal of Behavioral Science,* **8,** 132–144.

Stuart, R.B. & Tripodi, T. (1973) Experimental evaluation of three time-constrained behavioral treatments for predelinquents and delinquents. In R.D. Rubin, J.P. Brady, & J.D. Henderson (Eds.), *Advances in behavior therapy* (Vol. 4). New York: Academic.

Stuart, R.B., Tripodi, T., Jayaratne, S., & Camburn, D. (1976) An experiment in social engineering in serving the families of predelinquents. *Journal of Abnormal Child Psychology,* **4,** 243–261.

Stumphauzer, J.S., Candelora, K., & Venema, H.B. (1976) A follow-up of probation officers trained in behavior modification. *Behavior Therapy,* **7,** 713–715.

Tharp, R.G., & Wetzel, R.J. (1969) *Behavior modification in the natural environment.* New York: Academic.

Weathers, L., & Liberman, R.P. (1975) Contingency contracting with families of delinquent adolescents. *Behavior Therapy,* **6,** 356–366.

Weinrott, N.R. (1979) *Assessing the cost effectiveness of the teaching family programs.* Paper presented at the meeting of the American Psychological Association, New York.

Werner, J.S., Minkin, N., Minkin, B.L., Fixsen, D.L., Phillips, E.L., & Wolf, M.M. (1975) Intervention package: An analysis to prepare juvenile delinquents for encounters with police officers. *Criminal Justice and Behavior,* **2,** 55–83.

Willner, A.G., Braukmann, C.J., Kirigin, K.A., Fixsen, D.L., Phillips, E.L., & Wolf, M.M. (1977) The training and validation of youth-preferred social behaviors of child-care workers. *Journal of Applied Behavior Analysis,* **10,** 219–230.

CHAPTER 20

Failures in Behavioral Marital Therapy

ROBERT PAUL LIBERMAN
EUGENIE G. WHEELER
JULIE M. KUEHNEL

Success and failure in marital therapy are particularly difficult to determine, inasmuch as the criteria for defining a satisfactory outcome are multifaceted and conditional. The sophisticated behavioral marital therapist no longer seeks objective behavioral changes in a dyad as the sole criterion of outcome. Multimodal or multidimensional change—including affects, attitudes, and attributions; sexual intimacy; communication patterns and their attendant levels of satisfaction; family life and impact on children; leisure and recreational activities; even biophysiological status—is now the "name of the therapy game." Certainly, remaining married as opposed to obtaining a separation or divorce cannot be viewed, in isolation, as a measure of successful outcome in our modern world where individual fulfillment and mobility are so highly prized.

In Table 20.1 is an outline of three dimensions by which success in marital therapy might be measured. It is evident that subjective satisfaction with the marriage has priority over measurable overt changes. In fact, just as is the case with successful parent training in child management, a clinical intervention that positively reframes and improves the values and attributions of a couple toward their marriage can be considered a "success" even in the absence of demonstrable behavioral change.

This three-dimensional organization of outcome in marital therapy is obviously simplistic as it does not take into account important criteria such as impact on children and changes in self-esteem and individualistic fulfillment in other arenas of life. If, at the end of marital therapy, a couple separates and one partner interprets this outcome as wise, necessary, and satisfactory whereas the other depressively views it as rejection and failure, how should the therapy be evaluated? Thus the multimodal response of each spouse to the outcome of marital therapy

This chapter was prepared with the support of NIMH grant MH 30911-04 (Mental Health Clinical Research Center for the Study of Schizophrenia) and NIHR grant G008006802 (Rehabilitation Research-Training Center in Mental Illness).

Table 20.1.   Outcome Criteria for Determining Success or Failure in Marital Therapy

Marital Status	Satisfaction with Marital Status	Desirable Behavioral Change	Outcome
Remain married	Satisfied	Changes occurred	
Separated	Satisfied	No changes occurred	Success
Separated	Satisfied	Changes occurred	
Remain married	Satisfied	No changes occurred	
Remain married	Dissatisfied	Changes occurred	Questionable
Separated	Dissatisfied	Changes occurred	
Remain married	Dissatisfied	No changes occurred	Failure
Separated	Dissatisfied	No changes occurred	

is as important as the response of the couple as a dyad. A further complexity in developing a unitary conceptualization of success in marital therapy derives from the fact that the husband, the wife, and the therapist have their own set of goals at the outset of therapy and their own views and experiences of success at the time of termination.

Before writing this chapter, the authors polled leading practitioner-researchers in the field of behavioral marital therapy regarding their views of outcome. All agreed that separation or divorce alone would not reflect failure and that even therapy dropouts might represent a "healthy" or adaptive response to the interventions used. One expert stated that "achieving behavioral change which is satisfactory to the couple while failing to achieve attitudinal and meaningful change should be counted a failure." The example given was a wife who complied with her husband's requests to improve household maintenance. This change may have satisfied him, but in so doing, she reinforced her "traditional" wifely role as homemaker and sacrificed her individualism. Most of the experts indicated that behavioral marital therapy, by hastening the clarification of the positive and negative features of the relationship and the degree of difficulty in changing the negative features, might accelerate separation and divorce decisions to the potential benefit of the spouses.

Outcomes in the behavioral treatment of phobic disorders cannot be considered successful when increases in approach behavior and exposure to feared situations occur in the absence of reduction or elimination of subjectively experienced anxiety. Similarly, the outcome of marital therapy, when overt behaviors and communication patterns change without concomitant satisfaction with the changes, cannot be viewed as success.

In this chapter, we will define failure in behavioral marital therapy as a lack of demonstrable improvements in desired relationship patterns and interactions together with a lack of meaningful rise in marital satisfaction. Employing this combined criterion, case studies of behavioral marital therapy with 36 couples have yielded cumulative failure rates of only five percent where failure is defined as both lack of objective changes in desired areas and lack of improved satisfaction with the relationship (Greer & O'Zurilla, 1975). Experimental studies of behavioral marital therapy reported in the past five years have further documented the cumulative results of uncontrolled case studies with about 90 percent of couples showing significant improvements in their relationship as measured by both self-reported marital satisfaction as well as more direct observations of marital interaction (Liberman, Levine, Wheeler, Sanders, & Wallace, 1976; Jacobson & Margolin, 1979). This failure rate was echoed by the educated guesses proffered by the experts polled by the authors based upon a sample of over 400 couples treated.

Inasmuch as the research literature has not amassed large enough samples to permit analyses of correlates or predictors of failure in behavioral marital therapy, we will focus our discussion of failure around clinical cases that each of us has treated. It is hoped that the speculative and inferential links we have drawn from our clinical experiences may contribute heuristically to future research that will more conclusively identify patterns and predictors of failure and ways of reducing them.

NONCOMPLIANCE BY ONE SPOUSE WITH THERAPEUTIC ASSIGNMENTS REINFORCED BY THE MARTYR ROLE

Mrs. J. was being seen for several sessions of individual behavior therapy for her compulsive eating and self-induced vomiting problems, associated with depression about her weight. When it became apparent that she was experiencing frustrations in her relationship with her husband, we decided that some improvements in this area would be helpful. Her husband agreed to come in for six sessions to work on their relationship. Her husband was very involved in his work and his relationships at work. He commuted over 100 miles per day, leaving home at 7:30 in the morning and often not returning until 8:00 or later in the evening. They had two children, ages 8 and 10.

In the initial interviews Mr. J. stated that he was committed to the marriage and was fairly happy in the relationship. He explained that his long hours at work enabled him to relax and socialize with his associates. Mrs. J. was angry and frustrated with his coming home late and at different hours while she waited with dinner and handled the children alone. They both expressed a need for more physical affection from one another. During the late evenings and weekends they spent little time together alone and rarely communicated. Often, her efforts to reach out and talk were met with withdrawal by her husband. Expressions of anger or resentment by the wife were met with pouting on her husband's part.

The goals for marital therapy were to increase positive reciprocity, to increase each partner's ability to express feelings and ask for changes in the relationship, to improve their listening skills, and to increase their recreation time together. This was to be done through practice during the sessions and homework assignments. Although the husband expressed agreement and cooperation during the sessions, he routinely did not complete homework assignments and would come into the sessions playing the role of the naughty little boy who hadn't done his homework. This further reinforced his wife's feelings that she had little priority in his life. When she expressed these feelings during the session he charmingly agreed that this must be true or he would have had the time to do his assignments. Getting Mrs. J. to express her anger in a direct way led to silent withdrawal by her husband.

When the "payoff" for him of pouting and withdrawing was brought up, he acknowledged that it gave him a lot of power in the relationship and was a very effective way of punishing his wife. He also sabotaged structured exercises on communication during sessions. During one session, when they were learning to make requests of each other, they were instructed to stay away from requests with a high emotional charge. At his turn, he requested that his wife stop her binge eating; this statement devastated his wife. He apologetically said that her binge eating was the only thing he wanted her to change.

Their relationship was not progressing and it was apparent that the therapy was being used by the husband to act out towards his wife in a passive-aggressive manner. When confronted with the interpretation that his refusal to meaningfully participate in the therapy was helping to maintain his wife's problems, he acknowledged that he could see that. When asked what the payoff for him was of keeping his wife "sick," he responded that it made him the "good but long-suffering husband." In the eyes of his and her parents, he became a "saint."

This is an example where behavioral marital therapy was ineffective in improving a relationship. In fact the therapy was actually manipulated by the husband into a vehicle for acting out his passive-aggressive role and maintaining his identity as a martyr in the relationship. Paradoxical instructions and other types of strategic interventions might have been useful in altering this husband's defeatism. The therapist's approach, instead, was to terminate the couple sessions and continue working with the wife alone on her gaining assertiveness with her husband and establishing alternative outlets, relationships, and activities that did not require her husband's cooperation. With gradually increasing independence, the wife gained more control over her symptoms and the marriage also improved.

COVERT INTENTION FOR SEPARATION SABOTAGES THERAPY

Mr. and Mrs. M. had been married for 10 years and came for counseling initially because of problems with their teenage daughter. After five sessions, Mrs. M. said that they would like to work on marital concerns and Mr. M. concurred. Mrs. M. had three major complaints regarding the marriage:

Lack of sexual activity because of husband's poor performance.
Lack of initiative by her husband for planning family and recreational activities.
Lack of emotional supportiveness and responsiveness from her husband.

Mr. M. agreed that there were sexual problems although he was less concerned about them than his wife. She was very unhappy about their lack of sexual activity and even made veiled threats that she might not be willing to sustain their relationship in its present state for much longer. Mr. M. agreed to begin sexual therapy for what was diagnosed as secondary impotence. His major complaint in the marriage was her incessant criticism of him, but he down-played his complaint by saying he was generally happy with the relationship.

Therapy began with work aimed at improving communication skills and positive reciprocity through behavioral rehearsal and structured homework assignments using methods described in the *Handbook of Marital Therapy* (Liberman, Wheeler, de Visser, Kuehnel, & Kuehnel, 1980). Mr. and Mrs. M. also began a series of sensate focus exercises at home for the sexual problem.

The homework assignments were done sporadically, accompanied by a variety of excuses and explanations by the couple for their not having completed the assignments. They would agree on a specific assignment, but then fail to carry it out. Mrs. M. complained that her husband hadn't put a priority on the sexual and communication exercises. The therapist adopted and modeled a "shaping attitude," reinforcing and prompting Mrs. M. to, in turn, positively acknowledge her husband's efforts.

Regarding the other exercises, Mrs. M. complained that the only time they got done was when she initiated the practice at home. She pointed out that her husband's failure to complete his assignments reflected his lack of commitment to the marriage. He denied that the assignments were unimportant to him, and blamed his lack of follow-through on his being too tired, too busy, or too preoccupied with problems at work or with his daughter. Mr. M. finally agreed to initiate more exercises and the therapist again coached Mrs. M. to reinforce his efforts rather than to criticize his inadequacies. However, she was unable to shift to positive acknowledgements for his efforts and they limped along for several weeks.

It became apparent that Mr. M.'s passivity was being reinforced by his wife's emotional reactions in a classic coercive interaction pattern. He obtained his power in the relationship and expressed his anger by withholding behaviors that were important to his wife. The therapist decided to focus on helping Mr. M. become more assertive and direct in expressing his unhappiness and anger. He was instructed to monitor instances when he felt annoyed or hurt during the week. Unfortunately, he reported he never felt that way. He was then prompted to express his annoyed or hurt feelings during the sessions when his wife criticized or threatened him indirectly. He was able to do this with some laboriousness. The therapist actively coached Mrs. M. to reinforce her husband's fledgling expressions of annoyance during the sessions, but she found this difficult.

It was later revealed that Mrs. M. would verbally abuse Mr. M. for his fledgling efforts at assertiveness after the therapy sessions at home. The therapist's repeated remonstrations on the harmful effects of Mrs. M.'s criticism did not have much impact. Changes in her husband, Mrs. M. averred, were not occurring fast enough. It also became clear that Mrs. M. had a "hidden agenda" to terminate the marriage. Her participation in marital therapy enabled her to partially quell guilt she was experiencing about dissolving the relationship, inasmuch as it "proved" he was unable to change. When the hidden agenda is divorce, marital therapy will likely fail regardless of therapeutic strategy. To minimize unproductive focusing on marital improvement and to switch such couples more appropriately toward divorce, counseling requires an initial assessment that includes the motivation of each partner. Even a simple 10-point scale of "commitment to this marriage" can be revealing at the start of the treatment. Tapping underlying motivation should be done individually to protect a spouse who has high commitment from the emotional shock of hearing about a partner who declares low commitment. Assessing motivation separately also makes honest responses more likely. Once obtained, these motivational indicators can be used by the therapist to skillfully steer the therapy toward more realistic goals.

An example of the way in which intent to terminate a marriage can masquerade as a plea for marital therapy was a husband who, in his individual session for initial evaluation, explained that he had no intention of staying married. However, he wanted to be sure that his wife was involved in some type of therapy when he left her so she would not fall apart and he wouldn't feel guilty. This information was helpful to the therapist who was able to use the couple sessions to buffer the trauma of an impending separation and to redefine the relationship to permit the partners to work collaboratively for the good of their children.

MARITAL THERAPY COMES TOO LATE

Failure can occur when marital therapy is introduced too late. For example, Barbara wrote to her former marital therapist, "Our marriage had gone past the point of no return—the point at which counseling would have helped." Her husband, Joe, had fallen in love with another woman while he was traveling on his job. Barbara could have forgiven him and was willing to try again; however, Joe was unwilling to give up his new love. An outside affair can produce a situation where the partner who is reluctant to involve himself or herself in the therapy "plays games" with marriage counseling. Therapists must distinguish between lip service and genuine expressions of interest in marital therapy. This can be done by scheduling individual sessions and by confronting partners early with the realistic limitations of therapy.

MARITAL THERAPY COMES TOO SOON

An extramarital liaison does not necessarily spell failure. After the ground rules prohibiting affairs were explained to Mr. and Mrs. S. in a conjoint session, Mr. S. requested an appointment to be seen individually. He told the therapist that he was involved sexually with his secretary. He felt he would be unable to participate fully, honestly, or comfortably in marriage counseling until he could end this affair. He knew his limitations in resisting temptation, so he decided to fire his secretary as the only way he felt he could end their relationship. The therapy was postponed for three months, much to Mrs. S.'s distress and bafflement, inasmuch as no satisfactory explanation for the delay was ever made to her. At the end of the three-month period, a course of marital therapy was undertaken and was satisfactorily completed three months after that.

Also in the case of Mr. and Mrs. X., marriage counseling was introduced too early. It would have been easy to "write them off" inasmuch as they had been married for 48 years and neither was very motivated to change his or her pattern of constant bickering. It might well have seemed too late rather than precipitous, especially when Mrs. X. kept reiterating that, "It's too late after all these years. There's too much garbage over the dam."

The issues seemed banal. They involved Mr. X. eating too many sweets, Mrs. X's backseat driving, his not opening the car door for her, and her nagging. Some modification of these behaviors through training in basic communication and reinforcement skills seemed a reasonable goal. Although current favorable attitudes about aging precluded seeing their advanced years as a major detriment in the prognosis, Mr. & Mrs. X had been at each other almost daily for nearly 50 years.

Progress was painfully slow. They withdrew from therapy and went back to their mutually coercive pattern of interaction. It wasn't until a crisis occurred two and one half years later that they became truly motivated for therapy that aimed at their learning new ways of interacting. Mr. X.'s gambling had not been perceived as a major issue by the couple or by the therapist, but when he became deeply in debt and stood to lose their security, he finally recognized that he was addicted. He subsequently joined the self-help group, Gamblers Anonymous, and triumphantly reported to the marital therapist the positive impact this program was having on their marriage. He explained concepts learned in his group, such as taking responsibility for oneself and not trying to change the other person. These concepts had fallen on deaf ears when the therapist had tried to communicate them during their earlier course of therapy.

Readiness for therapy is not always easy to assess or anticipate. It may or may not follow crises or "divine discontent." About all that is certain is that it cannot be measured in years of marriage, duration of the problem, or the age of the partners. To reduce failure in marital therapy, the types of interventions have to be focused by the timing and precipitants of the call for help. It behooves the therapist to help the couple choose their goals for therapy based upon their motivations—overt and covert—and their marital and individual life-span, developmental phases. The goals of a couple suffering from the "empty nest syndrome" should be different than the goals of a couple coping with retirement.

WHEN ONLY ONE PARTNER WILL PARTICIPATE

There are, of course, many situations where only one partner will seek help, the other partner being totally unready. Often the willing client will give up at that point. A skillful therapist will never take the reluctant partner's refusal as final and will continue treatment with the willing partner, whether he or she calls it marital therapy or individual therapy, pending the possibility of conjoint sessions. If conjoint sessions are never achieved and the partner who has received treatment has grown, decides to leave his or her spouse, and has no regrets about his or her decision to terminate the marriage, is this success or failure? Suppose, on the other hand, one partner never comes in, but the other gets involved in therapy that is totally focused on marital communication. This partner learns how to communicate his or her feelings and ask for what he or she wants, learns how to avoid being caught up in some of the spouse's games and to counter the spouse's put-downs so that the relationship improves; is this marital or individual therapy?

Building and sustaining a positive supportive relationship with both spouses is the challenge and the most significant ingredient in marital therapy. Many treatment programs fail because one partner feels that the therapist is more identified with the other partner. Individual sessions have to be planned in the context of maintaining this balance. If a wife has a women's support group and the husband has nothing comparable, and if, in the conjoint sessions with a female therapist, he feels as if two aggressive, articulate women are ganging up on him, a male cotherapist can provide an effective, albeit expensive, solution.

Perhaps some failures are attributable to a partner's refusal to be involved, to the lack of availability of the counselor for supplementary individual sessions, to inappropriate questions in conjoint sessions, or to a faulty sense of timing. Appropriate timing can depend upon many factors from concrete matters such as money, time, and babysitters to the most subtle kinds of resistance.

INABILITY TO MOVE FROM THE PAST

In successful marital therapy, the vicious circle of accusations, defensiveness, and retaliation is broken. Mutual support replaces mutual bickering. Even with intensive behavioral marital therapy, some people do not easily give up the coercive pattern of interaction. When certain sensitive "buttons" are pushed, the values and self-esteem of one spouse are so threatened that he or she cannot have empathy with the mate who has pushed that button, outgrow the hurt and bitterness, or reach a new workable beginning. Behavioral therapy fails if there is insufficient time and effort given by the therapist to help the couple deal with these residual factors of recimination.

One tragic example was a husband who could never get past his feeling that their child's death was due to his wife's negligence, despite 10 sessions of marital therapy. Whether more time and/or therapy would have served to salvage their marriage will never be known. Other examples of failure to move away from the past include situations where a partner has felt betrayed, such as when one spouse has had sex with the mate's best friend, testifies against him or her in court, or betrays some confidence in other areas.

An example was the case of Mrs. D. She had come from an affluent background when she married Mr. D., who was an accountant. He came to feel that her happiness, their lifestyle, and their marriage depended on his bringing in a larger income than his salary afforded. When an opportunity to embezzle arose, he was not able to resist it. Although it was an act of desperation followed by monumental remorse, Mrs. D. perceived it only as an act of extreme disloyalty and could never trust him again. Even after efforts at cognitive restructuring, their marriage ended.

Other situations which come under the rubric of the "unforgiven" or the "unforgivable" are cases of incest and/or sexual abuse by parents of their own or stepchildren. Although these cases also may fall into the category of coming to therapy too late, much more than timing is involved. Here, therapy sometimes fails because therapists are not cognizant of the need for consultation from specialists, such as lawyers and experts in the field of child abuse and protective services. Some couples are not able to use marriage counseling to improve their current relationship because one partner's perception of the other is so negative, distorted, and static that it puts a ceiling on any hope for growth or change.

For example, Mr. and Mrs. J. married when she was a "wild" teenager—wilder than he realized when he married her—and he was a serious automobile mechanic. When he was asked what he felt would improve their marriage, he said that he believed that if his wife would "grow up," "settle down," stay home, and have dinner on the table when he got home at six o'clock each night, then maybe they could make it. Mrs. J. had become a licensed vocational nurse, responsible, and keenly interested in a career. Mr. J. saw her as she had been in the past and interpreted her unwillingness to be a "homebody" as due to the same "wildness" or immaturity that had been part of her unstable past. He equated her desire for social life—any kind of social life—as part of the same wildness. Their fights were stormy. Because of his traditional homemaker expectations, Mrs. J. grew increasingly alienated and angry. Her heated and defensive responses represented his self-fulfilling prophecy. That is, he pointed to her angry tirades as evidence that she was "acting like a teenager."

This couple used marital therapy for permission to split. Mr. J. did not want Mrs. J. as she had been in the past and could not see her as she was in the present. His undervaluing her current strivings for a career, combined with the strength of his expectations that she was acting like an adolescent led to their decision to separate. One approach to marriage counseling when there is much ambivalence on both sides is to suggest that the couple use the therapy to make the relationship as good as it can possibly be. Then it usually becomes clear whether it is "good enough" or not. Mr. and Mrs. J. could not sustain their motivation even long enough to test how much their marriage could be improved, and that, in itself, was sufficiently revealing for them to make the decision to separate. With the therapist's help in alleviating guilt, they both felt comfortable with the decision.

One of the greatest pitfalls for the marital therapist is to remain blind to the expectations and attitudes cast in the bronze of the past and to embark on fruitless paths to change the present and future. Only with a thorough history and exploration of past patterns can the therapist discover the desires of the spouses in therapy—to end the marriage, to punish the partner, to reform the partner, to obtain permission to assert oneself, or to gain a platform for trumpeting recriminations.

A couple's expectations of each other and of their respective roles in the marriage are often involved in their inability to move away from the past. How the parents of the counseled spouses carried their roles is significant and relevant to these expectations. The therapist needs to elicit generational patterns and expectations such as the wife who should cook like the husband's mother used to, or the man who should always do the yard work and discipline of the children like the wife's father used to. Very directive approaches toward helping both partners modify these expectations are not likely to meet with quick behavioral changes.

When Mrs. F. became 50 years old, she let it be known that she no longer intended to iron or do much of the cooking. She was especially tired of cooking huge feasts for the frequent gatherings of the extended family. Her mother had worked outside the home and Mrs. F. enjoyed many restaurant meals as a child. She felt a responsibility to set the stage for a graceful, satisfying aging process, and this was her way of doing it. Mr. F.'s childhood memories were highlighted by his grandmother's and then mother's traditional holiday family celebrations. The women in his childhood spent endless hours in the kitchen and waited on the men. Mr. and Mrs. F. had only one son who often took his father's side in this value conflict. Mrs. F. was feeling more and more put upon and scapegoated. The therapist's role was to help them sort out what was negotiable in their expectations of each other and what was nonnegotiable. In marital therapy, an assessment has to be made of the motivation to compromise, as well as the potential for learning the skills of negotiation on the part of both the husband and wife.

Role expectations can sometimes emerge in later, rather than earlier, stages of marriage when conflicting images of aging, retirement, or other phases of living are reached. Expectations of a young bride, or a young husband can be very different from expectations of a coparent, or a cograndparent; thus marriages can face obstacles in later years that were totally unforeseen. Now that we all tend to live longer there will be increasing opportunities to practice marital therapy with older couples. Attitudes toward aging become attributes of the therapist that need examination. If older clients are seen as threatening authority figures, "old crocks," cute little old types that couldn't really be interested in sex, or in any stereotypical way, the therapy may fail, regardless of the power of the behavioral methods.

Marriage failures are very often due to expectations that are too high to be attainable. Failures in marital therapy are sometimes attributable to the therapist's overlooking the significance of unreasonable expectations or his or her inability to help the clients reorder their expectations to be more in line with present reality. Role reversals can sometimes help to soften attitudes and expectations rooted in the past or even in past generations. When Mr. Y., a former marine drill sergeant and super macho Hispanic-American husband and father, took the part of his wife who wanted to get a job and spend some social time with her girlfriends, his previous intransigence melted away in a tearful realization of his unfair expectations.

CHANGES IN ONE SPOUSE REQUIRE PAINFUL ADAPTATION IN THE OTHER

When a husband and wife grow to want different things, the process of clarifying their newly felt needs may result in growth for some and disappointment for others. Some partners may get what they ask for through marriage counseling and then discover that it was not what they really wanted after all.

Mr. T. was the kind of lawyer that reminded one of *What Makes Sammy Run?* He was quick—on the tennis court, in the courtroom, in bed. Both he and his wife viewed the problem in their marriage as stemming from differences in pace. Mrs. T. was slow, passive, apathetic, dependent, and, according to her husband, uninteresting. She has been ambivalent about having a child, and her subsequent depression was the precipitating reason for their requesting therapy. Mr. T. felt that his wife needed psychiatric treatment. Mrs. T. wanted her husband's participation in the therapy inasmuch as decisions regarding parenthood were at issue. With counseling, Mrs. T. became assertive in expressing herself both at home and in the world of work. She "blossomed" during therapy, decided she preferred a career to motherhood, and dropped much of her passivity. She started to communicate much more directly as she learned that her passive resistance to her husband had been an indirect way of saying, "No." Mr. T. was uncomfortable with the changes in the "new Mrs. T." and could not make up his mind whether sharing the limelight was what he really wanted. Sensitivity on the part of the therapist led to the realization that Mr. T. needed more support than could be provided in the marital therapy. Would an offer of individual therapy jeopardize the emerging balance in the marriage or be too threatening for him? Separate cocounseling with male and female therapists worked in this situation. In meeting individually with a male therapist, Mr. T. was able to accept and reinforce his wife's new assertiveness. A potential failure in marital therapy was averted by the female therapist's active collaboration with the male therapist to whom Mr. T. was referred.

CAN FAILURES BE PREVENTED?

Although behavioral marital therapy has rapidly developed a wide base of assessment and intervention approaches and has become empirically the "treatment of choice" for marital conflict, failures occur with spouses remaining dissatisfied in the relationship whether or not they separate. Behavior therapists have gone beyond the facile "Look Ma, no hands!" phase of reporting their successes, and this book, *Failures in Behavior Therapy,* is testimony to the maturing of the field.

There are some caveats that can be offered to the behavioral clinician working with distressed marital couples. In dealing with the couple who have difficulty moving away from the coercion and recriminations of the past, it is mandatory that a number of sessions be scheduled to thoroughly review these feelings during the initial stage of therapy. Catharsis and abreaction are encouraged. Only after they've fully spewed out their anger and hurt feelings and have become satiated with them, the couple is moved into a future-seeking, problem-solving mode. Once the problem-solving phase begins, it is necessary to set stringent ground rules and remind the couple firmly that they are not allowed to drag the old skeletons out of the closet. One of us has used a policeman's whistle to stop verbal brawling and to snap the couple out of their recriminations.

Another concept that is helpful in minimizing the failure rate in marital therapy is "flexible levels of intervention." This refers to the gradual increase in the amount, type, and frequency of intervention to meet the needs and resistances of the couple. A modular approach to using flexible levels of intervention is depicted in Figure 20.1. Some couples may need only the initial sessions of catharsis and relationship building; others may require intensive work on communication skills. The modular approach is described more fully by Liberman et al. (1980); however, a brief case example will suffice to demonstrate the importance of escalating the amount of intervention to bring about desired therapeutic outcomes.

After six months of weekly sessions aimed at Mr. and Mrs. A.'s sexual problems and explosive rages, there was slight but disappointing progress. They were not practicing regularly their sensate focus exercises and only sporadically employed their communication skills at home between sessions. Mrs. A. had demonstrated her ability to make positive requests during the therapy sessions and her husband also was able to express his intimidated and angry feelings when supervised by the therapist. Although more frequently scheduled sessions or even home visits could have been ways to increase the level of intervention, the therapist instead chose to increase prompts and reinforcement for home practice by means of the phone. Three times a week, in between the weekly sessions, phone calls were initiated by the couple to the therapist who used the brief five-minute phone conversation to elicit their reports of home practice, to acknowledge their progress and efforts, and to engage them in problem-solving activities. This ploy led to a marked improvement in their adherence to their homework assignments.

Behavioral marital therapy that utilizes standardized intervention strategies without attention to the "process" issues and dynamics that are part of the therapy is to be eschewed. Experienced and sophisticated behavioral therapists employ strategies of assessment and intervention that build upon their sensitive clinical intuition (the "third ear") regarding the distribution of power, status, control, affection, rejection, passivity, and action within the family system (Birchler & Spinks, 1980). The use of covert strategies such as paradoxical instructions can sometimes help to get couples back on the therapeutic track by undercutting the abundant reinforcement that maintains their resistance in their sometimes unconscious efforts to defeat the therapist and their marriage partners.

Birchler and his colleagues have synthesized the behavioral and family systems approaches to marital therapy in a cogent manner.

If hidden agendas are present (e.g., control issues), therapists would expect to encounter resistance: couples' apparent inability to perform communication exercises in the sessions, incompleted homework, a vague picture of how one or both partners actually feel about the presenting problem, crises between sessions. Note that before hidden agendas can be implicated as resistance to therapy, a determined effort is

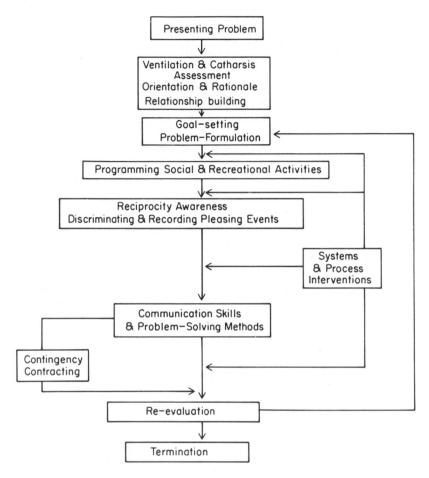

Figure 20.1. Modular approach to individualizing behavioral marital therapy through "flexible levels of intervention."

made to rule out competing explanations; for example, inappropriately designed homework, poor timing of therapeutic interventions, the therapist–patient relationship, and others. However, once therapists can rule out other explanations, it is assumed that there are as yet unidentified or unlabeled system problems which are blocking progress. It is incumbent upon therapists to recognize these signals, digress from the behavioral plan, and deal with the existing process issues. When such resistances are encountered, subsequent interventions consist of helping the clients identify the unlabeled hidden agendas and possibly interpreting for clients the therapists' observations. Such a digression from the behavioral framework may last for a few minutes within one session, or it may take several sessions.

Failures to produce mutually agreed upon satisfaction in marriage as well as to engineer mutually desired changes in relationship behaviors will continue to mark the efforts of behavior therapists who work with couples in conflict. Clinical failures are opportunities to develop new methods of understanding and intervention that will improve our therapeutic armamentarium and advance the field.

REFERENCES

Birchler, G.R., & Spinks, S.H. (1980) Behavioral-systems marital and family therapy: Integration and clinical application. *American Journal of Family Therapy,* **8,** 6–28.

Greer, S.E. & D'Zurilla, T.J. Behavioral approaches to marital discord and conflict. Journal of Marriage and family Counseling, 1, 299–315.

Jacobson, N.S. & Margolin, G. (1979) *Marital Therapy.* New York: Brunner/Mazel.

Liberman, R.P., Levine, J., Wheeler, E., Sanders, N., & Wallace, C.J. (1976) Marital therapy in groups: A comparative evaluation of behavioral and interactional formats. *Acta Psychiatrica Scandinavica,* Supplementum 266, 1–34.

Liberman, R.P., Wheeler, E., de Visser, L., Kuehnel, J., & Kuehnel, T. (1980) *Handbook of marital therapy.* New York: Plenum.

CHAPTER 21

Failure in Treating
Sexual Dysfunctions

WALTER T. A. M. EVERAERD

The literature on heterosexual dysfunctions focuses almost exclusively on success with various methods of therapy. A well-known exception is the report on failure by Masters and Johnson (1970).

By now, many investigators have had about 10 years of experience with sex therapy for heterosexual dysfunctions. In the course of these years, views on what is called "sexual response" have changed. Desire and emotional satisfaction as components of this response have been added to the arousal and orgasm components suggested by Masters and Johnson. This addition has led to a more accurate analysis of dysfunctions and to an improved specification of outcome criteria (Levine, 1980). At the same time, the feminist movement made important contributions to a further analysis of treatment goals that have resulted in a reevaluation of the "orgasm-through-coition" criterion.

SUCCESS AND FAILURE IN SEX THERAPY

Many authors of outcome studies claim that directive short-term treatments of sexual dysfunctions are very effective (Masters & Johnson, 1970, 1979; Kinder & Blakeney, 1977; Reynolds, 1977). Others (Wright, Perreault, & Mathieu, 1977) are considerably less enthusiastic. They posit that in the face of the diversity of success rates (39 to 98 percent), the recovery of patients in control groups, and insufficient specification of patients in the studies, no strong claims for general effectiveness are justified at present.

Follow-Up Studies

Masters and Johnson (1970) reported that changes following treatment have been maintained up to five years. Kilmann (1978) and Zilbergeld and Evans (1980),

---

Joost Dekker, Gail Pheterson, Deirdre Pronk-Lordan, and Paul Emmelkamp made useful suggestions during the preparation of this chapter.

however, pointed out that only a small portion of the original sample was followed up. Of course, this imposes serious limitations about the conclusions that can be drawn from these results; no generalizations about the entire group can be made.

Patients' motives for participation in a follow-up can vary widely. For example, couples treated by an adapted version of the Masters and Johnson's method did not show the same response to an invitation for evaluation as did couples treated by communication training (Everaerd & Dekker, 1981). Couples who were treated along the lines of Masters and Johnson (as measured at posttest) and who were satisfied with the results came to the follow-up interview, whereas the less satisfied couples did not. In the group who received communication training the reverse was seen: couples reporting for follow-up session were dissatisfied with the results at posttest. Inasmuch as the couples were not asked to specify their reasons for participation in the follow-up session, the cause of this difference cannot be ascertained. In any event, one can assume that there is a high degree of selectivity in the patients who participate in follow-up studies.

Arentewicz and Schmidt (1980) reassessed their couples two and one half to four years after completion of therapy. Of the 114 couples invited, 67 (64 percent) cooperated, but only 50 percent completed questionnaires. Twenty (18 percent) had moved to unknown destinations, and 21 (18 percent) refused cooperation. Arentewicz and Schmidt established that those reporting for follow-up did not differ from those who did not participate in the follow-up assessment. The initially positive outcome showed a slight decline after two and one half to four years. During this period 14 percent of all couples had been divorced and 28 percent had dropped out without positive therapy results. A rough estimate indicated 11 percent improvement, 17 percent marked improvement, and 31 percent "cure." About one quarter of the couples was still sexually dysfunctional. They regarded this 25 percent as their actual failure rate.

In a study conducted by us on 140 patients who had applied for sex therapy five to eight years ago, 88 couples (63 percent) cooperated: 12 couples had moved to unknown destinations; 16 failed to respond; 24 couples refused to answer questions by phone. Of those who responded, in 6 couples only one of the partners completed the questionnaire, and 13 couples sent a letter instead of the completed questionnaire. This means that quantitative data were available for analysis on 69 couples (49 percent).

Reassessment of our couples at follow-up showed a slight relapse as compared with results at posttreatment. Of the 112 couples for whom this could be established, 23 (20 percent) are now divorced. Of the 69 couples who returned completed questionnaires, 13 were divorced and 10 received additional therapy during the follow-up period. Thus only 46 couples who were not divorced and did not receive additional therapy completed the questionnaire. Self-reports on satisfaction with the sexual relationship were obtained from 45 couples. The results indicate that, of 35 couples who improved during therapy, 10 showed further improvement during the follow-up period, 12 remained unchanged, and 13 showed some slight relapse. Of the 10 couples who failed to improve during therapy, 3 did improve during the follow-up period, 4 remained unchanged, and 3 showed some relapse. For the reasons discussed earlier we do not feel that these results can be extrapolated to the entire sample.

ASSESSMENT OF FAILURES

Sex therapy generally aims at acquisition or restoration of the sexual response. An essential feature in the definition of the sexual response is "orgasm through coition." Patients—individually or as couples—usually expect that as a result of therapy their expectations, fantasies, and illusions about making love will be realized. Clinical practice is essentially a process of reducing the distance between expectations, fantasies, and illusions on the one hand, and the reality of love making on the other.

Treatment focuses mainly on the acquisition of skills that enable the patient to achieve the sexual response alone or with his or her partner. The principal elements of treatment are the supplying of information, exercises in sexual skills and communication skills, and discussion of attitudes and emotional barriers.

Masters and Johnson (1970) defined initial failure as the "indication that the two-week rapid treatment phase has failed to initiate reversal of basic symptomatology of sexual dysfunction for which the unit was referred to the Foundation" (pp. 352–353). Inasmuch as the authors did not define the meaning of "to initiate reversal," the degree of improvement their patients showed remains unclear. Thus the degree of sexual functioning is not reported, and no information on the patients' satisfaction with the results of treatment is provided.

Most researchers use the ability to achieve orgasm through coition as an outcome measure of sex therapy. However, sexual performance is not always related in a linear fashion to satisfaction with sexual interactions. The most commonly applied criterion, therefore, does not seem to be valid for all couples. There is some evidence that neither specific performance (coition) nor specific experience (orgasm) is required for satisfaction with the sexual relationship (Frenken, 1976; Morokoff, 1978; Schiavi, Derogatis, Kuriansky, O'Connor, & Scharpe, 1979, pp. 185–186).

A related issue is the relationship between self-report and actual behavior. LoPicollo and Hogan (1979) pointed out that the relationship between patients' self-report and the actual sexual interactions has not been ascertained. These authors reject the use of direct observation of sexual interactions or the exploration of sexual stimulation, as in the "sexological exam," inasmuch as stimulus control plays an important role in these assessment methods. Moreover, many patients will refuse to participate in observation and examination procedures. Finally, there are some obvious ethical problems in conducting such observations.

In our view, the patients' satisfaction with the result of treatment should be the principal outcome criterion. The limited data now available indicate that partners show high agreement regarding sexual satisfaction. In a study comparing three different methods of treating sexual problems (Everaerd, 1977), the results of therapy were judged separately by patients and by therapists. The patients (couples) entered treatment for female orgasmic dysfunction. After 12 sessions we asked both the couples and the therapists to rate degree of improvement. On a number of 5-point scales a sizeable agreement among spouses about the degree in satisfaction was found (*pm* correlation, $r = .64$, $p < .01$). The therapists ($n = 7$) showed more agreement in their evaluation of the male patient ($r = .61$, $p < .01$) than of the female ($r = .08$, n.s.). The female therapists did not differ significantly in their evaluation from the female patients; the male therapists rated improvement of female patients to be less than the patients' ratings of themselves.

Similar results were reported by Arentewicz and Schmidt (1980) who found high agreement between female therapists and female patients. They interpreted this as a tendency of the female therapists to protect the female patients from excessive male demands. Lassen (1976) proposed that this conflict of values is especially strong for female therapists. Our findings do not confirm this proposition. In our experience male therapists also introduce their values into therapy.

For couples entering treatment because of dysfunction in the male, we found that the original complaints generally showed little improvement. Yet, the majority of these couples indicated improved satisfaction with their sexual functioning. Arentewicz and Schmidt (1980) established that only about 50 percent of patients whose symptoms have "objectively" disappeared report that their sexual problems have, in fact, disappeared. Restoration of sexual functioning as such does not imply that patients will regard the therapy as successful. The failures that are perceived by patients may reflect discontent with the low level of goal differentiation established for sex therapy. This, in turn, may be a consequence of an oversimplified definition of sexual behavior.

FAILURE RELATED TO CONCEPTUALIZATION OF SEXUAL BEHAVIOR

Sexual arousal and orgasm have long been considered as the main goals in the treatment of sexual problems. The basic assumption was that an intact organism responds to adequate sexual stimulation by arousal and orgasm. In the experiments of Masters and Johnson (1966, 1979), several methods of stimulation—using the hand, the mouth, live and artificial genital organs—proved to be effective in producing arousal and orgasm. Those authors observed a high level of similarity of response in their experienced nondysfunctional male and female subjects who volunteered for the study. In contrast, a wide variation in response to stimulation was evident in sexual dysfunctional patients; they did not always respond effectively to stimulation. Other investigators reported similar results (Reynolds, 1977; Wright et al., 1977).

In the sensate focus procedure developed by Masters and Johnson (1970), stimulation of the entire body was initially separated from that of the genitals and the female breasts. This separation was introduced primarily in order to promote acceptance of sensory perceptions. Subsequently, expansion to explicitly sexual perceptions was effected by including the stroking and stimulation of the genitals in the exercises. The use of this separation can be seen also as promoting discrimination of sexual feelings, or as a way to teach sexual feelings. For some patients, caressing the entire body is acceptable but that of the genitals is averted. This means that therapy fails for some patients because they avoid these caresses or maintain that they "feel nothing" when subjected to them.

In recent years, these problems are no longer ascribed exclusively to the couple's interaction problems, but rather to problems with sexual motivation: inhibited sexual desire, low sexual desire, or sexual aversion (Kaplan, 1977; Kolodny, Masters, & Johnson, 1979; LoPicollo & Hogan, 1979; Masters & Johnson, 1979). When the patients' learning history is analyzed, it can be demonstrated that either positive expectations with regard to sexual interactions were not learned or negative ones were installed.

Sexual motivation can be defined as the expectation, based on past experience, that interactions characterized as sexual can produce pleasant sensations, usually arousal, and often also orgasms (Frenken, 1976; Kinsey, Pomeroy, Martin, & Gebhard, 1953). In many cases, however, sexual motivation is based on very few experiences and an accordingly small behavioral repertoire. Furthermore, motivation does not always become actualized within the range of behavioral alternatives offered in therapy as exemplified in the sensate focus program of Masters and Johnson. Sexual motivation seems to depend largely on learning experiences (Money, 1980). But its conceptualization is still in a fairly primitive phase of development; not only behavioral and cognitive information, but also information on somatic backgrounds are as yet inadequate (Schiavi & White, 1976).

The deficiencies in knowledge of sexual motivation are reflected in the way in which patients (but also therapists) think about sexual complaints. They tend to regard sexual motivation as a kind of natural disposition, especially in heterosexual relationships. When one enters a relationship, it is only natural that one has sex with his or her partner. The ban on premarital sex and masturbation especially prevent people from viewing sexuality as a learning process.

In the early 1960s, McGuire, Carlisle, and Young (1965) stressed the importance of masturbation in the learning of sexual behavior. LoPicollo and Lobitz (1972) were the first to include masturbation in the treatment of sexual problems. That enabled therapists to analyze complaints of couples in terms of both interactional and individual factors and to treat them accordingly. In retrospect, it is rather striking that we neglected to consider masturbation as a treatment option earlier in the history of sex therapy. Presumably, when failures in couple therapy occurred, masturbation was not taken into consideration because the norm dictated that sexuality involves interpersonal relationships.

Masturbation as a method of learning sexual behavior can be used in many different ways. Riley and Riley (1978) used this method to facilitate orgasmic release. Zeiss, Rosen, and Zeiss (1977) proceeded from masturbation to attain orgasm through coition. Barbach (1975) and also LoPicollo and Lobitz (1972) used it to teach people how to derive pleasure from sex thus enabling them subsequently to enter pleasant interactions.

These developments paved the way toward more differentiated views of sexual problems but at the same time made therapy more complicated. The behavior sequence with coition as the specified behavior, and orgasm through coition as outcome criterion, are no longer accepted uniformly. Instead, people's motivations for sex are viewed as widely varied. Also, we have learned to see that arousal and orgasm can result from widely varying stimulation programs. As a result, treatment programs are no longer comprised of canned procedures but show marked intraindividual and even more marked interindividual variations.

An important consequence of this development is a change in our criterion of failures on the basis of the orgasm-through-coition criterion. We are now placing greater emphasis on the learning history, and we catalogue behavioral alternatives that people have learned in the course of time. Individuals for whom sexuality has no meaning are very seldom encountered. It is always possible to find some stimulus source for arousal and possibly also for orgasm. But there are very marked differences in the extent to which people believe they can make passive or active use of these sources. Anyone who is able to produce a stimulus by fantasies, by one's behavior, or by behavior of others, is able to be sexually active. Those who are affected only by stimulation are at a disadvantage because they themselves cannot produce the stimulus.

One of the purposes of sex therapy is to make the relation between stimulation and arousal more explicit. In some cases this is very difficult, and one may resort to physiological registration methods (Heiman, 1978). As soon as the patient has learned to discriminate arousal, the question arises as to what the patient wants to do with it. Researchers who apply the orgasm-through-coition criterion disregard this problem and may promote failure: They claim to know the goal of therapy better than the patients.

The definition of orgasm through coition as the desired behavior is understandable in view of our cultural backgrounds, but is obviously biased. Coition is generally more effective for males than for females in achieving orgasm (Hite, 1976; Kinsey et al., 1953). The observation that more females than males suffer from sexual dysfunction (coital anorgasmy) is, therefore, misleading. Males show dominant behavior in heterosexual interactions and produce self-stimulation in coition (Masters & Johnson, 1979). The male dominance is sex-specific behavior, which plays a role also outside sexual interactions. Females who are unable to break the male dominance in a sexual interaction receive no adequate stimulation. Inability to break the male dominance, however, does not constitute female sexual inability! Individuals who have an adequate repertoire of sexual behavior are not always able to produce sexual stimulation in every situation. The causes of this inability often lie outside the context of specific dysfunctions. Failures on the basis of the orgasm-through-coition criterion, therefore, do not always provide an accurate picture of what has been achieved in therapy.

REFUSAL TO ENTER TREATMENT AND DROPOUTS

Several reports about treatment refusal and about dropping out of treatment are available (Arentewicz & Schmidt, 1980; Fordney-Settlage, 1975; Kilmann, 1978).

Many patients fail to show up for the first appointment, some patients do not accept the treatment offer, and others discontinue treatment prematurely (dropouts). Only a small number of the original patients are available for follow-up in most studies. Fordney-Settlage (1975) reported that, of 339 couples requesting therapy, 142 refused the treatment offered to them; of the remaining 197 couples, 147 completed therapy (25 percent dropouts). Thus treatment was completed by 44 percent of the entire intake sample. A higher percentage was reported by Arentewicz and Schmidt (1980) who found that 202 of 275 couples registered in the intake started therapy; 164 couples completed therapy (20 percent dropouts). Of those referred, therefore, 60 percent attended therapy. The marked difference in number of dropouts reported is probably due to differences in the selection criteria applied in the various centers (Arentewicz & Schmidt, 1980).

Treatment Refusal

Although few data are available on refusal to enter treatment, there are some indications that females more readily accept treatment than males. Fordney-Settlage (1975) reported that males show more resistance to therapy than females. In the discussion about this paper, LoPicollo reported that 80 percent of women referred to his clinic phone for an appointment, whereas only 10 percent of men do so. In his opinion, males show more resistance to identification of their sexual problems with psychological causes than females. In our experience, men often expect brief somatic treatment without having to be involved psychologically in it. Some men, in fact, forbid their partner to seek medical or psychological advice.

Dropout

Among dropouts the male/female difference is less pronounced. Comparing dropout rates of couples who enter treatment for female dysfunctions with those who do so for male dysfunctions, there are only slight differences reported in the literature. Arentewicz and Schmidt (1980), Everaerd (1977), and Nunes and Bandeira (1980) found slightly more dropouts in the treatment of female dysfunctions. The difference found by Nunes and Bandeira is negligible which is the more remarkable because of the high dropout rate (42 percent) reported.

Several factors seem to be related to dropping out of sex therapy. The most frequently offered motive for dropout is relationship problems (Arentewicz, & Schmidt, 1980; Fordney-Settlage, 1975; Kilmann, 1978; Kinder & Blakeney, 1977; LoPicollo & Hogan, 1979). The resistance of partners to solving their sexual problems together can have several different backgrounds. Often, this resistance may constitute an attempt to avoid a much more serious problem by focusing on their sexual interaction. In therapy, these patients usually show massive resistance to following instructions and sometimes they act with vehemence. For others, the sexual problems are the only remaining substance of the relationship.

Through therapy for sexual problems, these patients attempt to inform each other that they do not wish to continue the relationship.

Individual problems of one of the partners may also lead to dropout. Our experience indicates that this factor plays a role when the homework assignments give rise to problems that have so far been avoided. We have very frequently observed this in women with a history of unpleasant or traumatic sexual experience. Contrary to their expectation, they are unable to separate the situation with the present partner from that in which they had the unpleasant experiences. Next, they avoid the experiences that may be broached in the exercises; therapy is, then, impeded and individual treatment is required.

The way by which an individual's problems may impede sex therapy and may lead to premature termination can be illustrated by a man who applied for treatment to solve his erection problems. The man had previously been married twice; both wives died of uterine carcinoma. He had experienced slight erection problems with his second wife. With his present partner he failed to have an erection. The obvious interpretation (unprocessed mourning and fear of recurrence) was decisively rejected by the client; he did not want to discuss his previous partners and terminated therapy. In some cases interference of individual problems in the therapy process is not readily predictable. Many patients attach such great importance to restoration of their sexual functioning that they conceal problems. Even when such information is revealed, therapists sometimes tend to underestimate its interference with therapeutic outcome. The lack of attending to personal problems increases the probability that treatment will be discontinued prematurely.

In summary, the short-term effect of sex therapy can be described as fairly satisfactory. Due to the scanty follow-up data, it is more difficult to evaluate the long-term effect. Evidently, many problems are still unsolved both with respect to refusal to enter treatment and to drop out of treatment. We cannot go beyond the general conclusion that couples who are unwilling to cooperate with each other are likewise unwilling or unable to do so in sex therapy.

TREATMENT FAILURES

Numerous factors can affect outcome of therapy. Fordney-Settlage (1975) listed 10 factors that need to be assessed before treatment planning: deficient sexual information, deficient sexual experience, deficient sexual communication, negative sexual experience, regressive sexual behavior, destructive reaction patterns, nonsexual interpersonal distress, intrapsychic factors, inadequate sexual self-concept, and damaged self-concept. She used a weighted evaluation to predict whether sex therapy was indicated. In addition, she predicted the areas for which individual therapy was required. Although Fordney-Settlage presented some descriptions of predictions, she did not provide quantitative data on prognosis. Other authors reported results on variables related to the failure in sex therapy (e.g., Cooper, 1981; Reynolds, 1977). In the following section we shall review this information.

Patient Variables

Data from outcome studies led several authors to conclude that there are systematic differences between specific dysfunctions and the degree of success in sex therapy. Generally, female dysfunctions are more easily treated than male dysfunctions, presumably because of differences in socialization of sexuality for males and females. LaPlante, McCormick, and Brannigan (1980) tested the hypothesis that students would stereotype initiation of sexual intercourse as a masculine activity, and refusal to have sex as a feminine one. Their findings confirmed the hypothesis and they concluded: "The traditional sexual script dictates that men should use any strategy to influence dates to have coitus and that women should either passively acquiesce to their dates' sexual advances or use any strategy to influence a date and to avoid sexual intercourse" (p. 338).

When dysfunctions are classified into primary and secondary dysfunctions, significant differences between males and females are found. Although the definitions of "primary" and "secondary" dysfunction are usually operationalized as never having shown a given response (orgasm) or never having responded to a particular method of stimulation (coition); a dysfunction is labeled "secondary" when these responses are situationally determined.

Female Dysfunctions

Primary dysfunctions in women are easy to treat (Kilmann, 1978; Kinder & Blakeney, 1977). Secondary problems produce more failures. This is usually ascribed to factors in the couple's interaction. Several authors suggested that a direct approach to secondary anorgasmy should be supplemented by traditional psychotherapy (Kinder & Blakeney, 1977). In cases of secondary problems there is no dysfunction in the strict sense of the term inasmuch as the desired response can be elicited under certain conditions of stimulation.

With secondary dysfunctional females, the ignorance about stimulation techniques was found to be a major factor in only a few cases; in most cases the interpretation of the sexual dysfunction in terms of interactional problems was sufficient to restore effective responses (Everaerd & Dekker, 1981).

Male Dysfunctions

The distinction between primary and secondary dysfunction in males relates less to failure than that found in females. However, Cooper (1981) reported that males who had never been able to respond (primary dysfunction) were less easily treated than those who had lost this ability (secondary dysfunction). Cooper also suggested that duration of the problem is associated with failure: Dysfunctions of longer duration are resistent to change. Duration of dysfunction seems to be less important in females. Further, an acute-onset dysfunction has a better prognosis than an insidious-onset one (p. 213).

In our opinion (Everaerd, 1982), dysfunctional males have several ways to avoid sexual feelings. Such avoidance may lead to premature ejaculation. Actually, premature ejaculations are avoiding further interaction with their partner. In some cases this evokes enormous hostility in the female partner. When such a partner is given a responsible role in therapy (e.g., in the squeeze technique), it can easily lead to failure. Males with retarded or deficient ejaculation (or erectile impotence developed on this basis) often avoid all forms of direct stimulation, sometimes by overconcentrating on the stimulation of their partner. In both groups, the men are more difficult to treat when they no longer believe in the possibility of change, and particularly when their sexual motivation is seriously diminished as a result.

Sociological Factors and Psychopathology

Age and social class do not seem to be associated with failure (Ansari, 1976). Although religion is often considered as an important etiological factor, it does not seem to predict success or failure. The presence of psychopathological symptoms is regarded as a contraindication in selecting patients for sex therapy (Reynolds, 1977; Wright et al., 1977), although only few data are available. Obviously, persons with serious nonsexual problems can hardly be expected to cope with the tasks set in sex therapy. Moreover, Kinder and Blakeney (1977) mention the "hypothesized danger of precipitating a psychiatric disturbance in cases in which either the symptomatic patient or the spouse suffers from concomitant psychiatric illness of major proportions" (p. 527).

Treatment Variables

Masters and Johnson (1970) have made a substantial contribution to the treatment of sexual dysfunctions and their treatment program is now widely used. The interventions of Masters and Johnson (1970) are very well operationalized. Yet, the strict application of their instructions sometimes poses problems in therapy and may lead to failure. The rapid-treatment format in which patients receive treatment on 14 consecutive days allows for extensive control over the therapy. This is not the case when patients are treated in an outpatient setting and sessions are spaced over a longer period.

In spaced sessions, both authoritative instructions to avoid goal oriented performance (genital and female breast stimulation, coition and orgasm) and sensate focus instructions pose specific problems. These interventions are intended to reduce performance anxiety and spectatoring, and to promote concentration on feelings. In our experience, a simple discussion of the rationale behind the instructions is sufficient to abolish the problems of some patients, even though their dysfunctions were of long duration. Other patients interpret the ban on intercourse as a paradoxical message. The next time they proudly tell the therapist that they succeeded in having intercourse and derived much pleasure from it. These patients do not need further analysis of their interaction that takes place during sensate focus exercises. These exercises pose serious problems in couples who use their destructive interaction strategies to prevent each other's progress. In some cases one or both partners become so discouraged that they discontinue treatment.

Failure of therapy with the method of Masters and Johnson may be prevented by restricting sensate focus to the perception of feelings. When sessions are spaced, the ban on intercourse may reduce motivation to engage in sexual behavior. Inasmuch as there is evidence that postponement of genital stimulation or coition do not contribute to more effective responding (Huey, Kline-Graber, & Graber, 1981), it seems advisable to shorten the sensate focus phase.

When patients are familiar with the conditions for sexual functioning, simple communication exercises may be sufficient to restore sexual responding (Everaerd & Dekker, 1981). However, it is important to note that communication exercises may be "misused" if through these exercises, the partner most apprehensive of sexual interactions can postpone sex. The same applies to instructions to avoid goal oriented performance. It is not easy to determine whether avoidance of sex occurs; therefore, the therapist must remain aware of this possibility throughout the course of sex therapy.

Although masturbation training is an effective treatment, there are some contraindications. To some patients, separation of exploration of their own sexuality from sex with a partner is acceptable. But others cannot or will not agree to such separation. When the latter nevertheless participate in group training in which self-exploration and masturbation training are included, therapy is bound to fail.

A number of factors discussed in this section on patient variables may give rise to resistance in therapy. We prefer to discuss such resistance, but others may be more inclined to actively intervene as suggested by Cooper (1981): "Inertia or reluctance in one or both partners can be countered by threatening termination of treatment or suggesting that if no further progress is made they will have to consider seriously the alternatives open to them, including separation or a sexually abstinent relationship" (p. 208). The execution of a therapy program is a complex process in which interventions should be chosen to achieve a set of goals. In this context the "threatening" proposed by Cooper represents minimal technique, with a risk of failure.

Functional Analysis

The above problems with treatment technique and the possible failures resulting from them may be avoided as soon as research provides more precise indications for the best match between the complaint, the treatment, and the therapist. Clinically, more detailed analysis of problems is recommended. In our experience, a functional analysis of sexual problems should specify first the independent variables and then individual sexual responding as the dependent variable. Next, attention should be given to the skills required to produce sexual stimulation. In many cases the analysis will lead to an effective treatment program for restoring sexual responding. The analysis may reveal that some patients are unwilling to use their sexual skills for themselves or their partners.

Therapist Variables

Little is known about the influence of therapist variables on the outcome of sex therapy. A dual-therapist team (Masters & Johnson, 1970) is often recommended.

A male and female therapist are assumed to be capable of sex-specific interventions. The sex-specific understanding of problems plays an unmistakable role as does sex-specific hostility. However, neither understanding is essential for success of therapy (Arentewicz & Schmidt, 1980), nor does hostility breed failure. Novices as well as more experienced therapists often use their own norms and feelings as a reference in handling the patients' problems. In addition to training in assessment and treatment methods, insight into one's own attitudes and insecurities concerning sex seems to be an essential requirement for becoming an effective therapist.

SUMMARY AND CONCLUSIONS

Sex therapy is reasonably successful in the treatment of heterosexual dysfunctions, but some relapse is noted at follow-up. Refusal to enter treatment and dropout during treatment were reported so frequently as to reflect unsatisfactory clinical practice.

It is advisable to give patients who apply for sex therapy more accurate information about what they can expect of treatment. Moreover, research will have to pay more attention to the reluctance shown by males to discuss their sexual problems and to seek help for their dysfunction.

Definition of failure, like definition of success, proves to be complicated. Patients and therapists may have different views on both. What is perceived by the therapist as failure may be perceived by the patients as success and vice versa. Changes in the conceptualization of sexual behavior also have a bearing on the definition of failure which often stems from the treatment goals set by the therapist. These failures can be prevented by focusing more on patients' goals and adjusting outcome criteria accordingly.

Various factors contributing to failure have been described. Research into prognostic factors and variables related to treatment method and therapist has so far yielded insufficient data to establish the best complaint-treatment-therapist match.

REFERENCES

Ansari, J.M.A. (1976) Impotence: prognosis (a controlled study). *The British Journal of Psychiatry*, **128**, 194–198.

Arentewicz, G., & Schmidt, G. (1980) *Sexuell gestörte Beziehungen.* Berlin: Springer Verlag.

Barbach, L.G. (1975) Group treatment of pre-orgasmic women. *Journal of Sex and Marital Therapy*, **1**, 139–145.

Bentler, P.M. (1968a) Heterosexual behavior assessments I: Males. *Behaviour Research and Therapy*, **6**, 21–25.

Bentler, P.M. (1968b) Heterosexual behaviour assessments II: Females. *Behaviour Research and Therapy,* **6,** 27–30.

Cooper A.J. (1981) Short-term treatment in sexual dysfunction: A review. *Comprehensive Psychiatry,* 22, 206–217.

Everaerd, W. (1982) Current research on sexual dysfunctions. In J. Boulougouris (Ed.), *Learning theory approaches in psychiatry,* New York: Wiley.

Everaerd, W. (1977) Comparitive studies of short-term treatment methods for sexual inadequacies. In R. Gemme, & C.C. Wheeler (Eds.), *Progress in sexology.* New York: Plenum.

Everaerd, W., & Dekker, J. (1981) A comparison of sex therapy and communication therapy: Couples complaining of orgasmic dysfunction. *Journal of Sex and Marital Therapy.,* 7, 278–289.

Fordney-Settlage, D.S. (1975) Heterosexual dysfunction: evaluation of treatment procedures. *Archives of Sexual Behavior,* **4,** 367–387.

Frenken, J. (1976) *Afkeer in seksualiteit* (Sexual aversion). Deventer: Van Loghum Slaterus.

Heiman, J.R. (1978) Uses of psychophysiology in the assessment and treatment of sexual dysfunction. In J. LoPicollo, & L. LoPicollo (Eds.), *Handbook of sex therapy.* New York: Plenum.

Hite, S. (1976) *The Hite report,* New York: Dell.

Hogan, D.R. (1978) The effectiveness of sex therapy: a review of the literature. In J. LoPicollo, & L. LoPicollo (Eds.), *Handbook of Sex Therapy.* New York: Plenum.

Huey, C.J., Kleine-Graber, R.N., & Graber, B. (1981) Time factors and orgasmic response. *Archives of Sexual Behavior,* **10,** 111–118.

Kaplan, H.S. (1977) Hypoactive sexual desire. *Journal of Sex and Marital Therapy,* **3,** 3–9.

Kilmann, P.R. (1978) The treatment of primary and secondary orgasmic dysfunction: A methodological review of the literature since 1970. *Journal of Sex and Marital Theory,* **4,** 155–176.

Kinder, B.N., & Blakeney, P. (1977) Treatment of sexual dysfunction; A review of outcome studies. *Journal of Clinical Psychology,* **33,** 523–530.

Kinsey, A.C., Pomeroy, W.B., Martin, C.E., & Gebhard, P. (1953) *Sexual behavior in the human female.* Philadelphia: Saunders.

Kolodny, R.C., Masters, W.H., & Johnson, V.E. (1979) *Textbook of sexual medicine.* Boston: Little, Brown.

LaPlante, M.N., McCormick, N. & Brannigan, G.G. (1980) Living the sexual script: college student's views of influence in sexual encounters. *Journal of Sex Research,* **16,** 338–355.

Lassen, C.L. (1976) Issues and dilemmas in sexual treatment. *Journal of Sex and Marital Therapy,* **2,** 32–39.

Levine, S.B. (1980) Conceptual suggestions for outcome research in sex therapy. *Journal of Sex and Marital Therapy,* **6,** 102–108.

LoPicollo, J., & Hogan, D.R. (1979) Sexual dysfunction. In P. Ovide, & J.P. Brady (Eds.), *Behavioral medicine, theory and practice.* Baltimore: Williams and Wilkins.

LoPicollo, J., & Lobitz, W.C. (1972) The role of masturbation in the treatment of orgasmic dysfunction. *Archives of Sexual Behavior, 2,* 153–164.

Masters W.H. & Johnson V.E. (1966) Human sexual response. Boston: Little, Brown.

Masters, W.H., & Johnson, V.E. (1970) *Human sexual inadequacy.* London: Churchill.

Masters, W.H., & Johnson, V.E. (1979) *Homosexuality in perspective.* Boston: Little, Brown.

McGuire, R.J., Carlisle, J.W., & Young, B.G. (1965) Sexual deviation as a conditioned behavior: A hypothesis. *Behavior Research and Therapy, 3,* 185–190.

Money, J. (1980) *Love and love sickness.* Baltimore: Johns Hopkins.

Morokoff, P. (1978) Determinants of female orgasm. In J. LoPicollo, & L. LoPicollo (Eds.), *Handbook of sex Therapy.* New York: Plenum.

Nunes, J.S., & Bandeira, C.S. (1980) A sex therapy clinic in Portugal: Some results and a few questions, In R. Forleo, & W. Pasini (Eds.), *Medical sexology.* Littleton: PSG.

Reynolds, B.S. (1977) Psychological treatment models and outcome results for erectile dysfunction: a critical review. *Psychological Bulletin, 84,* 1218–1238.

Riley, A.J., & Riley, E.J. (1978) A controlled study to evaluate directed masturbation in the management of primary orgasmic failure in women. *The British Journal of Psychiatry, 133,* 404–409.

Schiavi, R., Derogatis, L.R., Kuriansky, J., O'Connor, D., & Sharpe, L. (1979) The assessment of sexual function and marital interaction. *Journal of Sex and Marital Therapy, 5,* 1969–224.

Schiavi, R., & White, D. (1976) Androgens and male sexual function: A review of human studies. *Journal of Sex and Marital Therapy, 2,* 214–228.

Wright, J., Perreault, R., & Mathieu, M. (1977) The treatment of sexual dysfunction. *Archives General Psychiatry, 34,* 881–890.

Zeiss, A.M., Rosen, M.R., & Zeiss, R.A. (1977) Orgasm during intercourse: A treatment strategy for women. *Journal of Consulting and Clinical Psychology, 45,* 891–895.

Zilbergeld, B., and Evans, M. (1980) The inadequacy of Masters and Johnson. *Psychology Today,* August, 29–43.

CHAPTER 22

Failures in Child Behavior Therapy

ANTHONY M. GRAZIANO
DIANE LEE BYTHELL

Failure is an event, and bound up with this event are our reactions to it. Our traditional American response to failures is to reject them, to consign them, metaphorically or actually, to the refuse heap where they are expected to decay and disappear into our tolerant environment like all of our wastes and useless by-products. We tend not to recycle our failures and process what may be valuable in them, to examine the conditions under which they occur so as to make appropriate adjustments in our procedures.

In science and technology, we expect to progress step-wise from our successes, but seldom discuss our failures or negative findings as useful. Any failure, it seems, is scrapped and we quickly turn "back to the old drawing board." That hackneyed phrase is valuable, however, for while implying a rejection of failures, it also advises us to examine the nature of the failure in redesigning for future success. In science and technology, the ideal model holds that failure provides opportunity to redesign, generating informational feedback that helps to eliminate rival hypotheses and develop alternative predictions and procedures. In contrast to this scientific ideal, the tradition in applied mental health towards its failures appears to have been quite different, and the ideal self-corrective functions of failure have not operated.

What seems important to understand here when we consider our field's apparently characteristic refusal to admit negative evidence is that the applied mental health field owes only part of its allegiance to the values of empirical research, and many of its decisions are based upon political needs. When arguing for more public support, for example, or in the continuing status conflicts between disciplines, it is not in the profession's or individual discipline's political best interest to be actively self-critical and to point out its own weaknesses and failures. Ignoring negative evidence has thus become a basic political survival tactic. One may raise the question, for example, as does Wolpe (1981) of how to explain the continued ascendance of psychoanalysis in light of the continually accumulating evidence that a variety of behavioral approaches appear to be more effective. Recognizing the political nature of the field helps to answer Wolpe's question, for we can see that it is in the political best interest of the psychodynamic adherents to ignore negative evidence.

We maintain, then, that refusal to admit negative evidence constitutes functionally effective professional behavior and has become characteristic of the traditional applied mental health field in general. The present chapter is not appropriate for further development of this argument. It has been presented briefly to point out that this exploration of failures in behavior therapy has been undertaken against the general background of the mental health field's traditional evasion of its failures and the attendant loss of opportunity for corrective feedback. It also points out that behavior therapy, embedded in clinical procedures and values, faces the same problems. In time and with growing status, behavior therapy runs the risk of becoming as politically self-defensive as the rest of the field. However, we believe behavioral models are less likely than traditional models to fall so deeply into the self-defensive trap of ignoring negative evidence. Their strong empirical tradition keeps us not too far away from the scientific willingness to base our decisions on objective data and to discard unproductive lines of inquiry.

Webster's tells us that failure means, "an inability to perform a normal function . . .a lack of success" But what is meant by failure in behavior therapy? Is it an outcome event, a phase in a process? Does it occur when the client and therapist try their best, but to little or no avail; when the client refuses from the start to accept the basic behavioral values and approaches or to invest the necessary effort and, therefore, drops out; when change is successful but incomplete, or when relapse later occurs? Is it when the therapist is not sensitive to potential value conflicts with clients, agencies, or other professionals—conflicts that can reduce the likelihood of success? Failure in behavior therapy is all of these; it is a complex variable occurring at many levels.

Our working definition of failure, then, is not to be limited to outcome events alone. Rather, we will develop the idea that failure can occur at any point in the behavior therapy process. Further, because it is the therapist who offers the service and assumes major control over the relevant treatment variables, we assign responsibility for those failures to the therapist and not to the clients or to society's inadequate supports for the mental health professions.

Two major categories of failure will be discussed, contextual failures and technical failures, with several examples presented in each.

CONTEXTUAL FAILURES

Ours is a multivalued world and the objective empiricism and outcome emphases of behavior modifiers are but selective examples of society's many divergent values and procedures. Value issues in behavior modification have been discussed by many writers (e.g., Graziano, 1975; London, 1972; Reppucci & Saunders, 1974). Every therapeutic effort is carried out within a context that is necessarily larger than the immediate goals and procedures of behavior change. That context includes the physical and social setting in which the treatment is carried out, as well as the divergent values, beliefs, and goals not only of the clients, but also of other professionals, supporting staff, the agency, and the community as a whole. The context exerts powerful control over treatment based on any theoretical model, and when the therapist is insensitive to the complexities of the surrounding context, failure may be likely. Contextual failures, then, are those occurring when nontherapeutic control, exerted by some aspect of the surrounding context, takes precedence and diverts the behavior therapist from desired behavior change goals.

The most obvious examples of contextual failures are those in which treatment is disrupted because behavior modification values come into conflict with surrounding value systems. In the applied settings, each based upon and operated with a diversity of value systems, every new application of behavior modification is potentially in conflict with the surrounding sets of values held by others, and such value conflicts have often been severe enough to bring about failures, even to the dissolution of entire programs. One of the early descriptions of value conflicts in an applied child-treatment setting was by Graziano (1969, 1974) who described the professional-political issues involved in an early 1960's attempt to initiate a behavior modification treatment program for autistic children in a community dominated by traditional psychiatric agencies. The program operated for six years but in spite of its apparent therapeutic successes, it ended in a flurry of value conflicts, and the state lost its only alternative to traditional services for autistic children. The failure of this program to survive has been discussed at length by Sarason (1972) as an example of the professionals' failures to appreciate and accommodate the historical and social context within which the new behavioral program was attempting to function as a change agent.

Similarly, Reppucci (1977) and Reppucci and Saunders (1974) discussed the variety of issues that hampered behavioral programming in a residential setting for children, some 10 years after the initiation of the program described above. Behavior modifiers, they noted, were perceived by mental health staff and administrators as espousing values and procedures that were so radically different from the traditional ways of working with children that the psychologists seemed even "to speak a different language." Such communication barriers are further illustrated by Wolfolk and Wolfolk (1975). Replicating earlier work, they found that describing a film of standard public school procedures in the language of "human growth" resulted in more favorable evaluation by undergraduate and graduate education majors than when the same procedures were described in behavioral science terminology. They suggest, as have others (e.g., Wilson & Evans, 1978) that some "humanizing" of the behavior modification language might help its general acceptance.

A similar issue was described by Balaschak (1976) who reduced severe seizures in an 11-year-old epileptic girl through a teacher-administered contingency management program. Balaschak observed that although organically based, the seizures appeared to be under operant control, triggered by academic and social pressures, and maintained by various forms of parent, teacher, and peer attention. The teacher was taught to provide positive reinforcement for seizure-free time periods, monitoring progress with a "good times" chart. The girl became quite involved in the challenge of self-controlling her seizures. The seizures decreased in school and later at home, after the mother initiated a similar contingency management program. Unfortunately, the child then had several weeks' absence from school because of an infectious illness. When the girl returned, the teacher eliminated the program and refused to reinstate it in spite of its earlier success both at home and in school. Over the remaining two months of school, under the teacher's refusal to carry out the program, the girl's seizures climbed back up to their pretreatment rate. In this case a technically successful behavioral intervention for a problem that had no other demonstrable means of solution turned out to be unsuccessful because another professional refused to cooperate. Although the reasons for the teacher's decision were not made clear, there appears to have been conflict between the teacher's educational values and the behavior change values of the consultant. The teacher, Balaschak suggests, believed that focusing on behavior change conflicted with the values and goals of intellectual and academic growth, and would inhibit the child's development.

Thus value conflicts can occur between the principles and procedures of behavior modification and the multivalued surrounding reality that forms the contexts for our interventions. Those conflicts can reduce a behavioral program's effectiveness and threaten its survival. Behavior modification with children suffers contextual failures when its designers do not adequately recognize the multivalued nature of society and do not anticipate, avoid, or resolve value conflicts.

Another type of contextual failure involves not the direct conflict between values but, rather, the subverting of the therapist's values by those of the context. This may be best seen in classrooms where, as discussed by Graziano (1975), teachers and children are participant observers of behaviors that range from amusing to bizarre. In their complex daily interactions, teachers and pupils alike function smoothly, often with good humor, enjoyment, and success. They also become bored, upset, lose control, and behave irrationally and disruptively—but only the children are "corrected" for such behavior.

Behavior modification has been used in such "correctional" service and has been criticized for too readily serving some questionable goals (Kanfer, 1973; Winett & Winkler, 1972). Considering the many criticisms of those goals (e.g., Silberman, 1970), behavior modifiers may have in some ways impeded improvements in education. Winett and Winkler found that many of the recent behavioral studies carried out in schools focused on such goals as reducing disruptive or inappropriate behavior (e.g., out-of-seat, running, talking to peers, etc.), and increasing what was considered to be appropriate behavior (e.g., attending to the teacher, remaining seated, working quietly, etc.). This use of new behavioral technology to support old goals and values is not surprising, inasmuch as the behavior modifiers are in the schools at the invitation of the school personnel who define or at least transmit the goals.

Finally, examples of contextual failures are those behavioral programs in which failure occurs not because of value conflicts, but because the therapist fails to assess whether the context can provide the basic supports necessary to carry out behavioral programming. Fine, Nesbitt, and Tyler (1974) for example, reported failure of programming in a school to improve an eight-year-old's behavior. The behavioral consultants recognized, but too late, that they had not adequately trained the teacher to carry out the specific programming procedures. The teacher's original doubts and misunderstandings had never been clarified, and training in how to systematically reinforce and record behavior had not been carried out. In addition, the time and attention required for these proved to be "excessive for the teacher." The researchers noted their "case accentuates the importance of the teacher in the behavior modification process. Yet it is disconcerting to note that actual problems such as those noted in (their) paper seem to be treated very lightly in the literature" (p. 17).

A large-scale school intervention program in which the context did not provide necessary supports was reported by Rogeness, Stokes, Bednar, and Gorman (1977). Their two-year intervention with an entire school "as a social unit," provided mental health and behavioral consultation "so that behaviors and attitudes that promote learning could be consistently reinforced throughout the school" (p. 246). Their data revealed improvements in anxiety, impulse control, and behavior problems among the students during the program's first year. The second year, however, not only showed little improvement, but posted some significant changes in the opposite directions; that is, anxiety and problem-solving increased, and impulse control decreased.

Among the researchers' major speculations about the reasons for the second year's disappointing results was their own failure to recognize and understand the school social system's characteristics and values before implementing the program. A requisite open, trustful working relationship and good communication among faculty and with administrators, and the teachers' "sense of being in control of their classes" were belatedly seen as necessary elements that were lacking in that system. An initial preparatory program aimed at some of those variables might have improved the program's success. "Before attempting a similar program in a school," they noted, "it would be important to understand the organization of the school and what is being reinforced by that organization" (p. 254).

Contextual failures are not limited to school systems but occur also in the context of the home, and particularly when parents become the behavioral change agents. There is little doubt that one of the major developments in behavior therapy with children has been its application in the natural environment of the child's home, with the active and often directive participation of the parents trained in behavior change methods. An astonishing amount of research has been carried out in the relatively short period of the past 15 years (Graziano, 1977).

Any form of behavior therapy used in an outpatient clinic, where the child is seen by a therapist for only one or two hours per week, must direct a major effort towards changing the behavior of the parents, who control the reinforcing contingencies that shape the child's behavior. But contextual failures occur here too, and we find some published cases in which behavior therapy at home failed because the parents either refused or were unable to carry out the behavioral programming. For example, Doleys (1977) reviews treatment for nocturnal enuresis and reports that the most common reason for failure of the urine alarm method, probably our most widely used behavioral treatment, was lack of parental cooperation. Four studies will be presented as examples of failures of the therapist to assess the context when training parents in child behavior modification.

Salzinger, Feldman, and Portnoy (1970) trained parents of brain-injured children in operant conditioning procedures in an extensive program. Training included behavior observation skills and instruction in operant conditioning principles, a detailed manual on which each parent was tested, development of specific program packages to apply to each family's problems, and individual and group sessions to monitor the actual execution of the treatment. Successful changes were reported in every case where the parents carried out the procedures as designed (four families), limited success for families who carried out only parts of the program (four families), and no change in behavior for parents who did not carry out the procedures (seven families).

Ferber, Keeley, and Shemberg (1974) trained parents in seven families with noncompliant children in a parent training program. They reported short-term positive changes in three of the families, based on a parent interview four weeks following treatment, and success at one-year follow-up for only one of the families. The rest all reported serious problems with their children.

In a study by Bernal, Klinnert, and Shultz (1980), therapists trained the parents of conduct-problem children aged 5 to 12 in either behavior management skills or client-centered therapy. They found significant improvement in parents' reports of problem behavior for the behavioral treatment and waiting-list control groups immediately following treatment, although no differences were found at this time in home observations of the children's behaviors. Upon follow-up at 6 and 12 months, parents' reports indicated no differences between the client-centered and behavioral treatment groups. The authors interpret these findings as indicating no actual improvement in the behavior therapy treatment group as compared to the other two groups at posttreatment, as shown by the home observation data. They explain the favorable parent report for the behavioral treatment group as due to the fact that these parents were "tuned in" to specific behaviors they had been monitoring as part of the treatment, and rated them as changed due to a "cognitive dissonance" effect. Some support for this conclusion comes from the fact that the more global ratings of child behavior, more likely to be rated as changed by the client-centered group, did not differ between the groups immediately after treatment. The general finding of this study, then, is that training parents in behavior modification procedures failed to bring about change in their children's behaviors.

Finally, Cole and Morrow (1976) trained small groups of parents whose children exhibited management problems. Ten sessions of step-by-step behavior modification were carried out. Although they described their program as generally successful in modifying one or more specific behaviors identified by the parents, these authors also identified parent behaviors that led to some failures to bring about behavioral change.

One reason cited by Cole and Morrow for failure of their program was the inability of parents experiencing marital discord to cooperate in the treatment. Problems included failure of parents to agree on designated behaviors or the level of severity of the behaviors, and inability to consistently carry out the planned interventions. Ferber et al. (1974) also cite marital problems as a factor contributing to parents' inability to carry out their treatments. The problem of marital discord affecting the success or failure of behavioral treatment was studied by Oltmanns, Broderick, and O'Leary (1977), who found that parents of children being treated for behavior problems were significantly more likely to have marital problems than a control group, although in this study level of marital adjustment was not related to efficacy of the behavioral treatment.

Cole and Morrow (1976) also cite a pattern of parent behavior described as "authoritarian" as contributing to failure of some parents to carry out the treatment procedures. These parents were characterized as punitive, judgmental, unable to focus on their children's positive behaviors, and insistent on immediate obedience to their authority. They were often unwilling to carry out the techniques step by step, and refused to continue techniques that did not show immediate achievement of therapy goals.

Salzinger et al. (1970) suggest that intelligence, verbal ability, and a high level of formal education are important predictors of therapy success. Those parents who scored high on tests of knowledge and understanding of operant principles were also more likely to be at least partially successful in carrying out the treatment in their study.

The reasons for parents' refusal to carry out behavior modification procedures may include a lack of understanding of their own contribution to the child's problem and a desire for the therapist to "fix up" the child, hostility to the therapist, hostility to the concepts of behavior modification, or hostility toward the child (Ferber et al., 1974). As Salzinger et al. (1970) report,

> Parents show strongly conditioned behaviors incompatible with those necessary to change their children's behavior in the desired direction. (p. 22)

> Parents' (behavior), no less than their children's behavior is subject to reinforcement contingencies, and in a number of cases we clearly could not provide suitably strong reinforcement through our method of training. (p. 20)

Behavior modification with children thus can fail even when it has been technically successful in changing specified behavior. The critical elements in those failures are the values and goals of the surrounding historical, social, and personal contexts within which therapy is carried out versus those of the behavior therapy model. When the therapist is so grossly immersed in behavioral technologies and values as to be insensitive to the realities of the context, then the probability for value conflicts, values subverting, and for proceeding in insufficiently prepared or supportive settings, increases. Technical expertise in behavior analyses and modification is not sufficient for success; knowledge of and sensitivity to the surrounding contexts is also needed. We suggest that such contextual failures are particularly apt to occur in working with children, because children as a class, compared with our adult clients, are far more subject to daily and detailed control by social contexts. When behavior modifiers add their own values to the already crowded controls over children, the chances of conflicts, and thus failure, are increased.

It must be emphasized that although we identify significant variables here as extratherapeutic, the failures arise only when those values are juxtaposed with those of the behavior modifier. The responsibility for the failure is still the therapist's, upon whom the demands are rightly made to operate with sensitivity to the details of each programming context, and to assess the levels of skill and commitment of significant adults within those contexts.

TECHNICAL FAILURES

Generalization and Maintenance

The processes involved in behavioral analyses, modification, generalization, and maintenance are complex, and in programming for even a single child there are many points at which technical errors can be made. Technical failures are here thought of as those made by the behavior therapist, and are independent of the surrounding context. For example, successfully bringing about behavior change without systematic inclusion of program elements to generalize those changes across settings and over time (i.e., maintenance) are technical failures that could occur in any context. Generalization and maintenance failures have been documented, lamented, and frequently reviewed in most areas of behavior therapy, and work with children is no exception. Reporting maintenance and generalization data is rare, as noted by Keeley, Shemberg, and Carbonell (1976). They found that in only 8 of the 146 operant studies they reviewed, were "hard" follow-up data of at least six months posttreatment reported.

Focusing on token systems, Levine and Fasnacht (1974) and Levine, Fasnacht, Funabiki, and Burkart (1979) reported that generalization and maintenance failures are common events in token reinforcement systems, whatever the nature of the client. The immediate effectiveness of token systems has been demonstrated many times: children have demonstrably improved their social and academic behavior in school and at home; the aversive qualities of mother–child interactions in many families have been reduced with tokens; and positive, cooperative parent–child interactions have been developed. However, despite such successes, Levine and Fasnacht express "trepidations about the long-range value" of token systems. Token programs, they argue, follow the same laws of extinction as do all other reinforcement systems. They and many others (e.g., Koegel & Rincover, 1977) note that in order to insure generalization and maintenance of gains, appropriate procedures must be specifically programmed into the treatment.

In an interesting analysis Levine et al. (1979) reviewed 12 studies of token systems that claimed maintenance of behavioral gain. They criticized the studies for having follow-ups that were too brief, for failure to control for maturation of subjects, for lack of control groups, and for the confounding effects of social reinforcers. With this latter point, the reviewers were able to suggest an alternative explanation of maintenance when it did occur; that is, in carrying out the token system the personnel may have learned the value of contingent social reinforcement and may thus have changed their own patterns of reinforcement. Thus the maintenance of treatment gains, they suggest, might not have been due to the reinforcing power of the tokens over the subjects but, rather, due to the altered behavior of the staff in posttreatment periods. Token systems then, might have maintenance value, but that maintenance may have been erroneously attributed to the effects of the tokens upon the clients. Their alternative explanation remains feasible, they maintain, inasmuch as the methodological errors made in most token research have not eliminated this, and perhaps other, alternative hypotheses.

Clinical or Personal Significance

In addition to the goals of behavior change, generalization, and maintenance, therapists are also responsible for bringing about change that is clinically or personally significant for the clients. Change, even if it is large, generalized, and maintained, is of little value if it does not make some real improvement in the life of the child or the family. This goal appears to be so basic as to be unquestionable and yet we do find instances of successful change that is of doubtful personal significance.

Some behavioral research has focused on a specific clinical population, identified some of the excess and deficit behaviors that differentiate the group of children from "normal" controls, and then have used behavioral techniques to bring about changes in these specific behaviors. It is assumed that changing these specified behaviors will then lead to changes in the behaviors that categorize the children as members of a clinical population and thus remove them from that population. Some examples are found in behavior therapy with "inattentive" children, socially withdrawn or isolated children, juvenile delinquents, and with child-abusing parents. These studies have demonstrated changes in children's behavior but these changes have not led to improvements in the more basic problems that determined their initial categorization within a clinical population. The studies demonstrate change, and in many cases also demonstrate generalization and maintenance of the changes, but fail to appreciably alter the child's problem.

For example, behavioral treatments to improve on-task academic behavior of children have used behavioral techniques to train self-instruction, self-monitoring, and other such behaviors that have been identified as differentiating "normal" school children from those with attention disorders, such as retarded children with attention problems. Many of these studies have demonstrated change in children's attentional behavior, but rarely do they lead to improvements in the subjects' academic performance, the major problem that was supposedly to be addressed. One such study was reported by Shemberg, Keeley, Gill, and Garton (1972). These authors used contingent reinforcement (M & Ms) given on a two-minute, fixed-interval schedule, to increase the classroom attending behavior of six mildly retarded children, ages 8 to 10, during arithmetic class. Designated behaviors of staying in their seat, not talking out in class, looking at the teacher, and looking at the materials were found to increase significantly upon reinforcement. However, the increase in attending behavior did not affect performance on arithmetic problems, and the authors suggest that, in fact, the high rate of reinforcement may have interfered with learning of arithmetic. The children, they suggest, may have learned a set of visual–motor attending behaviors that had no relationship to learning arithmetic, and were reinforced by higher valence reinforcers than those given for correct responses.

In a more recent study, Burgio, Whitman, and Johnson (1980) developed a self-instructional package to increase attending behavior in mildly retarded children. These researchers found significant improvement in attending behavior, and decrease in off-task behavior based on classroom observations following treatment. Again, however, no significant change was reported in the children's academic performance following training.

These studies illustrate a common finding with retarded children, that changes in a child's attending behavior will not necessarily affect academic performance. As Shemberg et al. (1972) conclude,

> Thus, if researchers and practitioners are interested in contingency controlled attentional behaviors for anything other than behavioral management, then much further work is needed to define more clearly the relationship between such attentional behaviors and the acquisition of academic skills. (p. 625)

There is a growing interest in social skills training for socially withdrawn, or "isolated," children. Assuming that intervention is needed, teachers and researchers have applied a variety of behavioral techniques that include modeling, flooding, direct social skill training of children, and training teachers. Studies often cite as justification the work by Cowan, Pederson, Babigian, Izzo, and Trost (1973), that found a child's popularity with peers to be the strongest predictor of later emotional adjustment. Social skills training programs have been aimed at improving a large number of behaviors with the goal of improving a child's popularity in the classroom. They have demonstrated changes in a wide variety of social skills, but have not found changes in sociometric peer ratings of popularity, the measure found by Cowan et al. (1973) to be the best predictor of later adjustment. Two recent examples illustrate this point: La Greca and Santogrossi (1980) trained third, fourth, and fifth graders with low-peer-acceptance as measured by sociometric ratings. The training focused on social skills, including greeting, conversing, sharing, smiling, and complimenting. They found the children in the four-week treatment group to be significantly better at verbal social skills, a role-play assessment of skills, and classroom behavioral observations of initiating behavior and positive social skills, as compared to both a waiting list and placebo control groups. No change was found on the sociometric ratings due to the treatment.

Another recent example is a study by Whitehill, Hersen, and Bellack (1980), in which four socially isolated children, chosen in a four-step criterion process that included sociometric ratings, behavioral measures of conversational skills, teacher ratings of social isolation, and classroom behavioral observations, were trained in social conversation skills. The three-week training program led to marked improvement over the baseline scores in all designated behaviors: number of informative statements, number of open-ended questions, and number of requests for shared activity, as well as improvement in overall conversational ability. These treatment gains generalized to the classroom, where treated children were found to spend less time in isolated free play immediately following the treatment and at four- and eight-week follow-up than at baseline. Again, however, there was no change in peer sociometric measures, or in teacher ratings of popularity of the children. The authors suggest that "criteria for peer acceptance (or rejection) may have only little to do with the targeted verbal skills" (p. 224).

Other studies of withdrawn children since 1975 include four controlled experimental studies treating a total of about 176 children. All of these studies have selected children from regular classrooms (Evers-Pasquale & Sherman, 1975; Gottman, 1977; Gottman, Gonso, & Shuler, 1976; Weinrott, Corson, & Wilchesky, 1979). There have been three case studies dealing with 11 children and these studies have selected withdrawn children with additional problems (Kandel, Ayllon & Rosenbaum, 1977; Strain, 1977; Strain & Pierce, 1977). Thus a sizeable number of children have been identified as withdrawn, and included as subjects in behavior change studies.

In a recent review, however, Shenfeld (1980) questions what she views as the too easily made assumptions about the nature of the "quieter" children and the desirability of intervention. Shenfeld writes

> That treatment strategies are being devised for these children suggests that professionals are concerned with the current or future adjustment of isolated and withdrawn children. This statement, however self-evident, introduces the crucial question whether treatment is in fact warranted for these different populations. No doubt, there is something intuitively disturbing about the withdrawn child who interacts infrequently with his peers. Similarly, it is tempting to infer that the child who has few friends or is outwardly rejected by his peers must be sad and lonely. Nonetheless, since children do not usually have the freedom to choose whether to accept treatment and typically do not volunteer for such programs, it is incumbent upon the researcher or treatment provider to demonstrate that these children actually could benefit from, or are in need of, treatment. (pp. 5–6)

Shenfeld discusses some of the major assumptions made about the less interactive children. These include assumptions that the child whose social interaction rate is low necessarily lacks social skills, that the child would "really" prefer to be more interactive and thus would welcome the intervention, that such children are mildly "unhappy" or dissatisfied, that solitary play for preschoolers (the group for whom most of the "social isolation" research has been developed) is less desirable than socially interactive play, and that such children will have greater future problems in adjustment. These are all, according to Shenfeld, only assumptions, largely untested, and in some cases, challenged by data. Researchers and teachers would be prudent to concern themselves with the issues raised and discussed by Shenfeld.

Thus children considered by their teachers or by psychologists to be socially withdrawn have been approached through a variety of behavioral techniques. The goal has typically been to increase the children's interactive social behavior and is based on a number of assumptions about children who are observed to be relatively inactive in social situations. The assumptions need verification and researchers are cautioned against too quickly interpreting these children's adjustment as "problematic." In this area the most important future research might not be in attempts to sharpen our ability to modify children's behavior towards increasing rates of social interaction but, rather, in sharpening our ability to differentially select from among the "quieter" children those whose relative social inactivity is, in fact, problematic *for the child;* that is, that the changes brought about are, in fact, of personal or clinical significance.

A great deal of behavioral programming with juvenile delinquents has been carried out during the past two decades, with considerable success in changing the youths' behavior. However, three reviews (Davidson & Seidman, 1974; Emery & Marholin, 1977; Graziano & Mooney, in press) of work from 1968 through 1980 concluded that positive changes have involved primarily institutional or academic behavior, that is, improved academic performance, improved housekeeping behavior, reduced fighting in cottages, more positive self-statements in group discussion meetings, and so on. Although presumably of value for many youths, those changes have not been associated with convincing demonstrations of impact upon delinquent behavior per se, and there is as yet no convincing indication that such improvements have had any effects in reducing juvenile delinquency. In their review Emery and Marholin (1977) noted that of all designated behaviors reported from 1968 to mid-1976, less than 4 percent were delinquent behaviors as such. Further, they noted, few studies involved individual functional analyses, and the vast majority of designated behaviors were predetermined by the investigators, apparently assumed to be characteristic and significant problems for all members of the group. Thus even when changes were brought about, the question must be asked, "Were those changes of personal and/or clinical significance for the youth involved?" In our view, many of the behavior modification studies of juvenile delinquency are examples of the failure of personal and/or clinical significance.

Our final examples in this section are drawn from a new area of behavioral research, child abuse. This is a difficult and distressing problem and, except for medical studies of injuries, little systematic research has been carried out although there is a voluminous literature on social service programs and case descriptions.

The typical case-by-case approach of most social service agencies is a combination of immediate medical care of the child when necessary, temporary protective custody of the child followed by return to the parents, and psychological counseling and economic and other support for the parents. There are serious limitations to this standard approach: It has no primary prevention value, there is little evidence that the psychodynamic-based therapies or economic supports are effective in reducing child abuse, and little or nothing is done to protect the child, who often must remain with the possibly still abusive parent. Finally, in the typical program virtually no immediate or long-term psychological, social, or educational support is given to the child to mitigate the effects of the abusive early history.

Recently, more behaviorally oriented approaches have been reported. They utilize functional behavior analyses to identify conditions under which abuse occurs and to plan treatment for the parents' abusive behavior. For example, papers by Crozier and Katz (1979), Denicola and Sandler (1980), and Sandler, VanDercar, and Milhoan (1978) described similar behavioral treatments for abusive parents in their homes. Other reports involving some aspects of behavioral approaches are those by Ambrose, Hazard, and Haworth (1980), Doctor and Singer (1978), Mastria, Mastria, and Harkins (1979), and Reavley and Gilbert (1979). Although improvements were reported, the major problem in this work is failure to provide objective physical evidence that the children's abuse had, in fact, been decreased. In only one study, Tracey and Clark (1974), which can be considered only minimally "behavioral," were the children regularly monitored and examined for physical signs of abuse and neglect in posttreatment follow-ups. In the other studies changes were reported in parent–child interactions, parent attitudes, and parental self-reports of use of punishment. However, if the major goal of therapy for child abuse is to eliminate the adult's abusive behavior towards the child, then neither the traditional social service programs nor the more recent behaviorally based interventions appear to have succeeded. Here then are examples of possible failures of clinical or personal significance.

Negative Effects of Treatment

Psychological treatment has many possible effects upon clients, intended and unintended, ranging from negative through positive (Graziano & Fink, 1973). These authors maintain that therapists do not sufficiently monitor possible negative effects of their interventions. The assumption is too easily made that our clients will either be helped or, at least, unchanged by our interventions. In fact, clients might become worse as a result of our treatment, and such unintended negative effects constitute another category of failure in behavior therapy. This failure is compounded in cases where negative effects occur but the therapist remains unaware of them. Several examples of unintended negative effects of behavioral treatments of children will be presented. In these examples, the authors did become aware of the problems.

A possible consequence of monitoring undesirable specified behaviors may be an increase in these behaviors. An example of this can be found in a report of a token program to increase on-task and decrease off-task behaviors in learning disabled and emotionally disturbed children in a day treatment classroom (Wasserman & Vogrin, 1979). A behavioral checklist consisting of six on-task and four off-task behaviors was used to assess behavior during each class period. Children earned tokens for on-task behaviors, and lost tokens for off-task behaviors or for failing to do appropriate on-task behaviors. The 30-week program led to a significant increase in the number of tokens lost due to inappropriate behaviors over the course of the treatment. The authors suggest that with the introduction of a token program, all designated behaviors, both appropriate and inappropriate, increased, and the addition of a response-cost component to the program was not sufficient to curtail the undesirable increase.

Another negative side effect of using tokens to increase behavior has been discussed by Levine and Fasnacht (1974). These authors warn that using tokens to increase desirable behaviors with "normal" children might decrease the intrinsic reinforcing value of those behaviors. They cite three studies in which it was found that rewarding a group of children for performing some activity led to less interest in and lower subjective ratings of enjoyment for the activity as compared to a no-reward group. Levine and Fasnacht argue that external reinforcers should not be used for any behaviors that may have intrinsic interest, because using tokens might lead to a decrease in interest. This notion is supported by the results of the study by Shemberg et al. (1972) which we reported previously, that suggested that use of reinforcers within a classroom may lead to an emphasis on learning the appropriate behavior to obtain the reinforcers, rather than on learning for its own sake.

Punishing undesirable behavior can also have negative effects. Treatments to eliminate self-injurious behavior in severely retarded and psychotic children have reported negative side effects using punishment procedures. Overcorrection, a procedure by which a client repeatedly performs an exercise involving the part of the body that performed the self-injury, in response to its occurrence, has been reported in some instances as leading to increases in other undesirable behaviors (Clements & Dewey, 1979) or other forms of self-injury.

Treatment of severe self-injurious behavior by the use of electric shock has also led to negative side effects. At least eight studies have reported negative emotional behavior such as fear and avoidance of the shock apparatus, and crying and withdrawal in response to the shock (summarized in Lichstein & Schreibman, 1976). In a study using a shock prod contingent on the occurrence of the self-injurious behavior, Bucher and Lovaas (1968) reported one subject who exhibited more aggressive behavior. Galbraith, Byrick, and Rutledge (1970), using a remote-control shock device to decrease chronic vomiting, reported high rates of new forms of self-injurious and other inappropriate behaviors, which were subsequently brought under control by the staff. Prochaska, Smith, Marzilli, Colby, and Donovan (1974) reported an increase in the self-injurious behavior of head-snapping after application of shock to punish head-banging and face-slapping. Prochaska et al. (1974) and Romanczyk and Goren (1975) all report the problem of equipment failure leading to temporary increases in self-injurious behavior. Ball, Sibbach, Jones, Steele, and Frazier (1975) describe a case of adaptation to shock in one study, and also report that the use of a jacket with pressure-sensitive switches to punish self-hitting and pinching led to the inhibition of all arm movement, including sign language.

A final example of negative effects is given in a paper by Herbert, Pinkston, Haydon, Sajwaj, Pinkston, Cordua, and Jackson (1973). Six mother–child pairs were included in a program to train parents in the use of contingent attention to their children as differential reinforcement to increase desirable child behavior and decrease deviant behavior. The children, all in special education classes, exhibited fairly severe behavior problems at pretreatment. Unfortunately, the training results were negative. The authors reported that the children's deviant behaviors did not decrease under the differential parental attention procedure but, in four of the six children, "actually increased in substantial and durable manner." The increased disruptive behavior was by no means trivial, including that of four children who began assaulting their mothers, another who "rammed a pencil into his nose and bled profusely," and one who became more enuretic. One of the children who had become assaultive towards her mother also began to scratch herself severely.

In discussing their findings of such negative impact of the use of differential parental attention, the authors question the common assumption that "parental attention is a positive reinforcer and that its systematic use in a differential reinforcement procedure will control undesirable behaviors." The researchers urge more careful study to identify the limiting conditions for the successful application of such "elementary" interventions, and greater caution in too avidly applying such principles.

SUMMARY AND CONCLUSIONS

Given the limited space of one chapter, our consideration of failures in child behavior therapy has been, of necessity, tentative, a beginning statement that must leave more development for a later opportunity. These considerations have been set against a background of a general unwillingness of the mental health profession to monitor its effectiveness and to examine its own failures. We have argued that the field of applied mental health services characteristically ignores its failures primarily because of political professional gains to be had by doing so. Behavior therapy, because of its conceptual alignment with empiricism may be more likely to avoid the self-defensive professional trap of minimizing or ignoring failures while maximizing perceptions of successes. However, the potential for falling into that same self-defensive trap is real, and behavior modifiers should be alert to and guard against that possibility.

We have argued that failures can occur at any point in treatment, and are not limited to only outcome events. Further, when failures do occur, they must be attributed to the actions of the behavior therapist and not to some extra therapeutic factors, as is commonly attributed in psychodynamic treatment models. Because failures can occur at any point in treatment, a variety of conditions controls their many forms. For the present discussion, two major categories of failures were suggested, contextual failures and technical failures. The former occur as a result of the therapist's inadequate assessment of the contexts within which the treatment occurs. Those treatment contexts include the physical and social settings in which treatment is carried out as well as the divergent values, beliefs, and goals not only of the clients, but also of other professionals, supporting staff, the agency, and the community. The contexts exert powerful control over treatment based on any theoretical model, and when the therapist is insensitive to the complexities of the surrounding contexts, failures may be likely. Contextual failures may be of particular importance when working with children because they, more than adults, are under the control of a variety of powerful social contexts—that is, parents, school, social agencies, and so on. Examples of contextual failures were discussed.

Technical failures were discussed as those that are largely independent of the context, and they include problems such as poor generalization and maintenance of behavior changes, failure to specify and bring about changes that are of clinical or personal significance for the child, and failure to guard against unintended negative effects of the treatment. Examples in the literature of technical failures in child behavior therapy were discussed.

We believe that the behavior therapist has a special responsibility to guard against failures when working with children because children, unlike many adult clients, do not have skills to monitor their own progress and to constructively assert to the therapist that changes in the interventions are needed.

REFERENCES

Ambrose, S., Hazard, A., & Haworth, J. (1980) Cognitive behavioral treatment for abusive families. *Child Abuse and Neglect,* **4,** 119–125.

Balaschak, B. A. (1976) Teacher-implemented behavior modification in a case of organically based epilepsy. *Journal of Consulting and Clinical Psychology,* **44,** 218–223.

Ball, T., Sibbach, L., Jones, R., Steele, B., & Frazer, L. (1975) An accelerometer-activated device to control assaultive and self-destructive behaviors in retardates. *Journal of Behavior Therapy and Experimental Psychiatry,* **6,** 223–228.

Bernal, M., Klinnert, M., & Shultz, L. (1980) Outcome evaluation of behavioral parent training and client-centered parent counseling for children with conduct problems. *Journal of Applied Behavior Analysis,* **13,** 677–691.

Bucher, B., & Lovaas, O. (1968) Use of aversive stimulation in behavior modification. In M. R. Jones (Ed.), *Miami symposium on the prediction of behavior, 1967.* Coral Gables, Fla.: University of Miami.

Burgio, L., Whitman, T., & Johnson, M. (1980) A self-instructional package for increasing attending behavior in educably mentally retarded children. *Journal of Applied Behavior Analysis,* **13,** 443–459.

Clements, J., & Dewey, M. (1979) The effects of overcorrection: A case study. *Behavior Research and Therapy,* **17,** 515–518.

Cole, C., & Morrow, W. (1976) Refractory parent behaviors in behavior modification training groups. *Psychotherapy: Theory, Research, and Practice,* **13,** 162–169.

Cowan, E., Pederson, A., Babigian, H., Izzo, L., & Trost, N. (1973) Long-term followup of early detected vulnerable children. *Journal of Consulting and Clinical Psychology,* **41,** 438–446.

Crozier, J., & Katz, R. (1979) Social learning treatment of child abuse. *Journal of Behavior Therapy and Experimental Psychiatry,* **10,** 213–220.

Davidson, W.S., & Seidman, E. (1974) Studies of behavior modification and juvenile delinquency: A review, methodological critique, and social perspective. *Psychological Bulletin,* **81,** 998–1011.

Denicola, J., & Sandler, J. (1980) Training abusive parents in child-management and self-control skill. *Behavior Therapy,* **11,** 263–270.

Doctor, R., & Singer, E. M. (1978) Behavioral intervention strategies with child-abusing parents: A home-intervention program. *Child Abuse and Neglect,* **2,** 57–68.

Doleys, D. (1977) Behavioral treatments for nocturnal enuresis in children: A review of the recent literature. *Psychological Bulletin,* **84,** 30–54.

Emery, R. E., & Marholin, D. (1977) An applied behavior analysis of delinquency: The irrelevancy of relevant behavior. *American Psychologist,* **32,** 860–873.

Evers-Pasquale, W., & Sherman, M. (1975) The reward value of peers: A variable influencing the efficacy of filmed modeling in modifying social isolation in preschoolers. *Journal of Abnormal Child Psychology,* **3,** 179–190.

Ferber, H., Keeley, S., & Shemberg, K. (1976) Training parents in behavior modification: Outcome of and problems encountered in a program after Patterson's work. *Behavior Therapy,* **5,** 415–419.

Fine, M. J., Nesbitt, M. A., & Tyler, M. M. (1974) Analysis of a failing attempt at behavior modification. *Journal of Learning Disabilities,* **7,** 12–17.

Galbraith, D., Byrick, R., & Rutledge, S. (1970) An aversive conditioning approach to the inhibition of chronic vomiting. *Canadian Psychiatric Association Journal,* **15,** 311–313.

Gottman, J. (1977) The effects of a modeling film on social isolation in pre-school children: A methodological investigation. *Journal of Abnormal Child Psychology,* **5,** 69–78.

Gottman, J., Gonso, J., & Schuler, P. (1976) Teaching social skills to isolated children. *Journal of Abnormal Child Psychology,* **4,** 179–198.

Graziano, A. M. (1969) Clinical innovation and the mental health power structure: A social case history. *American Psychologist,* **24,** 10–18.

Graziano, A. M. (1972) In the mental health industry, illness is our most important product. *Psychology Today,* **5,** 12–18.

Graziano, A. M. (1974) *Child without tomorrow.* Elmsford, N. Y.: Pergamon.

Graziano, A. M. (1975) *Behavior therapy with children: Volume II.* Chicago: Aldine.

Graziano, A. M. (1977) Parents as behavior therapists. In M. Hersen, R. M. Eisler, & P. M. Miller (Eds.), *Progress in behavior modification.* New York: Academic.

Graziano, A. M., & Fink, R. (1973) Second-order effects in mental health treatment. *Journal of Consulting and Clinical Psychology,* **40,** 356–364.

Graziano, A. M., & Mooney, K. C. (in press) *Children and behavior therapy: Research and applications.* New York: Aldine.

Herbert, E., Pinkston, E., Haydon, M., Sajwaj, T., Pinkston, S., Cordua, G., & Jackson, C. (1973) Adverse effects of differential parental attention. *Journal of Applied Behavior Analysis,* **6,** 15–30.

Kandel, H., Ayllon, T., & Rosenbaum, M. (1977) Flooding or systematic exposure in the treatment of extreme social withdrawal in children. *Journal of Behavior Therapy and Experimental Psychiatry,* **8,** 75–81.

Kanfer, F. H. (1973) *Behavior modification in education: A few opinions on critical issues.* Unpublished manuscript, University of Illinois.

Keeley, S. M., Shemberg, K. M., & Carbonell, J. (1976) Operant clinical intervention: Behavior management or beyond? Where are the data? *Behavior Therapy,* **44,** 297–299.

Koegel, R. L., & Rincover, A. (1977) Research on the difference between generalization and maintenance in extra-therapy responding. *Journal of Applied Behavior Analysis,* **10,** 1–12.

LaGreca, A., & Santogrossi, D. (1980) Social skills training in elementary school students: A behavioral group approach. *Journal of Consulting and Clinical Psychology,* **48,** 220–227.

Levine, F. M., & Fasnacht, G. (1974) Token rewards may lead to token learning. *American Psychologist,* **29,** 816–820.

Levine, F. M., Fasnacht, G., Funabiki, D., & Burkart, M. R. (1979) Methodological considerations regarding the evaluation of maintenance of gains due to token programs. *Psychology in the Schools,* **16,** 568–575.

Lichstein, K., & Schreibman, L. (1976) Employing electric shock with autistic children. A review of the side effects. *Journal of Autism and Childhood Schizophrenia,* **6,** 163–173.

London, P. (1972) The end of idiology in behavior modification. *American Psychologist,* **27,** 913–918.

Mastria, E., Mastria, M., & Harkins, J. (1979) Treatment of child abuse by behavioral interventions: A case report. *Child Welfare,* **43,** 253–261.

Oltmanns, T., Broderick, J., & O'Leary, K. (1977) Marital adjustment and the efficacy of behavior therapy with children. *Journal of Consulting and Clinical Psychology,* **45,** 724–729.

Prochaska, J., Smith, N., Marzilli, R., Colby, J., & Donovan, W. (1975) Remote-control aversive stimulation in the treatment of head-banging in a retarded child. *Journal of Behavior Therapy and Experimental Psychiatry,* **5,** 285–289.

Reavley, W., & Gilbert, M. (1979) The analysis and treatment of child abuse by behavioral psychotherapy. *Child Abuse and Neglect,* **3,** 169–175.

Reppucci, N. D. (1977) Implementation issues for the behavior modifier as institutional change agent. *Behavior Therapy,* **8,** 594–605.

Reppucci, N. D., & Saunders, J. T. (1974) Social psychology of behavior modification: Problems of implementation in natural settings. *American Psychologist,* **29,** 649–660.

Rogeness, G. A., Stokes, J. P., Bednar, R. A., & Gorman, B. L. (1977) School intervention program to increase behaviors and attitudes that promote learning. *Journal of Community Psychology,* **5,** 246–256.

Romanczyk, R., & Goren, E. (1975) Severe self-injurious behavior: The problem of clinical control. *Journal of Consulting and Clinical Psychology,* **43,** 730–739.

Salzinger, K., Feldman, R., & Portnoy, S. (1970) Training parents of brain-injured children in the use of operant conditioning procedures. *Behavior Therapy,* **1,** 4–32.

Sandler, J., VanDercar, C., & Milhoan, M. (1978) Training child abusers in the use of positive reinforcement practices. *Behavior Research and Therapy,* **16,** 169–175.

Sarason, S. B. (1972) *The creation of settings and the future societies.* San Francisco: Jossey-Bass.

Shemberg, K., Keeley, S., Gill, K., & Garton, A. (1972) A note on the inhibitory effects of the initiation of a behavior program. *Behavior Therapy,* **3,** 622–626.

Shenfeld, M. (1980) *The behavioral treatment of social withdrawal and isolation in children.* Unpublished manuscript, State University of New York at Buffalo.

Silberman, C. (1970) *Crisis in the classroom.* New York: Random House.

Strain, P. (1977) An experimental analysis of peer social initiations on the behavior of withdrawn preschool children: Some training and generalization effects. *Journal of Abnormal Child Psychology,* **5,** 445–456.

Strain, P. S., & Pierce, J. E. (1977) Direct and vicarious effects of social praise on mentally retarded preschool children's attentive behavior. *Psychology in the School,* **14,** 348–353.

Tracey, L., & Clark, E. (1974) Treatment for child abusers. *Social Work,* **19,** 338–342.

Wasserman, T., & Vogrin, D. (1979) Long-term effects of a token economy on target and off-task behaviors. *Psychology in the Schools,* **16,** 551–557.

Weinrott, M., Corson, J., & Wilchesk, M. (1979) Teacher-mediated treatment of social withdrawal. *Behavior Therapy,* **10,** 281–294.

Whitehill, M., Hersen, M., & Bellack, A. (1980) Conversation skills training for socially isolated children. *Behaviour Research and Therapy,* **18,** 217–225.

Wilson, G. T., & Evans, W. I. M. (1978) The therapist–client relationship in behavior therapy. In A. S. Gurman, & A. M. Razin (Eds.), *The therapist's contribution to effective psychotherapy: An empirical approach.* New York: Pergamon.

Winett, R. A., & Winkler, R. C. (1972) Current behavior modification in the classroom: Be still, be quiet, be docile. *Journal of Applied Behavior Analysis,* **5,** 499–504.

Wolberg, L. R. *The technique of psychotherapy.* (1954) New York: Grune & Stratton.

Wolfolk, R. L., & Wolfolk, A. E. (1975) Modifying the effect of the behavior modification label. *Behavior Therapy,* **10,** 575–578.

Wolpe, J. (1981) Behavior therapy *vs* psychoanalysis: Therapeutic and social implications. *American Psychologist,* 36, 159–165.

Author Index

Abrahms, E., 159, 165, *171*
Addington, H. J., 247, *261*
Adkins, D., 247, *262*
Adkinson, D., 125, *136*
Agras, W. S., 10, *34, 346, 351*
Agulnik, P., 62, *78*
Ahern, D. K., 7
Alavi, A., 27, *33*
Albala, A. A., 222, *228*
Alberti, R., 121, 122, 125, 133, *135,* 138, 149, *155*
Albin, R. W., *155*
Alexander, J. F., 363-365, *373, 376*
Allen, D. J., 338, 343, *350*
Allen, G. J., 273, *287*
Allen, R. P., 366, *375*
Alterman, A. I., 246, *261*
Altschul, A. M., 266, *285*
Ambrose, S., 418, *421*
Amit, Z., 186, *195*
Anderson, T. P., 315, *332*
Andrasik, S., 356, *376*
Andrew, J., 183, *190*
Andrews, J. D. W., 59, *78*
Andrews, W. R., 94, *102,* 186, *193*
Ansari, J. M. A., 401, *403*
Applebaum, A., 140, *155*
Arentewicz, G., 393, 395, 397, 398, 403, *403*
Argras, W. S., 305, *309*
Armor, D. J., 245, 246, 249, *260, 262*
Ascher, L. M., 290-292, 296, 298, 299, 304, 307, *308, 309*
Ascione, F., 338, *350*
Atkinson, C., 339, *351*
Atkinson, M. B., 141, *155*
Atthowe, J. M., 338, 343, *350*
Atwater, J., 358, *375*
Augusto, F., 264, *285*
Austin, S., 57
Ayala, H. E., 358, *373*
Ayers, W., 266, *285*

Ayllon, T., 337, 341, 343, 344, *350,* 416, *423*
Azrin, N. H., 337, 341, 343, 344, *350*

Babigian, H., 415, *422*
Backland, F., 90, *99*
Baer, D. M., 83, *99*
Baer, R., 338, 347, *350*
Bailey, J. E., 283, *286*
Bailey, J. S., 358, *374*
Baker, B. L., 186, *191,* 305, *309*
Baker, H., 336, 339, *350, 351*
Balaschak, B. A., 408, 409, *421*
Ball, P. B., 137, *155*
Ball, P. G., *155*
Ball, T., 419, *421*
Ballering, M. L., *155*
Bandeira, C. S., 398, *405*
Bandura, A., 1, 2, *8,* 83, *99,* 231, *244,* 268, 278, 279, 281, *284*
Baptiste, S., 318, *333*
Barbach, L. G., *403*
Bard, J. A., 159, *171*
Barlow, D., 1, *9,* 10, *34,* 173, 189, *191,* 305, *309*
Barnard, J. D., 364, *374*
Barnett, L. W., 229, *244*
Barrera, M., Jr., 181, 184, *191, 195*
Barrett, C. L., 84, *99*
Barrett-Lennard, G. T., 72, *78*
Barry, W. A., *155*
Bartman, E., 132, *135*
Barton, C., 363, 365, *373, 374*
Barton, M. C., 357, *373, 375*
Basmann, R. L., 345, *351*
Bass, R., 187, *191*
Bassett, J. E., 342, 344, *350,* 356, *374*
Bassiakos, L., 10, *32*
Battalio, R. C., 345, *351*
Battle, M., 90, *101*
Beach, L. R., 145, *156*
Beavin, J. H., 61, *81*

425

Beck, A., 48, *56*, 197, *215*, 217-219, 225, 227, *227, 228*
Beck, S., 70, *78*, 305, *308*
Bednar, R. A., 410, *423*
Beech, H., 50, *56*
Behles, M. W., 370, *374*
Bellack, A., *135*, 141, 145, *155*, 182, *191, 424*
Bencomo, A., 132, *135*
Bendfeldt, F., *261*
Bennett, P., 343, *351*
Bentler, P. M., *403, 404*
Bergin, A. E., 72, *78*, 165, *171*
Berman, S., *155*
Bernal, M., 411, *421*
Bernstein, D. A., 306, *308*
Best, J. A., 187, *191*
Beutler, L., 292, *308*
Bianchi, G. N., 69, *78*
Biglan, A., 197, *216*
Birchler, G. R., 389, *391*
Birky, H. J., 343, *350*
Bixler, E. O., 289, *309*
Black, J. D., *157*
Black, J. L., 176, *193, 194*
Black, R. G., 317, *332*
Blakeney, P., 392, 398, 400, 401, *404*
Blanchard, E. B., 342, 344, *350*, 356, *374*
Bland, K., 62, 63, 70, *78*
Blau, J., 95, *100*, 150, *156*
Blechman, E., 140, 148, *156*
Block, A., 311, 317, 318, *332, 333*
Blumetti, A. E., 318, *332*
Boersma, K., 10, *31*
Bootzin, R., 289, 290, 292, 293, *308*
Borden, B. L., 186, *192*
Boren, J. J., 338, *350*
Borkovec, T. D., 2, *8*, 25, 26, *31, 33*, 91, 99, 297, 307, *308*
Boudewyns, P. A., 84, *103*
Boulougouris, J. C., 10, 19, 21, 23, 24, *31, 32, 34*, 58, 71, 72, *80, 81*
Bowen, R. C., 69, *78*
Boyd, J., 159, *171*
Bozarth, J. D., 70, *81*
Brady, J. P., 247, *262*
Braiker, H. B., 249, *262*
Branch, L. G., 229, *244*
Brannigan, G. G., 400, *404*
Braukmann, C. J., 335, *352*, 358, *374-377*
Bray, G. A., 268, 271, *284*
Brena, S. F., 318, 331, *332*
Bridge, G., 339, *350*
Brightwell, D. R., 282, *285*

Brockway, B. S., 144, *156*
Broderick, J., 412, *423*
Bromet, E. J., 245, *261*
Brougham, L., 59, *80*
Broverman, D. M., 140, *156*
Broverman, I. K., 139, *156*
Brown, C. J., 314, *333*
Brown, G. D., 338, *353*
Brown, J. M., 338, *352*
Brown, J. S., 290, *308*
Brown, L. B., 73, *81*
Brown, R. A., 199, 202, 206, 213, *215*
Brownell, K. D., 187, 188, *191*, 230, *244*, 265, 266, 268, 270, 272, 273, 277, 278, *285, 287, 288*
Bryant, B., 106, *120*
Bucher, B., 419, *421*
Buglass, D., 62, 73, *78*
Burchard, J. D., 4, 7, 356, 358-360, 363-366, 370, *374*
Burgio, L., 415, *421*
Burkart, M. R., 413, *423*
Burkhart, B. R., 370, *374*
Bushell, D., Jr., 335, 340, 341, *350, 351*
Butler, P., 138, *156*
Butler, R. J., 340, 343, *351*
Butt, J., 183, *195*
Byrick, R., 419, *422*

Caddy, G. R., 247, 248, 250, *261*
Cain, R. B., *261*
Cairns, D., 314-316, *332*
Camburn, D., 366, *377*
Campbell, D. T., 299, *308*
Candelora, K., 370, *377*
Carbonell, J., 413, *423*
Carkuff, R. R., 24, *34*, 70, *81*
Carlin, A. S., 243, *244*
Carlisle, J. W., 396, *405*
Carroll, B. J., 222, *228*
Cartwright, R., 90, *99*
Carver, J., 125, *135*
Casto, G., 338, *350*
Catalan, J., 98, *101*
Catts, S., 10, *32*
Cavior, N., 343, *351*
Cawley, R., 16, *32*
Cayner, J. J., 343, *351*
Cesa, T. A., 181, *191*
Chamberlain, K., 182, *193*, 277, *286*
Chambless, D. L., 25, 29, *32*, 61, *78, 79*
Chambliss, J. E., 343, *350*
Chandler, T., 140, *156*
Chaney, E. F., 233, *244*

Chapman, C. R., 317, *332*
Chapman, S. L., 268, 277, *285*
Charles, E., 346, *353*
Cheek, D., 124, *135*
Choban, M. C., 343, *351*
Christensen, A., 184, *191*
Christenson, A., 150, *156*
Christie, M. M., 82, *102*
Christoph, P., *9*
Christophersen, E. R., 364, *374*
Ciminero, A. R., 176, *193*
Clark, E., 418, *424*
Clarke, C., 346, *353*
Clarke, J., 62, *78*
Clarkson, F. E., 140, *156*
Clausen, J. D., 266, 282, *285*
Clayton, S. H., 349, *351*
Cleary, P. D., 177, 183, 184, *193, 230, 244*
Clement, P. F., 275, *286*
Clement, P. W., 336, *353*
Clements, J., 419, *421*
Cleveland, S. E., 245, *262*
Coates, T. J., 178, 181, *191*
Cobb, J., 10, *33, 34, 57*
Cohen, D. C., 186, *191*
Cohen, E. A., 187, *191*
Cohen, F., 183, *191*
Cohen, H. L., 357, *374*
Colby, J., 419, *423*
Cole, A., *334*
Cole, C., 411, 412, *422*
Cole, T. M., 315, *332*
Coleman, J. C., 83, *100*
Colletti, G., *191*
Collins, R. L., 8, 236, 243, *244, 282, 285*
Colman, A. D., 338, *350*
Cook, B., 140, *156*
Cooke, C. J., 186, *194, 272, 274, 375, 285*
Coombs, J., 266, *285*
Coombs, R., 87, *100*
Cooper, A. J., 399, 400, 402, *404*
Cooper, C. M., 94, *102*
Coopersmith, M. L., 277, *286*
Cordua, G., 341, *351, 420, 423*
Corson, J., 416, *424*
Coryell, W., *228*
Cotter, S. B., 186, *191*
Cowan, E., 415, *422*
Cox, G. B., 317, *332*
Creel, J., 344, *353*
Creel, L., 344, *353*
Crisp, A. H., 61, 71, *78*
Cristol, A. H., *9*
Crowe, R., 87, *103*

Crozier, J., 418, *422*
Curran, J. P., 144, *156, 344, 351*
Currey, H. S., 274, *287*
Currie, D. W., 82, *102*
Curtis, G. C., 222, *228*
Cuvillier, C., 186, *194*

D'Angelo, C. M., *333*
Davidson, A., 187, *191*
Davidson, W. S., 356, 358-360, 368, *374,*
    417, *422*
Davies, D. L., 245, *261*
Davis, M., 27, *32*
Dean, C. W., 356, *374*
Dekker, J., 10, *31,* 392, 393, 400, 402, *404*
de la Pena, 292-299, 304, 307, *308*
Delateur, B. J., 314, *332*
Delateur, D., 314, *332*
DeLong, D. R., 183, *191*
Dement, W. C., 297, *308*
den Hengst, S., 10, *31*
Denicola, J., 418, *422*
Denney, D. R., 187, *191, 192*
Derogatis, L. R., 394, *405*
deSilva, P., 50, *56*
deSilva, R., 25, *34*
Dever, S., 154, *158*
deVigue, J. P., *228*
DeVine, M. D., 357, *375*
deVisser, L., 382, *391*
De Voge, J. T., 70, *78, 305, 306*
Dewey, M., 419, *421*
DeWolf, V. A., 140, *157*
DeZalera, E. K., 357, *375*
DiGiuseppe, R., 159, 167, *171*
DiTomasso, R., 7, 289-291, 298, *309*
Dixon, D. N., 172, 174, *191*
Dobroski, B. J., 172, 173, *194*
Doctor, R., 418, *422*
Dodd, D. K., 187, *191*
Doerfler, L. A., 182, *191,* 214, *215*
Doleys, D., 410, *422*
Donner, L., 186, *192*
Donovan, W., 419, *423*
Doppelt, H. G., 28, 30, *32*
Downing, R. W., 89, *103*
Drabman, R. S., 336, *351*
Dubbert, P., 6, 7, 264, 265, 280, *285*
Dubrow, M., 154, *156*
Dugovics, D., 140, *156*
Dunbar, J., 268, *285, 306, 309*
Duncan, G. H., 319, *332*
Dunlop, R. A., 348, *352*
Durham, T. W., 266, *286*

Durksen, D. L., 318, *334*
Dyrenforth, S. R., 267, *288*
D'Zurilla, T., 140, *156, 157,* 187, *192*

Edwards, G., 246, 249, *262*
Efron, J. S., 290, *308*
Egan, K., 136, 140, 143, 145, 146, 154, *157*
Eggeraat, J., 59, *79*
Eichenbaum, L. A., 153, *156*
Eisler, R., 128, *135,* 140, 145, *156, 157,*
    346, *351*
Elliott, C. H., 187, *192*
Ellis, A., 159, 165-168, 170, *171*
Ellis, E. M., 152, *156*
Emery, G., 217, *227*
Emery, R. E., 417, *422*
Emmelkamp, P., *392*
Emmelkamp, P. M. G., 2, 6, 7, *8,* 10, 12, 16,
    19, 24, 28, *31, 32,* 58-63, 67-69, 77, *78,*
    79, 91, 93, *100*
Emmelkamp-Benner, A., 58, 60, 67, *79*
Emmons, M., 121, 122, 133, *135,* 138, 149,
    155
Emrick, C. D., 230, *244*
Endicott, J., 197, *216*
Epstein, L. H., 176, *192*
Epstein, S., 183, *192*
Evans, M., 392, *405*
Evans, P. D., 58, *79*
Evans, W. I. M., 408, *424*
Everaerd, W., 393, 394, 398, 400, 402, *404*
Evers-Pasquale, W., 416, *422*
Ewart, C. K., 181, *192*
Ewing, J., 248, 249, 259, *261*
Eysenck, H. J., 200, *216*

Farbry, J., 183, *195*
Fasnacht, G., 413, 419, *423*
Feighner, J. P., 197, *216*
Feinberg, M., 222, *228*
Feingold, L., 346, *351*
Feldman, R., 411, *424*
Fenz, W. D., 183, *192*
Ferber, H., 411, 412, *422*
Ferdun, G. S., 357, *374*
Fiedler, D., 122, *135,* 145, *156*
Fiegenbaum, E., 347, *353*
Fiester, A., 90, *100*
Filipczak, J., 357, 365, *374, 375*
Finch, B., 132, *135*
Fine, M. J., 410, *422*
Fink, R., 418, *422*
Fischer, S. C., 19, *33, 100*
Fishbein, C., *156*

Fisher, E. B., Jr., 268, *286,* 345, *351*
Fisher, L. B., 174, 175, 188, *192*
Fitzhugh, K. B., 338, *352*
Fitzhugh, L. C., 338, *352*
Fixsen, D. L., 335, 347, *352,* 358, *373-377*
Fleischman, M. J., 364, 365, *375, 376*
Fo, W. S. O., 371, *376*
Foa, E. B., 7, 10-12, 14, 16, 18, 19, 21, 23-
    25, 27-30, *32, 33,* 40, 41, 43-48, 53, *56,*
    69, *79,* 84, 94, 95, *100*
Foa, U. G., 10
Fodor, I. G., 87, *100,* 138, 144, 145, 147,
    150, 152, *156, 158*
Follick, M. J., 7, 311, 314, 315, 327, 331,
    332
Fontana, M. E., 87, *103*
Ford, D. E., *333*
Fordney-Settlage, D. S., 397-399, *404*
Fordyce, W. E., 311, 312, 314, 316, 320,
    324, 329, *332*
Foreyt, J., 264-266, 278, *285, 286*
Foster, D., 282, *285*
Fowler, R. S., 314, *332*
Fox, R., 245, *261*
Frank, J., 20, *34,* 89, 90, *101, 103*
Frankl, V. E., 291, *309*
Franks, C. M., 268, *285*
Frazier, J., 125, *135*
Frazier, L., 419, *421*
Frederiksen, L. W., 145, *156*
Frenken, J., 394, 396, *404*
Frese, M., 10
Friedan, B., 146, *156*
Friedman, R. M., 365, *375*
Friesen, D. D., 348, *351*
Fry, W. F., 62, *79*
Fullerton, D. T., 343, *351*
Funabiki, D., 413, *423*

Gaind, R., 25, *34*
Galassi, J., 68, *79,* 125, *135*
Galassi, M., 125, *135*
Galbraith, D., 419, *422*
Gambriel, E. D., 144, *156*
Gant, B. L., 364, *374*
Garber, S., 344, *350*
Garfield, S. L., 2, 4, *8, 9,* 64, *79,* 89, *100,*
    165, *171*
Garlington, B., 315, *333*
Garlington, W. K., 338, *352*
Garron, D. C., *333*
Garton, A., 414, *424*
Gauthier, J., 82, 83, 86, 93, 94, *100, 102*
Gay, M. L., 68, *79*

Gaylor, M., 311, 317, *332, 333*
Gebhard, P., 396, *404*
Geesey, S., 345, 347, *352*
Gelder, M., 15, *34,* 58, 60, 68, 70, *79, 80,*
88, 98, *100*
Gelfand, D. M., 187, *191*
Genest, M., *334*
Ghia, J. N., 319, *332*
Gilberstadt, H., 317, *332*
Gilbert, F. S., 144, *156*
Gilbert, M., 418, *423*
Gilbert, T. F., 189, *192*
Giles, D. E., 223, *228*
Giles, D. K., 347, *354*
Giles, T., 7
Gill, K., 414, *424*
Ginor, M., 339, *352*
Glanz, L., 182, *191*
Glasgow, R. E., 172, 179, 186, 187, 189,
191, *192, 195*
Gleser, G. C., 245, *262*
Goldfried, A. P., 145, *157*
Goldfried, M. R., 106, *120,* 140, 145, *156,*
157, 173, 179, 187, *192*
Goldman, E., 249, *261*
Goldstein, A., 10, 12, 16, 24, *32,* 61, *78,*
79, 84, 87, *100,* 305, *309*
Goldstein, M. K., 314, *334*
Gonso, J., 416, *422*
Goodrick, K., 264, *285*
Gordon, A., 82, 83, *102*
Gordon, J. R., 174, 177, *193,* 230-232, 235,
244, 269, 279, 281, 283, *286*
Goren, E., 419, *423*
Gormally, J., 278, 279, 282, *285*
Gorman, B. L., 410, *423*
Gortney, C., *195*
Gotestam, K. G., 345, *352*
Gottheil, E., 246, 249, *261*
Gottlieb, H., 314, 315, *333*
Gottman, J., 145, *158,* 181, *192,* 416, *422*
Gotto, A. M., 264, *285*
Gottschalk, L. A., 245, *262*
Graber, B., 402, *404*
Grayson, J., 18, 25-28, 30, *31-34,* 41, 43,
56, 297, *308*
Graziano, A. M., 407-410, 417, 418, *422*
Greden, J. F., 222, *228*
Green, C. J., *333*
Green, D. R., 358, *375*
Greenberg, D. J., 348, *351*
Greenberg, J., 27, *33*
Greer, L., 174, *192*
Greer, S. E., 379, *391*

Gregg, J. M., 319, *332*
Grey, S., 10, 26, *33, 34,* 48, *56*
Grieger, R., 159, *171*
Grimm, L. E., 172, 175, *193*
Grinker, R. R., 197, 201, 204, 205, *216*
Groves, G., 21, 27, *32, 100*
Groves, P. M., 27, *33*
Grzesiak, R. C., 313, *333*
Guerny, B. E., Jr., 186, *192*
Guire, K., 278, *287*
Gullickson, G., 315, *332*
Gur, R. C., 27, *33*
Gur, R. E., 27, *33*
Gurman, A., 150, *157,* 264, *285*
Guze, S. B., 197, *216*

Hadley, S. W., 14, *33,* 71, *79,* 340, *353*
Hafner, J., 62, 63, 70, *81*
Hafner, R. J., 58, 59, 61-63, *79, 80,* 83-85,
87, 92, *100, 101*
Hagen, R. L., 186, *192,* 266, *286*
Hakstian, A. R., 201-203, 206, 215, *216*
Hall, J., 336, 339, *350, 351*
Hall, J. R., *157*
Hall, R. E., 186, *192*
Hall, R. F., 181, *194*
Hall, S. M., 186, *192*
Hallam, R. S., 62, 63, 70, *78,* 88, *101*
Hamilton, M., 201, *216*
Hammen, C. L., 181, *194*
Hand, I., 63, 67, *80,* 98, *101*
Hanley, E. L., 347, *354*
Hanna, C. F., 271, *286*
Hanson, R., 132, *135,* 186, *192*
Hanvik, L. J., 317, *333*
Hare, N., 94, 95, *101*
Harig, P. T., 356, 358, 364, *374*
Harkins, J., 418, *423*
Harper, T. M., 358, *376*
Harris, G. G., 138, *157*
Harris, M. B., *286*
Harris, R., 314, *332*
Hart, J., 25, *33*
Hartcett, R. F., 222, *228*
Hartmann, D. P., 339, *351*
Hartsook, J. E., 140, 145, *157*
Haskell, W. I., 283, *286*
Hawkins, R. C., 275, *286*
Haworth, J., 418, *421*
Hayden, M., 341, *351*
Haydon, M., 420, *423*
Hayes, C. S., 187, *191*
Hayes, S. C., 265, *285*
Hazard, A., 418, *421*

Headley, E. B., 245, *262*
Healy, S., 289, *309*
Heaton, R. C., 366, *375*
Heckerman, C., 187, 191, 265, *285*
Hedberg, A., 336, *353*
Hefferman, T., 182, *192*
Heiman, J. R., 397, *404*
Heitler, J. B., 66, *80*
Henderson, A. S., 62, *78*
Henderson, J. M., 137, *157*
Heppner, P. P., 172, 174, *191, 192*
Herbert, E., 341, *351*, 420, *423*
Herman, E., 317, 318, *333*
Herman, P., 278, *286*
Herman, S., *157*, 341, *351*
Hersen, M., 1, *9*, 128, 129, *135, 136*, 140, 141, *155, 157*, 179, *192*, 346, *351*, 416, *424*
Hester, R. K., 229, *244*
Hingson, R., 249, *261*
Hirsch, A. A., 274, *287*
Hite, S., 397, *404*
Hobbs, T. R., 356, *375*
Hockersmith, V., 314, *333*
Hodgson, R., 10, 12, 16, 20, 21, 23, 24, *33, 34*, 35, 39, 40, 42, 43, 50, *57*, 84, 88, 90, *101, 103*, 245, *261*
Hoen-Saric, R., 90, *101*
Hofmeister, J. F., 349, *351*
Hogan, D. R., 394, 396, 398, *404*
Hollandsworth, J., Jr., 140, 153, *157*
Hollandsworth, J. G., 68, *79*
Hollon, S. D., 217, 228, 358, *375*
Holt, N. M., 356, *375*
Holt, S., 175, *195*
Homer, A. L., 172, 179, 180, *192*
Hops, H., 347, *353*
Horne, A. M., 88, *101*
Horwitz, B., 183, *195*
Horwitz, M., 42, *56*
Howard, J. R., 359, *375*
Hudgens, A., 315, *332*
Hudson, B., 62, 63, 80, 87, *101*
Hudson, T., 143, *157*
Huey, C. J., 402, *404*
Hull, D. B., *157*
Humphrey, L. L., 181, *193*
Hung, D. W., 346, *351*
Hunt, J. G., 338, *352*
Hunt, W. A., 229, 230, *244*
Hursch, C. J., 289, *310*
Hutchinson, K., 339, *350*

Ignelzi, R. A., 314, *333*

Imber, S., 90, *101*
Izzo, L., 415, *422*

Jack, G. B., 137, 141, 143, 144, *158*
Jackson, C., 341, *351*, 420, *423*
Jackson, D., 61, *81*, 87, *101*, 143, *157*
Jacobson, N. S., 2, 9, 380, *391*
Jacobsson, H., 73, *81*
Jakobowski-Spector, P., 138, 144, 146, *157*
Jakubowski, P., 121, *136*
James, N. M. I., *228*
Jamieson, R., 27, *34*
Jancis, M., 317, *332*
Janoun, L., 68, *80*, 98, *101*
Jayaratne, S., 366, *377*
Jeffrey, B., 268, 277, *285*
Jeffrey, R. W., 182, *192*, 273, 274, 276, *286*
Jellinek, E. M., 246, *261*
Jenkins, W. O., 357, *375*
Jensen, J., 187, *191*
Jerremalm, A., 1, *9, 56*, 106, *120*
Jesness, C. F., 357, 363, 369-371, *375*
Johansson, J., 1, *9, 56*, 106, *120*
Johnson, M., 415, *421*
Johnson, V. E., 118, 392-397, 401, 402, *404, 405*
Johnson, W. G., 268, *283*
Johnston, D. W., 3, *9*, 14, *34*, 59-61, 68, *80, 81*, 88, 98, *102, 186, 194*
Jones, B. A., 87, *103*
Jones, H. H., 364, *374*
Jones, R., 359, 360, *375*, 419, *421*
Jones, S. L., 7
Jordan, H. A., 277, *286*
Joyce, M. A., 249, *261*

Kagel, J. H., 345, *351, 352*
Kales, A., 289, *309*
Kandel, H., 416, *423*
Kanfer, F. H., 172, 173, 175-179, 182, 186, *192, 193*, 409, *423*
Kanter, N. J., 106, *120*
Kantor, J., 77, *80*, 87, *101*
Kaplan, H. S., 151, 396, *404*
Karacan, I., 289, 293, *308, 310*
Karol, R. L., 187, 188, *193*
Karoly, P., 173, 175-177, 180, *193*
Kass, D. J., *193*
Kass, W. A., 338, *353*
Katch, F. I., 273, *286*
Katkin, E. S., 26, *33*
Katz, R., 418, *422*

Kazdin, A. E., 2, 7, 9, 20, *33*, 91, 93, *101*, 159, *171*, 264, *286*, 323, *333*, 335, 337, 339, 340, 345, 347, 348, *352*
Keefe, F. J., 314, 326, *333*
Keeley, S., 411, 413, 414, *422-424*
Kellam, A. M. P., 58, *79*
Kelly, B., 140, *158*
Keltner, A., 90, *101*
Kendall, P. C., 358, *375*
Kenigsberg, M., 264, *287*
Kerr, T. A., 69, *81*
Kershaw, P. W., 245, 249, *262*
Kevenkron, J. C., 268, *286*
Khatami, M., 227, 315, *333*
Kiecolt, J., *157*
Kiesler, D. J., 296, 300, *309*
Kifer, R. E., 358, *375*
Kilmann, P. R., 392, 397, 398, 400, *404*
Kinder, B. N., 392, 398, 400, 401, *404*
King, L. A., 347, *354*
Kinsey, A. C., 396, 397, *404*
Kinsinger, J., 338, *352*
Kirigin, K. A., 335, 340, 350, *352*, 358, 360, *374, 375, 377*
Kirschenbaum, D. S., 180, 181, *193, 195*
Kirschner, N., 128, *135*
Kleeman, M., 314, *333*
Klein, D. F., 87, *101, 103*
Klein, H., 339, *352*
Klein, N. C., 364, *376*
Klein, N. M., *157*
Klerman, G. L., 200, 201, 206, *216*
Kline-Graber, R. N., 402, *404*
Klinnert, M., 411, *421*
Koch, D. L., 318, 331, *332*
Koegel, R. L., 413, *423*
Kohout, J., 69, *78*
Koller, R., 314, *333*
Kolodny, R. C., 396, *404*
Kopel, S. A., *191*
Koshland, E., 344, *350*, 356, *374*
Kovacs, M., 200, 201, *216*, 217, *228*
Kraanen, J., 12, 24, *32*
Krasner, A. T., 338, 343, *350*
Krasner, L., 1, *9*, 345, *351*
Krauft, C. C., 71, *81*
Kreitman, N., 62, *78*
Kremer, E., 311, 317, *332, 333*
Kremer, M. E., 344, *353*
Kronfel, Z., 228
Krusen, E. M., *333*
Kuehn, F. E., 364, *374*
Kuehnel, J., 382, *391*
Kuehnel, T., 382, *391*

Kuipers, A., 59-61, 69, *79*
Kulich, R. J., 314, *332*
Kupfer, D. J., 223, *228*
Kuriansky, J., 394, *405*
Kurz, M., 89, *100*

Lachowicz, J., 347, *354*
Lader, M., 26, *33*, 42, 43, *56*, 58, *80*
LaGesse, D., 189, *193*
LaGreca, A., 415, *423*
Lambert, M. J., 72, *78*
Lamontagne, Y., 63, 67, *80*, 98, *101*
Lamparski, D., *155*
Lancashire, M., 60, *80*
Lane, T. W., 4, 7, 358-360, 363-366, 370, *374*
Lang, P., 25, 28, *33*, 48, 49, *56*
Lange, A., 121, *136*
Langenbucher, J., 264, *285*
Lansky, D., 174, *193*, 268, *286*
La Plante, M. N., 400, *404*
Lassen, C. L., 395, *404*
Last, R., 339, 343, *352*
Latimer, P., 10, 30, *32*, 95, *100*
Lazarus, A. A., 138, *157*
Lazarus, R. S., 183, *191*
Leavitt, F., 317, *333*
LeBow, M., 273, 277, *286*
Lee, I. A., 289, *309*
Lee, R., 122, *135*
Lee, S., 282, *285*
Lehmann, J. F., 314, *332*
Leitenberg, H., 305, *309*
Lemere, F., 245, *261*
Lentz, R. J., 335, 340, 344, 345, *351, 353*
Leon, G. R., 182, *193*, 277, *286*
Levenkron, J. C., 174, *192*
Leventhal, H., 177, 183, 184, *193*, 230, *244*
Levine, B. A., 94, *103*
Levine, F. M., 413, 419, *423*
Levine, J., 380, *391*
Levine, S. B., 392, *404*
Levis, D. J., 93-95, *101, 103*
Leviton, L. C., 149, *157*
Levitz, L. S., 277, 278, *286*
Levy, R., 23, *34*
Lewinsohn, P. M., 197-199, 202, 203, 213, *215, 216*
Lewis, M. A., 358, *375*
Lewis, S., 283, *286*
Lewittes, H. J., 153, 154, *157*
Liberman, R. P., 336, 338, *352*, 364, *377*, 380, 382, 389, *391*

Lichstein, K., 419, *423*
Lietaer, G., 72, *80*
Likierman, H., 25, *33,* 50, 54, 55, *56*
Lindstrom, H., 73, *81*
Linehan, M., 137, 140, 143, 145, 146, 154, *157*
Lipinski, D. P., 176, 179, *193, 194*
Lipsedge, M., 40, *57*
Lloyd, K. E., 338, *352*
Lloyd, R. W., 248, *261*
Lloyd, S., 90, *99*
Lobitz, W. C., 396, *405*
Lockard, H. R., 357, *374*
Locke, H. J., 273, *286*
Loesser, J. D., 311, *333*
Logan, D. L., 338, *352*
Lohr, N., *228*
London, P., 407, *423*
Lo Picollo, J., 394, 396, 398, *404, 405*
Loro, A. D., 174, *192,* 271, *286*
Loro, A. D., Jr., 268, *286*
Lovaas, O., 419, *421*
Lovibond, S. H., 247, 248, 250, *261*
Lowe, M. R., 174, *193*
Lowental, U., 339, *352*
Luborsky, L., 2, 7, *9*
Ludwig, A. M., *261*
Lundwall, L., 90, *99*
Lydgate, T., 371, *376*
Lykken, D. T., 26, *33*

McArdle, W. D., 273, *286*
McConaghy, N., 10, *32*
McCormick, N., 400, *404*
McCreadie, R. G., 348, *352*
McCubbin, R. J., 26, *33*
MacDonald, B., *57*
McDonald, B., 10, *34*
McDonald, R., *33*
McFall, R. M., 174, 175, 181-184, 187, *192-194,* 269, *287*
McGee, D., 264, *285*
McGrath, E., *157*
McGuire, R. J., 396, *405*

McKay, H. B., 357, *376*
McKee, J. M., 344, *350,* 356, 357, *375, 376*
McKinney, F., 189
McLaren, S., 59, *80*
McLaughlin, T. F., 347, *352*
McLaughlin-Reidel, T., 343, *351*
McLean, P. D., 198, 201-203, 206, 215, *216*
McNamara, J. R., 356, *376*

McNeill, T. W., *333*
McPhee, M., 314, *334*
McPherson, F. M., 59, 61, *80*
McReynolds, W. T., 172, 175, 177, 181, *194, 195*
Madorsky, A., 314, *333*
Magaro, P. A., 338, 343, *350*
Mahan, J., 357, *374*
Mahoney, K., 264, 286, *287*
Mahoney, M. J., 91, *101,* 175-177, 179, 186, 189, *193, 195,* 264, 266, *286, 287,* 369, *376*
Main, C. J., 348, *352*
Malaby, J. E., 347, *352*
Malcolm, R. J., 274, *287*
Malett, S. D., 181, *193*
Maloney, D. M., 358, *374, 376*
Mannogian, N., 283, *286*
Margolin, G., 380, *391*
Marholin, D., 417, *422*
Marks, I., 4, *9,* 10, 12, 16, 21, 23-25, 28, *33, 34,* 40, *57,* 58-60, 64, 67, 69, *79-81,* 84, 89-91, 98, *101,* 105, *120,* 264, *286*
Marlatt, G. A., 8, 174, 175, 188, *193,* 230-236, *244,* 269, 279, 281-283, *286, 309*
Marset, P., 58, *80*
Marshall, J., 87, *102*
Marshall, W. L., 82, 83, 86, 89-95, *100-103,* 186, *193*
Marston, A. R., 181, 182, *193*
Martin, C. E., 396, *404*
Maruta, T., 314, 315, 317, *333, 334*
Marx, R. D., 243, *244,* 270
Marzilli, R., 419, *423*
Marzillier, J. S., 6, 104, 105, 109, *120*
Mascitelli, S., 345, *352*
Massimo, J. L., 368, *376*
Masters, J. C., 83, *103,* 291, *309*
Masters, M. J., 180, *193*
Masters, W. H., 118, 392-397, 401, 402, *404, 405*
Mastria, E., 418, *423*
Mastria, M., 418, *423*
Mather, M. D., 23, *34*
Mathews, A. M., 14, *34,* 60, 68, 71, *80,* 88, 93, 98, *102*
Mathieu, M., 392, *405*
Matter, S., 282, *288*
Matthews, A., 186, *194*
Maudsley, H., 37, *56*
Mauger, P., 125, *136*
Mawson, D., 10, *33, 34, 57*
Mayo, J., 87, *102*
Meagher, R. B., 318, *333*

Meichenbaum, D., 94, *102,* 176, *194,* 313, *333*
Melamed, B. G., 25, *33*
Melin, G. L., 345, *352*
Mello, N. K., 246, *261*
Melvin, K. B., 344, *353*
Melzack, R., 311, *333*
Mendels, J., 222, *228*
Mendelson, J. H., 246, *261*
Menges, R. J., 172, 173, *194*
Menninger, K., 129, *136*
Mersch, P. P., 59, *79*
Meyer, V., 23, *34,* 70, *80*
Meyers, A., 186, *194,* 272, 274, 275, *285*
Michaelis, M. L., 341, *351*
Migler, B., 346, *351*
Mikulas, W. L., *193*
Milan, M. A., 344, *350, 356, 376*
Milby, J. B., 18, *32,* 94, *100,* 346, *353*
Milhoan, M., 418, *424*
Miller, B. A., 245, *262*
Miller, I., 197
Miller, P., 128, *135,* 140, *157,* 176, *192*
Miller, W. R., 184, 186, *194,* 229, *244,* 245, 248-250, 253, *261, 262*
Milliones, J., 129, *136*
Millon, T., 318, *333*
Mills, C. M., 367, *376*
Mills, H. L., 10, *34*
Mills, J. R., 10, *34*
Milton, F., 62, 63, 70, *81*
Minkin, B. L., 358, *377*
Minkin, N., 358, *373, 377*
Mintz, J., *9*
Mishara, B. L., 337, 343, *353*
Mitchell, K. M., 70, *81*
Mitchell, K. R., 181, 187, *194*
Mitchell, R. E., *285*
Modesti, M. M., 318, *332*
Money, J., 396, *405*
Monroe, L. J., 290, *309*
Montgomery, I., 289, *309*
Monti, P., 187, *191,* 265, *285*
Mooney, K. C., 417, *422*
Mooney, T. L., 314, *332*
Moos, R., 245, *261*
Moran, E. L., 338, 343, 349, *353*
Morgan, C., 140, *333*
Morganstern, K. P., 83, *102*
Morokoff, P., 394, *405*
Morris, L. M., 186, *194*
Morris, R. J., 71, *81,* 305, *309*
Morrow, W., 411, 412, *422*
Muehlenhard, C., 144, *157*

Muller, J. B., 357, *375*
Munby, M., 3, *9,* 59-61, 68, *80, 81,* 98, *101, 102,* 186, *194*
Munjack, D. J., 89, *102*
Munoz, R. F., 197-199, 203, *216,* 253, *262*
Munz, D. C., 338, *353*

Nadolny, A., 93, 94, *102*
Nash, E., 90, *101*
Naylor, C. S., 282, *285*
Neill, J., 87, *102*
Nelson, R. O., 176, *193, 194*
Nesbitt, M. A., 410, *422*
Nevid, J. S., 140, *158*
Newman, R. I., 315, *333*
Nicassio, P., 289, 292, *308*
Nicholas, M. P., *156*
Nicol, D. C., 150, *156*
Nunes, J. S., 398, *405*
Nunn, R., 197, *216*
Nunnally, J. C., 197, *216*

O'Brien, G. T., 91, *99,* 297, *308*
O'Brien, T., 268, *286*
O'Connor, D., 394, *405*
Odell, B. N., 367, *376*
O'Donnell, C. R., 371, *376*
O'Gorman, J., 27, *34*
Olch, D. R., 140, *157*
O'Leary, K., 412, *423*
O'Leary, M. R., 233, *244*
Olivean, D. C., 305, *309*
Oltmanns, T., 412, *423*
O'Neill, P. M., 274, *287*
Oppenheimer, E., 246, 249, *262*
Orchard, J., 273, *287*
Orford, J., 246, 249, *262*
Orne, M., 90, *102*
Osborn, S. M., 138, *157*
Ost, L., 1, *9,* 49, *56,* 106, *120*
Owen, L. E., 187, *191*
O'Zurilla, T. J., 379, *391*

Pace, J. B., 314, *332*
Padias, N. S., 200, *216*
Pariser, S. F., 87, *103*
Parker, C. R., 223, *228*
Parker, G., 73, *81*
Parker, L., 94, *102*
Parkinson, L., 42, 46, 50, 53, *56*
Parloff, M. B., 70, 72, *81*
Parsons, B. V., 363, 364, *373, 376*
Pasino, J. A., 314, 316, *332*
Patterson, G. R., 364, *376*

Pattison, E. M., 245, *262*
Paul, G. L., 1, *9,* 172, *194,* 335, 340, 344, 345, 350, *351, 353*
Pauls, D., 87, *103*
Pearce, J. W., 273, 278, *287*
Pederson, A., 415, *422*
Peele, S., 183, *194*
Penick, S., 230, *244,* 277, *287*
Pereira, M., 283, *286*
Perissaki, C., 24, *34*
Perkins, D., 247, *261*
Perkins, G., 289, *309*
Perreault, R., 392, *405*
Perri, M. G., 182, 187, *194, 195*
Perris, C. J., 73, *81*
Perris, H., 73, *81*
Persson, L., 269, *287*
Pertschuk, M., 247, *262*
Petersen, C. H., 172, *191*
Peterson, G. L., 145, *156*
Peterson, L., 172, 179, 180, *192*
Pheterson, G., 392
Phillips, E. A., 347, *353,* 358, *374*
Phillips, E. L., 335, 347, *352, 353,* 358, *373-377*
Piatowski, O. E., 181, *194*
Pierce, J. E., 416, *424*
Pinkston, E., 341, *351,* 420, *423*
Pinkston, S., 341, *351,* 420, *423*
Pinta, E. R., 87, *103*
Pisa, A., 348, *351*
Pisor, K., 344, *350*
Plochy, I., 12, *32*
Pokorny, A. D., 245, *262*
Polich, J. M., 245, 249, *260, 262*
Pomerleau, C. S., 182, *194*
Pomerleau, O., 182, *194,* 247, 250, *262*
Pomeroy, W. B., 396, *404*
Popham, R. E., 249, *262*
Portnoy, S., 411, *424*
Powell, G., *57,* 150, *157*
Power, D., 271, *286*
Power, M., 140, *158*
Presley, A. S., 62, *78*
Presse, L., 186, *193*
Prochaska, J., 95, *103,* 419, *423*
Pronk-Lordan, D., 392
Prout, M., 95, *100*
Prumo, F. M., 366, *375*
Prusoff, B. A., 200-203, 206, *216*

Rabavilas, A. D., 19, 24, *34,* 71, 72, *81*
Rabkin, J. G., 87, *101*
Rachman, S., 2, *8,* 10, 12, 13, 16, 20, 21, 23-28, *33, 34,* 35, 36, 39, 42, 43, 45-50, 53-55, *56, 57,* 84, 85, 88, 90, *101, 103,* 264, *287*
Rathus, S., 125, *136,* 140, *158*
Reavley, W., 418, *423*
Reese, S. C., 365, *375*
Reimherr, F., *334*
Reinhardt, L., 315, 318, *333*
Reivich, M., 27, *33*
Repucci, N. D., 305, *309,* 356, *374,* 407, 408, *423*
Reynolds, B. S., 392, 395, 399, 401, *405*
Rich, A., 128, *136,* 145, *158*
Richards, C. S., 172, 174, 175, 181, 182, 184, 185, 187, *191-195,* 214, *215*
Richey, C. A., 144, *156,* 184, *195*
Rickard, H. C., 344, *353*
Rickels, K., 88, 89, *103*
Riddle, F. E., 274, *287*
Rigsby, L., 10
Riley, A. J., 396, *405*
Riley, E. J., 396, *405*
Riling, M., 290, *309*
Rimm, D. C., 83, *103,* 291, *309*
Rincover, A., 413, *423*
Risley, T. R., 83, *99*
Roberts, A. H., 315, 318, 327, *332, 333*
Roberts, M. D., 344, *350*
Robins, E., 197, *216*
Robinson, M. J., 368, *374*
Rocchio, T. D., 318, *334*
Roemer, R. A., 10
Roffwarg, H. P., 223, *228*
Rogeness, G. A., 410, *423*
Rogers, T., 264, 270, 271, 273, *287*
Romanczyk, R., 419, *423*
Ronning, R. R., 172, *191*
Roper, G., 10, 25, *34*
Rosen, A. D., 27, *33*
Rosen, G. M., 172, 179, 181, 186, 187, 189, *191, 192, 195*
Rosen, M. R., 396, *405*
Rosenbaum, M., 416, *423*
Rosenkrantz, P. S., 140, *156*
Rosenthal, B. S., 243, *244,* 271, 273, 279, 281, 282, *287*
Rosenthal, D., 20, *37,* 89, *103*
Roshenow, D. J., 234, *244*
Ross, J., 68, *81*
Ross, R. R., 357, *376*
Roth, M., 69, *81*
Rothblum, E., 282, *285*
Rousaville, B. J., 201, *216*
Rouse, B., 248, 249, 259, *261*

Ruderman, A. J., 234, *244*
Rudestam, K., 90, *100*
Rush, A. J., 7, 217, 219, 220, 223, 227, *227, 228*, 315, *333*
Rush, J., 272, *287*
Russell, C. D., 338, *354*
Russell, R. K., 94, *103*
Russell, S., *334*
Rutledge, S., 419, *422*
Rybstein-Blinchik, E., 313, *333*

Sabshin, M., 197, *216*
Safer, D. J., 366, *375*
Sajwaj, T., 341, *351*, 420, *423*
Salter, A., 122, *136*, 138, *158*
Salzberg, H. C., 248, *261*
Salzinger, K., 411, 412, *424*
Sand, P. L., 314, *332*
Sanderd, N., 380, *391*
Sanders, S. H., 314, 326, *334*
Sandler, J., 418, 422, *424*
Santogrossi, D., 415, *423*
Santrock, J. W., 180, *193*
Sarason, S. B., 408, *424*
Sartory, G., 10, 26, *33, 34*, 48, *56, 57*
Saunders, J. T., 186, *191*, 407, 408, *423*
Saunders, K. J., 314, *334*
Saunders, W. M., 245, 249, *262*
Schaefer, H. H., 344, *353*
Schapira, K., 69, *81*
Scharpe, L., 394, *405*
Scheckenbach, A. F., 349, *351*
Schiavo, R., 363, *373*, 394, 396, *405*
Schlesser, M. A., 222, *228*
Schmidt, G., 393, 395, 397, 398, 403, *403*
Schmidt, W., 249, *262*
Schnurer, A., 23, *34*
Schreibman, L., 419, *423*
Schroeder, H., 128, *136*, 145, *157, 158*
Schuler, P., 416, *422*
Schultheis, K. R., 182, *194*
Schwartz, R. M., 145, *158*
Scotch, N., 249, *261*
Scott, D., 314, *333*
Scott, L. W., *285*
Scott, S. B., 348, *351*
Sechrest, L., 342, *354*
Seegal, J. L., 154, *158*
Segal, Z., 91, *103*
Seidman, E., 356, 358, *374*, 417, *422*
Serber, M., 142, *158*
Seres, J. L., 315, *333*
Sexauer, J. D., 274, *287*
Sexton, T., 175, *195*

Shah, P., 87, *100*
Shaw, B. F., 7, 217, 227, *227, 228*
Shaw, M., 264, *287*
Shaw, P., 15, *34*, 60, 68, *80*, 88, 93, 98, *102*, 106, *120*, 186, *194*
Shealy, C., 314, *334*
Shealy, M., 314, *334*
Shelton, G., 338, *352*
Shelton, J. L., 129, 132, *136*
Shemberg, K., 411, 413-415, 419, *422-424*
Shenfeld, M., 416, 417, *424*
Sherman, M., 152, 416, *422*
Sherry, G. S., 94, *103*
Shipley, R., 84, *103*, 183, *195*
Shore, M. F., 368, *376*
Shulman, R., 87, *100*
Shultz, L., 411, *421*
Sibbach, L., 419, *421*
Sides, J., 25, *31*
Silberfeld, M., 73, *81*
Silberman, C., 409, *424*
Silfen, M., 266, *285*
Simon, K. M., 268, 278, *284*
Simon, R., 182, *191*
Singer, E. M., 418, *422*
Singer, J. L., 83, *103*
Sipich, J. F., 94
Sjoberg, L., 269, *287*
Sjostrom, L., 273, 275, *287*
Skolada, T. E., 246, *261*
Sloane, R. B., 2, *9*
Slye, E., 289, *309*
Smith, B. S., 346, *351*
Smith, G. A., 93, *101*
Smith, N., 419, *423*
Smith, W. L., 318, *334*
Snyder, J. J., 348, *353*
Sobel, H. J., 331, *334*
Sobell, L. C., 247, *262*, 344, *353*
Sobell, M. B., 247, *262*, 344, *353*
Solyom, C., 73, *81*
Solyom, L., 73, *81*
Spevak, P. A., 188, *195*
Spinks, S. H., 389, *391*
Spinnato, N. C., 366, *375*
Spitzer, R. L., 197, 201, 213, *216*, 218
Stahley, G. B., 151, *158*
Stalgaitis, S., 186, *194*
Stambul, H. B., 245, *260*
Stamford, B. A., 282, *288*
Stampfl, T. G., 93, 95, *103*
Stanley, J., 299, *308*
Staples, F. R., *9*
Star, B., 151, *158*

Stauss, F., 193
Stebbins, C. A., 140, 154, 158
Steele, B., 419, 421
Stefanis, C., 19, 34
Steffy, R. A., 343, 353
Steger, J. C., 329, 332
Stein, G. R., 314, 334
Steiner, M., 228
Steinmetz, S., 150, 158
Steketee, G., 11, 18, 19, 21, 27, 28, 30,
    32-34, 41, 43, 56, 94, 100
Stern, R., 10, 33, 40, 57, 59, 60, 81
Sternbach, R. A., 314, 333, 334
Stoian, M. S., 94, 102
Stokes, J. P., 410, 423
Stone, A., 90, 101
Strain, P., 416, 424
Strassberg, D. S., 318, 334
Stringer-Moore, D., 137, 141, 143, 144, 158
Strite, L. C., 314, 333
Strupp, H. H., 2, 9, 14, 33, 71, 79, 90, 103,
    341, 353
Stuart, R. B., 172, 182, 195, 278, 287, 366,
    376, 377
Stumphauzer, J. S., 370, 374, 377
Stunkard, A., 174, 184, 186, 187, 195, 230,
    244, 263, 266, 268, 272, 273, 277, 278,
    285, 287, 306, 309
Suckerman, K. R., 71, 81, 305, 309
Sutherland, E. A., 186, 195
Swanson, D. W., 314, 315, 317, 333, 334
Swenson, W. M., 314, 315, 317, 333, 334

Taritca, J., 228
Taulbee, E., 90, 103
Taylor, C. A., 186, 194, 248, 262
Taylor, C. I., 274, 287
Teasdale, J., 68, 80, 98, 102, 186, 194
Terhune, W. B., 73, 81
Tharp, R. G., 176, 196, 371, 377
Thomas, C. R., 186, 194
Thomas, L., 314, 332
Thompson, R. F., 27, 33
Thorensen, C. E., 178, 181, 191
Thornby, J., 292, 308
Thornton, C. C., 246, 261
Tiebout, H. M., 245, 262
Tillmanns, A., 11, 33
Timbers, G. D., 358, 374, 375
Timmermans, G., 314, 333
Tolor, A., 140, 158
Tomarken, A. J., 180, 181, 195
Tracey, L., 418, 424
Tramontana, J., 341, 351

Trieschmann, R. B., 314, 332
Tripodi, T., 366, 376, 377
Trost, N., 415, 422
Trower, P., 106, 120
Truax, B. B., 70, 81
Truax, C. B., 24, 34
Tucker, R. D., 336, 351
Tupling, H., 73, 81
Turk, D. C., 313, 331, 333, 334
Turner, C., 187, 191
Turner, R. M., 7, 10, 19, 30, 32, 33, 100,
    289-292, 296, 298, 299, 304, 307, 308,
    309
Turner, S., 141, 155
Tyler, M. M., 410, 422
Tyler, V. O., 338, 353

Ullmann, L. P., 1, 9

Van Dercar, C., 418, 424
van der Helm, M., 12, 32
van der Hout, A., 7, 16, 32
van Hasselt, V., 129, 136
Van Italie, T. B., 271, 288
van Zanten, B. L., 12, 32
Vaughn, M., 50, 56
Venables, P. H., 26, 33
Vender, M., 182, 192
Venema, H. B., 370, 377
Venkatesh, A., 87, 103
Vicklund, J., 90, 99
Vogel, S. R., 140, 156
Vogrin, D., 419, 424
von Knorring, L., 73, 81

Wade, T. C., 180, 196
Wagner, A. R., 27, 32
Wagner, J., 314, 333
Walen, S. R., 159, 167, 171
Walker, C. E., 336, 353
Walker, H. M., 347, 353
Wall, K., 140, 153, 154, 157, 158
Wallace, C., 132, 135, 380, 391
Wallace, K. M., 273, 286
Walter, T. L., 367, 376
Walton, D., 23, 34
Ward, M., 334
Wasden, R., 343, 350
Waskow, I. E., 70, 81
Wasserman, T., 419, 424
Watkins, J. T., 220, 228
Watson, D. L., 176, 196
Watson, J. P., 25, 34, 60, 81
Watts, F., 48, 57

Watzlawick, P., 61, *81*
Weathers, L., 364, *377*
Webb, M. P., 357, *374*
Webb, W. B., 289, *310*
Webster, A. S., 62, 73, *81*
Webster, J. S., 176, *192*
Weerts, T. C., 297, *308*
Weiner, A., 186, *195*
Weinrott, M., 416, *424*
Weinrott, N. R., 359, *375, 377*
Weiss, A. R., 272, 274, 275, *288*
Weissman, M. M., 200, 201, 206, *216*
Weitz, S., 139, *158*
Weltman, A., 282, 283, *288*
Wender, P., 90, *102*
Werner, J. S., 358, *377*
Wessels, H., 19, *32,* 60, *79,* 93, *100*
Wessler, R. A., 159, 167, *171*
Wessler, R. L., 159, 167, *171*
Westlake, R. J., 265, *285*
Westlake, R. V., 187, *191*
Wetzel, R. J., 371, *377*
Wheeler, E., 380, 382, *391*
Whipple, K., *9*
White, A. W., 311, *334*
White, D., 396, *405*
White, M. J., 348, *353*
Whitehead, A., 200, *216*
Whitehill, M., 416, *424*
Whitehurst, R., 151, *158*
Whiteley, J. M., 159, 165, 167, 170, *171*
Whitman, T., 415, *421*
Wikler, A., *261*
Wilchesk, M., 416, *424*
Wilcoxon, L. A., 20, *33,* 91
Wildman, H. E., 268, *286*
Wilkes, L. I., 318, *334*
Wilkins, W., 91, *103*
Willcutt, H. C., 346, *353*
Williams, R. L., 289, *310*
Willner, A. G., 358, *377*
Wilson, G. T., 6, 7, 159, *171,* 230, 234, *244,*
    264-266, 268, 270, 272, 277, 278, 282,
    285-288, 340, *352,* 408, *424*
Winett, R. A., 409, *424*
Wing, L., 26, *33,* 42, *56*
Wing, R. R., 182, *192,* 273, *286*
Winkler, R. C., 345, 346, *351-353,* 409, *424*
Winokur, A., 89, *103*
Winokur, G., 197, *216*
Winter, C., 273, *287*
Winter, K., 6, 104, 105, 109, *120*

Wise, D., 289, *309*
Witherspoon, A. D., 357, *375*
Woerner, M., 87, *103*
Wolberg, L. R., *424*
Wolf, M. M., 83, *99,* 335, 339, 347, *352-*
    354, 358, *373-377*
Wolfe, B. E., 70, *81*
Wolfe, J. L., 138, 144, 145, 147, 150, *156,*
    158
Wolff, H. H., 58, *79*
Wolfolk, A. E., 408, *424*
Wolfolk, R. L., 408, *424*
Wolfred, T. R., 359, 360, *374*
Wolpe, J., 1, *9,* 83, *103,* 122, 131, *136,* 138,
    158, 167, *171,* 292, *310,* 406, *424*
Wood, P. D., 283, *286*
Woodruff, R. A., 197, *216*
Wooley, O. W., 267, *288*
Wooley, S. C., 267, 268, 272, 275, 282, 284,
    288
Woolfolk, R., 154, *158*
Worthington, E. L., 175, *196*
Wright, J., 392, 395, 401, *405*
Wright, L., 336, *353*
Wrobel, P. A., 341, *351*
Wyman, E., *155*

Yalom, I., 87, *101,* 123, *136*
Yardley, K., 106, *120*
Yates, A. J., 1, *9*
Yeaton, W. H., 342, *354*
Yorkston, N. J., *9*
Yospe, L. P., 315, *333*
Youkilis, H. D., 331, *334*
Young, B. G., 396, *405*
Young, E. A., 87, *103, 228*
Youngren, M. A., 199, *216*

Zeiss, A. M., 7, 197-199, 203, 206, 213,
    216, 396, *405*
Zeiss, R. A., 186, *196,* 396, *405*
Zeldis, S., 77, *80,* 87, *101*
Ziesat, H., 314, *333*
Zilbergeld, B., 392, *405*
Zimmerman, E. H., 338, *354*
Zimmerman, J., 338, *352, 354*
Zitrin, C., 77, *80,* 87, *101, 103*
Zitter, R. E., 7, 314, *332*
Zuckerman, D. M., 200, 201, 206,
    216
Zung, W. W. K., 68, *81*
Zwerling, I., 245, *262*

Subject Index

Abstinence rate, 230
Abstinence violation effect (AVE):
  and cognitive restructuring, 242
  and intervention, 233
  and relapse prevention, 232, 235, 281
Academic performance, 415, 417
Achievement Place program, 347
Acrophobics, 93, 94
ACTH, 222
Adrenergic alerting reactions, 296
Adult offenders, 338
Age, 68, 343
  and insomnia, 295
Agoraphobia:
  characteristics of, 4
  exposure in vivo, 68-70
  and interpersonal conflict, 61-63
  nonacceptance of treatment for, 64-68
  and perceived parental characteristics, 73,
    74
  prognostic variables, 59, 60
  and therapeutic relationship, 70-72
AIDS, 233
Alcoholics Anonymous, 246, 259
Alcoholism:
  and controlled drinking, 249, 250
  and relapse determinants, 269
  treatment of, 229, 234, 245
Allergies, 296
Alpha-methyl-dopa, 220
Amitriptyline, 200, 222
Anhedonia, 197
Anticipation, negative, 218
Anticipatory fear, 13
Antidepressants, 296
Anxiety:
  and chronic pain, 312
  and cognitions, 42
  and depression, 22
  and environment, 108
  and insomnia, 296
  and irrational belief, 45

  management of, 106
  and MMPI, 292
  performance, 290, 292, 294
  physiological signs of, 107
  reduction of, 18, 25, 83, 121
  social, 104-120
    adaptive value of, 119
  stimuli of, 19
  and systematic desensitization, 233
  treatment of, 1, 29
Appearance, 108
Arousal:
  characteristics of, 26, 27, 93
  levels of, 42, 46
Arousal increasing intervention, 304
Arousal reducing intervention, 298, 304
Arousing instruction, 298
Assertiveness training:
  assessment of, 125
  behavioral assumptions of, 122
  and canned procedures, 127, 128
  characteristics of, 59, 66-68, 76, 175
  and client characteristics:
    aggression, 130
    anxiety, 131, 132
    attitudes and beliefs, 130, 131
    resistance to change, 129, 130
    skill deficits, 131
  client choice in, 123
  and cognitive mapping, 127
  and contraindications, 126
  definition of, 122
  follow-up, 121
  group vs. individual, 124
  holistic-eclectic treatment, 133, 134
  and motivation, 123
  outcomes of, 121
  and referral, 124
  and screening, 124
  and transfer of training, 123
  and women:
    battered women, 150, 151

behavioral measures, 140
behavior rehearsal, 142
behavior therapy, 138
cognitive restructuring, 144
deficit behavior, 138, 139
desensitization, 142
and discrimination, 143, 144
dropouts, 137
and environmental reinforcement, 146
feminist therapists, 138
follow-up, 137
goals of, 138
and homework assignments, 148
roles, 139, 142
screening, 141
self-esteem, 137
and sexual harassment, 144
and significant others, 149, 150
stereotypes, 154
and support networks, 146
and therapist, 152-154
and women's movement, 138
and work, 151, 152
Attitude shaping, 382
Attrition, 266
Automatic arousal, 294
Aversive conditioning, 247, 250
Avoidance, behavioral or cognitive, 25, 26

BAC, 257
Barbituates, 290
Basal metabolic rate, 273
Beck Depression Inventory, 207-212
Behavioral analysis:
  and chronic pain, 320
  as information gathering, 86
  and insomnia, 292, 304
  and social anxiety, 108
  and therapist, 3
  and treatment strategy, 106
Behavioral-employment intervention, 367
Behavioral intervention, 317, 321
Behavioral management, 313, 314, 322,
    415
Behavioral marriage therapy, 2, 379, 381
Behavioral medicine, 311
Behavioral programming, 408, 410
Behavior modification:
  and children, 409
    parent training in, 411, 412
  community-based, nonresidential:
    employment, 367-369
    family, 363-365
    mediated, 371

probation, 369-371
school, 365-367
community-based, residential, 358-363
and delinquency, 355
and institutional behavior, 357
language, 408
values, 408
Behavior therapy, 159, 380
adherence to, 268
Benzodiazepines, 88, 97, 110, 289
Between-group studies, 2
Between-session practice, 38
Bibliotherapy, 202, 248
Biophysiological status, 378
Bipolar illness, 221. See also Manic-depres-
    sive illness
Body fat, 271
Borderline patients, 218
Boredom, 296
Breathalyzer, 252
Brevital, 89
Buddy system, 371

California Youth Authority, 357
Caloric restriction, 282
Cardiovascular health, 271, 282
Catharsis, 388
Central nervous system, 293
Chemotherapy, 87, 88
Child abuse, 386, 394, 414, 418
Children, 378
  inattentive, 414
  isolated, 414-416
  retarded, 415
  socially withdrawn, 414, 416, 417
Chlordizepoxicde, 289
Chlorpromazine, 348
Chronic Pain Syndrome, 324
Circadian dysrhythmia, 294
Client characteristics, 342
Clinicians, empirical, 291
Clomipramine, 28, 43, 47
CNS, 296
Cognitions, 269, 279
Cognitive behavior therapy, 159, 264
Cognitive dissonance, 232, 411
Cognitive Restructuring:
  and addictive behavior, 234, 236
  and agoraphobia, 58, 59
  and anxiety reduction, 67
  and assertiveness training, 121, 128
  characteristics of, 51, 52
  conducted by former phobics, 68
  and dropout, 66

and marital therapy, 386
and nonacceptance of treatment, 64
and therapist dissatisfaction, 76
see also Rational-Emotive therapy
Coition, 394, 396, 397, 401
Commitment, 20
Communication exercises, 389
Communication patterns, 378
Communication skills, 382, 384, 394
Communication training, 393
Community acceptance, 361
Compliance, 84
Compulsion, 36, 39, 48, 90
Conduct-problem children, 341
Consequence sharing, 346
Contamination, fear of, 13
Contingency contracting, 369
Conversation skills, 416
Coping, 270, 279, 281
Coping response, 238
Coping strategy, 251
Cotherapists, 68
Criminals, 356

Delinquent youth:
   and behavioral programming, 417
   and self-instruction training, 348
   and token economy, 338-340
   treatment of, 414
Deposit-refund contingency, 266
Depression:
   agitated, symptoms of, 26
   and agoraphobia, 68
   and alcohol abuse, 254
   and assertiveness training, 198, 208
   behavioral model of, 198
   behavioral treatment of, 198, 217-227
   and changing treatment goals, 6
   characteristics of, 21
   and dropouts, 199, 203, 205-208
   endogenous, 7, 201, 202, 218
   and homework assignments, 206
   and insomnia, 292, 296
   and intelligence, 219
   and life stress, 202
   and marriage therapy, 388
   medication for, 46, 47
   melancholic, 218, 222
   and multiple sclerosis, 220, 221
   and noncooperators, 199, 206, 208
   and nonresponders, 199, 203, 206, 209
   and obsessions, 39
   and obsessive-compulsives, 27, 40-43
   reactive, 201, 213

and relapsers, 199, 206
and relaxation training, 198, 201, 208
and self-control, 182
situational, 201, 213
and social skills, 198, 213
symptoms, 197
and systematic desensitization, 198
and treatment outcome, 29
and trust, 219
unresponsive, 221-223
Desensitization:
   and extraversion, 88
   and flooding, 82, 97
   self-administered, 186
   and stress, 47, 51, 52
   systematic, 58, 91, 93, 105
Detoxification, 254
Dexamethasone suppression test (DST),
      222, 223
Diagnostic error, 6
Diazepam, 289
Diets, 266, 283, 296
Dipenhydramine, 290
Disadvantaged students, 340
Discongruent treatment expectations, 64
Discriminant Function Analysis, 203
Disease phobia, 69
Dismissal training, 52
Distraction training, 52
Divorce, 378, 379
Dreaming, 96
Driving, fear of, 96
Driving while Intoxicated (DWI) program,
      250
Dropout:
   and agoraphobics, 66
   characteristics of, 4, 8
   and delinquents, 364, 366, 367
   and drinking, 254
   and flooding, 82, 84
   and obesity, 266, 267, 269
   and obsessive-compulsives, 12
   and preparation for treatment, 89, 91
   and sexual dysfunction, 397-399
Drugs:
   antidepressant, 47, 254
   anxiety-reducing, 46
   and insomnia, 289, 290, 296
   and obesity, 266, 283
   previous use of, 68
   psychotropic, 37
   and token economy, 348
   in treatment, 51
Dysphoria, 197

Economic variables, 345
Electric shock, 247
Electroconvulsive treatment (ECT), 222
Electroencephalogram (EEG), 223, 292, 297, 300
Emotional processing, 25, 26, 47-49
Environment:
    preparation of, 92
    social, 108, 114, 118
EPIN scale, 72
Erection problems, 399
Ethclorvyno, 290
Expectancy, 20
Expectations, of patient, 117
Exposure:
    duration of, 93
    failure of, 68-70
    in imagination, 11, 17, 18, 95
    in vivo, 11, 17, 18, 58, 62
    and obsessions, 44
    and phobia, 7
Extinction, 88, 95
Extraversion, 88

Family intervention, 363-365, 367, 372
Family relationship, 74, 378
Family support, 273
Fat cell, 273
Fear-reduction, 52
Fear Survey Schedule, 300
Female orgasmic dysfunction, 395
Flooding, 82-99
    imaginal, 94
    and relapse, 97-99
Flurazepam, 289
Functional analysis, 77

Generalization, 83, 413, 414
    lack of, 113
Glutethimide, 289
Goal-setting, 268
Grief, 94
Grinker factors, 204, 205
Group therapy, 118

Habituation:
    and agoraphobia, 69
    and anxiety reduction, 25
    and depression, 28, 31, 43, 44
    and exposure sessions, 27, 29, 93
    and intrusive thoughts, 42
    and obsessions, 45, 51-55
    and obsessive-compulsives, 41
    and phobias, 26

    between sessions, 30, 43-45, 69, 94
    within sessions, 43-45, 69, 94
    and stress, 46
Handbook of Marital Therapy, 382
Height phobia, 94
Heroin, 229
High-risk clients, 276
High-risk situations, 231-233, 235, 281
Hodgkins disease, 87
Home-practice, 91, 98
Homework assignments:
    and assertiveness training, 127, 129
    and depression, 226
    and dropout, 399
    in marriage therapy, 382, 389
    and self control, 188
    and social anxiety, 119
    and therapeutic cooperation, 380, 381
Hopelessness, 224
Hyperarousal, 292, 294
Hypersomnia, 293
Hyperventilation, 77
Hypnosis, 283
Hypochondria, 69
Hypothyroidism, 221

Idiopathic insomniacs, 297
Imipramine, 21, 87
Implosion, 84
Implosive therapy, 84
Incest, 386
Information dissemination, 4
Institute for Rational-Emotive Therapy, 161
Interpersonal conflict, 61, 62
Interpersonal Psychotherapy, 200
Intervention, flexible levels of, 389
Introverts, 88
Intrusive cognitions, 42
IQ, 343

Lean Line, 283
Leisure, 378
Leucotomy, 51
Lipoproteins, 282
Lithium, 211
Long-term follow-up, 3

Maintenance:
    and addictive behaviors, 229
    and child behavior therapy, 413, 414
    and chronic pain, 329
    and delinquency, 366
    and insomnia, 306, 307
    and obesity, 279

and relapse prevention, 230, 231
and treatment approach, 243
as treatment component, 304, 306
Maladaptive beliefs, 107
MANCOVA, 201
Manic depressive illness, 221. *See also*
    Bipolar illness
Marital adjustment, 412
Marital adjustment test, 273, 274
Marital complications, 68, 77
Marital discord, 412
Marital relationship, 76
Marital satisfaction, 63
Marriage, 378
Masturbation, 396, 402
Maudsley Personality Inventory, 200
Measurement:
    of depression, 215
    and emotional processing, 47, 48
    in obsessive-compulsives, 17
    of treatment effects, 2
    of treatment outcome, 6
Medical disorders, 220
Memory impairment, 220
Mentally retarded, 338
Metabolic rate, 273
Methaqualone, 290
Methypaylon, 290
Mismatch theory, 296
Mitral valve prolapse syndrome, 77, 87
MMPI:
    and chronic pain, 318
    and depression, 204, 205
    and dropouts, 205
    and insomnia, 292, 300
    and treatment failure, 317
    and treatment success, 205
Modeling, 47, 51, 52
Monroe's Daily Sleep Questionnaire, 299
Mother, discipline of, 77
Motivation:
    and controlled drinking, 252, 254, 256
    and depression, 218
    lack of, 14
    and obesity, 266
    and social anxiety, 107, 108
    therapist influence on, 90
    for therapy, 180, 214, 253

Neuroticism Scale, 200
Nitrazepam, 289
Nocturnal enuresis, 410
Nocturnal myoclonis, 293
Noncompliance, 267, 304, 305, 380

Nonresponders, 5, 8
NREM, 294
Nutrient intake, 282

Obesity, 230, 239-243. *See also* Overweight-
    ness; Weight reduction
Obsessions, 35-55, 90
    and depression, 40-42
    and overvalued ideation, 43-47
    and stress, 42, 43
Obsessive-compulsives:
    and agoraphobia, 69
    and anxiety, 22
    attitude toward treatment, 12-14
    characteristics of, 10-31
    and depression, 21, 43
    dropouts, 12
    and exposure, 24-28
    and flooding, 98
    and imaginal exposure, 19
    medication for, 28
    and overvalued ideation, 23
    refusals, 11
    and "the return of fear," 48
    and therapist characteristics, 14, 15
Orgasm, 394-397, 401
Outcome data, 313
Overload/Underload Mismatch Theory of
    Insomnia, 292-298, 307
Overvalued ideation:
    and agoraphobia, 69
    measurement of, 23
    and obsessions, 43-48
    preventing therapeutic progress, 53
    and response prevention, 14
Overweightness, 271. *See also* Obesity;
    Weight reduction

Panic reactions, 84, 87
Paradoxical intention, 296
Parental characteristics:
    controlling, 73, 74
    overprotectiveness, 73, 74
    rejection, 73, 74
Parental cooperation, 411
Partner, 66
Patient uniformity myth, 296
Personality, 88
    characteristics of, 7
Pharmacotherapy, 200, 201, 207, 254
Phenobarbital, 290
Phenothiazine, 84
Phobias, 8, 44
    duration of, 68

Physiological dysfunctions, 87
Pimozide, 348
Piperidinedime derivatives, 289
Placebo treatments, 234, 292
Play, 417
Population variables, 249
Premarital sex, 396
PREP, 365
Pretherapy training, 67
Probation, 369, 370
Process research, 358
Prognostic model, 29
Prognostic variables, 2, 21, 59, 60
Programmed learning, 357
Pseudoinsomniacs, 297
Psychodynamic theory, 95
Psychologically naive, 220
Psychophysiological responses, 25
Psychosis, diagnosis of, 43
Psychotherapy, insight oriented, 201
Public-speaking, distress of, 94
Punishment, 356, 360

Quasiexperimental design, 299

Rand Report, 245, 249
Rapid eye movement (REM), 223, 290, 294, 296
Rational-Emotive therapy (RET):
   and anxiety, 161
   and behavior therapy, 167
   and depression, 161
   and dissatisfaction with therapist, 76
   and dropouts, 169
   and EST, 170
   and frustration tolerance, 163, 164, 166
   and homework assignments, 165
   and hostility, 161
   Institute for, 161
   and neurotic traits, 162
   and phobia, 97
   and psychosis, 163
   and self-pity, 161
   and therapist behavior, 168, 169
   see also Cognitive Restructuring
Reactivity, 26-28
Recidivism:
   and behavior modification programs, 356, 365
   and duration of program, 357
   and employment programs, 368
   as measurement of change, 339
   and positive family interaction, 364
   and probation programs, 370

and teaching-family vs. nonteaching family youths, 359
   and therapist skills, 363
   and token economy, 349
Record keeping, 281
Recreational activities, 378
Recruitment, 264
Refusals:
   characteristics of, 4, 11
   and flooding, 89
   and obsessive-compulsives, 12
   and preparation for therapy, 90
   and sexual dysfunction, 398
Rehospitalization, 339
Reinforcement, 341, 347, 356, 360
   backup, 344, 346
   magnitude of, 344
Reinforcer sampling, 344
Relapse:
   and addictive behavior, 229, 231
   and agoraphobia, 63
   characteristics of, 5, 7, 8
   and controlled drinking, 258, 259
   counteraction of, 232, 236, 242-244
   determinants of, 231, 235, 238, 241, 269
   and flooding, 82, 84
   and high-risk situations, 281, 282
   and imaginal exposure, 19
   and maintenance, 230
   and obesity, 269, 270, 277-280, 283
   and obsessive-compulsives, 12
   programmed, 233
   and stressful events, 39
Relapse Prevention Model, 230-234
Relationship Inventory, 72
Relaxation training:
   and arousal level, 28
   and insomnia, 292, 296
   and intrusive cognitions, 42
   and phobia, 95, 96
   progressive, 301-303
   and social anxiety, 109
   and underload client, 298
Research Diagnostic Criteria, 201
Research strategies, 1
Response prevention:
   and checking compulsions, 39, 40
   and exposure, 18, 28, 52
   and flooding, 83
   and obsessive-compulsives, 10, 11, 17
   and phobia, 44
   and ritualistic behavior, 18
Restrained Eating Scale, 278
Risk factors, 271

Ritalin, 296
Rituals, 11, 18, 23
Role expectations, 387
Role-play, 415
Role reversal, 387
Rutgers Weight Control Program, 265, 267-
    269, 273, 279

Satiation, 45
Satiation training, 39, 45
Schizoaffective disorders, 218
Schizophrenia:
    delusion of, 37
    diagnosis of, 43
    patients, 337, 340, 346, 349
Seconbarbital, 290
Secondary gain, 66, 76
Sedative-hypnotics, 289, 290
Self-acceptance, 272
Self-contracting, 176-178
Self-control programs, 298
Self-criticism, 224
Self-efficacy, 231
Self-esteem, 272
Self-evaluation, 173-175
Self-injurious behavior, 419
Self-instruction, 414
Self-monitoring:
    characteristics of, 175, 176
    and child behavior therapy, 414
    and negative contingencies, 179
    and obesity, 268
    and self-control, 182, 184
Self-observation, 314
Self-punishment, 179
Self-regulation, 247, 250
Self-reinforcement, 180-182, 184,
    185
Self-speech, 94
Sensitization, 84
Separation, 378, 379
    covert intention for, 381
Sexological exam, 394
Sexual abuse, 386
Sexual arousal, 395, 397
Sexual intimacy, 378
Sexual motivation, 396
Sexual response, 392, 394
Shopping, fear of, 98
Side effects, 84, 272
Skills training, 233, 236, 239
Sleep apnea, 293
Sleep environments, 295
Sleeping behavior, 292

Smoking cessation:
    and reinforcement, 185
    and relapse, 229, 236-239
    and self-evaluation, 173, 174
    and self-monitoring, 179
    success rates during treatment, 230
    and supportive intervention, 188
    and treatment orientation, 183
Social Adjustment Self-Report Scale, 201
Social anxiety:
    behavioral treatment of, 105, 106
    characteristics of, 104, 105
    environmental factors, 108
    motivational factors, 107, 108
    and personal appearance, 108
    and social skills, 108
Social cohesion, 67
Social-marital problems, 256
Social phobia, 105
Social skills training, 106, 108, 121, 415
Social-support, 273
Social system, 227
Sociometric ratings, 415
Specificity theory, 311
Spider-phobia, 89
Spouse support, 280
Spouse training, 265
Stimulus content, 95
Stimulus control:
    and insomnia, 296, 298, 301-303
    and obesity, 281
    and relaxation therapy, 292
    and sleep disturbance, 290
Stimulus overload, 294, 296
Stress, 42, 47, 269
Strictness, 77
Subject selection, 264, 265
Suicide, 254
Symptoms:
    age at onset, 22, 29
    duration, 23
    emergence, 62
    obsessive-compulsive, 23
    severity, 23
Systems—behavioral approach, 363

Teaching-family model, 358-361
Teaching-parent, 369
Temple Insomnia Clinic, 299
Tension, 290
Therapeutic process, 2
Therapist:
    and amount of client contact, 185-187
    and assertiveness training, 132, 133

behavioral, 106
characteristics of, 14, 217, 218
client perception of, 67, 76
conceptualizations of, 85-89
female, 395
and flooding, 85
implosive, 93, 95
incorrect identification by, 37
and obsessive-compulsives, 14, 15, 24
and patient reassurance, 45
psychodynamically oriented, 290
relationship with clients, 7, 8, 70-72, 74,
    77, 111, 117, 304, 305
  and agoraphobia, 71
  see also Working alliance
and "rules of safety," 45
skills of, 365
and thought-stopping treatment, 40
Thought-blocking, 50
Thought-dismissal, 50
Thought-stopping, 40, 45, 51
Three-concept analysis, 49-53
Token systems, 413, 419
Tranquilizers, 289
Transference, 71, 77

Unassertiveness, 61, 63
Underload deficits, 294

Unresponsiveness, 337, 341, 349
Urine alarm method, 411

Verbal skills, 416

Weight reduction, 173, 174
  and age of obesity onset, 275
  and age of subject, 274
  biological boundaries of, 272
  and dieting history, 275
  and exercise, 279, 282
  and menopause, 275
  predictor of, 273
  and sex of subject, 274
  see also Obesity; Overweightness
Weight Watchers, 278, 283
Wilks lambda group, 204
Willoughby Personality Schedule, 300
Withdrawals, 91
Working alliance, 117. See also Therapist,
    relationship with clients
WRAT, 366

Yale University, Depression Research Unit
    of, 200

Zuckerman Sensation-Seeking Scale,
    296

Psychology and Psychiatry in Courts and Corrections: Controversy and Change
   by Ellsworth A. Fersch, Jr.

Restricted Environmental Stimulation: Research and Clinical Applications
   by Peter Suedfeld

Personal Construct Psychology: Psychotherapy and Personality
   edited by Alvin W. Landfield and Larry M. Leitner

Mothers, Grandmothers, and Daughters: Personality and Child Care in
Three-Generation Families
   by Bertram J. Cohler and Henry U. Grunebaum

Further Explorations in Personality
   edited by A. I. Rabin, Joel Aronoff, Andrew M. Barclay, and Robert A. Zucker

Hypnosis and Relaxation: Modern Verification of an Old Equation
   by William E. Edmonston, Jr.

Handbook of Clinical Behavior Therapy
   edited by Samuel M. Turner, Karen S. Calhoun, and Henry E. Adams

Handbook of Clinical Neuropsychology
   edited by Susan B. Filskov and Thomas J. Boll

The Course of Alcoholism: Four Years After Treatment
   by J. Michael Polich, David J. Armor, and Harriet B. Braiker

Handbook of Innovative Psychotherapies
   edited by Raymond J. Corsini

The Role of the Father in Child Development (Second Edition)
   edited by Michael E. Lamb

Behavioral Medicine: Clinical Applications
   by Susan S. Pinkerton, Howard Hughes, and W. W. Wenrich

Handbook for the Practice of Pediatric Psychology
   edited by June M. Tuma

Change Through Interaction: Social Psychological Processes of Counseling and
Psychotherapy
   by Stanley R. Strong and Charles D. Claiborn

Drugs and Behavior (Second Edition)
   by Fred Leavitt

Handbook of Research Methods in Clinical Psychology
   edited by Philip C. Kendall and James N. Butcher

A Social Psychology of Developing Adults
   by Thomas O. Blank

Women in the Middle Years: Current Knowledge and Directions for Research and Policy
   edited by Janet Zollinger Giele

Loneliness: A Sourcebook of Current Theory, Research and Therapy
   edited by Letitia Anne Peplau and Daniel Perlman

Hyperactivity: Current Issues, Research, and Theory (Second Edition)
   by Dorothea M. Ross and Sheila A. Ross

Review of Human Development
   *edited by Tiffany M. Field, Aletha Huston, Herbert C. Quay, Lillian Troll,
   and Gordon E. Finley*

Agoraphobia: Multiple Perspectives on Theory and Treatment
   edited by Dianne L. Chambless and Alan J. Goldstein

The Rorschach: A Comprehensive System, Volume III: Assessment of Children and Adolescents
   by John E. Exner, Jr. and Irving B. Weiner

Handbook of Play Therapy
   edited by Charles E. Schaefer and Kevin J. O'Connor

Adolescent Sexuality in a Changing American Society: Social and Psychological Perspectives
for the Human Service Professions (Second Edition)
   by Catherine S. Chilman

Failures in Behavior Therapy
   edited by Edna B. Foa and Paul M.G. Emmelkamp